HISTORY AND LIFE

THE WORLD AND ITS PEOPLE

2nd Edition

T. Walter Wallbank

Arnold Schrier

Donna Maier

Patricia Gutierrez-Smith

The cover of this book shows a
statue of Pharaoh Ramses II
at Abu Simbel, Egypt.

HISTORY AND LIFE

THE WORLD AND ITS PEOPLE

2nd Edition

T. Walter Wallbank, *University of Southern California*

Arnold Schrier, *University of Cincinnati*

Donna Maier, *University of Northern Iowa*

Patricia Gutierrez-Smith, *Roberto Clemente High School, Chicago, Illinois*

Scott, Foresman and Company

Editorial Offices: Glenview, Illinois

Regional Offices: Palo Alto, California •
Tucker, Georgia • Glenview, Illinois •
Oakland, New Jersey • Dallas, Texas

About the Authors

T. Walter Wallbank is the author of numerous articles and books in the field of world history. He pioneered the development of civilization and world history courses in high schools and colleges and has studied and taught extensively in Europe, Africa, and Asia.

Arnold Schrier has written extensively in the field of European and world history. He is an authority on Russian history and does research and teaching on the subject in this country and abroad. He also works with public high schools in the development of social studies curriculum.

Donna Maier has served as an African studies consultant for encyclopedia and trade book publishers. She has traveled and studied in Africa and Europe. She is the author of a number of articles dealing with African culture and is presently lecturing in African history and world history.

Patricia Gutierrez-Smith has participated widely in the formation of curriculum materials for urban schools and students. She has been a social studies teacher in several Chicago high schools and is presently teaching world history and Latin American history.

Teacher Consultants

Sister Mary Brian Bole, SSND
Chairwoman, Social Studies Department
Bishop Dunne High School
Dallas, Texas

William C. Driskell
Social Studies Teacher
Lakeside High School
DeKalb County, Georgia

Jeanette S. Gasbarro
Social Studies Teacher
Oakcrest High School
Mays Landing, New Jersey

Sharon L. Green
Coordinator, Multi-Ethnic Curriculum
Seattle Public Schools
Seattle, Washington

Frank Vlach
World History Teacher
Einstein Junior High School
Sacramento, California

Ronald Wiltse
History Teacher
San Antonio ISD
San Antonio, Texas

Academic Consultant

Dr. Gerald A. Danzer
Associate Professor of History
University of Illinois at Chicago Circle

The section entitled "Acknowledgements" is an extension of this page.
ISBN: 0-673-13480-6

CONTENTS

How To Use This Book

History and Life has been organized to make it easy to use. Chapters follow a regular structure you can depend on. Special features— Geography: A Key to History, Someone You Should Know, Points of Interest, and A Mystery in History—occur in each unit. Another special feature—What's in a Name?—appears in each chapter. The Table of Contents, Map List, Glossary, and Index can help you find what you want to know.

The Units

The nine units of *History and Life* correspond to well-defined historical periods. The unit introduction gives an overview of the main ideas in the unit. Time lines show you the chronology of events in the chapters within a unit; you can see when events in one chapter happened in relation to events in the other chapters. At the end of each unit is a test you can use to check your understanding of the material in the unit.

The Chapters

Below are the first and last pages of typical chapters. All chapters have the same elements: **A** a chapter numeral, title, and time span of events, **B** a chapter introduction, **C** a list of the sections of the chapter, **D** section headings, and **E** subsection headings. The section and subsection headings together make a sentence outline of the main ideas in a chapter. Another common element in each chapter is the feature called "What's in a Name?" As in **F**, it tells the origin of a content word in that chapter.

World history includes many foreign place names and proper names. Wherever one occurs in text, it will be followed by its pronunciation. Page 111 below gives pronunciations for Tacitus [tas'ə tus] and Tiber [tī'ber]. In addition, world history has its own vocabulary—words that have specific meanings related to concepts under discussion. On page 111, *Pax Romana* is defined. Vocabulary words are defined in text right after their first use, and they appear in the glossary.

A chapter **6**   750 B.C.–395 A.D.

THE ROMAN EMPIRE

The Romans decorated the plaster walls of their homes with paintings, much as we use wallpaper. This portrait from the city of Pompeii shows a husband and wife—both educated. He holds a papyrus scroll, she a writing stylus and tablet.

B To Edward Gibbon, an 18th-century English historian and author of *Decline and Fall of the Roman Empire*, "the period in the history of the world during which the condition of the human race was most happy and prosperous" was the 2nd century A.D. It was during this century that the Roman Empire reached its greatest extent and was, according to Gibbon, "governed by absolute power, under the guidance of virtue and wisdom." A Roman subject of the 2nd century agreed and had this to say about the era in which he lived:

> . . . The whole world keeps holiday; the age-long curse of war has been put aside; mankind turns to enjoy happiness. Strife has been quieted, leaving only the competition of cities, each eager to be the most beautiful and the most fair. Every city is full of gymnastic schools, fountains and porticos, temples, shops, and schools of learning. The whole earth is decked with beauty like a garden.

There were those who would disagree. Some thought Roman rule was a mixed blessing at best. Others felt it was oppressive and tyrannical. The famous modern-day historian, Arnold J. Toynbee, has called the 2nd century A.D. a time of stalemate when the world "lay more or less passive in the pall" of Roman power. The 2nd-century Roman historian Tacitus [tas'ə tas] agreed: "They [the Romans] make desolation, which they call peace."

A difference of opinion is a good point at which to begin to look at Roman history. In truth, military conquest made Rome a world state. The boundaries of the empire expanded as the Roman armies scored victory after victory. Yet force alone was not enough to maintain a unified state. Skillful diplomacy, effective government, a flexible system of law, a widespread network of roads and commercial towns—all these factors helped bring together a great number of peoples of varying customs and races. For over two centuries, from 27 B.C. to 180 A.D., the Romans maintained the *Pax Romana*, or "Roman Peace," throughout their far-flung domain.

The story of how Rome grew from a small city-state on the central Italian peninsula to a vast empire controlling the whole Mediterranean is told in this chapter as follows:

C
1. The Roman Republic arose on the Italian peninsula.
2. The republic became a world state.
3. The empire lasted for five centuries.
4. The Romans preserved Greek culture.

1 **D** The Roman Republic arose on the Italian peninsula

Between 2000 and 1000 B.C., about the time that the Greek-speaking tribes were moving into their future homeland, another branch of Indo-Europeans moved south through the Alps into the Italian peninsula. Most important were the Latins, a group of tribes who settled along the west coast of the central Italian peninsula in the lower valley of the Tiber [tī'bər] River. About midpoint in the 8th century B.C., they built a small settlement on the Palatine, a hill near the Tiber. The city of Rome grew from this modest beginning.

F

WHAT'S IN A NAME?
ROME
Legend has it that Rome is named for Romulus. He and Remus were brothers who, the story goes, were raised by a wolf. More likely, the city's name comes from *roma*, a Latin word meaning "crossroads."

E **Early Rome was ruled by the Etruscans.** In the 7th century B.C., the Latin tribes were conquered by their powerful neighbors to the north, the Etruscans. Little is known about the Etruscans. It is thought that they came originally from Asia Minor. They drained the marshes around Rome, encouraged trade,

110

111

End-of-Chapter Material

Every chapter ends with two pages like the ones shown here of Chapter 12. In **G**, paragraphs summarize the chapter, section by section; **H** asks you to recall the important terms, people, events and dates in the chapter; **I** gives questions that call for in-depth thinking about the main ideas; **J** suggests activities to help you learn more about the material in the chapter, and **K** is a short chapter quiz.

The Map Program

Each chapter contains a map lesson. These lessons discuss such things as map skills, geographical information, and the historical development of map-making. Each map lesson has questions for you to answer. In all, there are more than 85 maps in the text. At the back of the book is an Atlas of the Contemporary World. There you will find 7 more maps.

Geography: A Key to History

In order to understand why civilization developed in a certain way in a certain place, it is often necessary to understand geographic aspects of the place. In each unit, a one-page essay with a map explains some aspect of geography that has affected history.

Someone You Should Know

World history is filled with interesting people who have led exciting lives. A biography in each unit tells more about one such person who has been mentioned there.

Points of Interest

Many of the places talked about in this book are still in existence today. In each unit, a one-page, illustrated essay tells you some things you would learn if you had the chance to visit one of these places yourself.

A Mystery in History

Historians are like detectives. They seek clues in government records, diaries, newspapers, ballads, paintings, and objects that lie buried in the ground. Sometimes vital clues are missing. One page in each unit sets forth a historical mystery with its clues and interpretations.

---

12 chapter review   ❖ ❖ ❖

G Section Summaries

1. Much of Africa is desert and savanna. The continent of Africa has several different ecological regions. In the north and south are narrow regions of fertile coast. Farther inland are deserts—the Sahara in the north and the Kalahari in the south. Camels have ensured African trade and contact across the Sahara. The deserts of Africa merge into large regions of savanna where populations have prospered because of the farming and herding that are possible there.

2. Other features of geography made Africa a land of variety. In the west-central section of the continent is the rain forest. Fruits and vegetables grow well here, but the tsetse fly has prevented the raising of cattle and horses. The rivers of Africa connected the villages and cities that dot the valleys. Canoes and barges carried trading goods on the rivers. In East Africa, ancient earthquakes and volcanoes formed a mountain, valley, and lake region called the Rift Valley. Legends of the glorious Chwezi kings suggest that people have lived in this pleasant and fertile region for centuries.

3. The peoples of ancient Africa developed many practical skills. Useful farming methods, specialized cattle-raising, and ironworking helped Africans grow more food and control their environment. The Bantu migrations populated central and southern Africa. One of the earliest ironworking sites in Africa developed in the ancient kingdom of Kush.

4. Ancient Africans developed distinctive societies and cultures. Tribal groups and lineages formed the basis of African societies. Every person was expected to act in a way proper for his role. Priests became important in some groups, while in other groups political chiefs became powerful. Law and history were memorized and passed from generation to generation. Griots in West Africa had the job of studying history and remembering it for the whole community. Cultural advances were also made in early Africa.

Some societies had long traditions of art, particularly sculpture. The clay heads of Nok and the bronze sculpture of Ife and Benin are considered to be some of the best sculpture in the world.

Who? What? When? Where? **H**

1. Write an identifying sentence for each of the following groups:
a. Asante   e. Kulango
b. Bantu   f. Kushites
c. Chwezi   g. Nyamwezi
d. Gonja

2. Write a sentence for each of these terms that tells its importance:
a. caravan   f. lineage
b. cattle   g. oases
c. compound   h. plantain
d. fallow   i. tribe
e. griots   j. tsetse fly

3. Make a time line that shows the following events:
a. The people of Nok began making clay sculpture.
b. The Bantu migrations took place.
c. Farming began in the Niger River Valley.
d. The Kingdom of Kush flourished.
e. Bronze sculpture was first made in Ife.
f. Ironworking became common in Egypt.

4. What are the four major ecological areas of Africa?

Questions for Critical Thinking **I**

1. Why were the Kulango unable to adjust to life in Asante? Can you think of any difficulties people might be having today in trying to start life again in a new place? Explain.

2. What might be some reasons little has been known about African history and culture until recently?

---

3. In what ways do people of different occupations exchange goods today similar to the cooperation between farmers and herders of the African savanna?

4. Has studying this chapter changed your ideas about Africa? If so, how?

5. How does the geography of an area encourage people to develop special skills? Give specific examples from African history and from life today.

J Skill Activities

1. Read *Plays from African Folktales* by Carol Karty to find out more about the cultures of Africa. (Charles Scribner's Sons, 1975)

2. Find out what is happening in the countries near the borders of the Sahara today. Is the size of the desert still changing? Why? What effect is this having on the people who live there?

3. Show the four ecological areas of Africa on a map. Find pictures illustrating the different ways of life followed in these areas today.

4. Discuss in class the responsibilities of families toward their members today and compare these responsibilities with the traditional African lineage system.

5. Write an African folk tale based on the ways of life explained in this chapter.

6. Find pictures of different examples of African sculpture and wood carving. How are they different from modern art? How are they the same?

---

chapter **12** quiz

K Section 1

1. True or false: The Sahara always has been an impassable boundary between North and South Africa.

2. An important animal to the people of the Sahara was the: a. cow, b. camel, c. donkey

3. Most African people have lived in the: a. desert, b. savanna, c. forest

Section 2

4. Cattle cannot be raised in the African forest because of: a. lions, b. tsetse flies, c. custom

5. An important forest kingdom was that of: a. Niger, b. Benin, c. Masai

6. True or false: Plantain and yams became important crops to forest people.

Section 3

7. A pastoral society is one whose culture is based on: a. herding, b. farming, c. fishing

8. True or false: Archaeologists have learned about the Kushites from their hieroglyphics.

9. Farmlands in Africa were cultivated with: a. hoes, b. plows, c. shovels

Section 4

10. In African society, a group of people who are descended from the same person is a: a. tribe, b. lineage, c. compound

11. The lost-wax process was used to make: a. candles, b. iron tools, c. bronze sculptures

12. True or false: The priests were the most important leaders in all African societies.

Map List

UNIT ONE CIVILIZATION BEGINS

How did it all come about? Today we see and read about many nations and all kinds of people with different ways of life and government. How did people come to be this way? For an explanation, we must look at history—at the story of how people lived, what they did and said, how they solved their problems, and what ideas and customs they developed.

For the earliest people, life was difficult. They faced basic needs: make shelter, get food, protect themselves from wild animals, and build societies that would make group living possible. The way in which people live and work to satisfy these needs is called their *culture*.

A great advance in human culture came when people began to farm, form governments, use metals, live in cities, and use writing. This kind of human living is called *civilization*. People who lived before writing was invented are said to be *prehistoric*, because they left no written records.

Civilization started in four river valleys. Along the shores of the Nile and the Tigris [tī′gris]-Euphrates [yü frā′tēz] rivers in the Middle East, civilization began as early as 7,000 years ago. Between 2500 and 2000 B.C., civilization also developed in the Indus [in′dəs] River Valley in India and along the Hwang Ho [hwäng′ hō′] in China. This unit tells how humans lived in these early times and finally reached civilization.

The Time Line.   The time lines on the following two pages give an indication of the very long periods of time between different stages in human progress toward civilization. The top time line shows the events discussed in the first chapter of this unit. The red area at the far right represents just 5 thousand years in the 4 million-year story. To show the events in those years, the time line at the bottom uses a different scale. Thus, the small red line in the top time line stands for the entire time line at the bottom.

Stonehenge, in southern England, is the most famous of all the prehistoric monuments. Its exact use is not known today.

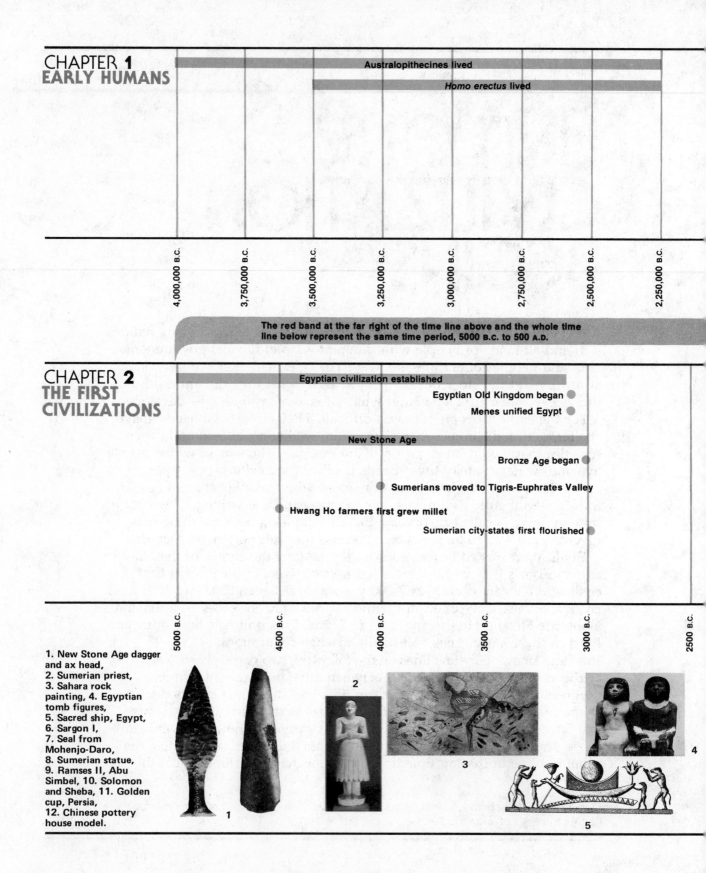

CHAPTER 1
EARLY HUMANS

Australopithecines lived

Homo erectus lived

4,000,000 B.C.	3,750,000 B.C.	3,500,000 B.C.	3,250,000 B.C.	3,000,000 B.C.	2,750,000 B.C.	2,500,000 B.C.	2,250,000 B.C.

The red band at the far right of the time line above and the whole time line below represent the same time period, 5000 B.C. to 500 A.D.

CHAPTER 2
THE FIRST CIVILIZATIONS

Egyptian civilization established

Egyptian Old Kingdom began ●

Menes unified Egypt ●

New Stone Age

Bronze Age began ●

● Sumerians moved to Tigris-Euphrates Valley

● Hwang Ho farmers first grew millet

Sumerian city-states first flourished ●

5000 B.C.	4500 B.C.	4000 B.C.	3500 B.C.	3000 B.C.	2500 B.C.

1. New Stone Age dagger and ax head,
2. Sumerian priest,
3. Sahara rock painting, 4. Egyptian tomb figures,
5. Sacred ship, Egypt,
6. Sargon I,
7. Seal from Mohenjo-Daro,
8. Sumerian statue,
9. Ramses II, Abu Simbel, 10. Solomon and Sheba, 11. Golden cup, Persia,
12. Chinese pottery house model.

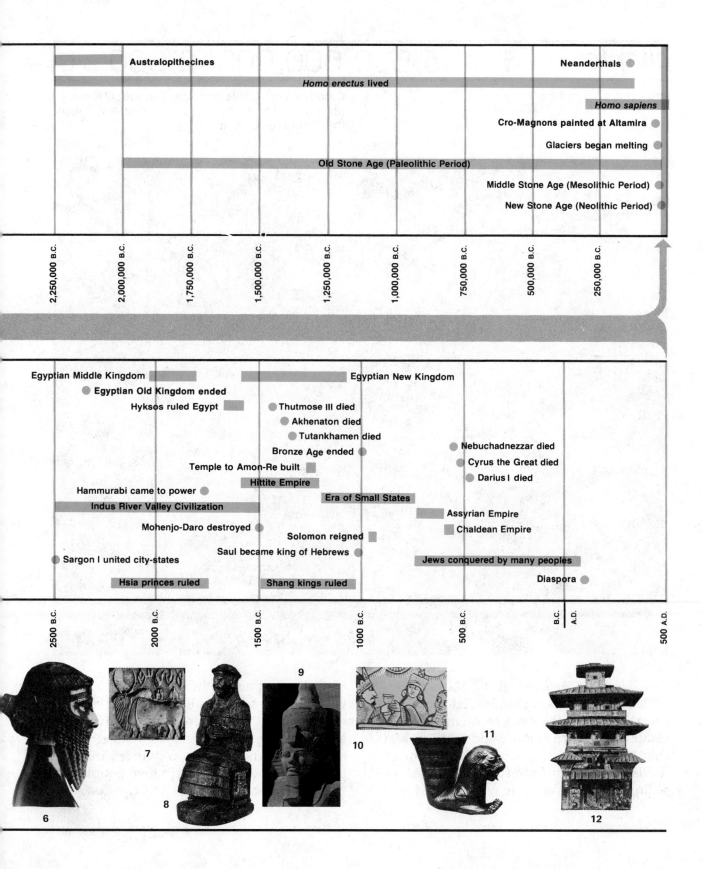

Australopithecines

Neanderthals

Homo erectus lived

Homo sapiens

Cro-Magnons painted at Altamira

Glaciers began melting

Old Stone Age (Paleolithic Period)

Middle Stone Age (Mesolithic Period)

New Stone Age (Neolithic Period)

2,250,000 B.C.
2,000,000 B.C.
1,750,000 B.C.
1,500,000 B.C.
1,250,000 B.C.
1,000,000 B.C.
750,000 B.C.
500,000 B.C.
250,000 B.C.

Egyptian Middle Kingdom
Egyptian New Kingdom
Egyptian Old Kingdom ended
Hyksos ruled Egypt
Thutmose III died
Akhenaton died
Tutankhamen died
Bronze Age ended
Nebuchadnezzar died
Cyrus the Great died
Temple to Amon-Re built
Darius I died
Hittite Empire
Hammurabi came to power
Era of Small States
Indus River Valley Civilization
Assyrian Empire
Mohenjo-Daro destroyed
Chaldean Empire
Solomon reigned
Saul became king of Hebrews
Sargon I united city-states
Jews conquered by many peoples
Diaspora
Hsia princes ruled
Shang kings ruled

2500 B.C.
2000 B.C.
1500 B.C.
1000 B.C.
500 B.C.
B.C.
A.D.
500 A.D.

9

7

8

10

11

6

12

3

EARLY HUMANS

Called the Dame of Brassampouy [brä sᴀɴ pü′ē], this prehistoric ivory carving was found in Europe. It is about the size of a human thumb.

One day in 1879, five-year-old María de Sautuola and her father, Don Marcelino de Sautuola, explored the cave of Altamira on his estate in northern Spain. Suddenly Don Marcelino heard her cry out, "Toros! Toros!" (Bulls! Bulls!) He found her staring at the ceiling of the cavern. It was covered with huge bison, painted in red and black. They were drawn so skillfully that they seemed almost alive. Elsewhere in the cave Don Marcelino found pictures of horses, deer, and wild boars. He was convinced that the pictures were made by primitive people.

María's discovery made the cave of Altamira famous. But scientists claimed that the pictures could not have been painted by primitive people, for they were as well done as paintings by modern artists. The scientists said that an artist who had visited Don Marcelino probably painted the pictures and that the Spanish nobleman was trying to fool people.

In 1895, a French scholar reported the discovery of prehistoric paintings on the walls of a cave in France. During the next two years other cave paintings were discovered. By 1900, scientists generally accepted cave art as the work of primitive people. Don Marcelino had been right all along. The lifelike and colorful cave paintings at Altamira were at least 20 thousand years old.

Many of the discoveries relating to early people are the work of scientists called *anthropologists*. They study the origin, races, and customs of people, both ancient and modern. *Archaeologists* are the scientists who specialize in a branch of anthropology. They excavate, classify, and study the remains of ancient cultures.

Paleontologists [pā'lē on tol'ə jists] study *fossils*, the hardened remains of life forms. All of these specialists may be included in a scientific team. Together they work out theories about what early people were like and how they lived. This chapter tells how:

1. Life began on ancient Earth.

2. People developed basic skills in the Old Stone Age.

3. People made great advances in the Middle Stone Age and the New Stone Age.

4. Important inventions appeared during the Bronze Age.

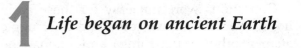

1 *Life began on ancient Earth*

How old is Earth? How long have people lived on it? In the past few years, scientists have found much to help answer these questions.

Earth was formed. Most geologists believe that Earth is approximately 4.5 to 5 billion years old. According to their theories, the planet began as a flaming mass of gas and steam that slowly cooled and hardened. For millions of years, clouds dropped rain onto the hot surface. The heat turned the rain to steam, which rose to become part of the overhanging clouds. As Earth cooled still more, the falling water filled hollows. These became the deep oceans and shallow seas that covered most of the planet.

It was in these oceans and seas that living things first appeared. And with them begins the story of life on Earth.

Living things developed from simple to more complex forms. Most scientists believe that the first living things—which existed at least 3.5 billion years ago—were simple, one-celled, water-dwelling plants and animals. These tiny bits of living matter had no bony structures. More advanced life forms then developed which were composed of more than one cell. Jellyfish, worms, snails, crabs, and then fish appeared in the water.

All the earliest animal life forms lived in water. From them developed amphibians [am fib'ē ənz], which could live on land as well as in water. Later, such reptiles as snakes and lizards appeared. And, after a long time, birds and more complex animals developed. Each of these stages of animal development took millions of years.

5

Conditions were not easy for these early life forms. To survive, they had to struggle against other living things and against the strong forces of nature. Many plants and animals could not survive. Others became stronger as new generations changed to meet changing conditions on Earth. Some animals changed a great deal. For example, millions of years ago horses were only about 1 foot (30 centimeters) high. They had four-toed front feet and three-toed hind feet. Today, horses are from 5 to 6.5 feet (150 to 195 centimeters) tall and have only one toe on each foot.

Skeletons gave clues to the appearance of early humans. There are many theories about the origin of human beings. However, most scientists believe that *Homo sapiens* [hō'mō sā'pē enz], modern human beings, came into being about 300 thousand years ago, which is quite recent in the long development of life on Earth. Ancient skeletons suggest that other beings, similar to humans,

lived before that time. No complete skeletons have been found. However, the anthropologists who study these ancient bones have developed ideas about what these creatures looked liked. They have also made assumptions about their diet and culture from the plant and animal remains and tools they found with the skeletal remains.

Scientists have called one group of early near-humans *Australopithecines* [ô'strə lō-pith'ə sēns]. Remains of Australopithecines have been found in Africa. The first were found in 1924 at Taung [tä ung'] in South Africa. Then in 1959, a British husband-and-wife team of anthropologists, Louis and Mary Leakey, pieced together a complete skull from fragments found at the Olduvai [ōl'dü vā] Gorge in Tanzania. This individual had a low brow and long face, with large, deep jaws. Since then, the skeletal remains of many Australopithecines have been found. Scientists who studied the bones think these creatures walked upright.

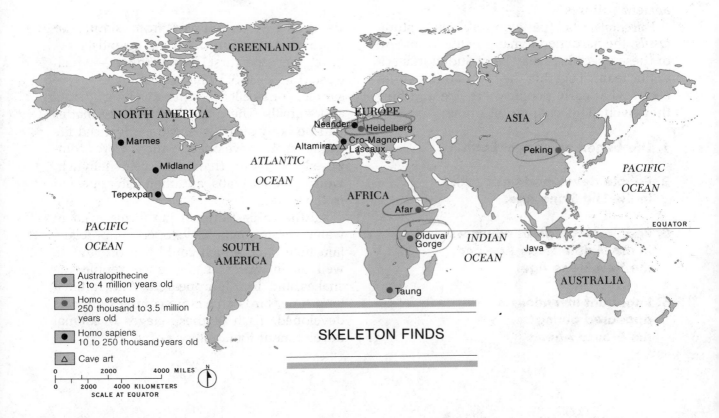

SKELETON FINDS

Australopithecine
2 to 4 million years old

Homo erectus
250 thousand to 3.5 million years old

Homo sapiens
10 to 250 thousand years old

△ Cave art

0   2000   4000 MILES
0   2000   4000 KILOMETERS
SCALE AT EQUATOR

Early people often carved pictures on pieces of animal bones. This carving shows fish and deer.

Living at the same time as some of the later Australopithecines were creatures more like modern humans. Scientists call them *Homo erectus* [hō′mō ə rek′təs]. The word *Homo*, from the Latin word for *man*, is the scientific term for humans. The word *erectus* means they walked upright.

The first remains of *Homo erectus* were found in 1891 by Eugene Dubois [Y zhen′ dʏbwä′], a Dutch surgeon and anthropologist. He found the top of a skull, three teeth, and a left thighbone in a dry river bed on the island of Java. From these remains, and others found in China, Africa, and Europe, anthropologists conclude that *Homo Erectus* was less than five feet (1.5 meters) tall. The head hung forward on the chest, and the strong teeth and jaws stuck outward. The skull was small and very thick, and the forehead sloped back. The oldest known *Homo erectus* fossil is the skull of a 2- or 3-year-old baby. It was found on Java and is presumed to have lived 1.9 million years ago. Other important discoveries were made in China near Peking and in Germany near Heidelberg [hī′dlbèrg′].

The study of skeletal remains suggests that changes took place over thousands of years. The brain became larger, the teeth became smaller, and the legs became longer and straighter enabling individuals to stand more erectly. Finds from the Neander Gorge in Germany and the Cro-Magnon [krō-mag′nən] cave in France show these changes. Scientists label these skeletons *Homo sapiens*, which means "thinking man."

section review 1

1. According to most geologists, how old is Earth? How were the oceans formed?

2. According to most scientists, what were the first living things? Where did these early life forms dwell?

3. How were Australopithecines and *Homo erectus* different from modern human beings? What physical changes apparently took place in human development?

4. What kind of remains have been found at the Neander Gorge and the Cro-Magnon cave?

2 People developed basic skills in the Old Stone Age

Generally, the time from about 2 million B.C. to about 3000 B.C. is called the Stone Age because people of this time made many of their weapons and tools of stone. Of course,

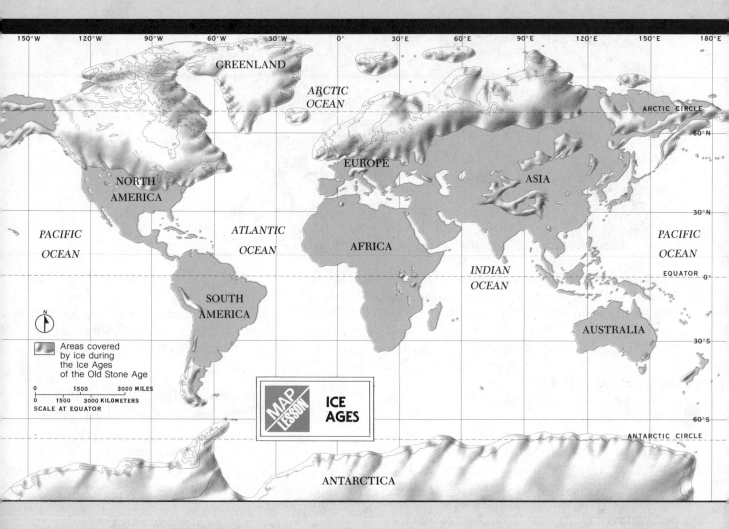

150°W 120°W 90°W 60°W 30°W 0° 30°E 60°E 90°E 120°E 150°E 180°E

GREENLAND

ARCTIC OCEAN

ARCTIC CIRCLE

60°N

NORTH AMERICA

EUROPE

ASIA

30°N

PACIFIC OCEAN

ATLANTIC OCEAN

AFRICA

INDIAN OCEAN

PACIFIC OCEAN

EQUATOR 0°

SOUTH AMERICA

AUSTRALIA

30°S

Areas covered by ice during the Ice Ages of the Old Stone Age

0   1500   3000 MILES
0 1500 3000 KILOMETERS
SCALE AT EQUATOR

MAP LESSON

ICE AGES

60°S

ANTARCTIC CIRCLE

ANTARCTICA

■ MAP LESSON 1: ICE AGES

1. During the Ice Ages, vast amounts of Earth were covered by ice. Study the map to determine which areas had the greater amount of surface covered by ice sheets:

  a. North America or South America
  b. Africa or Europe
  c. Asia or Antarctica
  d. North America or Asia
  e. South America or Africa
  f. Asia or Australia
  g. Europe or Asia
  h. Greenland or Australia
  i. Alaska or Arabia
  j. Siberia or Scandinavia

2. This map uses a Mercator projection to show the world. This is a basic map form that is used today. It always shows true directions and accurate shapes, but it greatly distorts areas above 60° latitude. Look at the map and determine which area is more distorted:

  a. Antarctica or Europe
  b. Alaska or Arabia
  c. Greenland or Australia
  d. areas along the equator or areas within the Arctic Circle
  e. areas within the Antarctic Circle or Europe
  f. Greenland or Madagascar
  g. Iceland or Australia
  h. Iceland or Africa

people who lived in this period did not know it was the Stone Age. It is a term that modern archaeologists use. They divide the Stone Age into three periods according to the kinds of stone-working done in each period. The earliest is called the Old Stone Age, or *Paleolithic* [pā′lē ə lith′ik] period. It lasted until about 8000 B.C. The Middle Stone Age, or *Mesolithic* [mes′ə lith′ik] period, lasted from about 8000 B.C. to 6000 B.C. The New Stone Age, or *Neolithic* [nē′ə lith′ik] period lasted from about 6000 B.C. to 3000 B.C.

During these very long stone ages, humans progressed more than all other living things. They were able to learn from experience and devise ways of doing things, and they were able to exchange ideas with others. Such capacities have helped humans live in a variety of environments and make steady advances in their ways of living.

Early people developed tools and skills. One of the first advances was the development of crude tools and weapons. People found ways of shaping rocks to sizes and forms that were helpful to them. They made the fist hatchet, an early tool and weapon, by using one rock to chip another. One end of a rock was left thick so that it would fit into one hand, and the other end was chipped to a point or edge that could be used for striking or cutting. With such weapons, people could hunt animals larger than those they could kill with their hands and teeth alone.

People found uses for fire. Most anthropologists believe that it took thousands of years for people to learn to use fire. People knew of fire because they saw grass or forests burning where lightning struck. If the fire was small, they were not afraid of it. They may have picked up burning sticks and used them to frighten off dangerous animals. This gave people another weapon for use against their natural enemies. Later, people learned to keep a fire burning by adding wood or

leaves. They learned to cover the fire with ashes at night so there would be coals glowing in the morning for rekindling the flames. An even longer time passed before people learned to start a fire.

Glaciers affected the way people lived. Fire became very important to people in regions affected by *glaciers*. These giant masses of ice covered much of the Northern Hemisphere during four different periods in the Old Stone Age. In each period, called an Ice Age, the polar ice caps gradually expanded toward the equator, eventually melted, and retreated toward the poles. The map called Ice Ages shows the greatest extent of land covered by ice during the Ice Ages of the Old Stone Age. Ice covered much of northern and central Europe, northern Asia, and North America.

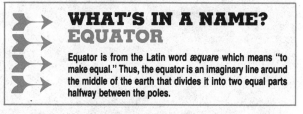

WHAT'S IN A NAME?
EQUATOR

Equator is from the Latin word *æquare* which means "to make equal." Thus, the equator is an imaginary line around the middle of the earth that divides it into two equal parts halfway between the poles.

As the ice moved south, it pushed millions of tons of gravel, boulders, and stones ahead of it. In North America, glaciers gouged out what became the Great Lakes, and water from melting ice formed the Ohio and Missouri rivers. About 50 thousand years ago, the glaciers stopped moving; about 20 thousand years ago, they began melting.

During the Ice Ages, many people and animals died from exposure or starvation. Some animals moved to warmer areas; others adapted to the cold. Some developed thick hides or coats of fur. Among these were the woolly mammoth and woolly rhinoceros.

Some people also adapted to the cold world. They lived in caves and learned to wear animal skins for warmth. To make such clothing, they had to invent new tools—stone knives for skinning and bone tools for

Southwestern France is pretty country where for tens of thousands of years small, swift rivers have cut through the limestone hills to form countless ridges, grottoes, and caves. One of the rivers, the Vesere in the Dordogne valley, served as a highway for prehistoric people. And these early people used the nearby caves, too. The most famous cave in the area, the Lascaux Cave, is dramatic evidence of this prehistoric use. As often happens, the cave was rediscovered by accident in modern times.

On the morning of September 12, 1940, five teenage boys living near Lascaux took their rifles and dog and went hunting for pheasants and rabbits in the nearby hills. While in the woods around Lascaux, they lost their dog. After much whistling and calling, they at last heard muffled barks coming from a large, deep hole in the ground. Carefully, the boys climbed down to save their pet. About 25 feet (7.5 meters) down, they came to the darkened opening of a cave. The boys lit some matches and advanced into the gloom.

Peering around, they saw that they were standing in an oval room some 60 feet (18 meters) long and about 30 feet (9 meters) wide. A vaulted ceiling curved above them. And covering the sloping walls were dozens of drawings of animals. There were horses and stags, sprawling bulls, oxen with elongated bodies full of slow movement, deer with delicate, branching antlers, sturdy ponies, fawn-colored horses, and strangely spotted bulls. All the animals were painted in shades of black, brown, yellow, and crimson. It was an awe-inspiring sight.

The boys' matches burned for about twenty seconds. In that fraction of a minute, they had stepped back twenty thousand years. They had looked upon some of the oldest paintings known. What they had seen had been hidden from human eyes for thousands of years.

Altogether, the Lascaux Cave contains more than 80 pictures that represent a wealth of prehistoric art. Archaeological experts have determined that the Lascaux pictures were drawn by New Stone Age people and that the Cave was probably used for magic rites. The Cave soon became famous, and tourists began to visit it. Today, the Lascaux Cave is under the care of the French government and is open to the public.

Above is the cave at Lascaux. It shows how the ceiling was used for drawings. *Below* are two of the types of drawing styles found in the cave.

scraping the flesh and fat from the inner side of animal skins. They invented spears, and later the bow and arrow, which served hunters and fighters until the gun came into use about 1300 A.D.

Neanderthal people advanced beyond their ancestors. The Neanderthal [nē an'dər täl] people were one Old Stone Age type that adjusted to the cold. They used fire, lived in caves wherever possible, and made clothing from animal skins. By studying the tools and weapons that Neanderthal people used, anthropologists know that these people learned to fasten handles to chipped stones to make crude knives and spears. Such a small pointed stone is called a microlith [mī'krə lith]. Neanderthal people also had religious beliefs. For instance, the food and weapons found in graves suggest that they believed in some kind of life after death.

Cro-Magnon people used art. Late in the last Ice Age, about 30 thousand years ago, a group of people lived near the Cro-Magnon cave in southern France. They invented better tools and weapons than did Neanderthals. Cro-Magnon people made spears with fine flint points and harpoons of reindeer horn and bone. To sew skins together, they developed bone needles. The Cro-Magnon people were also artists. They carved figures of animals from horn and bone, molded statues in clay, and carved and painted the walls of caves. On the ceiling of the cave of Altamira, discovered by Don Marcelino and his daughter, are many such drawings of animals. Anthropologists believe this Cro-Magnon art had a religious purpose.

Early people populated the world. During the long Old Stone Age, people migrated to various parts of the world. Little is known about this travel. By about 30,000 B.C., however, modern humans lived in Europe, Australia, Asia, and Africa, and had crossed the Bering Strait into the Americas.

section review 2

1. Into what three periods have modern archaeologists divided the Stone Age?

2. What kinds of tools and weapons did people make in the Old Stone Age? How did these new weapons and tools change people's lives?

3. How did people probably learn about fire? How did fire change their way of living?

4. List three ways Neanderthal people adapted to living in the Ice Age.

3 People made great advances in the Middle Stone Age and the New Stone Age

Toward the end of the Old Stone Age, the glacial ice receded to the north, and forests and grasslands grew in its place. About 8000 B.C., another stage in people's progress toward civilization began. This was the Middle Stone Age, or the Mesolithic period.

An important Mesolithic advance was the first crude pottery. Pots made of sun-baked clay were used to store food. By about 7000 B.C., kiln-fired bowls and jars were used to store water. Since many Mesolithic peoples lived along the shores of rivers, lakes, and seas, fish and shellfish were their main foods. Middle Stone Age people invented the fishhook and many types of nets and learned how to hollow out logs to make boats.

During Mesolithic times, people tamed the wild dogs, such as jackals, that followed groups of humans. Dogs became valuable for hunting and for guarding property.

About 6000 B.C., the Middle Stone Age gradually gave way to the New Stone Age. New Stone Age peoples learned to sharpen stone tools and weapons by grinding them against gritty stones instead of by chipping them. However, this is only one of many advances that made New Stone Age peoples different from those of the Old Stone Age.

People began to farm. New ways of getting food were among the most important discoveries of the New Stone Age. Neolithic people learned to tame such wild animals as sheep, goats, pigs, and cattle so they could have meat when they needed it. When herds and flocks of these *domesticated*, or tamed, animals ate most of the grass supply near a camping place, the people and animals

Daily Life

The tools used by ancient people tell much about the way those people lived. These tools are all made of stone or bone. This tells us that ancient people made tools from the hardest materials they could easily obtain. The three harpoons *below left* are made of bone and are about five inches (13 centimeters) long. The stone scraper, *below center*, was probably used to skin animals and scrape hides. The spear thrower *below right* was carved from an antler and was decorated with a bird. The spear thrower gave a hunter greater force and distance in a throw.

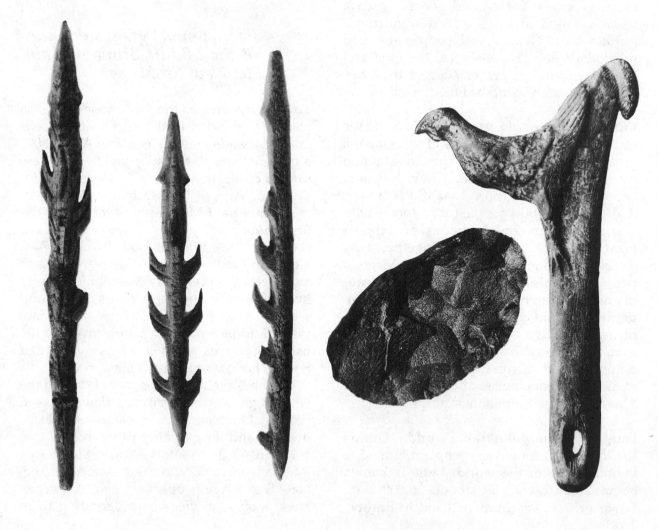

moved to fresh grazing lands. This way of life is called *nomadic* [nō mad′ik], and the people who travel from pasture to pasture are called *nomads*.

About this same time, one of the greatest discoveries of all time was made. People found that a seed planted in the earth would grow into a plant that would furnish food and many more seeds. In this way, people learned to grow food—to farm.

With this new knowledge of herding animals and raising plants, people could produce their own food supply. They no longer had to depend on luck in hunting animals or in finding edible fruits, roots, and seeds. People became less likely to starve. With a reliable food supply, people could turn their attention to improving other ways of living.

New Stone Age people developed other skills. During the New Stone Age, people learned to spin and weave. Linen fabrics dating from about 5000 B.C. have been found in Egypt. Linen is made from *flax*, a plant, whose long stalk fibers are spun into thread and then woven into cloth. Later, other people learned to spin the fleece from sheep into thread and weave it into woolen cloth. During this period, people also learned to press and roll animal hairs together to make felt blankets.

Important discoveries were made at an ever faster rate. Farming led to the invention of hoes and other stone tools for cultivating the soil. Milling stones were invented for grinding grain. Pottery-making was improved by heating the clay in a fire so that the pots were stronger. In time, potters learned to make a wide variety of cups, bowls, and plates and to decorate them with paint.

People learned to live in communities. Far back in the Paleolithic period, people had learned to help each other in hunting and fishing. Groups of families joined together for this purpose and formed a simple type of community. When farming began, many people established permanent settlements. Some farmers began to think of the land they farmed as belonging to them or their group. To protect their fields and animals, groups of New Stone Age farmers formed villages or small towns for safety against enemies.

As people began to live together in larger groups, they began to realize the need for rules. These rules served as laws to protect individual life, the community's food and water supplies, and important property. People developed governments to enforce these laws. Historians believe that in the earliest food-producing societies, the government was controlled by a small group of armed men, each of whom had a voice in the government.

In the more advanced food-producing societies, irrigation was very important. The government was controlled by members of the families who lived closest to the river. These families could become powerful because they could control the water supply for the entire community and for the crops. Often, the people looked to an important member of such a family to serve as the ruler and decision-maker for the whole group.

Anthropologists believe that behavior among Stone Age people was governed by custom. Different groups of Stone Age people developed their own ways of arranging marriages, bringing up children, distributing food, and showing respect for different members of the group. Anyone who broke these rules was considered a wrongdoer.

Stone Age people probably punished most wrongdoers by humiliating them. Anyone who cheated or injured another person was scorned and ridiculed by all the members of the group. People living in small groups were very dependent on each other for survival; unpopularity was a severe form of punishment. Even within small groups, however, some offenses, such as murder or treason, were punished in more drastic ways. After the group decided a person was guilty, the wrongdoer could be executed or be banished from the group and made to try to live alone. As people began to farm and groups became larger, more offenses were punished formally. Laws usually included the punishment to be given for each offense.

Religion, too, became more elaborate as the size of groups increased. People turned to certain men and women in their group who seemed to be skilled at praying and understanding what others needed. These special persons often became kinds of priests. It was their job to pray and try to keep droughts, famines, floods, and plagues from happening. To gain favor with the spirits of nature, people of the New Stone Age developed religious ceremonies, particularly dances. These ceremonies often were carried out for the purpose of producing good crops. In some groups, the powers of nature were believed to be gods. To gain favor with the gods, people prayed to them and offered them gifts.

section review 3

1. Name two or more advances people made in the Mesolithic period.

2. What improvements did New Stone Age people make in their tools and weapons? What new skills did they develop?

3. Why was the herder or farmer safer from starvation than the hunter?

4. How did farming change ancient people's way of living?

4 Important inventions appeared during the Bronze Age

As long as people were dependent upon stone tools, they were limited in the kinds of work they could do. Stone tools and weapons often broke easily. To make better tools, people needed a longer-lasting material that could be molded more easily into different sizes and shapes.

People learned to make tools and weapons of metal. Toward the end of the New Stone Age, people in the Middle East found that they could use copper in an almost pure metallic state to make tools and weapons. At first, they hammered the copper to shape it. Later, they learned that they could melt it, pour the liquid metal into molds, and make tools and weapons in desired sizes or shapes.

Early metalworkers made another advance when they discovered that tin and copper melted together in the right amounts made a metal called bronze. Bronze was easier to shape, was harder, and gave a sharper cutting edge than copper alone. Because bronze was the chief metal for about 2,000 years, the period in which it was used is called the Bronze Age. This age began about the year 3000 B.C.

Progress was made in farming, transportation, and commerce. Along with metal tools came other inventions. One of these was the plow drawn by animals. At first, farmers planted seeds in holes made with a digging stick. Then they learned to make a simple hoe that they pulled through the soil with a rope. The next step was to harness animals, such as the ox, to an improved hoe that became a plow. This invention enabled farmers to cultivate large fields instead of

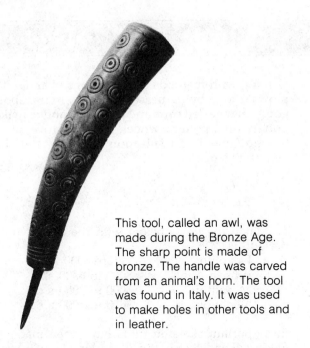

This tool, called an awl, was made during the Bronze Age. The sharp point is made of bronze. The handle was carved from an animal's horn. The tool was found in Italy. It was used to make holes in other tools and in leather.

small plots. Another aid to farming was the development of better ways to control and use water for crops. In places where there was little rainfall, farmers learned to *irrigate*, that is, to bring water to their fields by digging ditches to lakes and streams. They also learned to build dikes to protect their fields from floods.

One problem for early people was finding ways to transport heavy loads. Middle Stone Age people used a crude sled. Later, an ox was used to pull the sled. Someone may have learned that a sled could be pulled more easily if poles or logs were put under it so that it moved forward as the logs rolled along the ground. Many experiments were made before people invented the wheel.

Just as early people found easier ways to move heavy loads on land, they also found easier ways to carry these loads safely across water. One of the most important early inventions was the sailboat. Sailors discovered how to take advantage of the winds that always blew in the same direction, called *prevailing winds*. They also found the shortest sea routes from one place to another.

Bronze Age people also learned to build a *potter's wheel*. This small, flat wheel was set on top of a vertical axle, called a spindle. The potter threw a lump of wet clay onto the wheel and then, while turning the wheel, shaped the clay with his or her hand. The potter's wheel made possible the production of more pots of a more uniform shape and size than had been possible to make before this time.

All of these new discoveries called for specialized services or kinds of labor. *Commerce*, or trade, began when people turned to one another for certain goods and services. As the supply of food increased and surpluses were produced, workers were freed for other jobs. No longer were all people hunters, gatherers, herders, or farmers. Some became metalsmiths, sailors, potters, or tradespeople.

Different peoples passed through the prehistoric ages at different times. People around the world did not advance from one stage of prehistoric development to the next at the same time. Some people remained hunters and gatherers while others became herders and farmers. Today, there are a few isolated areas where people are still living in the Stone Age.

section review 4

1. In what ways was bronze better than copper for making tools and weapons?

2. What improvements in farming, transportation, and pottery-making took place during the Bronze Age?

3. What is commerce? How did it begin?

4. Did all people pass through the stages of prehistoric development at the same times?

SECTION SUMMARIES

1. Life began on ancient Earth. According to geologists, Earth was formed about 4.5 to 5 billion years ago from a flaming mass of gas and vapor. Seas and oceans formed, and gradually early forms of life appeared in them. As living things developed from simple to more complex forms, land plants and animals appeared. This took millions of years. Scientists believe that *Homo sapiens* came quite late in the long span of the development of life on Earth. From skeletal remains, anthropologists have learned about the changes that occurred from Australopithecines and *Homo erectus* to Cro-Magnon, the first modern human beings.

2. People developed basic skills in the Old Stone Age. Because people could think, remember, and talk, they were able to make advances in their ways of living. During the Old Stone Age, which lasted from about 2 million B.C. to about 8000 B.C., people learned to make stone tools and weapons by chipping one stone against another. They discovered uses for fire. Neanderthal people learned to live in caves and to make clothing of skins, thereby adapting to the Ice Age. Cro-Magnon people made advances in tools and weapons and painted pictures on the walls of caves.

3. People made great advances in the Middle Stone Age and the New Stone Age. About 8000 B.C., the Middle Stone Age began, following the end of the Ice Ages. During this period, people tamed the dog, made the first pottery from sunbaked clay, and hollowed out logs to make crude boats. In the New Stone Age, which began about 6000 B.C., people learned to make sharper stone tools, to spin and weave, and to fire clay to make pots. They became food producers by domesticating animals and growing plants from seed. When people began to farm, they settled down to live in one place. They formed towns for protection, made laws, created governments, and developed elaborate forms of religion.

4. Important inventions appeared during the Bronze Age. Bronze Age people learned to make metal tools and weapons, to improve farming with methods of water control and with plows drawn by harnessed animals, to transport goods in wheeled carts and sailboats, and to make pottery on a potter's wheel. Such improvements brought about specialization in work and the beginnings of trade.

Who? What? When? Where?

1. Match the items below with the correct time period:

a. Paleolithic	before 8000 B.C.
b. Bronze Age	8000 to 6000 B.C.
c. Mesolithic	6000 to 3000 B.C.
d. Neolithic	3000 to 1000 B.C.

2. Important skeleton finds have been made at Peking, Heidelberg, the Neander Gorge, Afar, and the Olduvai Gorge. Look at the map called Skeleton Finds in this chapter. On what continent is each site located?

3. Match the people with the location of their find:

a. María and Don Marcelino	Altamira
b. the Leakeys	Java
c. Eugene Dubois	Olduvai

4. Use each of these terms in a sentence that explains its meaning. Example: A geologist is a scientist who studies Earth's crust.

a. anthropologist	e. irrigate
b. archaeologist	f. geologist
c. domesticated	g. nomads
d. *Homo sapiens*	h. potter's wheel

Questions for Critical Thinking

1. Explain how specialization of labor began. Why did this make important changes in the lives of people? Are people today becoming more specialized in the work that they do? Give examples.

2. How did the inventions of farming and weaving by prehistoric people help civilization to progress?

3. Why do you think groups of prehistoric people remained hunters while others went on to become herders or farmers? Why are there a few areas today where people are still living in the Stone Age?

4. What might be some of the difficulties that modern archaeologists face in doing their work? Make a list of the difficulties.

Skill Activities

1. Read *Lucy: The Beginnings of Humankind* by Donald Johanson and Maitland Edey to learn more about this anthropologist's work in his own words. (Simon and Schuster, 1981)

2. Make a time line with pictures showing the order in which scientific theories say these events took place:
   a. jellyfish, worms, snails, crabs, and fish developed
   b. modern humans (*Homo sapiens*) developed
   c. Earth was a flaming mass of gas and steam
   d. simple, one-celled, water-dwelling plants and animals appeared
   e. Earth cooled and hardened
   f. birds and more complex animals developed

3. Imagine that you are an archaeologist digging in a lava bed 7,000 years old and you have found a crude clay pot, fishhooks, and a hollowed-out log. How would you interpret your find?

chapter **1** *quiz*

Section 1

1. Scientists who excavate the remains of ancient cultures are called: a. geologists, b. amphibians, c. archaeologists

2. According to most scientific theories the earliest forms of life began in the: a. deserts, b. oceans, c. atmosphere

3. Modern humans belong to the group called: a. Australopithecines, b. *Homo sapiens*, c. *Homo erectus*

Section 2

4. True or false: Two qualities that make humans superior to other animals are their abilities to think and talk.

5. Food found in ancient graves suggests that early people believed in: a. leaving records for later peoples, b. life after death, c. moving often from place to place

6. True or false: Cro-Magnon people painted on cave walls for religious reasons.

Section 3

7. An achievement of the New Stone Age was: a. use of fire, b. bow and arrow, c. farming

8. True or false: Neolithic people learned to domesticate animals such as sheep and cattle.

9. True or false: Stone Age people had few if any religious beliefs.

Section 4

10. The first metal used by most early peoples was: a. iron, b. copper, c. bronze

11. An invention of the Bronze Age was: a. bow, b. potter's wheel, c. hoe

12. True or false: The digging stick was an example of the improved tools made during the Bronze Age.

THE FIRST CIVILIZATIONS

Although Pharaoh Tutankhamen was not very important in real life, the splendor of his tomb attests to the glories of ancient Egypt. This gold panel from the tomb shows Queen Ankhesenamun rubbing scented oil on the pharaoh.

The first civilizations developed along rivers in Egypt, the Middle East, India, and China. The rivers were so important to the lives of the people who lived along them that they were worshiped as gods. These lines from a hymn to the Nile were sung 4,000 years ago.

Praise to thee, O Nile, that issueth from the earth, and cometh to nourish Egypt. Of hidden nature, a darkness in the daytime . . . .

That watereth the meadows, he that [the sun god] hath created to nourish all cattle. That giveth drink to the desert places, which are far from water: it is his dew that falleth from heaven.

Egypt is a model birthplace for civilization. If you were to head south into the countryside from Cairo [kī′rō], the modern capital of Egypt, you would soon be in a narrow valley. You would see fields, vivid green with fine crops. You would also see the vast expanse of dry, golden brown desert that borders this river valley. The Nile River makes this contrast possible. Without the river, all would be desert. Every September, the Nile floods, bringing huge amounts of water that can be used for irrigation. At the same time, the soil is made richer by deposits of Nile mud and silt, the fine particles of earth and sand that are carried by moving water. These conditions have been the same for thousands of years. This fertile soil gave rich harvests.

In times past, abundant harvests encouraged the population to grow. Everyone did not have to work at getting food; some people were free to spend their lives in other kinds of work. In this kind of situation, over hundreds of years, people developed what we call civilization.

Civilization is the advanced stage of human life in which people have cities and organized governments. People have different occupations. Some are merchants, others are soldiers, farmers, weavers, and so on. Most civilized people have writing to communicate with and to keep records and a calendar to keep track of time. They have numbers to keep track of how much is spent, how much is paid, and how much is owed. History really begins with civilization, and Egypt is one of the places where civilization began.

The same favorable conditions for human progress existed in Mesopotamia, the land between the Tigris [tī′gris] and Euphrates [yü-frā′tēz] rivers. In what is today Pakistan and western India, the Indus River performed the same services as the Nile.

In China, around the Hwang Ho (Yellow River), conditions also encouraged progress. Here, strong winds from Central Asia had deposited rich dust or light soil, called *loess* [les], forming a great plain. The area was excellent for farming.

In civilization, people improved their ways of living. This chapter tells how:

1. Civilization developed in Egypt.

2. City-states and empires flourished in Mesopotamia.

3. An ancient city revealed early Indus civilization.

4. Chinese civilization developed along the Hwang Ho.

1 Civilization developed in Egypt

By 5000 B.C., New Stone Age people living along the Nile had learned to farm barley and wheat and to raise cattle. From this modest beginning developed one of the first civilizations in the world.

Egyptian farmers took the first steps toward civilization. The farmers of Egypt relied on the September flood of the Nile to bring new soil and water to their fields. The new soil kept the land fertile for growing crops. During other months, farmers dug irrigation ditches to get Nile water to their fields.

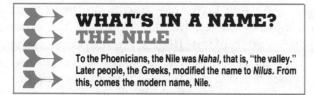

WHAT'S IN A NAME?
THE NILE

To the Phoenicians, the Nile was *Nahal*, that is, "the valley." Later people, the Greeks, modified the name to *Nilus*. From this, comes the modern name, Nile.

In order to dig the ditches, keep them in repair, and build dams for the benefit of all, the farmers formed groups. Each group had a leader, or *administrator*, who directed the work and made rules for the workers to follow. In time, as the work became more complicated and the groups contained more people, the leader grew more important and more powerful. He directed the work of planting and harvesting crops, and he decided whether to store or distribute crop surpluses. These early cooperative efforts, accompanied by the rise of an administrative class, probably were the earliest form of local government in Egypt.

Because the farmers needed to keep track of the passage of time in order to plan for planting and harvesting, they counted the days between the arrivals of the Nile floods. They studied the paths of the sun, moon, and stars to learn when to expect the spring planting season. Their studies led to the invention of a calendar that first came into use around 4000 B.C.

The Egyptians noticed that on one day each year about flood time a bright star—now known as Sirius [sir′ē əs]—appeared in the eastern sky before sunrise. By counting the days between appearances of this star, they figured that the length of a year is 365 days. They divided the year into twelve months and gave each month thirty days, with five days added at the end of the year. Although a year is actually about one-quarter day longer than 365 days, the calendar served the Egyptians well.

The development of irrigation, the rise of local governments, and the invention of a calendar took place between 5000 and 3100 B.C. During this time, the Egyptians also developed a system of writing and discovered how to make copper tools. They invented the plow, which greatly increased crop production, and much later, around 2000 B.C., they learned to make bronze by combining copper and tin.

The Old Kingdom began with the unification of Egypt (3100–2270 B.C.). At first, Egypt simply consisted of a number of independent, separate villages. In time, local rulers won control over nearby villages and then over larger areas. As generations passed, a ruling class of nobles and princes emerged. Perhaps because these nobles lived in large and luxurious houses, the Egyptian word *pharaoh* [fer′ō], which means "great house," also became the word for king.

By 3100 B.C., two separate kingdoms had developed. King Menes [mē′nēz], the ruler of one, united Egypt and made Memphis the capital city. The reign of King Menes marked the first time in history that a strong government ruled so large an area. He also founded the first Egyptian *dynasty* [dī′nə stē], that is, the first series of rulers belonging to the same family. With the unification of Egypt, a great period called the *Old Kingdom* began.

During the Old Kingdom, trading ships sailed up and down the Nile, and expeditions left the Nile Valley to trade with peoples in other parts of Africa and the Mediterranean. Artisans carved fine statues, wove soft linen cloth, and made pottery with the use of a potter's wheel. Workers continued to use stone tools, but they also made some tools from copper.

The Pyramids were built during the Old Kingdom as tombs for the pharaohs. The largest pyramid, built at the town of Giza [gē′zə] for Pharaoh Cheops [kē′ops], is about 450 feet (135 meters) high. Each of its four

GEOGRAPHY
A Key to History

NILE CURRENTS AND ETESIAN WINDS

About 5,000 years ago, the Egyptians learned to use the regular summer winds to move sailboats. As a result, they greatly expanded trade and travel along the Nile River.

In the summer, the air above the north African desert becomes very hot. As the air heats, it expands, becomes lighter, and rises. The air above the Mediterranean stays cooler than that above the desert. The cooler air stays near the ground, because it is heavier. It flows south to replace the hot air rising from the desert. This flow of air toward the desert forms the winds.

Etesian [ē tē′shən] is the name given to the winds that blow across the Mediterranean Sea into Egypt each summer. They begin in about the middle of May and continue until mid-October. During the day, the winds sometimes reach speeds of 40 miles (64 kilometers) an hour. During the cooler nights, the winds die down, since not as much hot air rises from the desert.

By harnessing the winds' power, the Egyptians carried on a two-way trade along the Nile. The river current carried boats north (downstream) toward the Mediterranean. The Etesian winds pushed sailboats south (upstream) toward Thebes and Karnak.

Thus, the Egyptians found a way to solve the problem that faces all river-traders: how to move goods upstream, against the current. For the times, the system offered a quick and easy way to travel. And it allowed Egyptian traders to do business all up and down the river.

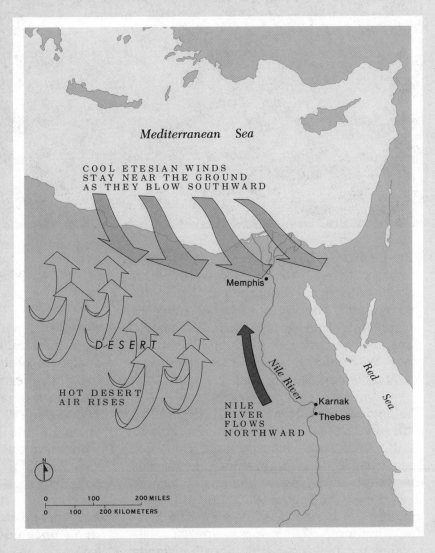

COOL ETESIAN WINDS STAY NEAR THE GROUND AS THEY BLOW SOUTHWARD

Mediterranean Sea

Memphis

DESERT

HOT DESERT AIR RISES

NILE RIVER FLOWS NORTHWARD

Nile River

Karnak

Thebes

Red Sea

N

| 0 | 100 | 200 MILES |
| 0 | 100 | 200 KILOMETERS |

More than 80 pyramids were built during the Old Kingdom. These at Giza are guarded by the Great Sphinx, a huge figure with a man's head and lion's body.

sides measures 756 feet (226.8 meters) long at the base. It is said that it took twenty years and the work of 100 thousand people to build this pyramid. The largest stone blocks weigh several tons (megagrams) each. To quarry, transport, and raise these huge blocks into place with almost no machinery was a remarkable engineering feat.

The Middle Kingdom arose (2060–1785 B.C.). In 2270 B.C., civil war brought an end to the Old Kingdom. For more than 200 years, rival leaders fought among themselves for wealth and power. Eventually princes from the city of Thebes [thēbz] reunified the kingdom. This period is known as the Middle Kingdom. The princes from Thebes became the new pharaohs, and they made Egypt strong and prosperous. They encouraged art and literature. They began new irrigation projects that greatly increased the crop area. Pharaohs of the Middle Kingdom built a canal that joined the business centers of the Nile Valley with the Red Sea.

About 1680 B.C., while weak from internal disorder, Egypt was conquered by invaders from Asia called the Hyksos [hik'sos]. An ancient record speaks of them savagely burning cities, destroying Egyptian temples, and treating the people with great cruelty. The Hyksos ruled Egypt harshly for about 100 years. But the Egyptians learned how to fight wars with horses and chariots like the Hyksos. This knowledge was useful to the Egyptians later.

Egypt freed itself during the New Kingdom and became an empire (1580–1085 B.C.). Thebes provided leaders who drove the Hyksos out and restored Egyptian rule to Egypt. This victory marked the beginning of the New Kingdom, or Empire. When a group of people conquers other very different groups of peoples and rules these new lands and peoples, we call this expanded nation an *empire*. During the New Kingdom, the phar-

? A MYSTERY IN HISTORY

THE CHEOPS BOAT

People from earliest times have been enticed by rivers, lakes, and oceans. To be able to navigate on water gave your ancestors the ability to fish for food, to transport heavy loads more easily, and to avoid long travels over land. Possibly they enjoyed being on water just for the fun of it. So they hollowed out logs, fashioned boats from reeds and twigs, and made crude canoes.

How far had this boat building skill progressed by about 2500 B.C.? An answer to this question may have been found in 1954 A.D. in Egypt. Workmen clearing a great pile of sand and rubbish from one of the sides of the great Cheops pyramid, near Cairo, uncovered 41 huge stone blocks serving as a cover for a large pit. An archaeologist, remembering that the decayed remains of a boat had been found in a pit nearby, began to chisel through the stones. He soon chipped a hole large enough to reveal a boat oar.

Over the next 18 months, the heavy stone covering was slowly removed, revealing a jumble of boat pieces, some 1,224 in all. They were well preserved, laid out in 13 criss-cross layers, and ready to be put together. But how to put the boat together was a puzzle. It was as though the archaeologist had discovered a giant do-it-yourself kit with no instructions.

An expert restorer of old relics was employed. He spent many months studying the designs of boats that had been chiseled on tombs and pyramids. He talked to old boat builders along the Nile who had ideas about how the craft should be assembled. Finally, after four years, the task was finished: a beautifully shaped boat 143 feet (40.8 meters) long, powered by ten rowing oars, each to be pulled by two people.

The discovery of the boat set off a dispute among scholars as to what the boat had been used for. One opinion was that it had been used as a floating hearse to carry the pharaoh's body from his capital at Memphis to his tomb at Giza. It had been rowed upstream and deposited in the pit beside the pyramid of Cheops. Another view held that the boat had never been used at all, but was buried near the pharaoh so it would be ready for voyages in his afterlife.

To add to the mystery, other archaeologists argued that in a closed pit nearby there was a second boat. This one would be equipped with sails instead of oars, enabling the craft to sail up the Nile as well as downstream. But so far, the second boat pit has not been excavated. The Cheops boat has deteriorated so much since its discovery that scientists worry about harm to a possible second boat.

A special museum was built for the Cheops boat. But the boat has not done well there. In fact, the boat stayed in better condition during its 46 centuries in the pit than it has during the few decades since its discovery. The special museum needs all new, heat-resistant windows and air-conditioning. But such special care is very expensive, and there is no more money. So the Cheops boat slowly disintegrates, and the second boat pit remains unopened.

Meanwhile, the questions continue. Will the second pit hold a boat, or will the pit be empty? Will the possible second boat be like the Cheops boat, or will it have large sails, as some believe? Will the second pit contain something as yet not thought of? Someday, when the preservation money is available, the second pit will be opened. Then the questions may be answered for all of us to know.

Daily Life

Much is known about everyday life in ancient Egypt. A lot of this knowledge comes from the wall paintings and objects found mostly in tombs. The wooden statue *below* of two farmers plowing a field shows much about agricultural methods and levels of technology of the time. For example, the two oxen are held together by a long board across the backs of their necks. It was many centuries before people developed the collar to fit completely around animals' necks. The colored glass vase, *right,* in the shape of a fish is less than 6 inches (14 centimeters) long. Its small size and intricate work give clues to the technological levels of artisans as well as to artistic styles. The painting of two musicians, *bottom right,* shows how women dressed, how they wore their hair, and what kinds of musical instruments they might have used. Transportation can be studied by looking at the boat painting, *center right,* while clothing of the wealthy can be studied by looking at the painting of dinner guests, *below left.*

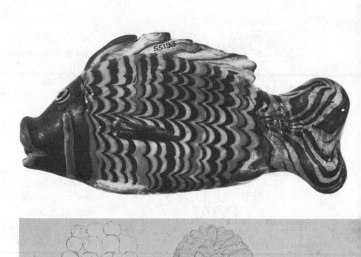

aohs created an empire that extended Egyptian rule into western Asia, far beyond the Nile River Valley.

For about 450 years after 1580 B.C., increased trade and booty from conquered countries made Egypt rich. The capital, Thebes, became a city of statues, temples, and palaces. Egyptian ships carried products, such as wheat and linens, across the Mediterranean to Europe and Asia. The ships returned with lumber and metal weapons, which Egypt needed but did not produce.

By 1100 B.C., Egypt had again grown weak from quarrels among its leaders, rebellions among its conquered peoples, and costly battles with foreign enemies. Years of civil war and foreign invasions followed.

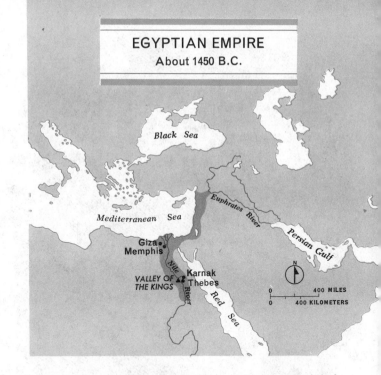

EGYPTIAN EMPIRE
About 1450 B.C.

The power of the pharaohs was absolute. The pharaohs had absolute power over their subjects—partly because most of these rulers governed justly, but primarily because the people believed that the pharaohs were descended from a god and were gods themselves. A government in which the religious leader rules the state as a god's representative is called a *theocracy* [thē ok′rə sē]. In theory, the pharaoh owned all the land, commanded the army, and controlled the irrigation system. Since no one person could administer such a huge kingdom, the pharaoh appointed officials to assist him. However, he made all the important decisions of government. Beginning with the Old Kingdom, Egyptians created a complicated but efficient government that supported the absolute power of the pharaoh.

Egyptian society was divided into three classes. The upper class of people was made up of priests, court nobility, and landed nobility. The men and women who were priests performed religious ceremonies,

especially those having to do with the burial of the dead. The court nobles advised the pharaoh and the queen and carried out their orders. The landed nobility managed their great estates. Women of this class were especially important because land and property were passed from mother to daughter.

The middle class included men and women who became rich through trade. Skilled artisans, who made furniture and jewelry, worked with leather and cloth, and directed the building of tombs and palaces, were also in the middle class. So were professional people such as teachers, artists, doctors, and scribes. *Scribes*, who wrote letters and documents for a living, held an important place in Egyptian life because few people could read or write.

The lower class, to which the great mass of Egyptians belonged, was made up of two groups—slaves and free laborers. The slaves were usually prisoners of war. Like the free laborers, they worked on farms, irrigation systems, roads, and building projects. The

Egyptian tombs contained many different kinds of items, including paintings of the deceased. The wall painting of Queen Nefertari shows her with very dark eyes and skin to stand for death.

free laborers, heavily burdened by taxes, had few political rights. They lived poorly in small, mud-brick homes with few furnishings. However, it was possible for smart and ambitious young Egyptians to rise to higher rank. Sometimes loyal and able slaves were given their freedom. On a few occasions, a talented slave rose to become a government official.

Religion in Egypt was concerned with life after death. Egyptians reasoned that just as plants decline in the autumn and reappear in the spring, so also people must have life after death. They believed that the human body should be preserved after death, as a mummy, in order for the soul to live on. Preserving the body became a highly skilled art. Beliefs about the afterlife led the Egyptians to build large tombs in which to keep the mummified bodies of their dead rulers.

Good conduct was also thought necessary for immortality, or life after death. In the *Book of the Dead*, one of the early Egyptian writings, the soul of a deceased man says to the god of the underworld:

Here am I: I come to thee; I bring to thee
    Right and have put a stop to wrong.
I am not a doer of wrong to men.
I am not one who slayeth his kindred.
I am not one who telleth lies instead of
    truth.
I am not conscious of treason.
I am not a doer of mischief.

The Egyptians worshiped many gods. This practice is called *polytheism* [pol'ē thē'iz'əm]. The most important gods were Amon-Re [ä'mən rā], the sun god, and Osiris [ō sī'ris], the god of the underworld and lord of the afterlife. However, during the reign of Pharaoh Akhenaton [ä'kə nä'tn] in the New Kingdom, a new faith was born. Akhenaton, who ruled from 1379 to 1362 B.C., believed in one supreme god, rather than in many gods. The supreme god, Akhenaton thought, was Aton [ä'ton], the sun. Akhenaton outlawed the worship of all gods but Aton and took government support away from the priests of other gods.

Yet the priests were many and powerful. They succeeded in terrifying the already fearful people into believing that if they obeyed Akhenaton they would suffer the anger of the gods. While Akhenaton lived, his orders were not openly disobeyed. After his death, however, the priests persuaded Egyptians to return to polytheism. In this way, the first attempt at belief in one god died with Akhenaton.

Hieroglyphic writing was developed. Between 4000 and 3000 B.C., the Egyptians developed a kind of picture writing known as *hieroglyphics* [hī'ər ə glif'iks]. The first writings consisted of pictures of objects. Gradually, picture signs came into use for ideas as well as objects. For example, a picture of an eye could mean "sight" or "eye." In time, writers also used picture signs to indicate sound. These developments were only the beginnings of an alphabet. A true alphabet is a set of letters, each representing one or more sounds.

The first Egyptian books were written as early as 4000 B.C. on the material made from *papyrus* [pə pī'rəs], a reed plant. Papyrus is the origin of the English word "paper." Egyptian books consisted of long rolls of papyrus pasted together. Most books were about religion, but some adventure stories were written. These works were probably the first storybooks ever published.

Mathematics and medicine advanced. Because Nile floods washed away markers for land boundaries, the Egyptians surveyed the land often, using geometry to measure the boundaries. Their engineers also used mathematics to work out the precise measurements necessary in the construction of the Pyramids and temples. The Egyptians were good builders in stone, and both sculptors and engineers liked to think big. Religion inspired the building of Egyptian tombs and temples. The most famous temple was that of the god Amon-Re, at Karnak [kär'nak], built between 1290 and 1224 B.C. Part of this great temple still stands. Its hall is larger than a football field and 80 feet (24 meters) high. The roof was supported by rows of giant columns.

As Egyptians studied ways to preserve the human body after death, their doctors became familiar with its anatomy and the healing properties of certain herbs. They also knew how to set broken bones and how to heal wounds.

section review 1

1. How did the farming methods of the early Egyptians lead to the beginning of local governments?

2. What two important things did King Menes do for Egypt?

3. Why can Egyptian government, beginning with the Old Kingdom, be called a theocracy?

4. What kind of writing system did the Egyptians develop? On what kind of material were the first Egyptian books written?

2 City-states and empires flourished in Mesopotamia

About the same time that civilization arose in Egypt, it also emerged in the valley of the Tigris and Euphrates rivers. This region is known as Mesopotamia, or "land between the rivers." Mesopotamia was a part of the Fertile Crescent, a large area that extends in an arc from the southeastern end of the Mediterranean Sea to the Persian Gulf (see the map called the Ancient Middle East on the opposite page).

Many of the peoples in the Fertile Crescent were nomadic herders. They lived, with their flocks, in family groups, or *clans*. When several clans recognize ties with other clans of the same ancestry, this large group is called a *tribe*. A tribe is made up of the people of the clans, their slaves, and some adopted strangers. All the people of a tribe share the same language, religion, and customs. Much of life in the Fertile Crescent was tribal. However, during the years covered in this Section (4000–300 B.C.), some of these tribes settled and built cities.

This book deals mainly with civilized groups whose activities had some influence on the way people live today. But it is important to remember that there were other groups of people busy pursuing other ways of living.

Civilized living in the Fertile Crescent first emerged in a small area of lower Mesopotamia in what is now Iraq [i rak']. The area extended about 500 miles (800 kilometers) northwest from the Persian Gulf. The Bible calls this area the Plain of Shinar [shī'när]. Some authorities believe that one of the earliest civilizations in the world began here.

The Sumerians lived in city-states (4000–2500 B.C.). About 4000 B.C., a tribe known

as the Sumerians [sü mir'ē əns] moved down from the hill country of the northeast into the fertile area of the Tigris and Euphrates rivers. Like the Egyptians, the Sumerians dug canals to control the spring floods and to irrigate the land for farming.

Unlike the Egyptians, who formed a unified nation under the Old Kingdom, the Sumerians created a number of *city-states*. Each city-state included a city and the farmlands and villages around it. The city-states were most prosperous from 2900 to 2400 B.C. During this time, Sumerian farmers raised barley, oats, and dates. Some city dwellers were skilled in crafts, and their products were traded as far away as India and Egypt.

Each city-state was a theocracy. The local god, believed to be the real ruler of the city-state, was represented by an earthly ruler who served as high priest and city governor. The ruler performed administrative duties, such as supervising the irrigation system. Like the Egyptian pharaoh, he was all-powerful, with absolute authority over the people, but he was not considered a god himself, as the Egyptian pharaoh was.

The Sumerians made several important contributions to the civilization of Mesopotamia. One was a form of writing. The Sumerians did not have paper. They used a *stylus*, or pointed stick, to make impressions on soft clay bricks or tablets. The tablets were then baked to give them permanent form. The Sumerians' type of writing is called *cuneiform* [kyü nē'ə fôrm], meaning "wedge-shaped," because of marks made by the stylus. Each combination of marks stood for a syllable. Sumerian cuneiform writing was later used by other peoples of the Fertile Crescent.

The Plain of Shinar lacked stones for building, but clay was everywhere. The Sumerians used it to build their houses and temples. Their invention of the arch continues to be important to architecture, because an arch

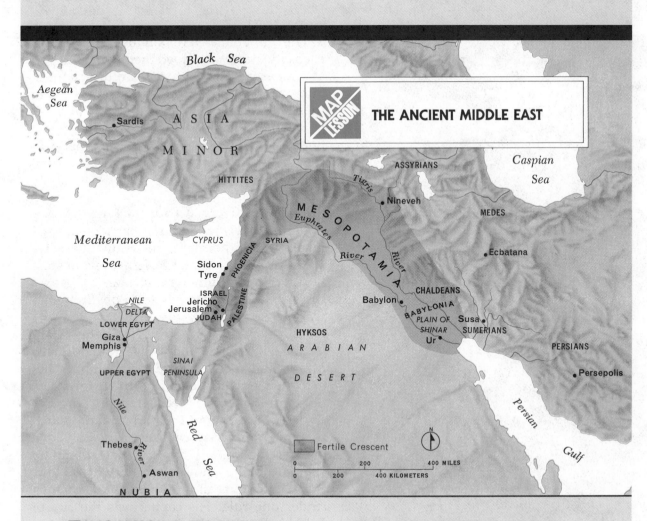

The map shows the Ancient Middle East. Labels include:

Black Sea, Aegean Sea, Caspian Sea, Mediterranean Sea, Red Sea, Persian Gulf

Sardis, ASIA MINOR, HITTITES, ASSYRIANS, MEDES, Nineveh, Ecbatana, Tigris, Euphrates, River, MESOPOTAMIA, CHALDEANS, Babylon, BABYLONIA, PLAIN OF SHINAR, SUMERIANS, Ur, Susa, PERSIANS, Persepolis

CYPRUS, SYRIA, PHOENICIA, Sidon, Tyre, ISRAEL, Jericho, Jerusalem, JUDAH, PALESTINE, NILE DELTA, LOWER EGYPT, Giza, Memphis, UPPER EGYPT, SINAI PENINSULA, HYKSOS, ARABIAN DESERT, Nile River, Thebes, Aswan, NUBIA

MAP LESSON: THE ANCIENT MIDDLE EAST

Fertile Crescent

0   200   400 MILES
0   200   400 KILOMETERS

N

■ MAP LESSON 2: THE ANCIENT MIDDLE EAST

1. Water has always been important to civilization. People have used seas, lakes, and rivers, such as those shown here, in different ways to meet different needs. The Nile River flows northward while the Tigris River and the Euphrates River both flow southward. All three of these rivers have been used both for irrigation and transportation. Into which bodies of water do these three rivers flow?

2. In ancient times, the Tigris River and the Euphrates River both had mouths to reach the sea, as this map shows. Today, the rivers join on the Plain of Shinar to form one river. How might this change have come about? How might it have affected living conditions on the Plain of Shinar?

3. Transportation has always been a major use of water systems. Look at the journeys listed below and decide which of them would have been possible in ancient times and which would not:

a. to sail from Egypt to the Black Sea
b. to travel from Babylon to Nineveh by rivers alone
c. to sail from the Mediterranean Sea to the Persian Gulf
d. to follow an all-water route from Sardis to Aswan

This religious object came from Ur, an important Sumerian city on the Euphrates River. It was made of gold, silver, lapis lazuli, and limestone. Seashells were used to make the goat's woolly fleece. The statue was made sometime between 3000 B.C. and 2340 B.C.

The Sumerians were polytheists. People of each city-state worshiped their own local god as well as gods brought in by other peoples. Sumerian religious beliefs were reflected in their literature. The epic poem *Gilgamesh* [gil′gə mesh′] tells a fascinating story of a flood like the story of Noah and the Ark, explained perhaps by the ever present possibility of river floods.

Hammurabi wrote a code of laws. Mesopotamia had few natural barriers against invasion. Furthermore, the individual city-states were easy to attack. However, in spite of invasions, Sumerian civilization lasted because the conquerors took on Sumerian ways.

About 2500 B.C., the city-states were united by Sargon I, an invader from northern Mesopotamia. He built a great empire that extended east to Persia, north to the Black Sea, and west to the Mediterranean. Sargon's dynasty lasted about 160 years and did much to spread Sumerian civilization.

Later, about 1760 B.C., Hammurabi [ham′ú rä′bē], who came from what is now Syria, brought all of lower Mesopotamia under one rule. His capital was the city of Babylon [bab′ə lən], and all of lower Mesopotamia became known as Babylonia [bab′ə-lō′nē ə].

Hammurabi's most important gift to civilization was his written code of laws. It was discovered in 1901 by a team of French archaeologists digging at Susa [sü′sə], Iran [i-ran′]. They found three pieces of black stone with a long series of writings on them. Put together, the stones made one block nearly 8 feet (2.4 meters) high. The discovery of this block of stone excited archaeologists and historians because the writing gave the earliest record of laws set down by a government. The Code had nearly 300 sections and covered in detail the everyday relations of the

can support very heavy structures even over the openings of doorways and windows. Also, the Sumerians probably were the first to make wheeled vehicles (although the wheel was invented earlier), and they taught the Egyptians to do the same.

Hammurabi's Code was carved on a column of diorite with some 3,600 lines of cuneiform writing.

people who lived in Hammurabi's empire. The following laws show that in Babylonia, human life was considered to be of less value than personal property.

If a man has stolen goods from a temple or house, he shall be put to death; and he that has received the stolen property from him shall be put to death.

If a man has broken into a house, he shall be killed in front of the place where he broke through and buried there.

If a man has committed highway robbery and has been caught, that man shall be put to death.

Penalties varied according to the social position of the injured: "If a man has

knocked out the eye of a noble, his eye shall be knocked out," whereas if the same man knocked out the eye of a commoner, he was only required to pay a fine. There are other parts of the Code that are more like modern justice. They bear out Hammurabi's claim that the Code would "prevent the strong from oppressing the weak." For instance, slavery for debt was limited to four years, and dishonest business practices were punished. Laws governing the fees of doctors and veterinarians allowed poor people to pay less for medical and surgical services than the rich. A woman's right to keep her marriage dowry and to control slaves was guaranteed.

Hammurabi's Code was not the first of its kind. He used existing laws and revised another code that was already 300 years old. But his Code became the basis for other legal systems long after his death. Since law is one of the main ways that people establish and keep social order, the Code represents a great advance in civilization.

After Hammurabi's death, mountain tribes invaded his kingdom from the east and north. The Hittites [hit'īts], one of these invading tribes, became powerful in the Fertile Crescent.

With iron weapons the Hittites ruled a powerful empire (1600–1200 B.C.). The Hittites lived in an area to the northwest of Babylonia in Asia Minor. (Today this is the country of Turkey.) They had just and humane laws, and their architecture was notable. Their most important discovery, however, was the knowledge of how to work iron. They refined iron ore and used it to make tools and weapons.

The Hittites were also stubborn and fierce fighters. Shortly after 1600 B.C., they conquered Babylonia and became rulers of the area once governed by Hammurabi. The Hittites were greatly aided in battles over the years by their iron weapons, which were harder and stronger than the bronze weapons used by their enemies. They also moved southward into Syria, in the western part of the Fertile Crescent.

These conquests alarmed the Egyptian pharaohs, who sent armies north to challenge the Hittites. Thus began a long struggle that weakened both the Hittite and Egyptian empires.

Civilization advanced during an era of small states (1200–750 B.C.). By 1200 B.C., the Hittite kingdom was beginning to collapse, and Egypt had also lost much of its power. In this situation, several small states were able to develop and maintain their freedom. A small state was often made up of just a few cities near each other. Two small states, the Phoenician and the Hebrew, made important contributions to later western civilizations.

The Phoenicians [fə nish'ənz] had been desert nomads who moved westward into an area of the Fertile Crescent bordering the eastern Mediterranean. There they became sea traders and built the great trading cities of Tyre [tīr] and Sidon [sīd'n]. Their ships sailed to Greece, Italy, North Africa, Spain, the west coast of Africa, and possibly even to faraway Britain. The Phoenicians set up many distant trading colonies, the greatest of which was Carthage, in North Africa.

To keep track of their trading operations, the Phoenicians developed a more advanced system of writing than that used by the Egyptians or Sumerians. They used letters or signs that represented sounds to make an alphabet. The word *alphabet* comes from their first two letters—"aleph" and "beth." The Phoenician alphabet was made up of twenty-two consonant symbols. Later, when the Greeks adopted the alphabet, they introduced vowel signs. From this combination of consonant and vowel signs came the alphabet we use today.

In Palestine was the country of the Hebrews, or Jews. Much of the history of this people is told in the Old Testament of the Bible. It tells how the Hebrews, under their leader Abraham, came from the eastern part of the Plain of Shinar. They searched for a "Promised Land" in which to settle and after years of wandering came to Canaan [kā'nən], or Palestine. The Book of Exodus in the Bible tells how some of the Hebrews were enslaved by the Egyptians. After a long captivity, a great Hebrew leader named Moses led his people back to Palestine. Jewish scriptures relate how Moses gave the Jews the Ten Commandments that God had revealed to him on Mount Sinai [sī'nī].

According to the Old Testament, the Hebrews had to fight the Canaanites and later the Philistines [fil'ə stēnz'] for possession of Palestine. Around 1025 B.C., Saul became the first king of the Hebrews. He was followed on the throne by David who, scriptures say, had killed the Philistine giant, Goliath, with a stone hurled from a slingshot. After defeating the Philistines, David established a kingdom with Jerusalem as its capital.

The Hebrew kingdom reached its height under David's son, Solomon, who reigned from about 977 to 937 B.C. He built a temple to God in Jerusalem and sent his ships to trade in distant countries. His expenses caused such high taxes that the Hebrew tribes in the north grew unhappy with Solomon's reign. After his death, they set up an independent kingdom. The land of the Hebrews divided into two parts: the Kingdom of Israel in the north and the Kingdom of Judah in the south. Thus weakened, the Hebrews were open to invaders. Between 722 B.C. and 66 A.D., the Jews were conquered by several different peoples.

DailyLife

Artifacts tell much about life in Mesopotamia. The relief, *top left,* describes home life. It shows a woman spinning thread while a slave stands behind and fans her. On the table is a fish for dinner. The many statues, *below,* represent a religious ceremony. The two largest figures may be a god and goddess while the clean-shaven man is a priest. The rest are thought to be worshippers. They were made about 2500 B.C. They were found in Tell Asmar, Iraq. The cuneiform map, *middle,* was made about 1300 B.C. It depicts the fields and canals of Nippur in Sumer. This shows the complex governmental system used by people of Mesopotamia. (The drawing of the map shows the fields and canals more clearly.)

The cruelty of the Assyrians can be seen in this sculpture showing them at war against their enemies.

In 66 A.D., the Jews staged a revolt against their Roman rulers. The Romans destroyed Jerusalem in 70 A.D. and drove many of the Jews from Palestine, and they scattered to many different parts of the world. In spite of this *Diaspora* [dī as'pər ə], or "scattering," the Jews clung to their religion and customs and dreamed of someday returning to the Promised Land.

Compared with the Egyptian, Babylonian, and Hittite empires, the Hebrew kingdom was an unimportant state. It is in the areas of religion, literature, and justice that they made lasting contributions to civilization. The religion that the Hebrews developed is called *Judaism* [jü'dē iz'əm]. With its *monotheism* [mon'ə thē'iz'əm], or belief in one god, and teachings of the Old Testament, Judaism formed the base of two other great religions of the world—Christianity and Islam. From an early worship of many gods, the Hebrews developed the idea of one god for their own tribe. This idea, over a long period of time, developed into the idea of one loving Father who ruled over the whole universe. Building upon the Ten Commandments, prophets developed some of the noblest rules of human behavior, as shown in the following short passage from the Holy Scriptures (Micah 6:8).

It hath been told thee, O man, what is good, And what the Lord doth require of thee: Only to do justly, and to love mercy, and to walk humbly with thy God.

The Assyrians ruled the largest empire the world had seen (750–605 B.C.). The era of small states ended with the rise of the Assyrians [ə sir'ē ənz]. Their original homeland was a highland region north of the upper Tigris River. Shortly before 1000 B.C., they began a series of attacks on their neighbors. Babylonia fell to them in 729 B.C. and Israel in 722 B.C. By 700 B.C., the Assyrians had created the largest empire yet. It included the Fertile Crescent, the area surrounding it, and Egypt.

The Assyrians ruled their empire by developing an advanced system of political administration and by building a well-trained army equipped with iron weapons. First, Assyrian bowmen weakened the enemy, using bows with vicious iron-tipped arrows as their main weapon. Then came attacks by horsemen and charioteers who were wearing helmets and breastplates. Bearing iron spears, swords, and bows, they smashed the ranks of the enemy and drove them from the field of battle.

Few conquerors in history have been so

Babylon was surrounded by a huge wall pierced by eight gates. The most famous of these was the Ishtar Gate, built by Nebuchadnezzar. This reconstruction, *left*, of part of the gate shows its size. The gate was made of enameled blue bricks. The fragment, *right*, showing a dragon is from the real gate.

cruel and heartless in war. The Assyrians terrorized conquered peoples and forced them to bow to Assyrian will. They frequently burned people alive or cut off their heads. However, the Assyrians' fine library of clay tablets in their capital, Nineveh [nin'ə və], helped preserve much of the knowledge of their day.

In 612 B.C., Nineveh was captured by the Chaldeans [kal dē'ənz] from Babylonia and the Medes from Persia. People throughout the empire rejoiced when their cruel Assyrian masters were overthrown.

A new Babylonian empire arose (605–550 B.C.). With the fall of Nineveh, Babylonia became powerful for the first time since Hammurabi. The Chaldeans, guided by their strong king Nebuchadnezzar [neb'yə kədnez'ər], built the Chaldean Empire by conquering the Fertile Crescent. Nebuchadnezzar rebuilt Babylon. Among its many marvels were the famous hanging gardens which were built on the rooftops of buildings.

The Chaldeans, building on the work of earlier peoples, studied the stars, as well as the sun, the moon, and the planets. Without any telescopes or accurate time-recording instruments they used mathematics to work out detailed tables of the movements of these

bodies and thus made important contributions to the science of astronomy.

The Chaldeans believed it was possible to tell the future through a study of the stars. They used charts of the movements of stars to help them make important decisions. Thus they began the study of astrology.

With Nebuchadnezzar's death in 562 B.C., the Chaldean Empire began to decay. It was eventually succeeded by the Persian Empire.

The Persians built a vast empire (525–331 B.C.). Among the different peoples of the Assyrian Empire were two related groups, the Medes and the Persians. After the Medes had helped the Chaldeans defeat the cruel Assyrians, they built a prosperous kingdom that included the Persians. The capital of this kingdom was at the city of Ecbatana [ek bat'ə nə].

In 550 B.C., a Persian general named Cyrus the Great led the Persians in a successful attack against the Medes. His troops captured Ecbatana, then the neighboring kingdoms, and finally the entire Chaldean Empire. At the time of Cyrus' death in 529 B.C., Persian rule extended east to the borders of India, west to the Aegean Sea, and south to Egypt. Cyrus' successors conquered

Someone You Should Know

Cyrus the Great

As with other famous rulers of ancient times, there are legends about the childhood of Cyrus the Great. When Cyrus was born, his grandfather Astyages was king. The most famous legend says that Astyages dreamt that Cyrus would one day lead a revolt against him. Fearing revolt, Astyages ordered his adviser to have the baby slain. The adviser, though, secretly gave the infant to a shepherd to raise. When Cyrus was ten, his many outstanding qualities led to his discovery, and Astyages let the boy live. It was a mistake. When he grew up, Cyrus did lead a successful revolt against Astyages in about the year 550 B.C.

Cyrus is remembered as a wise and courageous ruler who tolerated many religions and cultures. When he captured Babylon he allowed the 40,000 Jews there to return home and to practice their own beliefs. The legends about Cyrus's youth, whether true or not, are a way to explain his continuing importance and verify his greatness. And this importance is still seen today. In 1971 A.D., Iran celebrated the 2,500th anniversary of his monarchy.

Egypt in 525 B.C. and even won land in southeastern Europe. Unlike the Assyrians, however, the Persian kings sought to give the different peoples in their empire equal rights and responsibilities. They allowed conquered peoples to worship their own gods, to use their own languages, and to keep their own customs.

The Persian government, like the Assyrian and Chaldean governments, was a *despotism*, or rule of a king with unlimited power. Such a ruler is called a *despot*. Under Darius I, who ruled from 521 to 486 B.C., the Persian Empire reached its greatest size. Four capitals—Susa, Ecbatana, Babylon, and Persepolis [pər sep'ə lis]—were set up in different parts of the empire. The whole empire was divided into districts, each governed by a representative of the king. To keep himself informed on how well his officials governed, Darius employed inspectors, called "The Eyes and Ears of the King," who traveled from district to district, reporting their findings personally to him.

To improve communications throughout the huge empire, the Persian kings maintained a network of fine roads. Along these highways rode the king's messengers, changing horses every 14 miles (22 kilometers). Relays of these horsemen could cover 1,500 miles (2,400 kilometers) in a little more than a week; ordinary travelers took three months to travel the same distance.

The Persian kings protected farming and helped trade in the whole empire, partly because they wanted all districts to be able to pay taxes. The tax burden, however, was not heavy. Throughout the empire, a money system of gold and silver coins was used.

The fair treatment of other peoples by the Persian kings was partly due to the Persian religion. Founded by the teacher Zoroaster [zôr'ō as'tər] in the 7th century B.C., this religion asks its followers to choose Ahura Mazda [ä'hûr ə maz'də], the god of good, over Ahriman [är'i mən], the god of evil. In

Persepolis was begun by Darius about 518 B.C. The Tachara Palace, *left*, lies in ruins now but was once one of the most elegant buildings in the capital. It is believed that Darius used the palace only for ceremonial occasions. The relief, *below*, is from the Treasury. It shows Darius seated, with his son and successor, Xerxes, behind him.

. . . Ahura Mazda bore me aid . . . because I was not an enemy, I was not a deceiver, I was not a wrong-doer, neither I nor my family; according to justice and rectitude I ruled.

section review 2

1. Name two or more important contributions made by the Sumerians to the civilization of Mesopotamia.

2. What is important about Hammurabi's code of laws?

3. What is the religion of the Hebrews? Name the other two great religions based on its beliefs.

4. Name two or more ways in which Persian rule was different from Assyrian rule.

time, the Zoroastrians believed, the world would come to an end. Ahura Mazda would win over Ahriman. At that time, there would be a last judgment, and the righteous would go to heaven and the wicked to hell. In describing one of his victories, Darius I showed how he was influenced by the Persian religion:

3 An ancient city revealed early Indus civilization

More than 4,000 years ago, people living in the Indus River Valley in what is now Pakistan and India had a highly organized way of

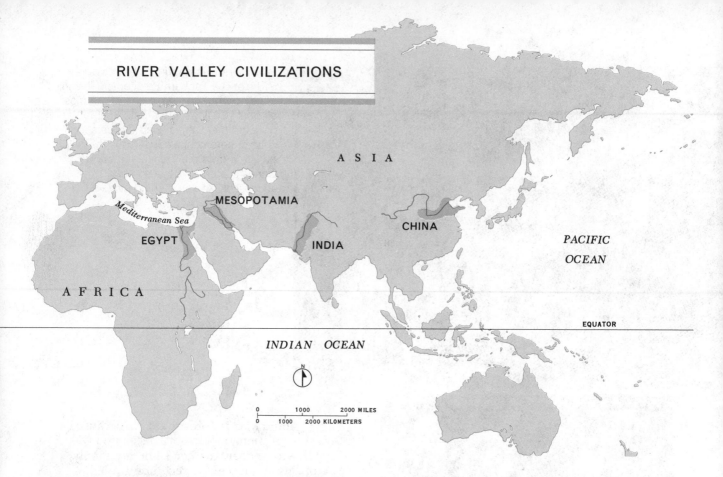

RIVER VALLEY CIVILIZATIONS

ASIA

MESOPOTAMIA

Mediterranean Sea

CHINA

EGYPT

INDIA

PACIFIC
OCEAN

AFRICA

EQUATOR

INDIAN OCEAN

N

0   1000   2000 MILES
0   1000   2000 KILOMETERS

life. Yet practically nothing was known about this early river valley civilization until recent times.

Archaeologists discovered a lost city. In the 1850s, engineers began to build a railroad in the Indus Valley. As workers prepared the area, they uncovered large numbers of bricks. These they promptly used in laying the railroad bed. They also uncovered many ornaments and small figures, which were mostly ignored or carried off as mementos by the local villagers. Little did they know that they were actually destroying the evidence of an ancient way of life that had existed many centuries before.

No one thought much about these discoveries for 70 years. Then in the 1920s, the British government began to study the area. Archaeologists discovered enough remains to learn that there, where the railroad work-

ers had found bricks, had once been the city of Harappa [hə rap'ə]. They found red limestone sculpture and delicate jewelry, graveyards, pottery, and tools. The people of this city had developed an advanced civilization at about the same time as the Egyptians and Sumerians. This civilization covered a huge area from the Arabian Sea to what is now the city of Delhi [del'ē].

In the years since Harappa was discovered, British, American, and Indian archaeologists have learned much about this ancient culture. Remains of 60 villages and towns have been found. The best source of information is Mohenjo-Daro [mō hen'jō dä'rō], a city 400 miles (640 kilometers) southwest of Harappa. (See the map called Ancient India on page 54 of Chapter 3.)

Life in Mohenjo-Daro was highly organized. The city of Mohenjo-Daro was laid out in blocks. The streets were paved with bricks and lined with shops. The windows of houses faced interior courtyards, not the street. Light and fresh air came through window grills made of red clay or *alabaster*, a white marble-like stone. Staircases led to the roof tops where the families enjoyed the cool night air. Most houses had indoor toilets, and some of the larger houses had baths. Neat brick-lined sewers along the streets carried off bath and rain water.

In the center of the city was a thick-walled, mud-brick fort, or *citadel* [sit′ə del], that guarded the city. Inside the citadel were public buildings: a great bath, probably used for religious bathings, and a granary where carts could drive right up to deposit the harvest for the year.

Life for members of the upper-class was luxurious. Their two-story houses had rooms for servants and guests. Waterproof tiles lined their bathtubs. Their wooden furniture was decorated with bone, shell, and ivory inlays. They also had ornate pottery, bronze tools, silver pitchers, and gold jewelry.

Numerous toys and stamp seals have been found. Toy birds, animals, bulls tethered to small carts, marbles, balls, and rattles amused the children of Mohenjo-Daro. The stamp seals were small pieces of stone with carefully detailed carvings. It is thought they were pressed into soft material—wax or clay—to show ownership. Most had small rings on the back and could be worn on thongs as ornaments.

The people of Mohenjo-Daro had an elaborate religion. Many female statues have been found, showing that the people worshiped a goddess. She is shown adorned with necklaces, bracelets, and a girdle, or belt, around her exaggerated hips. Sculpture and carvings on the seals also show that the people burned incense or candles to their goddess and that animals were included in their religion. The great bath house, with its

This haughty figure with his carefully trimmed beard and fancy cloak is believed to represent a high-ranking priest.

huge public bathing area surrounded by smaller private baths, also had living quarters. These private baths and living quarters suggest that a priest class lived in luxury and celebrated ritual bathings.

Farming and some trade formed the economy of this ancient civilization. Farming was the basis of life. There were huge round platforms in the city where an organized labor force pounded grain. Trade was important, too. Quartz weights, many of them exactly the same size, have been found. These indicate that the people used standard weights to measure goods in their business deals. Some weights are so small they must have been

DailyLife

Trade was an important part of life in the Indus Valley. Grain was stored and transported in pottery jars such as the one at *right*. The jar kept the grain dry and safe from pests. Merchants used stamp seals like the one, *below right,* to mark their goods. Goods with Indus Valley seals have been found along the caravan route to Mesopotamia. The characters at the bottom of the seal may stand for the owner's name. This terra cotta bull, *below left,* is a child's toy. The head can be moved by pulling the bull's string tail. Other Mohenjo-Daro toys, such as carts, are evidence that these people used wheels and animals to pull heavy loads.

used to weigh gold. Others were used by grocers who sold spices. The largest ones, made of stones so heavy they had to be hauled into place by ropes, may have been used to weigh large amounts of grain.

The ancient Indus Valley civilization had two port cities, recently excavated. Today, these cities are 30 miles inland from the Arabian Sea. However, huge piers and warehouses indicate that the cities must have once sat right on the water. The shape of the Indian subcontinent has been changing. Layers of rock deep in the earth's surface have shifted, raising up mud to become land where it was once coastline.

Evidence indicates that Indus Valley people traded with many distant groups. The port cities received ships from the Sumerians. Sailboats of the Indus Valley people traveled the Arabian Sea. Camels and ox-drawn carts carried goods overland.

History is silent about the end of these people. The people of this ancient Indus culture had writing, but scholars have not yet learned to read it. Little is known about what happened to these people. The city of Mohenjo-Daro seems to have been slowly overrun by mud from a nearby lake, formed from the earth's shifting surface. Over and over, houses were rebuilt on platforms raised to higher, safer levels. Some archaeologists believe this constant work reduced the will and energy of the people. We do know that the oldest buildings, found 40 feet (12 meters) below the mud surface, were much better built than those above. Dikes and banks seem to have been neglected, and prosperity declined.

Then disaster struck. About 1500 B.C., some terrible misfortune hit Mohenjo-Daro and possibly all the Indus River people. Skeletons were found in groups, some showing axe or sword cuts, as though these long-dead people had huddled together for comfort in the face of a terrible catastrophe. But what happened is still a mystery. The name Mohenjo-Daro means "the place of the dead."

section review 3

1. What happened to much of the historical evidence at Harappa?

2. In what ways did some people of Mohenjo-Daro have very comfortable lives?

3. Describe the religious practices of people in the Indus Valley.

4. What evidence shows that the shape of the Indian subcontinent has changed in the last 4,000 years?

4 Chinese civilization developed along the Hwang Ho

The Chinese have many myths and legends about ancient times. They are very tall stories that have to be taken with several grains of salt. Many other groups have similar stories. Early peoples often had creation myths to explain their beginnings in ways that made sense for their values. One Chinese story tells of the first man, P'an Ku, who used a hammer and chisel for 18 thousand years to make the universe. The job was finished 2,229,000 years ago!

More definite information tells us that from 2205 to 1766 B.C., princes, called the Hsia [hə sǐ'] ruled over a number of little kingdoms. Yu, the first prince, is remembered as brave and strong. He is said to have fought a mighty river to save his people from floods. According to an early Chinese saying, the people claimed that, "But for Yu, we should all have been fishes." Such legends are unreliable as historical evidence, but it is true that people of a New Stone Age culture settled in the Hwang Ho Valley. (See the map on page 74 of Chapter 4.)

Neolithic Chinese were farmers. The early people of China were farmers. In the cold, dry areas of northern China were great plains of fertile loess. The Hwang Ho ran through these plains carrying large amounts of coffee-colored silt. It continually built up the river bed until its banks became higher than the surrounding plain. From time to time the river overflowed, causing tragic floods, so that the river came to be called "China's Sorrow." In spite of this, its waters brought life. Forests did not grow in the plains and the land did not need to be cleared for farming. It was on these plains that the Chinese began to farm.

As long ago as 4500 B.C., Chinese farmers were growing *millet* [mil'it]. (This cereal grass, with tufts that look like fuzzy caterpillars, is eaten today by about a third of the world's population.) A thousand years later, soybeans were cultivated, and pigs were raised for food and for scavenging, to keep farmyards clean.

By 3500 B.C., Chinese women were raising silkworms, spinning the unraveled cocoons into fine silk thread, and weaving silk cloth. Throughout history, people have considered Chinese silk among the best cloths in the world.

About 3000 B.C., the people in the southern, semitropical climate at the mouth of the Yangtze [yang'tsē] River learned to grow rice. Because rice needs to have its roots underneath water, these people developed the elaborate farming methods still used in much of Southeast Asia today. They made artificial pools, called *paddies*, by building dikes around low-lying land and diverting water from nearby streams. Then, they sowed the rice seeds in dry land and trans-

This jade pendant was made between 1300 B.C. and 1030 B.C. and demonstrates the artistic skills of early Chinese people. It was carved so that it can be hung from the small hole on the outside of the tail but still remain vertical. Jade was highly prized by early Chinese and probably could be owned only by persons of the highest rank.

planted them to the paddies by hand, a plant at a time, when the shoots were about a foot high. Later, as more land was needed, they learned to build paddies on hillsides.

These early Chinese lived in villages near their fields. Walls of pounded earth protected their villages. Their houses were mud-and-grass walled cones placed over circular areas dug out of the ground. The roof was

This bronze ceremonial vessel was made during the Shang dynasty. Its decoration of animal forms and curls are typical of the types of decorations on many Chinese bronzes.

supported by six posts cut from tree trunks, and it was made of wooden beams which were covered with straw and earth. The whole structure was between 12 and 17 feet (3.6 and 5.0 meters) in diameter. The doorway was an opening in the roof.

Shang kings were religious leaders (1500–1027 B.C.). The written history of China begins about 1500 B.C. with the rise of the Shang dynasty. Their capital was north of the Hwang Ho, near the present city of Anyang. The Shang kings controlled only a small area around their capital, while strong nobles ruled the more distant parts of the kingdom. However, the nobles recognized the Shang king as the head of the armies and as the religious leader of the whole group. They believed that he governed by the command of heaven. As high priest, the king paid homage to his ancestors and made animal sacrifices to the gods as a way of asking for good harvests in the future.

Much of the knowledge of Shang history comes from excavations, begun in 1928, of sites near Anyang. Archaeologists here found no great monuments or palaces. Stone was scarce in China, and buildings were made from perishable wood and packed earth. A poem from the *Book of Odes*, the oldest collection of Chinese poetry, tells how the people built:

He called upon his overseer of public works,
He called upon his Minister of Education,
And charged them to build dwellings.
They leveled all the land by skillful measuring,
They built wooden frames which rose straight and high,
The temple of our ancestors grew mightily.
Armies of men brought earth in baskets
And, shouting joyfully, poured it into the frames.
They rammed it in with great ringing blows,
They leveled off the walls and these resounded mightily,
They built up five thousand cubits at once,
And so well did they labour
That the rolling of the great drum
Would not cover the noise thereof.

One important source of information about the early Chinese is the writing on pieces of animal bones and tortoise shells. Priests wrote questions about the future on the bones and shells. Then they heated the bones and interpreted the cracks that appeared as answers from gods or ancestors.

This bone from 1300 B.C. was used for record-keeping rather than predicting the future. The bone says "On the seventh day of the month . . . a great new star appeared in company with Antares." It is the oldest known record of the astrological event now called a nova.

Questions were asked on many subjects, and they tell us much about the Shang civilization. The bones ask about what to sacrifice to the spirits, when will be a good day for an important journey, and when will be a good time for the army to attack. Priests asked about the harvest and the weather, about when the time was good to go hunting or fishing. Also, the priests told the spirits about their enemies' misdeeds, about how many people had been killed or taken prisoner, so the spirits could punish their enemies. The inscriptions show that Chinese writing was well advanced at this time. Shang writing had about 2,000 symbols. In addition to writing on bones and shells, the people kept records on tablets of wood and bamboo.

The people of the Shang period are best known for their fine bronze work. Artisans made bronze vases of different shapes for different purposes. A slender, rectangular vase, the *ting* vase, stood on four legs and was used for honoring ancestors. Another vase stood on three legs and had large, hollow feet. Another was built in two sections, like a modern double-boiler, with space for water in the bottom part and food in the top. These vases were beautifully shaped and elaborately decorated with scrolls, spirals, and the faces of dragons and other fabulous creatures.

In addition to the bronze work, pieces of carved ivory and jade, marble sculptures, dagger-axes, and chariot fittings have been found at Shang sites. These discoveries show a high level of technology. The Shang people, however, were conquered in 1027 B.C. by a less civilized group of nomads who invaded the country from the northwest.

section review 4

1. What is an ancient Chinese legend of the origin of the universe?

2. Name three major crops grown by early farmers in China. What kind of cloth did the Chinese become famous for?

3. Why did the strong nobles accept the Shangs as kings?

4. What are the people of the Shang period best known for?

Section Summaries

1. Civilization developed in Egypt. Farmers in the Nile Valley formed local governments to control irrigation. They developed a calendar and the plow. By 3100 B.C., a strong king, Menes, unified Egypt, marking the beginning of the Old Kingdom. Egyptian religion involved many gods, pharaoh-worship, good conduct, and belief in afterlife. The Pyramids were built; trade flourished; and society was divided into different classes. Princes from Thebes ruled during the Middle Kingdom. Following 100 years of Hyksos rule, the New Kingdom began, and Egyptian power grew into a great empire. Books were written on papyrus rolls. Mathematics, medicine, and architecture advanced.

2. City-states and empires flourished in Mesopotamia. The Sumerians were the first nomadic tribe to build cities in the Tigris-Euphrates Valley. Like the Egyptians, their government was a theocracy. They developed cuneiform writing, invented the arch, and used wheeled vehicles.

When Hammurabi conquered lower Mesopotamia and ruled from Babylon, he wrote a code of laws and made the government responsible for enforcing them. The Hittites conquered Babylonia with iron weapons and ruled a large empire. Egypt engaged the Hittites in a lengthy war that weakened both empires. An era of small states followed. Two lasting achievements, the Phoenician alphabet and the Hebrew religion, developed in this time. Large empires ruled by despots came next. The Assyrian Empire was held together by efficient administration, an excellent army, and terrorism. The Chaldeans were noted for their developments in astronomy and astrology. Finally, the Persians built a vast empire run by a highly organized government. Zoroastrian beliefs led the Persians to rule with consideration and justice.

3. An ancient city revealed early Indus civilization. Excavations at Mohenjo-Daro revealed a civilization based on farming and trade. Indus people developed sophisticated cities, traded with groups such as the Sumerians, and made elaborate jewelry and furniture. They also worshiped a goddess and some animals. How this civilization ended is not known.

4. Chinese civilization developed along the Hwang Ho. Early Chinese civilization was based on farming. Also, silk worms were domesticated, and the silk trade was begun. The first Chinese dynasty was the Shang. Shang kings were high priests recognized by nobles in the Hwang Ho Valley. The Shang people are known for their cast bronze pottery, their advances in writing, and their use of bones and shells to tell the future.

Who? What? When? Where?

1. Find the time during which each of the following events took place:

4000–3001 B.C.	1500–1001 B.C.
3000–2001 B.C.	1000–501 B.C.
2000–1501 B.C.	

  a. Sargon I united the city-states of Mesopotamia.
  b. The Egyptians developed hieroglyphics.
  c. The Shangs ruled China.
  d. Hammurabi ruled Babylonia.
  e. Solomon ruled the Hebrew kingdom.
  f. The Egyptians built the temple of Amon-Re at Karnak.
  g. Cyrus the Great conquered the Chaldean Empire.

2. Name the civilization that:

  a. built the pyramid at Giza
  b. asked questions on bones and shells
  c. believed P'an Ku made the universe
  d. used cuneiform writing
  e. invented the arch
  f. brought horses and chariots to Egypt
  g. developed an alphabet
  h. wrote the Old Testament

3. Write sentences to show you understand these terms:

a. despotism	e. papyrus
b. dynasty	f. polytheism
c. empire	g. scribes
d. monotheism	h. theocracy

4. What archaeological evidence is there for each of the following:

    a. the ways buildings were made in China during the Shang period
    b. religious practices of the Indus people
    c. Egyptian belief in life after death
    d. property valued more highly than life in Mesopotamia

Questions for Critical Thinking

1. What does Hammurabi's Code tell about life in ancient Mesopotamia?

2. What did the Egyptians learn from other peoples? Why is it important that people have contact with others not like themselves?

3. What are the major differences between Egyptian hieroglyphics, Sumerian cuneiform, and the Phoenician alphabet?

Skill Activities

1. Read *Discovering Tut-ankh-Amen's Tomb* edited by Shirley Glubok to learn more about the treasure of the Egyptian boy-king. (The Macmillan Co., 1968.)

2. Write sentences telling who wrote these and what they are about: *The Book of the Dead*, *Gilgamesh*, and the *Book of Odes*.

3. Choose Thebes, Babylon, or Mohenjo-Daro. Then write two or more paragraphs telling why you would rather live in that city at its height rather than one of the other two.

chapter 2 quiz

Section 1

1. The Egyptians developed a kind of picture writing known as: a. papyrus, b. hieroglyphics, c. cuneiform

2. The beginning of government in Egypt was helped by: a. religion, b. despotism, c. irrigation projects

3. The famous pyramids of Egypt were built during the: a. Old Kingdom, b. New Kingdom, c. Middle Kingdom

Section 2

4. A famous code of laws was developed by: a. Sargon I, b. the Hyksos, c. Hammurabi

5. After Solomon's death, the Hebrew kingdom was divided into: a. Israel and Judah, b. Israel and Canaan, c. Judah and Egypt

6. The city that was *not* a Persian capital was: a. Memphis, b. Babylon, c. Ecbatana

Section 3

7. Mohenjo-Daro arose in the broad river valley of the: a. Hwang Ho, b. Indus River, c. Nile River

8. People of the Indus Valley used stamp seals to: a. mark their property, b. decorate their walls, c. weigh gold

9. True or false: Remains of their culture show that the Indus Valley people had contact with other early civilizations.

Section 4

10. The Chinese became famous for their: a. silk cloth, b. calendar, c. army

11. The first Chinese dynasty was the: a. Shang, b. Hsia, c. Harappa

12. The rich soil of the great plain in China is made of: a. silt, b. loam, c. loess

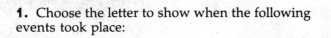

1. Choose the letter to show when the following events took place:

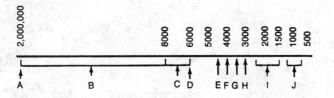

```
2,000,000                 8000 6000 5000 4000 3000 2000 1500 1000 500

  A         B            C  D     E F G H    I     J
```

____The years of the Old Stone Age
____A calendar was being used in Egypt
____The years of the era of small states
____Australopithecines lived in Africa
____The years of the Middle Stone Age
____The Bronze Age began
____Farming began in the Hwang Ho Valley

2. Match these terms with the correct meanings from the list below:

anthropologists	irrigation
despotism	Mesolithic
empire	monotheism
fossils	Paleolithic
geologists	polytheism
hieroglyphics	prehistoric
Homo sapiens	theocracy
Ice Ages	

a. The kind of writing developed by the Egyptians
b. Time before the invention of writing
c. A belief in more than one god
d. A government ruled by one person with absolute power
e. Modern human beings; thinking man
f. The hardened remains of ancient plants or animals
g. Scientific term for the Old Stone Age
h. A government in which the ruler is also the head of the official religion
i. Scientists who study ancient and modern peoples
j. The supplying of water to farmland
k. Periods when glaciers covered large parts of Earth
l. Different peoples under the rule of a strong nation
m. Scientists who study Earth's crust and its layers
n. Belief in one, all-powerful, god
o. Scientific term for the Middle Stone Age

3. Two important rivers in China's early history are: a. the Hwang Ho and the Indus, b. the Hwang Ho and the Yangtze, c. the Tigris and the Nile

4. Egyptians developed a calendar in order to: a. use the summer winds effectively, b. regulate the reigns of their rulers, c. plan for planting their crops

5. The alphabet we use today comes from: a. the Phoenicians and the Greeks, b. the Greeks and the Hebrews, c. the Egyptians and the Sumerians

6. Match the letters on the map with the place names of the four river valley civilizations:
____China
____Mesopotamia
____Egypt
____India

UNIT TWO
CLASSICAL
CIVILIZATIONS

All human beings have certain things in common. People raise families, build societies, and organize governments. They develop rules of conduct and create beautiful art and architecture. They find ways to explain the mysteries of nature and the purpose of life. And most people leave written records that future generations can read. No other creatures on Earth can do all the things humans can. However, human beings pursue these activities in different ways.

Around 1000 B.C., at least four major civilizations began to emerge in India, China, Greece, and Italy. The peoples in each of those areas had their own ideas, and the civilizations have gone through many changes. But they are still thought of as a kind of standard, or ideal. That is why they are called *classical*.

Each of the four classical civilizations made important contributions. During India's classical times, customs developed that still shape Indian village life. And Indian religion and architecture spread throughout Southeast Asia. In its classical period, China became a vast empire. The religions of Confucianism and Taoism began, and a tradition of reverence for things of the past arose.

Greece was the home of democracy. Western ideals of freedom, equality before the laws, individualism, and public involvement in government have their roots in classical Greek thought. The great Roman Empire preserved Greek culture and spread it throughout Europe and the Middle East. Roman military strength, legal system, and governmental genius influenced European rulers of many later centuries. In addition, all four civilizations made contributions to science, technology, education, art, and architecture.

Athena, the Greek goddess of wisdom, was the ruler of storms, patron of peace and war, and guardian of cities, especially Athens.

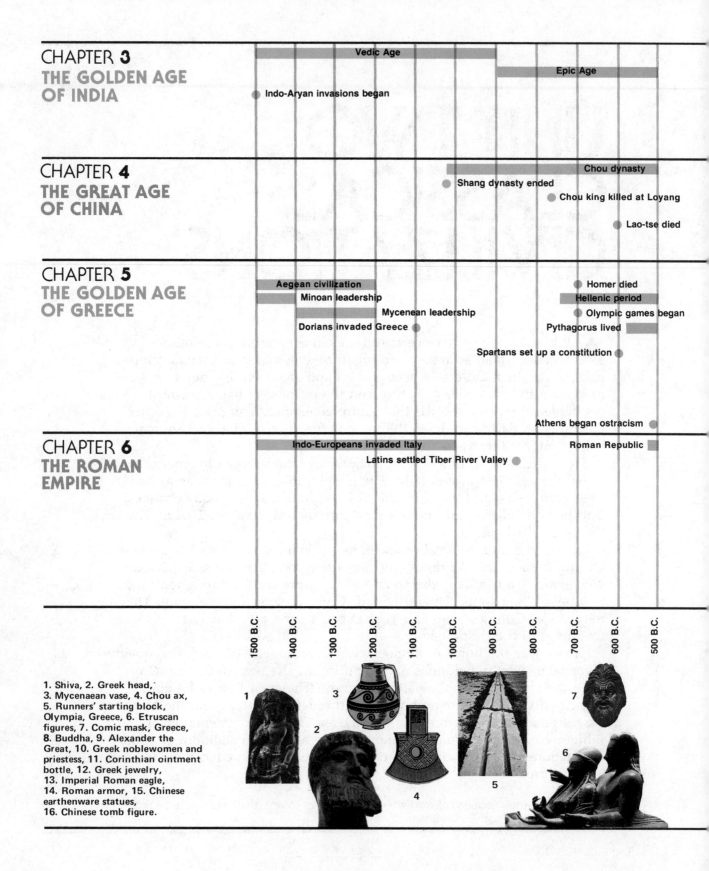

CHAPTER 3
THE GOLDEN AGE OF INDIA

Vedic Age

Epic Age

● Indo-Aryan invasions began

CHAPTER 4
THE GREAT AGE OF CHINA

Chou dynasty

● Shang dynasty ended

● Chou king killed at Loyang

● Lao-tse died

CHAPTER 5
THE GOLDEN AGE OF GREECE

Aegean civilization

Minoan leadership

● Homer died

Hellenic period

Mycenean leadership

● Olympic games began

Dorians invaded Greece ●

Pythagorus lived

Spartans set up a constitution ●

Athens began ostracism ●

CHAPTER 6
THE ROMAN EMPIRE

Indo-Europeans invaded Italy

Roman Republic

Latins settled Tiber River Valley ●

1500 B.C. 1400 B.C. 1300 B.C. 1200 B.C. 1100 B.C. 1000 B.C. 900 B.C. 800 B.C. 700 B.C. 600 B.C. 500 B.C.

1. Shiva, 2. Greek head,
3. Mycenaean vase, 4. Chou ax,
5. Runners' starting block,
Olympia, Greece, 6. Etruscan
figures, 7. Comic mask, Greece,
8. Buddha, 9. Alexander the
Great, 10. Greek noblewomen and
priestess, 11. Corinthian ointment
bottle, 12. Greek jewelry,
13. Imperial Roman eagle,
14. Roman armor, 15. Chinese
earthenware statues,
16. Chinese tomb figure.

1   3   7

2   4   6

5

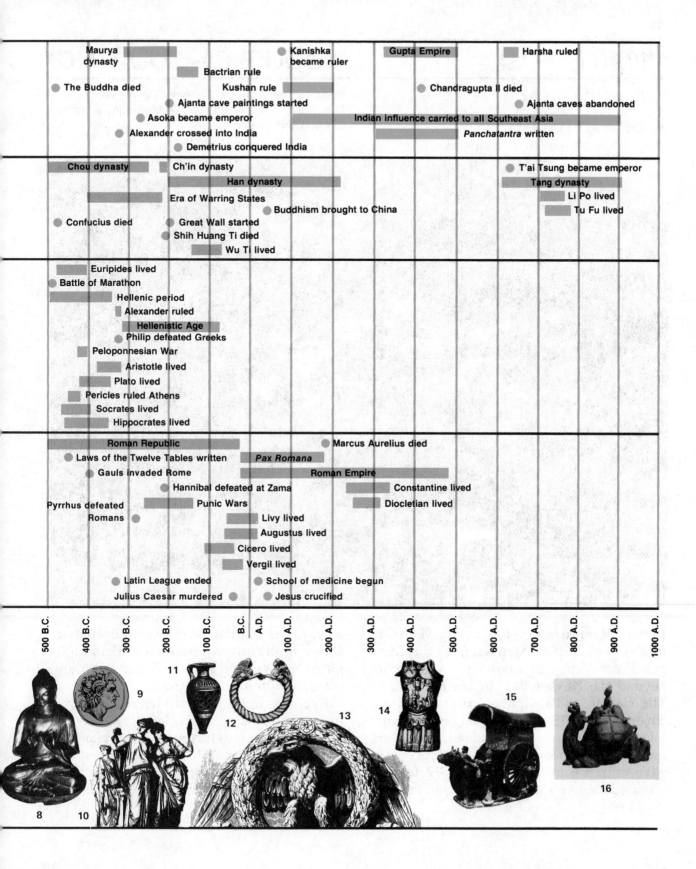

Maurya dynasty

Bactrian rule

Kanishka became ruler

Gupta Empire

Harsha ruled

The Buddha died

Kushan rule

Chandragupta II died

Ajanta cave paintings started

Ajanta caves abandoned

Asoka became emperor

Indian influence carried to all Southeast Asia

Alexander crossed into India

Panchatantra written

Demetrius conquered India

Chou dynasty

Ch'in dynasty

T'ai Tsung became emperor

Han dynasty

Tang dynasty

Era of Warring States

Li Po lived

Buddhism brought to China

Tu Fu lived

Confucius died

Great Wall started

Shih Huang Ti died

Wu Ti lived

Euripides lived

Battle of Marathon

Hellenic period

Alexander ruled

Hellenistic Age

Philip defeated Greeks

Peloponnesian War

Aristotle lived

Plato lived

Pericles ruled Athens

Socrates lived

Hippocrates lived

Roman Republic

Marcus Aurelius died

Laws of the Twelve Tables written

Pax Romana

Gauls invaded Rome

Roman Empire

Hannibal defeated at Zama

Constantine lived

Punic Wars

Diocletian lived

Pyrrhus defeated Romans

Livy lived

Augustus lived

Cicero lived

Vergil lived

Latin League ended

School of medicine begun

Julius Caesar murdered

Jesus crucified

500 B.C. | 400 B.C. | 300 B.C. | 200 B.C. | 100 B.C. | B.C. | A.D. | 100 A.D. | 200 A.D. | 300 A.D. | 400 A.D. | 500 A.D. | 600 A.D. | 700 A.D. | 800 A.D. | 900 A.D. | 1000 A.D.

8 9 10 11 12 13 14 15 16

THE GOLDEN AGE OF INDIA

Buddhism began in India and moved to other lands from there. This very large statue of Buddha is on the island of Sri Lanka.

In the 4th century B.C., the mighty Mauryan [mä′ùr yən] Empire extended from the Ganges River Valley in northeastern India to beyond the Khyber Pass in the northwest. The capital, at Pataliputra [pä′tə li pü′trə], covered some 18 square miles (46.8 square kilometers) and was surrounded by a deep moat and a wooden wall. Sixty-four gates gave entrance to the city, and 572 towers guarded it. Streets were laid out in an orderly way. At the heart of the city stood the palace, a beautifully carved wooden structure. Its pillars were plated with gold and silver and covered with intricate designs.

Chandragupta Maurya [chun′drə gùp′tə mä′ùr yə], the king, rarely left his palace. But on special holidays he toured the capital city. A Greek visiting in 302 B.C. described one such colorful procession. First came the monarch, riding an elephant.

Then came a great host of attendants in holiday dress, with golden vessels, such as huge basins and goblets six feet broad, tables, chairs of state, drinking and washing vessels, all of Indian copper, and many of them set with jewels, such as emeralds, beryls, and Indian garnets. Others wore robes embroidered in gold thread and led wild beasts, such as buffaloes, leopards and tame lions, and rare birds in cages.

The visitor was favorably impressed by the prosperity and wealth of the empire. All land belonged to the state, and a tax on farm products was the chief source of government income. Farmers used irrigation and crop rotation to increase crop yield. Famine was almost unknown in the land. Trade and handicraft industries thrived. Artisans made textiles, cutlery, and farm tools for export. Products from southern India, China, Mesopotamia, and Asia Minor were sold in markets in Pataliputra, Taxila [tak si′lə], and other cities of the empire.

The Mauryan Empire was one of the first large, well-protected, and well-run states in history. It was divided into three provinces. Each was governed by a *viceroy*, the king's representative in the province, who had his own staff of civil servants. In Pataliputra, government committees guarded the rights of craft workers, recorded all births and deaths, regulated the quality of goods for sale, and collected taxes. The Mauryan army had 600 thousand infantrymen and 30 thousand cavalrymen. They used 9 thousand war elephants in much the same way that modern armies use tanks. Excellent roads, with markers showing distances, connected the many villages and towns. One road extended for 1,200 miles (1,920 kilometers) from Taxila to Pataliputra.

After the fall of the Mauryas in the 2nd century B.C., influences from outside India helped bring about changes in the way of life. Five hundred years passed before the Gupta [gup′tə] Empire began. Chapter 3 shows how:

1. **Geography shaped history in India.**

2. **Many features of Indian life began in early times.**

3. **Strong rulers built empires in India.**

4. **Gupta rule launched a golden age.**

1 *Geography shaped history in India*

Geography has greatly influenced the history and lives of people in India. Ancient India included the land that is now India, Pakistan, and Bangladesh. This area of 1.6 million square miles (4.2 million square kilometers) is about half the size of the United States. It is called a *subcontinent*, because it is so large and is so isolated from the rest of the continent of Asia. India is shaped like a triangle, with its eastern and western sides on the sea. Its third side, on the north, is a great mountain wall formed by the Himalayas [him′ə lā′əz] and the Hindu Kush [hin′dü kush′] Mountains.

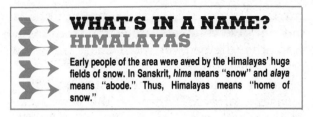

WHAT'S IN A NAME?
HIMALAYAS

Early people of the area were awed by the Himalayas' huge fields of snow. In Sanskrit, *hima* means "snow" and *alaya* means "abode." Thus, Himalayas means "home of snow."

Mountain passes are doorways into India. The Himalayas make up the largest part of the mountain wall. The Hindu Kush Mountains, which are in the northwest, have openings, called passes, through them. For some 4,000 years, invaders have pushed through these passes into India. Best known is the

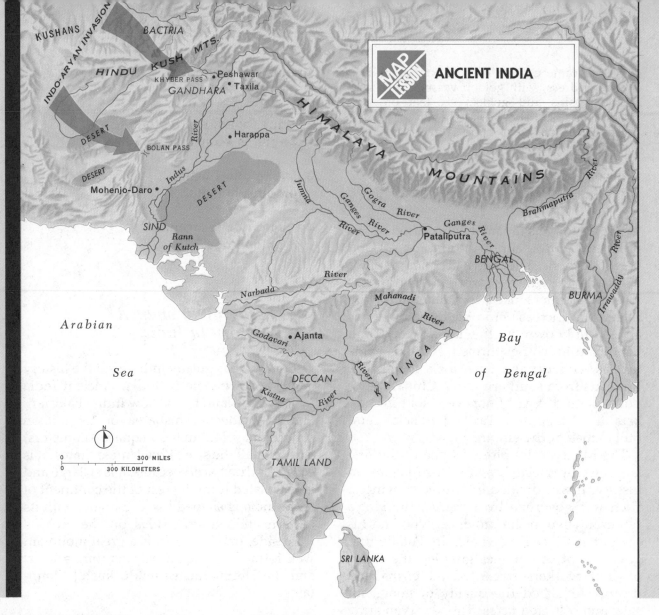

Khyber [kī′bər] Pass. While the mountains did not give complete protection from invasion, they helped set India apart from the rest of the world.

India's history is a story of succeeding invasions of people through the passes. As each group came, it gradually mingled with the people who had come before. The modern people of India are so intermixed it is difficult to distinguish the different races. However, the people of India can be divided into groups according to the languages they speak.

The largest group of people in India speak Indo-Aryan [in′dō er′ē ən] languages. Another major group speak Dravidian [drə-vid′ē ən] languages. Members of this group lived in India before the Indo-Aryans came. Some historians believe the Dravidians may be descendants of the people of Mohenjo-Daro. Another group is made up of people who speak Tribal languages. The ancestors of these hardy people once lived all over India. Some of these people were absorbed in advancing civilizations. Others were pushed into the hills and jungles. Modern Tribal people continue to follow the fishing and food-gathering cultures their ancestors began

■ MAP LESSON 3: ANCIENT INDIA

1. Rivers are always of great importance on historical maps. The Ganges is known as the sacred river of India. Why might this be so? Note that the Ganges delta is very large. The delta also receives the waters of the Brahmaputra River.

2. The Indus River is much like the Nile; both flow through a desert and end in a major delta. However, the two rivers flow in opposite directions. Into what body of water does the Indus flow?

3. Locate Pataliputra, the center of the Mauryan Empire. Why was this a good location for a capital city? Today this city is called Patna.

4. A ridge of mountains, the Western Ghats, runs along the west coast of India. Thus, no major rivers flow into the Arabian Sea for about 1,000 miles (1,600 kilometers). How might this affect coastal life?

5. East of the Indus delta is a large bay of the Arabian Sea. This is called the Rann of Kutch. In ancient times, it was a shallow bay, but today it is a vast sea of mud. How might this affect the way it is shown on maps?

6. Locate the Himalaya Mountains. To the north of the mountains, the Brahmaputra River flows past permanent ice fields for hundreds of miles (kilometers). Then it knifes through the barrier, cutting a deep canyon southward to bring its waters down to a lush rain forest. Into what body of water does the Brahmaputra flow?

Even today, the Khyber Pass is still a major travel route through the Hindu Kush Mountains.

thousands of years ago. A fourth group is made up of Mongoloids [mong′gə loidz], who live in the mountains in the far north. Their ancestors came to India from central Asia, bringing a Mongol language with them. Of these four main groups, the Indo-Aryan and the Dravidian are most important to the history of India.

Rivers and monsoons bring life-giving water.

Two great river systems that cross India have also been important to Indian history. In the northwest is the Indus, where one of the first civilizations began. Life in the arid northwest depends upon the Indus. The Ganges [gan′jēz′] River, in the east, is sacred to the Indians, who call it "Mother." The Ganges has been the difference between food and famine.

The climate has been as important as the physical features in shaping the lives of the people. Generally, India is an extremely hot land. The south is warm year-round; the average monthly temperature is always above 65°F. (18°C.). Rain, not temperature, distinguishes one season from another. Summer is the wet season; winter, the dry. In the northern plains, temperatures are more extreme. Summer highs of 125°F. (51°C.) have been recorded. In the winter, the temperature may reach the freezing point (32°F., 0°C.).

Above all, life in India has been dependent upon its seasonal winds, called *monsoons* [mon sünz′]. The summer monsoons that blow from the Arabian Sea and the Indian Ocean carry much moisture. If these monsoons fail, crops do not grow well and famine results. Lack of water has caused terrible crop failures and famines throughout Indian history, bringing much suffering and death. Thus, great efforts have been made to guard

GEOGRAPHY

A Key to History

MONSOON WINDS AND INDIAN HISTORY

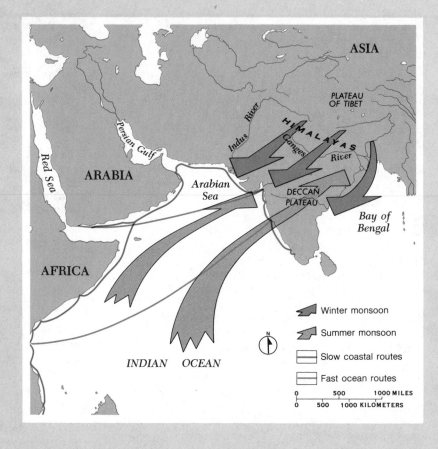

Like most other parts of southern Asia, India has been greatly affected by the seasonal winds called monsoons. As early as 300 B.C., people in India were writing about the monsoons.

The summer monsoon winds are mainly caused by seasonal changes in air pressure. From March to June, extremely hot air accumulates above the Indian subcontinent, forming a low-pressure area. From June through September, cooler air from the Indian Ocean sweeps across the subcontinent into this low-pressure area.

The cooler air brings heavy rains. The heaviest rains fall in the northeast corner of the subcontinent. There the clouds drop their remaining moisture before they reach the Himalayas. The rainwaters often flood the Ganges River Valley.

India gets about 90 percent of its yearly rainfall from the summer monsoons. The people rejoice at the sight of the first great drops of rain. Without the rains, crops wither and die, and the people may starve. In good years, the summer monsoons bring the right amount of rain at the right time. In bad years, the monsoon rains are too heavy and wash away the crops or come too early or too late. The monsoon rains are so important that many Indian languages use the same words for "year" and "rain" or "rainy season."

From October through January, the winter winds blow southwest from the Himalayas to the Indian Ocean. The winter monsoons are the trade winds, which blow throughout the tropical part of the Northern Hemisphere. The winter winds are cool and dry.

The monsoons have affected transportation and trade, too. During the 1st century A.D., a sea captain named Hippalus discovered that the winds in the Indian Ocean regularly blew in certain directions. By using the summer winds, ships could sail directly across the Indian Ocean from the Red Sea or Africa, rather than following the coast. This route cut the sailing time from twelve months to two months. The winter monsoons enabled ships to make a rapid return journey. With this discovery, sea trade between India and Africa increased.

The monsoons also affected warfare. Invaders waited for the dry season before attacking. The muddy conditions during the wet season brought fighting to a halt.

water supplies. Thousands of ponds have been dug to hold rainfall for use during the dry season.

All in all, India's geography is a picture of contrasts. There are great deserts and heavy rainfalls. There are lands of permanent snow in the north and baking plains in the south. The highest mountains in the world have flat plains at their base. The Indian landscape is varied, but the climate has been difficult to live with. This fact has influenced all aspects of Indian life.

section review 1

1. Name the modern countries that make up what was once ancient India.

2. What two mountain ranges divide India from the rest of Asia? Describe two effects these mountains have had on Indian history.

3. What makes the four major groups of Indian people different from each other?

4. What are the two major river systems in India?

2 Many features of Indian life began in early times

During the time from 1500 to 500 B.C., the Indian people developed ways of living that are still followed today. Strict rules of social behavior and two great religions, Hinduism and Buddhism, developed then. The people began following customs that even today influence how villagers make a living, worship, dress, and eat.

Indo-Aryans invaded from the northwest. About 1500 B.C., tribes of invaders began pouring through the mountain passes into northwest India. These were the Indo-Aryans, groups of people who spoke Indo-European languages. The Indo-Europeans came originally from central Asia. In ancient times, one branch of this large group moved westward into Greece, Italy, and western Europe. Others moved into Asia Minor and the Middle East.

The Indo-Aryans were hearty eaters and drinkers who fought hard and led simple lives. They did not have writing or cities. They lived mainly by herding cattle and by farming small plots of ground. The richest families were those who had the most cattle. (The Indo-Aryan word for war meant "a desire for more cows.") Usually, the richest man in a tribe was the ruler, or *rajah* [rä'jə].

When the Indo-Aryans came into India, they found the Dravidians already living there. The Dravidians had created a strong, well-organized society in India, especially in the south. They had built large cities and castles, and they traded with Babylonia. Although the Indo-Aryans defeated the Dravidians, they took on many Dravidian customs and ideas, including certain parts of the Dravidian religion.

Village life took shape in the Vedic Age (1500–900 B.C.). The first Indo-Aryan civilization lasted some 600 years, and this period is called the *Vedic* [vā'dik] (meaning "knowledge") *Age*. Information about the Indo-Aryans is found in the *Vedas*, which are collections of writings on religion, philosophy, and magic.

Indian village life then followed much the same pattern as it does today. There was a village leader, called the headman. Sometimes he inherited the post. Sometimes he was elected to it. An elected council of village men and women distributed land and collected taxes. The villagers were farmers or craft workers, or both. Their houses had mud

Among the parts of traditional Indian village life that continue today are the village council and ritual bathing in the sacred Ganges River. At *left*, a village council meets to decide community issues. At *right*, Indians bathe in the waters of the Ganges, thus following a practice begun by their ancestors thousands of years ago.

walls, clay floors, and thatched roofs. A man's chief garment was a wraparound skirt, the end of which he threw over his shoulder. A woman wore a similar garment, usually wrapped tightly under her arms. Another piece of cloth covered her head.

The family was the center of social and religious life. Families were often large. When the older sons married, they brought their wives into the family home. The grandfather was the head of the family. All males of a family group were consulted on serious matters, because property belonged to the family group as a whole. Marriage was very important, because it joined families and their property. Each person's wishes were thought to be less important than the family's interests. For thousands of years, the interests and safety of the family group dominated the life of India's villagers.

Indo-Aryans set up the basis of the caste system. At the time of their first invasions, some Indo-Aryans married Dravidians. Soon, however, the invaders began to feel that if they continued to intermarry, in a few generations they would be indistinguishable from the Dravidians. In addition, they feared that Dravidians might enter into the high government positions that the Indo-Aryans wanted for themselves. To prevent this, the Indo-Aryans developed a system of rigid social groups. Dravidians were not allowed to marry Indo-Aryans or even to associate closely with them.

For some time, the system was just a simple division between the two groups of peoples. Gradually, however, five distinct groups appeared among the Indo-Aryans: (1) *Brahmans*, who were priests and their families; (2) warriors and their families; (3) traders and landholding farmers; (4) serfs, and (5) *pariahs* [pə rī'əz], also called the *untouchables*. Other Indians believed that the touch, or even shadow, of a pariah would contaminate them. For a long time, the warriors ranked first. But as warfare declined and religion became more important, the Brahmans became most important.

From this beginning, the people of India developed even more rigid and complex divisions called the *caste* [kast] *system*. Hundreds of divisions were based on skin color, politics, place in society, kind of work, wealth, and religion. The members of each caste had to follow its rules for marriage, work, and religious rites. There were even rules for eating and drinking. People had to marry within their own caste. No amount of success or achievement would allow a person to move from one caste to another.

Indian writing developed. Over a period of a thousand years, the Indo-Aryans in India developed a written language called *Sanskrit* [san'skrit], which had its own alphabet. By 300 B.C., spoken Sanskrit had become differ-

ent from the written forms of the language used by priests and poets.

Knowledge of Sanskrit did not reach Europe until more than 3,000 years later, in the 18th century. It then became the basis for a comparative study of languages. Many words in Greek, Latin, English, German, Persian, and other languages are also found in Sanskrit. The Sanskrit word *mata*, for example, became *mater* in Latin, *mutter* in German, and *mother* in English. The English words *brother*, *sister*, *daughter*, and *son* are directly related to the Sanskrit words *bhrata*, *svasir*, *duhita*, and *sunu*.

The most important Sanskrit literature is the *Rig-Veda* [rig vä'də], meaning "Hymns of Knowledge." It has 1,028 hymns of praise to different gods that were passed down by word of mouth from generation to generation. Scholars wrote many notes and explanations, called the *Upanishads* [ü pan'ə-shadz], about the *Vedas.* These collections of religious writings deal with the beginning of the world and the meaning of life.

Hinduism began. The Indian religion of Hinduism had its beginnings in the Vedic Age. The early Indo-Aryans sacrificed animals to a number of gods. The *Rig-Veda* verses tell of the greatest god, Indra, who— like the main god in other religions at the time—threw thunderbolts, ate bulls by the hundred, and drank lakes of wine. But the *Rig-Veda* hymns tell about something more than the gods; they tell about a moral law that rules both gods and people. Hinduism gradually moved to a belief that the universe and everything in it was God, or Brahma. The many gods were like different faces of Brahma. During the Vedic Age, three gods

This copper statue of Siva was made in the 1400s A.D. The figure is made to stand for both the destroying and preserving forces in the universe.

emerged as the most important: Brahma (the creator), Siva (the destoyer), and Vishnu (the preserver).

City-states developed during the Epic Age (900–500 B.C.). The Indo-Aryans had been gradually pushing east to the valley of the Ganges River and south toward the Narbada [när bä'də] River. Settlement reached these river banks about 900 B.C., marking the beginning of the 400-year-long *Epic Age*. Our knowledge of this time comes from the long poems, or epics, which were written during the period.

By the beginning of the Epic Age, the Indo-Aryans had formed many city-states. These states were almost always at war with each other. Cities of this time were protected by moats and walls. Each city had its own rajah, who had much greater power than any village headman. The rajah lived in a palace in the center of the city. He kept an army and consulted a royal council made up of relatives and other nobles. His power extended over the villages in the countryside beyond the city walls. Villages paid taxes to the rajah.

A new social class began to develop as some city people became rich through trade. They formed a middle class between the villagers and the nobles. As trade increased, people needed some form of money and credit. Copper coins came into use, and by 500 B.C., banking had developed.

Literature was developed. The Epic Age produced two great epic poems, the *Mahabharata* [mä hä'bə rä'tə] and the *Ramayana* [rä'mä yä'nə]. Unlike the *Vedas*, which were religious, the epics tell about the adventures of heroes of the early wars. The *Mahabharata* tells of a great war and is probably the work of many poets. Its most famous part is a long poem, the *Bhagavad-Gita* [bug'ə vəd gē'tə],

meaning "The Lord's Song," which emphasizes that one must never shirk duty nor fear death. The *Ramayana* tells of a hero's wanderings and the patient wait of his faithful wife.

Hinduism stressed rebirth. Much can be learned about Hinduism from the epics. Verses tell of the religious wish to escape from the physical world into a world of the spirit. True happiness and peace come when a person's soul is taken by the "world-soul." The belief is that individual existence is an illusion, as all people are part of the "world-soul." As people come to see this, they become part of it.

The following lines from the *Bhagavad-Gita* show how Hindus see little difference between life and death. To them, the end of life is like going to a new place. They believe that after death they will be born into a new body. This belief is called *reincarnation* [rē'in-kär nā'shən].

> All that doth live, lives always! To man's frame
> As there come infancy and youth and age,
> So come there raisings-up and layings-down
> Of other and of other life-abodes
> Which the wise know and fear not.

By the Epic Age, Hinduism had been developing for 1,000 years. The ideas expressed in the *Bhagavad-Gita* continue to have a profound effect on peoples' lives today, and Hinduism has made many great contributions to world culture. Because Hinduism recognizes many paths to truth, it has encouraged religious toleration, that is, the freedom to follow one's own beliefs. Hinduism has encouraged scholarship, work, love, meditation, and civic responsibility. And it has developed a deep appreciation for art and beauty.

This seated Buddha was made about 300 A.D. and is 36 inches (90 centimeters) high.

Buddhism originated in India. Some Indian thinkers disagreed with the elaborate rites of Hinduism and with the caste system. One of these was Siddhartha Gautama [sid′är′thə gô′tə mə], who lived from 563 B.C. to 483 B.C. Gautama was the son of a king whose land lay close to the Himalayas. When Gautama was twenty-nine, he left his wife and child and his easy life to search for an answer to the question, Why do people suffer pain and sorrow? He lived with holy men, fasted, and denied himself material comforts. This freed his mind for concentration on religious thoughts. Then, one day as he sat meditating under a sacred tree, he felt that the truth had come to him. Thereafter, he was known as the Buddha [bü′də], a name meaning ''The

Enlightened One.'' He taught and preached for the rest of his life, and he formulated these beliefs, the Four Noble Truths:

1. Human life—from birth, through old age, sickness, and death—is full of pain and sorrow.
2. Pain is caused by a longing for life, passion, and pleasures.
3. Pain can be stopped.
4. The way to stop longing and thus to end pain, is to travel the *Eightfold Path*. One must practice (a) right belief, (b) right intention, (c) right speech, (d) right action, (e) right livelihood, (f) right effort, (g) right thinking, and (h) right meditation.

The Buddha believed that by following these rules the soul would finally be freed of the bondage of rebirth and would enter *nirvana* [nir vä′nə]. Nirvana, according to the Buddha, cannot be defined, but it is the end of all earthly desires when the soul finds perfect peace.

As a reformer of the Hinduism of his time, the Buddha preached against the teachings of the priests and broke with their rules of caste by treating all people alike. He also attacked the extremes of some holy men who tortured their own bodies in order to deny their physical nature and heighten their spiritual life. The Buddha taught the Middle Way, or moderation in all things.

This simple and humble teacher claimed no godlike powers. He left some of the most noble and beautiful rules for right conduct:

Hatred is never ended by hatred at any time; hatred is ended by love.
Let people overcome anger by love, let them overcome evil by good.
Everyone trembles at punishment, everyone loves life. Remember that you are like unto them, and do not cause slaughter.

During the Buddha's lifetime, his teachings spread over all central and northern India. He founded several orders of *monks*, holy men who live apart from society. These monks built monasteries [mon'ə ster'ēz] that became centers of learning. The Buddha's followers continued his work after his death. The religion called Buddhism is based on his teachings.

section review 2

1. What are the years of the Vedic Age? Why is the early Indo-Aryan period called the Vedic Age?

2. What were the reasons behind the origin of the caste system? What changes took place in the system?

3. What was the main subject of the *Vedas?* What were the subjects of the epics?

4. What Hindu beliefs and practices did the Buddha attack? What beliefs and practices did he encourage?

3 Strong rulers built empires in India

Shortly after the end of the Epic Age, India was threatened by a new attack from the northwest. These attackers were led by Alexander the Great, a Greek general who became one of the great conquerors of the world. He had defeated Persia in 328 B.C. Two years later, hoping to conquer still more land, he crossed the Indus River into India. He defeated an Indian army and pushed on toward the east. However, his soldiers refused to go farther, and he had to turn back.

The Mauryan dynasty brought unity and peace (321–184 B.C.). Alexander is said to have met and influenced a young Indian named Chandragupta Maurya (chun'drə-gŭp'tə mä'ŭr yə]. In 321 B.C., Chandragupta seized an Indian kingdom and made himself ruler from its capital, Pataliputra [pä'tə li-pu'trə]. His power grew, and in the years following, he conquered all of northern India. He was the first of the Mauryan dynasty.

In 273 B.C., Chandragupta's grandson, Asoka [ə sō'kə], became emperor. He led a military campaign that enlarged the Mauryan Empire to include all but the southern tip of India. But the cruelty of battle horrified him, and he never fought again. Asoka explained how he came to this decision. He had the following words carved on a rock for all to see:

> Kalinga was conquered by his Sacred and Gracious Majesty [Asoka] when he had been consecrated eight years. 150,000 persons were thence carried away captive, 100,000 were slain, and many times that many died. . . . Thus arose [Asoka's] remorse for having conquered the Kalingas because the conquest of a country previously unconquered involves the slaughter, death, and carrying away captive of the people.

Asoka determined to give his people peace rather than war.

At about this time, he became a Buddhist. His new religion may well have helped turn him away from warfare. Asoka commanded his people to be kind and truthful. He had rules of conduct carved on stone pillars 30 or 40 feet (9 to 12 meters) high. Some of these still stand today. A strong believer in not hurting people or animals, Asoka stopped the religious sacrifice of animals in Pataliputra. He encouraged nobles to make holy trips to Buddhist shrines instead of going on hunting parties. Asoka ate no meat and encouraged his people to be vegetarians. Although a devout Buddhist, he allowed other religions in his empire.

Asoka sent Buddhist missionaries north to the lands of the Himalayas, to the southern tip of India, east to Burma, and west across

Syria and Egypt to Cyrene in North Africa. As a result, Buddhism became the religion of a large part of the world.

Asoka, one of the outstanding rulers in history, gave India unity and peace. But soon after his death in 232 B.C., his empire began to fall apart. The last Mauryan emperor was assassinated in 184 B.C., and a series of attacks brought northern India under foreign rule.

Greek kings ruled in India (183–130 B.C.). In the eastern part of Alexander's empire, bordering northern India, was the Greek kingdom of Bactria. Demetrius [də-mē'trē əs], a Bactrian ruler, conquered part of northern India in 183 B.C. He ruled an area stretching from Persia to the middle of the Ganges Valley, including Pataliputra. Demetrius believed in joining East and West on an equal basis. Coins during his rule had Greek writing on one side and Indian on the other.

An important development that came from this mixing of cultures is seen in the religious art, called Gandharan [gand här'ən]. Because the Buddha had taught against worship of idols, artists up to this time had never shown him in human form. In Gandharan art, the Buddha is shown in a beautiful form; his face is graceful and peaceful.

In 130 B.C., Bactria, with its majority of Indian people and a ruling Greek class, was attacked by nomads from central Asia. Greek rule in India came to an end.

As part of his devotion to Buddhism, Asoka commissioned this building during the first century B.C. It was made to hold the relics of Saripatta and Mahamogalana, two of Buddha's most famous pupils. The building is in Sanchi, India. At *right* is the top of a pillar also commissioned by Asoka. The wheel underneath the lions is the Wheel of Law which Buddha set in motion through his teachings. Today, this pillar is a national symbol of modern India.

63

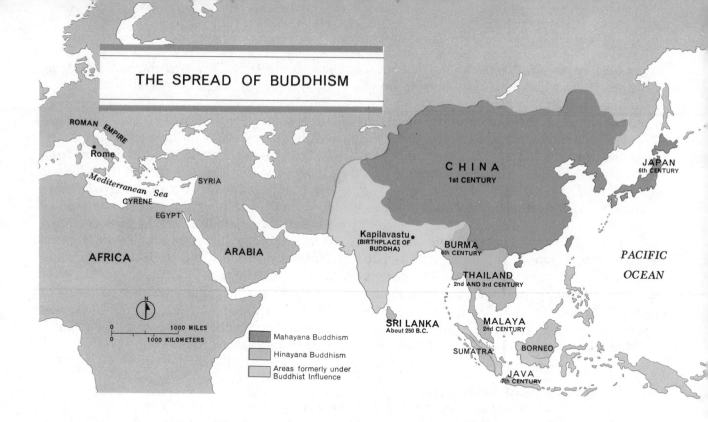

THE SPREAD OF BUDDHISM

ROMAN EMPIRE

Rome

Mediterranean Sea

SYRIA

CYRENE

EGYPT

AFRICA

ARABIA

CHINA
1st CENTURY

JAPAN
6th CENTURY

Kapilavastu
(BIRTHPLACE OF
BUDDHA)

BURMA
6th CENTURY

THAILAND
2nd AND 3rd CENTURY

PACIFIC

OCEAN

SRI LANKA
About 250 B.C.

MALAYA
2nd CENTURY

SUMATRA

BORNEO

JAVA
4th CENTURY

0   1000 MILES
0   1000 KILOMETERS

Mahayana Buddhism
Hinayana Buddhism
Areas formerly under
Buddhist Influence

Kushan rulers (78–200 A.D.) helped spread Buddhism. A period of many wars and different rulers followed the fall of Bactria. But by the 1st century A.D., an Asian tribe called the Kushans [kù shanz'] had proved themselves to be the most important of the invading tribes.

The most powerful Kushan king, Kanishka [kə nish'kə], became ruler about 78 A.D. He ruled over a large area of Asia, including what is now Afghanistan and northwestern India. He pushed his boundaries south, perhaps as far as the Narbada River. He built fine buildings in his capital, Peshawar [pə-shä'wər]. One of his best-remembered buildings was an immense wooden tower, said to be 600 feet (180 meters) high. It was decorated with many figures of Buddha and was still standing as late as the 6th century A.D. Foreign visitors called it one of the wonders of the world.

Kanishka was a Buddhist. During his reign, Gandharan art flourished. Many statues were carved to honor Buddha. In a secluded valley of what is now Afghanistan, carvings were made on the face of a rock cliff. One image of Buddha is 115 feet (30 meters) high, another is 170 feet (51 meters) high. A person standing by the second carving only comes up to the toe of the image.

Kanishka called a council of 500 monks. They developed the Mahayana [mä'hə yä'nə] school of Buddhism. The believers of this school added to Buddhist traditions. One addition is belief in a great number of minor gods who help people reach nirvana. Mahayana Buddhism spread through much of northern Asia, China, Mongolia, Tibet, and Japan. The traditional, or Hinayana [hē'nə-yä'nə] Buddhism, was strongest in Burma, Thailand, Malaya, and on the island of Sri Lanka.

Southern India traded with Rome. During the Kushan period, India carried on a flourishing trade with the western world. By this time, the enormous Roman Empire had grown up along the Mediterranean Sea. With its capital at Rome, it included the northern coast of Africa, Spain, Europe to the Rhine River, and many of the eastern lands that Alexander had conquered. There was a great exchange of goods between the Kushan and Roman empires. Most of it passed through the ports of southern India.

The people of the south, the Tamils [tam'əlz], were descendants of the Dravidians. They had built several independent kingdoms that were often at war with each other. Especially important was the Tamil kingdom at the tip of the Indian peninsula. The Tamils were great sailors. Their ships could travel the dangerous waters of the Arabian Sea and Red Sea.

Tamil ports were well-equipped with wharves and warehouses. Lighthouses guided merchant ships safely into their harbors. Roman ships brought gold, wine, glass, and pottery to southern India. They took back with them silks, pearls, rice, and spices. The spices of India—pepper, ginger, and cinnamon—were highly valued by the Romans. Food spoiled fast in those days before refrigeration, and rich-tasting spices covered up the bad taste of spoiling food. The silks that went in and out of these ports came either by a long journey overland across central Asia or by sea in Chinese ships, called *junks*.

Harbors on the west coast of Tamil land were crowded with merchants, caravan leaders, and sailors. There were so many outsiders that special settlements were built to house them. With this incoming population came a number of Arabs, Jews, and Christians whose descendants live in south India today.

section review 3

1. Why was Asoka's first military campaign also his last? How did he encourage Buddhism?
2. During what years did Greeks rule a part of India? What effect did this rule have on Indian religious art?
3. What is the name of the new form of Buddhism that grew up under Kanishka? Where is it practiced today?
4. What goods were traded by the Indians and the Romans?

4 Gupta rule launched a golden age

After the fall of the Kushans about 200 A.D., northern India broke up into many small states. This period of cultural decline lasted about 100 years. Then in the 4th century, a new line of kings, the Guptas, came to power. Their reign is called the golden age of Hindu culture. The first Gupta king became ruler of the Ganges Valley about 320 A.D.

The people prospered during the Gupta Empire (320–500 A.D.). The Gupta emperors ruled strongly and fairly. Their income came from port duties, the royal lands and mines, and a tax on farm produce. Trade and manufacturing flourished. So good was life in the Empire that a Chinese Buddhist who went to India wrote:

> . . . The people are many and happy. They do not have to register their households with the police. There is no death penalty. Religious groups have houses of charity where rooms, couches, beds, food, and drink are supplied to travelers.

Buddhism, however, was no longer one of

During the second century B.C., Buddhist monks began to build a fantastic monastery in the Indhyari Hills, a short distance from the village of Ajanta. For the monks, the remote location, with the nearby Waghora River for fresh water, was an ideal spot in which to meditate.

The monastery is actually a group of 29 caves carved by hand into the sides of basalt cliffs that form a horseshoe-shaped ravine. Built over several hundred years, many of the caves were carved with vaulted ceilings inside and porches outside. All had steps leading down to the river. Four of the caves were designed as chapels; the rest were living quarters for the monks.

All the caves were decorated with paintings, however. And it is these fragile paintings that have brought Ajanta its greatest fame. Painted on a thin layer of plaster over the basalt, many of the colorful drawings show stories about the Buddha. At the same time, they also tell much about life in ancient India. There are bull fights, dancing girls, hunting parties, and scenes of life among the nobles of the day.

About 650 A.D., the caves were abandoned as Buddhism declined in India. Then the destruction began. Bats, monkeys, tigers, insects, peacocks, and other animals all came to inhabit the caves. Porches collapsed, and stairs turned to rubble. Hermits moved into the caves and damaged the paintings with smoke from their cooking fires.

For more than 1,000 years, the caves were known to the Ajanta villagers and few others. Then in April, 1819, a local youth showed the caves to a group of British soldiers on a tiger hunt. Soon tourists began to come. They chopped out pieces as souvenirs. Guides splashed varnish on the paintings to make the colors brighter for important visitors. The varnish slowly dried to become a thick, dusty film.

Finally, the government of India stepped in. Some of the most seriously damaged caves were closed to tourists. More guards were posted to stop the looting and vandalism. Caves were fumigated to get rid of the insects. And advanced techniques of restoration were begun. It now seems that careful work can save these treasure houses of ancient art.

Above *left* is a Buddhist saint from the wall painting in Cave 1. Above *right* is Cave 19 showing some of the elegant carving. *Below* is the basalt cliff of Ajanta and the scaffolding put up by restorers.

Dancers in the temple inspired this Gupta sculpture.

the chief religions. In time, Indian Buddhism became so much like Hinduism that it was looked upon as a sect of Hinduism. This caused a steady decline. People began to feel that Hinduism was a more truly Indian religion. Gupta rulers also aided Hinduism by supporting its priests.

Learning and art flourished. Learning and science grew under the Guptas. The astronomer and mathematician, Aryabhata [är′yə-but′ə], wrote verses about the value of pi (π), and the rotation and spherical shape of Earth. Other Indians calculated the size of the moon and wrote on gravitation.

The contributions of Indian mathematicians to world civilization are among the greatest of any people. They developed the number symbols that served as the basis for our own numerals. (It is because these symbols were adopted and carried westward by Arab traders that we call them Arabic numerals.) Gupta scholars also worked out the decimal system and were among the first—along with the Maya Indians of the Yucatan Peninsula—to use the zero.

Indians found new uses for chemistry in manufacturing. Their steel was the best in the world. They were the first to make cashmere and such cotton fabrics as calico and chintz. Gupta doctors were among the best doctors of the time. In special schools begun during this time, physicians learned to clean wounds, do surgery, and treat snake bites.

Gupta literature is famous for its fairy tales and fables. The most famous storybook of the time is the Panchatantra [pan′chə-tan′trə]. This collection of eighty-seven stories was written between 300 and 500 A.D. Other Indian writings included the world-famous story of Sinbad that finally found its way into *The Arabian Nights.* Some Indian fables were later translated into European languages and were used by such authors as Chaucer, the Grimms, and Kipling. Much excellent poetry and drama also came from the Gupta period.

During this time, Indian painters and sculptors also freed themselves from Greek influences to create a distinctly Indian art. Artists, inspired chiefly by Hinduism, produced dignified and restrained work. The Ajanta cave paintings, for example, are well known for their beauty.

Indian culture influenced other peoples. From about the 2nd to the 10th centuries A.D., Indian emigrants, traders, and armies carried their way of life to many distant places. The influences were gradual but eventually reached as far away as Madagascar and Taiwan.

Indian influence was strongest in such places as Sri Lanka, Burma, and what is now central Thailand. Here the cultures became almost entirely Indian. In more distant places such as Java, Cambodia, and southern Indochina, Indian influence was weaker, and Indian culture blended with local ways.

Indian art, however, made a strong impression on all of Southeast Asia. In central Java, the world's largest Buddhist shrine shows Indian influence. About the same time, Hindus in Cambodia began one of the greatest religious buildings in the world, the temple of Angkor Wat [ang′kōr wät′].

Angkor Wat is one of the world's finest examples of a blend of architecture and sculpture. The temple was begun by Suryavaram II, king of the Khmer people, to honor the Hindu god Vishnu. Although damaged during a 1970s war, the temple is a glorious reminder of the technical skills and artistic genius of its builders.

Centuries of disunity followed Gupta decline. Gupta power began to decline after Chandragupta II died in 413 A.D. The Huns, a fierce people from the central Asian plains, invaded northwestern India near the end of the 5th century. By the middle of the 6th century, the Gupta Empire was ended.

Small states continued to make war on one another until early in the 7th century when a ruler named Harsha brought order. Between 606 and 612, he made himself master of most of the area of the Gupta Empire. Harsha was a patron of the arts, a poet, and a good military leader and administrator. He was a despot, though a kindly one. When he died in 647, he left no one trained to take his place. All of northern India again fell into warfare.

Not only did strong government disappear, but other areas of life also suffered. There was little progress in literature or science. The Hindus had become satisfied with what they were. As a 10th-century visitor to India wrote:

The Hindus believe that there is no country but theirs, no nation like theirs, no religion like theirs, no sciences like theirs. . . . If they traveled and mixed with other nations they would soon change their mind, for their ancestors were not so narrow-minded as the present generation.

This Indian attitude not only halted progress, it also weakened the country. Their self-imposed isolation kept them from learning of new methods of warfare. Because of this weakness, the Indians could not defend themselves against a new wave of attacks.

section review 4

1. Why did Buddhism lose most of its followers in India?

2. What contributions did Gupta scholars make in science, technology, mathematics, and literature?

3. Where in Southeast Asia was Indian influence strongest? Where did it have less effect?

4. What attitude weakened India after 647?

68

Section Summaries

1. Geography shaped history in India. Surrounded on two sides by water, India traded with both east and west. The mountains on the north protected it, but there are passes through which warring tribes attacked. Two great river systems provided fertile soil for the development of civilization. A hot climate, wet and dry seasons, and the monsoons have influenced the way Indians farm, trade, and wage war.

2. Many features of Indian life began in early times. Indo-Aryan invaders defeated the Dravidians and pushed them towards the south. But the mingling of cultures produced some basic features of Indian culture. Among the most important were the village community, the caste system, and the Hindu religion. In the first stage of this development, the Vedic Age, Sanskrit writing became well developed, and religious writings were produced. In the following Epic Age, city-states grew strong, a middle class developed through trade, and great poems were produced. Another Eastern religion, Buddhism, was also begun in India at this time. Its founder, Gautama Buddha, wanted to reform Hinduism. Instead, his followers made a religion of his teachings after his death.

3. Strong rulers built empires in India. Shortly after an invasion by Alexander the Great, northern India was united under the Mauryan dynasty. Asoka, an important ruler of this dynasty, brought peace and spread Buddhism. The decline of the Mauryas in the 2nd century B.C. was followed by other invasions. Rule by Greeks from Bactria gave rise to an important Buddhist art style, called Gandharan, which spread to parts of Asia. The Kushans, who controlled northern Indian areas for 200 years, also aided the growth of Buddhism. During the Kushan period, a lively trade with the West moved through Tamil ports.

4. Gupta rule launched a golden age. The Gupta Empire was a prosperous time. Contributions to the world included the numerals now used in most of the world, and the decimal system, as well as advances in astronomy and medicine. Writers and artists also made important contributions to the civilization of India. Indian influence in art and religion reached the people of Southeast Asia. However, because Gupta rulers favored Hinduism, Buddhism almost disappeared from the land of its birth.

After the Guptas, India was thrown into discord. During a brief period in the 7th century, Harsha provided strong rule. Following his death, there was a 800-year-long period of isolation and decline.

Who? What? When? Where?

1. Write sentences telling what role each of these played in Indian history:

    a. Alexander the Great
    b. Aryabhata
    c. Asoka
    d. Chandragupta Maurya
    e. Demetrius
    f. Harsha
    g. Kanishka
    h. Siddhartha Gautama

2. Write sentences that show the importance of each of these terms to the Hindu religion: *Rig-Veda*, Brahma, Siva, Vishnu, reincarnation.

3. What question was Gautama trying to answer when he left his family?

4. In which of these time periods did each of the following events occur:

1500–1001 B.C.
1000–501 B.C.
500–1 B.C.
1–500 A.D.
501–1000 A.D.

    a. Harsha brought peace to India.
    b. Gautama Buddha died.
    c. Gupta rule began.
    d. The Vedic Age began.
    e. The *Mahabharata* was written.

5. Using the map on page 54, describe the areas of the Indian subcontinent covered by each of the following at the time given:

    a. Mauryan Empire, about 270 B.C.
    b. Bactrian Empire, in 183 B.C.
    c. Kushans, about 70 A.D.
    d. Tamils, about 100 A.D.

Questions for Critical Thinking

1. Compare traditional Indian family life and marriage with that in the United States. In what ways are they different?

2. What are some of the original sources of information about early Indian life mentioned in this chapter?

3. Why do you think the caste system is not followed in the United States?

4. What often happened when an important leader, such as Asoka or Harsha, died?

5. How are Hinduism and Buddhism alike? How are they different? If you were an Indian ruler, which would you choose to follow? Why?

Skill Activities

1. Read *The Wonder that Was India* by A.L. Basham to learn more about India before 1000 A.D. (Grove Press, 1959)

2. Pretend you are a visitor to India during the Gupta Empire and write a letter home describing your experiences.

3. Read one or both of the excerpts from the *Bhagavad-Gita* and Buddha's *Four Noble Truths*; write a paragraph telling what these writings mean to you.

4. In encyclopedias, research the Brahmaputra, Ganges, or Indus river. Find out how long it is, where the major source is, and what major cities are along its route.

chapter 3 quiz

Section 1

1. The great mountains to the north of India are the : a. Himalayas, b. Alps, c. Ganges

2. The people of India are divided into groups by their: a. height, b. language, c. race

3. True or false: The two great rivers of India are the Gupta and the Ganges.

Section 2

4. The first group to live in India were the: a. Indo-Aryans, b. Tamils, c. Dravidians

5. In Indian family life, the most important group is the: a. family unit, b. parents, c. children

6. True or false: The three most important Hindu gods are Brahma, Siva, and Vishnu.

Section 3

7. True or false: Alexander the Great conquered India in 330 B.C.

8. True or false: The peace and unity of Asoka's empire lasted 100 years.

9. The first art form to show Buddha as a human was: a. Malayan, b. Gandharan, c. Mahayanan

Section 4

10. By 1000 A.D., Indians were weak because they were: a. conquered by other nations, b. ill from diseases, c. too satisfied with their lives

11. True or false: Gupta rule was a time of great prosperity and advance.

12. Gupta power declined after the rule of: a. Harsha, b. Panchatantra, c. Chandragupta II

THE GREAT AGE OF CHINA

These terra cotta soldiers are two from the thousands that were found in the 1970s in China. They come from the tomb of Shih Huang Ti. The larger figure is that of an officer. The inset shows the hairdo of an infantryman. The way the hair was braided told the man's rank.

Astronauts orbiting Earth can see many of the planet's natural features. With the unaided eye, however, they are able to recognize only a few humanmade features. One of them is the Great Wall of China. It is the longest wall in the world. It extends for 1,500 miles (2,400 kilometers), crossing mountains and blocking narrow valleys. The building of the Wall was begun in the 3rd century B.C. A Chinese ruler decided that the empire needed a defensive barrier against the Huns, tribal nomads who periodically attacked China's northern borders.

Building the Wall was an amazing undertaking. The forced labor of thousands of men was used. Huge blocks of stone had to be cut

The Great Wall extends for hundreds of miles (kilometers) across China. In the foreground of this picture is a watchtower. In the east, the Wall is made of earth and stone and faced with brick. In the west, the Wall is made only of earth.

and moved from quarries and then fitted into the wall. Many men died in accidents. It is said that every block cost a human life.

When it was completed, the Wall was 40 to 50 feet (12 to 15 meters) high, and its base measured 15 to 30 feet (4.5 to 9 meters) wide. In some places, it consisted of three different walls, built one behind the other for better defense. Every few miles there were tall watch towers where guards could look across the countryside for signs of invaders. Behind the Wall were permanent camps for soldiers.

The Wall gave the Chinese long periods of safety. Over the years, various rulers have repaired or improved the wall. And only a handful of invaders have been able to break through it. The Wall has been called one of the wonders of the world. It is to China what the Pyramids are to Egypt.

The course of Chinese history described in this chapter covers about 2,000 years. During this long period, China profited from important inventions, such as printing and the making of paper. It developed the first civil service system in the world, and it produced fine philosopher-teachers, great poetry, and matchless painting. In this chapter, you will find that:

1. **Geography helps explain the Chinese story.**

2. **The Chou dynasty ruled longest in China.**

3. **Two dynasties united China.**

4. **The Tang dynasty gave China a golden age.**

1 *Geography helps explain the Chinese story*

In every country, geography influences how people live. However, different aspects of geography have different importance in different countries. In India, for example, climate is the most striking geographic influence. In China, it is the land itself.

Natural borders isolated China. China covers an area a little larger than that of the 50 United States. China's borders of sea, jungles, mountains, and deserts are natural barriers that have hampered invaders from other parts of the world. Until the 19th century, the wide salt marshes on the seacoast and the lack of harbors stopped invaders from the east. To the south, mountains and the thick jungles of Indochina also made a natural border. At the west, the rugged Plateau of Tibet, more than 10 thousand feet (3,000 meters) above sea level, and the towering Himalayas protected China.

Only at the north and northwest have outsiders been periodically successful at invading China. There, the Gobi [gō'bē]—the huge desert of Mongolia [mong gō'lē ə]—and other parts of central Asia have been home to nomadic tribes called the Huns for thousands of years. In these dry regions, there was little farming. The Huns moved their settlements each season as their herds grazed on the vast but scanty grasslands. In dry years, there would be little grass for the herds. Then the tribes would begin to push south into the fertile valleys of China.

The isolation of China and the fact that many of the neighboring peoples lived as nomads rather than as farmers or as city people led the Chinese to think of themselves as superior. They spoke of their country as the Middle Kingdom and considered it to be the center of the world. The people who lived in the barren wastes of central Asia were said to live in the Outer Kingdoms.

Within China itself, natural features isolated different parts of the country from each other. The rough, hilly land made it difficult to build roads across China. Mountain ranges such as the Tsinling [ching'ling'] and Altai naturally separate China into parts. Northern China is relatively dry and has seasonal changes in temperature similar to those in the northeastern United States. Southern China is relatively wet, because monsoon winds from the Pacific Ocean bring large amounts of rain. The temperatures are similar to those in the southeastern United States.

WHAT'S IN A NAME?
ALTAI MOUNTAINS

The name Altai comes from the Mongolian words *Altain ula*, meaning "mountain of gold." In the 700s A.D., people believed these mountains were rich in gold and silver.

Fertile valleys aided the growth of civilization. High in the western mountains, less than 100 miles (160 kilometers) apart, are two streams. One flows northeast, the other, southeast. These streams are the headwaters of the two biggest river systems of China— the Hwang Ho and the Yangtze [yang'tsē]. Both rivers carry rich silt as well as water. Chinese civilization developed in the fertile valleys formed by these rivers. The valley of the Hsi [shē] River, in the south, has also been important in Chinese history.

The Hwang Ho meanders through the loess-filled plains of northern China. Because the river often floods, through the centuries the Chinese have built dikes, or *levees*, to keep it within its banks. In the process, they also created irrigation systems. Governments developed in part because of the need to build and maintain the dikes and irrigation systems.

Chinese civilization developed first in the Hwang Ho Valley. Since the river is shallow and unsuitable for navigation by large boats, the valley has been more important as a millet- and wheat-growing area than as a trading center. As the population grew, people moved past the hills to settle in the Yangtze Valley.

The Yangtze flows through the rough, hilly land of southern China. Much of its course lies in the so-called lake plains. Here small rivers and lakes expand and contract, depending on the season and the amount of rainfall. The small bodies of water ultimately flow into the Yangtze, making it a river that varies greatly in width. For instance near

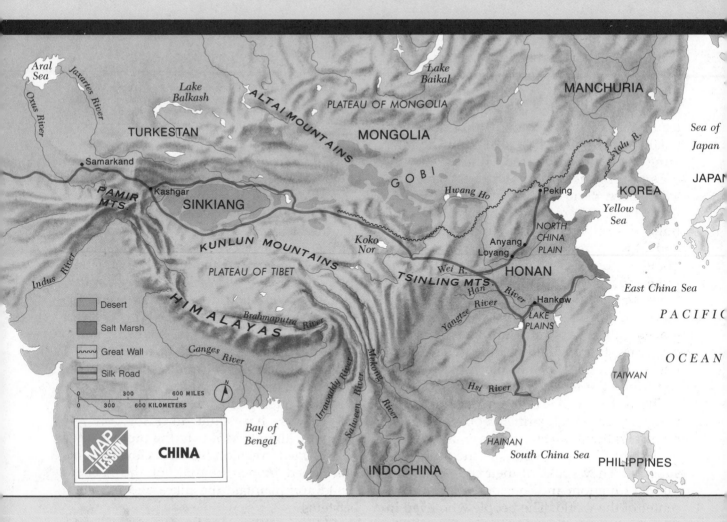

CHINA

■ MAP LESSON 4: CHINA

1. The Hwang Ho originally flowed into the sea by a more northerly course. About 602 B.C., it shifted and entered the Yellow Sea south of the peninsula. About 70 A.D., it again moved north of the peninsula in its present bed. In 1938, the Chinese returned the river to its southern bed to forestall a Japanese invasion. In 1947, they steered the river back to its present course. The Hwang Ho has no great city near its mouth. Why might this be so?

2. The Pacific coast of China is divided into several areas. Into what seas do the Hwang Ho, Yangtze, and Hsi flow? What direction are these seas from the rivers?

3. What direction is the Gobi from the Great Wall? Why might this be so?

4. Koko Nor is a large salt lake in Outer China, a name given to the sparsely settled areas away from the coast and lake plains. The densely settled plains may be called Inner China. Which direction is Koko Nor from the Silk Road?

5. The Silk Road has three end points in Inner China. What direction is the Peking end point from the end point along the Hsi River?

Hankow, where the Han River flows into the Yangtze, the river is ¾ mile (1 kilometer) across in the dry season and 5 miles (8 kilometers) across in the wet season. The Chinese have developed irrigation systems that use this water to grow rice.

The culture of southern China is quite different from that of the north. Food, language, clothing, housing—all reflect the isolation of the two areas and the differences in climate and land. The Yangtze is navigable for 600 miles (960 kilometers) inland, and it was an early trade route.

In the southernmost part of China is the Hsi Valley, which is farmable year-round. It is isolated from the rest of China by rough hills. The point where the river empties into the South China Sea is one of the few natural harbors in China. The villages near the river's mouth developed as trading centers.

section review 1

1. Name the four types of geographic barriers that have kept China separated from other parts of the world. Tell where each barrier is found.

2. What led the Chinese to think of themselves as superior?

3. Name three rivers that have been important in the history of China.

4. How is the culture of southern China different from that of northern China?

2 The Chou dynasty ruled longest in China

The Shang dynasty had arisen about 1500 B.C. in the region of the Hwang Ho Valley—the most northern of the three major river valleys in China. Their era ended, like many others in Chinese history, with a successful invasion by a less civilized people. In 1027 B.C., the Shang were conquered by a group of people who lived on the northern edge of the Shang territory. The leader of this less civilized group was known as Chou [jō]. The dynasty named after him lasted until 256 B.C.—almost 800 years.

Strong nobles ruled feudal states. During the first 250 years or so of the Chou dynasty, the kingdom was made up of more than 1,000 *feudal* [fyü'dl] states. (A feudal state is ruled by a noble who gets his authority from the king. In return, he owes the king soldiers to keep order and to protect and enlarge the kingdom.) At first, the nobles were loyal to the king. Toward the end of this period, however, the nobles used their soldiers to fight among themselves and increase the size of their own states. Finally in 771 B.C., some of the nobles joined together and marched on the Chou capital at Loyang [lō'yäng'] in the province of Honan [hō'nan']. There they killed the king.

A new Chou king was allowed to take the throne, but he had little power. He became hardly more than a high priest who performed state religious rituals and tried to keep peace among the nobles. During this period (771 B.C.– 456 B.C.), the Chinese moved into and settled the richly fertile river valley of the Yangtze. The stronger nobles gained control over the land of the weaker nobles. As a result, the number of feudal states decreased, but those that survived increased in power.

The last 200 years of the Chou period are sometimes called the Era of Warring States. During this time, the strong nobles were constantly battling with one another. They invented catapults to break down the mud walls of enemy towns. For the first time, small groups of archers riding on horses, which gave the advantage of surprise, were used to make attacks.

Life for the rich merchants and nobles was luxurious and elegant. This was in sharp con-

Bronze pots were an important type of Chinese art for centuries. This one was made about 700 B.C. It is 46.5 inches (118 centimeters) high and weighs 141.5 lbs. (64.2 kilograms).

trast to the poverty among the peasants and unskilled workers. The poor lived in mud huts with thatched roofs of straw. The rich had homes that were groups of buildings with courtyards, gardens, and tile roofs. In the north, the poor lived on millet. In the south, they ate rice. Everywhere, rich people had huge banquets using the "five flavors"— sweet, sour, salty, spicy, and bitter.

The rich developed an elaborate social code in the nobles' courts. They took part in archery contests that were accompanied by music and were more like ballets than sporting events. In their free time, they played checkers, gambled with dice, hunted, fenced, and trained horses and dogs. The peasants had few comforts, paid taxes to the rich, served as soldiers, and had no political rights. The nobles were separated from the peasants by land ownership and family descent—a system that lasted for centuries.

The Chou period made lasting achievements. Even though there was much confusion and fighting among the nobles, the 800 years of Chou rule were perhaps the most important in Chinese history. This time is often called the classical period because many basic parts of Chinese civilization began during that time.

During the Chou period, economic life in China changed greatly. Towns grew in size and number as many people became merchants or artisans. Skilled workers who had the same trade started organizations to help each other and to improve the quality of their work. Canals were dug, and better ways of irrigating the land were found. Even though farming methods improved, many farmers found it hard to make a living. The farms were often too small to produce crop surpluses for use when the harvests were bad.

Because the family unit was very important in Chinese culture, family members stayed together. As the population grew, more and more people had to be supported from the harvests of farms that were already too small. This problem, which began during the Chou dynasty, remained until the Chinese communist government in the 20th century broke up farm holdings and redistributed the people.

Trade grew during the Chou dynasty, although most of it took place within the Chou kingdom itself. The goods traded included jade ornaments, bronze mirrors and vessels, iron tools, silks, furs, and furniture. During the Chou period, small coins with square holes were being made and used in trade. These continued as the basic coinage until late in the 19th century.

The Chou era was also an important time for the government of China. The Chinese, like the Egyptians, believed that their ruler was divine. Beginning with the Chou period, the Chinese called their king the *Son of Heaven*. Unlike the Egyptians, however, the Chinese limited the power of their kings. When the Chous came to power, they said that they were right in taking over because the Shangs had not ruled well and therefore had lost the support of the gods. In this theory, called the *Mandate of Heaven*, all rulers were expected to govern justly and to look after the well-being of the people. If a king did not do this, he would no longer have the support and favor of the gods and could be overthrown by his people. This belief made people feel that revolution was sometimes necessary and right.

The king was aided by a chief minister and six department heads. They were chosen for their intelligence rather than their birth. They headed the departments of agriculture, public works, war, religious affairs, finance, and justice. Thus, the Chinese had a tradition of using intelligent policy makers in government, unlike other cultures in which such positions were often the reward for military service or the accident of birth.

Confucius was a great Chinese teacher.
During the Chou period, great thinkers and teachers drew up rules of conduct for the Chinese people. These leaders decided what should be worn for special occasions, how to serve and eat food, and the way in which people talked to one another. Even the conduct of a son toward his father, a wife toward her husband, a friend toward a friend, and other social relationships were regulated. This code of politeness changed little until recent times.

One of the greatest Chinese teachers, Kung-fu-tzu, is better known in the West today as Confucius [kən fyü′shəs]. He is the most honored and revered person in all of Chinese history.

Confucius was born in 551 B.C., only a few years after the Buddha. He began to teach when he was 22 years old. However, his goal was to hold high political office. But he never reached this goal. His greatest success came as a teacher.

Confucius did not think of himself as an inventor of new ideas. He thought of himself as one who passed on the ideas of others. He is believed to have preserved the literature of China for later times. Because he lived during a troubled era, Confucius feared that the literature would be lost. Therefore, he gathered earlier writings together into what are called the "Five Classics."

Unlike the Buddha, Confucius did not seek to escape from the world. Instead, he wanted to find a way for people to be happy on Earth. Confucius taught that human nature is good, not bad. If people would think and act properly, he believed, most evils would disappear. His teachings held that individuals should be tolerant and kind and have respect for older people and ancestors. In government, he believed that the ruler was like the father in a family. The ruler directed the government, but was responsible for the welfare of his people. Confucius also stressed the importance of education, good manners, and respect for the ways of the past.

Many of the sayings of Confucius are in a book called the *Analects*. These samples show his wisdom and understanding of human nature:

A man who has committed a mistake and doesn't correct it is committing another mistake.

A man who brags without shame will find great difficulty in living up to this bragging.

He was asked, "What do you think of repaying evil with kindness?" Confucius replied, "Then what are you going to repay kindness with? Repay kindness with kindness, but repay evil with justice."

A gentleman blames himself, while a common man blames others.

To know what you know and know what you don't know is the mark of one who knows.

The teachings of Confucius gave a useful standard of correct behavior for the people of China and had a great influence on them. His followers combined his teachings with their religious ideas about ancestor worship to make a religion called *Confucianism* [kən-fyü′shə niz′əm], which continues today.

The Chinese religion, unlike that of the people of India, has little to do with the mystery of the afterlife. As Confucius once said, "While you do not know life, what can you know about death?" The main concern of the Chinese since the days of the Chou has been how to have a happy, well-balanced life in this world. They have always respected learning and have given the highest roles and respect to scholars and philosophers.

Great as Confucius was, he may not have been altogether good for China. He loved tradition and the past. He stimulated in the Chinese a strong dislike for change. This dislike had serious consequences in later years.

Taoism grew out of Lao-tse's teachings. Chou China produced another great teacher, Lao-tse [lou′ tse′]. Very little is known about him as a person, but his teachings make up a religion known as *Taoism* [dou′iz′əm]. It has had a great influence on China. This religion holds that the best way to live is according to nature. The word *Tao* means "way." Taoists believe that those who follow this way, as taught by Lao-tse, will learn the meaning of the universe. The religion holds that people should be kind, free from pride, humble, thrifty, and should return an injury with a great kindness. Confucius had stressed the importance of good government. Lao-tse, however, believed that the less people are governed, the better off they are.

Over the centuries, simple Taoism became buried under a great deal of superstition and magic. Many Taoist teachers claimed they had supernatural powers. They could foretell the future and prolong life "through breathing exercises and diets of powdered dragon bones, moonbeams, and mother of pearl." Sorcery, fortune telling, and charm selling eventually became important activities of Taoist believers. But early Taoists, because of their stress on nature and inner peace, made important contributions to Chinese thought. Taoism provided a simple, acceptable philosophy that greatly strengthened the Chinese social order and internal peace.

Art and literature flourished. Chinese artists produced some of the world's greatest art. Much art from the Chou period has been excavated. This includes handsome bronze vases used in religious ceremonies and many pieces of carved jade, lacquer ware, and pottery. Chou artists carved jade and ivory very well. *Jade* is a semiprecious stone that is usually whitish or soft green in color. But the most prized stones are emerald green or pure white. When Confucius was asked why the Chinese liked jade so much, he said:

> It is because, ever since the olden days, wise men have seen in jade all the different virtues. It is soft, smooth, and shining, like kindness; it is hard, fine, and strong, like intelligence; its edges seem sharp but do not cut, like justice . . . the stains in it, which are not hidden and which add to its beauty, are like truthfulness.

The Chinese developed writing. Chinese writing has been in use for over 3,500 years and is the oldest living language in the world. Long before the Chous rose to power, the Chinese had a system of writing. By the end of Chou rule, this system was so well developed that it has come down to the present with few changes.

The Chinese have a very complicated language, although individual words have only one syllable each. A single word may have several meanings. For example, the word *fu* can mean "rich," "store up," or "not." The speaker's tone of voice gives the meaning. As a result, spoken Chinese varies in tone and has a rhythmic quality.

Chinese writing, like that of the Egyptians, developed from picture writing. But unlike the Egyptians, the Chinese continued to use one symbol for each word or idea. Today, there are about 50,000 Chinese word symbols. Only a few scholars learn all of them. For many centuries, the great majority of Chinese people never learned to read or write because there were too many word-symbols to memorize.

section review 2

1. Why did the Chou rulers have trouble keeping peace in their kingdom?

2. What was the goal of Confucius' teachings?

3. Why might Confucius' teachings have hindered change for the Chinese?

4. What type of writing did the Chinese develop?

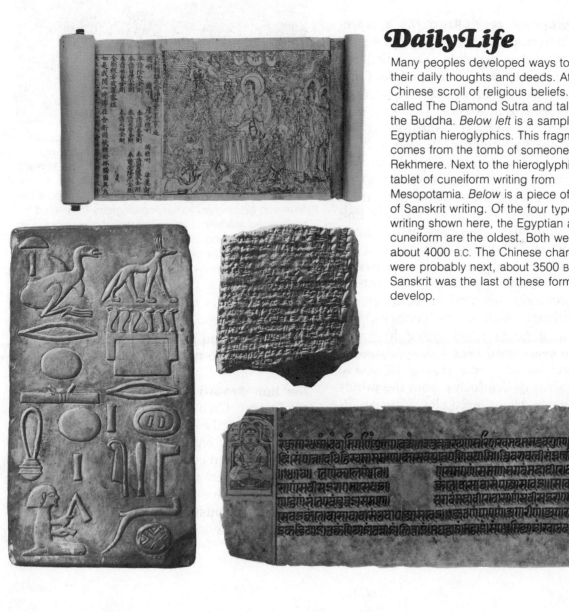

Daily Life

Many peoples developed ways to record their daily thoughts and deeds. At *left* is a Chinese scroll of religious beliefs. It is called The Diamond Sutra and talks about the Buddha. *Below left* is a sample of Egyptian hieroglyphics. This fragment comes from the tomb of someone named Rekhmere. Next to the hieroglyphics is a tablet of cuneiform writing from Mesopotamia. *Below* is a piece of a scroll of Sanskrit writing. Of the four types of writing shown here, the Egyptian and the cuneiform are the oldest. Both were begun about 4000 B.C. The Chinese characters were probably next, about 3500 B.C. The Sanskrit was the last of these forms to develop.

3 Two dynasties united China

In the last years of the Chou dynasty, many of the feudal states were at war with one another. The king of Ch'in [chin], one of these states, emerged as the most powerful ruler. The Chou dynasty fell in 256 B.C. After a power struggle among several states, the Ch'in ruler seized control in 221 B.C. He began a new dynasty, and it is from this dynasty that China got its name.

A Ch'in emperor centralized the government. Ch'in rule lasted only until 206 B.C., but its control was absolute. The ruler had complete authority over all the people. Only a very able, strong man could have brought about such a state of affairs. This man was called Shih Huang Ti [shir'hwäng'tē'], which means ''first emperor.''

Shih Huang Ti extended China's boundaries south. He united the country by making Ch'in laws the laws of the whole nation. He set up a uniform system of weights and measures and built a network of tree-lined roads. Most important, he strengthened the central government by ending the power of the nobles. He then divided China into 36 military provinces, each governed by an appointed official. With a few changes, this basic form of government lasted for more than 2,000 years until 1912 A.D.

To bolster his rule, Shih Huang Ti tried to erase the ideas of Confucius from the minds of the Chinese. He ordered all Confucian literature burned because it favored tradition and called the old Chou system good and just. However, many books survived and were later collected and saved.

Shih Huang Ti wanted to protect the northern and western border areas from the frequent invasions of the Huns. To do this,

This gilded bronze lamp was probably made about 173 B.C. It is almost 19 inches (48 centimeters) high and weighs almost 35 lbs. (16 kilograms). The servant girl's sleeve is hollow so that candle smoke will go into it rather than into the room. The round walls of the lamp can be opened to varying degrees to give off the needed amount of light. The girl's timid expression and simple clothing are fitting of her low social position. The whole lamp reflects the elegant creativity and mechanical resourcefulness of artisans of the time.

he added to and joined together several protective walls to make the Great Wall.

The Han dynasty extended the boundaries of China. Civil war broke out in China shortly after the death of Shih Huang Ti in 210 B.C. After eight years of fighting, a new dynasty gained control. It took the name *Han* because its first ruler had once led an army on the Han River. The Han dynasty was one of the most outstanding in Chinese history. Some Chinese still call themselves ''sons of

Han." The Hans ruled for more than 400 years—from 202 B.C. to 220 A.D. During Han rule, China grew as large and prosperous as the Roman Empire of the same period.

The greatest Han ruler was Wu Ti [wü' dē'], who lived between 140 and 87 B.C. He drove the Huns back from the Great Wall and took over part of Korea. He extended the empire south to Indochina and west to central Asia and brought an era of peace to all of central and eastern Asia. Later Han rulers pushed the boundaries to the borders of India and Persia.

During Han rule, the Chinese made several cultural advances. They invented the first *yoke*, or shoulder collar, for draft animals. This made it possible for animals to pull heavier loads. (Europeans did not have a similar device for another 1,400 years.) By 100 A.D., the Chinese had invented paper. They also wrote the world's first dictionary and the first history of China based on facts rather than legend.

China met other civilizations. The expansion of China during Han rule brought the country into contact with other peoples. Trade did well, especially along the "Silk Road." This route ran from China through central Asia, crossing deserts and mountains, to the edges of the Middle East. Along the way, probably in Chinese Turkestan,

merchants from the West met Chinese trade caravans. The Chinese had luxury goods—silks, spices, and furs—that were highly prized by the merchants from the West. The two groups traded ideas as well as goods and exchanged much information.

People of the West learned about such fruits as peaches, apricots, and rhubarb from the Chinese. Western influence led the Chinese to take a more lifelike approach to art and design and possibly learn new ideas about music and chemistry. From central Asian peoples, the Chinese learned about grapes and alfalfa.

Chinese contact with India led to the introduction of Mahayana Buddhism in China. A Chinese mission went to the Kushan Empire and brought back the religion about 67 A.D. After that, it spread rapidly in China.

section review 3

1. What dynasty gave China its name? Name some of the accomplishments of that period. How did these accomplishments help unite China?

2. Why did Shih Huang Ti try to destroy Confucianism?

3. What were the accomplishments of Wu Ti?

4. What did the West learn from the Chinese? What did the Chinese learn from other peoples?

Daily Life

Tomb figures from Han times tell about how people lived then. In this terra cotta village, the wealthiest family has a house with a balcony and also lives closest to the town well. The trading caravan passing through town uses horses and camels to carry loads.

4 The Tang dynasty gave China a golden age

The glory of the Hans faded in the third century A.D. Strong nobles seized parts of the empire, and the last of the Hans was overthrown in 220 A.D. China broke up into little warring kingdoms. Barbarians broke through the Great Wall. Science, art, invention, and trade stood still or declined. China, like Europe at the same time, went through a period of darkness and confusion. Chinese recovery began in 618, when the Tangs [tängs], came to power.

For almost 300 years the Tangs gave China a golden age. The country was prosperous and free from invasion. Its people made progress in education, literature, and the arts. New canals were built, and foreign trade grew. The population grew to 50 million. At its height, the Tang Empire was the strongest, most advanced, and best governed in the world.

A great emperor governed wisely. A great Tang ruler, T'ai Tsung [tī' dzung'], became emperor in 627, when he was only 21 years old. He pushed back invaders and enlarged the borders of China.

After several wars, T'ai Tsung concentrated on the peaceful internal development of China. He strengthened the government, stopped the growth of large estates, and tried to make taxes more equal. He valued history and once said: "By using the past as a mirror, you may learn to foresee the rise and fall of empires."

T'ai Tsung did not believe harsher laws were the way to stop crime. He explained that to "diminish expenses, lighten the taxes, and employ only honest officials . . . will do more to abolish robbery than the employment of the severest punishments." He knew that he owed it to his people to govern wisely. One day, when in a boat with his son, he said: "The water bears up the boat, but it can also overturn it. So with the people—they uphold the prince but they can also overthrow him!"

Education strengthened Chinese government. The Chinese were the first to fill *civil service* jobs, that is, government jobs, by public examination. The system, which began during Han rule, was strengthened by the Tangs.

Education had an important place. Good students were sent from local schools to the colleges of their provinces. The best students then went to the imperial school in the capital, where several thousand of them studied for the civil service. This system gave China intelligent and well-trained officials. They were highly thought of and had many duties. They collected taxes, kept order, punished wrongdoers, conducted tests for government service, and ran the postal service. Other countries of Asia also sent their young men to China to be educated. As a result, Chinese influence spread beyond its borders.

Thousands of officials of the Chinese government belonged to the civil service. They were chosen after taking written tests that were given every three years. Each candidate sat in a small, separate room, like a phone booth. In some towns, there were acres of these booths in long rows. The test took three days. Food was brought in by servants. Officials watched from high towers to see that no one cheated. The test was so important that some candidates went mad or even died of exhaustion. The final examination tested knowledge of current events, Confucian classics, creative writing, law, and math. Candidates could take the tests many times.

Bright young men from very poor families

THE GROWTH OF CHINA

- ▢ Chou, 1027–256 B.C.
- ▢ Chin, 221–206 B.C.
- ▢ Han, about 100 A.D.
- ▢ Tang, 618–907

0   500   1000 MILES
0   500 1000 KILOMETERS

One of the greatest and certainly one of the most carefree of the Tang poets was Li Po [lē' bô']. One of his poems, called "The Moon over the Mountain Pass," reads:

> The bright moon soars over the Mountain of
>   Heaven,
> Gliding over an ocean of clouds.
> A shrill wind screaming ten thousand li away,
> And a sound of whistling from Yu-men pass.
> The imperial army marches down White
>   Mound Road.
> The Tartars search the bays of the Blue Sea.
> The warriors look back to their distant homes:
> Never yet has one been seen to return.
> Tonight, on the high towers she is waiting.
> There is only sorrow and unending grieving.

could take the easiest test. If successful, they could enter the lowest civil service rank. With more study and experience, they could be promoted to the highest posts. Thus, in Chinese government there was the kind of "log cabin to White House" idea that is found today in the United States.

This Chinese system of selecting government workers lasted until the early 1900s. Although it was more advanced than any other such system in the world, it did have a serious fault. The candidates were tested mainly on the old classics. Not enough attention was paid to new ideas. Therefore, civil servants chose to support old ways rather than to prepare their country for change. This weakness became very serious in modern times, when China was not able to meet the challenges of a rapidly changing world.

Many poets wrote during the Tang period. A common saying about the Tang period held that "Whoever was a man was a poet."

These pottery figures show dancers and musicians entertaining a princess. Such entertainments in the Tang court often began after dinner—a great feast of tortoise, duck, and other delicacies.

These two figures both come from tombs of the Tang era. The camel comes from the tomb of a merchant who was involved in trade with Persia and Turkestan. The horse figure is made of glazed pottery. Although the saddle is heavily decorated, it has no stirrups for the rider's feet—they were not invented until several centuries later. Thus, the rider held on by gripping very tightly with his knees.

The Chinese invented printing. Literature flourished under the Tangs. This was not only because the people were prosperous and the government stable, but also because of the invention of printing. Ink had been used as early as 1200 B.C., and paper made from wood pulp had been invented during the Han dynasty.

Early Chinese printing done during the Tang era is called *block printing*. The printer carved raised characters on a block of wood, wet the surface of the characters with ink, and pressed sheets of paper against them. Chinese printers in the 11th century invented movable type made of baked clay. These characters could be rearranged to form different words and so be used over and over again. But because of the difficulty in making the nearly 50 thousand characters in the Chinese alphabet, most Chinese printers continued to use block printing.

Most early Chinese books were really printed on rolls of paper. Gradually, however, the Chinese made books with pages and covers. They also invented paper money and printed playing cards.

section review 4

1. After the fall of the Han dynasty, what did China have in common with Europe of the same period?

2. Why were the years of the Tang Empire a golden age in China?

3. What was the major fault of the Chinese civil service system?

4. Name the major kind of printing used in China. Why was it used so much?

Section Summaries

1. Geography helps explain the Chinese story. Natural barriers have isolated China from other centers of civilization. Within China, the Tsinling Mountains have separated the peoples of the north and south. Different ways of life developed in these two regions. The Yangtze River provided a good trade route with the interior. The Hsi River promoted year-round farming, and a port city developed at its mouth.

2. The Chou dynasty ruled longest in China. In the history of China, the Chou period, from 1027 to 256 B.C., is called classical. This is because many basics of Chinese civilization were formed at this time. A group of fine thinkers, especially Confucius, wrote lessons that guided personal actions and behavior for the next 2,000 years. Taoists followed another "way." Also during this time, a feudal government arose that limited the king's power. Towns and trade grew. The people designed fine art and formed lasting customs.

3. Two dynasties united China. In the 3rd century B.C., the Ch'in dynasty united the feudal states. Under Shih Huang Ti, laws were standardized and the country was divided into 36 provinces. The Great Wall was built as a barrier against invaders. After the Ch'in dynasty, the Hans ruled China from 202 B.C. to 220 A.D. They won control of eastern and central Asia and provided an era of peace. Contact with the world beyond the borders of China led to increased trade with the West and brought Buddhism from India.

4. The Tang dynasty gave China a golden age. Emperor T'ai Tsung expanded China and ruled with wisdom and justice. For 300 years, the Tangs held the empire together. Education and a civil service system were improved, great poetry was written, and printing was developed.

Who? What? When? Where?

1. Match the dynasty (Ch'in, Chou, Han, or Tang) with the years of its rule:

a. 623 A.D.–900 A.D.
b. 1027 B.C.–256 B.C.
c. 221 B.C.–206 B.C.
d. 202 B.C.–220 A.D.

2. Match the correct dynasty (Han, Chou, Tang, or Ch'in) with the statements below:

a. This dynasty was named after a river.
b. Li Po lived then.
c. The last years of this dynasty are called the Era of Warring States.
d. The "First Emperor" built the Great Wall.
e. Printing was invented.
f. It ruled only fifteen years.
g. This was China's "golden age."
h. This dynasty lasted for almost 800 years.
i. Shih Huang Ti tried to destroy the works of Confucius.
j. Ideas and goods were traded with the West.
k. Confucius began his teaching.
l. This dynasty was as large and prosperous as the Roman Empire.
m. It was the "classical" period.
n. Mahayana Buddhism was introduced in China.
o. This dynasty gave China its name.

3. What barrier did the Chinese build to keep out strangers? Who were these strangers?

4. In what ways did Chinese life change very little for 2,000 years?

5. Give evidence to prove that Shih Huang Ti was not able to completely destroy the ideas of Confucius.

6. Name some Chinese improvements or inventions in these areas: government, farming, and printing.

Questions for Critical Thinking

1. China was weakened by not changing for 2,000 years. Why didn't the leaders realize that they were hurting themselves?

2. A common saying in the Tang period was: "Whoever was a man was a poet." How does this idea fit in with our society's ideas of manliness?

3. How did trade help the Romans and the Chinese improve their lives? Why is contact between people with different ideas and life-styles important?

4. List some ways in which our lives have been improved by inventions of the Chinese.

5. For what common reason did different Chinese dynasties rise and fall?

Skill Activities

1. Read *Ancient China* by Robert Knox to learn more about this land and its past. (Watts, 1979)

2. In everyday language, explain the sayings of T'ai Tsung. Was T'ai Tsung a wise leader?

3. Discuss the *Mandate of Heaven*. Is there any way in which it is like our ideas about government today?

4. Describe two or more types of Chinese art mentioned in this chapter. What materials were used? What were some subjects shown by the artists? What outside influences changed Chinese art styles? How?

5. On a map of China, sketch in and label the ocean, jungle, mountain, and desert areas that have protected it from the rest of the world. Add the great rivers, and show where various crops are grown. Indicate the "Outer Kingdoms" of Mongolia and Sinkiang, and draw arrows representing invasions.

chapter **4** *quiz*

Section 1

1. The Huns invaded because: a. they needed new grazing lands for their herds, b. they needed more farmland to feed a growing population, c. they hated the Chinese

2. To control the Hwang Ho floods, the Chinese built: a. levees, b. the Great Wall, c. canals

3. True or false: The Plateau of Tibet and the Himalayas form two of China's natural borders.

Section 2

4. True or false: The early centuries of the Chou dynasty saw a kingdom made up of feudal states.

5. True or false: There was a sharp contrast between the lives of the rich and the poor during the Chou dynasty.

6. The person who gathered earlier writings together into what are called the "Five Classics" was: a. Wu Ti, b. Li Po, c. Confucius

Section 3

7. The religion that is not native to China but came to be widely practiced is: a. Confucianism, b. Buddhism, c. Taoism

8. An important advance of the Han era was the: a. yoke for draft animals, b. sale of luxury goods, c. burning of Confucian literature

9. True or false: Shih Huang Ti was a firm believer in Confucianism.

Section 4

10. T'ai Tsung was a: a. great emperor of the Tang era, b. major poet who also founded a great religion, c. civil servant who invented block printing

11. Civil service officials were chosen by a system that was based on: a. election, b. family name, c. ability

12. True or false: Chinese printers preferred movable-type printing.

THE GOLDEN AGE OF GREECE

This face mask is made from a thin sheet of solid gold. The face is thought to be that of Agamemnon, the leader of the Greeks in the Trojan War.

In ancient Greece, it was thought an honor to be able to die in battle. A famous *funeral oration*, or speech given in honor of the war dead, is remembered because it describes not the soldiers, but the way of life they fought to preserve.

Our government is not copied from our neighbors. We are an example to them. Our constitution is called a *democracy* because power is in the hands not of the few but of the whole people. When it is a question of settling private disputes, everyone is equal before the law. No talented man is kept out of public service because he is poor or from the wrong class. We have no dark words or angry looks for our neighbor if he enjoys himself in his own way. We are open and friendly in our private, day-to-day relations with each other. In our public affairs we keep strictly to the law.

Our city is so large and powerful that all the wealth of all the world flows in, and our own products seem no more homelike to us than the works of other nations. The gates of our city are flung open to the world. We let visitors see or discover anything, even though it might help an enemy, because we trust not in military equipment, but in our own good spirit in battle.

The speaker was Pericles [per′ə klēz′], a famous general and statesman of the Greek city-state Athens. The speech was what we today call *propaganda*, that is, its main purpose was to spread ideas or beliefs. In it, Pericles described effectively the things that he felt made the Athenians better than their enemies, the Spartans. Of more importance to us, his praise for his native city described the contributions of ancient Greece to civilization. These contributions include:

1. The Greek government, in which citizens were equal before the law, became a model for Western democracy.

2. Public service was thought to be an honorable and necessary part of every citizen's life.

3. Individuals were free to live their own lifestyles, to come and go as they pleased, to speak their minds openly.

4. An awareness of beauty enhanced Greek life. As Pericles said: "Our love of what is beautiful does not lead to extravagance; our love of the things of the mind does not make us soft."

5. Public debates were held before the state took action. As Pericles also said:

". . . we decide or debate carefully and in person all matters of policy. We do not think there is an incompatibility between words and deeds. The worst thing is to rush into action before the consequences have been properly debated."

These five qualities of the best in Athenian society make up what is often described as the Greek view of life.

Western civilization owes much to the Greeks. The classic forms of architecture, sculpture, history, philosophy, drama, and poetry come from Greek originals. Modern science began with the study of Greek writings on physics, mathematics, biology, and medicine.

How was it that these talented people were able to leave such magnificent gifts to civilization? Historians cannot agree on any one answer. There are many points to consider: the origin of the Greeks, the relative isolation of their individual city-states, the freedom and individualism fostered by their society, the competition and rivalry among the city-states, and their conflicts with outsiders. This chapter tells how:

1. Aegean civilization depended on sea trade.

2. The Greeks established the basic principles of democracy.

3. The Greeks were threatened by Persia and by city-state rivalries.

4. The Macedonians united Greece and the Hellenistic Age began.

5. Greek civilization formed the basis for Western culture.

1 *Aegean civilization depended on sea trade*

To early people, the sea meant mystery and danger. In their small boats, they ventured upon it with caution. They stayed close to the shoreline by day and took refuge in harbors at night. Little by little, the sea became more important as a highway for trade. The Phoenicians were among the early traders who dared to sail the open waters. Others who met the challenge of the deep were the people who lived on the islands of the Aegean [i jē′ən] Sea and along its shores.

Crete developed a flourishing culture. It is believed that the island of Crete [krēt] was settled as early as 6000 B.C. by Neolithic peoples from southwest Asia. About 3100 B.C., Egyptians also immigrated to Crete. Between 1600 and 1400 B.C., Crete became a power in the ancient world. The island served as a stop on the trade routes between Europe and Africa and between Africa and Asia. The civilization that developed on Crete is called *Minoan* [mi nō′ən] for King Minos [mī′nəs]. According to mythology, he ruled Crete.

Ancient Greek legends include a number of references to Minoan civilization. One of the best-known stories concerns the Minotaur [min′ə tôr], a monster with the head of a bull and the body of a man. The Minotaur was an object of worship and was kept beneath the royal palace in a *labyrinth* [lab′ə-rinth′], an intricate and bewildering series of passageways. Every year, the Minotaur was offered a human sacrifice of seven boys and seven girls from Athens. Finally, it was killed by the Greek hero, Theseus [thē′sē əs]. He escaped from the labyrinth by following a thread given him as a guideline by Minos' daughter.

Until the end of the 1800s, little was known about Minoan civilization. But in 1894, Sir Arthur Evans, an English archaeologist, began excavations on Crete. He found inscribed clay tablets and jewelry. These showed that the Minoans had a system of writing. Copper and bronze tools and weapons showed an advanced stage of technology. An important find was the ruin of the

This wall painting shows the sport of bull dancing. The painting is on a wall at the Palace of Knossos.

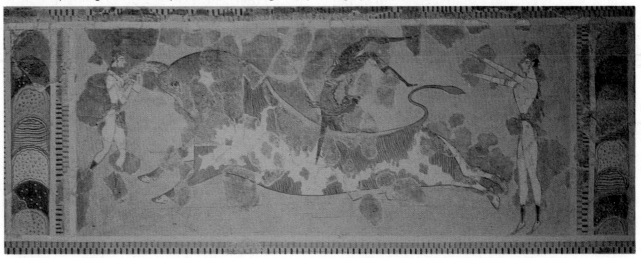

royal palace at Knossos [nos′əs], the capital city. It was an amazing building, covering 6 acres (2.4 hectares). Like a giant labyrinth, it had many living quarters, corridors, tunnels, storerooms, and an ingenious underground plumbing system.

Crete became rich from its overseas trade and metalworking industries. Minoan manufactured goods included decorated clay vases, bronze weapons, and locks and keys. These were traded for gold, silver, and grain.

Egyptian influences can be found in much Minoan art, but the island people also had their own forms of architecture, painting, and sculpture. Their art reveals their love of athletics and the world of nature. Many of the wall paintings show the dangerous sport of "bull dancing." The idea of this sport was to meet the bull head-on, grab his horns, and somersault over his back to safety. Women as well as men participated in these events.

About 1900 B.C., people from the area around the Caspian [kas′pē ən] Sea invaded the Greek peninsula. The newcomers are known as Mycenaeans [mī′sə nē′ənz]. They spoke an early form of Greek. The Mycenaeans built fortified cities and began to engage in trade and manufacturing. They did especially well at the cities of Mycenae [mī sē′nē] and Tiryns [tī′rinz]. About 1500 B.C., the Mycenaeans captured Knossos. During the following century, they attacked and destroyed other cities on Crete. However, in 1400 B.C., the Minoans succeeded in driving the Mycenaeans off the island. Minoan trade and city life revived somewhat, but commercial leadership in the Aegean had passed to Mycenae. The island of Crete no longer was the main center of trade.

Mycenae and Troy became centers of Aegean civilization. From 1400 to 1200 B.C., Mycenae was the most important power in the Aegean community. During this time, all the people of the Aegean area developed a feeling of fellowship. They spoke a common language and believed in the same gods. Zeus [züs], the strongest god, ruled over a family of gods and goddesses. These gods and goddesses were believed to live on Mt. Olympus.

Aegean civilization also included parts of Asia Minor. The city of Troy was especially important. It was strategically located on the Hellespont [hel′i spont], a *strait*, or narrow channel, connecting two major bodies of water. (The Hellespont is now called the Dardanelles [därd′n elz′].) Because of its location, Troy controlled the trade between the two seas.

After about 1300 B.C., Mycenaean trade began to decline. The reasons for this decline are still not fully understood. Trade contacts with Egypt and the east coast of the Mediterranean were cut. This time of crisis is revealed in the *Iliad* [il′ē əd] and the *Odyssey* [od′ə sē], two epic poems thought to have been written in the 800s B.C. by the blind poet Homer.

The *Iliad* tells of the anger of a warrior named Achilles and its tragic results, an episode in a war between some Mycenaeans and Troy. The *Odyssey* describes the many adventures of the soldier Odysseus [ō-dis′ē əs] on his 20-year trip home after the end of the Trojan War.

The most famous story of how Troy was taken was written more than 700 years after Homer's time by the Roman poet Vergil (70 B.C.–19 B.C.). His epic poem, the *Aeneid*, was based on Greek sources. It told how the Mycenaean invaders built a huge wooden horse outside the city gates and then went away. The Trojans were impressed with this statue. They moved it into their city only to discover—too late—that enemy soldiers were hidden inside this Trojan horse.

One entrance to the city of Mycenae is famous for its lion figures.

This view of the Trojan horse is on a large pottery vase.

section review 1

1. Why did Crete's geographical location make it a power in the ancient world?

2. Who were the Mycenaeans and what effect did they have on Minoan life?

3. Where was Troy? Why was this an important location for a city?

4. What are Homer's two epic poems, and what stories do they tell?

2 The Greeks established the basic principles of democracy

Throughout its existence, the Aegean civilization had been threatened by invaders. About 1100 B.C., the warlike Dorian people from the north began moving into the Greek peninsula. The Mycenaeans were driven from their cities. Many of the survivors fled east and settled in and around the city of Athens [ath'ənz]. Others moved to the islands of the Aegean and the strip of seacoast in Asia Minor known as Ionia [ī ō'nē ə]. But in time, a peaceful mingling began to take place. From this mixture of different groups emerged the Greeks. During this time of transition—from the first invasions to about the middle of the 700s B.C.—the basis for Greek civilization was made.

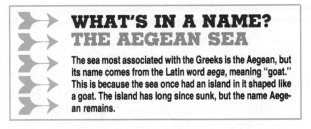

WHAT'S IN A NAME?
THE AEGEAN SEA

The sea most associated with the Greeks is the Aegean, but its name comes from the Latin word aega, meaning "goat." This is because the sea once had an island in it shaped like a goat. The island has long since sunk, but the name Aegean remains.

Little is known about this time. Trade stopped and people lived in small farming communities. Slowly, the people of Athens and other cities began to cooperate with each

This part of the famous Greek statue, called Nike of Samothrace, is a good example of Greek artistic skills. Although made of marble, the figure's clothing seems to be blowing in the breeze.

that followed the time of transition is called the *Hellenic* [he len'ik] *period.* It lasted from about 750 to 338 B.C.

Independent city-states were formed on the Greek peninsula. Early Greek society was simple. The people grouped into clans ruled by a king or tribal chief. Each clan founded a settlement, known as a *polis* [pō'lis], where the people would be safe from attack. The country around the polis was used for farming and grazing. The geographic isolation of these settlements led to the growth of small, independent city-states. The members of a city-state were proud of their home city. And each city-state was jealous of its independence. The city-states rarely cooperated with each other except when invaders threatened.

One of the greatest contributions of the city-states to civilization was democratic government. It is a government controlled by its citizens. But in early Greek society, only male landowners born in the city-state could become full citizens. Democratic government evolved gradually. The first step was most often the formation by the nobility of an *oligarchy* [ol'ə gär'kē], or government or rule by the few, that replaced the ruling king or tribal chief. With their increased power, the nobles wrote law codes. No longer was justice a matter of whim or guess. Penalties were set by law rather than by a judge, and the laws were available for all to see. Thus, the common people benefited from the law codes.

Greek traders set up colonies and trade routes. By the middle of the 700s B.C., the nobles who ran the Greek world had so much power that they became corrupt. They had increased their wealth through control of the farmland. Small farmers had been forced to mortgage their land or sell themselves into slavery to pay their debts. Many farmers gave up the land in favor of small-scale man-

other for protection and for religious festivals. From these contacts came the famous Olympic games, beginning in the 8th century B.C. They were held every four years in honor of Zeus. Little by little, the people reestablished the feelings of cultural unity, or *brotherhood,* that had existed when Mycenaean power was at its height.

The Greeks called themselves Hellenes [hel'ēns] after Hellas, an area in the northern and western part of Greece. The great era

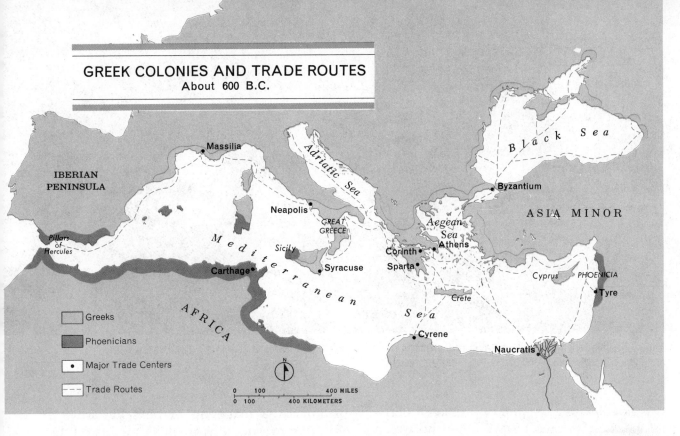

GREEK COLONIES AND TRADE ROUTES
About 600 B.C.

Black Sea

Adriatic Sea

IBERIAN PENINSULA

Massilia

Byzantium

ASIA MINOR

Neapolis

GREAT GREECE

Aegean Sea

Athens

Pillars of Hercules

Mediterranean

Sicily

Corinth

Sparta

Cyprus

PHOENICIA

Carthage

Syracuse

Crete

Tyre

AFRICA

Sea

Cyrene

Naucratis

Greeks

Phoenicians

• Major Trade Centers

--- Trade Routes

N

0   100   400 MILES
0   100   400 KILOMETERS

ufacturing. Poor soils and a lack of good land also led to the decline of farming.

The making of pottery, textiles, and bronze weapons and tools developed rapidly. It was not long before the Greeks needed more markets for their goods. A growing population put even greater demands on the available food supply, so new sources of food were needed. Migration would give the people a chance to get rich or have more political freedom. For these reasons, the Greeks began to set up colonies.

Each new colony was bound by social and religious ties to its parent city-state. Thus the city-states became less isolated. Colonies were established in the north Aegean and the Black Sea areas, and in what is now Egypt, Sicily, Italy, and southern France.

The power of the nobility was challenged by tyrants. The colonies did not end the discontent in Greece, however. A number of trends brought about the fall of the nobility. The first was the growth of a heavily armed *infantry* of citizens. The power of this infantry grew until they were a match for the *cavalry* of the nobles. (Infantry are foot soldiers, and cavalry are soldiers mounted on horseback.) The infantry demanded better living conditions for the common people. Second, the development of coinage in Lydia [lid′ē ə], a country in Asia Minor, quickly spread to Greece. With money, a family could become rich without owning much land. Third, an important new group appeared: a business class of merchants, owners of ships, weavers, potters, and blacksmiths. They were unhappy with the rule of the nobility and wanted a voice in government.

From about 650 to 500 B.C., a number of revolutions took place in Greece. Many city-states came under the rule of *tyrants* who had taken power unlawfully. To the Greeks, tyranny simply meant one-man rule. A tyrant

The Acropolis in Athens still contains many of the most famous buildings from ancient times. At *left* is the temple of Athena Nike; at *right* is the Parthenon.

was not always a cruel or oppressive ruler—as the word means today. Often he was a noble who had become democratic in outlook and to whom the people turned for leadership. In Greece, the rise of tyrants was the first step toward government by the people.

The first democracy grew in Athens. On the dusty coastal plain of Attica [at'ə kə] in southeast Greece lay the city of Athens. The city hugged the slopes of a hill known as the Acropolis [ə krop'ə lis]. It was here that the Athenians built their forts and temples. Sailors and merchants from far-away countries brought money and many different ideas to Athens.

From the 700s to the 500s B.C., the government in Athens was controlled by a council of nobles. The most important public official was the chief magistrate, who was elected every year from among the nobles. During these two centuries, different groups of citizens in Athens became more and more unhappy with their conditions. One of these

groups was made up of peasant farmers. They were struggling to make a living on the hills or had become sharecroppers on the nobles' rich farmland. Many were so badly in debt that they had become like slaves to the nobles who supported them.

The council of nobles finally realized that if they did not heed the people's cries for reforms, they would probably be overthrown by a tyrant, as had been happening in other Greek city-states. In 594 B.C., the nobles elected Solon [sō'lən] to be chief magistrate and gave him broad powers to make changes. Solon was a noble who had both an understanding of the farmers' needs and a strong sense of justice. He made middle-of-the-road reforms. His name has come down in history as a byword for wise statesmanship.

Solon canceled the farmers' debts. He outlawed the practice of debt slavery. However, he resisted the farmers' demands to redistribute the land. He enlarged the council and included not only the nobles but also rich property owners. This Council of 400 drew up new laws, and an assembly of all citizens voted on them. Solon offered citizenship to craftsmen who had not been born in Athens if they and their families would settle there. He encouraged trade. Solon did not create democracy, but his rule opened a new chapter in the history of Athens.

However, there was still discontent in Athens. The shepherds were unhappy because they owned no land. They found a leader in Pisistratus [pī sis′trə təs], a distant relative of Solon. Pisistratus took over in 560 B.C. and ruled as tyrant for over thirty years. He solved the economic problems by banishing many nobles and distributing their lands among the poor. He encouraged trade and the arts.

The next important tyrant in Athenian history was Cleisthenes [klīs′thə nēz], who came to power in 508 B.C. Under Cleisthenes, *ostracism* was begun. Ostracism was a system that gave the 6,000 citizens a chance once a year to banish any officials they thought were dangerous to the Athenian state. Cleisthenes strengthened the growth of democracy. He set up new political districts and increased the number of members in the council to 500. These changes allowed more people to take part in politics and a greater variety of local interests to be represented in government.

Solon, Pisistratus, and Cleisthenes were champions of the people. With their reforms, Athens took large steps toward becoming a democracy. Other city-states followed the lead of Athens. By 500 B.C., democratic governments were being set up in most city-states.

Sparta became a warrior state. The city-state of Sparta was an important exception to the trend toward popular government. Sparta lay on the Peloponnesus [pel′ə pə-

nē′səs], the peninsula that makes up the southern part of Greece. When the ancestors of the Spartans came to the Peloponnesus, they subdued the natives, whom they called *helots*. Allowed to remain on the land as farmers, the helots grew food for the conquerors but the helots could not become citizens. In the 700s B.C., the Spartans took over neighboring Messenia [mə sē′nē ə]. Sparta then had enough land and was not attracted

This bronze statue shows a Spartan warrior dressed for battle.

by colonization and trade. Of greatest importance in shaping the Spartan government was the never-ending threat of rebellion by the Messenians and the helots.

In about 600 B.C., the Spartans set up a constitution. Its purpose was to keep up the military strength of the state. An assembly of citizens was created, but it had little power. Control of the state was held by a small group of citizens called the Council of Elders. The council made laws for the assembly to vote on and appointed magistrates.

Sparta was set up much like a military camp. To keep up high health standards, all weak or deformed children were killed. Only the strong and healthy were allowed to live. At age seven, boys were taken from their homes and sent to real military camps. There they got strict training in gymnastics and military exercises. Each year, they were flogged to test their powers of physical endurance. At age 20, the young men became field soldiers, and were then allowed to marry, but they continued to live in the barracks. At age 30, men were admitted to the assembly and given various government posts. Girls were trained to be strong, healthy mothers of warriors. As their men marched off to war, Spartan women said goodby with the following words: "Come back with your shield or on it." To this day, the English word *spartan* means "sternly disciplined."

The helots were looked upon as state property and were little better than slaves. They could not be citizens and were governed harshly. To spy on them and to stop revolt, the Spartans set up a secret police force. Once a year, the government made it legal to kill any helot so that troublemakers were always wiped out.

The highly trained Spartan army was used against its neighbors with some success. But it was diplomacy, backed by force, that allowed Sparta to extend its influence. In the

■ MAP LESSON 5: ANCIENT GREECE

1. A merchant sailing from Athens to a Black Sea port would follow the traditional border between Europe and Asia. Through which four bodies of water would such a merchant travel?

2. Islands were very important in ancient Greece. Locate Crete, Rhodes, and Samothrace. How might the many islands of the Aegean both aid Greek civilization and hinder Greek unity?

3. Mount Olympus, the home of the gods, is located south of Macedonia. The Olympic Games, however, were held at Olympia on the Peloponnesus. What direction is Mount Olympus from Olympia?

4. The marathon race in the Olympic Games today is named for the Battle of Marathon. The news of the Greek victory was brought by a runner from the battle site to Athens. In what direction did the runner go?

5. What direction is Corinth from Athens? Sparta from Delphi?

500s B.C., Sparta formed the Peloponnesian League, a military alliance with nearby states in the south of Greece, that increased Sparta's power.

section review 2

1. When and what was the Hellenic period?

2. Why did many Greek city-states set up colonies?

3. What reforms of Solon, Pisistratus, and Cleisthenes helped bring Athens closer to democracy?

4. Why was it important to the Spartans to have a strong army? How did they make sure they would stay strong?

ANCIENT GREECE

3 The Greeks were threatened by Persia and by city-state rivalries

The Greeks came into contact with other peoples as they expanded their colonies and their power. The Persian Empire was the most dangerous enemy. Bad feelings between the Persians and the Greeks began when Cyrus [sī′rəs] of Persia attacked and defeated Croesus [krē′səs], the king of nearby Lydia, in 546 B.C. Cyrus stayed on the attack until he had beaten most of the Ionian Greeks in Asia Minor.

The next Persian ruler to threaten the Greeks was Darius I, who came to power in 522 B.C. One of his most important acts—the reorganization of the empire into administrative districts—made the Ionian Greeks very angry. Although they were a part of one of these districts, they felt they had been given a lesser role in the empire. In 499 B.C., the Ionian Greeks attacked the Persians. Athens sent ships to help the Ionians, but the Greeks were defeated decisively at the naval battle of Miletus [mī lē′təs] in 494 B.C. The city of Miletus was burned by the Persians. This act of revenge made the Athenians angry. They began to build a navy to protect their city. However, Darius was determined to take the Greek mainland and punish the Athenians for helping the Greeks in Asia Minor.

The Greeks were victorious at Marathon and Salamis. In 492 B.C., Darius tried to crush the people of Thrace [thrās], an area north of

Greece. At the same time, he tried to punish Athens, but his navy was almost destroyed by a storm. Two years later, a Persian army and navy crossed the Aegean Sea to the Bay of Marathon, about 25 miles (40 kilometers) from Athens. The Greeks were ready for this move. Athens and Sparta had earlier agreed to an alliance to fight the Persians. But when the Athenians sent a runner to Sparta to tell of the Persians' approach, the superstitious Spartans refused to march until the next full moon. Without aid from Sparta, the Athenians were outnumbered by the Persians two to one. The Greek historian, Herodotus [hə-rod'ə təs], described the battle:

> So when the battle was set in array, and the victims showed themselves favorable, instantly the Athenians . . . charged the barbarians at a run. Now the distance between the two armies was a little short of a mile. The Persians, therefore, when they saw the Greeks coming on at speed, made ready to receive them, although it seemed to them that the Athenians [had lost] their senses, and [were] bent upon their own destruction; for they saw a mere handful of men coming on at a run without either horsemen or archers . . . the Athenians in close array fell upon them, and fought in a manner worthy of being recorded. . . .

The Greeks, with their superior weapons and sheer courage, won the battle. The Persians lost 6,400 men while the Athenians lost only 192.

The success of the battle of Marathon in 490 gave the Greeks confidence and touched off rebellions in other parts of the Persian Empire.

Ten years later, Xerxes [zèrk'sēz'], the son of Darius, attacked Greece. Athens and the Peloponnesian League took on the main job of defense. The Persians defeated the Spartan army at Thermopylae [thər mop'ə lē] in 480 B.C. Next, Xerxes took Athens and burned the Acropolis, but the Athenians were not so easily defeated. They took to their ships and fought the enemy in the har-

bor of the island of Salamis [sal'ə mis]. This sea battle was a disaster for the Persians. Xerxes returned to Asia Minor.

The Greeks had proved themselves the masters of the Aegean. A major result of their victory was that the budding city-states had a chance to develop their democratic systems of government.

Athens became the leading city in Greece. After the defeat of the Persians, Athens took the lead in holding many of the city-states together in a loose federation called the Delian [dē'lē ən] League. The power and wealth of Athens was based on a thriving trade, supremacy at sea, and prestige. Led by Pericles, Athens reached the high point of its democracy. His rule from 460 to 429 B.C. is called the Golden Age of Pericles. During this time, the Parthenon [pär'thə non]—a beautiful temple to the goddess Athena—was built, and the arts and literature flourished.

The real power of government lay in the assembly. All male citizens over 18 years old

Pericles

Daily Life

Artists of ancient Greece were interested in the details of ordinary life. The plate *above left* shows a dinner party. The men reclined on couches to eat and amused themselves with singing, dancing, and playing musical instruments. The bearded man is drinking from a shallow bowl; his friend is playing a tune on double pipes. In the cobbler's shop at *left* the shoemaker is cutting a piece of leather to fit his customer's foot. In the fabric shop *above* weavers are spinning thread.

were members. The assembly passed laws, decided important issues, and elected an executive board of ten generals. The generals were controlled by the assembly. It could reelect them, exile them, or put them to death. Pericles was president of the board.

The Council of 500, which drew up laws for the assembly to pass on, was divided into committees dealing with matters such as public buildings and street repair. Everyone serving the state was paid for his work. This meant that even poor men were able to serve. The juries of the court were also paid. The juries were made up of as many as 2,001 jurors, too many for anyone to bribe. To pre-vent corruption, judges and juries were chosen by lot.

Athenian democracy was based on the principle that all citizens were equal before the law. This made it possible for nearly every citizen to hold one or more public offices during his life. The mass participation of citizens in political life is known as *pure* or *direct democracy*. Governments in which the citizens elect representatives to act for them are called *representative democracies* or *republics*.

Not all people in Athens could be citizens, however. Women, foreigners, and slaves could not be, and these groups far outnumbered the citizens. Therefore, limits to the idea of equality did exist.

The Athenians either bought their slaves or captured them as prisoners of war. The slaves who worked in the silver mines did so in chains and suffered greatly. House slaves, however, were often treated well, almost as members of the family. Some slaves even became free noncitizens. There were about 100,000 slaves in Athens. This huge number made possible the Hellenic idea of leisure. While slaves did most of the work, citizens had time to cultivate their minds and beautify their environment.

A liberal education was stressed. Education in Athens was important in keeping up a healthy democratic government. The aim of Athenian education was to help students develop fine bodies and an appreciation for the arts, to learn to think for themselves, and to become good Athenians.

Parents were expected to educate their sons. However, the state did not provide schools, so parents hired tutors to teach their sons. Most tutors taught large groups of children. Even so, tutors were poorly paid. Athenian boys started school when they were 6 years old and continued until they were 16 or older. Most boys learned to play musical instruments, such as the flute or lyre [līr], an ancient stringed instrument, somewhat like a small harp. Then, at age 14, boys began going to a gymnasium. Here they were trained in running, wrestling, boxing, and other athletic skills. Here, too, they studied geometry, astronomy, natural history, geography, and public speaking.

Women in Athens did not take part in political affairs, so the training of girls was more limited. Women did not have any standing in court. If a woman wanted the protection of the law, she had to find a male citizen to represent her in court. Girls did not attend school as the boys did. However, girls were taught in their homes to read, write, and play a musical instrument. Girls were also taught many skills, such as weaving and pottery making. Athenian homes were often self-sufficient workshops run by women.

City-state rivalries undermined Greek power. Athens kept the Delian League from becoming a true union of Greek states. City-states in the Delian League were forced to pay taxes to Athens. And farmers in other city-states were often forced off their land by Athenian settlers. Athenian traders kept the best commercial advantages for themselves.

During the last years of Pericles' rule, the other city-states tried to bring about the downfall of Athens. In addition, corruption crept into the government of Athens. Pericles' successors did not have his intellect or high morals. They used the ruling bodies for their own gain.

In 431 B.C., the resentment of the other city-states brought open war. With Sparta in the lead, the city-states fought Athens in the Peloponnesian [pel'ə pə nē'shən] War. In 404 B.C., Sparta defeated Athens after a long and costly struggle. Wars among the city-states went on, however, and brought about the collapse of Spartan leadership. The disastrous Peloponnesian War left the Greeks weakened and divided. Meanwhile, to the north, a new power was gaining strength.

section review 3

1. Why were the battles of Marathon and Salamis important?

2. In what ways was Athenian government democratic? Undemocratic?

3. In what ways did the training of an Athenian boy differ from that of an Athenian girl?

4. What caused the decline of Athens?

4 The Macedonians united Greece and the Hellenistic Age began.

To the north of Greece lay Macedonia [mas'ə dō'nē ə], which was inhabited by hardy mountain people. Philip, their king, was an excellent military strategist. When Philip came to power in 359 B.C., he organized a standing army of professional soldiers. They were drilled in cavalry and infantry tactics and kept in trim through a rigorous program of athletics. Philip was also a ruthless leader. He was willing to use bribery, lies, and other treacherous ways to reach his goals. He was determined to unite the Greeks under his rule. Little by little, he brought outlying Greek areas under his control. Yet Philip wanted the friendship of the Greeks and at first avoided the use of force. As a youth he had been a hostage in the Greek city of Thebes [thēbz] and had learned to respect Greek culture.

Philip's conquest of the Greeks ended the Hellenic period.

Early in 338 B.C., Athens and Thebes formed an alliance to protect themselves from the Macedonian threat. In the summer, they attacked Philip. But the Macedonian king almost destroyed the Greek army. This fight marked the end of the power of the city-states. All of the Greek peninsula except Sparta quickly came under Philip's rule.

Within a year, Philip called together delegates from the major city-states of Greece (except Sparta) at Corinth. There the so-called Hellenic League was formed. The city-states got a large degree of self-government, but agreed to give Philip military support against any of them who threatened the general peace. Then, in 336 B.C., Philip died suddenly.

Fortunately, Philip was one of the few kings of ancient times who had prepared his successor for the task of ruling. His son, Alexander, had been given the finest education available. This included tutoring by the famous Greek philosopher, Aristotle [ar'ə stot'l]. While Alexander was still in his early teens, Philip had shared state secrets with him. At age 16, Alexander took command of an elite guard. On taking the throne at age 20, he proved himself a strong leader by crushing a revolt by Thebes.

Alexander conquered the Persian Empire.

The young Alexander decided to carry out his father's plan to conquer Persia. He admired Hellenic civilization and wanted to spread it abroad. Also, he believed that it was his destiny to rule the world. In 334 B.C., with more than 30 thousand infantry and 5 thousand cavalry, he marched east. It was a journey from which Alexander would never return.

In 334 B.C., Alexander won a great triumph at the battle of Granicus. This victory encouraged the Greeks in Asia Minor to revolt against their Persian masters. The next year, Alexander's forces met the armies of the Persian ruler, Darius III at Issus [is'əs]. Though outnumbered three to one, Alexander's army roundly defeated the Persians. Darius fled from the field of battle and cheated Alexander of the chance to defeat him once and for all. Then Alexander made a successful trip to Egypt, where he founded the city of Alexandria. After this, he swung north to face Darius again. In 331, in the battle of Arbela [är bē'lə], Alexander again defeated Darius's troops, and Darius again got away. It was clear, however, that the Persian ruler could no longer rally his forces against Alexander's army, and Darius was later murdered by one of his own men. Alexander marched on to Babylon and then Persepolis, where he took his seat on the throne of Persia. So ended

Someone You Should Know

Alexander The Great

Even as a boy, Alexander was fearless, strong, and self-confident. When he was twelve, his father, King Philip of Macedon, bought a large black horse named Bucephalus. But at its first workout the horse bucked and reared so much that no one could mount it, and Philip ordered it taken away.

Alexander burst out that it was a shame to lose so fine a horse just because nobody had the skill to handle it. He took the horse by the bridle and turned the animal toward the sun. He had noticed that the horse did not like the sight of its shadow dancing about on the ground. Running quietly by the horse's side, Alexander held the bridle in one hand and patted the horse's neck with the other. When he saw his chance, he swung himself onto the horse's back. He rode off across the field and then galloped back to where Philip was standing.

Alexander liked the horse so much that he kept it as his own. Over the next 20 years, he rode Bucephalus to places as far away as India.

almost two hundred years of Persian threats to the Mediterranean world.

Alexander then moved east through Persia to India. However, his homesick, weary soldiers made him turn back. In 323 B.C., he died in Babylon, a victim of fever. Many of his military successes were due in part to the disorganized state of the Persian Empire. But Alexander in his own right was a skillful general and a gallant leader of men.

To later generations, Alexander's idea of "one world" was of great importance. He planned a blend of Greek and Persian culture with the Greek language and Greek law as strong bonds. Marriages between his soldiers and native women were encouraged. Alexander himself married two Persian princesses. One system of money was used throughout the lands he conquered. The Persian system of administrative districts was kept almost the same. Over seventy new cities were founded. Their governing bodies were staffed by Persians as well as Greeks and Macedonians. In short, Alexander believed in the creation of a strong world government in which all peoples were equal.

Commerce and culture spread during the Hellenistic Age. With the death of Alexander, the empire was left with no heirs to govern it. As a result, it was divided into three parts, each ruled by one of Alexander's generals. Antigonus [an tig'ə nəs] ruled the kingdom of Macedonia, which had partial control over Greece. Egypt was ruled by Ptolemy [tol'ə mē]. Syria and Persia were ruled by Seleucus [sə lü'kəs]. Dynasties were established in these kingdoms, and the three parts made up what was called the *Hellenistic world.* The period of these kingdoms, called the *Hellenistic Age,* lasted for almost two hundred years after Alexander's death.

The Hellenistic Age was a time of great economic growth and of cultural exchange between East and West. The network of cities founded by Alexander made new markets for

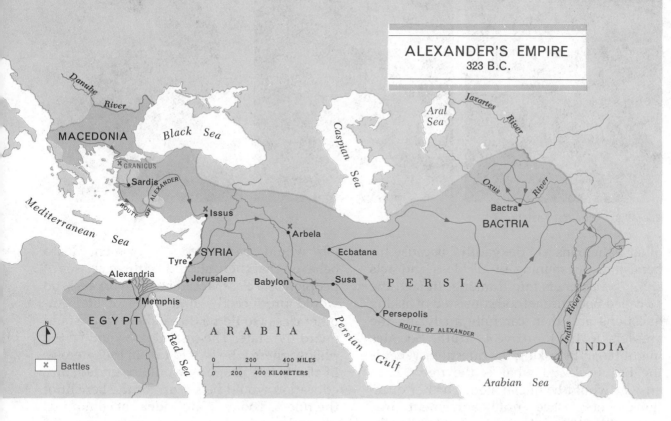

MACEDONIA

Black Sea

Danube River

Mediterranean Sea

× GRANICUS

Sardis

ROUTE OF ALEXANDER

× Issus

× Arbela

SYRIA

Tyre

Alexandria

Jerusalem

Babylon

Memphis

EGYPT

ARABIA

Red Sea

Ecbatana

Susa

Persepolis

ROUTE OF ALEXANDER

PERSIA

Caspian Sea

Aral Sea

Jaxartes River

Oxus River

Bactra

BACTRIA

Indus River

INDIA

Persian Gulf

Arabian Sea

N

× Battles

0   200   400 MILES
0   200   400 KILOMETERS

---

a variety of goods and acted as centers for the spread of Greek culture. The greatest city of all was Alexandria, Egypt, with a population of more than half a million people. The city had wide, beautiful streets and a great library of 750 thousand books. A lighthouse nearly 400 feet (120 meters) high was judged by the Greeks to be one of the Seven Wonders of the World.

section review 4

1. Why was Philip able to conquer the Greek city-states? What was the result of his victory?

2. What was unusual about Alexander's early training in leadership?

3. How did Alexander try to form a "one world" culture in the areas he conquered?

4. What was the Hellenistic Age?

5 Greek civilization formed the basis for Western culture

The Hellenic and Hellenistic phases of Greek civilization were different from each other in one basic respect. During the Hellenic Age, Greek culture was confined to the Greek peninsula. In the Hellenistic Age, the later of the two, Greek culture spread to those parts of the world known to the Greeks at that time, especially the Middle East, India, China, and North Africa. But in both the Hellenic and Hellenistic phases, Greek culture was firmly based on its great philosophic traditions.

Athens had great philosophers. The three greatest Greek philosophers were Socrates [sok′rə tēz′], Plato, and Aristotle. Socrates lived in the 5th century B.C. He was known to

Socrates, Plato, and Aristotle

other Athenians as "the gadfly" because his persistent questioning of all ideas and acts stung his listeners into thinking. In fact, the so-called Socratic method consisted of asking questions and then carefully analyzing the answers to try to arrive at truth. Socrates might begin by asking the question, What is the beautiful and what is the ugly? Each answer would be questioned. Further questions were asked until agreement was reached by the participants about the exact meaning of the terms. Socrates' advice to everyone was "know thyself."

Some Athenians believed that Socrates was a bad influence on his students, because he encouraged young men to question practices of all kinds. He even questioned the acts of Athenian leaders. This led the Athenians to put Socrates on trial, charging him with corrupting the youth of the city. He was sentenced to death and made to drink hemlock, a poison. Socrates accepted the verdict calmly. His friends urged him to escape. Socrates refused, because he insisted that people must obey the laws of the state.

The most famous pupil of Socrates was Plato, who lived from 430 to 347 B.C. He started the Academy, a famous school in Athens that existed for almost nine hundred years. His best known work is *The Republic*. It is a book that describes an imaginary land in which each person does the work that suits that individual best. All young people would be given twenty years of education, and no job would be closed to women. Plato believed that there should be three classes of people. One class would be the workers who would produce the necessities of life. Another class would be the soldiers who would guard the state. The final class would be the philosophers who would rule in the interests of all. Private property would be ended, and education would be set up for the benefit of the rulers. Today, Plato's ideas of communal life and a rigid class system seem harsh and like Spartan ideas. However, *The Republic* is an important work because it was the first attempt to devise a planned society.

Plato's most famous pupil was the 4th-century philosopher, Aristotle. He was a brilliant thinker with wide interests. He wrote about biology, astronomy, physics, ethics, logic, and politics.

Like most Athenians, Aristotle believed that a person could be happy by being moderate in most things. He taught that people should strike a balance, or mean point, between rash action and inactivity. According to this Doctrine of the Mean, the best way to meet danger is through brave action— brave action being the mean between foolhardiness and cowardice. In his *Politics*, Aristotle wrote about the good and bad features of different kinds of governments: monarchy, aristocracy, and democracy. Unlike Plato, he did not describe an imaginary state, nor did he find a single ideal system. *Politics* serves to point out an important difference between Plato and Aristotle. Plato often appears to deal only with abstract ideas. Aristotle seems more down-to-earth.

Hellenistic philosophers sought the good life. Two major schools of Greek philosophy came out of the Hellenistic Age. These were Epicureanism [ep′ə kyü rē′ə niz′əm] and Stoicism [stō′ə siz′əm]. The first was developed by Epicurus, a man who believed that a life free of extremes was best for lessening pain and increasing pleasure. Some of his followers misunderstood his ideas about pleasure. They thought he meant that one should only eat, drink, and be merry. For this reason, Epicureanism is often misinterpreted as meaning that pleasure, instead of the mental activity that Epicurus emphasized, is a way of gaining inner peace.

Zeno [zē′nō] developed a philosophy known as Stoicism. He taught that true happiness, or inner peace, can be reached by people when they find their proper places in nature. His followers were called *Stoics*, because they often met on a *stoa*, or porch. Believing all nature to be good, the Stoics thought that people must accept poverty, disease, and even death as the will of God. This philosophy led them to an indifference toward all kinds of experience, good or bad. Today, the word "stoic" means a person who does not show feelings or emotions.

The Greeks made many advances in science. In the Hellenic Age, Aristotle contributed to the development of the natural sciences. Other Greeks made important discoveries also. Pythagoras [pə thag′ər əs], a philosopher, set up the geometric rule that bears his name, the Pythagorean [pə thag′ə rē′ən] theorem. Hippocrates [hi pok′rə tēz′] founded a medical school. "Every disease has a natural cause," he said. His work helped end some of the superstitions and belief in magic that had stood in the way of the study of disease. Physicians today swear an oath of ethical conduct based on one that Hippocrates drew up. It is called the Hippocratic oath.

During the Hellenistic Age, Euclid [yü′klid] wrote his textbook, *The Elements*. It is still the basis for the study of plane geometry, and Euclid is often called "the father of geometry." Archimedes [är′kə mē′dēz] figured out a way to measure the circumference of a circle. He also discovered the rule of specific gravity. He noticed that the water in his bathtub overflowed when he lowered himself into it. From this experience, he wrote what is known as Archimedes' law: "A body floating in a liquid is held up by a force equal to the weight of the liquid displaced." Another scientist, Aristarchus [ar′is tär′kəs] discovered that the earth rotated and revolved around the sun. Eratosthenes [er′ə tos′thə nēz] made a fairly good estimate of the circumference of the earth. He also drew the first longitudes and latitudes on a map of the world. Thus, more than 1,700 years before Columbus, Hellenistic scientists had learned that the earth is round.

Scientists of the Hellenistic Age made many machines that used levers, cranks, and geared wheels. A Greek named Hero made a steam engine but used it as a toy. Other inventions were siphons and derricks.

Herodotus and Thucydides were famous historians. So far as is known now, the word *history* was first used for a description of past events by Herodotus, a 5th-century B.C. Greek who was born in Halicarnassus, Asia Minor. As a young man, he was exiled from his home town for taking part in a minor revolution. He traveled to Greece, Egypt, and the lands of the Persian Empire to gather information for his masterpiece, *History of the Persian Wars*. The work is filled with anecdotes, legends, and many entertaining bits of odd information that are not always reliable as historical evidence. However, Herodotus let the reader know when he was describing events that he could not verify. This allowed

his readers to decide whether the events were fact or fiction. Herodotus's basic belief was that the gods punish people who have excessive pride. To his mind, the Persians were guilty of great pride and were destroyed by the gods. In spite of its rambling style, the *History* has caused Herodotus to be called "the father of history."

Like Herodotus, Thucydides [thü sid'ə-dēz'] lived in the 5th century B.C. and was also an exile. Also like Herodotus, Thucydides wrote only one book, the *History of the Peloponnesian War*. Here, however, the similarities between the two men end. Thucydides only used material that he felt was important to the history. He judged evidence and only used facts he had carefully checked. He said:

> Of the events of the war I have not ventured to speak from any information, nor according

to any notion of my own; I have described nothing but what I either saw myself or learned from others of whom I made the most careful and particular inquiry.

Thucydides looked for the human causes of the Greek wars. He did not believe that human events could be explained as fate or as acts of the gods. *History of the Peloponnesian War* became a model for other historians.

The Greeks invented drama. Greek drama began as part of religious rites that were held at festivals honoring the god of wine, Dionysus [dī'ə nī'səs]. A chorus of men chanted hymns and performed stately dances in praise of the god. In the 6th century B.C., changes in the rites eventually led to the development of drama. Individual actors were separated from the chorus and given roles to play. Dialogue was used. Most

The open-air theater at Epidaurus at *left* was shaped much like the theater of Dionysus. At Epidaurus, important people sat in the front row. Their seats had back rests; the other seats did not. The theater had 55 rows of seats altogether. The limestone mask *above* is a copy of a mask of comedy made in the 4th century B.C..

important was the use of new themes based on heroic tales not related to Dionysus.

Greek tragedy often expressed religious ideas, and poetic language was thought to be the proper form. The chorus was a basic part of the play, commenting on the action as it took place. Both men's and women's roles were played by men. Most important, tragedy dealt with serious matters—people's destinies and the problems of good and evil. Tragedies had unhappy or disastrous endings. The most famous authors of tragedies were three Athenian poets who lived in the 5th century: Aeschylus [es′kə ləs], Sophocles [sof′ə klēz′], and Euripides [yu̇ rip′ə dēz′].

Comedy, which is a play with a nontragic ending, also began in the festivals of Dionysus. The greatest comic author was Aristophanes [ar′ə stof′ə nēz′], another 5th-century Greek. Since no laws protected Athenians from false or damaging statements, Aristophanes often ridiculed important citizens in his plays.

The open-air theater of Dionysus sat on the slopes of the Acropolis. It was semi-circular in shape and seated 14 thousand people. Various devices were used to make a play understandable to the large audiences. The actors wore thick-soled shoes to make them taller. They carried painted masks showing grief, horror, and other strong emotions. Speaking tubes were used to make the actors' voices louder.

Greek architecture and sculpture were widely copied. Most Greeks, even those who were rich, lived in simple clay-brick homes. However, they built beautiful temples of marble for their gods. The finest of these temples was the Parthenon in Athens. It is judged to be one of the most beautifully proportioned buildings of all time. Many modern buildings use features created by the Greeks.

Early Greek sculptors made bronze and marble figures that were stiff and formal. But later workers, including the famous Phidias [fid′ē əs] of the 5th century used the natural lines of the human body. In the 4th century B.C., Praxiteles [prak sit′l ēz′] carved figures that equaled or surpassed those of Phidias in grace and poise.

section review 5

1. Who were the three greatest Greek philosophers?

2. What were the contributions of Pythagoras and Hippocrates?

3. What is the difference between history as written by Herodotus and by Thucydides?

4. How did Greek drama originate? What was the purpose of the chorus?

Section Summaries

1. Aegean civilization depended on sea trade. The first civilization, the Minoan, developed on Crete. Later Mycenae and Troy became important centers. In time, this civilization fell to a warlike people, the Dorians. They settled in the Peloponnesus and drove the Mycenaeans into Attica and Ionia. Gradually, the Dorians and the original inhabitants intermarried to become the Greeks.

2. The Greeks established the basic principles of democracy. Though the Greeks had a common language and customs, they formed city-states rather than one nation. The two most important city-states were Athens and Sparta. From a council of nobles and a weak assembly, Athens developed a democratic government. Sparta developed a militaristic state to prevent the downtrodden Messenians and helots from uprising. Athens and many other city-states set up colonies and trade routes in the Mediterranean region.

3. The Greeks were threatened by Persia and by city-state rivalries. During the Hellenic Age, 750–338 B.C., the Greeks beat off invasions of the Persians. Athens became the most powerful city-state, and the head of the Delian League. Athens reached its height during the Golden Age of Pericles. Then jealousy and fear of Athens led to the Peloponnesian War.

4. The Macedonians united Greece and the Hellenistic Age began. Weakened by wars among themselves, the city-states were prey to Philip of Macedonia. His conquest of Greece ended the Hellenic Age. Philip's son Alexander surpassed his father in military and political achievements. Using Greek and Macedonian forces, Alexander conquered the Persian Empire. He then spread Greek culture throughout his lands. His death was followed by the division of his empire.

5. Greek civilization formed the basis for Western culture. The Greeks of the Hellenic Age left magnificent examples of sculpture, architecture, drama, and poetry. Outstanding contributions to philosophy and science were made. The Greeks' democratic government inspired democratic movements the world over. In the Hellenistic Age, new centers of Greek culture arose in the Middle East, especially in Alexandria. The chief contributions of this time were in science, technology, mathematics, and philosophy.

Who? What? When? Where?

1. Match the items below with the correct years:

1500–1001 B.C.   500–401 B.C.
1000–501 B.C.   400–301 B.C.

   a. The Golden Age of Pericles took place.
   b. Philip of Macedonia conquered Greece.
   c. The Dorians drove the Mycenaeans into Attica.
   d. Alexander began his attacks on the Persians.
   e. The first Olympic Games were held.
   f. The Mycenaeans captured Knossos.
   g. Sparta set up a military state.
   h. Athens won the battle of Marathon.

2. Give the years of the Hellenic Age. Of the Hellenistic Age.

3. Who said, "Come back with your shield or on it"? To whom was it said and when?

4. Divide these men into the correct groups of philosophers or playwrights: Zeno, Sophocles, Socrates, Plato, Euripides, Aristotle, Aristophanes, and Aeschylus.

5. How was the education of an Athenian boy different from that of a Spartan boy?

6. Write sentences describing each of these:
   a. Council of Elders
   b. Council of 500
   c. Delian League
   d. Hellenic League

7. Name the author and tell what each of these books is about:
   a. *The Elements*
   b. *History of the Peloponnesian War*
   c. *History of the Persian Wars*
   d. *Politics*
   e. *The Republic*

Questions for Critical Thinking

1. Compare Athenian democracy with democracy in the United States. Could the United States be a pure democracy? Why or why not?

2. What do you think are the greatest things accomplished by the Greeks? Tell why you think so. Why were the Greeks able to do so much?

3. Why weren't the Greeks able to avoid being conquered by Macedonia? What should they have done?

4. Given a choice, would you rather grow up in Athens or in Sparta? List reasons for your choice.

5. Which philosophy do you think would have more appeal in the United States today, the Epicurean or the Stoic? Why?

Skill Activities

1. Read *The Parthenon* by Peter Green to learn more about this famous temple. (Newsweek Books, 1973)

2. Find out what the English word *marathon* means and why.

3. Write "historical" paragraphs in your own words using the methods of Herodotus or Thucydides.

4. Debate the good and bad points of Athenian democracy or Spartan militarism.

5. Act out the life of Socrates, his teaching, arrest, trial, and death. Discuss whether or not he should have tried to escape.

6. Make a chart that shows the differences and the similarities between the Hellenistic Age and the Hellenic Age.

chapter 5 *quiz*

Section 1

1. The earliest civilization on Crete is called: a. Minoan, b. Aegean, c. Mycenaean

2. True or false: There is evidence that shows there was contact between Egypt and Crete.

Section 2

3. The Greeks called themselves: a. Aegeans, b. Minoans, c. Hellenes

4. The Greeks were the first to develop: a. city-states, b. democracy, c. trade routes

Section 3

5. True or false: At the battles of Marathon and Salamis, the Greeks defeated the Phoenicians.

6. At the end of the Peloponnesian Wars, the leading city in Greece was: a. Athens, b. Corinth, c. Sparta

7. The Golden Age of Pericles was from: a. 460 to 429 B.C., b. 610 to 583 B.C., c. 331 to 323 B.C.

Section 4

8. The leader who dreamed of "one world" was: a. Philip, b. Alexander, c. Pericles

9. True or false: Greek culture spread throughout the known world during the years known as the *Hellenic* period.

Section 5

10. The philosopher who refused to escape death was: a. Aristotle, b. Plato, c. Socrates

11. A person who does not show his or her feelings to others is called a: a. stoic, b. Spartan, c. scientist

12. Drama began as part of the Greek festivals that honored: a. Aeschylus, b. Dionysus, c. Eratosthenes

THE ROMAN EMPIRE

The Romans decorated the plaster walls of their homes with paintings, much as we use wallpaper. This portrait from the city of Pompeii shows a husband and wife—both educated. He holds a papyrus scroll, she a writing stylus and tablet.

To Edward Gibbon, an 18th-century English historian and author of *Decline and Fall of the Roman Empire*, "the period in the history of the world during which the condition of the human race was most happy and prosperous" was the 2nd century A.D. It was during this century that the Roman Empire reached its greatest extent and was, according to Gibbon, "governed by absolute power, under the guidance of virtue and wisdom." A Roman subject of the 2nd century agreed and had this to say about the era in which he lived:

> . . . The whole world keeps holiday; the age-long curse of war has been put aside; mankind turns to enjoy happiness. Strife has been quieted, leaving only the competition of cities, each eager to be the most beautiful and the most fair. Every city is full of gymnastic schools, fountains and porticos, temples, shops, and schools of learning. The whole earth is decked with beauty like a garden.

There were those who would disagree. Some thought Roman rule was a mixed blessing at best. Others felt it was oppressive and tyrannical. The famous modern-day historian, Arnold J. Toynbee, has called the 2nd century A.D. a time of stalemate when the world "lay more or less passive under the pall" of Roman power. The 2nd-century Roman historian Tacitus [tas'ə təs] agreed: "They [the Romans] make desolation, which they call peace."

A difference of opinion is a good point at which to begin to look at Roman history. In truth, military conquest made Rome a world state. The boundaries of the empire expanded as the Roman armies scored victory after victory. Yet force alone was not enough to maintain a unified state. Skillful diplomacy, effective government, a flexible system of law, a widespread network of roads and commercial towns—all these factors helped bring together a great number of peoples of varying customs and races. For over two centuries, from 27 B.C. to 180 A.D., the Romans maintained the *Pax Romana*, or "Roman Peace," throughout their far-flung domain.

The story of how Rome grew from a small city-state on the central Italian peninsula to a vast empire controlling the whole Mediterranean is told in this chapter as follows:

1. **The Roman Republic arose on the Italian peninsula.**

2. **The republic became a world state.**

3. **The empire lasted for five centuries.**

4. **The Romans preserved Greek culture.**

1 The Roman Republic arose on the Italian peninsula

Between 2000 and 1000 B.C., about the time that the Greek-speaking tribes were moving into their future homeland, another branch of Indo-Europeans moved south through the Alps into the Italian peninsula. Most important were the Latins, a group of tribes who settled along the west coast of the central Italian peninsula in the lower valley of the Tiber [tī'bər] River. About midpoint in the 8th century B.C., they built a small settlement on the Palatine, a hill near the Tiber. The city of Rome grew from this modest beginning.

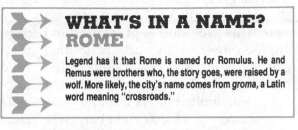

WHAT'S IN A NAME?
ROME

Legend has it that Rome is named for Romulus. He and Remus were brothers who, the story goes, were raised by a wolf. More likely, the city's name comes from *groma*, a Latin word meaning "crossroads."

Early Rome was ruled by the Etruscans. In the 7th century B.C., the Latin tribes were conquered by their powerful neighbors to the north, the Etruscans. Little is known about the Etruscans. It is thought that they came originally from Asia Minor. They drained the marshes around Rome, encouraged trade, and taught the Latins to use arches in their buildings.

Many important features of Roman government developed under Etruscan rule. A king of Etruscan descent ruled the state and was elected to his office by the Latin tribal chieftains. He served as high priest as well as chief magistrate. The king chose a group of nobles known as the *senate* to advise him. These high-ranking freemen were usually large landowners and were known as *patricians* [pə trish'əns], or fathers of the state. The common people—small farmers and tradespeople—were known as *plebeians* [pli-bē'əns].

The Roman Republic was established. In the 7th and 6th centuries B.C., an Etruscan family named Tarquin ruled Rome. A bitter rivalry for power developed in the family. One member, Tarquin the Proud, murdered the king and then himself ruled as a tyrant. Despised by the people, he was finally deposed by the senate in 509 B.C. They then set up a *republic,* a state in which the citizens elected representatives to run the government. As in the early oligarchies of Greece, power in the Roman Republic was not in the hands of the people but was held tightly by the men at the top of the social scale.

The new republic was governed by two chief magistrates, called *consuls,* and the senate. The consuls could serve for only one year. This provision kept them from becoming too powerful. In wartime or other emergencies, a *dictator,* or absolute ruler, could rule in place of the consuls, but his term of office was limited to six months. The senate was made up of 300 members who were appointed for life by the consuls. The senate proposed the laws and nominated the consuls for office. Only patricians could become consuls or serve in the senate.

The plebeians had their own assembly that passed laws for their class. At first, however, the assembly was not very important in Roman government.

Rome expanded within the Italian peninsula. Soon after Tarquin was overthrown, Rome and the nearby Latin tribes got together to form the Latin League. By the beginning of the 4th century B.C., Rome and the league controlled the central Italian peninsula.

Two setbacks to Roman expansion occurred. The first was the invasion in 390 B.C. by the Gauls. These fierce, fair-haired warriors came from what is now France and northern Italy. The Gauls burned Rome to the ground. Although they left after they were paid a *tribute,* or tax, the damage to Roman prestige was serious. The second setback took place in 340 B.C., when other members of the Latin League, jealous of Rome, revolted. Two years later, Rome defeated them, dissolved the league, and forced each tribe to sign a separate treaty. The Romans then turned north and conquered the Etruscans, who were weak from repeated attacks by the Gauls. For protection against the Gauls, a defensive line on the Arno River was set up to stop future attacks.

The only serious rivals to Roman rule left on the Italian peninsula were the Greeks in southern Italy. They had settled colonies there and on the island of Sicily [sis'ə lē] during the 8th century B.C.

The Greeks became alarmed at the growing power of Rome. They called upon Pyrrhus [pir'əs], a relative of Alexander the Great and an ambitious military leader from northern Greece, to help them. In 280 B.C., with an army of 25 thousand men and twenty elephants, he defeated the Romans in battle. He then invited the former members of the Latin League to join forces with him against Rome. They refused. Stunned, he made a peace offer to Rome. It was rejected.

Pyrrhus then launched a second successful attack. But his losses were so great that he exclaimed, "Another such victory and we are lost." To this day, a costly victory is known as a *Pyrrhic victory*.

Pyrrhus returned to Greece, and the Romans quickly conquered the Greek holdings on the Italian peninsula. By 270 B.C., less than 250 years after the founding of the republic, Rome was master of all the central and southern Italian peninsula.

The values of the early Romans helped strengthen the republic. Most of the early Romans were farmers. They lived simply, worked hard, and fought well. The Roman family was a close-knit group. It was held together by affection, the necessities of a frugal life, and the strict authority of parents. Both parents played important roles in family activities. They taught their children the virtues of loyalty, courage, and self-control. Most Romans took their civic and religious duties seriously. They strengthened the laws and customs of the republic.

The stern virtues prized by Roman family life were a source of strength to the early republic. In later years, when increasing power and wealth began to undermine Roman family life, some people were unhappy about the passing of the old order. "Rome stands built upon the ancient ways of life," warned a poet of the 3rd century B.C.

Military strength was combined with wise rule. The success of the Roman conquests was due largely to the well-trained army of citizen-soldiers. The basic military unit was the legion [lē'jən]. This infantry force had 6,000 men at full strength. The legions were divided into groups of 120 men each called *companies*. As Rome expanded, the need for soldiers increased. Conquered tribes were forced to supply troops for the army.

Pyrrhus used war elephants to help him in his battles with the Romans. This Roman dinner plate shows two soldiers riding one of the war elephants. A baby elephant follows behind.

The Romans had great talents for organization. They gave full privileges of Roman citizenship to some of the conquered. These conquered could vote and hold political office in Rome. Others were given less important rights, such as the right to own property in Rome.

Rome granted a large measure of independence to the peoples it conquered. They were free to run their own affairs, set up their own assemblies, and elect their own magistrates. Rome controlled the administration of justice and handled city-to-city affairs. As a result, the Roman Republic maintained stability even in its expansion.

The plebeians wanted equal rights within Rome. Soon after the founding of the republic, the plebeians began to demand a greater role in government. As Rome's need

The Roman Forum grew from a market place to be the center of the city's civic life. In the open space were statues of important rulers and generals as well as the great platform where speeches were made. Around the open space were imposing buildings.

for loyal and well-trained citizen-armies grew, the plebeians were able to gain a greater voice.

In 494 B.C., two plebeian officials, called *tribunes*, were appointed to protect the members of their class from injustice. Anyone, even a consul, who tried to harm a tribune, could be killed. In time, the number of tribunes was increased to ten. The tribunes sat in on senate discussions. They could not take part in the debates or vote. But if they felt the laws under discussion would not be in the plebeians' favor they could cry out "*Veto*," that is, "I forbid." At first, the veto did not stop the senate from passing laws, but it encouraged senators to rethink unpopular legislation.

About 450 B.C., the plebeians won the right to have laws put in writing. This prevented judges from making different decisions on similar cases. These written laws were called the Laws of the Twelve Tables. They were carved on twelve bronze tablets hung in the *forum*, a central, open-air meeting place. One of the laws prohibited marriage between plebeians and patricians, but by 440 B.C., such intermarriage had become legal.

Little by little, the plebeians made more gains. The veto power of the tribunes became effective. By the 4th century B.C., one of the consulships was held by a plebeian. At the end of that century, plebeians could become members of the senate. In 287 B.C., a law made the plebeian assembly into a popular assembly for the entire state. The old distinctions between patrician and plebeian were wiped away. However, the struggle for political power and social equality did not come to an end. In the centuries ahead, differences in wealth and status played an important part in the story of the internal affairs of Rome.

section review 1

1. Describe the government of the early Roman Republic.

2. What role did Pyrrhus play in the Roman conquest of the Italian peninsula?

3. Describe early Roman family life. How did the Roman family help keep the government strong?

4. Tell the steps by which the plebeians won more rights in the republic.

2 The republic became a world state

The story of Roman expansion turns next to Carthage, on the north African coast. The city of Carthage had been founded in 814 B.C. by Phoenicians. Carthage had grown rich from the sea trade in the western Mediterranean. The Carthaginian domain included territory in north Africa and the Iberian peninsula (present-day Spain) and important trading centers on the islands of Sardinia, Corsica, and Sicily. The strong Carthaginian navy blocked Roman expansion in the Mediterranean region. Between 264 and 146 B.C., Carthage and Rome fought three wars, known as the Punic [pyü'nik] Wars. (The word *Punici* is Latin for "Phoenicians.")

The Punic Wars strained the resources of Rome. Sicily was the prize of the First Punic War. The contest was clearly unequal. The odds favored Carthage, which was rich in gold, manpower, and ships. The Romans were not a seafaring people, but they realized that Carthage could be defeated only if its navy were smashed. With amazing determination, the Romans built up a navy. While the ships were being built, the Romans trained their soldiers as oarsmen on shore. Several Roman fleets were destroyed with great loss of life. Finally, the Romans were able to defeat the Carthaginians off the coast of Sicily in 241 B.C.

Sicily became the first Roman province. It was made to pay an annual tribute of grain to Rome. Three years after the end of the war, Sardinia was conquered; later, Corsica. In 227 B.C., both were made into a single province. No longer was Roman power restricted to the Italian peninsula. The Roman navy was the strongest in the western Mediterranean. Although the First Punic War had exhausted Rome and Carthage, both made ready for another struggle.

The Second Punic War has been called a "conflict between the nation Rome and the man Hannibal." Hannibal was a Carthaginian general whose military genius has been rated as equal to that of Alexander the Great. Hannibal began the war in 219 B.C. by attacking a Roman ally, the city of Sagento on the Iberian peninsula. With cavalry, war elephants, and about 40 thousand infantrymen, Hannibal then crossed through southern Gaul and over the Alps into the Italian peninsula. The difficult journey cost him about half of his men, much of his equipment, and all but one elephant. With the Gauls of the northern Italian peninsula as allies, Hannibal began to march south.

To meet the emergency, the Romans made Fabius Maximus dictator. He was a cautious leader who refused to risk an all-out battle. His so-called *Fabian policy* of watchful waiting frustrated Hannibal. However, it was unpopular with many Romans. They wanted a face-to-face battle with Hannibal. It came at Cannae [kan'ā] in the southern Italian peninsula. There, in 216 B.C., the Carthaginian general encircled the Romans and wiped out a force at least a third larger than his own. But Hannibal dared not lay siege to Rome without reserves of manpower and supplies. He was cut off from these by Roman armies in the Iberian peninsula and on Sicily.

Finally, the Romans decided to open up another front. Under the leadership of Scipio the Elder, Roman forces invaded north Africa. Hannibal had to return home to defend Carthage. At Zama [zā'mə] in 202 B.C., Hannibal was defeated. He fled to the east to save his life. The peace terms dictated by the Romans were harsh. Carthage gave up its navy, lost its freedom in foreign affairs, paid annual tribute to Rome, and surrendered the Iberian peninsula. Still, the Romans were afraid Carthaginian power would grow again.

This fear was well founded. In 150 B.C., the Carthaginians attacked a Roman *ally*. (An

DailyLife

Today, much is known about the lives and times of the Romans. A lot of this knowledge comes from buildings, sculpture, books, and paintings. Some knowledge, though, comes from artifacts. The leather shoe, *right,* and the two hair combs, *below,* are some of the artifacts. The shoe is open on the top to make it cool to wear; it laces up the back. The two combs are carved from wood. The sculpture *below right* shows a young boy with his tutor. It became fashionable for wealthy Romans to hire Greek tutors for their sons. The shop *right* sells pillows, cloth, and scarves. In this scene the shopkeeper is selling a piece of cloth to a customer while his wife and children look on. *Above right* is a fabric shop where two clerks are displaying a large piece of cloth for several customers. *Above left* is a butcher shop. The wife is the cashier; her husband is responsible for cutting the meat.

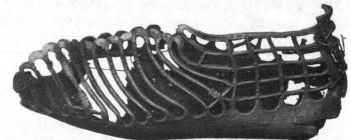

ally is one country that supports the policies and actions of another.) The Romans replied by attacking North Africa one year later. They laid siege to Carthage and kept food from coming into the city. Most of the people starved to death. When the Romans entered Carthage, they burned the city to the ground. Then they destroyed the fertility of the soil by throwing salt into the plowed land outside the city. The Carthaginians who were left were sold into slavery. Thus, in 146 B.C. the Third Punic War ended. Rome made the former Carthaginian holdings in north Africa into the Roman province of Africa.

Roman armies were victorious in the east. Shortly after the end of the Second Punic War, the Roman legions turned eastward. After a series of wars, they defeated the Macedonians. In 146 B.C., Macedonia became a Roman province. In the same year, the Romans burned Corinth and made the other Greek city-states subject to Rome.

When the king of Pergamum in Asia Minor willed his kingdom to Rome in 133 B.C., the Romans began to take over lands in the Middle East. Egypt and other countries allied themselves with Rome and later became Roman territories. By 100 B.C., all land bordering the Mediterranean, except for the Atlas Mountains region of northwest Africa, was under Roman control.

Roman expansion led to changes within the republic. During the Punic Wars and the conquest of Mediterranean lands, changes were taking place in the republic. These changes made the years from 150 to 31 B.C. stormy ones.

As Rome became increasingly involved in foreign affairs, the senate grew in power and prestige by conducting state negotiations. The popular assembly had the power to *ratify* treaties, that is, to approve them, and to declare war. However, this body acted merely as a rubber stamp for the decisions of the senators. The tribunes became yes-men of the senate. Political power had become concentrated in the senate. Corruption in government increased, particularly in the provinces. Officials sent to the provinces often used their jobs to make themselves rich. The senate decided from whom the army would buy supplies and who could collect taxes in the provinces. Men who wanted these jobs often bribed senators to get them.

The wars hurt farming in the Italian peninsula. The southern peninsula had been devastated by Hannibal's army. The farmers from this region drifted to Rome in search of jobs. But there were none. The big landowners used slaves captured in wars to work their land, and there was no large-scale industry to give these farmers jobs. An unhappy, out-of-work mob was created that could easily be made to riot.

As the riches of war poured into Rome, some people became rich for the first time. This new wealth changed Roman attitudes toward the state. The traditions of public duty and self-discipline gave way to greed and soft living.

Civil War weakened the republic. Two brothers, Tiberius [tī bir′ē əs] and Gaius [gī′yəs] Gracchus [grak′əs], came to the support of the masses. In 133 B.C., Tiberius was elected tribune. He proposed a law that would divide the farmlands gained in war among the out-of-work farmers. He also wanted to make it against the law for any person to own more than a certain amount of land. His proposal would have taken away land from some of the richest families. To stop him, a group of rich men had him murdered. They also had 300 of his followers killed, saying these followers were public enemies.

Ten years later, Gaius was elected tribune. He was able to pass a land reform bill, and the wealthy were again alarmed. Many of Gaius's supporters were attacked and killed. Gaius committed suicide.

Rome was now the scene of bitter rivalry between the People's party, supported by the plebeians and the masses, and the senate, the agent of the rich patricians. The country was divided by violence and civil war. Hundreds of Romans were killed. Finally, Sulla [sul′ə], a victorious general, restored order. He doubled the size of the senate and limited the power of the veto. Sulla's changes wiped out many of the gains made by the plebeians in their long struggle for equality. In 79 B.C., Sulla retired. He had brought peace, but his changes were not to last.

Julius Caesar became dictator of Rome.

During the time of civil strife, the army had changed. Traditionally, the Roman army had been made up of citizens who fought because of duty to the state. Now the army included volunteers from the landless class. These soldiers expected to get rich from the gains of war. They were willing to serve for long periods of time and were loyal to their leader. It was easy to see that a popular general could use his military power to gain political power. Such a man was the brilliant general Julius Caesar [sē′zər].

After a successful military career in the Iberian peninsula, Julius Caesar joined with Pompey, another military hero, and Crassus, one of the wealthiest men in Rome. Their support made it possible for Caesar to become consul. In 60 B.C., the three men formed a union, called the First Triumvirate [trī um′və rāt′], to rule the state jointly.

From 58 to 51 B.C., in the Gallic Wars, Caesar conquered Gaul and extended Roman borders northward to include most of modern France and Belgium. He also led his legions across the English Channel to invade Britain. These accomplishments made Cae-

Julius Caesar

sar popular with the Roman masses. But the jealous senate, fearing his growing power, ordered him to return to Rome without his army. Caesar knew that to obey meant imprisonment or death. Crassus was dead, and Pompey, he knew, had conspired with the senate to ruin him.

On January 10, 49 B.C., Caesar brought his army across the Rubicon River into the northern part of the Italian peninsula. Afraid of the legions who were friendly to Caesar, Pompey and most of the senators fled to Greece. Caesar followed and defeated them. When Caesar returned to Rome, he became dictator. In 44 B.C., he became dictator for life.

During his five years of rule, Caesar made moderate reforms. He weakened the power of the senate, but at the same time increased its membership to 900. Roman citizenship was extended to persons living outside the Italian peninsula. In the provinces, taxes were adjusted and the administration improved.

The senate became afraid that Caesar meant to make himself king and begin a dynasty. A group of men, including Marcus Brutus, one of his best friends, joined in a plot to murder Caesar. On March 15, 44 B.C., a day known as the "Ides of March," the plotters surrounded Caesar on the floor of the senate building and stabbed him to death.

Augustus became the first Roman emperor.
Before his death, Julius Caesar had made his grandnephew and adopted son, Octavian, his *heir*. (An heir is the person who gets or has the right to someone's property or title after that one dies.) The eighteen-year-old Octavian joined with Mark Antony, Caesar's chief lieutenant to restore order in Rome and to punish the murderers. They attacked Brutus and his fellow conspirators, defeating them in the Battle of Philippi in 42 B.C.

For the next ten years, Octavian and Antony shared absolute power in the republic. Octavian ruled Rome and the western part of the empire. Antony ruled Egypt and the eastern part. While Octavian was shrewdly increasing his power in Rome, Antony had fallen in love with Cleopatra, the glamorous queen of Egypt. Word reached Rome that Antony had given Roman territory to Cleopatra and was plotting to seize the whole empire. Octavian persuaded the Romans to declare war on Egypt.

In 31 B.C., at Actium, a cape on the western coast of Greece, Octavian's fleet clashed with that of Antony and his queen. When Cleopatra fled the battle, Antony deserted his men and followed her to Egypt. The following year, Octavian landed in Egypt. Antony and Cleopatra, unable to get a navy to fight him, committed suicide. Egypt became a Roman province.

This coin shows Cleopatra on one side and Mark Antony on the other. It calls Cleopatra the "goddess manifest."

Octavian returned to Rome and proclaimed that he would return the government from a dictatorship to a republic. Although he was careful to observe the forms of republican government, he kept the final power in his own hands, largely through his control of the army. He was called *imperator* from which the word "emperor" comes. In 27 B.C., the senate gave Octavian the honorary title of Augustus, meaning "The Majestic." From then on, he was known by that name. After a century of civil war, Rome at last had been united under one ruler. The reign of Augustus began the Roman Empire.

section review 2

1. What happened to Carthage as a result of the Punic Wars?

2. How did government, farming, city life, and attitudes of the people change as Rome became a world power?

3. Why was Julius Caesar popular with the Roman people? Why did the senate fear him?

4. How did Octavian become the supreme ruler of Rome?

3 The empire lasted for five centuries

Augustus ruled a mighty world state. The empire extended east to the Euphrates River and west to the Atlantic Ocean, north to the Rhine and Danube rivers and south across the Mediterranean to north Africa and the sands of the Sahara. By the 2nd century A.D., the empire included 100 million people of different races, faiths, and customs.

Generally speaking, the first two and a half centuries of the empire were peaceful and prosperous. This period, from 27 B.C. to 180 A.D., is known as the *Pax Romana,* or "Roman Peace." Within the empire, business grew as conditions for trade improved. Bandits and pirates were hunted down. Roads and sea lanes were cleared for commerce. Ostia, at the mouth of the Tiber River, served as a sea-

■ MAP LESSON 6: THE ROMAN EMPIRE ABOUT 117 A.D.

1. This map uses different colors to show change over time. Note that over time, the Romans brought all of the Mediterranean world into one political organization. Which of the following provinces—Egypt, Dacia, Gaul, Thrace, Britain—were added after 14 A.D.?

2. In 14 A.D., the northern frontier was defined by two major European rivers. What were they? What happened after 14 A.D.?

3. Since this is a historical map, seemingly minor geographic features are named because they have historical importance. Note, for instance, the four rivers identified in Italy. Use this chapter to indicate the importance of the Tiber River and the Rubicon.

4. Locate Rome. Is it about in the center of its empire? What city is located at the mouth of the Tiber?

This statue of Augustus stood in the villa owned by his wife, Livia. The marble was originally painted to look more lifelike.

port for the city of Rome. Egypt, North Africa, and Sicily furnished grain for the entire empire. Timber and various farm products came from Gaul and central Europe. The Iberian peninsula supplied gold, silver, and lead; Britain, tin; Cyprus, copper; the Balkans, iron ore and gold. Outside the empire, Rome carried on a thriving trade with distant lands, such as India and China.

Augustus was the architect of the Pax Romana. Augustus proved to be a wise ruler. He improved the government of the provinces and did away with corruption there. A census was taken and tax rates were adjusted. A program of public works was begun; and roads, bridges, and aqueducts were built.

Augustus was not successful in his attempts to restore the old ideas of Roman simplicity and home life. Laws were passed

The Roman Empire about 117 A.D. map labels:

WALL OF ANTONINUS
WALL OF HADRIAN
BRITAIN
London
English Channel
GAUL
Lyon
TEUTOBURG FOREST
Rhine River
Danube
DACIA
ALPS
Po River
Massilia
Arno R.
Rubicon R.
Corsica
IBERIAN PENINSULA
Sagento
Cordova
Ostia
Rome
Tiber R.
Cannae
BALKANS
THRACE
MACEDONIA
PHILIPPI
Byzantium
Black Sea
CAUCASUS MTS.
Caspian Sea
Sardinia
Mediterranean
Sicily
Syracuse
Sparta
ACTIUM
Athens
Corinth
Ephesus
Pergamum
ASIA MINOR
Euphrates River
Antioch
Babylon
ATLAS MTS.
Carthage
Zama
Crete
Cyprus
Tyre
Damascus
Sea
Cyrene
Jerusalem
Petra
Alexandria
AFRICA
Memphis
EGYPT
ARABIA
Thebes
Red Sea
SAHARA

Roman Empire in 14 A.D.
Provinces added after 14 A.D.
Frontier Provinces
× Battles

0 250 500 MILES
0 250 500 KILOMETERS

N

to encourage large families and to limit luxurious living—but with little lasting effect. He made the old religious rituals again a part of the affairs of state. In time, worship of the emperor began, and as the years went by, served as a bond for all peoples within the empire.

Both bad and good rulers followed Augustus. When Augustus died in 14 A.D., the senate voted the title of imperator to his stepson, Tiberius. It was during his reign, which lasted until 37 A.D., that Jesus was crucified in Palestine. From the time of Tiberius to the end of the empire in 476 A.D., Rome was ruled by a wide variety of emperors, some improved the government and some thought only of selfish interests. For instance, Nero, judged the most wicked and worthless ruler ever to mount the throne, murdered his wife and his mother. He was accused of setting

fire to Rome in 64 A.D. This nine-day catastrophe destroyed half the city.

In spite of incompetent rulers, the empire held together. Efficient administrators at many levels of responsibility kept justice and order. Commercial strength helped keep the empire stable. Only when economic decline and social unrest set in did the lack of good leadership at the top harm the empire.

During the 2nd century A.D., the empire enjoyed the rule of a group of good emperors. Trajan, who ruled from 98 to 117, was an ambitious military leader. Before his death, the empire reached its greatest extent. His successor, Hadrian, ruled from 117 to 138. Hadrian made it his policy to strengthen the frontiers. Traveling throughout the empire, he supervised the building of many public works. One of the most famous projects was Hadrian's Wall in Britain. This wall was built as a protection against the unfriendly tribes

A MYSTERY IN HISTORY

Time Capsules on Planet Earth

Time capsules are usually buried in the ground or in the cornerstone of a building. Some time capsules have been in place for a hundred years or more. Inside the time capsule, which is usually a hollow cylinder or block, are things people have put there to show future generations what their way of life was like. What might you find in a time capsule? Could an entire city be put in a time capsule? In a way, that's what happened to Pompeii, Italy, some 1,900 years ago.

Until August 24, 79 A.D., the city of Pompeii [pom pā′] was a bustling, fun-loving place. It was bounded on one side by mountains and on the other by the sea. In between were gently curving streets and gracious houses. Beautiful wall paintings, cool interior gardens and fountains in the houses gave pleasure to their owners.

Streetside was another story. Graffiti covered the blank outside walls of buildings. Children wrote the alphabet up as high on the walls as they could reach, and boys scribbled their girlfriends' names. Pompeians even left messages for each other: "Samius to Cornelius—Go hang yourself!"

The city had a huge sports arena where the government staged free entertainment. Gladiatorial contests were the favorites. And Pompeii did well in business. Trade in wine, olive oil, and clothing were all very successful.

Founded about 800 years earlier, this city of nearly 20,000 people prospered. They never paid much attention to Vesuvius, the volcanic mountain that loomed over them. Then suddenly Vesuvius blew up. Volcanic cinders and ash began to fall in the streets and on the houses like rain. By August 26, Pompeii was buried under 20 feet (6 meters) of lava chunks and ash. More than 75 percent of the people were dead.

The volcano was a good preserver. It made a time capsule that was not opened until 1748. In that year, archaeologists found Pompeii. They found hollows in the ash where Pompeians had fallen, dying from the poisonous fumes or the rocks that Vesuvius shot out. Plaster was poured into the hollows, and casts were obtained, some of pet dogs and their owners. Coins were recovered from cafe counters where they had been dropped. Surgical instruments, a little pig in a roasting oven, and brushes in the bath lay where they were abandoned.

Are there other time capsules like Pompeii? Very likely. One of them may be the "lost continent" of Atlantis that Plato wrote about in 355 B.C. Others may lie buried deep in the earth and long forgotten. Our planet may be full of time capsules waiting to be discovered.

Many of the villas of Pompeii had beautiful paintings on the interior walls. This scene of the city shows that some villas had large porches facing the sea to take advantage of the cool breezes.

Parts of Hadrian's Wall still snake across the British countryside.

living in what is now Scotland. Marcus Aurelius, who ruled from 161 to 180, won both the respect and admiration of his people. His volume of essays, called *Meditations,* is one of the best expressions of the Stoic philosophy ever written. It is one of the ironies of history that this scholarly, bookish man was forced to spend most of his rule as a soldier, defending the frontiers of the empire in the north and east.

Economic decline and political instability weakened the empire. By the end of the 2nd century A.D., attacks on the frontiers came more and more often. To meet these threats, the empire doubled the size of its army. The drain on the supply of men and resources brought on an economic crisis that was made more severe by other factors. Poverty and unemployment were on the rise. Trade started to fall off. In an attempt to save valuable metals, the emperors reduced the gold and silver content of the money in circulation. Because money was worth less, people charged higher prices. Thus inflation and further hardship came about.

Business was hurt by crime of all kinds which, in turn, was caused by political instability. Meetings of the senate and the popular assembly had become formalities. These two groups were no longer effective in governing the state. Political power was held by the emperor, who himself was often at the mercy of the army. Peaceful succession to the imperial throne was rare. The death of an emperor signaled a free-for-all struggle. Of the twenty-nine emperors who ruled between 180 and 284 A.D., only four died of natural causes. The others were murdered by army officers or by rivals for the throne.

The soldiers had the real power to select the new emperor. As a result, emperors often followed the cynical advice of Emperor Septimius Severus, who is said to have told his sons, ''Make the soldiers rich and don't trouble about the rest.'' To keep the legions at full strength, barbarians were recruited and war captives were forced to enlist. These new legionnaires cared for the empire only so long as they were paid. However, the empire was still strong and had lasted a very long time. In 248 A.D., Emperor Philip celebrated the 1,000th anniversary of Rome's legendary founding on April 21, 753 B.C.

Two emperors tried despotism to save Rome. After a century of decline and civil disorder, two emperors were able to halt the disintegration of the empire. The first was Diocletian [dī ə klē′shən], who reigned from 284 to 305 A.D. He set up a full-fledged *despotism*, or government by a ruler with unlimited power. Harsh laws controlled all business.

Constantine was the next emperor and he enforced even more despotic control over his subjects. He also moved the capital of the empire from Rome to Byzantium, which he renamed Constantinople after himself.

Diocletian and Constantine halted civil war and economic decline for a time. Yet, as a cure, despotism proved worse than the ills from which the empire suffered. State regulation of business killed individual initiative. The secret police choked off reform. Trade came to a standstill in many places, and the amount of wealth available for taxation decreased. After the death of Constantine in 337, rivals for the throne butchered one another. The last ruler of a united Roman Empire was Theodosius I. At his death in 395, the empire was divided between his two sons: one son ruled the western half, the other son ruled the eastern half.

section review 3

1. How did Augustus improve the government and economy of the provinces?

2. Why was the empire able to survive during periods when there were bad rulers?

3. What problems weakened the empire between 180 and 284 A.D.?

4. What did Diocletian and Constantine do to stop the empire from falling apart? Why was despotism not the answer to Rome's problems?

4 The Romans preserved Greek culture

The roots of Western civilization can be traced to the blend of Greek and Roman culture, known as *classical culture*, that flourished during the *Pax Romana*. The Romans admired Hellenic culture and borrowed widely from the Greeks. In the process, certain elements of the culture were changed. For example, Roman sculpture became more lifelike than the Greek; Roman architecture, more elaborate. In addition, the Romans themselves made many contributions of their own that, when added to the Greek heritage, helped form a truly Greco-Roman culture. Perhaps the greatest single achievement of the Romans was the creation of a body of laws suitable for governing a world state.

Roman law held the peoples of the empire together. In modern-day Italy, France, Spain, and Latin America, law codes based on Roman legal principles are still in use. Law in the modern English-speaking countries was also greatly influenced by Roman law.

Roman law developed from the Laws of the Twelve Tables—those written laws won by the plebeians so that they would know how they would be ruled. As Rome expanded, laws governing noncitizens were added. The *legal interpretations*, or decisions, of different magistrates in the provinces were kept, and these helped other judges decide cases. Sometimes, the existing laws of a conquered place influenced the magistrate's decision. In this way, local rules and customs became a part of the larger body of Roman law. Roman laws became international, particularly the laws dealing with commerce. When Augustus was emperor, professional law schools were established to teach the law. Later, in the 6th century A.D., Justinian, emperor of the eastern empire, had this huge body of laws *codified*, that is, organized into a system that could more easily be used.

The Latin language was a lasting gift to civilization. The Romans spoke a language called Latin. It is one of the Indo-European languages, as are German, Slavic, Greek, and Sanskrit. The Romans did not develop writing until the 7th century B.C., when they adopted an alphabet used by the Etruscans. Writing with an alphabet is much easier than writing with picture forms, as in Chinese, the oldest system of writing still in use. Today, the so-called Roman alphabet is the most widely used alphabet in the world.

During the years of Roman civilization, two forms of Latin developed. One was literary Latin, the form used in writing. The second was the *vernacular* [vər nak'yə lər], or simplified, spoken language used in people's everyday dealings with each other. Literary Latin continued to be more formal and is highly prized for its logic and exactness.

Latin was the official language of business, education, government, and the arts throughout the empire. It formed the basis of the modern Spanish, Portuguese, Romanian, French, and Italian languages and contributed many words to English. All of these languages are written in the Roman alphabet, as are German, Dutch, Polish, Czech, Hungarian, Finnish, Swedish, and Turkish. Literary Latin was preserved for centuries after the end of the Roman Empire because it was the official language of the Roman Catholic Church. Today, it still uses Latin for all official documents. However, Latin is no longer used as an everyday language.

The Romans were great engineers and architects. A network of roads knit together the Roman realm. They were built to help speed the movement of armies and military supplies, but the roads were free to the public for travel and commerce. Built of several layers of stone, the Roman roads were super-

The aqueduct at Segovia, Spain, shows off the building skills of the Romans. The water ran through pipes at the top. Huge stone arches helped even out the countryside to a slight downward tilt so that gravity could move the water along.

ior to any highways constructed in Europe until the 1800s. Roman engineering skill was used throughout the empire in the construction of numerous dams, bridges, drainage systems, and *aqueducts*—bridgelike structures that held water pipes.

From the Etruscans, the Romans learned how to build arched constructions called *vaults*. Little by little, the Romans improved vault forms so that large interior spaces could be enclosed. To roof these areas, domes were often used. To make the structures solid and lasting, Roman architects used cement and concrete as basic materials. Exteriors were faced with marble or stucco and decorated with sculpture. The Romans preferred decoration to the simplicity of Greek architecture.

Roman public buildings were both magnificent and practical. The public baths were multilevel structures that included steam rooms, different bathing and swimming pools, gardens, gyms, and libraries. The Roman baths, which were like modern athletic clubs, served as popular meeting places for social and business purposes. By the 4th century A.D., the city of Rome boasted 1,000 public baths. The huge Colosseum in Rome seated 50 thousand persons and was the scene of bloody gladiatorial combats and even mock naval battles. At the Circus Maximus, a stadium in Rome that seated 150 thousand, chariot races were held.

The Romans are justly famous for city planning. Provincial cities and towns were usually built around a forum that would be close to the crossing of two main roads. The main civic buildings and the marketplace were centrally located in the forum area, and building codes were enforced to keep architectural styles uniform. The logical planning in the provinces was in strong contrast to the capital city of the empire. Rome had narrow, winding streets, a poor drainage system, and was overcrowded. In the 2nd century A.D., the city's population of more than a million persons was jammed into 9 square miles (23.4 square kilometers). Augustus claimed that he had found the city of brick and had left it of marble. However, the splendid public buildings built or repaired under his direction were often flanked by dark and flimsy tenement houses. Throughout the lifetime of the empire, Rome remained a sprawling, bustling city of magnificence and squalor.

The Romans used Greek models for literature. Throughout the history of Rome, Greek literature remained the most important influence on Latin literary works. An educated Roman was expected to know Greek as well as Latin. Wealthy families often owned Greek slaves who served as tutors for the children of the household. With Greek models to imitate, the Romans developed a literature of the first rank. While it was the Greek genius to speculate brilliantly about destiny and the universe, the Romans had a gift for describing less abstract ideas, using literature to point out important ethical concepts.

The wealth and leisure resulting from Roman conquests provided a growing audience for literature. From about 100 B.C. to 14 A.D.—the years from the last century of the republic through the reign of Augustus—Latin literature was at its best. This period has been called the Golden Age of Latin literature.

One of the leading writers of the Golden Age was the master statesman and polished orator, Cicero [sis'ə rō']. His speeches, letters, and essays showed a wide-ranging intellect and noble character. The respect he commanded as spokesman for the senate made Mark Antony jealous. Antony had Cicero put to death in 43 B.C. Julius Caesar contributed to Latin literature. His military history, *Commentaries on the Gallic Wars*, is famous for its careful descriptions and vigorous style.

The greatest poet of the Golden Age was Vergil [vėr'jəl]. He has been called the "Homer of Rome" because the *Iliad* and the *Odyssey* served as models for his epic, the *Aeneid* [i nē'id]. The chief character in Vergil's work was Aeneas, the legendary Trojan hero who overcame many obstacles before founding the city of Rome. The most outstanding aspect of the *Aeneid* is Vergil's patriotism; the glories of Rome were praised in poetry. Another patriotic writer was Livy [liv'ē], whose history of Rome was called *From the Founding of the City*. By picturing the past greatness of Rome in glowing terms, he hoped to convince his readers to return to the simple ways of their ancestors.

The Roman historian Tacitus [tas'ə təs] is best known for *Germania*, his study of the

The Colosseum took twelve years to build and could seat 50,000 people. Water pipes in the floor could turn the arena into a lake for naval exhibitions.

German tribes that lived north of the imperial frontiers in central Europe. Like Livy, Tacitus urged a return to traditional Roman values. His work contrasts the strength and simplicity of the Germans with the weakness and immorality of upper-class life in Rome.

Another important writer was the Greek biographer Plutarch [plü'tärk]. His masterpiece, *Parallel Lives*, paired forty-six biographies of Greek and Roman statesmen, orators, or warriors whose careers and talents were similar. Plutarch did not flatter the Greeks at the expense of the Romans. His accounts were well balanced and his judgments of character sound. His descriptions of people and events are so colorful that *Parallel Lives* proved to be an invaluable source for later writers. The famous English playwright Shakespeare drew heavily on Plutarch's biographies when writing *Julius Caesar* and *Antony and Cleopatra*.

Greeks in the empire made important scientific discoveries. During Roman times, most of the noted men of science were Greeks. Alexandria, Egypt, the former Greek colony, was a center for research and experimentation, with its famous museum and library. One famous Greek scholar was the astronomer Ptolemy [tol'ə mē]. Between 127 and 151 A.D., he brought together in one book all that was then known about astronomy. For 1,500 years, Ptolemy's views were generally accepted by educated people. Unlike Aristarchus before him, he believed that the sun revolved around the earth. Also a

In 63 B.C., a senator named Catiline plotted a revolt when he lost an election. In this fresco, Catiline sits alone as fellow senator Cicero fires accusations at him.

map maker, Ptolemy was the first to draw the earth as round, although Greek astronomers had known it was round since the 3rd century B.C.

The Greek physician Galen [gā′lən], who lived in the 2nd century A.D., also studied in Alexandria. Next to Hippocrates, he was the most famous doctor of ancient times. He discovered that arteries contain blood. Before then, they were thought to be filled with air.

The Romans themselves made few contributions to scientific knowledge. However, they were skillful in applying Greek findings in medicine and public health. The Romans built the first hospitals, some of which gave free medical care to the poor. About 14 A.D., the first school of medicine was begun in Rome. It was there that Celsus [kel′səs], a Roman-born physician, wrote and taught.

One of his books describes surgical procedures for removing tonsils and cataracts, as well as the steps involved in elementary plastic surgery.

section review 4

1. In what countries of the world today are the laws based on Roman law?

2. What language did the Romans speak? In what ways did it continue to be used after the end of the empire?

3. What types of buildings did the Romans erect? What materials were used? How was Roman architecture different from that of the Greeks?

4. Name three or more of the greatest writers of the Golden Age of Latin literature and some of their works.

Section Summaries

1. The Roman Republic arose on the Italian peninsula. Conquered by the Etruscans in the 7th century B.C., the Romans overthrew their Etruscan king in 509 B.C. and set up a republic that lasted until 31 B.C. After a long struggle for equal rights with the high-born patricians, the plebeians got some control over the government. From 509 to about 100 B.C., the Roman state expanded. By 270 B.C., the Italian peninsula was conquered.

2. The republic became a world state. Rome defeated Carthage in the Punic Wars. Further military campaigns in the Middle East resulted in Roman control by 100 B.C. over lands bordering the Mediterranean. Although conquest brought wealth to Rome, it also created serious problems for the republic. Graft and corruption increased. Rich officials bought up the land of the little farmers, who then went to Rome vainly seeking work. The population became divided into the many poor and the few very rich. The tribunes Tiberius and Gaius Gracchus were unsuccessful in their attempts to reform the state, and civil wars broke out, lasting for about 100 years. Finally, after the Battle of Actium in 31 B.C., Octavian (later known as Augustus) became ruler of Rome. He was a strong ruler whose reign marked the beginning of the Roman Empire.

3. The empire lasted for five centuries. The first 250 years of the empire were peaceful and prosperous, and the *Pax Romana* was extended from Britain to the Euphrates, from the Rhine to North Africa. By the 3rd century A.D., the Roman Empire had begun to show signs of decay. Poverty increased, business activity declined, and the authority of the central government weakened. Diocletian and Constantine chose despotism as a way to strengthen the government, but civil wars followed their reigns.

4. The Romans preserved Greek culture. The Romans developed a legal system that was effective in holding together the many different peoples and customs of the empire. Engineers and architects built excellent roads, bridges, aqueducts, and massive public buildings. Literature flourished, particularly during the last century of the republic and the reign of Augustus. The Romans admired Hellenistic culture and blended it with their own achievements to form a truly Greco-Roman culture.

Who? What? When? Where?

1. Arrange the events in chronological order.

   a. The Roman Republic was begun.
   b. Diocletian set up a despotic government.
   c. Rome was founded.
   d. Caesar became dictator of Rome.
   e. Constantine moved the capital to Byzantium.
   f. The Romans destroyed Carthage.

2. Name three problems that led to the end of the Roman Republic. Tell how each of these men tried to deal with the problems: Tiberius and Gaius Gracchus, Sulla, Julius Caesar.

3. Name one important contribution to literature or science made by each of these men: Julius Caesar, Tacitus, Livy, Vergil, Celsus, Marcus Aurelius, Cicero, Galen, Plutarch, Ptolemy.

4. Tell what role each of these people played in the rise and fall of Rome:

   a. Cleopatra   d. Nero
   b. Constantine   e. Scipio
   c. Marcus Brutus   f. Trajan

Questions for Critical Thinking

1. What were the greatest accomplishments of the Romans? What mistakes did they make? List two of each.

2. How much responsibility for the end of the Roman Republic is Julius Caesar's? Why was he killed? Why didn't his death save the republic?

3. Describe the increases in the plebeians' power during the republic. What happened to increase the conflicts between the rich and poor? What kinds of reform were needed?

4. In Greco-Roman culture, which contributions were Greek and which Roman? Give specific examples. Why is it significant today that the Romans preserved Greek culture?

Skill Activities

1. Read *The Last Days of Pompeii* by Edward Bulwer-Lytton to learn more about this famous city at its height. (Van Nostrand Reinhold, 1979)

2. Choose a short paragraph from any book. Use a dictionary to look up the origins of the words.

How many are of Latin origin? Greek? Other origins? Show the original forms for the words you look up.

3. Report on or discuss how life must have changed for people when their land became part of the Roman Empire. Think of the conquered people's language, government, law, transportation, food, and other goods, etc.

4. Research the origins and meanings of the names for the months of the year.

5. Using the map in this chapter called Roman Empire About 117 A.D., name at least 10 cities studied in previous chapters that were part of the Roman Empire by 117 A.D.

6. Research the Colosseum and the forum, telling what they were like in Roman times and what remains today.

chapter **6** *quiz*

Section 1

1. The tribal group from which the Romans developed were the: a. Etruscans, b. Gauls, c. Latins

2. Upper-class Romans were called: a. plebeians, b. patricians, c. legions

3. The officials who protected the plebeians were the: a. tribunes, b. patricians, c. consuls

Section 2

4. The Punic Wars were fought between Rome and: a. Sicily, b. Carthage, c. Corinth

5. The "Ides of March" was the day that: a. Hannibal was defeated at Zama, b. Caesar was killed, c. Caesar crossed the Rubicon.

6. The first Roman emperor was: a. Octavian, b. Julius Caesar, c. Antony

Section 3

7. Hadrian's Wall was built in: a. Britain, b. Gaul, c. the Iberian peninsula

8. When some emperors reduced the amount of gold and silver in the coins, this caused: a. despotism, b. inflation, c. increased trade

9. The architect of the *Pax Romana* was: a. Diocletian, b. Nero, c. Augustus

Section 4

10. The author of *Parallel Lives* was: a. Plutarch, b. Vergil, c. Galen

11. True or false: The laws in many countries of the world today are based on Roman legal ideas.

12. True or false: Ptolemy believed the earth was round.

1. Match the correct identifying phrase with one of these: Alexander, Asoka, Buddha, Confucius, Herodotus, Julius Caesar, Socrates, Wu Ti

a. The son of Philip and student of Aristotle, he left the important idea of "one world" to later generations.

b. The cruelty of war horrified him, so he became a Buddhist and tried to bring peace and toleration to his people.

c. He taught a way to find peace through the Four Noble Truths.

d. A great military leader, he also wrote a history of the Gallic Wars.

e. Called the "Father of History," he wrote a rambling account of the Persian Wars.

f. His teachings gave his people a standard of behavior and a deep respect for the past.

g. The greatest of the Han rulers, he brought peace to central and eastern Asia.

h. A great teacher, he asked questions to arrive at the truth.

2. Choose the letter of the invention or development associated with these civilizations: India, China, Greece, Rome

a. aqueducts
b. Arabic numerals
c. block printing
d. caste system
e. civil service system
f. cotton cloth
g. democracy
h. drama
i. Gallic Wars
j. geometry
k. Great Wall
l. Hadrian's Wall
m. tribunes
n. reincarnation
o. silk
p. Stoicism

3. Tell which civilization—India, China, Greece, or Rome—the following quotations describe:

a. ". . . The whole world keeps holiday; the age-long curse of war has been put aside."

b. "[to] diminish expenses, lighten taxes, and employ only honest officials will do more to abolish robbery than . . . the severest punishments."

c. ". . . power is in the hands not of the few but of the whole people."

d. ". . . The people are many and happy. They do not have to register . . . with the police. There is no death penalty."

4. Match the letters on the time line with the events they stand for.

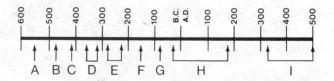

____Pericles was born.
____Rome destroyed Carthage.
____The Peloponnesian War ended.
____The *Pax Romana* existed.
____Asoka lived.
____Wu Ti died.
____Alexander the Great lived.
____The Guptas ruled India.
____Confucius was born.

5. Match the letters on the map with the places described below:

____Alexander's armies moved eastward to this region before turning back.

____Rugged mountains in this area separate India and China.

____The Roman Republic was founded in this region.

____A Ch'in emperor completed a protective wall in this area.

____The Greeks founded their first city-states in this area.

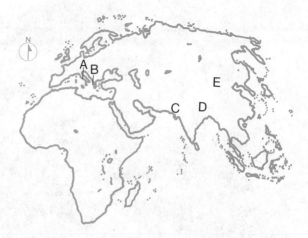

UNIT THREE
THE WORLDS OF CHRISTENDOM AND ISLAM

We now turn to two major civilizations that were largely shaped by religion—the world of Christendom and the world of Islam. Both had their origins in the Mediterranean area. They were often enemies, but there was also a great deal of interchange between them.

Christianity united peoples from Ireland to Russia and from Scandinavia to Sicily. Although there were other faiths, Christian laws and customs governed the way of life. Christendom was divided into two parts. Western Christendom looked to the head of the Church in Rome for leadership. Eastern Christendom looked to Constantinople.

The era of western Christendom, from the fall of Rome to the fourteenth century, was called by later people the "medieval period," or "middle ages." It seemed that nothing important had happened. But universities began and great art, architecture, and literature were produced.

In eastern Christendom, the Byzantine Empire flourished. Constantinople was a far more brilliant center of culture than Rome. Greek Orthodox Christianity was adopted by the Slavic rulers of the Black Sea and thus played a major role in the formation of Russia.

The world of Islam arose in the seventh century and created a powerful empire. From the Fertile Crescent, the world of Islam moved west to southern Spain and east to the Indus River. Held together by a common religion and language, Muslim civilization was based on widespread trade.

In both worlds, religious buildings reached their steeples, spires, or domes into the sky. And religion affected both the daily lives of individuals and the activities of governments.

Charlemagne symbolized the forces that shaped western Christendom.

CHAPTER 7
THE RISE OF CHRISTENDOM

Jesus lived   Edict of Milan ●   ● *City of God*
Christians persecuted   ● Council of Nicaea
● Paul the Apostle died   Saint Jerome lived   Gregory the Great was pope
● Rome burned   Ulfilas lived   Saint Patrick lived
Battle of Adrianople ●   ● Battle of Chalôns
Visigoths looted Rome ●   ● "Fall" of Rome
Theodoric became king of Ostrogoths ●   ● Clovis died
Saint Benedict lived
Christianity made official religion ●   Augustine sent to England ●
Attila died ●

CHAPTER 8
WESTERN CHRISTENDOM IN THE MIDDLE AGES

CHAPTER 9
BYZANTINE CIVILIZATION AND THE FORMATION OF RUSSIA

Constantinople made a Roman capital ●   ● Roman Empire split   Heraclius lived
Nika Revolt ●
Procopius lived
Justinian lived
Romans took Byzantium ●   Hagia Sophia begun ●
Theodora died ●

CHAPTER 10
THE RISE OF ISLAM AND THE MUSLIM EMPIRE

Mohammad lived
Hijra ●
Umayyad dynasty founded ●
Abu Bakr lived

CHAPTER 11
ISLAMIC CIVILIZATION

A.D. | 50 | 100 | 150 | 200 | 250 | 300 | 350 | 400 | 450 | 500 | 550 | 600 | 650 | 700

1. Jesus, 2. St. Luke, 3. Viking post head, 4. Hagia Sophia, 5. Justinian, 6. Mohammad, 7. Charlemagne, 8. Viking ship, 9. Russian sword, 10. Viking wagon, 11. Persian battle-ax, 12. French noble, 13. Crusaders, 14. European crossbow, 15. Medieval nobles, 16. Seige of Constantinople, 17. Russian sledge, 18. German musician.

2
3
5
4
1
6

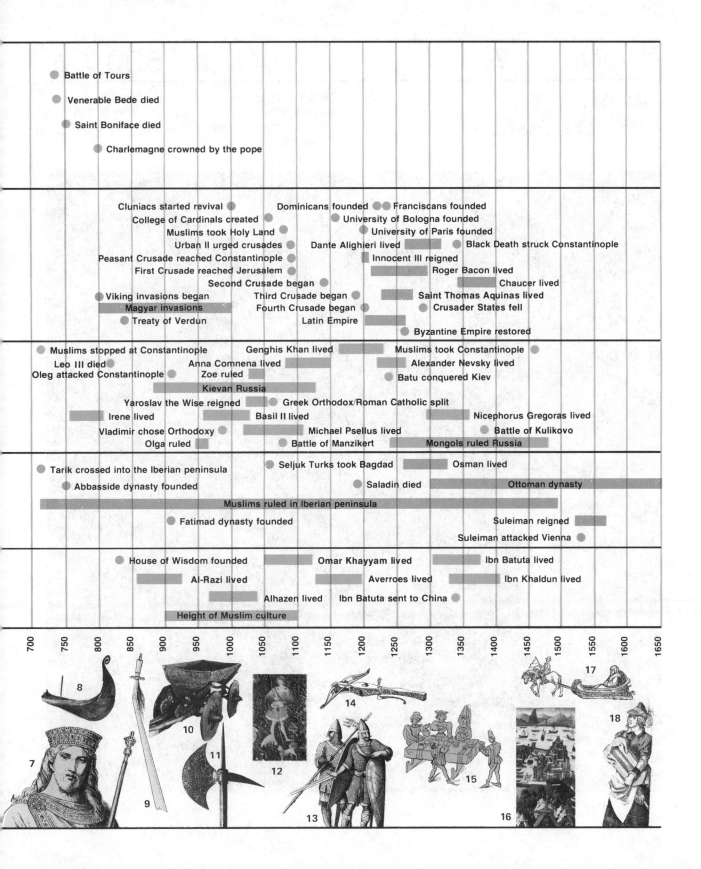

Battle of Tours

Venerable Bede died

Saint Boniface died

Charlemagne crowned by the pope

Cluniacs started revival ●   Dominicans founded ● ● Franciscans founded
College of Cardinals created ●   ● University of Bologna founded
Muslims took Holy Land ●   ● University of Paris founded
Urban II urged crusades ●   Dante Alighieri lived ● Black Death struck Constantinople
Peasant Crusade reached Constantinople ●   ● Innocent III reigned
First Crusade reached Jerusalem ●   ● Roger Bacon lived
Second Crusade began ●   Chaucer lived
Viking invasions began   Third Crusade began ●   Saint Thomas Aquinas lived
Magyar invasions   Fourth Crusade began ●   Crusader States fell
Treaty of Verdun ●   Latin Empire
Byzantine Empire restored ●

Muslims stopped at Constantinople ●   Genghis Khan lived   Muslims took Constantinople ●
Leo III died ●   Anna Comnena lived   Alexander Nevsky lived
Oleg attacked Constantinople ●   Zoe ruled   Batu conquered Kiev ●
Kievan Russia
Yaroslav the Wise reigned   ● Greek Orthodox/Roman Catholic split
Irene lived   Basil II lived   Nicephorus Gregoras lived
Vladimir chose Orthodoxy ●   Michael Psellus lived   ● Battle of Kulikovo
Olga ruled   Battle of Manzikert   Mongols ruled Russia

Tarik crossed into the Iberian peninsula ●   ● Seljuk Turks took Bagdad   Osman lived
Abbasside dynasty founded ●   ● Saladin died   Ottoman dynasty
Muslims ruled in Iberian peninsula
Fatimad dynasty founded ●   Suleiman reigned
Suleiman attacked Vienna ●

House of Wisdom founded ●   Omar Khayyam lived   Ibn Batuta lived
Al-Razi lived   Averroes lived   Ibn Khaldun lived
Alhazen lived   Ibn Batuta sent to China ●
Height of Muslim culture

700   750   800   850   900   950   1000   1050   1100   1150   1200   1250   1300   1350   1400   1450   1500   1550   1600   1650

7   8   9   10   11   12   13   14   15   16   17   18

THE RISE OF CHRISTENDOM

The Book of Kells is one of the most famous and beautiful illuminated manuscripts of all times. The Irish masterpiece is heavily illustrated. This page shows Jesus.

The rise of a great religion or the decline of a great empire happens slowly. The growth of Christianity and the decline of the Roman Empire both took centuries. Eventually they became a civilization called Christendom.

Why did the Roman Empire decline? There are many reasons. One was the internal corruption and immorality of the Romans themselves, which weakened the empire. Another was the powerful German tribes that threatened to overrun the empire.

As early as the 1st century A.D., Tacitus, one of Rome's greatest historians, sensed what might happen. An admirer of the republican form of government, Tacitus was extremely critical of the Roman emperors and the decline in Roman moral standards. In an effort to show how these were weakening, he wrote a work called *Germania* that described the German tribes to the north. Almost as a warning of the danger to Rome, he noted the German drive for constant military action:

> If their native state sinks into the sloth of prolonged peace and repose, many of its noble youths voluntarily seek those tribes which are waging some war, both because inaction is odious to their race, and because they win renown more readily in the midst of peril, and cannot maintain a numerous following except by violence and war. . . . Nor are they as easily persuaded to plough the earth and to wait for the year's produce as to challenge an enemy and earn the honor of wounds. Nay, they actually think it tame and stupid to acquire by the sweat of toil what they might win by their blood.

The Roman Empire survived for another three centuries. But the description of the Germans by Tacitus helps us understand why they were able to conquer Rome in the long run.

In the year 800, a Germanic king named Charlemagne was proclaimed emperor of a new Roman Empire. As a Christian warrior-king of German blood who admired the culture of the Roman Empire, he represented the forces that would reshape western Christendom. This chapter traces the rise of Christendom by describing how:

1. **Christianity became a strong religion in the Roman world.**

2. **German tribes attacked the Roman Empire.**

3. **The Church became the preserver of civilization.**

4. **An alliance of popes and Franks aided western Christendom.**

1 Christianity became a strong religion in the Roman world

By the middle of the 4th century, the once powerful and prosperous Roman Empire showed unmistakable signs of decay. The government was riddled by corruption. Barbarian tribes threatened the imperial frontiers. Heavy taxes burdened the citizens. And city mobs shouted for bread as food production continued to drop off. In the face of these problems, many Romans turned to their old gods—Mars, Jupiter, and Minerva. Other Romans looked to the teachings of Greek philosophy, chiefly Stoicism, which taught people to accept their fate with quiet courage. Still others turned to Mesopotamian religions.

Of greater significance in the history of Western civilization was the rise of a new faith that had been founded in Palestine in the 1st century A.D. This faith—Christianity—was the religion based on the teachings of a Jew named Jesus.

Christianity began with the teachings of Jesus. Solid historical information about Jesus is extremely scanty. Most of what is known about him comes from the Gospels, the first four books of the New Testament of the Bible. The Gospels were written years after Jesus's death, and despite much agreement, there are points on which they seem to disagree. According to the Gospels, Jesus was born in Bethlehem and reared in the village of Nazareth. He apparently stopped working as a carpenter at the age of thirty and began to travel throughout Palestine, preaching his doctrines.

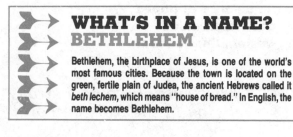

WHAT'S IN A NAME?
BETHLEHEM

Bethlehem, the birthplace of Jesus, is one of the world's most famous cities. Because the town is located on the green, fertile plain of Judea, the ancient Hebrews called it *beth lechem*, which means "house of bread." In English, the name becomes Bethlehem.

The teachings of Jesus had their roots in Judaism. Like other Jews, Jesus condemned violence and selfishness and taught doctrines based on brotherhood. Most Jews,

Early Christians buried their dead in underground tombs, called catacombs, outside Rome. The Catacomb of Priscilla, like the others, was decorated with paintings.

■ MAP LESSON 7: THE SPREAD OF CHRISTIANITY TO 1100 A.D.

1. This map shows change over time. In this case, different colors show stages in the spread of the Christian religion. Maps like this one are generalizations. Not everyone in each area became a Christian in the time shown. And the boundaries between different colors are approximations. Christianity first spread along the Mediterranean coasts. Then it spread inland. What city served as a dispersion point on the Greek peninsula? On the Italian peninsula?

2. Where was Christianity established first, in Ireland or Germany? In Spain or Norway? In Finland or Russia?

3. There is an "island" of early Christianity in the Rhone Valley in France, near what is now the city of Lyon. Here lived many Greeks who had come from Asia Minor. They brought Christianity with them before the end of the second century. During what period did the surrounding area become Christian?

however, did not accept Jesus's claim that he was the Messiah, the leader who was divinely chosen to usher in the great judgment at the end of time. (Messiah is a Hebrew word; in Greek it is Christ.)

The Gospels report that Jesus attracted crowds of people wherever he went. Both Roman rulers and Jewish authorities reacted against his preaching. To Jewish authorities, proclaiming oneself the Messiah was blasphemy [blas'fə mē]. To the Romans, concerned about political discontent in Palestine, it appeared to be a call to overthrow the government. Historians differ as to exactly what happened next. But in 33 A.D., Jesus was put to death by crucifixion on the order of Pontius Pilate [pon'shəs pī'lət], the Roman governor of Judea.

Finns 1100s

Norwegians
995-1030

St. Patrick
442-461 A.D.

North Sea

IRELAND   BRITAIN

ENGLAND

St. Boniface
719-755 A.D.

*ATLANTIC
OCEAN*

St. Augustine
596-604 A.D.

GERMANY

Poles
966-1034

Russians
988-1025

FRANCE

Magyars
950-1050

Constantine's Edict
of Milan 313 A.D.

Bishop Ulfilas
341-348 A.D.

Black   Sea

SPAIN

I T A L Y

Rome

Constantinople

Nicaea   ASIA
MINOR

Monte
Cassino

Troas

Mediterranean

Tarsus

Antioch

Corinth

Ephesus   Attalia

MALTA   *Sea*

Nazareth

Nazareth
PALESTINE

Jerusalem

To 200 A.D.

200-400 A.D.

400-800 A.D.

800-1100 A.D.

- - - Journeys of St. Paul

N

0   200   400 MILES
0   200   400 KILOMETERS

The New Testament tells how Jesus reappeared to his disciples following the crucifixion and confirmed his teachings of eternal life. A few followers set about to spread the news of the Resurrection. They became missionaries of the new faith. They called themselves "brethren," brothers, of "the way." Later, believers in "the way" were called Christians and their faith Christianity.

Paul spread the teachings of Jesus. The most important missionary was Paul, a well-educated Jew from the Hellenistic city of Tarsus in Asia Minor. As a young man, Paul believed that Christian teachings went against Judaism, and he took part in the persecutions of Christians. According to the Acts of the Apostles (9:1–5) in the New Tes-

tament, Paul was on his way to arrest any men or women whom he found to be followers of "the way," when he was suddenly surrounded by "a light from heaven." After this experience, Paul became dedicated to Christianity. Immediately, he set out to bring Jesus's teachings to as many people as possible—to Jews and Gentiles, non-Jews, alike. From about 37 A.D. until his death in the year 67, he journeyed to many cities around the eastern Mediterranean, spreading the Christian gospel. His great contribution helped Christianity grow from a small Jewish sect in Palestine to a world religion.

Christianity triumphed over persecution. Officials of the Roman government allowed many different religions to exist in the empire as long as the people accepted government authority. The Christians, however, refused to obey many of the Roman laws—particularly that of emperor worship. Roman officials, therefore, looked upon Christians as enemies of the state.

Nero blamed the Christians for the burning of Rome in 64 A.D. and punished them severely. Other emperors, seeking excuses for bad conditions during their reigns, used the Christians as scapegoats. They crucified Christians, threw them to wild beasts and mad dogs in arenas, or had them burned alive.

The first widespread persecution was carried on from 249 to 251 A.D. The last was ordered in 303. During these years, Christians lived a hunted existence. But the religion could not be wiped out. In fact, the courage with which Christians met death inspired a Roman writer of the 2nd century to say that "the blood of the martyrs became the seed of the Church."

In 311 A.D., Christianity was made a legal religion in the eastern Roman Empire. About two years later, Emperor Constantine in the western empire issued the Edict of Milan, which legalized Christianity throughout the empire. In 395, the Emperor Theodosius made Christianity the official religion.

Christianity was strengthened by a common creed. Early Christians held differing views of the substance of God and Christ. To resolve this conflict, the Emperor Constantine called the Council of Nicaea [nī sē'ə] in 325. This body put together a creed which said that God and Christ were of the same substance. All members of the council agreed to the Nicene [nī sēn'] Creed except a priest named Arius and his few followers. They maintained that God and Christ were of different substances. Arius and his followers were therefore banished from the Church as *heretics* [her'ə tiks]. (Heretics are persons who hold a belief different from the accepted

view.) However, many people continued to cling to Arian beliefs. As the years passed, the Nicenes and the Arians struggled for leadership in the Church. The Nicenes were finally victorious.

In addition to the Nicene Creed, the early Church developed an official book of sacred writings. To the holy writings of the Jews, which the early Christians called the Old Testament, were added religious writings collected after the death of Jesus. Twenty-seven of these collections, or books, were selected to make the New Testament. In his travels from place to place, Paul had kept in touch with Christians through letters of encouragement and advice. These letters, or *epistles*, make up some of the most important books of the New Testament.

The official teaching, or *theology*, of the Christian Church was systematized by a group of men known as the Church Fathers. Saint Jerome, one of the most famous, lived from about 340 to 420 A.D. From the Hebrew original, he made a Latin translation of the Bible, called the Vulgate, which is still used as the official version in the Roman Catholic Church. In 426, another of the Church Fathers, Saint Augustine finished *The City of God*. This book provided much of the foundation of Christian theology.

The Church established a well-knit organization. At first, Christians met in small groups, often in their homes. As time went by and more people became Christians, an organization developed, based on Roman governmental units.

Presbyters [prez'bə tərz], later known as priests, were ordained, or officially consecrated, to conduct the services and business of village churches. Several villages made up a diocese [dī'ə sis], which was placed under the direction of a bishop, a priest who administered the religious affairs of a church district. A number of dioceses made up a province under the authority of an archbishop.

Early Christians painted pictures of Jesus on cloth.

And a group of provinces made up a patriarchate. The title of patriarch [pā'trē ärk] was given to the bishop of a large city, such as Rome, Constantinople, or Alexandria. Gradually the Bishop of Rome assumed leadership as *pope*, from a Greek word meaning "father."

Church leadership developed in Rome partly because it was the capital of the empire. In addition, with the decline of the western part of the empire, the Roman bishops took on governmental leadership as it slipped from the hands of the weak emperors. Finally, the popes claimed supremacy through the Petrine Theory. This doctrine held that the Roman church had been founded by Peter, leader of Jesus's Apostles and was therefore the most important church. By the year 600, Rome was thought of as the capital of the Church and the successor of Peter as head of the Church.

section review 1

1. Name four problems of the Roman Empire in the 4th century.

2. Why did the Roman rulers and Jewish authorities in Jerusalem disapprove of Jesus's teachings?

3. How did Paul the Apostle help spread the Christian religion?

4. Why did Rome become the capital city of Christianity? By what year had this happened? What was the title of the leader of the Church?

2 German tribes attacked the Roman Empire

While the Church was growing stronger, the once mighty government of the Caesars was crumbling. Internal problems of the Roman Empire made it easier for external forces to destroy it. Thus came the final crushing blow—attack by Germanic tribes.

German tribes pressed against the Roman frontier. In the 4th century A.D., most Germanic peoples in Europe were living east of the Rhine and north of the Danube. To the west and north of the Black Sea, were the East Goths (Ostrogoths) and the West Goths (Visigoths). To the west of these tribes and extending over a large area east of the Rhine were the Vandals, Lombards, Alemanni,

By the 700s A.D., Germanic tribes decorated their tombs with pictures carved in stone.

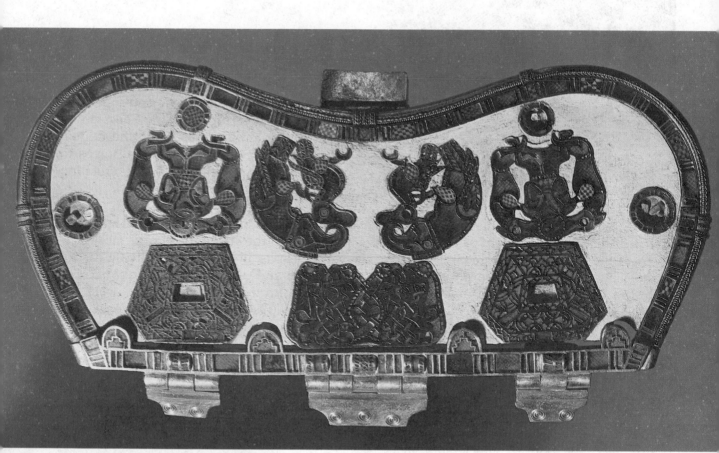

Daily Life

The treasure of Sutton Hoo, near Suffolk, England, is evidence of Saxon abilities. Sutton Hoo was a king's tomb. *Above* and *far left* are purse lids of gold. At *near left* is a helmet. Together, these pieces show the way nobles of the time lived.

Burgundians, and Franks. In and near present-day Denmark lived the Jutes, Angles, and Saxons.

These groups were partly nomadic, herding their flocks and tilling the soil. Large and vigorous, the people prized strength and courage in battle. They worshiped many gods, including Tiw, the god of war; Wotan, the chief of the gods; Thor, the god of thunder; and Freya, the goddess of fertility. (Their names are in the English words Tuesday, Wednesday, Thursday, and Friday.)

The Germans governed themselves with tribal assemblies made up of voting freemen. Their laws were based on long-established customs of the tribe. These political practices had a strong influence later in medieval England, where they laid a foundation for parliamentary government and English common law.

For hundreds of years, the Germans had fought the Romans on the borders of the empire. Long periods of war alternated with periods of peace. During the peaceful periods, the Roman and Germanic peoples mixed with each other. Some Germans entered the Roman Empire and settled on vacant lands. Others, captured in war, became slaves on Roman estates, and still others became soldiers in the legions. If this mixing had been allowed to continue, the Germans might have been gradually absorbed into the empire. However, outside forces suddenly turned the gradual infiltration into a rushing invasion.

German tribes forced their way into all parts of the western Roman Empire. In Asia, during the 4th century, fierce nomads called Huns were on the march from the East. Mounted on swift horses, they attacked all tribes in their path with lightning ferocity. Crossing the Dnieper [nē'pər] River, they conquered the Ostrogoths in eastern Europe. The Visigoths, fearing that the Huns would attack them also, begged Roman authorities for safety in the empire. The Roman officials agreed, promising the Visigoths lands to settle if they came unarmed.

Neither side lived up to the agreement. The Visigoths, without land and facing starvation, began to attack Roman settlements. In 378 A.D., the Roman emperor Valens led a great army against the Visigoths at the Battle of Adrianople. To everyone's surprise, the Visigoths defeated the Romans, scattered the imperial force, and killed the emperor. This battle is considered to be one of the decisive battles in world history because it left the Roman Empire defenseless. It was the first major battle that Rome had lost in hundreds of years. German tribes outside the empire began to round up their cattle, mobilize their fighting men, and move toward the Roman borders.

The German general Alaric led the Visigoths southwest. They reached Rome in 410 A.D. and looted the city. By that time, other German tribes—the Franks, Vandals, and Burgundians—were moving into the empire. And about 450 A.D., Germans from northwest Europe—the Angles, Saxons, and Jutes—sailed to Britain, where they killed or enslaved the Britons they found there and forced others to retreat into Wales and Scotland.

To add to the confusion, the Huns, led by Attila, had also invaded the empire and were threatening to enslave or destroy both Romans and Germans. Forgetting their own differences for a while, the Romans and Germans united against a common enemy. They fought together in Gaul (present-day France) and defeated Attila at the Battle of Châlons in 451. Shortly afterward, Attila died in Italy and his savage cavalry drifted apart.

The western empire collapsed. Meanwhile, the emperors in Rome had become so weak that they were mere puppets of the army. Many of the soldiers were of German birth, and one, Odoacer [ō′dō ā′sər], became a commander of the Roman armies. In 476, he deposed the last of the Roman emperors and became the first German ruler of Rome. This date—476—is often given as the date for the "fall" of Rome. In a strict sense, there was no "fall." The decline of Roman imperial power was slow and complicated. Weak emperors, corrupt officials, and the admission of German soldiers into the legions all played a part.

Since the early decades of the 4th century, emperors at Rome had sensed the growing weakness of the empire in the west. In the year 330 A.D., Emperor Constantine had moved his capital to the city of Byzantium, in the eastern part of the empire. By the end of the century, the Roman Empire had become permanently divided. One emperor ruled in the west and another in the east. Although separated, the two sections of the empire continued to be thought of as one.

However, the western part of the empire was breaking up. By the year 476, when Odoacer came to the throne, German kingdoms had been established in many former Roman provinces. The Anglo-Saxons were in England. The Visigoths had moved into the Iberian peninsula. In northern Africa, the Vandals had built up a kingdom, and by 486, the Franks controlled Gaul. The Italian peninsula was the scene of much warfare, and near the end of the 5th century, it fell under the rule of the Ostrogoths.

The Ostrogoths had been freed from the Huns after the death of Attila in 453. The Ostrogoths then built a settlement within the Roman Empire south and west of the Danube. In 471, they elected Theodoric [thē-od′ər ik] their king, and soon afterward he led a march toward the eastern part of the empire.

The emperor in the east tried to stop the Ostrogoths from moving into his lands. He encouraged Theodoric to invade the Italian peninsula instead and to overthrow Odoacer, who had ruled there since 476. Theodoric did so and established his capital at the city of Ravenna, in the northeast part of the Italian peninsula. His rule brought prosperity and peace to his kingdom, but at his death in 526, civil war began again. In the middle of the 6th century, a strong emperor at Constantinople, Justinian, won back Italian lands for a few years. Then the Lombards, another German tribe, conquered the Italian peninsula in 568 and stayed there for 200 years.

The eastern part of the empire, however, did not give way to internal decay and bar-

During the 500s, noble Saxon families built large forts in Britain.

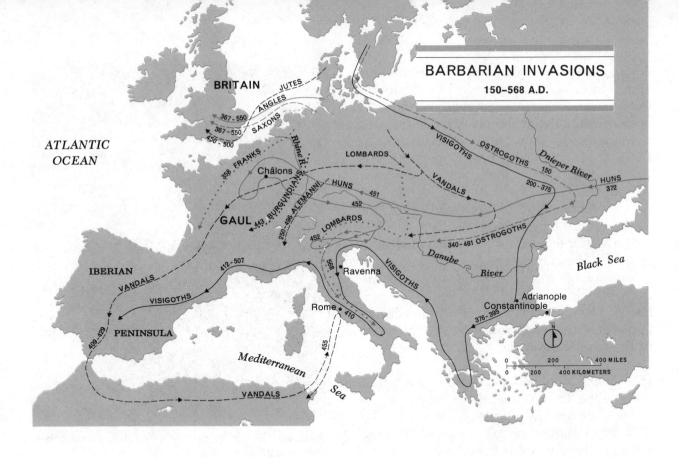

barian invasions. With its capital at Constantinople, it endured, carrying on the imperial tradition for a thousand years more. It preserved much of Greco-Roman culture and served as a buffer for western Europe against invasions from the Middle East.

section review 2

1. Why did the semipeaceful relationship between Romans and Germans change suddenly in the 4th century?

2. How did the Battle of Adrianople in 378 affect the Roman Empire?

3. What happened in 476 that is called the "fall" of Rome?

4. How long did the eastern part of the empire remain strong? Give two reasons why the eastern empire was important to western Europe after the fall of Rome.

3 The Church became the preserver of civilization

As the Roman Empire declined, a new pattern of civilization developed. This pattern combined the old Roman culture with the vigor of the Germanic tribes. The Christian Church became the main force in shaping this new pattern—preserving culture and civilizing the Germans.

During the German invasions, the Roman government gradually stopped providing services. City populations shrank and people turned to renting farm land. There they were protected by the landowners. But as the farmers fell behind in their rent payments, Roman law bound them to the land. These were long-range changes, though, and most persons saw little change in their daily lives.

About two-thirds of the land changed ownership, but usually only the wealthy landowners were affected. In a few regions, the Germans outnumbered the old inhabitants, but the newcomers soon took on the customs of the Romans. The blending of peoples that had been going on before the invasions continued. The Germans made use of some of the old Roman political forms and kept Latin as the official language.

Many of the invaders had been Christianized by missionaries. The invaders had come in too quickly to be absorbed, to appreciate Roman culture, or to care if the empire lasted. However, they respected the Church and were impressed and awed by the ritual of the Christian service.

The Church provided protection and order. During the invasions and confusion of the times, Roman law was not enforced. The Church took over the task of protecting the helpless and punishing the criminal. Persons fleeing for their lives could find safety, called *sanctuary*, in any church building.

As the Roman emperors became weaker, popes and their assistants took over governmental powers. They set up Church courts and took over the right to collect taxes. The governmental power of the Church was especially evident from 590 to 604, when Gregory the Great was pope. He supervised the police, directed the generals of the army, coined money, and kept aqueducts in repair.

Missionaries spread Christianity. As early as the 3rd century, fearless missionaries had carried the teachings of Christianity beyond the frontiers of the Roman Empire. One of the most important of these missionaries was Ulfilas [ul'fi ləs]. An Arian Christian, Ulfilas preached among the Gothic peoples. He invented a Gothic alphabet, which he used in translating the Bible. Another famous missionary, Saint Patrick, was born in Britain

Monks sometimes spent their whole lives illuminating a single copy of a book.

about 389. He journeyed to Ireland to convert the Celtic peoples to the faith and founded many monasteries that became famous as centers of learning. In 496, Pope Gregory sent a Roman monk, Augustine, as missionary to England. Augustine later became the first Archbishop of Canterbury.

In the early part of the 8th century, a young priest named Winfrid was sent to preach in Germany. He later changed his name to Boniface and became famous as the Apostle of Germany. There he founded churches and monasteries until his death in 755.

Monks helped preserve culture. During the years of the Roman persecutions, a few Christians went into the wilderness, giving up worldly interests and living alone. Others lived in groups, dedicating themselves to the service of God. Christian *monasteries*, places

where groups of monks lived apart from the world, were first set up in Egypt. Later, monasteries appeared in the eastern part of the Roman Empire. About the middle of the 4th century, monasteries also sprang up in the west.

When men went out to live a holy life alone, they were often too hard on themselves. Monasteries gave these men a way to live apart from society, to dedicate their lives to God, and yet live useful lives. About the year 520, Saint Benedict set up a monastery in Italy at Monte Cassino and drew up rules for the monks to live by. His rules required obedience and poverty, daily prayers, and at least six hours of useful work each day. The rules of the Benedictine order were widely adopted by other monasteries in western Christendom.

In German lands beyond the old frontiers, where life was rough, monks not only spread the teachings of Christianity but also advanced civilization. In wild and forested lands, monks often cleared the forests, drained the swamps, and introduced new crops. The few schools that existed in Europe during the early Middle Ages were run by monks. The monasteries also served as inns for travelers and as hospitals.

At a time when libraries were neglected and precious manuscripts were destroyed or lost in looting, copies of the Scriptures and some of the classics were made by monks and preserved in monasteries. Often, a monk spent his entire lifetime making just one copy of a book. Nearly all the important monasteries had a writing room where monks copied manuscripts by hand. These they illustrated, or *illuminated*, with decorative designs, borders, and initials done in gold and brilliant colors. The monks also kept historical records, called *Chronicles*. One, *The Ecclesiastical History of the English Nation*, written by Saint Bede in the early 8th century, is the best account available of nearly two hundred years of English history.

section review 3

1. Tell three ways in which the German tribes became like the Romans they invaded.

2. Why did the Church take on the role of government? What services did the Church provide after the collapse of Roman law?

3. Describe the work of the Christian missionaries.

4. How did the monks bring civilization to the German lands outside the empire?

An alliance of popes and Franks aided western Christendom

In the last part of the 5th century, the Franks, a German tribe, began to build a nation in the north and east of Gaul. This nation became the greatest empire of early medieval times.

Clovis united the Franks and extended the power of the Church. Clovis began his remarkable career as the ruler of a small Frankish kingdom. By 486 A.D., he had overcome the last remains of Roman authority in Gaul. He then turned against the other Frankish kings and crushed their forces. In 507, the Visigothic kingdom in southern Gaul was conquered, and the Visigoths fled to their relatives in the Iberian peninsula.

Clovis was converted to Christianity when he won a victory in battle after an appeal to the Christian God. As a result, not only Clovis but all his warriors were baptized into the Christian faith.

Clovis became one of the most powerful rulers in western Europe. He was the first important Germanic king to become a Roman Catholic, that is, to accept the Nicene Creed upheld by the pope in Rome. All other Germanic rulers and their subjects—except those in England—were Arian Christians. The pope considered them to be heretics. This gave Clovis an excuse to attack his Arian neighbors. He said, "I cannot endure that those Arians should possess any part of Gaul. With God's aid we will go against them and conquer their lands." He defeated the Arians, extending his lands and the authority of the pope at the same time.

Clovis died in 511, and his kingdom was divided among his four sons. They pushed Frankish authority into lands north and east of the Rhine, but their four kingdoms were poorly governed. The kings that followed were immoral, weak drunkards who were nicknamed the Do-Nothing Kings.

The Carolingian family won control of the Franks. Since the Frankish kings did not perform their duties, the office of Mayor of the Palace became politically important. One mayor, Pepin, took control of all Frankish lands and actually became the sole ruler. He also cooperated with the Christian church and supported missionaries sent by the pope. In 714, his son Charles inherited the office of mayor. Charles's greatest success was at the Battle of Tours in 732. Pitted against an army of Muslim invaders from the Iberian peninsula, he won a victory that saved the northern European continent for Christianity. After that, he was known as Charles Martel, or Charles the Hammer.

When Charles Martel's son, Pepin the Short, became Mayor of the Palace, he asked the pope to decide whether he or a Do-Nothing King should be considered the legal ruler of the Franks. The pope approved Pepin, and thus began the Carolingian [kar'ə-lin'jē ən] line of kings. In return, Pepin led an army against the Lombards, who were threatening the *papacy*, that is, the office and government of the pope. In 756, Pepin turned over to the pope a part of the territory the Lombards had controlled. This Donation of Pepin came to be known as the Papal States.

Charlemagne built an empire. In 768, Pepin's sons Charles and Carloman inherited the throne. Charles became the sole ruler in 771 when Carloman died. He was called Charles the Great, or Charlemagne. Charlemagne too led an army to protect the pope's interests. This time, the Lombards were completely beaten. In 774, Charlemagne took the title of King of the Lombards. He went on to win

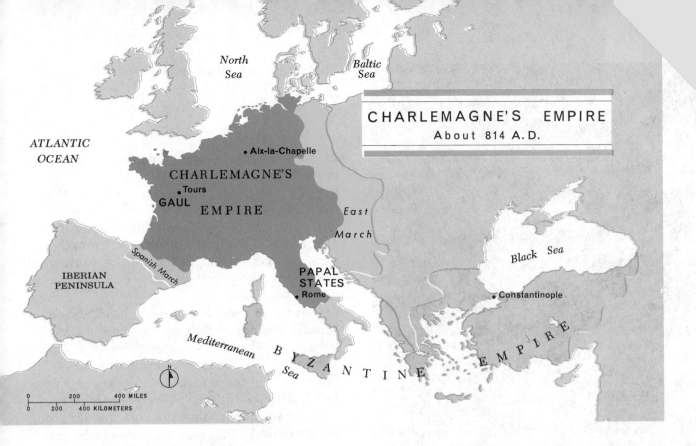

CHARLEMAGNE'S EMPIRE
About 814 A.D.

other battles against different German tribes. Eventually, he governed an empire stretching from the Danube to the Atlantic Ocean, from Rome to the Baltic and North seas. Priests traveled with his armies. While the armies made conquests for Charlemagne, the priests made converts for the Church.

Charlemagne appointed counts to run the *counties*, or districts, into which he divided his empire. He kept law and order through agents called *missi dominici*, or "messengers of the lord." The *missi*, traveling in pairs, visited every county annually, checked on the local courts, and reported their findings to Charlemagne. On the borders, he set up defense districts called marches.

Charlemagne modeled his capital at Aix-la-Chapelle (present-day Aachen, West Germany) on Roman cities and imported statues and marble from the Italian peninsula to improve the beauty of his city. Aix-la-Chapelle [āks'lä shä pel'] was also famous for the revival of learning, often called the Carolingian Renaissance. And Charlemagne urged priests to study and improve their education. He also sponsored a refinement of the system of handwriting then in use and generously supported Church schools. There boys were taught Christian doctrine, arithmetic, grammar, and singing. The rebirth of learning during Charlemagne's rule helped preserve Roman culture and continue the development of civilization in western Christendom.

Charlemagne was crowned by both Church and state. In the year 800, Charlemagne traveled to Rome. While he was attending Church services on Christmas Day, the pope placed a crown on the king's head and declared, "To Charles Augustus crowned of God, great and pacific Emperor of the

Charlemagne was a steadfast defender of Christianity who carried the religion throughout his vast empire.

of Charlemagne's rule. Charlemagne was emperor by the grace of God, with the Church on his side. However, it was not all a positive gain for the king. The coronation also showed that the Church had the right to say who was the Roman emperor. From that time on, popes and kings each claimed to have the highest authority.

Christendom emerged as a civilization. Most important of all, the crowning of Charlemagne by the pope completed the blending of two major ideas after a period of some 400 years. One of those ideas was the concept of political unity that was represented by the old Roman Empire. The other was the idea of religious unity that was represented by the new Christian Church. The mixture of the two ideas resulted in a civilization that can best be described as Christendom.

The world of Christendom was one in which Christianity was the single most powerful force that influenced the way people behaved and what they believed. People who lived in that world thought of themselves as Christians, not Romans. The religious unity of western Christendom was to last for more than 700 years.

Romans, long life and victory.'' Whether the pope planned this action with Charlemagne's knowledge is unknown. However, the ceremony proved that the idea of the Roman Empire was still alive, and that there was a strong desire to bring back the political unity of imperial Rome.

The coronation also illustrated another great theme of medieval history: the struggle between Church and state. By crowning Charlemagne, the pope showed his approval

section review 4

1. Why did Clovis's victories have religious importance?

2. What was the Donation of Pepin?

3. How did Charlemagne preserve Roman culture and civilization in western Europe?

4. What did Charlemagne's coronation signify for Christendom?

Section Summaries

1. Christianity became a strong religion in the Roman world. The Christian religion grew from the teachings of Jesus. Although he was crucified and his followers harshly persecuted, the small group of "believers" gathered strength through the work of missionaries, especially that of Paul. At first, the Romans outlawed Christianity and put many of its followers to death. But it grew in strength and finally became the official religion in the empire.

2. German tribes attacked the Roman Empire. German invasions, which had begun as early as the 2nd century B.C., increased in the 4th century A.D. At that time, Huns from Asia forced the German tribes to seek safety in the empire. Once inside, they increased their power and landholdings at the expense of the Romans. After the Visigoth defeat of the Roman army in 378 A.D., many German tribes moved onto Roman lands. In time, a German ruler, the general Odoacer, became the Roman emperor, and German kingdoms took hold in many former Roman provinces.

3. The Church became the preserver of civilization. As the western part of the Roman Empire crumbled, the Church at Rome, having become the head of all Christian churches, took over leadership in civil government. Christian missionaries carried the religion and Roman culture to the German tribes. In the monasteries, culture was preserved and education continued.

4. An alliance of popes and Franks aided western Christendom. In Gaul, about the year 500, the Frankish king Clovis grew powerful and extended his lands in the name of his new religion. The Do-Nothing Kings who followed Clovis allowed the Carolingian family to gain control. The greatest member of this royal house was Charlemagne, who expanded the Frankish Empire still farther. His reign was noteworthy for good government, for the encouragement of education, and for the extension of the power of the Christian church. When the pope crowned him emperor in 800, a tradition was established that would affect the relationships of popes and kings for many centuries. It also symbolized the completion of the process that resulted in the rise of Christendom.

Who? What? When? Where?

1. Why are these dates important in the Christian religion?

a. 33 A.D.
b. 37–67
c. 311
d. 313
e. 395
f. 325
g. 600

2. What effect did each of these people have on the growth of the Church?

a. Paul
b. Theodosius
c. Nero
d. Saint Jerome
e. Constantine
f. Pope Gregory the Great
g. Saint Patrick
h. Saint Augustine

3. What role did each of these people play in the Germanic invasions and the fall of Rome?

a. Valens
b. Attila
c. Odoacer
d. Theodoric
e. Alaric
f. Justinian

4. Give the years and the importance of:

a. the Battle of Adrianople
b. the Battle of Châlons
c. the Battle of Tours

Questions for Critical Thinking

1. Why is it not correct to say that Rome "fell" in 476?

2. What problems was the Roman Empire suffering from in the 4th century? Why do some people turn to religion in times of trouble? Give examples from this chapter and from the present.

3. Why did the Germanic invaders take on so many of the ways of the peoples whose lands they invaded?

4. Why did men enter monasteries such as the one set up by Saint Benedict in 520? Consider what life was like at that time in the outside world.

5. Why didn't the persecutions of the early Christians by the Romans destroy the Christian religion?

Skill Activities

1. Read *Stories of Charlemagne* by Jennifer West-wood to learn more about this famous ruler and his times. (S. G. Phillips, Inc., 1976)

2. Make a list of ways that the collapse of the Roman Empire might have been avoided.

3. Study the pictures and their captions in this chapter. Write a few sentences on three of the pictures explaining what the subject of the picture is, what materials the picture is made of, and (where possible) how old the picture is.

4. Describe the routes of the Germanic invasions, telling which countries the various tribes traveled through, the years of the invasions, and where the tribes settled.

5. Make a chart showing the way that Church government was set up. Which areas were run by priests, bishops, archbishops, patriarchs, and the pope?

chapter **7** *quiz*

Section 1

1. Most of what is known about Jesus is found in the: a. Old Testament, b. Gospels, c. Petrine Theory

2. The member of the Council of Nicaea who did not agree with the Nicene Creed was: a. Arius, b. Petrarch, c. Ulfilas

3. The capital city of the Christian religion was: a. Jerusalem, b. Rome, c. Alexandria

Section 2

4. The Germanic tribes pushed into the Roman Empire after they were attacked by the: a. Muslims, b. Norsemen, c. Huns

5. The first German ruler of Rome was: a. Attila, b. Odoacer, c. Theodoric

6. The capital city of the eastern empire was: a. Constantinople, b. Ravenna, c. Damascus

Section 3

7. After the fall of Rome, some civil government services were provided by the: a. Germans, b. Church, c. army

8. People looking for personal protection could go into any church building for: a. monks, b. libraries, c. sanctuary

9. An important Christian missionary to Ireland was: a. Ulfilas, b. Patrick, c. Benedict

Section 4

10. The first important German king to become a Roman Catholic was: a. Charlemagne, b. Pepin, c. Clovis

11. The Carolingian kings took over from the: a. weak Roman emperors, b. Arians, c. Do-Nothing Kings

12. The crowning of Charlemagne showed the strength of the: a. Church, b. emperor, c. army

WESTERN CHRISTENDOM IN THE MIDDLE AGES

Sometimes festivals in the Middle Ages involved mock military contests between knights trying to prove their bravery.

"In the name of God, Saint Michael, and Saint George, I dub thee knight. Be valiant." To a young man of the Middle Ages, these words, along with the tap of a sword blade on his neck or shoulder, meant that he had become a knight.

Knighthood reached its greatest importance in western Christendom during the Middle Ages, when law was in the hands of the nobility. Nobles, called *lords*, owned much of the land and ruled from the 9th through the 13th centuries.

The great unifying force in western Christendom was the Church. The Church held vast areas of land, and clergymen were involved in feudal rivalries. Also, the Church urged Christians to fight in religious wars called *crusades*.

In the early Middle Ages, most people lived and worked on manors in the countryside. In the 11th century, trade began to expand beyond the local markets of the manor, and town life revived. A middle class of people made up of carpenters, weavers, people in other crafts, and merchants began to develop.

Some members of the middle class grew so rich and powerful that they became rivals of the feudal lords. Many people of this middle class used their wealth to advance education, learning, and the arts. By the late Middle Ages, the civilization of western Christendom was at its highest cultural level. This chapter explains how:

1. **Feudalism arose in western Christendom.**

2. **The manor was the center of economic life.**

3. **The Church unified Christendom.**

4. **Town life revived in the later Middle Ages.**

5. **Education, learning, and the arts advanced.**

1 Feudalism arose in western Christendom

The kings who followed Charlemagne were not able to hold the reins of power. Strong nobles forced Charlemagne's weak successors to give them special rights. As a result, strong local governments, which had begun to form during the decline of Rome, again became important.

Division weakened the Carolingian Empire. In 843, Charlemagne's grandsons signed the Treaty of Verdun, which divided the empire into three parts. Charles the Bald got lands west of the Rhone River, called West Frankland. This land later became France. Louis the German got lands east of the Rhine, called East Frankland, which became modern Germany. A narrow strip of land between these two kingdoms was given to the eldest grandson, Lothair. Ever since, the ownership and government of this land have been the cause of many wars between Germany and France.

TREATY OF VERDUN
843 A.D.

North Sea

Rhine R.

Verdun • the middle kingdom

East Frankland to Louis the German

West Frankland to Charles the Bald

Rhone R.

to Lothair

Adriatic Sea

Mediterranean Sea

0 100 300 MILES
0 100 300 KILOMETERS

The three kingdoms were still thought of as parts of one great empire, but none of the three brothers had any real authority. Government and economic life were run by the local counts, dukes, and other nobles.

Vikings, Magyars, and Muslims attacked the empire. During and after Charlemagne's rule, the empire was invaded by bands of Scandinavian warriors. These people were known as Vikings, Northmen, or Norsemen. They sailed to Russia, England, the shores of western Europe, and into the Mediterranean. They set fire to towns, seized all movable riches, and sacked churches.

Some Vikings repeatedly raided the coast of West Frankland. So in 911, the Frankish king gave them the area, on the condition that they accept Christianity. These Vikings were known as Normans, and the area became known as Normandy. They developed a well-governed, Christian state.

At the end of the 9th century, another

group, the nomadic Magyars from Asia, attacked eastern Europe. By the late 10th century, they had formed settlements, adopted Christianity, and built a new state known as Hungary.

Meanwhile, another very powerful group was building an empire to the south. These were the Muslims, Arab followers of the religion of Islam. They pushed into the southern Italian peninsula and the southern coast of West Frankland. They sacked towns and sold their captives in the slave markets of North Africa. They built bases on most of the important islands in the Mediterranean and drove Christian traders out.

During these invasions, the Carolingian kings gave little protection to their people. In fact, no central government worthy of the name existed.

Feudalism, a new system of government, emerged. With the disappearance of a central government, a new system based on land ownership and personal service gave government services to the people of western Christendom. This system is called *feudalism* [fyü′dl iz′əm]. Landowning nobles became almost independent of kings and princes. They settled legal disputes, kept armies, controlled the food supply, and collected taxes.

Feudalism had its beginnings during the decline of Rome. Cities no longer gave good law enforcement, and small landowners turned over their property to larger landowners in return for protection. An early German tribal custom also contributed to the development of feudalism. German chiefs divided the spoils of war among their companions in return for pledges of loyalty and military service. These warriors became lords and passed out their lands for the same pledges. This process continued until at the bottom were land divisions just large enough to support one knight.

The person who received land from a lord was called a *vassal* and the land, in whatever large or small amount, was called a *fief* [fēf] or a *feud* [fyüd]. A feudal contract between the lord and the vassal laid out the rights and duties of each. The lord had to protect the vassal and his family, defend their honor, and give them justice in his court. The vassal had to provide military service, pay taxes, and sometimes give shelter, entertainment, and food to his lord.

Feudalism was complicated and clumsy because it divided western Christendom into thousands of local governments. For example, one lord might be the vassal of several other lords. Sometimes a king, with many vassals of his own, might also become a vassal of another king. For instance, King John of England, who held lands in France, was a vassal of the French king, Philip.

The Church entered into feudal contracts. Gifts of land to the Church often carried feudal obligations. The result was that a clergyman holding a fief was at the same time a servant of the pope and a vassal of a lord. Often he had to decide to whom he owed first loyalty. When a Church official died, the Church still held the land. Church lands grew until the Church owned about a third of the land in western Christendom.

Medieval society had fixed classes: nobility, clergy, and peasants. The nobility was made up of the kings, their vassals, and lesser lords. Their status was inherited.

Generally speaking, clergymen, or churchmen, were the only group educated in subjects other than warfare. Bishops and high-ranking clergy lived much like the rich lords. However, village priests came from the lower class and had only a little education.

The peasants were on the bottom of the social scale. They were by far the largest group of people. Nearly all of them were *serfs*, peasants who by law had to work the land they were born on. They depended on the nobles for their livelihood. A peasant could never become a noble. But a man from the peasant class might become a clergyman and rise within the Church.

A very small group of people were free-men. They rented their lands from the lord. They could hire someone to do their work or leave if they found a new tenant.

section review 1

1. Name two modern nations that began after the Treaty of Verdun.

2. List three steps in the development of feudalism in western Christendom.

3. How was feudalism a form of government?

4. Who were the serfs?

2 The manor was the center of economic life

The economic system of the Middle Ages was the *manorial system*. Almost all the goods and services necessary for life were produced on the manors, or estates, of the nobles. The manorial system developed at a time when towns in Europe had become few and small. Trade, which had flourished between different centers during the Roman Empire, had almost stopped. Throughout a great part of western Europe, most people lived on the manors of nobles.

Farming formed the basis of the manorial system. The fief of a large landowner might include several hundred manors that were widely separated from each other. The fief of a small landowner might be only one manor. Each manor was the center of the social and economic life of the people who lived on it. Just as the peasants depended on the lord for protection and provisions, so also the lord's power and wealth depended on the peasants who worked his estates.

The manor house was the heart of a manor. In many cases, the manor house was a large fortified building, even a castle. The lord's barns, stables, mill, bakehouse, and cookhouse were also on the estate. Nearby were the church, the priest's house, and the village where peasants' huts lined a narrow street. The lord divided up meadows and woodlands as he pleased. But he made a pasture available to everyone.

All the people of the manor shared the farmland. The lord usually took the best and let the peasants raise food for their families on the poorer land. The farmland was divided into long strips, most often separated only by dirt ridges. The peasants pooled their oxen and plows and worked all the fields together. By planting only some of the fields each year, they kept the farmland from being overworked.

Because the lord could live on only one of his estates at a time and was often busy fighting wars, the day-to-day running of the manors was left to certain officials. In England, these people were known as the *steward*, the *bailiff*, and the *reeve*.

The steward had the highest rank. He was a legal adviser to the lord and ran the manor court. He traveled from one manor to another, checking on conditions.

The bailiff supervised the work of the peasants and the farming of the land. He also checked the financial accounts and the collection of rents, dues, and fines.

The reeve helped the bailiff supervise farm work. A large manor might need many reeves just as a large factory today needs many foremen. The reeves oversaw the growing and storage of hay, the care of bees and herds, and the harvesting of crops. It was also the reeve's job to tell the lord of any complaints peasants had about officials.

Before they did their own work, serfs had to work two to three days a week on the lord's land. Even more time was required during planting and harvest. In addition,

Daily Life

Many people on a medieval manor worked at farming tasks. At *near right* a farmer sharpens tools used to cut grain. Immediately *below* workers use the tools to harvest the grain. *Below left* sheep are being sheared to use their wool for making cloth. *Below right*, men knock nuts off trees so the pigs can eat the nuts. In the village at *far right* the manor house sits on a hill overlooking the peasants' village.

they had to pay part of their own harvest in taxes. Most of the flour, bread, and wine made by the serfs in the lord's mill, oven, or wine press had to be given to the lord. Serfs could not leave the manor of their own free will. Nobles considered them to be property not much above cattle. They could not hunt in the woods, for the woodlands belonged to the lord, nor could they fish in his streams.

Literature of the times is filled with references to peasant ugliness, stupidity, and filthiness. Peasants had no education and believed in witches, magic, and ogres. Only from time to time were their dull lives brightened up by folk dances, church festivals, or rough athletic contests.

Women worked hard on the manor. Most women in the Middle Ages were housewives and mothers. They took care of the home and raised large families of children. They also worked on the estate.

Peasant women did every kind of farm work except heavy plowing. They planted

157

Sometimes medieval tournaments seemed more like wars than celebrations or festivals.

and harvested grain. They sheared sheep, milked cows, and took care of chickens. They thatched roofs by joining together many bunches of straw or rushes to form a solid covering.

Noble women, called *ladies*, inherited land and held honors and offices. Because there were so many wars, lords were often absent and the ladies ran the manor and defended it if it were attacked. If a lord were taken prisoner, his wife raised the ransom needed to save him. And noble women performed the medical services needed on the manor, as there were very few doctors.

Women of all classes married young, often by the time they were fourteen. Their fathers set up the marriages, sometimes while the girls were still babies. Every father tried to have a *dowry* for his daughter, some amount of money, land, or goods, that she took to her marriage. Without a dowry, it was almost impossible for a girl to marry. Letters and diaries of the time indicate that arranged marriages in the Middle Ages turned out well.

Living conditions in the castle were crude. The lord's manor house or castle was built mainly for defense against enemies. The great stone tower, or *keep*, provided a safe place during a siege. Other buildings—holding stables and supplies—were near the keep.

A high wall, often several feet thick, surrounded all the buildings. During a battle, defenders could stand on dirt walks near the top of the wall. Then they poured burning oil or dropped heavy rocks on the enemy below. A moat [mōt], or ditch filled with water, ran around the outside of the wall. Entrance to the castle was controlled by a drawbridge that was lowered across the water from inside a gate in the wall. A heavy iron grating that could be dropped quickly protected the drawbridge gate.

By modern standards, the castle had few

comforts. Rooms were dark, cold, and musty. In winter, hearth fires warmed only small areas. Since chimneys did not come into use until the 14th century, large rooms were often full of smoke. When eating in the great hall, nobles sat at boards placed on sawhorses. They threw food scraps over their shoulders to the dogs. Rushes, which were spread over the floor to lessen the cold, became filthy and evil smelling from the garbage that collected in them. Carpets were not used until late in medieval times.

The nobles' huge, heavy beds were often built on platforms. There were canopies on top and heavy curtains around the sides for privacy and protection from drafts. Falcons, dogs, and even farm animals slept in the same room as the family.

During the evenings, jesters and clowns entertained the nobles. Travelers were welcome, for they brought news and gossip from places beyond the manor. Welcome also were the traveling musicians who moved from one castle to another, bringing their poems and music of heroic deeds, love, and great adventures.

section review 2

1. In what ways was a manor self-supporting?

2. Who ran the manor? What were the different duties of different officials?

3. Describe the life of a noble woman of the Middle Ages.

4. What kind of living conditions did a castle of the Middle Ages provide?

3 The Church unified Christendom

The Church was the unifying force in the Middle Ages; most Europeans believed that only the Church could give eternal salvation.

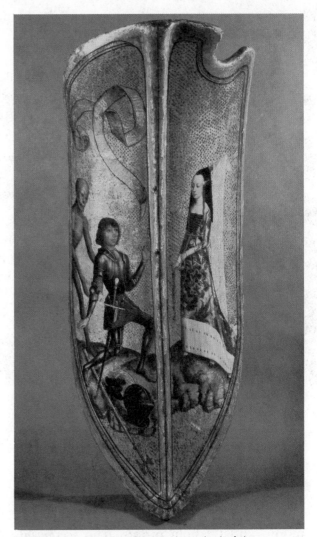

The Flemish Shield of Parade is typical of the romance of the Middle Ages. The scroll above the knight's head says "You or death."

Church influence was so strong that Europe was referred to as Christendom. Government services were provided by the Church, and its laws crossed political borders.

The Church had also grown very wealthy. Its income was more than that of all the important kings and princes put together. The Church constantly received large gifts of land in addition to the *tithe*, or tenth part of a person's income, that each member had to pay to the Church.

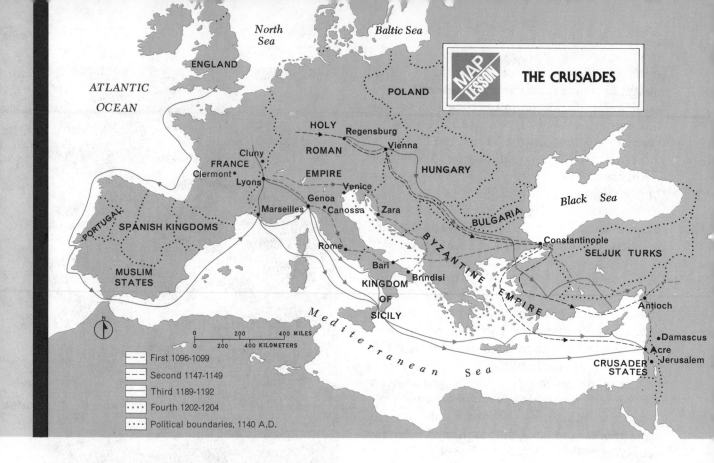

Map labels: North Sea, Baltic Sea, ENGLAND, ATLANTIC OCEAN, POLAND, HOLY, Regensburg, ROMAN, Vienna, Cluny, FRANCE, EMPIRE, HUNGARY, Clermont, Lyons, Venice, Black Sea, Genoa, Canossa, Zara, Marseilles, BULGARIA, Constantinople, SELJUK TURKS, PORTUGAL, SPANISH KINGDOMS, BYZANTINE EMPIRE, Rome, MUSLIM STATES, Bari, Brindisi, Antioch, KINGDOM OF SICILY, Mediterranean Sea, Damascus, Acre, Jerusalem, CRUSADER STATES

N

| | 200 | 400 MILES |
| 0 | 200 | 400 KILOMETERS |

- – – First 1096-1099
- – – Second 1147-1149
- — Third 1189-1192
- •••• Fourth 1202-1204
- •••• Political boundaries, 1140 A.D.

People looked to the Church for salvation. The Church had developed a body of beliefs that all Christians accepted. Most important were the seven sacraments: (1) baptism, (2) confirmation, (3) penance, (4) the Holy Eucharist, (5) extreme unction, (6) matrimony, and (7) holy orders. The *sacraments* were ceremonies believed to be necessary for salvation, but no one received all seven.

In *baptism,* a person—usually an infant—became a Christian. In *confirmation,* the individual crossed over from childhood to become an adult member of the Church. In *penance,* the individual confessed his or her sins and was forgiven. In the *Holy Eucharist,* a priest reenacted Jesus's Last Supper with his disciples and the people received consecrated bread and wine. *Extreme unction* was given by a priest to a dying person. All Church members received these five sacra-

ments. Of the two others, *matrimony* was the marriage ceremony, and *holy orders* were for men who became priests.

The Church enforced its rules. The Church had courts to help protect the weak and to punish those who had done wrong. It also tried clergymen and others for religious offenses. These people were judged by canon law—the law of the Church.

Heresy was the most horrible of all crimes. It was thought to be a crime against God, because it denied religious teachings. The Church looked for and punished heretics. One of the main weapons it used against offenders was *excommunication.* When a person was excommunicated, he or she was no longer a member of the Church and therefore could never go to heaven. So the Church usually tried to persuade heretics to give up

■ MAP LESSON 8: THE CRUSADES

1. Information on this type of historical map is condensed and simplified. Thus, the routes are approximations of major movements. If this map included all of the minor groups and routes, it would be so complicated that we would not be able to read it. The political boundaries are probably most accurate for which crusade?

2. Which crusade had a major army sail from England?

3. Regensburg and Vienna are both on the Danube River. Three crusades followed this route. Which were they?

4. The map shows that the Fourth Crusade never reached the Holy Land. Where did this crusade begin and end?

5. The Muslim States, the Spanish Kingdoms, and Portugal did not fight in any of the crusades because they were already fighting each other at home. Of the three groups, which one was fighting the other two?

their beliefs. If a heretic refused, he or she was usually burned at the stake.

The Church became stronger and more independent. During the 10th century, the papacy depended upon a German king for protection against feudal abuses, unruly Italian nobles, and Roman mobs. This arrangement led German kings to interfere in Church affairs, even in the election of popes.

During the 11th century, a great religious revival was begun by the monks at Cluny [klü′nē]. They spoke out against kings and princes who interfered in Church affairs. They started a reform program to remove all civil control over the pope, to forbid the sale of Church jobs, and to stop kings and nobles from choosing bishops. In 1059, the College of Cardinals was created. Its job was to elect a

successor to the pope who would be the choice of the Church, not of a king or mob.

The power of the Church grew under the reign of Pope Innocent III (1198 to 1216). Innocent claimed that his authority was above that of any other ruler and that the word of the Church was final. He forced King John to give England to the papacy and then take it back as a fief. This made John a vassal of the pope. Innocent also made vassals of other rulers.

During the 12th and 13th centuries, two religious groups, the Franciscans and the Dominicans, were begun. Unlike other groups, these two worked among the people. They preached in the towns and countryside to spread the gospel and fight heresy. Both groups became famous as university teachers. They had an important influence at a time when many people criticized the Church for being too interested in power and wealth.

The Church urged crusaders to save the Holy Land for Christians. For hundreds of years, Christians had visited the Holy Land to worship at places associated with the life of Jesus. In the 11th century, Muslim Seljuk Turks swept into Palestine. By 1089, they had taken Jerusalem and were threatening Constantinople, the capital of the Byzantine Empire. The Byzantine emperor asked the pope for help.

In 1095, Pope Urban II called a meeting where he urged thousands of knights to become *crusaders*, a word that means "marked with the cross." Urban promised the crusaders forgiveness for their sins, freedom from their creditors, and a choice of fiefs in the land to be conquered. His stirring speech created great enthusiasm. As Urban finished speaking, the audience roared, "God wills it!"

While the knights began to organize an

Preparing for a crusade was a major task. When the crusaders traveled by ship, many provisions, such as food and water, had to be brought with them.

army, preachers in France and Germany urged peasants to join the crusade. Thus aroused, mobs of poor, ignorant peasants started to Jerusalem, killing and pillaging thousands. Many victims were Jews, who were singled out as nonbelievers in Christianity. The peasants also murdered 4,000 Hungarians, mostly Christians. The peasants reached Constantinople in 1096 and began to burn and steal. After leaving Constantinople, they were attacked by the Turks; few ever got to Jerusalem.

WHAT'S IN A NAME?
JERUSALEM

Jerusalem comes from two Babylonian words. *Uru* means "city" and *Salim*, the "god of peace." Together, they are *Urusalim*, or "city of peace." Over the centuries, Urusalim became Jerusalem.

Unlike the Peasant Crusade, the First Crusade was an organized army. Led by Frankish princes and nobles, it included 3,000 knights and 12,000 infantry. In 1099, the army got to Jerusalem and mercilessly slaughtered Muslims, Jews, and some Christians. The crusaders seized land and created the Crusader States on a strip of land along the Mediterranean. Nearly fifty years later, Muslims attacked the Crusader States. A Second Crusade was begun in 1147. Again, after Jerusalem was taken by the Muslim leader, Saladin, a Third Crusade started in 1189. Both failed; Christians merely won the right to visit Jerusalem. But to gain that right the Third Crusade cost the lives of 300 thousand soldiers and countless civilians.

In 1202, a Fourth Crusade began. Instead of fighting the Muslims, however, the crusaders captured and sacked Constantinople. They set up their own government, the Latin Empire. In 1261, they were thrown out, and the Byzantine Empire was restored. But it never wholly recovered from the blow dealt it by the Fourth Crusade. Thirty years later, Acre, the last Christian stronghold in the Middle East, fell to the Muslims. This marked the end of the crusades.

The Holy Land was lost to Christendom. However, contact with the Middle East ended the isolation of Europe. Christendom had been exposed to a civilization that in many ways was superior to its own.

The crusades helped spread commerce and indirectly led to the growth of great ports and cities. Knowledge of the Middle East enriched Christendom's culture. New foods and fabrics were brought back to Europe.

In addition, the crusades reduced the number of Christian nobles. This weakened feudalism and thereby indirectly led to the rise of royal power in western Europe.

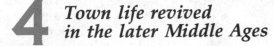

section review 3

1. Why did most people of western Christendom obey the rules of the Church?

2. How did the monks at Cluny and the College of Cardinals strengthen the Church?

3. What was the main reason for the crusades?

4. How did the crusades benefit western Christendom?

4 Town life revived in the later Middle Ages

During the 10th and 11th centuries, new towns and cities began to appear in Christendom and old cities began to revive. However, the fastest growth was in the 13th century when trade increased. The cities were places where new classes of people grew in wealth and power. Cities also became centers for education, literature, and the arts.

Trade increased between Italian cities and the Middle East. The Fourth Crusade ended in 1204. Then trade grew between the Middle East and Italian city-states such as Venice. People in western Christendom, especially the nobility, wanted to buy the spices and silks that Arab sea merchants brought back from Asia.

Large fleets of ships from Venice, Genoa, and other Italian cities sailed the Mediterranean, bringing luxury goods to England and northern Europe. As international trade grew, towns grew; as cities grew, trade expanded.

The use of money replaced barter. During the early Middle Ages, barter had been a common practice. Serfs bartered farm products or homemade goods in the local market. They traded a wooden spoon, for example, for some eggs. Local markets were held each week in the open squares near castles or churches.

As nonlocal trade increased, feudal lords set up annual fairs. These became meeting places for merchants from all over Christendom. The lords rented space and levied fines and taxes for income. People at the fairs used money, but they had different coins. So money changers set up booths and, for a small fee, exchanged different coins.

Soon, merchants and traders found that it was safe to leave large sums of money with the money changers. They, in turn, lent money to borrowers and charged interest. A merchant could also deposit money in one city, get a receipt, and collect the money in another city. This was a safe way to transfer money. In Europe, these simple forms of banking and credit developed first in northern Italy. The use of money helped break down the isolation of the era.

Many factors helped the growth of towns. The recovery of trade was very important in causing towns to grow. But there were also other reasons towns grew. Changes in farming had a marked effect on town growth. New farm methods and technology yielded bigger crops, bettered living standards, and led to an increase in population. At the same time, fewer people were needed to do the work on the manors. Three inventions—the tandem harness, the horse collar, and horseshoes—helped transportation and farming methods.

Daily Life

As towns grew, so did the numbers and types of jobs there. *Above right*, are a husband and wife in their carpentry shop. At the wife's feet is their small child who is collecting the wood shavings for later use as fuel. At *top* is a butcher shop that also sells meat pies. *Above left* is a dye shop where men of that guild dye cloth under the watchful eye of the guild master.

At the beginning of the 11th century, more land became available for farming as forests were cleared, swamps drained, and land reclaimed from the sea. The lords who developed many of these wilderness lands needed workers to dig ditches, build dikes, cut timber, and uproot tree stumps. To get workers for these new lands, the lords promised serfs their freedom and the right to rent land at fixed fees. The peasant with a little money could now choose to remain on the manor or move to the town.

Towns gained independence and grew in political stability. City living became increas-

A MYSTERY IN HISTORY

DID ROBIN HOOD REALLY EXIST?

Lithe and lysten, gentylmen,
That be of frebore blode:
I shall you tell of a good yeman.
His name was Robyn Hode.

So begins "A Lytell Geste [story in verse] of Robyn Hode" from an old manuscript preserved in the library at Cambridge University in England. Hundreds of these four-line stanzas tell of the courteous outlaw and his Merry Men who lived in Sherwood Forest. They stole from the rich and gave to the poor. And they were heroes of ballads as early as the 1200s.

Was Robin Hood a real person? Who was he, and when did he live? The answers are clouded in mystery.

A poem of the late 14th century speaks of the "rymes of Robyn Hode." Rymes were popular ballads based on legend. Since it takes time for a legend to become the subject of a ballad, if there really was a Robin Hood, he must have lived in the early 1200s.

Not until the 16th century did two historians try to prove he really existed. They had little to go on but early ballads and various graves that the people of the countryside had always believed to be the grave of Robin Hood—but there was more than one!

One historian suggested that Robin Hood was really a nobleman who had come on hard times. His theory became very popular. Today almost all films and stories about Robin Hood show him to be a knight or earl who lost his wealth. But medieval documents do not support this interpretation.

Several 19th-century historians tried to prove that a man named Robert Hood, who bought a plot of land in 1316, was the real Robin Hood. They had many impressive pieces of evidence to support their case. But the date is too late. In fact, a charter in 1322 makes it clear that Robin Hood was already a legendary figure by that time.

Historians will go on searching for the real Robin Hood because uncovering the past is what history is all about. But even if they never find him, the ballads will always be important for history.

They express the peasant discontent that raged in 13th- and 14th-century England. It was a time when English peasants bitterly resented the harsh demands of the landowners and the sheriffs who protected them. Robin was the peasant's ideal of someone who could give them justice.

ingly desirable, and serfs continued to leave the manors. This exodus lasted for hundreds of years and was one of the great social, political, and economic revolutions of history.

Town life had good and bad features. In their early stages, towns were rural in character. To leave the country and live in a city did not mean giving up fresh air. Even in the country, houses were built close together for protection and warmth. In the cities, rows of houses served as a protective wall, and the gardens they surrounded became space for playing games and growing food. A middle-class home might house the shop, workrooms, and family living space.

Opportunities to make money and gain personal freedom in the cities were more important than the discomforts and dangers of large populations. As cities grew larger, public health and safety laws to lessen these dangers began to appear. Over a period of about two hundred years, some cities began to have paved streets. Fireproof roofing was required in some cities. England forbade people to throw waste into ditches and rivers.

In 1347, an epidemic of bubonic plague began in Constantinople. In 1348 and 1349, it spread all over Europe, following the trade routes. The people of the times called it the Black Death, because the corpses of its victims turned a dark color. The Black Death struck hardest in the cities. Some records say that half the city population died from the disease.

Despite the Black Death, the cities recovered. Populations began to increase. By the middle of the 15th century, London had a population of 40 thousand and Brussels, 35 thousand. Paris had grown to 300 thousand.

New classes of people arose in western Christendom. With the rise of towns and the expansion of trade and industry, a powerful class of people had developed in Christendom. Unlike the nobility, their interest was in business rather than war. They were referred to as men of the burg, that is, *burghers* [bėr'gərz], or the *bourgeoisie* [bŭr'zhwä-zē']. At the top of the scale were the prosperous merchants and bankers. Their sons attended the universities and became important professional men, even advisers to kings. Feudal lords looked down their noses on the middle class as mere upstarts, but the bourgeoisie continued to prosper. They became patrons of the arts and established a kind of nobility of their own. In turn, they looked down on those beneath them on the social scale, such as the skilled workers. Thus, class distinctions were developing along lines of wealth rather than according to birth.

The economic life of skilled workers was regulated by organizations called *guilds*. Merchants and craftspeople had separate guilds. A guild strictly controlled its number of members and the quality of goods produced. Guild courts settled disputes and judged members. The guilds assisted needy members, built homes for the poor, and held banquets and other social events.

The bourgeoisie were the city landholders. They hired former serfs, but they did not let them own land in the cities, hold political office, or vote.

section review 4

1. What European cities were first affected by the increased Middle East trade?

2. What was the purpose of the fairs? How did they encourage the use of money?

3. What reasons other than trade helped towns become larger?

4. Describe the new class of people that lived in towns. What was the name of the class? What kinds of work did people of this class do?

5 Education, learning, and the arts advanced

By 600, formal education had almost ended in western Christendom. The few schools that did exist were run by the Church to train men to become monks. This situation lasted for 500 years. Then new conditions created a need for people with other kinds of training and education.

Universities were begun all over Christendom. During the 1100s, three things helped the growth of learning in Christendom: (1) the rise of cities and a rich middle class, (2) Church reforms, and (3) contact with other cultures. Both the Church and civil governments needed trained lawyers for courts, for drawing up documents, and for government. To meet these demands, teachers and students formed groups called *universities*. They had no set courses of study, no permanent buildings, and few rules. Students were granted rights, such as freedom from military service and from the jurisdiction of town officials.

One famous university was begun at Bologna [bə lō′nyə] about 1158. Another started at Paris about 1200. Bologna gained a reputation for the study of law. Student groups controlled the administration, hired teachers, and made the rules for the school. At Paris, the university was run by the administration and faculty, not the students. Other universities patterned themselves on one of these two systems.

Classrooms were cold in winter. Students wore heavy gowns and hoods and sat on floors covered with straw for warmth. They went to one or two classes every day, each class being several hours long. Once darkness fell, studies were stopped, for candles were expensive.

The most famous scholar of the Middle Ages was Saint Thomas Aquinas [ə kwī′nəs]. He lived from about 1225 to 1274. He joined the Dominicans as a youth and became a brilliant lecturer and writer. During his lifetime, a scholarly controversy over conflicts between faith and reason reached its height. Saint Thomas disagreed with both sides. He taught that a person's reason and faith are both gifts of God, that certain truths can be understood by powers of reasoning, while other truths, basic to Christianity, can be understood only by faith. So convincing were his arguments that his work *Summa Theologica* (The Highest Theology) is still an authority for the Roman Catholic Church.

Scientific knowledge made some progress in the later Middle Ages. Greek and Arab works flowed into Christendom, particularly after the beginning of the 12th century. Algebra from the Arabs, trigonometry from the Muslims, and Euclid's *Geometry* added to the scope and accuracy of math.

In the 1100s, the sailor's compass was invented, followed by the development of a better rudder for larger ships in about 1300. The 1300s also saw the introduction of the blast furnace and progress in iron-working. Greek and Arab writings on biology were popular among doctors and improved their techniques.

Roger Bacon, an English monk of the 1200s, advanced scientific knowledge. He felt that learning should be based not on faith, but on observation and experience. As a result, he was attacked by many of the learned men of his day. Toward the end of his life, he was put in prison for 15 years, and his works were condemned. But it was Roger Bacon who predicted the coming of power-driven ships, cars, and flying machines.

Popular languages replaced Latin. Among educated people, Latin was an international means of communication. Almost all the writings of the Church, the governments, and the schools were in Latin. However, most of the people in western Christendom could not speak or understand it, even though they came in contact with Latin in the Church. They spoke different local languages.

After the fall of the Roman Empire, changes in the spoken Latin developed that varied from geographic area to area. Latin-based languages now known as *Romance languages* appeared in Italy, France, Spain, and Portugal during the early Middle Ages. Several hundred Germanic words became part of the Romance languages from the time of the earliest barbarian invasions. Contact with the Middle East brought in words from the Greek, Persian, and Arabic languages as well.

Native German became the base of the Dutch and Scandinavian languages, as well as modern German. The major influence on English was Germanic, but hundreds of English words come from Latin. The Latin original and its variations can be seen clearly in the English words *study*, *letter*, and *city*:

Latin	Italian	French	Spanish
studiare	studiare	étudier	estudiar
littera	lettera	lettre	letra
civitas	citta	cité	ciudad

Literature of the Middle Ages took many forms. Latin was used both for serious works and for the saucy poetry written by university students. Traveling students sang happy, irreverent verses about the joys of wine, love, and song in exchange for food and housing.

The earliest form of native literature was the epic, a long poem that told of the adventures of great heroes. *Beowulf*, written in the Anglo-Saxon language in the 8th century, is an example of an early epic.

With the rise of the city and the influence of the middle class, a short story form became popular. These stories were comical, often scandalous. Also popular were animal stories, such as *Reynard the Fox*, and ballads, such as those about Robin Hood.

Dante and Chaucer were two great poets. Dante Alighieri [dan'tā ä'lē gyer'ē] was an Italian poet, philosopher, and student of politics. Born in Florence in 1265, he wrote a poem that later admirers called the *Divine Comedy*. This work shows the religious spirit of the times, telling of a mythical journey through hell, purgatory, and paradise. His writings in Latin and in the local Tuscan dialect were an inspiration for many poets who came after him.

Geoffrey Chaucer was born about 1340 in London, the son of a wine merchant. His best known work is *The Canterbury Tales*, which tells the story of thirty pilgrims on their way to Canterbury cathedral. It offers a vivid picture of England in Chaucer's time. The Midland dialect Chaucer used was the base from which English developed.

The arts served the needs of the Church. Most music in the Middle Ages was written for the Church. Church services were sung or chanted. Musicians used various instruments—organs, violins, dulcimers, and lutes.

Dramatizations of Bible stories and religious teachings were performed in the churches. At first, these stories were sung by the choir. Later, they developed into plays. In time, plays were performed in local languages and in public places outside of church buildings. But the plays kept their religious character and were called *morality plays*.

Artists and sculptors of the day were hired to decorate churches and cathedrals. Both the outside and inside walls were covered with pictures showing events in the life of

At *left top* is a Romanesque church in Milan. The supporting walls are thick, and the windows are few. At *left center* is a gothic style church in Amiens. Gothic style allowed many large beautiful windows to be used. At *left bottom* is one such window, the Rose Window in the Cathedral at Chartres.

Jesus, the saints, and scenes from Bible stories. The use of stained-glass windows, which dated from ancient times, became a fine art in the medieval period.

Between 1050 and 1200, the major style of architecture was *Romanesque*. Churches of this style were rather dark inside and had thick walls. Many large columns were needed to support the low ceilings.

Gothic architecture developed by the middle of the 12th century. Gothic churches used pointed arches for the roof. Outside supports, called *buttresses*, made it possible for these buildings to be taller than those built before. Throughout the 13th century, towns competed in building the highest cathedral in the area. Walls, no longer needed to support the roof, were thinner and were covered with stained-glass windows. In some churches, such as Sainte Chapelle in Paris, the sides of the building served mainly as a framework for the beautiful jewellike windows.

section review 5

1. Why was there an increased need for educated men in Europe during the 1100s? Who ran the university at Bologna? At Paris?

2. Name some of the scientific advances made in Europe during the Middle Ages. Which were based on ideas from the Greeks? From the Arabs?

3. What medieval literature gives an example of the English dialect of the Middle Ages? What was this dialect called?

4. How did medieval music, drama, and art help people learn about their religion?

Section Summaries

1. Feudalism arose in western Christendom. With no protection from a central government and in the face of repeated attacks by invaders, local governments became strong throughout Europe. Feudal contracts described the relationships among kings, nobles, knights, and peasants. The Church, too, was involved in feudal arrangements. Society was divided into fixed classes, and there was little social mobility.

2. The manor was the center of economic life. Self-sufficient manors supplied most of life's necessities for the people who lived on them—and the majority of people lived on manors. Supervised by officials, the peasants produced food and drink, clothing, and building materials. The manor house was the center of the manor and was built to withstand attacks. Life inside these houses or castles was crude by modern standards.

3. The Church unified Christendom. Almost all people in western Europe during the Middle Ages were Christians who believed the seven sacraments of the Church were necessary for salvation. This gave the Church enormous control over people's daily lives. In addition, the Church was the largest landowner of its day. The Church had its own laws and courts. Excommunication was its severest penalty. A religious revival, begun by monks at Cluny, helped strengthen the Church. It became even more independent of civil authority. During the 11th century, the Church urged its members to fight for Christian lands in Palestine. A series of holy wars, called the crusades, were marred by senseless killing and destruction. No permanent gains were made. However, the crusades brought Christendom into contact with the Arab world, and trade increased.

4. Town life revived in the later Middle Ages. As a result of increased trade and a new group of free peasants, towns began to grow. Money and banking replaced barter. Two classes of townsfolk, the bourgeoisie and skilled workers, developed and grew.

5. Education, learning, and the arts advanced. Universities began to supply learned men for governments and the Church. Advances in mathematics, navigation, iron-working, and medicine took place. Popular languages developed, and literature was written in them, rather than in Latin. Music, theater, and architecture were used to enhance church services, and these art forms progressed.

Who? What? When? Where?

1. Put these events or developments in chronological order from first to last:

  a. The Black Death spread throughout Europe.
  b. The Treaty of Verdun divided Charlemagne's empire.
  c. The College of Cardinals was created.
  d. A university was founded at Paris.
  e. The last crusade was undertaken.

2. Write sentences that tell what each of these means:

  a. steward   d. keep
  b. bailiff   e. dowry
  c. reeve   f. manorial system

3. Write sentences that tell an achievement of each of these men:

  a. Pope Urban II   d. Pope Innocent III
  b. Roger Bacon   e. Geoffrey Chaucer
  c. Charles the Bald   f. Saint Thomas Aquinas

4. Tell the effect each of the following had on the growth of towns in Christendom: a. crusades, b. trade with the Middle East, c. fairs

Questions for Critical Thinking

1. Why did the feudal system develop? What were some good and bad effects of feudalism on people's lives?

2. How did the Church make up for the lack of central government during the feudal period?

3. Why did Latin die out as the language of western Europe? How do languages change? Give some examples from this chapter and from your own experience with language today.

Skill Activities

1. Read *A Distant Mirror*, Chapter 5: "This Is the End of the World: The Black Death" by Barbara Tuchman to find out more about life and death during the plague years. (Alfred A. Knopf, 1978)

2. Use material in this chapter, including the pictures, to draw or write a description of a medieval manor. Show how the manor was self-sufficient. Include a castle, with its different parts, and the other buildings necessary for life on the manor.

3. Write a diary for a week in the life of a person during the Middle Ages. Write about a knight, village priest, lady, or woman serf.

4. Find pictures of Gothic and Romanesque churches in this book and in the library. What problems did architects have in the Middle Ages? What materials did they use? Name some churches that were built during the Middle Ages that can be visited today and plot the sites of these churches on an outline map of Europe.

5. Make a chart showing the differences and similarities between the lives of the serfs and the lives of the nobles.

6. Make a piece of art that illustrates some part of modern life that comes from developments of the Middle Ages.

chapter **8** *quiz*

Section 1

1. One thing that was not a reason for the breakdown of central governments was: a. weak rulers, b. barbarian invasions, c. crusades

2. Power during the feudal period was based on: a. land, b. money, c. education

Section 2

3. True or false: All fiefs had only one manor.

4. True or false: Noble women could not inherit land.

Section 3

5. Dominicans and Franciscans were: a. hermits, b. teachers, c. farmers

6. The crusades were formed to save: a. the Turks, b. Constantinople, c. Jerusalem

7. True or false: The word *crusaders* means "marked with the cross."

Section 4

8. The use of money as a system replaced the system of: a. barter, b. credit, c. bank

9. The power of the bourgeoisie was based on their: a. land, b. money, c. education

Section 5

10. During the Middle Ages, education was kept alive by the: a. nobles, b. governments, c. Church

11. Students themselves ran the university system at the city of: a. Florence, b. Paris, c. Bologna

12. Dante Alighieri wrote: a. *Beowulf*, b. *Divine Comedy*, c. *Reynard the Fox*

BYZANTINE CIVILIZATION AND THE FORMATION OF RUSSIA

Justinian brought back the fading glory of the Roman Empire. This mosaic portrait of the emperor and his court expresses that revival.

While western Christendom went through a long period of decline, Christian civilization in the east flourished. This eastern Christendom was known as the Byzantine Empire. Constantinople was its capital, and its wealth and culture attracted many visitors. One of those visitors was Rabbi Benjamin ben Jonah, a Jew from the Iberian peninsula, who visited Constantinople in 1161. He was wide-eyed with wonder, as we can see from this excerpt from the diary he kept during his life:

It is a busy city, and merchants come to it from every country by sea or land, and there is none like it in the world except Bagdad, the great city of Islam. . . .

The Greek inhabitants are very rich in gold and precious stones, and they go clothed in garments of silk with gold embroidery, and they ride horses, and look like princes. Indeed, the land is very rich in all cloth stuffs, and in bread, meat, and wine.

Wealth like that of Constantinople is not to be found in the whole world. Here also are men learned in all the books of the Greeks, and they eat and drink every man under his vine and his fig-tree.

The Byzantine Empire lasted for 1,000 years, produced new forms of art and architecture, and preserved the great contributions of ancient Greece and Rome.

Byzantine influence reached beyond the empire's borders and was felt by the Slavs living north of the Black Sea. Those Slavs, ancestors of the present-day Russians, adopted from the Byzantines their religion (Orthodox Christianity) and their written literature.

The early Russians did not build a state as strong as that of the Byzantines. The first Russian political organization was really a grouping of city-states under the leadership of the city of Kiev. For two centuries, Kiev had close ties with Christendom and it was through Kiev that Christianity spread to the rest of Russia. When civil war broke out among the ruling princes, the Kievan state became internally weak and was conquered by Mongols from Asia in the early 13th century.

The Mongols ruled Russia for more than two centuries. Their hold on the country was finally broken when a series of strong princes in Moscow, a city in central Russia, defeated them in battle and began to form a new Russian state. This chapter tells how:

1. The eastern empire survived the fall of Rome.

2. The Byzantines made important contributions in many fields.

3. Kiev became the first Russian state.

4. The Mongols conquered and ruled Russia.

1 *The eastern empire survived the fall of Rome*

In southeastern Europe, on a peninsula between the Black and Aegean seas, lies the modern-day city of Istanbul. On its site, a Greek colony called Byzantium [bi zan'tē-əm] was begun in the 7th century B.C. This colony fell under Roman control in 196 A.D.

Constantine, emperor of Rome from 306 to 337 A.D., ordered a new city built on the site of this Greek colony. In 330, it became the second capital of the Roman Empire. The city was named Constantinople, or the city of Constantine. It became a thriving metropolis and the center of a new civilization, usually called *Byzantine* [biz'n tēn'] after the original Greek settlement.

The Byzantine Empire was the continuation of the Roman Empire. After the death of Emperor Theodosius in 395, two emperors ruled the Roman Empire—one in the east at Constantinople and one in the west at Rome. While Germanic tribes invaded the western empire, the eastern empire stood firm.

Justinian restored Roman greatness. The eastern emperor Justinian, who ruled from 527 to 565, took back some of the crumbling western empire from the Germanic tribes. In

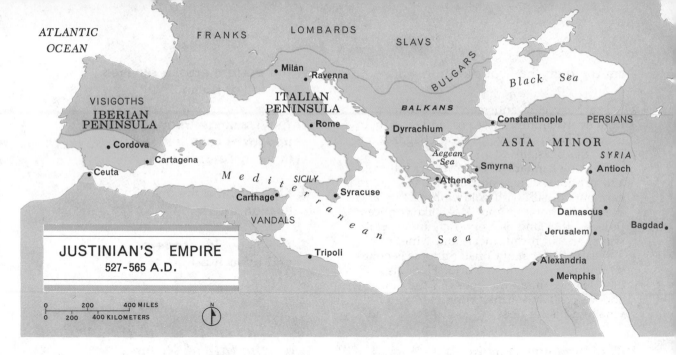

ATLANTIC OCEAN · FRANKS · LOMBARDS · SLAVS · BULGARS · Black Sea · Milan · Ravenna · VISIGOTHS · IBERIAN PENINSULA · ITALIAN PENINSULA · BALKANS · Constantinople · PERSIANS · Cordova · Rome · Dyrrachium · ASIA MINOR · SYRIA · Cartagena · Aegean Sea · Smyrna · Antioch · Ceuta · Mediterranean · SICILY · Athens · Carthage · Syracuse · Damascus · Bagdad · VANDALS · Sea · Jerusalem · Tripoli · Alexandria · Memphis

JUSTINIAN'S EMPIRE
527-565 A.D.

0   200   400 MILES
0   200   400 KILOMETERS
N

a brilliant campaign, Justinian's army destroyed the Vandal kingdom in North Africa and gained a foothold on the Iberian peninsula. He then fought the Ostrogoths on the Italian peninsula. After many years of desperate fighting, the Byzantines won. In the process, however, the Italian peninsula was devastated. Fields lay untilled, and cities fell into ruin. Famine and disease were everywhere. Justinian's triumphs were a hollow mockery to the people he had "rescued" from Germanic domination.

Justinian's most lasting contribution to western civilization was his organization of Roman law into a systematic form. A commission of lawyers revised and codified the laws.

Justinian also lavished money on roads, aqueducts, and other public projects. He helped make Constantinople one of the wonders of the Middle Ages, far larger and more beautiful than any city in western Europe.

At his death, Justinian left a realm that was dangerously weakened by his extravagant ambitions. The treasury was empty, and the western borders of the overextended empire were hard to defend. In reclaiming the lost territories of Rome, Justinian had neglected the eastern provinces of his own empire. Persians, Slavs, Bulgars, and others periodically attacked the eastern borders.

The eastern empire became Byzantine. After Justinian's death, the western empire was sliced away by further Germanic conquests. The idea of a united Roman Empire was never entirely discarded. However, by the 8th century, the eastern empire had developed a civilization that was more Greek and Middle Eastern than Roman.

The Byzantine population was largely Greek, but it included Slavs, Syrians, Jews, and others. Greek was the national tongue. The Greek classics formed the basis of Byzantine literature. (Latin was used for state documents until the 7th century when it was completely discarded.)

The Middle Eastern traditions in the Byzantine Empire came from the ancient empires of Persia and Mesopotamia. Eastern customs were reflected in the elaborate etiquette at the royal court and the lavish ceremonies associated with the semi-divine status of the emperor. Roman influence was obvious in the law and in the political power of the emperor. The empire was Christian, but the Byzantine church evolved in a pattern different from that of the church in Rome.

The Eastern Church split off from Rome. In western Christendom, the power of the church grew as that of the princes and kings declined. In the east, the relationship between church and state was not the same. The Byzantine emperor was supreme in church and state affairs. However, he customarily let the *patriarch*, the highest church official, run the church. And the emperor left the details of civil government to his chief advisers.

Increasingly poor feelings strained the relationship between the eastern and western churches. As early as 381 A.D., the church in Constantinople rejected the theory that the bishop of Rome was the highest church authority on Earth. A complete break came in 1054, when Pope Leo IX and Patriarch Michael Cerularius [ser'ū ler'ē əs] excommunicated each other. Then, after the crusaders plundered Constantinople in the Fourth Crusade, the *Eastern (Orthodox) Church* and the *Roman Catholic Church* went their separate ways.

The Byzantines withstood many invaders. Periods of imperial instability and economic decline alternated with periods of strength and prosperity. For ten centuries, the Byzantine capital fought off numerous attempts to destroy it. The outer provinces were sometimes taken. In the 7th century, the emperor Heraclius [her'ə klī'əs] beat the Persians and took back Syria, Palestine, and Egypt. However, a new menace—the Muslim Arabs— soon replaced the Persians. By the end of the 7th century, the Muslims had conquered North Africa, the eastern Mediterranean lands, and parts of Asia Minor. In the 7th century, the Bulgars, a nomadic people who spoke a Finnic language, attacked the northern Balkans. They overpowered the Slavs and settled what is now Bulgaria.

A Muslim army was repulsed at the very gates of Constantinople (717–718), and the Byzantine navy drove off the invader's fleet.

A major element in Byzantine naval success over the years was the use of "Greek fire." This was a flammable liquid containing lime, sulfur, and other chemicals that set fire to the enemy ships.

Under Leo III, who ruled from 717 to 741, the Byzantine Empire regained its strength. Leo increased the power of the emperor by weakening the power of the provincial governors.

Another outstanding emperor, Basil II, ruled from 976 to 1025. He revived the power and prosperity of the empire after a long period of decline. For his ruthless conquest of the Bulgars, Basil became known as the "Bulgar Slayer." On one occasion, Basil had thousands of Bulgars blinded and only a handful left with a single eye each to guide the rest home. The Bulgarian king is said to have died of shock when this sightless mul-

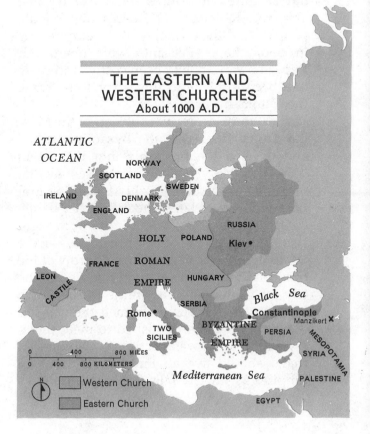

THE EASTERN AND WESTERN CHURCHES
About 1000 A.D.

titude returned. However, once the fighting was over, Basil gave the Bulgars self-rule within the Byzantine Empire.

After Basil's death, the empire fell into another era of decay. The city-state of Venice and other newly emerging centers offered serious competition to Byzantine trade in the eastern Mediterranean. And the Muslim Turks, a foe more powerful than any the Byzantines had faced to that time, appeared from central Asia. After the Turks beat a Byzantine army at Manzikert in 1071, the whole of Asia Minor was overrun by these hardy invaders.

Turks overwhelmed the Byzantine Empire.
The Byzantine Empire never fully recovered from the attack on Constantinople made by the crusaders of the Fourth Crusade. Even after they were thrown out in 1261, the empire did not have peace. Civil war broke out as different princes fought to become emperor. Religious differences divided the people. And the economy of the empire was in poor shape. Peasants were overtaxed. Repeated warfare had been costly, and trade had been hurt. Onto this sorry scene came the Ottoman Turks.

The Ottomans, former subjects of the Muslim Turks, by-passed the Byzantine capital and crossed the Bosporus into Europe in 1354. By 1445, Constantinople was all that remained of the once-mighty Byzantine Empire. Eight years later, the end came. Barely 8,000 defenders—many of them foreign-born troops serving only for their pay—were left to fight the besieging Turkish army of 160 thousand men. After eight heroic weeks, the city fell. Emperor Constantine IX died with his men. As the Turks stormed the walls of the city, the emperor rushed to meet them, crying out as he was cut down, "God forbid that I should live an Emperor without an Empire! As my city falls, I fall with it."

section review 1

1. Name three of Justinian's accomplishments.
2. In what ways was Byzantine civilization Greek? Middle Eastern? Roman?
3. Why did Pope Leo IX and Patriarch Michael Cerularius excommunicate each other?
4. What problems weakened the empire and led to its final collapse in 1453?

2 The Byzantines made important contributions in many fields

Byzantine civilization was superior to the civilization that existed in medieval Europe. Not until the 1300s were Byzantine standards of art and scholarship reached by the peoples of western Christendom. The amazing strength and endurance of Byzantine civilization was due to several factors. Two of these were a centralized government and a well-trained bureaucracy, or groups of workers who deal with specific kinds of government business. Also important were the efficient and well-led army and navy, the strength and leadership of the Orthodox Church, and a high standard of living from a strong economy.

Industry and trade thrived. With its strong commercial life, the Byzantine Empire was able to survive civil war and the steady attacks of foreign enemies. Sitting at the crossroads of Europe and Asia, Constantinople was the greatest center of trade at that time. In an era when the commerce of western Europe had almost stopped, the Byzantine capital was filled with merchants from many lands. A stable money system based on gold greatly helped the empire's economic position. Because money was scarce in the west, the gold coins of the Byzantines

GEOGRAPHY
A Key to History

STRATEGIC STRAITS

A body of water can both divide people and bring them together. If the body of water is wide, deep, or difficult to cross, it separates people. If it can be navigated and easily crossed, it can help bring them together. The straits and small sea that separate Asia from Europe are the latter kind. They have helped human contact and trade more than they have served as a barrier.

The Bosporus, the Sea of Marmara, and the Dardanelles separate Europe from Asia. But they also link the Black Sea to the Mediterranean. For several thousand years, some important city has controlled one or the other of the straits. Troy controlled the Dardanelles (which was called the Hellespont in ancient Greek times). Later, Byzantium and then Constantinople controlled the Bosporus. Indeed, control of the Bosporus helped make Constantinople great.

When Constantine founded Constantinople in 330 A.D., he chose the best site he could find. He selected a point of land above a natural harbor called the Golden Horn. The Golden Horn had a narrow, deep entrance. In the past,

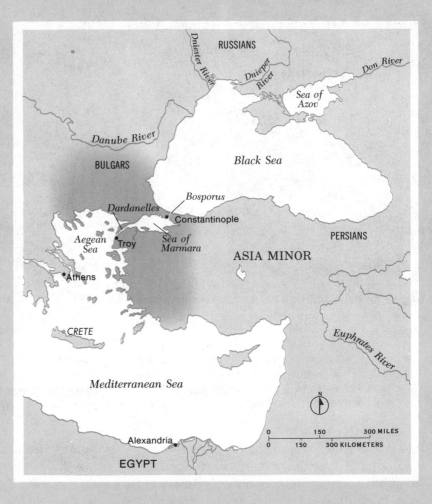

a chain was stretched across it to prevent enemy ships from entering. The Bosporus itself was so narrow that trade caravans could cross it easily by ferry.

Constantinople became the most important trading center between Europe and the East. From Persia and East Asia came spices, perfumes, jewels, and other costly goods. From Russia by way of the Black Sea came furs, fish, and honey. They were exchanged for wines, silks, fruits, glassware, and other luxuries.

Constantinople's wealth made it a place that many people wanted

to control. Arabs, Russians, Europeans, and Turks—all attacked Constantinople between the 7th and 15th centuries. The city's location helped it withstand these attacks. It was protected on three sides by water. Enemies approaching by water could be spotted easily. On its land side, the city was protected by fortified walls.

Eventually, Constantinople fell to the Turks. But the desire to control the straits continues. Today, Western European countries, the United States, and the Soviet Union have treaties to keep the straits open.

These three famous empresses of the Byzantine Empire led very different lives. Empress Theodora, *left*, was the daughter of an animal trainer in the circus. She became a trusted adviser to her husband, Justinian, whom she married in 523 A.D. Irene, *center*, lived from 752 to 803 A.D. Her husband died in 780, and she became regent for their son until 790, when he became emperor. But Irene had him deposed and blinded. In 797, Irene became empress. In 802, she was deposed and died in exile. Zoe, *right*, was empress from 1028 A.D. until her death in 1050. During this time, she had three husbands. Her first husband, Romanus III, was murdered. Many people think Zoe planned the murder.

became a basis for international exchange.

The government acted as a stern watchdog over all parts of the economy. Industry was rigidly controlled. Wages, prices, and working conditions were set. The quality of products was checked, and exports were subject to strict regulation. Jeweled ornaments, magnificent tapestries, carved ivory, and exquisite leather work were the pride of Constantinople. Cloth was the chief industrial product. About the year 550 A.D., silkworms were smuggled out of China. Thereafter, splendid silk fabric and clothing were made in Constantinople. The silk industry became a profitable state monopoly.

The lower classes did not share in the general prosperity. However, their standard of living, meager as it was, would have been envied by the peasants in western Christendom. The Byzantine economy was relatively stable. And governmental supervision of the great estates improved peasants' lives.

Rulers maintained a centralized government. Unlike the feudal system of western Europe, the Byzantine state was centralized. In theory, the emperor was a despot; however, custom and tradition limited his use of power. The weaker emperors were often overshadowed by strong governmental ministers or church patriarchs. An army of civil servants was responsible for the actual workings of government. Despite corruption and bribery, the administrative officials were generally conscientious and efficient.

As with the empire in Rome, a serious defect marred Byzantine political life. This defect was the lack of legal succession to the throne. Any upstart might become emperor. Many did so, and the story of the rise and fall of Byzantine emperors is a record of intrigue and violence. Of the 107 emperors who ruled between 395 A.D. and 1453, only 40 died a natural death in office.

The excitable city population of Constantinople added to the hazards of government. Popular uprisings were apt to break out at any time. The most famous of these was the terrible Nika Revolt in 532, during the reign of Justinian. Named for the rallying cry of the rebels (*nika* means "victory"), the revolt lasted for seven days. Before it was over, some 30 thousand people had died. Empress Theodora's bravery inspired her husband to stay in the city and crush the rebellion. She said to Justinian:

> If . . . it is your wish to save yourself, O Emperor, there is no difficulty. For we have much money, and there is the sea, here the boats . . . as for myself, I approve a certain ancient saying that royalty is a good burial-shroud.

Byzantine civilization spread throughout Europe. The Slavic peoples of Russia and the Balkans were the most deeply influenced by the Byzantine Empire. Missionaries carried Christianity to these tribes in the 9th century. The Orthodox faith became the major religion in Russia, Yugoslavia, Greece, and Bulgaria. The *Cyrillic* [si ril'ik] alphabet, used in the Russian, Serbian, and Bulgarian languages, is taken from the modified Greek letters of Byzantium. And much of the literature of early Russia, especially the lives of the saints, is Byzantine in origin.

Scholars preserved classical learning. Byzantium inherited the intellectual treasures of ancient Greece. The works of Plato and Aristotle were studied with deep respect. The most outstanding Byzantine scholar was Michael Psellus [sel'əs], an 11th-century professor who wrote widely on many subjects. Yet his writings had little originality, for, like other learned men of the time, he preferred to comment on the ancient classics rather than to think in untried areas. Only in the fields of history and theology did the empire produce works of real excellence. Anna Comnena [kom nē'nə], daughter of the 11th-

century emperor Alexius, wrote an important work on the life and times of her father. In the 1300s, Nicephorus Gregoras [nē'se-fôr'əs greg'ə rəs] wrote movingly of the declining empire. Probably the best-known historian, however, is Procopius [prō kō'pē-əs]. His notorious *Secret History* is a biased but fascinating account of Justinian's reign.

The libraries of the empire were rich in the masterpieces of Greek philosophy and literature. Even though priceless manuscripts were lost in the plunders of Constantinople, the works that did survive were important to cultural revival.

Architects and artists created domes, mosaics, and paintings. The creativity of the empire in art and architecture is in direct contrast to the imitativeness of its scholarship. In the church of Hagia Sophia, Byzantine genius in the arts came to full flower. It was a church, wrote Procopius, "the like of which

Hagia Sophia was begun on February 23, 532 A.D., during the reign of Justinian. It was completed in five years, ten months, and four days. The minarets, the four slender towers at the corners, were added later.

has never been seen since Adam, nor ever will be." Built in the shape of a Greek cross, which is about as long as it is wide, the church was surmounted by a huge dome suspended 179 feet (53.7 meters) above the floor. Hagia Sophia was both an artistic and engineering triumph.

In the decorative arts, Byzantines are best known for their use of *mosaics*—small bits of colored glass or stone formed into patterns and pictures. Mosaics were usually placed on the walls and ceilings of churches. Most of the designs were scenes of religious importance. Wall paintings and *icons*, images of sacred figures, usually painted, also added richness to church interiors.

The nonreligious art in the royal palaces was also done on a dazzling scale. Polished marble, inlaid bronze, rich fabrics, gold and silver dishes, and jeweled ornaments were all representative of the Byzantine genius.

section review 2

1. What factors led to the amazing strength and endurance of Byzantine civilization?

2. How did Byzantine government control the economy?

3. What were the two most serious problems that caused trouble in the empire?

4. What is Hagia Sophia? What is its significance?

3 Kiev became the first Russian state

The original homeland of the Slavs is unknown. It is thought that they were one of many peoples who migrated from Asia long before the Christian era. Three distinct groups eventually emerged: the southern or Balkan Slavs; the western Slavs, including the Czechs and the Poles; and the eastern Slavs, who much later became known as Russians, Ukrainians, and Belorussians. By the early 700s, the eastern Slavs had settled between the Baltic and Black seas. In the more isolated areas, they lived by farming, hunting, and fishing. In the growing towns they led an active commercial life. The Slavs did not have a central government, but were organized in city-states. In these, wealthy merchants made up the ruling class.

Viking invaders ruled the first Russian state. Viking raids along the coasts and inland waterways of Europe in the 800s also reached Slavic settlements. According to tradition, in 862 A.D., a Viking chief named Rurik [rur'ik] became ruler of Novgorod [nôv'gə rot'], an important city in the northwestern part of Russia. In 882, his successor, Oleg, captured Kiev [kē'ef], a city to the south. Later on, Oleg took Smolensk [smō lensk'], another city, and formed the first Russian state. The Vikings and Slavs intermarried, and their cultures mixed. The name Russia, which came into use much later, probably comes from *Rus'*, a term once used by foreigners to describe the Slavs and their Viking rulers.

For three centuries, Kiev was the capital of a loose confederation of city-states. Its site on the Dnieper [nē'pər] River made it a major stop on the trading route with the Byzantine Empire. Sometimes, the Russian traders were badly treated by the Byzantines. In 907, Oleg led a successful attack against Constantinople. Four years later, the Byzantine emperor agreed to a treaty giving Russian traders favorable treatment.

Russia adopted some of Byzantine culture. In 954 or 955, Olga, the ruling princess of Kiev and the first female ruler in Russian history, was converted to Christianity by Byzantine missionaries. Olga did not try to convert

180

In 957 A.D., Princess Olga visited the Byzantine court. She turned down the Emperor's marriage proposal but returned to Kiev with rich gifts—a sign of friendship between the two Christian rulers.

her people to Christianity. That was done in 988 by her grandson Vladimir [vlad'i mir]. In trying to decide which faith to choose, Vladimir sent out ten men to observe the Muslim Bulgarians, the Catholic Germans, and the Orthodox Byzantines. When they returned, they reported:

we journeyed among the Bulgarians. . . . there is no happiness among them, but instead only sorrow and a dreadful strench . . . . Then we went among the Germans . . . but we beheld no glory there. Then we went on to Greece . . . to the buildings where they worship their God, and we knew not whether we were in heaven or on earth. For on earth there is no such splendor or such beauty, and we are at a loss how to describe

it. We know only that God dwells there among men, and their service is fairer than the ceremonies of other nations.

Vladimir officially adopted the Orthodox faith for all his people. He ordered that the idols of the former gods be destroyed and that the whole population be baptized. However, it took several hundred years for Christianity to be accepted by most people.

The adoption of Orthodox Christianity was the single most important event in Russia's early history. Through the Church, Byzantine culture influenced the literature, art, law, manner, and customs of Kievan Russia. Orthodoxy also helped unify the country with a common religion. In addition, Russia stayed outside the Roman Catholic Church

Kievan Rus
Paying tribute to Kievan Rus
Often controlled by the Pechenegs
Major Trade Routes
Other Trade Routes

0   100   200   300 MILES
0 100 200 300 KILOMETERS

FINNISH TRIBES
Gulf of Finland
Neva R.
ESTONIANS
Lake Peipus
Novgorod
Baltic Sea
Pskov
Rostov
Vladimir
Kazan
LITHUANIANS
W. Dvina River
Smolensk
Moscow
PRUSSIA
Oder River
Vistula River
Bug River
Riazan
KIEVAN RUŚ
Kulikovo
POLAND
Turov
Dnieper River
Cracow
Kiev
Dniester River
Don River
CARPATHIAN MTS.
HUNGARY
PECHENEGS
Danube River
SERBIANS
WALLACHIA
BYZANTINE
BULGARS
Black Sea
CHAZARS
Volga River
CAUCASUS MTS.
Caspian Sea
Constantinople (Istanbul)
EMPIRE
URAL MOUNTAINS
Ural River

and was isolated from the Latin civilization of western Christendom.

Yaroslav was the Charlemagne of Russia.
Kievan Russia reached the top of its power during the rule of Yaroslav [yu ru slaf'] the Wise, from 1019 to 1054. Kiev became the religious and cultural center of Russia as well as the political capital. It also became one of the wealthiest cities of Christendom and was richer and more brilliant than Paris or London. Yaroslav founded schools and libraries to support scholars and artists. He issued the first Russian code of laws. With the help of Byzantine architects, he had a copy of the cathedral of Hagia Sophia built in Kiev. The Byzantine patriarch sent a bishop to head the Kievan Church.

Yaroslav extended his domain by defeating the Lithuanians [lith'ü ā'nē əns] to the west, the Finns and Estonians [e stō'nē əns] to the north, and the Pechenegs [pech'ə-

negz'] to the south. In 1036, the Pechenegs were beaten. Never again did they bother Kiev or block the road to Constantinople.

The empire of Yaroslav has been compared to that of Charlemagne. Russian unity was broken by civil war among Yaroslav's heirs. It was regained only briefly during the twelve-year rule of Vladimir Monomakh in the 1100s.

section review 3

1. Which of the three Slavic groups were ancestors of the Russian people? What kind of government organization did they have? Who were their rulers?

2. How did Oleg get favorable trade started between the Russians and Constantinople?

3. Why did Vladimir choose Orthodox Christianity for his people? How did it affect Russian culture?

4. Describe Kiev during Yaroslav's rule.

4 The Mongols conquered and ruled Russia

From the time of the Huns in the 5th century, periodic waves of invaders from Asia had swept into Europe. The Russians always managed to hold off the invaders and stay independent. But in the 1200s, a more powerful conqueror appeared. Led by Genghis Khan [jeng'gis kän'], these Mongol horsemen overran parts of China, Persia, and Russia. In 1240 A.D., Genghis Khan's grandson, Batu, captured Kiev as well as several other Russian states.

The Mongols created fear and terror. These horsemen were a fierce tribe who showed their enemies no mercy. Their savagery can be seen in the following description of Batu's capture of the city of Riazan in 1237:

They came to the Cathedral . . . and they cut to pieces the Great Princess Agrippina, her daughters-in-law, and other princesses. They burned to death the bishops and the priests and put the torch to the holy church. And they cut down many people, including women and children. Still others were drowned in the river. . . . And churches of God were destroyed, and much blood was spilled on the holy altars. And not one man remained alive in the city. All were dead. . . . And there was not even anyone to mourn the dead.

Mongol rule influenced Russian history. So widespread was the destruction in Russia and so great were the tributes, that some historians estimate that Mongol rule held back the development of Russia by 150 or 200 years. The Mongols also cut Russia off from Byzantium and in part from western Christendom for about 250 years. Russia's isolation increased.

The Mongols made very few positive contributions to Russian civilization. As the Mongols had adopted the Muslim faith, they kept apart from the Russians. They did not interfere with the Orthodox Church, but the Church had to support the Mongol power. The Mongols deserve some credit for bringing a postal system and a census to Russia, but they brought nothing important in philosophy or science.

Russian princes gradually grew stronger. Russia's national hero during the early years of Mongol rule was Prince Alexander of Novgorod. Known as Alexander Nevsky [nev'skē] for his defeat of a Swedish army on the Neva River in 1240, he also fought off other attacks from the west. His most notable victory was in 1242 over the Teutonic Knights, a German group of crusaders. Nevsky never dared challenge the Mongols, however. From his capital at Vladimir, he led the Russian nation from 1252 to 1263. His rule rested on the formal consent of the Mongols and also on a peace agreement he nego-

Daily Life

Travel in early Russia was not easy. In winter, people often had to use sleighs or skis. And soldiers needed heavy clothing to protect them from the cold. The Mongols, who moved frequently, had special problems. They had to find ways to move their villages. Sometimes, they put their homes on wheels.

tiated to protect his people from additional attacks by Mongol forces.

Daniel, Alexander Nevsky's youngest son, inherited the city-state of Moscow. It was hardly more than a few villages dominated by the Kremlin, a walled fortress protecting the inner city. Daniel and his successors built up Moscow's strength and gained control of the Moscow River, their road to the Volga and to the trade routes. Moscow became the new center of the Russian church when the bishop moved there in 1328.

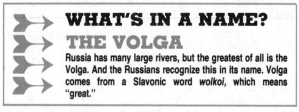

WHAT'S IN A NAME?

THE VOLGA

Russia has many large rivers, but the greatest of all is the Volga. And the Russians recognize this in its name. Volga comes from a Slavonic word *wolkoi*, which means "great."

The princes of Moscow were obedient and reliable servants of the Mongols. In return, they were put above the other Russian rulers. After the Mongol Empire began to disintegrate in the late 1300s, Russian forces under Moscow's leadership crushed a huge Mongol army at Kulikovo in 1380. The victory was short-lived, however. Mongol power was revived under Timur the Lame (Tamerlane). Moscow was sacked in revenge, and regular tribute was again exacted from the Russian princes. Not until 1480 was the Mongol threat ended forever. Then Moscow began to take over leadership of the Russian land.

section review 4

1. What effect did the Mongols have on Russia's history?

2. How did Alexander Nevsky get his name? What was Nevsky's real title?

3. How did the princes of Moscow become stronger than the other Russian princes?

4. What effect did Tamerlane have on Russia and on Moscow in particular?

Section Summaries

1. The eastern empire survived the fall of Rome. Christendom in the east became the Byzantine Empire. It inherited its territory and much of its political tradition from the Roman Empire. In costly warfare, the Byzantines fought to take back lands that the Romans had once ruled. The eastern empire drew its traditions from Greece, Persia, and Mesopotamia more than from Rome. The break between the churches strengthened this division. The Byzantines withstood many invaders, but finally fell to the Turks in 1453.

2. The Byzantines made important contributions in many fields. Constantinople, the strategically placed Byzantine capital, was a prosperous city that kept the best of Greco-Roman culture. Rulers maintained a strong central government that acted as a stern watchdog over all parts of the economy. Byzantine scholars tended to be imitative rather than creative. However, artists and architects created magnificent domes, mosaics, and paintings.

3. Kiev became the first Russian state. The eastern Slavs and their Viking rulers created the foundation of a new state—Russia. For three centuries, Kiev was the capital of a loose confederation of city-states. The single most important event of this era was the adoption of Orthodoxy by Vladimir in 988 for himself and all his people. Yaroslav the Wise, who ruled from 1019 to 1054 and has been compared to Charlemagne, brought Kievan Russia to the peak of its power. After his death, civil war broke out. Unity was regained only briefly during the rule of Vladimir Monomakh.

4. The Mongols conquered and ruled Russia. In the 13th century, the Mongol yoke was fastened upon the Russian people. Mongol rule seriously delayed Russia's development. The Mongols brought terror and destruction to Russia, along with demands of heavy taxes. Alexander Nevsky was the national hero of the time, although he never tried to drive off the Mongols. During the next hundred years, the principality of Moscow slowly grew in strength. In 1380, Russian forces under Moscow's leadership beat a huge Mongol army at Kulikovo. However, Timur the Lame sacked Moscow in revenge. Two centuries passed before the princes in Moscow were able to win independence for Russia.

Who? What? When? Where?

1. Put these events in order from first to last:
   a. Tartar rule ended in Russia.
   b. Justinian ruled the Byzantine Empire.
   c. Muslim Turks defeated the Byzantines at Manzikert.
   d. Oleg captured Kiev.
   e. Russia adopted Orthodox Christianity.
   f. The Byzantine Empire collapsed.
   g. Roman Catholic and Eastern Orthodox leaders excommunicated each other.
   h. The Russians got favorable trade agreements with Constantinople.

2. Give one event in Byzantine or Russian history that involved each of these groups:

   a. Bulgars   e. Ottoman Turks
   b. Lithuanians   f. Pechenegs
   c. Mongols   g. Teutonic Knights
   d. Muslim Turks   h. Vikings

3. Why was each of these persons important in Byzantine history?
   a. Anna Comnena
   b. Nicephorus Gregoras
   c. Justinian
   d. Leo III
   e. Procopius
   f. Empress Theodora

4. Write a sentence to describe the role played by each of these leaders in the history of Russia:

   a. Alexander Nevsky   d. Olga
   b. Vladimir Monomakh   e. Rurik
   c. Oleg   f. Vladimir

5. Define each of these terms:
   a. Byzantine   c. mosaic
   b. icon   d. patriarch

Questions for Critical Thinking

1. What were the successes and failures of Justinian's rule? What should he have done that he did not do?

2. How might the world be different today if Russia had become Roman Catholic instead of Eastern Orthodox in 988?

3. Why did the common people in Russia continue to practice their old religious customs for hundreds of years after the official conversion to Christianity?

4. Compare life in Constantinople at the height of the Byzantine Empire with life in Athens during the 5th century B.C.

Skill Activities

1. Read *Byzantium* by Philip Sherrard to learn more about the religion, culture, and art of the Byzantine Empire. (Time-Life Books, 1966)

2. Discuss how the people of a free nation might react if their government told them they had to follow a certain religion. Would it be easy or difficult for the government to change its people's religious beliefs?

3. On a map of Europe (you could trace one in the back of this book), show where the enemies of the Byzantine Empire came from. Label these enemies and give the years of their attacks. Draw a line around the empire at its greatest extent. Label Constantinople.

4. Using the map in the Geography a Key to History essay in this chapter, list four or more reasons why Constantinople was in a good location. Consider defense, transportation, trade, and communication within the country and with other nations.

chapter **9** *quiz*

Section 1

1. The language of the Byzantine population was: a. Latin, b. Greek, c. Oriental

2. The Byzantine emperor known as the "Bulgar Slayer" was: a. Basil II, b. Justinian, c. Constantine IX

3. At the Battle of Manzikert in 1071 A.D., the Byzantines were beaten by the: a. Persians, b. Turks, c. Romans

Section 2

4. True or false: Byzantine civilization was more advanced than that of western Christendom.

5. A serious problem of the Byzantine government was: a. disease, b. religion, c. power rivalries

6. Byzantine merchants traded with Russia across the: a. Red Sea, b. North Sea, c. Black Sea

Section 3

7. According to tradition, the Viking who came to rule Novgorod was: a. Vladimir Monomakh, b. Rurik, c. Oleg

8. The term *Rus'* was used by foreigners to describe the Slavs and the: a. Mongols, b. Byzantines, c. Vikings

9. The religion of the Russians was officially changed by: a. Vladimir, b. Olga, c. Yaroslav

Section 4

10. Russia was cut off from the rest of the world for more than 200 years by the: a. Byzantines, b. Mongols, c. Vikings

11. During Mongol rule in Russia: a. the invaders became Christian, b. the Russians became Muslim, c. each group kept its own religion

12. Alexander Nevsky defeated the: a. Mongols, b. German crusaders, c. Russian traders

THE RISE OF ISLAM AND THE MUSLIM EMPIRE

As with books in Christendom, early Muslim books were heavily decorated. This elaborate page shows Mohammad ascending to heaven.

The three men hid in the cave as their pursuers searched the hillside. At last, the searchers gave up, mounted their camels, and rode away. Mohammad [mō ham′id], his faithful father-in-law, Abu Bakr [ä′bü bäk′ər] and their guide stayed in the cave for three more days. Then, when they were certain it was safe to leave, they led their camels quietly out of the stuffy cavern. Although the city of Medina [mə dē′nə] was their destination, they rode off in the opposite direction. For ten days, they wound about the hot Arabian desert, zig-zagging back and forth to make sure that no one was following them. Finally, the three tired men rode into Medina and sank down in the shade of a tree. It was 622, and this was the end of the *Hijra*, the "migration" of the prophet of a new religion called *Islam*.

Within a few years, this new faith from Arabia spread far and wide. Today, more people are followers of Islam than of any other religion in the world except Christianity.

Mohammad and his first followers were Arabs. After Mohammad's death, his followers conquered huge territories beyond Arabia and converted many people to Islam. Because followers of Islam are called *Muslims*, the empire they established is known as the Muslim Empire. At its height, the Muslim Empire was larger than either the Byzantine or Roman empires had ever been.

By the 8th century, the empire included peoples of very different backgrounds and needs. As there was no government strong enough to hold the entire empire together, some smaller states broke away. Nevertheless, Islam and its culture gave unity to the Muslim world.

Eventually, the Arab dynasties that first ruled the empire were replaced by Turks, who were also Muslims. Turkish rule was long; a part of the empire continued to be ruled by Turks up to the early 1900s. This chapter tells of the growth of Islam and the spread of the Muslim Empire:

1. **Islam was based on Mohammad's teachings.**

2. **Arab caliphs conquered a huge empire.**

3. **The Muslim Empire divided.**

4. **Turks assumed leadership of the Muslim world.**

1 Islam was based on Mohammad's teachings

The Arabian peninsula is a land of deserts that was inhabited in early times by nomadic peoples. These nomads had no organized government but lived in small family groups, or clans, and depended on their flocks of sheep for food and clothing. Their religion consisted of worshiping the spirits that they believed lived in trees and rocks.

By the 7th century A.D., prosperous trading cities flourished on the Arabian coasts of the Red Sea and the Persian Gulf. Many caravans traveled the trade routes that connected India and China with the Byzantine Empire. The city of Mecca, near the Red Sea, was a busy caravan stop. It was in Mecca that Mohammad was born, and it was to Mecca that he returned triumphant. Mecca was to become a holy city for all his followers from the prosperous merchants to the nomadic shepherds to the people in lands beyond Arabia as well.

Mohammad gained many followers in his lifetime. About the year 570, Mohammad was born in Mecca. Little is known of his early life except that he was orphaned as a child and was raised by relatives. As a young man, he went to work for a wealthy widow who was engaged in the caravan trade through Arabia. He traveled with the caravans to manage his employer's transactions. In his travels he met many people of different cultures, including Jews and Christians. These contacts were to have a profound influence on the religion he later developed.

As Mohammad grew older, his employer's respect and love for him grew. Eventually, she married him, in spite of the fifteen years' difference in their ages. They had four children. Mohammad's marriage brought him economic security and social prestige. It also gave him leisure time, which he spent in meditation and prayer. By the time he was about 40, he began to have visions in which God and the Angel Gabriel were speaking to him. Mohammad became convinced that he was the appointed prophet of the one true God, called *Allah* in the Arabic language. At first, Mohammad made few converts beyond his own family.

As Mohammad's teachings became more widely known, he aroused opposition from the wealthy merchants who dominated Mecca. They feared that if many were converted to Mohammad's new religion, they would lose money. Mecca held a most important Arab shrine, the *Kaaba* (meaning cube). The Kaaba was a cube-shaped building that housed a sacred black stone and the images of several hundred tribal gods. Every year, many Arabs made pilgrimages to the Kaaba, and the money they spent in Mecca was an important source of income to the local merchants. These merchants also suspected that Mohammad wanted to become the ruler of their city, and they proceeded to make life miserable for him and his few followers.

In 622, Mohammad fled Mecca for a more promising field for his missionary work, the trade city of Medina. His departure is known as the Hijra [hi′ jər ə], meaning flight. It is so important to Muslims that it marks the beginning of the Muslim calendar, just as the birth of Jesus marks the first year of the Christian calendar.

Mohammad soon became Medina's political and religious leader. He formed an army and launched a successful holy war against his enemies. In 630 he returned to Mecca in triumph. The idols were taken out of the Kaaba, and it was preserved as a sacred temple of the Muslim faith. By Mohammad's death two years later, Islam had spread to most of the Arabian peninsula.

The Koran was the Bible of the Muslims. The teachings and sayings of Mohammad were set down in the *Koran,* the Muslim holy book. The official version was prepared by

This picture was made in the 1300s. It shows Mohammad setting the sacred black stone in place.

Daily Life

Life for a Muslim meant following the rules set down in the Koran, a page of which is shown *above*. Books of this time were copied by hand. The pages were often beautifully illustrated, as this one is. Muslims also prayed five times a day, facing toward Mecca, which is shown in the picture at *top*. The Sacred Mosque is the large walled building in the center. In the middle of it is the Kaaba. The duties set down in the Koran, which included the daily prayers, tied the Muslim world together.

Mohammad's followers soon after his death. They believed that the words of the Koran were inspired by Allah.

The Koran included laws on personal behavior which described five duties of a good Muslim. These are sometimes known as the Five Pillars of Islam. The first, and most important, was to believe and state publicly that there is only one God, Allah, and Mohammad is his prophet. The second duty was to pray five times daily, facing toward Mecca. Giving money to the poor and fasting during the daylight hours of the holy month, *Ramadan*, were the third and fourth duties. The fifth duty was to make a *Hajj* [haj], or pilgrimage, to Mecca. Many Muslims who lived far away from Mecca could never afford the trip. They were not punished, for it was only important that they wanted to go.

In addition to describing what good Muslims must do, the Koran stated those things which they must not do. Worshiping idols, gambling, drinking liquor, and eating pork were forbidden.

The Koran taught that there is a life after death. The faithful will be rewarded with the eternal joys of heaven; unbelievers will be condemned to the fire of hell. In the Koran, it is said that believers are:

In a high garden
Where they hear no idle speech,
Wherein is a gushing spring,
Wherein are couches raised
And goblets set at hand
And cushions ranged
And silken carpets spread.

The Koran also told what will happen to those in hell. They will be:

Toiling, weary,
Scorched by burning fire,
Drinking from a boiling spring.
No food for them save the bitter thorn-fruit
Which doth not nourish nor release from
   hunger.

Mohammad taught that all Muslims were equal. In the sight of Allah, there were no differences among believers. For this reason, there was no racism in the Muslim world. Arab, black, and European converts mingled freely in the mosques and marketplaces. Equality, however, extended only to Muslims. The ancient Arab custom of slavery continued, but one Muslim could not enslave another. It was considered a good deed to free a slave, but in practice, Arab culture depended on a large number of slaves.

While Muslim women had equal rights to the joys of heaven, their lives on Earth were dominated by men. Mohammad's teachings limited men to four wives (there had been no limit before), and Arab customs dictated that women's activities were restricted to the home. Arab women inherited property, however, which meant that some women became wealthy and influential in their communities. But, like a modern executive in a penthouse office, a wealthy Arab woman conducted business through others she appointed, all of whom were men.

Mohammad taught that an individual should communicate directly with God; no human could intervene between God and the individual. Therefore, no organized or privileged priesthood developed in the Muslim world. However, there were learned teachers, known as the *ulema* [ü'lə mä], who explained religious doctrine. Also, in each community a certain man, known as the *Imam* [i mam'] led the prayers. Praying together was especially important for the noon prayer on Fridays, the holy day of Islam.

Mosques were the churches of Islam. A *mosque* [mosk] was the place of prayer. It could be as simple as a circle of stones, or a vast, beautiful building decorated with fountains and mosaics. Mosques dominated the skylines of cities in the Muslim Empire just as churches did in Christendom.

Islam borrowed from many sources. The influence of Judaism and Christianity on Islam was great. Many figures in both the Old and New Testaments, including Moses and Jesus, are accepted as prophets. However, Mohammad is considered the last, and most important, prophet.

section review 1

1. Why did Mohammad leave Mecca in 622? How is this event remembered by Muslims today?

2. What are the Five Pillars of Islam?

3. Why was there slavery but no racism in the Muslim world?

4. Describe the life of a Muslim woman.

2 Arab caliphs conquered a huge empire

Mohammad's successors, called *caliphs* [kā' lifs], led Muslim armies in a series of holy wars. Mohammad had left the command-

All Muslims try to make the pilgrimage to Mecca. Here a wealthy woman sets out on the journey. She is riding in the golden tent on top of the camel. Some of her servants are going with her while others are wishing her a good trip.

ment to spread the faith, by the sword if necessary. This, and a growing population's need for new lands to settle, spurred on the Arab conquerors. Within 100 years of the Prophet's death, most of the peoples in the area from the Iberian peninsula through North Africa to India were living under Muslim rule.

Mohammad established a theocracy. Mohammad was the religious and political ruler of Medina, Mecca, and much of the Arabian peninsula. He controlled an army and made laws. He negotiated peace treaties with surrounding peoples and settled legal disputes. Many of the rules in the Koran deal with trade, taxation, slavery, and such military matters as war booty and prisoners.

When Mohammad died, he left no son to inherit his rule. Leadership passed to his companion on the Hijra, Abu Bakr. Abu Bakr took the title of Caliph, which means successor (of the Prophet). The caliph was Mohammad's successor in every way except that he could not change the religious beliefs. However, Muslims swore to obey the caliph, which was the same to them as obedience to Mohammad and to God.

The caliphs continued Mohammad's work of spreading the faith. Religious fervor was only one reason for Arab expansion. The Arabian deserts could not support large numbers of people. Yet, with the prosperity that trade through Mecca brought, the population of the peninsula grew. New places to settle and farm were needed, as well as new land to tax for revenue.

Arabs conquered much of the Byzantine and Persian empires. The weaknesses of the only other important states—the Byzantine and Persian empires—contributed to the early success of Arab armies. The Byzantines and Persians had been fighting each other for a long time, and the conquered peoples in these two empires were tired of the warfare and heavy taxes. They put up little resistance to Arab attack. They expected better government and treatment from the conquering Muslims.

One of the first places the Arabs attacked was Syria, at that time part of the Byzantine Empire. Its capital, Damascus, was easily conquered. From Syria, the Arabs moved west to Egypt and Alexandria. The Nile River Valley gave the Muslims a base from which to conquer all of North Africa.

At the same time, Arab armies moved northeast into the Persian Empire and took Iraq. They repeatedly beat the Persian army. And within ten years of Mohammad's death, they destroyed the Persian Empire.

The many peoples under Arab rule were given the choice of either becoming Muslims or paying a head tax, that is, a tax levied on each person. Jews and Christians were protected because the Muslims believed that they worshiped the same God, although in a different way. Nevertheless, they had to pay the head tax. As time passed, these heavy taxes caused many persons to convert to Islam. For the first hundred years of the empire, converts who were not Arabs were a kind of second-class citizens who did not have equal rights. Gradually over the centuries, Mohammad's teaching of equality came to be extended to all converts.

The Umayyad dynasty increased Arab lands (661–750). The first four caliphs were elected by the Muslims in Mecca and had all been associated with Mohammad. However, the expansion of Muslim territory yielded a new kind of ruler. The generals and governors of the new provinces became more powerful than the caliphs in Mecca. In 661, the Muslim governor of Syria declared himself caliph and made Damascus the capital of Muslim lands. This new caliph founded the Umayyad [ü mī′yad] dynasty, which lasted until 750. Under the Umayyad caliphs, Arab conquests continued.

Along the northwest coast of Africa, in northern parts of present-day Morocco, Algeria, and Tunisia, lived a nomadic tribal people, the Berbers. Arab armies, under Umayyad leadership, moved into this area, conquered the people, and converted them to Islam. In 711, a Muslim army of Arabs and Berbers, led by the able Berber commander Tarik, crossed the Strait of Gilbraltar into the Iberian peninsula. In less than ten years, Muslims crushed the Visigothic forces there. By 719, the Muslim army had crossed the Pyrenees [pir′ə nēz] Mountains that form the border between modern Spain and France.

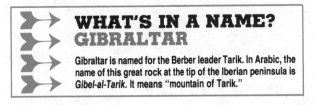

WHAT'S IN A NAME?
GIBRALTAR

Gibraltar is named for the Berber leader Tarik. In Arabic, the name of this great rock at the tip of the Iberian peninsula is *Gibel-al-Tarik*. It means "mountain of Tarik."

The southwest area of France was at that time a Christian stronghold, and its people feared a Muslim conquest. But in 732, the Frankish leader Charles Martel (grandfather of Charlemagne) defeated the Muslims at Tours. Muslim losses were heavy, and the remaining troops retreated during the night.

Muslim rule in Spain continued for over 700 years. The people of mixed Arab and Berber ancestry are known as Moors, and they developed a Moorish civilization in Spain. Islamic influences, especially in architecture, have remained strong in Spain down to the present.

The furthest eastern extent of the Arab empire was the region of Sind in the northwestern Indian subcontinent in what is now Pakistan. From 637 to 644, the Arabs sent several small naval expeditions to Sind. These the ruling Indian chiefs turned back. Next, between 650 and 700, Arab armies attacked Kabul and the Helmand Valley (in present-day Afghanistan) and Sind. They succeeded in capturing Sind in 712.

THE SPREAD OF ISLAM, 632–750 A.D.

SLAVIC PEOPLES

KINGDOM OF THE FRANKS

TOURS x

AVARS

CHAZARS

Black Sea

Constantinople

SPAIN
IBERIAN PENINSULA
Cordova

Rome

KINGDOM OF THE LOMBARDS

BYZANTINE EMPIRE

ARMENIA

Caspian Sea

KHORASAN

Kabul

Indus River

Strait of Gibraltar

Mediterranean Sea

SYRIA
Damascus

PERSIA

Helmand River

MAGRIB

Tripoli

Jerusalem

IRAQ

BERBERS

Alexandria

Cairo

SIND

EGYPT

Persian Gulf

AFRICA

Nile River

Red Sea

Medina

Mecca

ARABIA

OMAN

Arabian Sea

Islam at the death of Mohammed: 632

Moslem expansion under the first four Caliphs: 632-661

Moslem expansion under the Umayyad Caliphs: 661-750

x Battle of Tours, 732 A.D.

0   250   500 MILES
0 250 500 KILOMETERS

At first Arab control was loose, and local chiefs kept their power. But by 724, the Arab governors ruled Kabul, Sind, and the Helmand Valley as the caliph's representatives. The people of the area were converted to Islam and have remained so.

The Muslim navy and armies repeatedly attacked the Byzantine capital of Constantinople. In the famous seige of 717–718, Constantinople held off the Arab navy by stretching a great chain across the narrow entrance to the harbor of Constantinople. The Umayyads were never able to take the city.

For many centuries, the Pyrenees Mountains in the west and Constantinople in the east were the borders between the Islamic and Christian worlds. The Indus Valley was the border between the Islamic and Hindu worlds. The Muslim Empire thus included a vast group of peoples with different cultures, languages, and religions.

section review 2

1. In what ways was Muslim government a theocracy? How did the Koran support the idea that religion and government are the same?

2. What role did Abu Bakr play in the history of Islam?

3. What peoples came under Arab rule during the first four caliphs?

4. Who are the Moors?

3 The Muslim Empire divided

The vast Muslim Empire was difficult to rule. Communication and transportation were slow, and the peoples of different regions had very different problems. For efficient administration, regional governors were given the power to make many decisions on their own. As these regional governors grew in power, some refused to obey the caliph at Damascus. Eventually, three regions broke political ties with the empire.

The Abbassides overthrew the Umayyads. The Umayyad rulers and governors primarily occupied themselves with military affairs and left matters of trade and agriculture to the local peoples. As the Arab expansion halted, the Umayyads and their armies became less important. A government was needed that took an interest in the expansion of trade and agriculture.

The peoples of the empire were also ready for new rulers. Many of the non-Arab peoples in the empire were treated as second-class citizens by their Arab conquerors. This caused much dissatisfaction; these peoples felt they were just as good as the Arabs and many had become Muslims in hopes of receiving better treatment. They wanted to take part in the government, but the Umayyad dynasty would not allow it.

In 750 A.D., a revolution took place. It was very carefully planned and had been preceded by much propaganda: speeches, pamphlets, protests, and even such acts of terror as political murders. The Umayyads were overthrown, and new rulers called the Abbassides [ab'ə sīdz] came to power. Like the Umayyads, the Abbassides were Muslim Arabs, but the Abbassides promised that all Muslims—Arab and non-Arab alike—would be treated as equals. Many non-Arabs were made part of the new government.

The most famous Abbasside caliph was the 8th-century ruler Harun al-Rashid [hä rün' al-ra shēd']. His legendary deeds were recorded in the tales of the *Arabian Nights*, which include the popular stories of "Aladdin and His Lamp" and "Ali Baba and the Forty Thieves." Harun al-Rashid lived at the same time as Charlemagne, and the two exchanged gifts to encourage peace between their lands. The Muslim sent the Christian rich fabrics, perfumes, and even an elephant named Abu-Lababah, meaning the father of intelligence. Harun al-Rashid's relationship with the Byzantine emperor was not so cordial, and border conflicts between their empires erupted periodically.

The first Abbassides moved the capital from Damascus to a new city to the east, called Bagdad. Over 100 thousand workers labored for four years on the banks of the Tigris River to build Bagdad. Many trade routes crossed there, and fertile farmland surrounded the new capital. In Bagdad, the Abbasside rulers surrounded themselves with luxury, pomp, ceremony, and a culture with strong Persian influences. Bagdad became a world center of ideas, trade, wealth, and government.

The Muslims put up many splendid buildings on the Iberian peninsula. The Alhambra was a fortress and palace on a hill overlooking the city of Cordova. Its Lions' Court, with a dozen lions spouting water in the center fountain, is one of the most famous parts. Hundreds of years later, a Christian ruler looked around the Alhambra and remarked, "Ill-fated the man who lost all this." In Granada, the Great Mosque is famous for its interior striped arches. Today, people come from all over the world to visit these buildings and marvel at their beauty.

Moving the capital to Bagdad meant less control of North Africa and the Iberian peninsula by the Abbassides. Soon, the Muslim Empire split into several separate regions.

Iberian and North African Muslims broke with the Bagdad caliphate. During the revolution, the Abbassides had tried to kill all members of the Umayyad family. However, a young prince named Abd al-Rahman [ab' däl-rə män'] escaped by swimming across the Euphrates River. In a journey filled with danger, and pursued by Abbasside spies, he made his way to the Iberian peninsula. Once there, Abd al-Rahman gathered an army from among those who believed him to have a true claim to power. He took over leadership of the Iberian peninsula in 756, and Umayyad rule continued there until 1031.

Abd al-Rahman did not claim to be caliph but contented himself with the title *Amir* [ə-mir'], meaning leader. Nevertheless, his Muslim state, with its capital at Cordova, refused to recognize the authority of the Abbassides in Bagdad. Thus, it became the first part of the Muslim Empire to break away. Under the rule of Abd al-Rahman and his descendants, the Iberian peninsula enjoyed a period of peace and splendor that rivaled Bagdad's.

The Abbasside government became corrupt. In the luxury of their palaces at Bagdad, Abbasside rulers began to neglect the business of the empire. Court standards of morality lowered, and many rulers cared only about leading lives of pleasure. Throughout the empire, taxes rose to support the rich living of the caliph's court. These taxes were not collected fairly. The caliphs did little to protect the trade routes from bandits or to assure farmers a fair price for their produce.

Another result of the Abbasside life-style was the changing status of women. In the early years of Abbasside rule, many upper-class women had political influence. Some

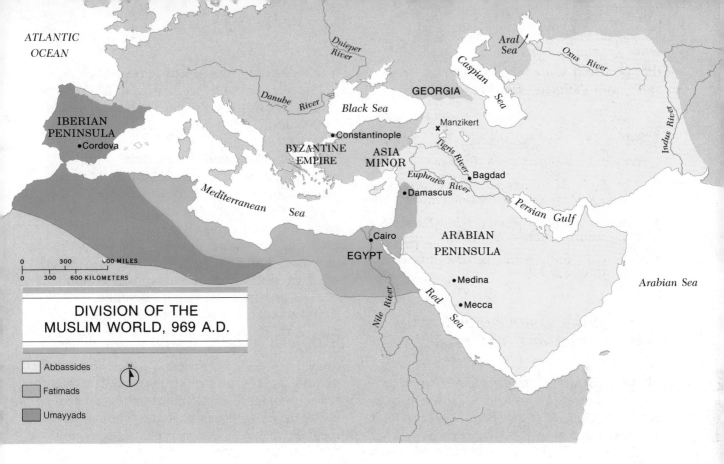

ATLANTIC
OCEAN

IBERIAN
PENINSULA
•Cordova

Mediterranean   Sea

Danube   River

Dnieper
River

Black Sea

•Constantinople

BYZANTINE
EMPIRE

ASIA
MINOR

GEORGIA

Aral
Sea

Oxus   River

Caspian
Sea

Manzikert
×

Tigris River

Euphrates River

•Bagdad

•Damascus

Persian Gulf

•Cairo

EGYPT

ARABIAN
PENINSULA

•Medina

•Mecca

Nile River

Red   Sea

Indus River

Arabian Sea

0   300   600 MILES
0   300   600 KILOMETERS

DIVISION OF THE
MUSLIM WORLD, 969 A.D.

☐ Abbassides

☐ Fatimads

☐ Umayyads

N

were educated and respected for their poetry, musical talent, and storytelling. Other women rode horses splendidly and even led troops to war. Under the later Abbassides, however, upper-class women were secluded in harems—rooms of palaces where only women were allowed. This custom never took hold in the villages in the empire. Women were needed to work in the fields and thus villagers could not afford to keep women out of men's sight.

In the early 10th century, small resistance movements began all over the Muslim Empire. The major resistance was in North Africa. The people there wanted a ruler who was a direct descendant of Mohammad's daughter, Fatima [fə tē′mə]. The Fatimads opposed the Abbasside rulers, whose relationship to Mohammad was through his uncle Abbas. In 908, a member of the Fatimad family was made ruler of what is modern-day Tunisia. The Fatimads called themselves caliphs and claimed to be rulers of the whole Islamic world.

One after the other, Fatimad caliphs led Berber armies in conquests of North African states. By 969, the reigning Fatimad, Al Muiz [äl mü iz′], had added all of Egypt to the Fatimad Empire. Al Muiz founded Cairo and made it the capital of an empire that extended from Morocco to Syria. The Fatimads were never able to overthrow the Abbassides, but neither were the Abbassides able to put down the Fatimad dynasty. Fatimad rule lasted until 1171.

Thus by 969, almost 300 years after its beginning, the Muslim Empire had split into three major sections: one centered in Bagdad, one centered in Cordova, and one in Cairo. All three, however, had similar governmental forms; a single religion, Islam; one written language, Arabic; and one legal system. Despite periods of insecurity, the advancements in culture, trade, and farming

197

that occurred under the Umayyads, Abbassides, and Fatimads were significant.

section review 3

1. Why did the Umayyads lose power?
2. Why did the Muslims on the Iberian peninsula break away from the Abbasside Empire?
3. How did the role of women in Muslim society change during Abbasside rule?
4. Why did North Africa become dissatisfied with Abbasside rule?

4 Turks assumed leadership of the Muslim world

About 1000 A.D., Turkish nomads from central Asia migrated into Abbasside territory in Persia. A great chieftain, Seljuk [sel'jûk], led these warring nomads, who became known as the Seljuk Turks. They became Muslims and before the end of the century dominated the world of Islam from the Mediterranean to China.

The Seljuk Turks ruled from Bagdad. In 1055, Bagdad was captured by the Turks. Although the Seljuk Turks could not read or write at first, they appreciated the high level of Abbasside civilization. Bagdad continued to be the center of Muslim culture in the east for another three centuries. The Seljuk rulers did not depose the Abbasside caliphs; instead they took the title of *sultan*. Although caliphs continued to reign, sultans were the real power in the Muslim Empire.

The Seljuks embraced Islam and Muslim culture whole-heartedly. They built mosques and libraries wherever they went and reconquered large areas.

The second Seljuk sultan, Alp Arslan [äl'-pär slan'], was a brilliant general. He conquered Georgia (on the east coast of the Black Sea), Armenia (south of Georgia), and most of Asia Minor. Alp Arslan defeated the Byzantine emperor at the Battle of Manzikert (Syria) in 1071. It was these Seljuk advances that prompted the First Crusade.

The Seljuks fought the crusaders. Both religious and economic reasons spurred the crusades. Christendom had watched with dismay as the Seljuk army captured Jerusalem from the easygoing Abbassides and swept into the Byzantine Empire. The Byzantine emperor wrote to the pope and princes of western Christendom for help in regaining his lost provinces and their holy land. But he did not expect the army of crusaders. When they arrived in Constantinople in 1096, he quickly turned them toward the Turks. The First Crusade was the most successful. The Seljuks were taken by surprise and the Christians managed to establish the Crusader States in Syria and Palestine. The Muslims recaptured Jerusalem in 1187 and the last of the Crusader States in 1291.

One of the greatest Seljuk leaders was the able soldier, Saladin [säl'ə dən]. Sultan of Egypt and Syria, he ended the Fatimad dynasty and founded his own. In 1187, Saladin attacked the Crusader States. This provoked the Third Crusade, led by three of the most famous medieval knights—Frederick Barbarossa of Germany, Richard the Lion-Hearted of England, and Philip Augustus of France. Frederick was drowned in Asia Minor. And after many quarrels with Richard, Philip returned home leaving Richard to challenge the Turks. Saladin and Richard grew to admire each other's statesmanship. Eventually, a truce was worked out, but it merely gave Christian pilgrims free access to Jerusalem, something Saladin would have granted at any time. By Saladin's death in 1193, the Crusader States were nearly destroyed.

Mongols broke up the eastern Muslim Empire. In the 1200s, the Mongols, under

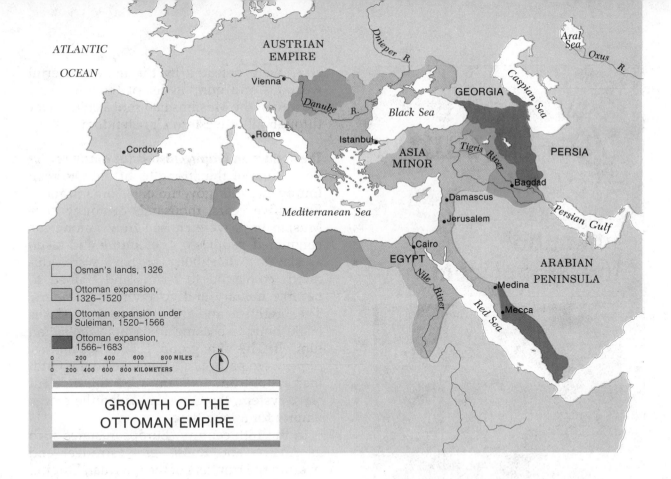

their famous leader Genghis Khan, swept into the Middle East. In 1258, his successors captured Bagdad, killed the caliph, and ended the Abbasside dynasty. The new invaders did not convert to Islam. The center of the Muslim world shifted to Egypt. There, in 1260, a powerful, professional army, the Mamluks, stopped the westward movement of Mongols.

Ottoman Turks made new conquests for Islam. The Ottoman Turks had once been vassals of the Seljuk Turks. Their fief was in Asia Minor, on the border of the weak Byzantine Empire. Through repeated attacks across the border, the Ottomans grew in wealth and power. Under their leader Osman, who lived from 1259 to 1326, the Ottomans took over from the Seljuks and moved west. They beat the Mamluks in Egypt and put a final stop to Mongol inva-

sion in the Middle East in general.

The Ottomans also conquered the Muslim lands of Iraq, much of the Arabian peninsula, Egypt, and all of the North African coast. Not since the Umayyads had this entire area been unified under one Muslim leader.

For two centuries, Ottoman power grew. In 1453, the Ottomans finally succeeded in capturing the Byzantine capital of Constantinople, the object of Muslim attacks for 750 years. They changed the city's name to Istanbul and from there pressed on into southeastern Europe.

The Ottoman Empire reached its height during the reign of Suleiman [sü lā män'] the Magnificent (1520–1566). In 1529, Suleiman led the Ottoman armies in an attack on Vienna. But it became difficult to continue to provide food and ammunition for his troops, and Suleiman was forced to withdraw. In 1683, the Ottomans again attacked Vienna.

Someone You Should Know

Suleiman The Magnificent

Christians knew and feared him as Suleiman the Magnificent. Muslims called him Suleiman the Lawgiver for the justice of his rule and the legal reforms he sponsored. But when it came to personal style, the title Magnificent fit him well, for Suleiman was a man who loved pomp and splendor.

In June, 1530, Suleiman put on a lavish, three-week celebration in honor of his four sons. He provided all sorts of amusements, invited the highest dignitaries, and generously distributed expensive gifts. When the celebration ended, Suleiman asked his chief minister, Ibrahim, which had been the more magnificent—the celebration or Ibrahim's own wedding. With quick wit, Ibrahim said that the wedding had been the more magnificent since it had been honored with Suleiman as a guest.

"Be a thousand times praised," replied Suleiman, "for having thus recalled me to myself."

They were defeated by the more powerful weapons and gunpowder of the Viennese. However, the Muslims had sent a chill of fear through all of western Christendom.

The Ottoman Empire lasted for many centuries. One of the strengths of the Ottoman Empire was its governmental organization. Every five years, thousands of young non-Muslim boys were chosen from among the conquered peoples of the empire and taken as slaves to Istanbul. The boys were educated, converted to Islam, and trained to become military and governmental leaders. The brightest and most industrious slaves could hope to become advisers to the sultan himself. This elite group, called the *Janissary corps*, were patriotically devoted to the Ottoman Empire and to Islam. With this efficient slave system, the Ottomans ruled their large empire for a long time.

In the 18th century, European states such as Austria and Russia grew stronger and overran the frontiers of the Ottoman Empire. At the same time, Ottoman provinces such as Egypt claimed independence. In the 19th and 20th centuries, there were attempts to reform the old, tottering empire, but without success. In World War I, the Ottoman Empire lost its many provinces and became the nation of Turkey. Despite weakness in the last years, Ottoman rulers led the Muslim world from the 13th to early 20th centuries.

section review 4

1. Where did the Seljuk Turks come from? How did they strengthen Islamic civilization?

2. What encouraged western Christendom to invade Muslim lands?

3. When and why did the center of the Muslim world move from Bagdad to Egypt?

4. What was the Janissary corps? How was it recruited? What did it do for the Ottoman Empire?

Section Summaries

1. Islam was based on Mohammad's teachings. During the 7th century A.D., an Arab named Mohammad inspired the religion of Islam. In 622, Mohammad's opponents forced him to flee from Mecca to Medina. He became the political and religious leader of Medina, launched a holy war against his enemies, and began a series of conquests that was to become an empire. Mohammad's teachings, recorded in the Koran, spell out the religious duties of a good Muslim. The Koran also includes rules for governing the Islamic world. Mohammad taught that all Muslims are equal.

2. Arab caliphs conquered a huge empire. Mohammad had established a theocracy. The caliphs who came after him continued to rule as heads of both the religion and the empire. Overpopulation of the Arabian peninsula and religious zeal led the Muslims to spread Islam. They first took Damascus in the Byzantine Empire. After the first four caliphs, power moved to the Umayyads. The empire was extended west to take in vast regions of North Africa. Arab armies moved east into the Persian Empire up to the Indus Valley. In 711, Tarik led an army into the Iberian peninsula. Six years later, it was conquered. The Muslim move into western Christendom was halted at Tours by Charles Martel. But a Moorish civilization was established that lasted 700 years. An 8th-century siege of Constantinople failed.

3. The Muslim Empire divided. The peoples of the empire grew dissatisfied with Umayyad rule. In a carefully planned revolution, the Abbassides overthrew the Umayyads. Bagdad became the capital of the empire. In the 8th century, Harun al-Rashid kept peace with Charlemagne's Christian empire. Border disputes marred relations with the Byzantine Empire. Abd al-Rahman took control of the Iberian peninsula, and his descendants ruled for several centuries. In north Africa, the Fatimads took control. By 969, the empire was divided into three parts. One religion, one written language, and one legal system continued to unite the world of Islam.

4. Turks assumed leadership of the Muslim world. In 1055, the Seljuk Turks captured Bagdad and ruled as sultans, allowing Abbasside caliphs to continue in title only. The Seljuks became Muslims and preserved Islamic culture. They reunited much Islamic land under one rule. Seljuk advances brought on the crusades. Saladin, the sultan of Egypt and Syria, ended the Fatimad dynasty. He fought the crusaders and regained most of the lands they won. Then, in 1258, new invaders, the Mongols, took Bagdad and put a final end to the Abbassides. The center of Islam moved to Egypt where it was protected by the Mamluks. Ottoman Turks took over from their former lords, the Seljuks, and stopped the Mongol attacks. The Ottoman Turks built up a huge empire. In 1453, they took Constantinople and changed its name to Istanbul. The Ottoman Empire lasted for many centuries and was finally broken up in the 20th century.

Who? What? When? Where?

1. Place these events in the correct order from first to last:
   a. Battle of Tours
   b. the Hijra
   c. Mohammad was born
   d. Mongols took Bagdad
   e. Muslims landed in the Iberian peninsula
   f. Ottomans took Constantinople
   g. Seljuks took Bagdad

2. Write sentences that tell what role each of these persons played in Muslim history.
   a. Tarik
   b. Harun al-Rashid
   c. Abd al-Rahman
   d. Saladin
   e. Suleiman
   f. Al Muiz

3. Tell how each of these terms applies to Islam:
   a. Koran   e. ulema
   b. Muslim   f . caliph
   c. Hijra   g. Ramadan
   d. Imam   h. mosque

4. Vienna, Manzikert, and Tours were important Muslim battles. Tell the years and the outcome of each.

Questions for Critical Thinking

1. What was the relationship between the lifestyle of the early Muslims and their ideas of heaven and hell as expressed in the Koran?

2. Why did Mohammad use the Kaaba as a holy place for Muslims after he returned to Mecca?

3. What reasons explain the rapid spread of Islam?

4. Was religion more important to people in the Muslim Empire than it is today? Defend your answer with specific examples.

Skill Activities

1. Read *Mosques and Minarets* by Doreen Ingrams to learn more about the teachings of Islam. (EMC Corp., 1974)

2. Compare the basic teachings of Christianity and Islam. How are they alike and different?

3. Write a report on the Muslim world today. What is its importance in world political affairs? Its resources? Use news articles for your report.

4. Draw (or trace) a map showing the areas controlled by Muslims from 650 to 1450. Label the areas held by the Umayyads, Abbassides, Seljuks, Mongols, and Ottomans.

5. Use the maps in the Atlas section of this book to find out what modern countries contain these cities: Cairo, Damascus, Mecca, and Vienna.

chapter **10** *quiz*

Section 1

1. The correct name of the religion begun by Mohammad is: a. Mohammadanism, b. Islam, c. Muslim

2. True or false: Once a year, Muslims fast during the feast of Fatima.

3. The holy book of the Muslims is called the: a. Kaaba, b. Allah, c. Koran

Section 2

4. True or false: Mohammad passed on his rule to his only son.

5. Islam was spread to other countries by: a. missionaries, b. teachers, c. holy wars

6. Christians and Jews in Muslim territories were: a. made to pay a special tax, b. treated like slaves, c. forced to leave the country

Section 3

7. The Umayyad and Abbasside dynasties were: a. Mongol, b. Arab, c. Turkish

8. True or false: The Abbasside dynasty made many non-Muslims part of the government.

9. True or false: When the Abbasside Empire split up, those who broke away were no longer Muslims.

Section 4

10. True or false: The Ottomans changed the name of Constantinople to Istanbul.

11. True or false: Before their conquest of Bagdad, the Turks had been Muslims.

12. The empire that lasted until World War I in the 1900s was the: a. Ottoman, b. Seljuk, c. Abbasside

ISLAMIC CIVILIZATION

In the 1200s, Arab traders traveled the seas in boats manned by slaves.

There is a story in the *Arabian Nights* about a beautiful slave girl named Towaddud. She had a good master, but he was very poor. As a solution to his problems, she suggested he sell her to the caliph, Harun al-Rashid, for 100 thousand pieces of gold. Her master reluctantly agreed and together they went to the palace. Harun al-Rashid was amused by their suggestion. He asked why they thought

she was worth such an enormous price. Towaddud replied that she could prove herself to be as wise and knowledgeable as all the caliph's most intelligent advisers. Her boast intrigued him; Harun al-Rashid sent for the most learned scientists, teachers, and scholars of the land.

For days, Towaddud was questioned about everything the learned people knew.

They asked her questions about the Koran and about grammar, poetry, history, mathematics, philosophy, astronomy, geography, law, and medicine. All were amazed to find that she could answer anything they asked. In addition she was a talented musician and poet. She even defeated the chess master of the empire three times.

Impressed by her many talents, the caliph agreed to pay Towaddud's price. Then he asked her if there was any favor she wished, but she only wanted to be restored to her master. So Harun al-Rashid made him an official at the palace, and Towaddud and her master no longer had to live in poverty.

The story of Towaddud's knowledge is obviously an exaggeration. But it was not unusual for slave girls and boys to receive some education when the Muslim Empire was at its height of culture, 900–1100. Those two hundred years are often called the golden age of Muslim learning. Poor children learned to read and write by memorizing the Koran. Wealthy persons received an extensive education and often devoted their adult lives to scientific study, writing, observation, and experimentation. Others pursued the arts by writing poetry, playing music, painting, weaving, or designing buildings. Throughout the Muslim world, scholars, scientists, and artists made outstanding contributions in their fields.

Chapter 10 discussed political developments in the world of Islam from 622 to about 1700. This chapter concentrates on Islamic cultural activities of that time:

1. Religion and government encouraged prosperity.

2. Vigorous trade spread Islamic culture.

3. Science and the arts flourished.

1 Religion and government encouraged prosperity

Religion and government in the Islamic Empire were inseparable. The caliph was the head of both, and the Koran, the holy book, dealt with both religion and government. Holy pilgrimages brought many different people in contact with each other. Agriculture advanced with the caliphs' support. Industry grew as artisans in the cities made their wares for trade.

Arabs preserved the cultures of the peoples they conquered. Often the Arab armies conquered regions in which the armies and governments were weak, but the peoples had strong cultures. The Arabs conquered much of the finest territory of the Byzantine and Persian empires. They had beautiful towns with thriving markets. They had poems and ballads, industries and productive farms. The Arabs had much to learn from the peoples they conquered, for the Arab armies were made up of simple nomads who had become warriors. They appreciated the cultures they encountered and did much to preserve them. The Arabs translated many of the classical works of the Greco-Roman culture into Arabic. Persian and Indian classics too were translated into Arabic. Huge libraries made these documents available to Muslim scholars.

Whenever a person converted to Islam, he or she learned Arabic in order to say prayers and read the Koran. All the laws and official correspondence of the Muslim world were in Arabic even in areas where most of the people spoke Persian or Greek. Although some civilizations have developed without writing, Arabic was definitely important to the development of the high level achieved in the Muslim world.

To all Muslims, one of the most important journeys of a lifetime is to Mecca, Saudi Arabia. The city is so sacred that only Muslims are allowed to enter. But pictures and descriptions are abundant, so it is not difficult for non-Muslims to learn what Mecca is like.

Today many pilgrims travel by plane to the city of Jiddah, near Mecca. Little else, however, has changed about the Hajj since Muslims began coming to Mecca in the 600s. In Jiddah, the pilgrims bathe and dress in the simple clothing which they will wear until their pilgrimages are finished.

Upon arrival in Mecca, pilgrims go to the huge Sacred Mosque in the center of town. Tall minarets tower in each corner of the mosque, and the Kaaba stands in the center, draped in black cloth. Imbedded in one corner of the Kaaba is the Black Stone, probably a meteorite. Muslims believe the Black Stone was sent by God.

One part of the pilgrimage is to see the Kaaba, walk around it seven times while praying, and touch the Black Stone. Sometimes, though, the crush of people makes this last act very difficult.

Muslims can—and do—go to Mecca anytime. In the last month of the Muslim calendar year, however, as many as 2 million pilgrims come from all over the world for special ceremonies. On the ninth day of that month, pilgrims gather at the Mount of Mercy, outside Mecca. They pray together and hear sermons from noon to sunset. Pilgrims say this is the most inspiring part of the Hajj.

On the tenth day, pilgrims travel to the nearby town of Mina. Three whitewashed pillars in the town are thought to represent devils. Pilgrims throw stones at the pillars to show their rejection of evil. Later, there is a great feast. Muslims all over the world have a great feast on the same day. Finally, when it is time to leave, pilgrims return to the Sacred Mosque to walk again seven times around the Kaaba as a farewell.

At *right* is the Kaaba during prayers. *Below* is the Sacred Mosque at dusk.

Daily Life

Muslims made everyday objects into beautiful pieces. This brass pitcher and astrolabe were both made during the 1200s. The pitcher is inlaid with silver. The Greeks had used simple astrolabes, but Arab scholars preserved and developed the idea. Artisans then created versatile and beautiful ones. Astrolabes helped determine the user's position on land or sea. Such instruments greatly aided travel. Artisans also made beautiful tapestries. This one was a saddle bag for a camel. The bags were filled with food, clothing, and sometimes children. Today, such items are prized as art objects.

Islamic civilization was made up of the contributions of a great variety of peoples of different races, backgrounds, and religions. Muslims, Christians, Jews, Arabs, Persians, Indians, Berbers and other Africans—each group brought its special crafts, customs, and ideas to the empire.

The pilgrimage encouraged the exchange of ideas. Each Muslim was supposed to make a pilgrimage to Mecca at least once in a lifetime. To a sincere Muslim, this was one of the high points of life. When pilgrims set out from their homes, large celebrations and feasts provided a proper send-off. The journey took as much as eight years as pilgrims traveled over land and sea, on camels, donkeys, in tiny boats, or on foot. Some travelers never returned home.

A Muslim tried to be in Mecca during the special pilgrimage month. During that month, Mecca was filled with hundreds of thousands of believers from all over the world. All the pilgrims in Mecca were dressed exactly the same, in a seamless white cloth. Thus rich and poor, kings and farmers could hardly be told apart. All the pilgrims prayed at the same time and performed the same devotions for 10 days.

The pilgrimage, called the Hajj, frequently inspired Muslims to reform their lives. Chiefs and kings were known to give up their rule after performing the Hajj. Upon return from Mecca, a Muslim was called Hajji [hä'jē], or pilgrim, for the rest of his or her life. This was a term of great respect.

For centuries people came together during the pilgrimage. They exchanged ideas and learned of the differences and similarities among all peoples. Pilgrims acquired a tolerance for differences and an openness to new ideas, and these attitudes were strengths for the Islamic world. When pilgrims returned home, they brought new ideas with them. People in the community were willing to listen to the new things the Hajji spoke about because a pilgrim was respected for completing an important religious act.

The caliphs improved farming methods and crop yields. The centuries of the Umayyad and Abbasside reigns were generally ones of peace within the empire. Islam provided a tie that helped keep Muslims from fighting each other. Also, the caliphs in Bagdad could usually prevent civil wars and revolts within their realm. This peace allowed agriculture and trade to expand without disruption.

The caliphs built vast irrigation projects. They extended the canals of ancient Mesopotamia and encouraged such scientific farming methods as crop rotation and the use of fertilizer. The arid regions of the Middle East and North Africa blossomed. Wheat and other grains grew in the Nile Valley. Cotton, flax, and sugar cane were cultivated in North Africa. Olives, fruits, and fine wines were produced in Spain.

Stock breeding flourished in Asia Minor, Persia, and Syria. New varieties of sheep furnished raw material for fine woolen cloth. Arabian horses, famous for their speed and endurance, were brought to full development. The camel, the "ship of the desert," became the chief means of land transportation across the Sahara.

Food for the empire was produced on great estates, which were worked by tenant farmers and serfs. Though slavery was common, most slaves were personal or household servants; slaves usually were not used for plantation labor. Small landholdings were common. Although the peasants seldom became rich, they had more independence than the serfs of Christendom.

Artisans made a variety of products. Muslim industry centered around the great cities of the empire, most of which specialized in the manufacture of certain products. Bagdad was noted for glassware, jewelry, silks, and luxury goods; Damascus for strong, tempered steel and "damask," or embossed linen; Cordova for leather products; and Toledo for fine steel.

Using the wool of sheep raised in Persia and Syria, workers made the beautiful, durable, hand-woven carpets, known today as "Oriental" carpets. Muslim artisans learned some of the secrets of Byzantine metalworking in gold, silver, and bronze. Papermaking was brought from China. Workers formed guilds that protected them, supervised the training of new artisans, and controlled most of the production and sale of goods.

Cities enjoyed a high standard of living. The heavily populated and well-planned urban centers of Islamic civilization had fountains, libraries, teeming markets, and proper drainage. They were in sharp contrast to the smaller, less healthy wooden villages and crude, cold stone castles surrounded by serfs' and peasants' huts in Christendom.

City life in the Muslim Empire was far better than that in western Christendom. Muslims could chose from a large variety of fruits and vegetables, the result of extensive agriculture and irrigation projects. People could also choose from a variety of foods introduced by the many different groups who lived in the empire. Fashions in clothing, such as baggy trousers, and new games, such as polo, chess, and backgammon, became popular. New conveniences like ovens, frying pans, and porcelain dishes made the work of servants in a Muslim household less dreary.

The common people as well as the aristocracy had some leisure time. It was often spent listening to lute players or reciting poetry. Public taverns and restaurants for men, and special hours at the public baths for women, were opportunities for social gathering. At a time when people in Christendom did not bathe once in a whole year, the people of Bagdad made frequent use of the thousands of public baths their city contained.

section review 1

1. How did the conquering Arabs react to the more advanced cultures they met?

2. How did the pilgrimage to Mecca help unify the Muslim Empire?

3. Describe farming and agriculture within the Muslim Empire?

4. What kinds of living conditions did Muslim cities provide?

■ MAP LESSON 11: MUSLIM TRADE ROUTES ABOUT 1000 A.D.

This map shows how the Muslim world was bound together by trade routes. These furnished connections between Europe, Africa, and Asia. Most routes used land and sea. Few, however, followed river courses because suitable streams were rare.

1. Most port cities were around the Mediterranean. Name the one at or near:
   a. the Strait of Gibraltar
   b. the mouth of the Nile River
   c. the straits between the Black Sea and the Aegean Sea

2. Other major trading centers had inland locations. Name the one which was:
   a. between Tashkent and Nishapur
   b. on the way from Acre to Raqqa

3. A merchant traveling by land from Tunis to Constantinople via the main trade route would pass through six major trading centers along the way. Name them in the proper order.

2 Vigorous trade spread Islamic culture

Islam had begun in Mecca, the major trade center of Arabia. Mohammad and his wife had been part of the caravan trade. Mohammad had traveled with the camel trains to trade in distant towns. Thus Muslims considered trading to be an honorable profession. Commerce was a bigger business than either industry or agriculture.

Many factors helped trade. Within the empire there were no trade barriers, such as taxes or import duties, between regions. Gold and silver coins were used in trade. Moneychangers and moneylenders were in every market. Business terms such as *bazaar*,

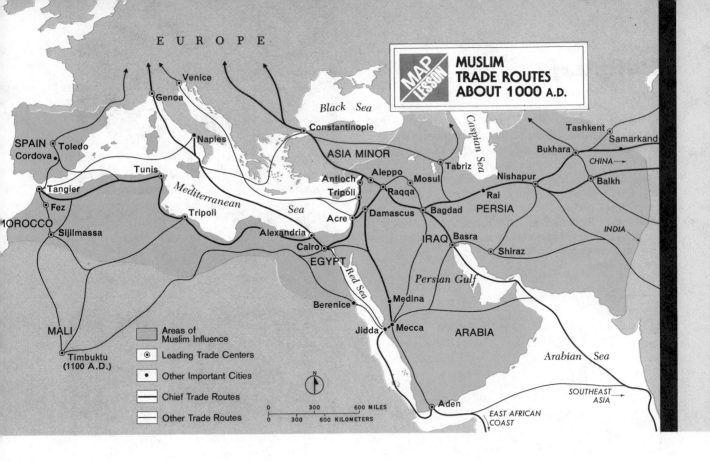

MUSLIM
TRADE ROUTES
ABOUT 1000 A.D.

EUROPE

Venice
Genoa
Black Sea
Constantinople
Caspian Sea
Tashkent
Samarkand
SPAIN
Toledo
Naples
ASIA MINOR
Bukhara
Cordova
Aleppo
Tabriz
CHINA →
Tunis
Antioch
Mosul
Nishapur
Balkh
Mediterranean
Tripoli
Raqqa
Rai
Tangier
Damascus
Bagdad
PERSIA
Fez
Tripoli
Sea
Acre
INDIA
MOROCCO
Alexandria
IRAQ
Basra
Sijilmassa
Cairo
Shiraz
EGYPT
Persian Gulf
Red Sea
MALI
Medina
Areas of
Muslim Influence
Berenice
Arabian Sea
Leading Trade Centers
Jidda
Mecca
ARABIA
Timbuktu
(1100 A.D.)
Other Important Cities
Chief Trade Routes
SOUTHEAST
ASIA →
Other Trade Routes
Aden
EAST AFRICAN
COAST

N

0   300   600 MILES
0   300   600 KILOMETERS

tariff, traffic, check, and *caravan* have come into English from Arabic.

A complex banking system grew in the Islamic world three centuries before it did in Christendom. Central banks were formed with branches in distant cities of the empire. The Muslims used a variety of business and banking practices, such as the use of receipts, checks, and letters of credit. This meant that a merchant who placed money in the care of a banker in Bagdad could draw on that money from the banker's relative or employee when he arrived in Damascus or some other Muslim city far from his home bank.

The Muslims also formed trade associations and developed joint-stock companies. These associations made it possible for several persons to pool their money and finance large trading expeditions. An expedition might take five or ten years to send goods to markets in a distant country and return with the profits. No single member of the association would have been able to afford such a large, long-term expense alone.

Muslim trade spread culture to foreign lands.
Trade flourished beyond the borders of the empire to China, India, Europe, Russia, and Central Africa. Daring explorers opened up new overland routes to East Asia. Sea voyages to India and China by way of the Persian Gulf, the Red Sea, and the Indian Ocean were undertaken by Muslim traders centuries before Western navigators discovered the Atlantic route to the East. New inventions—the compass and the astrolabe—helped sailors find their way.

Along with their goods, Muslim mer-

Daily Life

Life in Muslim cities was much the same everywhere. Slaves were bought and sold in many city markets. At *right bottom* the buyer chooses among black or white slaves. The slave dealer, on the platform carefully weighs a customer's gold pieces. Many Muslim cities also had public baths such as at *far right.* Men and women used the baths at different set times of the day. Carpenters as at *middle* drilled holes by pulling a bow back and forth. This way of turning wood is still used today. Rich people had luxurious lives. At *right top* a wealthy boy is tutored by a scholar. At the same time, servants bring food, play music, and provide entertainment.

chants carried their religion. Thus Islam spread to East and West Africa, India, parts of China, and Indonesia. Peaceful and energetic Muslim traders made converts in lands where the battles and swords of Islam had long ago failed.

The traders also acquired and passed on much new knowledge. Muslim traders learned about the numerals *1* through *9* from the Hindus in India and devised the important zero, later teaching these to the Europeans. These so-called "Arabic numerals" became the basis for all modern mathematics. In China, Muslim traders learned how to make paper and carried the secrets throughout the empire.

Ibn Batuta traveled widely. Perhaps no single person saw as much of the Muslim world as did Ibn Batuta (ib'ən ba tü'tä]. He was a living example of the cultural unity of Islamic civilization. Ibn Batuta was born in Morocco, North Africa. In 1325, when he was 21, he set out on the pilgrimage to Mecca. He was already highly educated and trained to be a judge in Islamic law; but by the time he reached Egypt, Ibn Batuta knew he wanted to learn more about the peoples and places of the world. He decided to travel and set himself the rule "never to travel any road a second time." By the end of his life, he traveled more than 75,000 miles (120,000 kilometers).

Ibn Batuta journeyed through Arabia, Syria, Persia, Iraq, and Asia Minor. He went from Samarkand to India. In India he worked for two years as a judge for a Muslim sultan. Then, in 1342, the sultan sent Ibn Batuta on an official mission to China. Travel was dangerous in those days, and it took Ibn Batuta several years to reach China. Robbery and

shipwreck accompanied his trip. Pirates attacked his ship in the Indian Ocean, and all his notes and diaries were lost. His mission was finally successful, and he returned home to Morocco.

But Ibn Batuta was still not content, for he wished to visit every Muslim country. So he set off for Spain. From Spain he journeyed south, across the Sahara to West Africa and visited the thriving Muslim African state of Mali in 1352. His account of Mali, describing everything from the advanced scholarship of the capital, Timbuktu, to the curious hippopotamuses in the Niger River, is one of the most valuable and unique sources for the history of Africa at that time. After traveling in Africa, Ibn Batuta returned to Morocco to live out his life and write his great book *Travels*.

Ibn Batuta was able to travel so far because the Islamic world at that time was large and peaceful. He was able to stop and work as a judge wherever he went because Islamic law was in use in most of the places he visited. He was always received with respect and was considered a most learned and religious man. As he traveled, he learned from others and spread his own knowledge. Ibn Batuta was an ambassador of Islamic culture.

section review 2

1. Why did Muslims consider trade an honorable profession?

2. Name three or more business practices that helped trade. Explain how they worked.

3. How did trade spread the Muslim religion and culture?

4. Why was Ibn Batuta able to travel so far and to find work wherever he went? In what ways was he an "ambassador of Islamic culture"?

3 Science and the arts flourished

The Arabs before the time of Mohammad had little knowledge of the physical and natural sciences. However, their desire for trade and their increased traveling promoted a need for more understanding of mathematics and astronomy. The Umayyad and Abbasside rulers were tolerant of new ideas. Early Abbasside caliphs encouraged and paid for the systematic translation of books. The science and philosophy of the Greeks were eagerly studied and the works of Aristotle, Euclid, Ptolemy, Archimedes, and Galen were translated into Arabic. The people of Europe rediscovered these classics in Muslim Spain and, during the Crusades, in Syria and Palestine. But, in addition to preserving Greek knowledge, Muslims contributed much original information and theory of their own. In medicine, mathematics, astronomy, chemistry, and physics, Muslim achievements were particularly noteworthy.

Muslim works on medicine were the most advanced of the time. Islamic medicine is perhaps the best known of the Muslim achievements, partly because it was only a century ago that Western schools of medicine stopped including Islamic medical practices and books as part of their requirements.

Well-equipped hospitals, usually associated with medical schools, were located in principal cities throughout the Muslim Empire. At a time when superstition still hampered the practice of medicine in Christendom, Muslim physicians were basing their practices on careful observation of the patient, the symptoms, and the effect of treatment. They diagnosed diseases, prescribed cures, and performed surgery. Pharmacies were common, and druggists had to pass an examination in order to practice.

Doctors also had to be licensed and were trained in medical schools and hospitals.

Caliphs were willing to pay for medical services to poor rural areas. They also supported the examinations and license system that made medicine and health care so highly developed in the Muslim world. The first hospital in Bagdad was established by Harun al-Rashid.

Probably the greatest of all Muslim physicians was the 9th-century figure, al-Razi, known in the West as Rhazes [rā'zēz]. He was the author of many scientific works, including a comprehensive medical encyclopedia and a pioneering handbook on smallpox and measles. Other Muslim doctors developed an early method of vaccinating against smallpox. It was first observed by Europeans in the early 18th century in Istanbul and was used in Europe and America until a better method was developed in England in the early 19th century. A 10th-century physician, Avicenna [av'ə sen'ə], wrote a huge *Canon of Medicine*, which was the standard guide in Muslim and European medical circles until the late 17th century. Portraits of Rhazes and Avicenna are in the great hall of the School of Medicine of the University of Paris today.

Muslim physicists founded the science of optics, the study of sight. Al-Hazen [al-hä'zen] who lived from 965 to 1039, challenged the Greek view that the eye sends rays to the object it sees. Al-Hazen said that one sees because the object sends rays of light to the eye.

Related to the field of medicine was that of alchemy [al'kə mē], an Arabic word that means "the art of mixing metals." Alchemy was an ancient study that went back to early Egypt and early China. Its followers melted and mixed different metals to make stronger or more beautiful objects.

Muslim alchemists searched for a way to change less valuable metals into more precious ones such as gold. Although they were never successful, in trying, they developed ways of analyzing materials that became the basis of modern chemistry. Such carefully controlled methods as distillation and crystallization, which include melting, boiling, evaporating, and filtering, were invented by Muslim alchemists. Through their experiments, they also discovered new substances such as alum, borax, nitric and sulfuric acids, carbonate of soda, cream of tartar, antimony, and arsenic.

Astronomy and mathematics advanced.
Pilgrims, traders, and sailors needed good ways of finding directions. Arab travelers provided geographers and map makers with a wealth of information. Muslim scholars made atlases of the heavens and the earth. The great poet Omar Khayyám [ō'mär kī-yäm'] worked out a calendar so accurate that it contained an error of only one day in 3770 years compared to an error of one day in 3330 years in the Gregorian calendar, now used in the Western world.

Calculations for determining the position of the planets, distances across land, and complex calendars, as well as the advanced Muslim banking system, gave rise to the need for better mathematics. Although the Arabs learned about numerals from the Hindus in India, scholars credit the development of the indispensable zero to Muslim mathematicians. Important advances were made in algebra, analytical geometry, and plane and spherical trigonometry.

The "Father of Arithmetic" was a Muslim by the name of al-Khwarizmi [al'kwə riz'mē] who lived in the mid-9th century in Bagdad. He wrote many books on mathematics and invented algebra, which comes from an Arabic word. In addition to scholarly books, al-Khwarizmi wrote a simplified book on calculation for people to use in everyday trade, in determining inheritances, and in surveying.

The caliphs encouraged many scholars. Throughout history, scholars, philosophers,

In the picture at *top*, a Muslim druggist is making cough medicine, perhaps for himself. The outdoor laboratory puts him near the leaves he needs to cook to make the medicine. Muslim scholars studied the heavens and the earth. In the observatory *above*, astronomers are using several types of instruments to study the sky. In the bottom of the same picture geographers are studying a globe that shows Asia, Africa, and Europe.

and poets have found it difficult to earn a living from their work. Today, such people often teach to earn money and then write or paint only in their spare time. In the past this was also true, but often rulers or wealthy upper- and middle-class people who enjoyed music, books, and works of art supported scholars and artists. These people who gave approval and support are called *patrons*.

The early Umayyad caliphs were patrons of the arts and scholarship. They encouraged people to write down the early nomadic poetry that up to that time had been passed on orally. In 830, the Abbasside caliph al-Mamun [al'mä mün'] established a House of Wisdom in Bagdad for the translation of the Greek classics. Here also was a library, a museum, and an academy where scholars taught students. Al-Khwarizmi lived and worked at the House of Wisdom. Avicenna was often in the employ of various lesser rulers and governors. But the palaces of the Muslim rulers were best known for their support of poetry, literature, and art.

Poetry was highly esteemed among Muslims. The Arab poets of the nomadic desert tribes had held positions of respect. They had been entertainers, historians, and mental record-keepers of political and judicial events. As a result they often had great political influence.

During the early Muslim Empire, poets began to write down poems. These works often reflected social situations and problems. A famous young poet, who was the wife of an early Umayyad caliph, expressed what many of the Arabs must have felt after they left their life in the desert to settle and govern in Damascus:

A tent with rustling breezes cool
Delights me more than palace high,
And more the cloak of simple wool
Than robes in which I learned to sigh.

Poetry was not just for the rich. Muslims enjoyed hearing poetry recited much as Americans enjoy listening to songs on the radio or watching a movie, for the verses told a story and were often accompanied by music. People who could compose good poems and recite them well were famous and popular in the Muslim world.

By the time of the Abbasside caliphs, Arabic poetry and literature were strongly influenced by Persian sources. The *Arabian Nights,* written in Arabic, includes many Persian and Indian stories. One of the most famous Persian poets was Omar Khayyám, who wrote the *Rubaiyat* [rü bī ät'] in the 12th century. Khayyám's poems, and those of many Muslims, were often full of the romance and leisure that surrounded the caliphs' courts, as these popular lines from the *Rubaiyat* show:

A Book of Verses underneath the Bough,
A Jug of Wine, a Loaf of Bread—and Thou
    Beside me singing in the Wilderness—
Oh, Wilderness were Paradise enow!

A Muslim in the time of the Abbassides would have declared that poetry and literature were the most important Islamic contributions and the marks of true civilization.

Philosophy was a common theme in Islamic books. Muslims, with their interest in religious matters, considered it necessary for every scholar to know philosophy. The Muslim thinkers, including the physician Avicenna, valued the works of the ancient Greek philosophers, such as Plato, and compared what the Greeks said with the teachings of Islam.

A century before Saint Thomas Aquinas tried to reconcile the teachings of Aristotle with those of Christianity, the most distinguished Muslim philosopher, Averroes [ə ver'ō ēz'], tried to bring together the principles of Aristotle and the faith of Islam. Averroes lived in Cordova, in Muslim Spain, in the 12th century. He was the personal doctor of the caliph there. Averroes is another example of the Muslim belief that every great scientist or scholar is also a philosopher. His books on Aristotle's works were read in

Christendom long before the original Greek texts were available.

Muslims also wrote excellent histories and biographies. Ibn Khaldun [ib'ən kal dün'] of Tunis, applied philosophical ideas to history. He produced a lengthy history of the Arab states, emphasizing Spain and North Africa. In this work he showed history as an evolutionary process in which societies and institutions change continually. Historical development depends on a number of things, according to Ibn Khaldun, including geography, climate, economics, and personalities, as well as moral and spiritual forces. Such ideas are not new today, but in Ibn Khaldun's time they were. Because of his attempt to see history in this broad, evolutionary way, Ibn Khaldun is often said to be the first modern historian and the founder of social science.

Muslim cities had beautiful buildings. The Arabs had originally lived in tents in the desert. As they conquered lands, they built mosques wherever they went. In the Byzantine territories they often built on the sites of old Christian churches. In time a distinctive Muslim style developed. This style used domes that had been used in Byzantine churches and added minarets [min'ə rets']— slender towers from which the faithful were called to prayer. The arcade and the horseshoe arch are other graceful features of Muslim architecture.

Soon the caliphs and wealthy Muslim citizens began to build beautiful palaces and homes for themselves. Great care was taken to make whole cities attractive and convenient for everyone. Damascus, for example, had a city water supply that is still in use today. Bagdad, constructed from builders'

Omar Khayyám was a mathematician as well as a poet. This page at *left* comes from his book called *Algebra*. It tells how to solve cubic equations by using conic sections. In the 700s, the much-loved fables of *Kalila and Dimna* became part of Arabic literature. The stories were meant to be a guide for young rulers as described by a wise adviser. This page *below* from the book shows a judge handing out punishment to the guilty.

plans, led the Muslim world in beauty, wealth, and services.

Second only to Bagdad was Cordova, the capital of Muslim Spain. By the 11th century, Cordova had paved streets with public lights, hot and cold running water in some homes, 80,000 shops and perhaps as many as 3,000 mosques. It had 113,000 homes, many suburbs, and a population of more than a million people. There were libraries, schools, and a university. A bridge with 15 arches spanned the river that ran through town. The royal palace, with quarters for thousands of slaves and guards, was surrounded by gardens with rare fruit trees, fountains, shade trees, and flowers. Other gardens were located throughout the city.

The Royal Mosque in Isfahan had a beautiful blue dome, floors of blue tiles, and a large central court that surrounded a pool. Both the dome and the two minarets were decorated with intricate patterns. Isfahan is in present-day Iran.

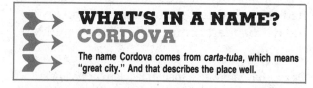

WHAT'S IN A NAME?
CORDOVA

The name Cordova comes from *carta-tuba*, which means "great city." And that describes the place well.

A typical middle-class home in Cordova was located on a narrow, clean street. The wooden doors and windows of the house were usually shut to keep out street noise. Inside, a long archway led into a sunlit central courtyard. All the rooms of the house opened onto it. The mosaiclike tile floor was easy to keep clean. In the center, beside some lemon trees or flowers, was a large clay pot filled with cool water and a cup for the thirsty to drink from.

In the far corner of the first floor was the kitchen. Bread baked in brick ovens and meat cooked over charcoal fires. Another, cooler room stored fruits, vegetables, milk, and yogurt. Colorful plates and dishes stood on pantry shelves. On the second story, sleeping rooms opened onto a balcony overlooking the courtyard. The rooms had pillows, linen sheets, carefully embroidered wool blankets, and feather mattresses on the floor.

Muslims enjoyed luxurious furnishings and elaborate designs. The decorative handicrafts of rug weaving, pottery making, jeweled metal work, and tiled mosaics showed exquisite workmanship. These products adorned the interiors of Muslim buildings. Because the followers of Islam believed that the representation of human and animal figures was a form of idol worship, Muslim artists concentrated on intricate geometric and floral designs in their architecture and crafts. Arabic script was used a great deal as decoration in art and on household objects too.

section review 3

1. List three or more practices that show the advanced level of Muslim medicine.

2. Name one or more Muslim advances in both mathematics and astronomy.

3. What were the great literary achievements of Omar Khayyám, Averroes, and Ibn Khaldun?

4. What are three major features of Muslim architecture?

Section Summaries

1. Religion and government encouraged prosperity. The large empire which the Arabs conquered in the 7th century soon became the foundation of a remarkable civilization and a surge of prosperity which lasted several centuries. The religion of Islam, the central government provided by caliphs, and the Arabic language gave unity to the many varied peoples of the Muslim Empire. The Hajj helped spread ideas throughout the empire. Improvements in agricultural methods provided abundant harvests, and trade brought variety to the dinner tables in Muslim cities.

2. Vigorous trade spread Islamic culture. Trade was an honorable profession in the Muslim world, and many factors encouraged its growth. No taxes between regions helped its activity, coins and banking practices eased the way, and joint stock companies made large, lengthy trade ventures possible. Islamic religion and culture went wherever Muslim traders went.

3. Science and the arts flourished. Muslim scholars in Damascus and Bagdad were very interested in science. They preserved and studied the ancient Greeks' works and added their own ideas and observations. Al-Razi, al-Khwarizmi, Avicenna, and al-Hazen made names for themselves in medicine and mathematics. The study of geography, philosophy, and history interested Muslim scholars too. Caliphs and wealthy governors were patrons of poets, scholars, and artists. The cities of Bagdad, Damascus, and Cordova were unequaled in wealth and splendor. Middle-class people enjoyed many comforts.

Who? What? When? Where?

1. Write sentences that describe the contributions these people made to Muslim culture.

a. al-Hazen   f. Avicenna
b. al-Khwarizmi   g. Harun al-Rashid
c. al-Mamun   h. Ibn Batuta
d. al-Razi   i. Ibn Khaldun
e. Averroes   j. Omar Khayyám

2. Define these words in terms of their importance to Muslim culture:

a. damask   d. minarets
b. guilds   e. patrons
c. Hajj

3. Give specific examples of how civilization has benefited from Arabic contributions in:

a. astronomy   d. language
b. business   e. literature
c. chemistry   f. mathematics

Questions for Critical Thinking

1. Why are math and science important to civilization? What is the importance of poetry and literature? Explain why you agree or disagree with the Muslim view that poetry and literature are the marks of a true civilization.

2. How did the life-styles of the Arab people change after they became Muslims? How much of this change was due to Mohammad? Explain whether or not they would have advanced as far if he had not been born.

3. Describe the ties that unified the Muslim peoples. What similar ties can be found in the United States today?

4. This chapter compares Christendom to the Muslim world. What are some reasons for the higher degree of accomplishment of Muslim civilization at this time?

Skill Activities

1. Read *Early Islam* by Desmond Stewart to learn more about Muslim life and the lands in which it developed. (Time-Life Books, 1967)

2. Trace the map of the Eastern Hemisphere in the atlas section of this book. Then draw the route of Ibn Batuta's travels. Label the cities he visited.

3. With a group of students, form a joint stock company to finance a caravan from one city in the Muslim Empire to a distant city. Where will your caravan go? Draw a map showing the route. How many miles does the route cover? Will someone from the company go with the caravan? Why? Will the caravan bring back goods? What ones? Make out the bill of lading you receive when the caravan reaches its destination.

4. Based on information in the chapter, draw a typical middle-class house in Cordova. Make a floor plan for the house. Find, or design yourself, a geometric pattern for decorating the courtyard floor.

5. Describe the goods and activities that would be found in a bazaar in Bagdad about 1000 A.D.

Where would the products have come from? What might the people at the bazaar be doing?

6. Name the modern nation in which each of these Muslim cities is located:

   a. Bagdad
   b. Cordova
   c. Damascus
   d. Mecca
   e. Samarkand
   f. Timbuktu
   g. Toledo
   h. Tunis

7. In chart form, compare and contrast life in a Muslim city about 1000 A.D. with life in feudal Christendom.

chapter 11 quiz

Section 1

1. True or false: In the Islamic Empire, the caliph was head of the government only, since government and religion were totally separated.

2. Muslim civilization was unified by trade, religion, and: a. nationality, b. language, c. race

3. Among the fine products of the Islamic world were damask, "Oriental" carpets, and: a. fine race horses, b. steel, c. corn

4. After a pilgrim made the trip to Mecca, he or she was called a: a. Hajji, b. Muslim, c. caliph

Section 2

5. Because Mohammad had been one, many Muslims became: a. mathematicians, b. farmers, c. traders

6. The inventions that guided Muslim sea voyagers were the compass and the: a. arcade, b. tariff, c. astrolabe

7. Muslim traders learned about the system of numbers we use today from the: a. Arabs, b. Persians, c. Hindus

8. True or false: Ibn Batuta wrote a book called *Travels*.

Section 3

9. Two famous Muslim scholars who are said to be the founder of social science and the "Father of Arithmetic" are: a. Avicenna and Averroes, b. Omar Khayyám and Ibn Khaldun, c. Ibn Khaldun and al-Khwarizmi

10. Muslim scholars preserved the classic works of the ancient: a. Christians, b. Greeks, c. Arabs

11. Muslim medicine was based on: a. superstition, b. observation, c. alchemy

12. Artists and scholars of the Muslim Empire were supported by: a. the caliphs, b. their own work, c. their relatives

1. Match the items below with the correct one of these civilizations: feudal Christendom, the Byzantine Empire, Russia, the Muslim Empire.

   a. The Umayyads, Abbassides, and Fatimads were important dynasties.
   b. Yaroslav and Alexander Nevsky were important rulers.
   c. Justinian had Hagia Sophia built.
   d. The Mongol conquest held back its progress by as much as 200 years.
   e. Muslims captured the capital in 1453.
   f. The people were mostly Greek, and they followed the Orthodox faith.
   g. Trade was an honored profession, and no taxes between regions hindered its growth; coins, banks, and joint-stock companies helped its spread.
   h. Vladimir chose the Orthodox faith.
   i. Stewards, bailiffs, and reeves helped run the manors.
   j. Ibn Batuta traveled a great deal here.
   k. After Urban II's speech, the crowd roared, "God wills it!"

2. Match the following statements with the correct one of these persons: Genghis Khan, Jesus, Mohammad, Odoacer, Olga, Saint Patrick, Theodora, Yaroslav.

   a. The New Testament tells how he reappeared to his disciples following the crucifixion.
   b. In 476, he deposed the last Roman emperor and became the first Germanic ruler of Rome.
   c. He journeyed to Ireland to convert the Celtic peoples to Christianity and began many monasteries.
   d. Refusing to escape during the Nika Revolt, she said, "I approve a certain ancient saying that royalty makes a good burial-shroud."
   e. During his rule, Kiev became the religious and cultural center of Russia.
   f. He led Mongol horsemen over China, central Asia, Persia, and southern Russia.
   g. He became convinced that he was the appointed prophet of the one true God.
   h. The first female ruler in Russian history, she was converted to Christianity by Byzantine missionaries.

3. Match the letters on the time line with the events they stand for:

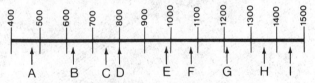

____Mohammad made the Hijra.
____The Ottomans took Constantinople.
____The Abbassides came to power.
____The Black Death struck Europe.
____Rome "fell."
____The Fourth Crusade began.
____The pope crowned Charlemagne.
____Vladimir chose the Orthodox faith.
____Seljuk Turks won the Battle of Manzikert.

4. Match the letters on the map with the places described below:

____The Islamic religion began here.
____The Crusader States were located here.
____These straits connect Europe and Asia.
____Charlemagne's empire centered here.
____The first Russian state centered here.

UNIT FOUR
THE WORLDS
OF AFRICA AND
THE AMERICAS

While cultures and civilizations were rising and falling in the Mediterranean and Asian worlds, people were creating important civilizations and empires in Africa and the Americas. For the most part, the rest of the world knew nothing about these peoples.

From the 9th century A.D. on, Muslims came in contact with African empires such as Mali, Songhai, and the East African city-states. In the 15th century, Portuguese traders made contact with the African coasts. Arab and Portuguese records have shed light on civilizations whose own records have not yet been deciphered.

In the Americas, too, documentary evidence is scanty or undeciphered for the centuries before the Spanish conquerors came. But ruined buildings and the sites of cities give archaeologists much evidence with which to piece together the story of the great Maya, Aztec, and Inca civilizations.

In places where people did not build with materials that last as long as stone and did not write, historians have difficulty discovering the past. It is our lack of knowledge that makes the worlds of Africa and the Americas seem remote. To know something about the history of all these peoples is to widen our understanding of the human experience.

Early people of both Africa and the Americas often made beautiful masks. This one, which has a leather top knot, was made by Eskimos.

CHAPTER 12
THE LANDS AND PEOPLES OF AFRICA

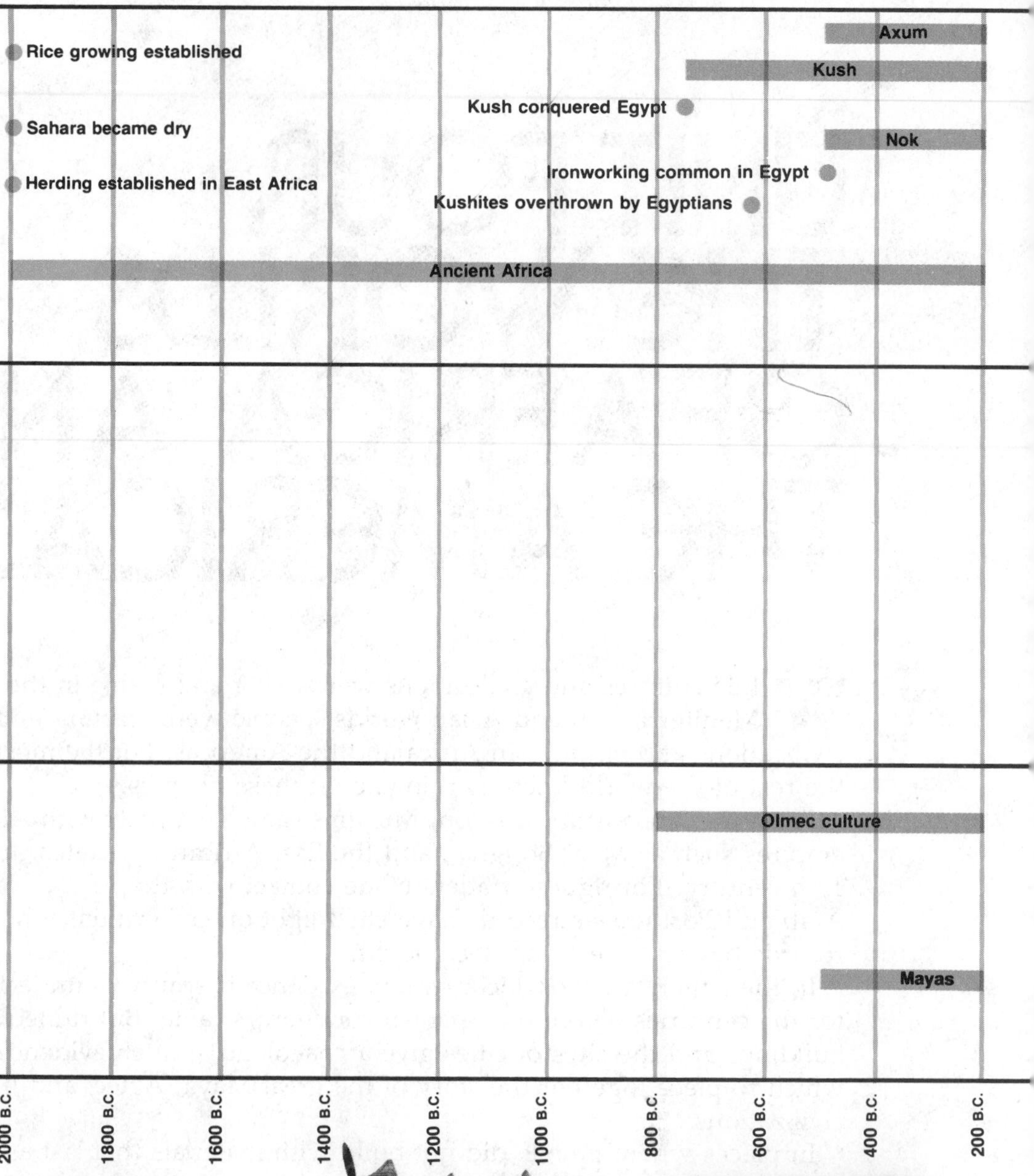

● Rice growing established

● Sahara became dry

● Herding established in East Africa

Kush conquered Egypt ●

Ironworking common in Egypt ●

Kushites overthrown by Egyptians ●

Axum

Kush

Nok

Ancient Africa

CHAPTER 13
AFRICAN CIVILIZATIONS SOUTH OF THE SAHARA

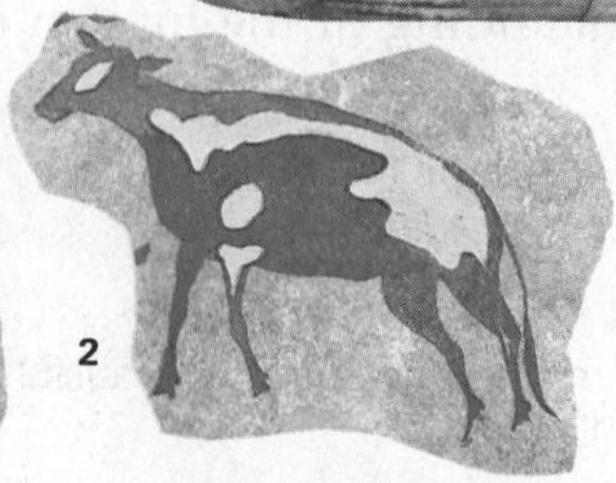

CHAPTER 14
EARLY CULTURES IN THE AMERICAS

Olmec culture

Mayas

2000 B.C.	1800 B.C.	1600 B.C.	1400 B.C.	1200 B.C.	1000 B.C.	800 B.C.	600 B.C.	400 B.C.	200 B.C.

1., 2. Tassili n'Ajjer frescoes, 3. Eskimo umiak, 4. Olmec head, 5. Maya figure, 6. Peruvian head, 7. Benin king sculpture, 8. Chichen Itza pyramid, 9. Aztec drawing, 10. Asante sword.

1

2

3

4

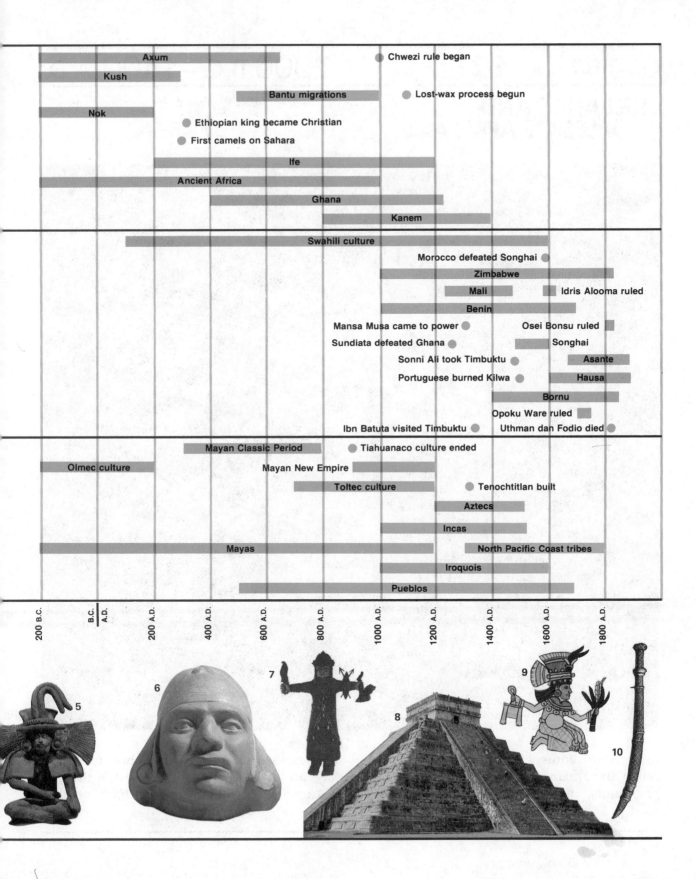

Axum

Kush

Bantu migrations

Nok

● Chwezi rule began

● Lost-wax process begun

● Ethiopian king became Christian

● First camels on Sahara

Ife

Ancient Africa

Ghana

Kanem

Swahili culture

Morocco defeated Songhai ●

Zimbabwe

Mali

Idris Alooma ruled

Benin

Mansa Musa came to power ●

Osei Bonsu ruled

Sundiata defeated Ghana ●

Songhai

Sonni Ali took Timbuktu ●

Asante

Portuguese burned Kilwa ●

Hausa

Bornu

Opoku Ware ruled

Ibn Batuta visited Timbuktu ●

Uthman dan Fodio died ●

Mayan Classic Period

● Tiahuanaco culture ended

Olmec culture

Mayan New Empire

Toltec culture

● Tenochtitlan built

Aztecs

Incas

Mayas

North Pacific Coast tribes

Iroquois

Pueblos

200 B.C.   B.C. | A.D.   200 A.D.   400 A.D.   600 A.D.   800 A.D.   1000 A.D.   1200 A.D.   1400 A.D.   1600 A.D.   1800 A.D.

5

6

7

8

9

10

THE LANDS AND PEOPLES OF AFRICA

The people of Benin carved statues and figurines from ivory.

In the 18th century, a small group of people called the Kulango lived in the *savanna*, or grasslands, of West Africa. They had few possessions other than their houses, clothing, and cooking utensils. Life was a struggle because they did not always have enough rain for their crops. But in the forest to the south of them was a wealthy country called Asante [ə sän'tē]. Some of the Kulango wanted to move there. The land was better, and rainfall was plentiful in Asante, they said. And the Kulango could benefit from the wealth in the capital city of Kumasi.

Some Kulango families went to Kumasi to beg the king, Opoku Ware, to give them a place to live. Pleased that the Kulango had heard of his wealth and power and wanted to settle in his kingdom, Opoku Ware gave them good land in his forest.

For several years, the Kulango lived in the Asante forest. They made farms and built houses. But try as they would, they could not adjust to life in the forest. It was simply too different from their savanna home. True, Asante was a wealthy kingdom with much trade and plenty of food. But the Kulango could not grow the same crops in the forest as they had grown in the savanna. They had to eat foods they were not used to and get along without donkeys and horses to carry their goods to market. Some of the Kulango people even died because they were not used to the food and climate.

Naturally, the Asante people, who had lived in the forest all their lives, liked the food and knew how to grow forest crops. They were very healthy. The Asante thought that the Kulango had very strange ways.

Finally, the Kulango went back to King Opoku Ware and explained to him that they could not adjust to forest living. He listened sympathetically and suggested that they move to a different part of Asante where there were grassy plains. This they did. They made new houses and farms like those they had had in the savanna, and they went back to the way of life they knew.

In Africa, there are many different climates and landforms. Each of the many regions has its own plants and animals. Over the centuries, the many different peoples of Africa have learned to adapt their ways of living to the climate, landforms, soils, vegetation, and animal life available in their own region. Some of these ways of living have developed so differently from others that the people of one region have great difficulty in adjusting to living in a different region.

In ancient Africa (from about 2000 B.C. to about 1000 A.D.), the people learned basic skills that helped them live in their sometimes harsh environment. These skills included ironworking, farming, animal breeding, house construction, and political organization. The skills provided firm foundations upon which African societies grew. This chapter explains that:

1. **Much of Africa is desert and savanna.**

2. **Other features of geography made Africa a land of variety.**

3. **The peoples of ancient Africa developed many practical skills.**

4. **Ancient Africans developed distinctive societies and cultures.**

1 Much of Africa is desert and savanna

Africa is the second largest continent in the world. It has four major ecological regions: coast, desert, savanna, and rain forest. At the very north and south of Africa are two narrow regions of fertile coast. A relatively short distance inland, these areas give way to deserts—the huge Sahara in the north and the Kalahari in the south. Where the deserts end, the savanna begins. Near the deserts, the savanna's bushes and grasses are short. Nearer the equator, the grasslands of the savanna give way to a lush rain forest.

The Sahara was not always the vast wasteland that it is today. The Sahara (which means "desert" in Arabic) is nearly as large in area as the United States. It covers about a fourth of the African continent and is the world's largest desert. Many areas of the Sahara are barren of plants, uninhabited, and unexplored. Spectacular sand dunes dominate the western and eastern thirds of the desert. However, much of the Sahara is hard dirt and rocky sand that supports patches of scrubby plants. These areas are lightly populated. Small groups of people live as nomadic herders, moving each week from one place to another in search of fresh grazing lands.

The Sahara was not always this way. Until about 2000 B.C., regular rainfall made it possible for plants, animals, and people to live there easily. Paintings in caves and on rocky sides of mountains show what life must have been like between 6000 and 1500 B.C. In these Mesolithic paintings, horses pull carts. Hunters give chase to giraffes, elephants, and hippopotamuses. People gather wild grain. And musicians play for women who wear elaborate hair styles and long robes and capes.

What happened to the nameless people whose artists decorated the Sahara caves? Scientists believe that about 2000 B.C., the Sahara became dry. Over the years, rainfall gradually stopped, and the people died or moved to more fertile areas. Some moved to the Nile Valley, some to the north African coast, and some south to the savanna.

Travel across the deserts was dangerous. Although most of the Sahara was no longer habitable, travel across it never stopped. It has always been a link between the Mediterranean world and the parts of Africa that are to the south. Through the ages, travelers followed trails across the Sahara, carrying goods, moving armies, and exchanging ideas. Many oases [ō ā′sēz′] helped keep the

As in the past, the oases of the Sahara still bring water and much life to the dry lands.

trails open. An *oasis* is a place in the desert where an underground spring comes close to the surface. People kept the oases habitable by digging wells and irrigating nearby land. Traders and travelers stopped at oases to rest and water their animals.

Just as the Sahara was sometimes called an ocean of sand, so the camel was called the "ship of the desert." Beginning about 100 A.D., people used camels to cross the Sahara. Camels were much better suited to the hot, dry climate than were donkeys or horses. They could travel fully loaded in the desert for four days without water. Traders, soldiers, travelers, diplomats, desert nomads—all used camels.

To guard against becoming lost and as protection against bandits, people crossed the Sahara in large groups, called *caravans*. Long lines of camels, sometimes as many as 10,000, carried the heavy goods, including leather bags of water. Caravans journeyed

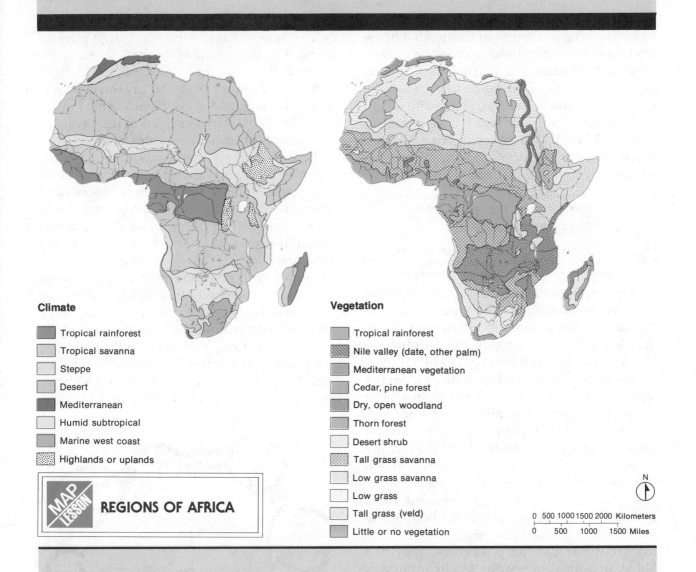

Climate

- Tropical rainforest
- Tropical savanna
- Steppe
- Desert
- Mediterranean
- Humid subtropical
- Marine west coast
- Highlands or uplands

Vegetation

- Tropical rainforest
- Nile valley (date, other palm)
- Mediterranean vegetation
- Cedar, pine forest
- Dry, open woodland
- Thorn forest
- Desert shrub
- Tall grass savanna
- Low grass savanna
- Low grass
- Tall grass (veld)
- Little or no vegetation

MAP LESSON REGIONS OF AFRICA

N

| 0 | 500 | 1000 | 1500 | 2000 | Kilometers |

| 0 | 500 | 1000 | 1500 | Miles |

■ MAP LESSON 12: REGIONS OF AFRICA

1. Climate is one of the most important factors in determining vegetation. That is why these two maps have many similarities. Compare, for example, the area of tropical rain forest climate with the tropical rain forest vegetation region. What symbols are used to show tropical rain forest climate and tropical rain forest vegetation?

2. Each of these maps is really two maps in one. The major purpose is to show the distribution of the various climate and vegetation regions in Africa. But the maps also show the modern boundaries of the nations of Africa. Algeria is the largest nation in area in North Africa. It borders the Mediterranean Sea. What three climate zones does Algeria have?

3. Locate the island of Madagascar and name three or more types of its vegetation.

4. Major rivers are also included on these maps. Find the Nile River on both maps and trace its course. It begins in the highlands and flows northward, ending in the Mediterranean Sea. Name four vegetation areas found along the Nile.

from Morocco or Tunisia in the north to large trading cities along the Niger [nī′jər] River, such as Timbuktu. The journey usually took two months. A skilled guide always led the caravan. He knew his way across the desert by following the stars and by watching for landmarks such as large rocks. No one dared leave the caravan, for to do so would probably mean becoming lost and dying of thirst.

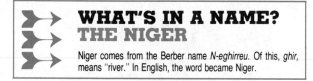

WHAT'S IN A NAME?
THE NIGER

Niger comes from the Berber name *N-eghirreu*. Of this, *ghir*, means "river." In English, the word became Niger.

Despite the dangers and hardships, caravans made great profits by guiding passengers across the desert and by selling the caravan's goods. Salt, copper, and cloth from North Africa brought good prices in the cities on the Niger River. And such items from the savanna and forests as gold, ivory, and hides were prized in Mediterranean markets.

The life of the people in the Kalahari Desert was quite different from that in the Sahara. They lived as hunters, often traveling great distances when stalking game. They also gathered roots, leaves, and seeds for food. They had no permanent homes and no draft animals like the camel. Entire hunting groups would camp wherever they had killed an animal; when the food supply was gone, they would move on. To survive their hostile environment, they had to become highly skilled hunters and gatherers.

Large populations flourished in the savanna.
South of the Sahara the savanna starts at the Atlantic coast and extends across the continent to the Indian Ocean. In the east, the grassland pushes south to the tip of southern Africa and thus covers almost half the continent. In the savanna, a dry season alternates with a rainy season. Prairie grass and scrub trees grow.

The savanna has supported large populations. For the past 2,000 years, farming villages and some large cities and towns have been scattered all over the savanna. People kept livestock and grew crops such as millet and rice. Most Africans lived in the savanna, and many African states were located there.

Few trees grew in the savanna. Savanna peoples used all available wood for supporting roofs and for making fires, tools, and weapons. The walls of buildings were made of a strong plaster of mud and straw. Sometimes, the mud and straw mixture was baked into bricks.

People built one-room houses and topped them with thatched straw roofs. Several of these one-room houses formed a circle, and a wall or fence around the houses gave protection and privacy. The many little buildings thus connected formed a bigger living area called a *compound*. A courtyard in the center provided an area for cooking and visiting.

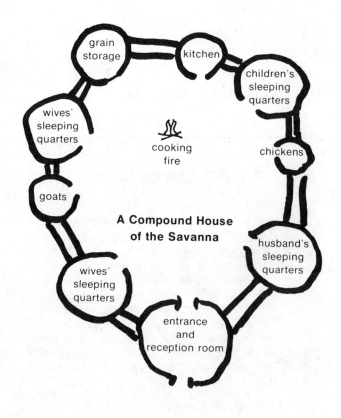

A Compound House of the Savanna

The straw roofs and thick mud walls of the houses kept out the sun, and the inside was as cool as modern air-conditioning might have made it. Houses are still being built in the savanna in the same way as they have been for the past 2,000 years.

Domesticated animals were important in the savanna. Some people in the savanna were nomadic herders who raised cattle, sheep, and goats. These herders moved their homes whenever their livestock needed new places to graze and drink. The herders' cattle and sheep provided much-needed meat for the farmers of the savanna. The farmers in turn sold grains to the herders for making bread and porridge.

The donkey was an important domesticated animal in the grasslands. While camels were vital for crossing the desert, they were not well suited to the savanna, for their soft hooves rotted in the wetter climate. Therefore, when a caravan reached the southern edge of the Sahara, the camels were unloaded, and donkeys were used for the trip across the grasslands.

The savanna was also the breeding ground of fine horses. Some of the savanna states had large cavalries. The powerful armies of these states controlled large areas inhabited by farming peoples, who had no way to defend themselves against the mounted soldiers.

section review 1

1. Name the four major ecological regions of Africa. In what general parts of Africa are these regions found?

2. What evidence is there that more people once lived in the Sahara? About when and why did the region become a desert?

3. What items were carried by the caravans that crossed the Sahara?

4. How did herders and farmers help each other?

2 Other features of geography made Africa a land of variety

Some people believe Africa to be covered with "jungles." In fact, however, the rain forests cover only about 20 percent of the African continent. Yet the forests have played a significant role in African history. Rivers, too, have presented opportunities and challenges to the peoples of Africa. And long, long ago, earthquakes left fertile land for the people of the Rift Valley to develop. The peoples of Africa acquired special skills to use these natural features.

The heavy rains influenced life in the forests. The rain forests begin along the southern coast of West Africa and push east and south into the savanna. Rainfall is heavy in all seasons; sometimes more than 7 feet (2.1 meters) of rain fall in a year. Rain and constant warmth make thick forests and towering trees. But the rain forests are not all impassable jungles. Pathways and clearings are common. The tall trees block out the sun's rays, and only a few shade-loving plants grow on the wet floor of the forest. "Jungles" of dense, entangling underbrush appear only where the trees have been cleared by nature or by people or along the edges of the rivers. Here the sun's rays hit the ground, and many, many low plants grow.

The peoples who developed civilizations in the forest had to acquire special skills to overcome the difficulties of living there. They worked hard to build their villages, clear fields, and cultivate small farm plots. Some crops could be grown in the forests that would not grow in the drier savanna. Plantains (a very nutritious type of banana) and yams (a kind of sweet potato) are good examples. Many kinds of fruit also grew in the forests.

The tsetse [tset'sē] fly affected life in the forest. This insect carries a disease known as African sleeping sickness. It kills cattle, horses, and once in a while people when they aren't careful. The tsetse fly probably has been present in the African forests for thousands of years. It thrives in the trees and shrubs of the rain forest.

The tsetse fly also affected transportation in the forests. Donkeys could not be used because they fell victims to African sleeping sickness. Horses could not survive either the disease or the forest climate. Therefore, in forest regions, goods were carried by people who are less susceptible to sleeping sickness than are animals. Africans found that the easiest way to carry a large bundle of heavy goods was by balancing it on their heads. In this way, the entire body, not just the arms or shoulders, supported the weight of the load. Wealthy traders or important chiefs of the forest regions often traveled with many porters who had large boxes or baskets balanced on their heads. This was also the only way that farm produce got to markets in the African forest regions.

The forest affected communication and warfare. Because the use of donkeys and horses was impossible, the African forest kingdoms, such as Asante and Benin, had to rely on foot soldiers in times of war. The soldiers fought hand-to-hand combat among trees and across rivers. They were disciplined and ready to act in case of a sudden change in the battle. They had to rely on their wits since messages reached them slowly.

Drums were sometimes used to send messages in the forest. These drums had strings on their sides which, if pressed in and out, changed the tension of the drumhead and made the sound of the drum higher or lower. The drums did not actually make the sound of a word, but worked more as a bugle does

The artists of Benin made elaborate statues of the tribe's warriors.

in modern armies. Everyone knew that certain patterns of sounds meant certain things, such as to advance, retreat, or prepare for the arrival of the king.

Great states developed among the isolated forest peoples. In the forest, large roads quickly became overgrown with vegetation. This meant that many small groups of people in the forest were isolated from each other. Villages were seldom visited by travelers, traders, or even tribute collectors.

However, large kingdoms were able to repair roads and make large clearings in the forest for their towns. The forest provided wood for strong houses, furniture, and tools. And the regular rainfall yielded good crops. As a result, for hundreds of years, many

A MYSTERY IN HISTORY

WHO WAS THE QUEEN OF SHEBA?

A story in the Bible (I Kings 10:1–13) tells of the visit of the beautiful Queen of Sheba to King Solomon of Israel.

The Queen wanted to see if Solomon was as wise and rich as people said he was. She found that he was more wise and wealthy than all the rumors had claimed, so she stayed and visited with him for several months. Solomon, the Bible says, enjoyed her company. When she was ready to return to her own country, he gave her many gifts and granted all her requests.

But where was the country of the Queen of Sheba? No one is certain. Some scholars say it was in the southern Arabian peninsula. But the people of Ethiopia in Africa believe it was their country and that the Queen of Sheba was their queen.

Ethiopian documents dating from the 4th century A.D. tell the story of Solomon and the Queen almost as the Bible does. But they add something. They say that the Queen's name was Makeda [mə kä′də], and that while she was in Jerusalem, Solomon fell in love with her. He asked her to marry him, but Makeda refused. Solomon then agreed not to marry her unless he could find her guilty of taking something from his palace.

Makeda consented to this arrangement, confident she would never take anything from Solomon.

But Solomon was very clever. That same night he served Makeda a very spicy, salty dinner. During the night she became so thirsty that she got up and took a drink of water. Solomon was watching. He leaped up and claimed his right to marry her immediately because she had taken water that was his. When Makeda later returned to her own country, she gave birth to a son of Solomon.

This son, the Ethiopians claim, was their first king, called Menelik I [me′nə lik]. When he grew up, he is said to have ruled justly and to have introduced the laws of Judaism into Ethiopia. All the kings of Ethiopia, even into the 20th century, claimed direct descent from Solomon and the Queen of Sheba, Makeda.

In about 330 A.D., the king of ancient Ethiopia converted to Christianity. After that, the story of Solomon and the Queen of Sheba became even more popular with the Ethiopian Christians. They believed the story provided an important link between themselves and the Jewish people and Jesus.

Could the details of the story be true? Could the Queen of Sheba have come from Ethiopia? There was a very powerful kingdom in Ethiopia from about 500 B.C. to 600 A.D. It was called Axum. Axum conquered many states, including Kush, traded with India, made its own gold coins, and had its own written language. An early queen of Axum could have traveled to visit the famous King Solomon in 900 B.C. Whether she did or not, historians may never know, but Ethiopians have been convinced of it for centuries.

Africans have lived in the forest. Powerful kingdoms such as Asante and Benin [bə-nēn'] developed.

Four rivers have been important to Africa's economic history. Four great rivers, the Niger, the Nile, the Zambezi [zam bē'zē], and the Congo, flow through the savanna and forest regions. Towns, farms, and markets dot the river valleys. Farmers settled near rivers because the yearly flooding renewed the fertility of the soil. Fishermen used the rivers to earn a living; traders used them for traveling.

Canoes were used for transportation on the rivers, and large barges carried loads of goods, animals, and people for long distances, especially on the Nile and the Niger. Flat-bottomed boats holding up to 100 tons of goods transported items for hundreds of miles (kilometers) along the Niger River. In other parts of Africa, rivers do not provide long, smooth stretches of water for boat travel. Rapids, waterfalls, and rocks interrupt their streams. Goods transported on these rivers had to be unloaded frequently and carried overland because of the poor water systems.

Civilization developed in the Rift Valley. In East Africa, a region called the Rift Valley was formed by earthquakes and volcanoes millions of years ago. High mountains tower over this deep valley that extends for hundreds of miles. So high are the mountains that snow and ice stay on them all year-round, even though they are located near the equator. In the valley, the soil is very fertile and the climate is pleasant. Large lakes provide a ready source of water year-round, as well as good fishing.

The great variety and quantity of foods available on the shores of Lake Victoria contributed to the growth of a healthy, agricultural population with strong government.

Legends tell about the people who were ruled by warrior kings called the Chwezi [chə wā'zē]. As long ago as 1000 A.D., say the legends, the Chwezi kings, more than 8 feet (2.3 meters) tall, ruled the land without fear. It was said you could not look a Chwezi in the face, because his eyes were so bright that it was like looking at the sun.

section review 2

1. About what percentage of Africa's land is covered by rain forests?
2. What effect did the tsetse fly have on the transportation methods of the forest societies of Africa?
3. Name the four major rivers of Africa. Why were many other rivers in Africa unsuitable for travel?
4. Why were many people able to live good lives in the Rift Valley?

3 The peoples of ancient Africa developed many practical skills

Early peoples of Africa hunted, fished, and gathered wild grain. The artists of the Sahara, whose rock-paintings show these ways of life, lived before the development of farming. However, after the Sahara dried up and some of the peoples moved south into the savanna, they developed farming methods and other skills.

African farmers learned to grow different crops in different areas. Farming probably began in Africa in the Nile Valley. However, wheat and barley, which were good crops along the Nile, did not grow well in the savanna. The savanna people of the Niger River Valley had to experiment to find plants they could cultivate. Beginning about 2000 B.C., they grew African rice, which does not need large amounts of water, and they grew millet. None of these crops, however, grew well in the forest. By 500 B.C., the forest peoples had learned to grow yams. About the same time, Indian sailors landed small boats in East Africa. They brought with them the plantain, which added more nutrition to the African diet. These new foods made it possible for larger numbers of people to live in Africa.

The soil in the savanna and forests of Africa was often not very fertile, because the rain and sun removed many of the nutrients that helped plants grow. African farmers observed this and learned to let the land lie fallow to regain the nutrients needed for another good crop. Also, African farmers had to find and clear new land continually, which required a lot of hard work.

For the past 3,000 years, farms in most of Africa have been cultivated by hoes, not plows. Farming with hoes requires much more work, but the plow is not suitable for the poor African soils, because it cuts too deeply. A plow turns up unfertile soil and increases erosion.

Herders brought domesticated animals to Africa. Cattle, sheep, and goats were not native to Africa. These animals were imported to northern Egypt and then south along the Nile River. By 2000 B.C., the people in East Africa had become herders. Some societies that developed were based entirely on herding and raising cattle. The life of people in such a society was *pastoral*, that is, it revolved around the care of the cattle.

Pastoral children learned at an early age to watch and tend cattle. They knew every animal in their family's herd by name. The children sang songs to the animals, much as cowboys of the American West sang songs to quiet their herds of cattle. One of these, sung today by African children, calls God the finest white cow who must protect the herd:

White cow of heaven, you have fed in rich
   pastures
And you who were small have grown
   great.
White cow of heaven, your horns have
   curved full circle
And are joined as one.
White cow of heaven, we throw at you the
   dust
Which your feet have trampled in our kraals
   [corrals]
White cow of heaven, give your blessing on
   the kraals
Which you have overseen
So that the udders of our cows may be
   heavy
And that our women may rejoice.

Adults in pastoral societies measured their wealth by how many cattle they owned. Cattle were important for milk and were considered too valuable to butcher regularly. But the occasional weak or aged animal was killed for meat.

The use of iron changed the lives of many Africans. About 500 B.C., ironworking became common in Egypt, where it had been introduced by the Hittites. Historians are not certain how Africans far away from Egypt learned to make iron. Perhaps the knowledge spread from Egypt along ancient trade routes. However, in western Africa along the Niger River archaeologists have found ironworking sites that date from about 400 B.C.— almost the same time that iron became common in Egypt. It is probable that the skill of ironmaking developed independently in western Africa about the same time that the Egyptians learned about it.

The use of iron caused major changes in Africa. Iron tools were stronger and longer-lasting than stone or wood ones. These stronger tools made it possible to grow more food and feed more people. Better hunting weapons meant more meat for the community. And strong weapons meant that people

As early as 3100 B.C., Kush noblemen visited Egypt. The wall paintings of Pharaoh Seti I show a parade of Egyptians and Kushites at Seti's funeral.

were not as afraid to venture into strange lands, because they could protect themselves. Between 100 A.D. and 1000 A.D., great migrations into central and southern Africa took place as population expanded. These are called the Bantu migrations, from the name of the group of languages that most of these people spoke. Much of Africa became settled by people as a result of the Bantu migrations and the use of iron.

Kush was an important ironworking center.
The African kingdom of Kush flourished from about 750 B.C. to 150 A.D. It was located south of Egypt on the Nile River, in what is today the country of Sudan. The Kushites had been Egyptian subjects. About 750 B.C., they invaded and conquered Egypt. The Kushite kings made themselves the 25th dynasty of the pharaohs of Egypt. By about 630 B.C., the Kushites were no longer able to defend Egypt against outside attacks and were driven back to their own land. There they continued to rule independently from their capital of Meroe [mə rō']. Around Meroe were valuable iron ore deposits that the Kushites learned to use. By the first century B.C., Meroe was carrying on a lively iron trade with Egypt, Arabia, India, what is now Ethiopia, and portions of Africa farther south.

Today, Meroe is uninhabited. However, the extensive heaps of iron refuse and ruins of brick palaces, pyramids, temples, and homes attest to Kush's greatness. Lovely jewelry and iron utensils and chairs have been found in the ruins. Kush kings and queens were buried with iron weapons and artifacts. Kush had its own hieroglyphics, which modern-day scholars have been unable to read. This makes it difficult to know exactly what happened in Kush during the centuries of rule from Meroe and what brought this kingdom to an end. However, Kush's importance as a trade, ironworking, and cultural center is certain from its archaeological remains.

The pyramids at Meroe are vivid examples of the city's former grandeur.

1. What kinds of crops were first grown in Africa?

2. Describe the importance of cattle in a pastoral society.

3. What were the Bantu migrations?

4. Why is little known about the details of the kingdom of Kush?

4 Ancient Africans developed distinctive societies and cultures

The increasing use of iron and the advances in tools, farming techniques, food plants, and trade laid the foundations for African civilizations over the centuries. In Africa, as in other parts of the world, improved farming meant more food. This meant that everyone in the community did not need to work at getting food. Therefore some people could pursue other occupations. Specialists such as miners, potters, metalsmiths, and political and religious leaders could devote all their time to developing their skills.

Lineage was the basis of tribal organization.
Government in African tribal societies was a matter of custom based on family relationships. Persons in a tribe belonged to subsections, called *lineages* [lin'ē ə jəz]. It was through a person's lineage that he or she had a place in tribal society.

A lineage is several generations of a people who are all descended from the same person—usually a great-great-great-great-grandfather though sometimes a great-great-great-great-grandmother. Most people in Africa belonged to the lineage of their father, although in some societies, people belonged to the lineage of their mother's brother instead.

A lineage took care of its own members. It gave food and money to those who were in

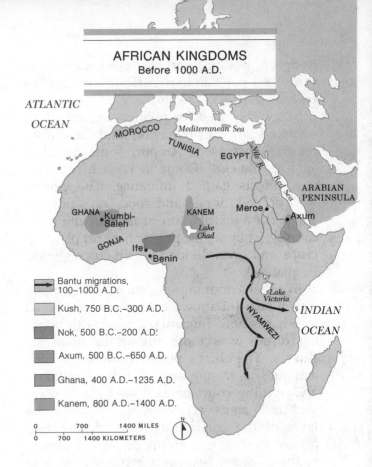

AFRICAN KINGDOMS
Before 1000 A.D.

Bantu migrations, 100–1000 A.D.

Kush, 750 B.C.–300 A.D.

Nok, 500 B.C.–200 A.D.

Axum, 500 B.C.–650 A.D.

Ghana, 400 A.D.–1235 A.D.

Kanem, 800 A.D.–1400 A.D.

trouble. If a person committed a crime, it was the responsibility of the lineage to pay the fine and make certain that the criminal was punished. Widows, orphans, the old, and the sick were taken care of by their lineage. Individuals knew their own status in the lineage and treated older members with respect. Tribes recognized a few of the oldest members, called elders, as their leaders. The kings, chiefs, and elders in a tribe often had to come from certain lineages.

A village in Africa was usually composed of several lineages. People in the same lineage lived in different houses. Most households were made up of small family groups. Especially in farming communities, a husband, his wife or wives, and their unmarried children lived together in one house. Each of these households worked their own farm separately. Special activities, such as house-building and some harvests, required other members of the lineage to help.

Religion, politics, and law became important. As sub-Saharan African societies increased in size and skills from the 1st century A.D. on, the need for political organization, accepted rules of behavior, and an official religion increased. Among some peoples, such as the early Gonja in West Africa, certain priests gained influence. The priests who prayed for rain and good crops came to control the distribution of land in the community. They set the proper time for planting crops and even decided which crops should be planted.

In other communities, such as the many Nyamwezi [nī'am wē'zē] groups who lived in what is now Tanzania, a chief with political duties was more important than the priests. The chief's power came from such activities as raising armies, collecting taxes, and settling court cases. Cases about taxes and trade were very common. Although the laws of the community were not written down, everyone knew the laws and agreed to them. These laws were remembered, and much care was taken to pass them on from generation to generation. A chief, although he was very powerful, had to conform to the laws of the community. Eloquent debating in court cases was a skill practiced by many young Africans who wanted to be leaders.

Historians were respected in West Africa. Knowledge of events and laws of the past became more important as societies grew larger and more complex. Kings wanted to know who their ancestors had been and what brave deeds they had done. Other people wanted to know how land had been divided and how taxes had been paid so they would not be cheated. In most of Africa, however, local languages were not written. Although the Arabic language was both written and spoken in Africa after about 650 A.D., most of Africa's peoples did not use it. As a result, history and laws were memorized.

In West Africa, a special group of people

called griots [grē'ōz] were the professional record keepers, historians, and political advisers to chiefs. Griots were living libraries of information about their society's past.

To become a griot, a young man underwent a long, careful education. He traveled from village to village, studying under famous griots, learning all they had to teach, memorizing everything. Kings and other important people in West Africa always had a griot attached to their families. He was given food, clothing, and shelter in exchange for poems about the family. Having a griot insured that the family's name and deeds would be remembered. The griot also entertained the family with poems and stories of the tribe's history. If a noble family fell on hard times, the members often would sell their horses and all their belongings before they would dismiss the family griot.

Through griots, history has been passed on from generation to generation for at least the last eight centuries. Some griots today can remember detailed family histories that go back more than 200 years and know the brave deeds of kings of 700 years ago.

Early Africans made outstanding sculpture. Sculpture and wood carvings depicting people and animals were the most common art form in ancient Africa. Sometimes, the carvings were decorated with ivory. Some were

The artisans of Benin, Nok, and Ife all made stylized statues of their kings, priests, and nobles. Some statues, such as at *left* were terra cotta; others, such as at *center* and *right* were bronze.

very realistic, while others showed people with exaggerated faces and bodies. Statues of kings and queens were sometimes covered with symbols of their reign; these were especially common in the area now called Zaïre.

Unfortunately, wood does not last long in the African climate. As a result, the oldest remaining wood carvings were made only 400 years ago. Clay, on the other hand, lasts much longer. Some clay sculptured heads have been found near the town of Nok, Nigeria. These sculptures were made as early as 500 B.C. The heads were made in a uniform style with exaggerated lips and eyes. But there is no doubt that they are human faces and were made by very skilled artists, probably for religious purposes.

About 1100 A.D., sculptors in the kingdom of Ife [ē'fā], in present-day Nigeria, began making beautiful bronze sculptures. These sculptors developed a method of bronze casting known as the *lost-wax process*. In this process, the artist made a model of the sculpture in wax. Because the wax was soft, it could be sculpted in delicate detail. The wax model was then covered with clay and heated. As the wax melted away, its form was left in the clay. Then, melted bronze was poured into the clay form. When the bronze cooled, the clay was washed away and an exact bronze copy of the wax original remained. The bronze sculptures of Ife, made by this pro-

cess, are some of the world's best sculpture.

The people of Benin learned the lost-wax process from the people of Ife. By the 15th century, the Benin people were not only making beautiful sculptures of peoples and animals, but also wall plaques, hundreds of which have been found. These plaques show military and historical events from Benin's past. Great heroes, famous battles, the coronations of kings, and wealthy traders were portrayed on the plaques.

These early African art objects are sought and prized by art collectors all over the world today. And the stylized form influenced modern artists such as Pablo Picasso.

section review 4

1. What function did lineage relationships play in African society?

2. From what group of people did leaders come in the Gonja community? In the Nyamwezi?

3. Why did West African kings need griots?

4. Describe the three steps in the lost-wax method of sculpture.

Section Summaries

1. Much of Africa is desert and savanna. The continent of Africa has several different ecological regions. In the north and south are narrow regions of fertile coast. Farther inland are deserts—the Sahara in the north and the Kalahari in the south. Camels have ensured African trade and contact across the Sahara. The deserts of Africa merge into large regions of savanna where populations have prospered because of the farming and herding that are possible there.

2. Other features of geography made Africa a land of variety. In the west-central section of the continent is the rain forest. Fruits and vegetables grow well here, but the tsetse fly has prevented the raising of cattle and horses. The rivers of Africa connected the villages and cities that dot the valleys. Canoes and barges carried trading goods on the rivers. In East Africa, ancient earthquakes and volcanoes formed a mountain, valley, and lake region called the Rift Valley. Legends of the glorious Chwezi kings suggest that people have lived in this pleasant and fertile region for centuries.

3. The peoples of ancient Africa developed many practical skills. Useful farming methods, specialized cattle-raising, and ironworking helped Africans grow more food and control their environment. The Bantu migrations populated central and southern Africa. One of the earliest ironworking sites in Africa developed in the ancient kingdom of Kush.

4. Ancient Africans developed distinctive societies and cultures. Tribal groups and lineages formed the basis of African societies. Every person was expected to know his or her position in the lineage and to act in a way proper for that role. Priests became important in some groups, while in other groups political chiefs became powerful. Law and history were memorized and passed from generation to generation. Griots in West Africa had the job of studying history and remembering it for the whole community. Cultural advances were also made in early Africa.

Some societies had long traditions of art, particularly sculpture. The clay heads of Nok and the bronze sculpture of Ife and Benin are considered to be some of the best sculpture in the world.

Who? What? When? Where?

1. Write an identifying sentence for each of the following groups:
   a. Asante
   b. Bantu
   c. Chwezi
   d. Gonja
   e. Kulango
   f. Kushites
   g. Nyamwezi

2. Write a sentence for each of these terms that tells its importance:
   a. caravan
   b. cattle
   c. compound
   d. fallow
   e. griots
   f. lineage
   g. oases
   h. plantain
   i. tribe
   j. tsetse fly

3. Make a time line that shows the following events:
   a. The people of Nok began making clay sculpture.
   b. The Bantu migrations took place.
   c. Farming began in the Niger River Valley.
   d. The Kingdom of Kush flourished.
   e. Bronze sculpture was first made in Ife.
   f. Ironworking became common in Egypt.

4. What are the four major ecological areas of Africa?

Questions for Critical Thinking

1. Why were the Kulango unable to adjust to life in Asante? Can you think of any difficulties people might be having today in trying to start life again in a new place? Explain.

2. What might be some reasons little has been known about African history and culture until recently?

3. In what ways do people of different occupations exchange goods today similar to the cooperation between farmers and herders of the African savanna?

4. Has studying this chapter changed your ideas about Africa? If so, how?

5. How does the geography of an area encourage people to develop special skills? Give specific examples from African history and from life today.

Skill Activities

1. Read *Plays from African Folktales* by Carol Karty to find out more about the cultures of Africa. (Charles Scribner's Sons, 1975)

2. Find out what is happening in the countries near the borders of the Sahara today. Is the size of the desert still changing? Why? What effect is this having on the people who live there?

3. Show the four ecological areas of Africa on a map. Find pictures illustrating the different ways of life followed in these areas today.

4. Discuss in class the responsibilities of families toward their members today and compare these responsibilities with the traditional African lineage system.

5. Write an African folk tale based on the ways of life explained in this chapter.

6. Find pictures of different examples of African sculpture and wood carving. How are they different from modern art? How are they the same?

chapter **12** *quiz*

Section 1

1. True or false: The Sahara always has been an impassable boundary between North and South Africa.

2. An important animal to the people of the Sahara was the: a. cow, b. camel, c. donkey

3. Most African people have lived in the: a. desert, b. savanna, c. forest

Section 2

4. Cattle cannot be raised in the African forest because of: a. lions, b. tsetse flies, c. custom

5. An important forest kingdom was that of: a. Niger, b. Benin, c. Masai

6. True or false: Plantain and yams became important crops to forest people.

Section 3

7. A pastoral society is one whose culture is based on: a. herding, b. farming, c. fishing

8. True or false: Archaeologists have learned about the Kushites from their hieroglyphics.

9. Farmlands in Africa were cultivated with: a. hoes, b. plows, c. shovels

Section 4

10. In African society, a group of people who are descended from the same person is a: a. tribe, b. lineage, c. compound

11. The lost-wax process was used to make: a. candles, b. iron tools, c. bronze sculptures

12. True or false: The priests were the most important leaders in all African societies.

AFRICAN CIVILIZATIONS SOUTH OF THE SAHARA

This map was made in 1347. It shows Mansa Musa, the wealthy king of Mali, waiting for the arrival of a trader. The map shows the North Africa coast much as it is but shows the Atlas Mountains as a rock wall.

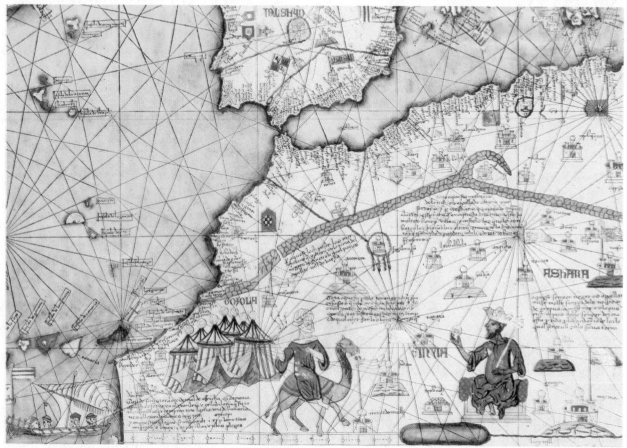

Dixon Denham did not know what to expect. He had heard contradictory stories about the kingdom of Kanem-Bornu, but no European had seen this part of Africa. It was 1823, and he would be the first.

Denham rode ahead of his companions toward the African kingdom. Suddenly, in front of him appeared several thousand cavalry. The soldiers were dressed in chain mail, and their horses were decorated with quilted cloth and metal coverings. The African cav-

alry remained steady until Denham's fellow travelers caught up with him. Then a shout rang out from the leaders of the force. Trumpets blew. And the cavalry charged to welcome them:

There was an appearance of tact and management in their movements which astonished me: Three separate small bodies, from the centre of each flank, kept charging rapidly towards us, to within a few feet of our horses' heads, without checking the speed of their own until the moment of their halt, while the whole body moved onwards. These parties . . . [were] mounted on small very perfect horses who stopped and wheeled from their utmost speed with great precision and expertness, shaking their spears over their heads, exclaiming "Barka! Barka! [that is] . . . Blessing, Blessing!"

Denham and his party were surprised to find so powerful a cavalry and so well-administered an empire in the interior of Africa. Europeans for centuries had had only wisps of information about Africa. Sometimes, it was hinted that there were cities of gold. Other rumors told of vast stretches of uninhabited rain forest. Yet, large empires had been rising and falling and replacing each other in Africa for centuries. These empires were based on trade, education, effective governments, and cities.

Long trade routes across the desert had been tapping the gold supplies of West Africa. And great empires flourished on this trade. Sea routes across the Indian Ocean kept East Africa in constant communication with India and China. Islam spread across West Africa in waves of religious revival that were both violent and inspiring. Powerful states developed in the rain forest. This chapter describes some of the highly developed civilizations south of the Sahara:

1. Famous empires grew in the West African savanna.

2. City-states flourished along the East African coast.

3. The kingdom of Zimbabwe developed in the interior.

4. Islam stimulated new states in West Africa.

5. The forest states developed strong governments.

1 Famous empires grew in the West African savanna

The Sahara can be compared to an ocean. It is crossed by the "ship of the desert," the camel. And, just as cities grow up on ocean coasts, cities grew up on the edge of the desert. The towns in the Sudan (a name for the northern savanna of Africa that should not be confused with the modern nation of that name) were much like port cities. For more than eight centuries, they took their turn as capitals of three powerful empires: Ghana, Mali, and Songhai.

Gold was exchanged for salt across the Sahara. A rich gold-mining area lay in a wide forest region called Wangara [wäng-gä′rə] near the sources of the Niger, Senegal, and Gambia rivers. Gold from Wangara was the basis for profitable trade as far back as ancient Roman times because it was prized by the rich and powerful of many nations.

Traders brought the gold through the forests to the savanna. There, they were met by other traders from the cities of the North African coast who exchanged goods for the gold and carried it across the Sahara to cities on the Mediterranean Sea. From there, much of the gold was shipped for sale in Europe and Asia.

One important item needed by the West Africans was salt. It is an essential item in people's diets; without it they will die. People who live in hot climates need even more salt than those who live in cooler places. There were very few salt deposits in West Africa except along the Atlantic coast and in places in the Sahara that once were salt lakes.

A place named Taghaza [tə gä′zə] developed near a salt deposit in the Sahara. It became a major stop on the trade routes. The gold mines of Wangara now are exhausted, but there is still plenty of salt near Taghaza.

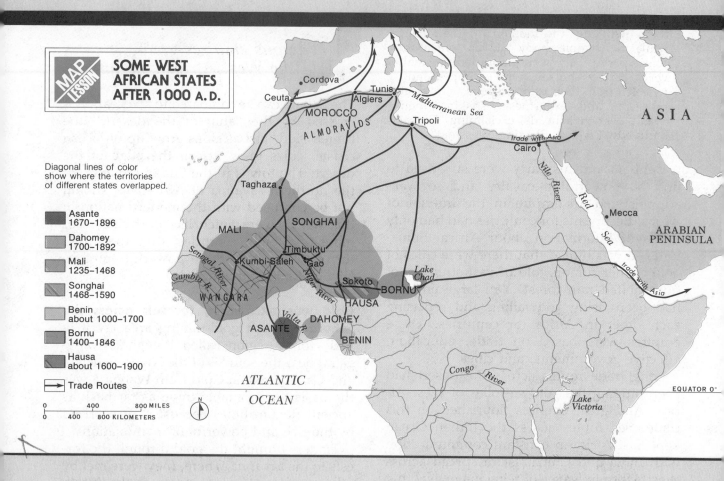

SOME WEST
AFRICAN STATES
AFTER 1000 A.D.

Diagonal lines of color
show where the territories
of different states overlapped.

Asante
1670–1896

Dahomey
1700–1892

Mali
1235–1468

Songhai
1468–1590

Benin
about 1000–1700

Bornu
1400–1846

Hausa
about 1600–1900

Trade Routes

0   400   800 MILES
0 400   800 KILOMETERS

N

ATLANTIC
OCEAN

Cordova
Ceuta
MOROCCO
ALMORAVIDS
Tunis
Algiers
Mediterranean Sea
Tripoli
ASIA
Trade with Asia
Cairo
Nile River
Red Sea
Mecca
ARABIAN
PENINSULA
Taghaza
MALI
SONGHAI
Senegal River
Gambia R.
Kumbi-Saleh
Timbuktu
Gao
Niger River
WANGARA
Sokoto
HAUSA
Lake Chad
BORNU
Volta R.
DAHOMEY
ASANTE
BENIN
Congo River
EQUATOR 0°
Lake
Victoria
Trade with Asia

■ MAP LESSON 13: SOME WEST AFRICAN STATES AFTER 1000 A.D.

1. This is really two maps in one. The first shows major trade routes during the thirteenth century. The second is a historical map showing the location of West African states over some nine centuries. It shows change over time. Particular areas belonged to one state at one time and to another state at a different time. Thus, the town of Sokoto belonged to Songhai during the 15th and 16th centuries and later belonged to the Hausa. During what years did the city of Taghaza belong to Songhai?

2. The cartographer has indicated change over time by combining colors in alternating strips. For example, the alternating green and orange strips show that Mali and Songhai controlled the same

territory at different times. Name three cities that were controlled by Mali and Songhai over the years.

3. Study the map and decide which of the following statements are true and which are false:

a. The Songhai controlled the largest area of all the states shown.

b. Bornu controlled Lake Chad during the time that Songhai controlled the Gambia River.

c. The state of Mali arose after the Hausa declined.

d. Asante arose at about the same time that Benin declined.

e. Most of the territory of the Hausa was later controlled by Dahomey.

Even today, caravans of camels and jeeps come to Taghaza to buy salt for the people in the savanna.

The 10th-century A.D. Arab geographer al-Masudi described what has come to be called the "silent trade." He said that traders from the north crossed the desert and came to a certain place in the Sudan, possibly on the banks of the Niger River. At this place every year, they laid their goods—salt, cloth, and copper—on the ground. Then, they beat their drums to let the people of the savanna know the market was ready, and withdrew a half-day's journey away.

Next, the savanna people came and placed piles of gold beside the goods in as large a quantity as they thought them worth. Then, they too went a half-day's journey away, beating drums to signal merchants from the north.

The North Africans returned, and, if they thought the price was right, they took the gold and left. If not, they withdrew again to wait for the savanna traders to put down more gold. The exchange went on for several days until both groups were satisfied with the price. Neither group of traders ever saw or spoke with the other. This trade probably developed because Africans wanted the goods of other regions but wanted to keep the source of their own valuable goods a secret from outsiders. Thus they prevented foreigners from learning about their country or even learning their language.

The silent trade took place in other parts of Africa as well. The 4th-century B.C. Greek historian Herodotus described it going on in the northwest coast of Africa. And a 6th-century A.D. Greek trader saw it in East Africa.

Ancient Ghana controlled the gold trade (400–1235). About 400 A.D., the kingdom of Ghana [gä'nə] began to develop in the Sudan. It should not be confused with the modern country of the same name, which is far to the south of ancient Ghana. Ancient Ghana grew near the marketplace of the gold traders, and its power came from its location.

By the end of the 7th century, the people of the Muslim world began to write about Ghana as the spread of Islam brought Arabs in contact with West Africans. From the writings of Arab geographers, we know that by this time Ghana was a large empire based on trade and agriculture. Its strong central government was ruled by a king who appointed the different officers of the kingdom and who was the final judge of all court cases. Ghana's ruler was believed to be partly divine and able to talk with the gods for the good of the empire.

The king claimed the right to own all the gold nuggets that came from the mines of Wangara. Other people could trade only in gold dust. With this right, the king of Ghana could control the economy by holding back gold nuggets from trade if the price was not right. In addition to owning all the gold nuggets, the empire taxed all goods, including salt and gold, entering and leaving Ghana.

The twin cities of Kumbi-Saleh [kŭm'bē-sä'lə] made up the capital of ancient Ghana. The king and his officers lived in one town; merchants and strangers lived in the other. The towns, located on the edge of the Sahara, were about 6 miles (10 kilometers) apart. Between the two towns were the small mud houses of the people who grew food to support the inhabitants of the capital.

The king's town was built like a fortress. Whenever the king appeared in public, he was surrounded by servants carrying gold swords. The princes and advisers of the empire, in splendid dress, accompanied him. Horses with gold cloth blankets and dogs with gold and silver collars were also part of his parade.

A powerful army protected the kingdom and helped the king control the large variety of peoples within its boundaries. In 1067, the

Arab writer al-Bakri wrote that the army was made up of 200 thousand warriors.

The traders' town was made up of two-story stone houses and public squares. After the 7th century A.D., mosques were built there because many of the traders were Muslim. The kings and farmers of Ghana, however, kept their old religious customs.

In the 11th century, a group of Muslim Berbers, the Almoravids [al'mə rä'vidz] lived northwest of Ghana. The Almoravids believed in living a very strict religious life. And they believed it was their mission to stamp out wickedness and convert people to Islam. In 1076, they attacked Kumbi-Saleh in order to make the people there better Muslims. The Almoravids occupied the capital for about ten years, and then the people of Ghana won it back.

Ghana never recovered from the occupation. Great damage had been done. The many provinces of Ghana no longer obeyed the weakened Ghana government. Many merchants moved from Kumbi-Saleh to other trading towns on the edge of the desert. Within fifty years, an army from one of the provinces conquered Ghana, and a new empire emerged that became larger and more prosperous than Ghana had been.

Trade and learning flourished in Mali (1235–1468). Sundiata [sùn'dē ä'tə] was the leader of a province of Ghana called Mali [mä'lē]. The king of Ghana had had eleven of Sundiata's brothers murdered so that the province would not be a threat to Ghana. But these measures did not stop Mali's ambitions. In 1235, Sundiata led his people to victory over the last king of Ghana.

During the years of his rule, Sundiata conquered vast territories and Mali became an empire. He brought the gold- and salt-mining areas under his control. Traders now penetrated deep into both these regions, and the silent trade died out everywhere as commerce flourished. Sundiata became a hero to his people much as George Washington is to the people of the United States.

One of the most famous *mansas*, or kings, of Mali was Sundiata's nephew Mansa Musa [män'sə mü'sə]. His rule began in 1307. Mansa Musa was a Muslim, for by this time the rulers of Mali were Muslim. Most of the common people, however, were not Muslim. It is said that the gold miners in Wangara once threatened to strike when Mansa Musa tried to force them to become Muslims.

In 1324, Mansa Musa set out on his pilgrimage to Mecca. It was an amazing journey. Records tell of thousands of servants, gifts of gold and ivory, and a caravan of camels, horses, and slaves. When his caravan reached Cairo, Egypt, it brought so much gold, spent so much, and gave so much to the poor that the value of gold in Cairo dropped for at least twelve years.

The gold trade brought Mali great wealth. The empire was the supplier of gold to Europe, though many Europeans did not know that this was where the gold was coming from. *Guinea* [gin'ē] gold was used for the coins of the northern Italian city-states of the fourteenth century. (*Guinea* is an old word for West Africa.)

The city of Timbuktu, located on the bend in the Niger River, was the cultural center of Mali. Scholars from the Muslim world came to study the manuscripts stored in its huge library. The conversion to Islam had brought the kings of Mali in contact with the Arabic language, both spoken and written. Mansa Musa's pilgrimage had served as an advertisement of the wealth of his country. Arab scholars and travelers came to Timbuktu to see Mali for themselves.

WHAT'S IN A NAME?
TIMBUKTU
The word *Timbuktu* means a "hollow." The city is built in a hollow among the sandhills, near the course of a dry creek.

The globe-trotting Muslim traveler, Ibn Batuta, visited Timbuktu in 1352 and stayed in Mali for eight months. He found that the people had a strong sense of justice; wrongdoers were quickly punished. Both the city streets and countryside were safer places than any he had noted in his wide travels. He also wrote about the women of Mali. Unlike many other places in the Islamic world, women here were not kept out of public sight and were not required to obey their husbands. He met Mali women who were educated. Ibn Batuta was impressed by the wealth, comfortable living, and great amount of trade that he saw.

When the first European saw Timbuktu in 1828, he marveled at the difficulties the city builders had overcome.

The Songhai Empire (1468–1590) replaced Mali. After Mansa Musa's death, Mali had a series of rulers who were not able to control the huge empire. Many provinces struggled to seize power. One was Songhai [song' hī] with its capital Gao [gow] not far from Timbuktu.

In 1468, Sonni Ali [son'ē ä lē'], the king of Songhai, attacked and captured Timbuktu. He then went on to capture many other cities of Mali. Sonni Ali ruled for thirty-five years. They were years of persecutions and warfare. At his death, one of his generals became head of the empire.

Sonni Ali had been a man of the countryside. He had failed to understand or help the people of the towns. He had judged their dissatisfaction as disloyalty and had been ruthless in his treatment of them. His reaction to a revolt in Timbuktu had been such widespread slaughter that he gained a permanent reputation as a ruthless tyrant. His successor reversed this policy.

Askia [äs kē'yə] Mohammad, Sonni Ali's successor, came to power in 1493. During his thirty-five-year reign, the empire grew to include most of the grasslands of West Africa. It reached from the Atlantic Ocean halfway across Africa to Lake Chad, from what is today the southern border of Algeria south to the edge of the rain forest. He was an able administrator who gave the empire an improved system of government.

Askia Mohammad understood that the wealth of the empire depended on the commerce of the towns. He set up a fair method of taxation and a good system of communication with the provinces. He encouraged the Muslim religion. Most of the townspeople, especially the traders, were Muslims. Timbuktu reached new heights as a center for scholarship. A visitor in the early 16th century wrote this description:

> The rich king of Timbuktu has many plates and sceptres of gold, some whereof weigh 1300 pounds; and he keeps a magnificent and well-furnished court. . . . Here are a great store of doctors, judges, priests and other learned men, that are bountifully maintained at the king's cost and charges. And hither are brought divers manuscripts of written books out of Barbary [North Africa] which are sold for more money than any other merchandise.

Songhai was probably the most highly organized and efficient of all the early West African states. Its wealth and power aroused the jealousy of Morocco in North Africa. The Songhai rulers who came after Askia Mohammad were not as powerful as he had been. In 1590, the king of Morocco equipped an army of about 5,000 men to cross the Sahara and attack Songhai. Only about 1,000 of the Moroccan soldiers survived the crossing. But they had brought with them guns and gunpowder, which were superior to the swords and spears of the Songhai army. The Moroccans were able to beat the Songhai army, but they were not able to hold the empire together. During the following years, large numbers of provinces, cities, and small groups broke away and began to govern themselves. This large and powerful empire in West Africa came to an end.

section review 1

1. What was the silent trade? What goods were traded? Who was involved? Why was it silent?

2. Name three sources of the king of Ghana's power. How did the empire of Ghana fall?

3. What was life in Timbuktu like during the Mali Empire? Describe the religion, education, economy, and role of women.

4. In what ways was Askia Mohammad a different kind of ruler than Sonni Ali?

2 City-states flourished along the East African coast

More than 2,000 years ago, people from India and Arabia sailed westward looking for new sources of trade. The monsoon winds, or trade winds, of the Indian Ocean blew steadily toward East Africa for months and then steadily back toward India for months giving sailors a safe, direct route. By about 120 A.D., a guide published in Egypt told where ports could be found along the East African coast.

The 7th-century expansion of Islamic trade caused the East African and Indian Ocean trade to boom. A distinctive culture developed in East African city-states blending Islamic and Asian cultures and languages with that of the native Africans. Then, in the 16th century, Portuguese traders nearly destroyed the economic life of the coast. But this distinctive culture has survived to the present.

International trade was the basis of East African civilization. As in West Africa, there were large supplies of gold in East Africa. Ivory, which came from the tusks of the African elephant, was another valuable trade item. It was strong but soft enough to be carved into objects that were both beautiful and useful. Chessmen and even thrones were carved from African ivory. Ivory was in great demand in the Muslim Empire, India, and China. A third item of export was East African iron, considered of high quality and carried to all the markets of Asia where it was made into strong, sharp weapons.

Asian and Arab traders brought cotton cloth and porcelain utensils to sell in East Africa. Chinese porcelain was especially prized; East Africans built small niches in the walls of their homes to display the finer pieces. Along the coasts of modern-day Kenya and Tanzania, broken pieces of very old Chinese cups, saucers, and vases lie in the sand, evidence of the trade that took place many centuries ago.

City-states developed from East African ports. In response to the centuries-old trade, coastal marketplaces developed into large cities. Traders from Africa and the Mid-

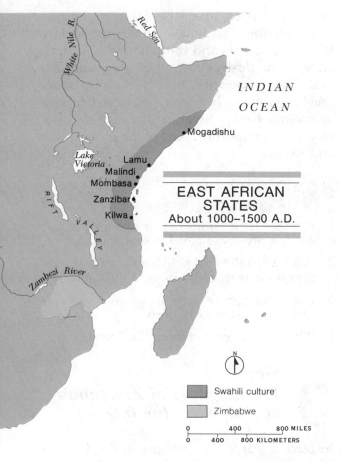

INDIAN
OCEAN

• Mogadishu

EAST AFRICAN STATES
About 1000–1500 A.D.

Lamu
Malindi
Mombasa
Zanzibar
Kilwa

Swahili culture
Zimbabwe

0   400   800 MILES
0   400   800 KILOMETERS

White Nile R.
Red Sea
Lake Victoria
RIFT VALLEY
Zambezi River

main palace of Kilwa stood on the very edge of a cliff overlooking the ocean. It had more than one hundred rooms and an eight-sided bathing pool in one of its many courtyards.

Kilwa was only one of several important trading towns. Each had its own ruler, government, laws, taxes, and small police force. The influence of each of these city-states spread a certain distance from the city itself, sometimes all along a trade route to the interior. Each city-state was in fierce competition with the others.

Swahili culture thrived in the city-states.
The African, Indian, and Arab traders who settled in the port cities intermarried and had large families. Eventually a way of living called *Swahili culture* grew up. Swahili [swä hē'lē] is the name of the language the coastal peoples spoke. It is an African language with many Indian and Arabic words mixed in. Swahili was written in Arabic script until modern times. (Today it is sometimes written in the English alphabet.) The Swahili people wrote poetry and stories in both Arabic and Swahili.

Life in the city-states was comfortable. People were free to practice the religious beliefs of their choice. The Arab influence caused some to convert to Islam. But most Swahili people kept to traditional African religions.

Swahili peoples kept in touch with distant lands seeking good trade relations. A Chinese painting shows a giraffe brought to the emperor of China in 1415 by the people of Malindi [mä lin'dē]. Malindi was one of the smaller city-states. Writing on the picture tells of the emperor's pleasure with the gift. He sent a fleet of ships and thousands of Chinese sailors with numerous gifts to accompany the Malindi traders back to their homes in Africa.

dle East built homes and settled in the port cities to act as agents for distant traders.

One of the richest cities was Kilwa. South of most of the other ports, Kilwa was closer to the gold fields of the kingdom of Zimbabwe [zim bä'bwā]. (Present-day Zimbabwe includes the area of the historic Zimbabwe kingdom.) The merchants of Kilwa controlled much of the gold trade and grew wealthy by imposing taxes on its sale.

Ibn Batuta visited Kilwa in 1331 and wrote that it was one of the most beautiful and well-constructed towns he had seen. Today, stone ruins of enormous palaces, mansions, mosques, arched walkways, town squares, and public fountains hint at what Kilwa once was. Coral and wood were used to make carved arches, doors, and windows. The

The Portuguese destroyed much of the East African trade. By the 12th century, the Christian kingdom of Portugal was established on the west coast of Europe. The Portuguese were a seafaring people. In the 15th century, Prince Henry the Navigator encouraged Portuguese sailors to seek new trade routes to Asia. In 1498, Vasco da Gama [väs′kō də gä′mə] sailed south from Portugal around the tip of Africa. For the first time, the Portuguese saw the East African coast.

They were eager for gold and wealth and were delighted to find the thriving city-states. Their descriptions give a picture of life in Kilwa as even more prosperous than when Ibn Batuta had visited. The common people dressed in imported cottons and silks. The wealthy wore gold, silver, and jeweled ornaments. Freshwater streams, orchards, and fruit gardens surrounded the towns.

The Portuguese wanted to participate in the rich trade, but they were scorned by the Swahili. The Swahili thought the Portuguese had bad manners, unclean habits, and cheap trading goods. But the Portuguese had something few Swahili had—guns.

Most of the Indian Ocean trade was fairly peaceful at that time. The East African city-states had few defenses. With the power of their muskets and cannon, the Portuguese began a campaign of piracy and looting. An expedition ordered by the king of Portugal in 1505 burned Kilwa. After capturing the town of Mombasa further north, the Portuguese sailors, swinging axes, broke into the houses and killed anyone who had not escaped before the attack. A Swahili poet later wrote of the ruin of his city:

> Where once the porcelain stood in the wall
>   niches,
> Now wild birds nestle their fledglings

The Portuguese built their own trade fort at Mombasa. But just as the Moroccans had been unable to hold the Songhai Empire together, the Portuguese could not replace the governments and trade networks of East Africa. The destruction, insecurity, and fear that they caused led to a decline in trade. Swahili culture, however, managed to survive. And today, Swahili language and poetry are an important part of life in Tanzania and Kenya.

section review 2

1. How did trade winds help the peoples of East African city-states develop economically?

2. What items did Arabs, Indians, and East Africans trade with each other?

3. List at least three ways in which Kilwa was typical of East African ports.

4. Why did the Swahili scorn the Portuguese?

3 ## The kingdom of Zimbabwe developed in the interior

In 1868, a European hunter stumbled across the massive stone ruins of a group of palaces, fortresses, and houses in the interior of southeast Africa near the Zambezi River. The impressive stone buildings of Zimbabwe, which means "royal dwelling," had been built by expert masons from the 10th through the 18th centuries. The buildings were made from oblong slabs of granite. They had walls 10 feet (3 meters) thick and 30 feet (9 meters) high. And these elaborately patterned walls were not held together by mortar. Instead, the rocks had been shaped to fit together exactly.

Zimbabwe grew from an iron-working settlement. The builders of Zimbabwe were descended from the iron-working peoples of the Bantu expansion. Historians believe that

The huge stone wall of the temple dominates the ruins of ancient Zimbabwe.

the Bantu probably originated in the Congo forest and migrated from there. By the 11th century, some Bantu peoples, called the Shona [shō′nə], had crossed the Zambezi River and pushed back or conquered any hunting and gathering peoples that lived there.

The Shona people found gold deposits near Zimbabwe. They mined the gold and traded it with the Swahili city-states. They imported such Asian goods as cotton, brass, and porcelain. By the 1400s, Zimbabwe was a strong state with a large population, much wealth, and a centralized government.

Gold formed the basis of Zimbabwe's economy. The Portuguese never saw Zimbabwe itself. But in the 16th century, they recorded conversations with the descendants of the Shona people. From these Portuguese records and from archaeologists' study of the stone ruins, historians have learned what Zimbabwe was like at its height in the 1400s.

Zimbabwe was ruled by a king who was believed to be semi-divine. His health was important for the welfare of the kingdom. If he became ill, he was supposed to commit suicide so that a healthy king could take his place and keep the country strong. The king made the necessary decisions, but only his closest advisers were allowed to see him.

One of the major stone buildings at Zimbabwe is thought to have been the palace where the king lived with his royal wives, advisers, and officers. About 1,000 people lived in the palace at one time. Cooks, servants, farmers, and soldiers lived with their families in smaller stone buildings surrounding the palace. Ruined buildings of this type have been found not only at the capital but all over the region. The larger sites were probably the homes of provincial chiefs.

Many of the common people were involved in gold mining. The mines were pits dug into the earth; some were as much as 50 feet (15 meters) deep. Men and women both worked in the gold mines and along the streams, where even more gold washed out of the ground.

In the early 1500s, the Portuguese tried to gain control of the gold regions, but the rulers of Zimbabwe prevented them from reaching even the capital. The Zimbabwe kings dictated to the Portuguese all rules concerning trade and taxes. Gradually, Zimbabwe's trade with the East African coast dropped off as a result of the destructive Portuguese actions there. Internal quarrels among brothers who all wanted to be king further weakened Zimbabwe. However, the kingdom survived until 1830. Then, it was attacked by Ndebele peoples from the south who were seeking land on which to settle. The great stone buildings were abandoned and large hordes of gold were left to be found and carried off by European prospectors in the later 19th century.

---

section review **3**

1. Who built Zimbabwe? Where did they come from? During what years were the stone buildings built?
2. From what two sources do we get our knowledge of 15th-century Zimbabwe?
3. Describe the royal palace at Zimbabwe.
4. Who attacked Zimbabwe in 1830? What was the result?

4 Islam stimulated new states in West Africa

When Songhai collapsed in the Moroccan invasion, the center of trade and political power in West Africa shifted south and east. The Muslim state of Kanem-Bornu emerged as the most powerful military state of the central Sudan. Fierce religious wars converted the people of the Hausa [hou′sə] states to Islam, and religious warfare continued in West Africa until the early 1800s.

Kanem-Bornu had a long history (800– 1846). The rich empires of Ghana, Mali, and Songhai overshadowed the lesser states of the Sudan before 1600. Yet, the history of these states goes back for centuries. About the year 800 A.D., a centralized state with a king emerged in Kanem [kä′nem] east of Lake Chad. This first king, Saif [sef], began a dynasty that ruled for a thousand years.

In 1085, the king of Kanem was converted to Islam. The kingdom continued to grow in strength, and Islam became firmly established among its rulers. Most of the agricultural population, however, continued traditional religions.

Like other states of the Sudan, Kanem engaged in trade across the Sahara. The people of Kanem exchanged cloth and leather goods for the salt of the north.

By 1400, civil war and attacks from the east had weakened Kanem. The king and his court moved west of Lake Chad to Bornu [bôr′nü], and the new state was called Kanem-Bornu.

After the fall of Songhai in 1591, Kanem-Bornu became the strongest state in the central Sudan. Its most famous ruler was Idris Alooma [id′ris ə lü′mə], who ruled from 1580 to 1617. He spread Islamic law throughout his territories and forced the common people

The bodyguards of the ruler of Kanem-Bornu were armed with fierce lances.

to become Muslims, something which had never been done in Ghana, Mali, or Songhai.

Idris Alooma built up the cavalry of Kanem-Bornu until it was the terror of the central Sudan. Both riders and horses wore chain mail and padded cloth coverings, like the knights and horses of western Christendom. Experts from Egypt and Asia Minor trained the army in the use of guns imported from North Africa. Idris Alooma personally led the cavalry. Thus, the horse became one of the basic requirements for any state in the Sudan that wanted to be strong. Many rulers of smaller states imitated Kanem-Bornu's cavalry. So important a state was Kanem-Bornu that ambassadors were sent to create good relations between Kanem-Bornu and the Ottoman Empire and to confirm that the state of Kanem-Bornu was part of the Muslim world.

The rulers who followed Idris Alooma were not as strong as he had been. The state gradually weakened. The last king of Kanem-Bornu was killed in 1846 in a religious war.

Trade flourished in the Hausa states. A people called the Hausa lived in trading cities in what is now northern Nigeria. The Hausa city-states did not unite with each other but remained individual states. Each had its own government, laws, and taxes.

The Hausa city-states were small and weak until the 15th century when Islam was introduced. After that, these cities enjoyed a lively trade with Mali, and later Songhai, as well as with the lesser states in the African forest.

The Hausa engaged in trade and manufacture. From the forest, they collected ivory, hides, and kola nuts to trade with North Africa. The kola nut was very popular with the Muslims, who chewed it like gum. The kola nut contains caffeine, which not only keeps one awake, but also helps one to go long periods of time without food or water. (Many modern soft drinks are made from the kola nut. However, the caffeine, which is linked with high blood pressure, has been removed from many of these drinks.)

In addition to trading forest products, the Hausa developed many handicraft industries such as leather manufacture and cloth weaving.

Uthman dan Fodio united the Hausa states. Living in the Sudan and the Hausa cities were a people called the Fulani [fü lä'nē]. Following the collapse of Songhai in the 1600s, the Hausa cities became more wealthy and powerful. The Fulani began to resent the control the Hausa people had over them. After more than a hundred years of discontent and minor uprisings, a leader arose in the early 1800s to lead the Fulani in a revolution against the Hausa.

Uthman dan Fodio [ùth'mən dan fō'dē ō] was a devoted Muslim who claimed that his revolution was a holy war, or *jihad* [jə häd']. It was fought to please God and to reform the lax behavior of the Muslim Hausa peoples. His writings are full of criticisms of the Hausa's careless religious practices as well as their high taxes, forced military service, and neglect of the rural peoples under Hausa control.

Uthman dan Fodio's revolution was successful. By the time of his death in 1817, he had established an empire over the disunited Hausa city-states. The capital was at Sokoto [sō'kō tō], and its ruler took the title of Sultan, as Muslim rulers of large territories were called all over the Islamic world. The Sultan of Sokoto believed in fair rule with no special privileges.

The jihad against the Hausa was not the only holy war in the Sudan. Earlier Muslim wars had spread across the western Sudan from the Senegal and Gambia river valleys to the valley of the Niger. New states formed wherever the Muslims were successful. Hundreds of thousands of people were converted to Islam in these jihads, and others who were already Muslim became increasingly devout. Uthman dan Fodio's jihad was one of the last and most successful. The warfare of this completely African revolution did not end until the late 1800s.

5 The forest states developed strong governments

The forest states of Benin, Dahomey, Kongo, and Asante flourished on agriculture and trade. One kind of trade, the trade in human beings, became a great source of wealth for these states. As the demand for cheap labor on the plantations of the West Indies increased, slave raids in Africa took an enormous toll. Eventually, the slave trade was stopped. Efficient governments continued to keep the forest states strong until the European conquests of the 1800s.

Strong kings helped Benin grow wealthy and powerful. The forest state of Benin, located in what is now southern Nigeria, had kings, called *Obas*. The first Oba [ō'bə] lived some time in the 11th century. Oba Ewedo [ə wā'dō], who ruled in the 14th century, strengthened the position of the Oba by weakening the power of the council of elders who helped him rule. Ewedo built a new capital, which he called Benin.

A 15th-century Oba, Eware [ə wä'rē] the Great, increased the strength of the Benin army. With this more powerful army, he expanded the state by conquering many villages in the area. He fortified the city of Benin with high wooden walls.

The Obas of Benin were religious rulers. They were responsible for all religious ceremonies and prayed to the gods for Benin's welfare. The reigns of the Obas were recorded on cast bronze plaques that were hung on the palace walls. Many of these have been preserved. They give historians details about Benin's past.

Europeans arrived in West Africa. In the late 1400s, sailors from Portugal came to the coast of West Africa looking for places to trade their country's manufactured goods. They brought muskets and metal utensils in exchange for gold and spices. The first visit of a Portuguese ship to Benin was in 1472.

By 1500, the English, French, and Dutch were also trading with Benin. Benin regulated trade with the Europeans. The foreign traders had to pay port taxes and import duties. They could only trade with chosen representatives of the Oba. Europeans were not allowed to live in Benin. They could visit it for a short time, but had to live on their ships anchored off the coast.

The Europeans brought new foods to Africa. The Portuguese brought corn and cassava (a plant also called manioc from which tapioca is made) from their colonies in the Americas. These foods grew so well in the African forest that within fifty years they had become staple items in the forest peoples' diet. The population increased as a result.

Many small forest states close to the coast traded gold, ivory, and later slaves with the Europeans. Through this trade, these forest states grew rich and powerful.

Slave trade produced wealth for the cities and terror in the countryside. African states had always had a form of domestic slavery. Prisoners of war, debtors, and convicts could be made into slaves. In addition, there was some international trade in slaves in the Muslim cities. But this slave trade was not based on race; both light- and dark-skinned people were offered for sale in slave markets. And slaves were not used as the basis of plantation labor. Slaves were usually treated well, though sometimes underfed. Some were able to gain freedom through hard work and marriage into free families. Some slaves even became advisers to kings.

By the early 16th century, the Europeans had begun sugar plantations in the West Indies. They needed many slaves to work

Someone You Should Know

Olaudah Equiano

In 1752, eleven-year-old Olaudah Equiano [ō lou'də ē'kwē ä'nō] was kidnaped from his village in what is now Nigeria. The kidnapers sold him to Europeans, and he was put on a ship. Olaudah thought the Europeans had long hair, strange-colored skin, spoke strange languages, and were extremely cruel. Their leaders beat the white sailors and black slaves alike. When the ship set sail, Olaudah and the other slaves were put below the deck in chains. They scarcely had room to move, many became sick, and some died.

Olaudah reached America alive and was bought and sold several times. But he managed to save a little money by trading on his own. Finally he was able to buy his freedom from a kind master for about $150.

Eventually Olaudah settled in England. He worked hard to end the slave trade by making speeches and writing his autobiography in 1789. But he was not to see the success of his efforts. He died in 1797, just ten years before the British outlawed slavery.

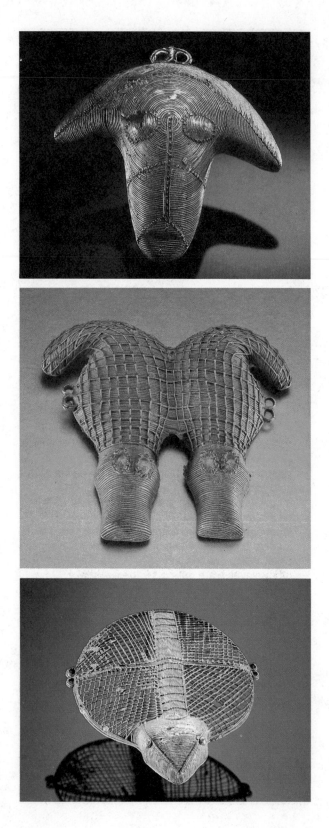

these plantations. These slaves were treated very cruelly and had almost no chance of gaining freedom. The Europeans came to the markets of West Africa to buy their slaves.

Many West African states, such as Benin, Dahomey [də hō'mē], and Asante [ə sän'tē] kept strict control over the slave trade in their countries. They made certain the Europeans did not leave the coast and capture slaves for themselves. These states grew very rich from the sale of captives from the interior of the continent.

African merchants raided isolated villages and kidnaped anyone they could find. Surviving first-hand accounts tell of the horrors of these raids. The autobiography of Olaudah Equiano is one such account. Most of the peoples who fell victim to the slave raiders did not have centralized governments to help protect them. Villages posted children in trees to act as lookouts for the approach of slave raiders.

In some places or states, such as the Kongo, so many people were enslaved and taken to the Americas that the population became dangerously small. In Benin, the slave merchants bought guns and challenged the Oba's army. The power of the Oba began to lessen. The people grew frightened. Taxes did not come in regularly. And laws could not be enforced.

The worst part of the slave trade was after the slaves were put on ships to America. The sea voyage lasted a grueling ten weeks or more and was called the Middle Passage. The slaves were packed in large numbers below the deck of the ship. They were often chained and fed mostly porridge. More slaves died from illness and unclean conditions on the Middle Passage than from cap-

The people of Asante created beautiful gold jewelry, often in the shapes of animals. These pendants show a cow, a pair of lizards, and a turtle.

ture in Africa or hard labor in America. Not until early in the 19th century was anti-slavery sentiment in America and Europe strong enough to finally end the slave trade.

Trade, taxes, and good government made Asante a strong state. About 1670, two great leaders united the many small clans who lived in the Asante forest. They were Osei Tutu [ô'sā tü'tü], the first king of Asante and his friend the priest Okomfo Anokye [ō-kōm'fō ə nō'chē]. Together they persuaded the clans to settle their differences and form a union. The union was then represented by a Golden Stool that Okomfo Anokye said had been sent from God.

The Golden Stool, a low wooden seat covered with gold, was a state symbol much like flags are to modern nations. It was displayed on official occasions. No one was allowed to sit on it except the king at a festival once a year. Kings could die or be removed from office, but the Golden Stool remained to represent the collective nation of Asante.

To further cement the new union, Okomfo Anokye introduced certain laws and customs. One famous rule stated that no Asante could talk about the place his or her ancestors came from. Thus, all Asantes would remember that they were Asante first and persons of a certain town or clan second. An idea of citizenship was formed.

A well-organized army helped Asante expand. All men could be called up for military service. And every clan and village had its assigned place in the army. There were orderly ranks for officers and systematic methods for giving orders in the field. Under the leadership of two kings, Opoku Ware (1710–1750) and Osei Bonsu (1801–1824), Asante conquered a large empire covering almost the same area as the modern nation of Ghana. The newly conquered peoples were expected to pay taxes to the Golden Stool in return for the benefits of law courts, protection, and good roads that the Asante government provided.

Trade in gold, kola nuts, and slaves gave Asante a good tax base. A bureaucracy of officials chosen for ability rather than noble birth or wealth managed the governing of the empire. This system had two advantages over government by an all-powerful king: (1) government could continue to operate even when the king died or was removed from office; (2) the bureaucratic departments accomplished more than the king could do by himself. One department made certain that taxes were paid. Another was responsible for seeing that messages got through. A different department saw that appeals from court cases were heard. Yet another enforced trade regulations with foreigners. One department kept the roads throughout the empire clear and safe for travelers. It enforced a law in the capital city of Kumasi [kü mä'sē] requiring persons to burn their garbage behind their houses every morning.

Asante was eventually conquered by the British in 1896 after several wars and the loss of many lives on both sides. But Asante was never destroyed. There is still a king who appears publicly with his court and the Golden Stool. He has his own judicial court and is influential in the politics of modern Ghana.

section review 5

1. How was the government of Benin strengthened in the 14th and 15th centuries?

2. What products besides slaves did the Europeans and West Africans trade?

3. How did the slave trade affect the forest states with strong governments? What happened in the isolated villages in the interior?

4. What helped Asante have good taxes and good government?

13 chapter review ❖ ❖ ❖

Section Summaries

1. Famous empires grew in the West African savanna. Ancient Ghana, Mali, and Songhai were three empires in the western savanna from the 9th through the 16th centuries. They were based on the gold and salt trade across the Sahara. They were wealthy empires, and their armies and governments controlled large areas. Cities of these empires, such as Timbuktu, became centers of scholarship in the 14th and 15th centuries.

2. City-states flourished along the East African coast. From the 7th through the 14th centuries, trading ships from Arabia, India, and China carried on a lively trade with the East African coast. Thriving city-states grew up there. These cities were inhabited by Africans and Asians. The combination of peoples gave rise to Swahili culture, which had its own language and tolerated many religions and life-styles. The Portuguese destroyed much of the East African trade after 1500.

3. The kingdom of Zimbabwe developed in the interior. In the interior of East Africa, other states were developing from the 11th century on. One was Zimbabwe, whose economy was based on gold. The extensive ruins of large stone buildings are evidence of the power and sophistication of this kingdom.

4. Islam stimulated new states in West Africa. Islam had a strong effect on West Africa as well as the Middle East. The rulers of Mali, Songhai, and Kanem-Bornu had been Muslims. In the 17th and 18th centuries, waves of Muslim reform movements spread over West Africa. Large numbers of the common people were converted to Islam, and small Islamic states were formed. Uthman dan Fodio united the Hausa states in a holy war in 1801.

5. The forest states developed strong governments. States such as Benin had begun to grow in the forests by the 11th century. The arrival in the 1400s of the Europeans in search of trade and slaves, and the foods brought from the Americas by the Portuguese, caused more states to expand and grow rich. However, the slave trade did much damage to many African communities until it was stopped in the 19th century. Complex governments like that of Asante developed in spite of the slave trade.

Who? What? When? Where?

1. Make a timeline that shows about when each of these arose:
   a. Asante
   b. Benin
   c. Ghana
   d. Kanem-Bornu
   e. Mali
   f. Songhai
   g. Zimbabwe

2. Write a sentence for each of these that explains its importance in Africa's history:
   a. Almoravids
   b. Asante
   c. Fulani
   d. Hausa
   e. Muslims
   f. Portuguese
   g. Shona
   h. Swahili

3. Write identifying sentences for these individuals:
   a. Askia Mohammad
   b. Ibn Batuta
   c. Idris Alooma
   d. Mansa Musa
   e. Okomfo Anokye
   f. Opoku Ware
   g. Sonni Ali
   h. Sundiata
   i. Uthman dan Fodio
   j. Vasco da Gama

4. Write descriptive sentences for each of these terms:
   a. Golden Stool
   b. Guinea gold
   c. *jihad*
   d. monsoon
   e. Oba
   f. silent trade

Questions for Critical Thinking

1. Why were gold and salt so important in early African trade? What do you feel are the most important items of trade today? What nations or regions are involved in this trade?

2. In what way was Swahili culture an international culture?

3. Why and how did the Portuguese destroy East African trade? Do you think this was right?

4. In what ways was the slave trade harmful to some African states? Which ones?

5. Why do you think African kings cooperated with European slave traders?

Skill Activities

1. Read *Nomads of the World* by the editors of the National Geographic Society for more information on the harsh living conditions of African nomads. (National Geographic Society, 1971)

2. On an outline map of the African continent, show where these ancient states were located: Asante, Benin, Kanem-Bornu, Dahomey, Mali, Songhai, and Zimbabwe. Also sketch in the Nile, Niger, and Congo rivers.

3. Suppose you were the king of a country that controlled a resource (like gold) wanted by people in other nations. What rules would you make for trade? Why? What would be the effect of those rules on the growth and wealth of your nation?

4. Use the *Readers' Guide to Periodical Literature* to find out about American trade relations with the oil-producing nations of Africa and the Middle East.

5. Pretend you are Ibn Batuta visiting your town. Write a page in your diary telling what you see. Include things that make outstanding impressions, such as strange customs you observe. Is it a rich place? A poor place? What do you think of the manners and food of the people you meet?

chapter **13** quiz

Section 1

1. True or false: The ancient Romans knew that gold was mined in West Africa.

2. The silent traders exchanged gold for: a. rice, b. slaves, c. salt

3. Mansa Musa's religion was: a. Christian, b. tribal, c. Muslim

Section 2

4. True or false: Chinese homes displayed very old African dishes.

5. The culture that is a blend of African, Indian, and Arab is: a. Benin, b. Swahili, c. Hausa

Section 3

6. The buildings at Zimbabwe were built by the: a. Shona, b. Swahili, c. Benin

7. Zimbabwe was destroyed in the year: a. 1412, b. 1783, c. 1830

Section 4

8. True or false: Idris Alooma was famous because he allowed freedom of religion in his kingdom.

9. The army of Kanem-Bornu was trained by experts from: a. India, b. Egypt and Asia Minor, c. China

Section 5

10. The history of Benin can be seen on: a. rock paintings, b. bronze plaques, c. stone carvings

11. True or false: Africans captured slaves from other African villages.

12. True or false: Slavery had harmful consequences everywhere in Africa.

EARLY CULTURES IN AMERICA

Early people of Central and South America made beautiful gold jewelry such as this pendant. It was made between 1100 and 1500 A.D. by people who lived in what is now Panama.

High in the Andes Mountains in Peru, almost always shrouded in cold mist, stands Machu Picchu [mä'chü pēk'chü], the deserted ruins of the last center of Inca civilization. This mountain fortress is believed to have been the last hiding place of the Inca nobles who fled the Spanish conquerors in the sixteenth century. No one knows how long the Inca nobles or their descendants may have remained there. Machu Picchu lay hidden away and forgotten for centuries, until it was discovered in 1911 by North American archaeologist Hiram Bingham.

Who were the Incas? Before the Spanish conquest, they ruled the largest empire in all the Americas. At its height, the Inca Empire stretched from Ecuador to central Chile—more than 2,500 miles (4,167 kilometers).

How did the Incas keep control over so vast an area? The secret of their success is partly revealed in the following excerpt, written by a Spaniard who traveled widely in Peru and interviewed many Incas in the 1530s and 1540s.

So great was the veneration that the people felt for their [Inca] princes, throughout this vast region, that every district was as well regulated and governed as if the lord was actually present to chastise those who acted contrary to his rules. This fear arose from the known valour of the lords and their strict justice. It was felt to be certain that those who did evil would receive punishment without fail, and that neither prayers nor bribes would avert it. At the same time, the Incas always did good to those who were under their sway, and would not allow them to be ill-treated, nor that too much tribute should be exacted from them.

Besides the Incas, there were many other Indian cultures in North and South America. Most cultures north of the Rio Grande (now the border between Mexico and the United States) were based on hunting, fishing, and food gathering and did not develop cities. South of the Rio Grande, two major civilizations in addition to that of the Incas developed—that of the Mayas and that of the Aztecs. This chapter tells how:

1. **American Indian cultures developed over many centuries.**

2. **The Mayas achieved a most complex civilization.**

3. **The Aztecs conquered much of central Mexico.**

4. **The Incas controlled a vast empire in South America.**

5. **Indians had distinctive customs.**

1 American Indian cultures developed over many centuries

When Columbus reached the Caribbean islands at the end of the 15th century, he mistakenly called the people he met "Indians," because he thought he had landed in the Indies in Asia. But the lands and people he found were not a part of the "Old World." Columbus had landed in a "New World" that had a long and complex history of its own.

We know very little of this history. Most of the Indian cultures were destroyed or greatly weakened by contact with Europeans. For example, the Spanish conquerors killed many of the Indian leaders, tore down their temples, and burned their books. Very few Indian writings survived. From these and from the often sketchy accounts of Indian life written by European conquerors has come much of our knowledge of 16th-century American cultures. Archaeologists know about earlier periods by studying the many artifacts left by early cultures. Of course, archaeologists are constantly uncovering evidence. Knowledge of ancient American cultures is being constantly revised.

The first American Indians probably came from Asia. Archaeologists believe that people have been living in the Americas as long as 10 to 30 thousand years. The first Americans probably came from Asia in many separate migrations over a long period of time. They may have come over the Bering Strait between Siberia and Alaska. The prehistoric people of the Americas had fire, stone tools, skin clothing, and the domesticated dog. Most of them lived as hunters or gatherers. During the centuries before the coming of the Europeans, descendants of these people settled in North and South America.

Most evidence indicates that the American Indians were isolated from the civilizations of the Old World. Some scholars believe, however, that daring seafarers crossed the Pacific or Atlantic oceans to America centuries before the Vikings or Columbus. Other authorities believe that the Indians developed their cultures independently. They maintain that similar inventions in the Eastern and Western Hemispheres indicate only that peoples often hit upon similar ideas when they face the same problems.

Farming changed Indian life. Perhaps as early as 7000 B.C., some Indians learned to grow crops. As time passed, the people developed new varieties of plant life. The most important of these was corn, which was developed about 3000 B.C. in Central America. Corn became as important in the Western Hemisphere as wheat was in the Eastern Hemisphere. Farming made it possible for people in America to settle in communities, to develop such skills as weaving and pottery making, and to set up a division of labor. These skills spread slowly throughout the Americas.

North American Indians had a variety of cultures. As people everywhere had done, the Indians of North America learned to live with their environment. Since the climate and geography of the huge North American continent is so varied, Indians in different parts of the continent developed different cultures.

Eskimos lived in the frozen lands of the extreme north. The short growing season made it impossible to grow crops. Instead, the Eskimos fished and hunted for food, particularly walrus, whales, seals, small fish, and caribou. They used the bone and ivory of some of these animals to make tools such as needles, knives, fishhooks, and harpoons. With the skins they made clothing and tents. They also learned to build houses out of snow and ice. Eskimos lived in small family

groups and never needed to develop a central government. The resources of the extreme north were not great enough to support a large, centralized population.

Farther south, in a heavily forested area that reached from southern Alaska to the present state of Washington, lived the North Pacific coast Indians. Like the Eskimos, they hunted and fished for food. But they also gathered wild berries from the forest. And, unlike the Eskimos, these Indians lived in villages. From the many woods available in the forests, they built wooden houses.

In front of their home, each family put up a *totem pole*. These wooden poles were carved with the figures of an animal whose spirit was considered special to the family. The totems identified families as belonging to the Beaver people, the Bear people, and so on. Strangers with the same totem were always welcome.

North Pacific tribes were divided into nobles, common people, and slaves, whom they captured from other tribes. One important custom of the nobles was a ceremony called *potlatch*. On major occasions, particularly those marking events in their children's lives, such as the day a daughter gathered her first berries, noble families would give a great feast. At the feast, the family would give away its most prized and beautiful possessions because it was considered a greater virtue "to give rather than to receive."

In the eastern part of the continent in the northeast woodlands, the Indians were not only hunters but also farmers. They lived in villages and built long, oval-shaped houses called wigwams out of poles covered with bark and skins.

Five Woodland tribes—the Seneca, Cayuga, Onondaga, Oneida, and Mohawk—formed a confederation called the League of the Iroquois, or the Five Nations. Through this political organization, the five tribes acted together on matters of common inter-

This elegant totem pole still stands in Neah Bay, Washington.

Pueblo Indians lived in cities. One of the oldest and most complex cultures north of the Rio Grande was that of the Pueblo tribes in what is now the southwestern United States. They used adobe [ə dō′bē], or sun-dried clay, to build several-storied houses that have been called the first American apartment buildings. In the Pueblo form of government, the people chose their own chiefs. These chiefs, in turn, were advised by a council of elders. No action could be taken unless all these leaders agreed.

Pueblo Indians were master farmers who developed a complex system of irrigation canals. Their main crop was corn. But they also gathered seeds and berries. As a safe-guard against drought, each family carefully built up a supply of food that was held in reserve. The Pueblo Indians produced excellent pottery, beautifully decorated blankets with geometric designs, and finely woven baskets.

Pueblo Indians, which included the Hopi and Zuni, were peaceful people. They fought wars rarely and only when necessary for survival. Returning warriors had to go through a long ritual to get rid of their "madness." The religion of the Pueblo Indians taught that people should live in harmony with nature, that they should respect the life of others and the traditions of the past, and that they should do things in moderation.

section review 1

1. Why is the term "Indian" not correct when describing the first people of the Americas?

2. About when was farming started by early Americans?

3. What were some differences between the cultures of the Eskimo and North Pacific Coast Indians? What did geography have to do with their cultural differences?

4. How were the people of the Five Nations different from those of the Pueblo?

est. Rivalry among them was strong and frequently erupted in war. By the 1700s, the League controlled an area from Lake Michigan to the Atlantic and from the St. Lawrence River to the Tennessee River.

Before the 1600s, most of the Indians who lived on the Great Plains in the central part of the North American continent made a living as farmers. After the Spanish brought horses to America, the Indians, such as the Sioux and the Cheyenne, became buffalo hunters.

2 The Mayas achieved a most complex civilization

Indians in Mexico and in Central and South America built more complex civilizations than their neighbors to the north. They began their development at about the time the Hans of China and the Romans were building their empires thousands of miles away. The Mayas in the Yucatan [yü'kə tan'] peninsula, the Aztecs of central Mexico, and the Incas in Peru had civilizations that in many respects rivaled those of ancient Egypt and Mesopotamia.

These cultures of the south developed further than those of the north probably because they had learned earlier how to raise corn. As a result, they had lived in one place for longer periods than the northern Indians. This allowed for more time to develop skills.

Mayan culture had two main periods. Beginning about 500 B.C., the Mayan Indians developed a high culture located chiefly in the peninsula of Yucatan (present-day southeastern Mexico, Belize, and Guatemala). By 1 A.D., the Mayas had writing, a system of numbers, and a very accurate calendar. These were impressive cultural achievements. By 300 A.D., in Honduras, north Guatemala, and nearby areas of Mexico, the Mayas had established a distinctive civilization. Its early phase, which lasted until the 9th century, is called the Classic period, or Old Empire. During this time, the Mayas built several cities and perfected their arts, science, and learning. Then, in the 800s, the people began to abandon these centers. Why they left remains a mystery. Some scholars have guessed that the population grew too great for the food supply. Others have suggested that epidemics and wars may have killed off many people.

After the Old Empire crumbled, large numbers of Mayas evidently moved northward and built new cities in the northern tip of the Yucatan peninsula. Around these new centers grew up city-states similar to those of other early peoples. Some scholars believe that the Mayan governments were theocratic since Mayan life seems to have been dominated by priests. This later Mayan phase, usually called the Post-Classic period or New Empire, flourished from about 900 to 1200 A.D. It is characterized by new cultural influences, particularly the worship of a feathered serpent god that probably began with a northern tribe called the Toltecs.

Toltec warriors conquered the Mayas of Yucatan in the 11th century and remained in control for about 200 years. After this time, the Mayan city-states seem to have gone into a long period of decline. Certainly, their cities were not as well built or as beautifully decorated as they had been in earlier times. But some scholars think the Maya were simply focusing their attention on economic activities such as trade rather than on religious affairs. At any rate, when the Spanish came to America in the early 16th century, most of the great Mayan cities of the Post-Classic period were no longer occupied and had long been covered by the dense growth of rain forest.

Mayan cities were trade and religious centers. Most Mayas were corn farmers who lived in thatched huts on the outskirts of cities. These cities were chiefly religious centers with huge stone pyramids, astronomical observatories, temples, and monuments. When a religious ceremony was to be held, the people would come from the nearby farm villages and gather in the great stone buildings.

Each city usually had a market square. There merchants and shoppers carried on business. People made cotton cloth and pot-

Chichen Itza is the site of the most extensive and best preserved ruins of Maya civilization.The city was founded by the Mayas about 250 A.D., but it reached its height between 1000 and 1200 A.D. In those years, the conquering Toltecs worked with Maya artisans to build the giant stone structures in Chichen Itza. The city was mostly a center of religion and government. But peasants flocked there to watch the suspenseful ball games, enjoy the market, and participate in religious ceremonies.

Today at Chichen Itza, the great pyramid, built about 1100 A.D., towers over all the other buildings. From its summit one can see the observatory and survey the vast Yucatan peninsula.

The Mayas knew much about the sun's movements, and this knowledge guided daily lives and religion. For example, the great pyramid is so carefully located that on March 21 and September 21, the spring and fall equinoxes, the shadows on one side of the pyramid form the image of a moving serpent on the steps.

Near the great pyramid is the ball court. It is a little smaller than a modern football field and has steep stone walls. The exact meaning of the ball court games is not yet clear to archaeologists. But the games may have been religious ceremonies.

Beyond the ball court is the sacred well. Chichen Itza means "the well of Itza." The well, a round, natural pool in the rock, was a major religious site. It is more than 60 feet (18 meters) from the top of the well to the beginning of its dark water. Into the well, priests threw valuable objects of all kinds as sacrifices to the gods. Bold archaeological divers have recently recovered gold and jade jewelry, copper plaques, sacrificial knives, and even human skeletons from the well bottom.

In the 1400s, Chichen Itza was suddenly abandoned, though scholars do not know why. And the purposes of many of the 50 remaining buildings and ruins is unknown. They stand there unmoved through the centuries, a proof of the skill of Mayan artisans and the complexity of Mayan civilization.

Above is the observatory with the great pyramid in the distance. *Below left* is part of the ball court. *Below right* is one of the statues at the temple of warriors.

tery at home and then brought their products to the central market to sell. Traders set up booths to display carved jade, jewelry made of shells, and brilliant feather headdresses to be used for special ceremonies. Women ran restaurant stalls where they sold hot tortillas [tôr tē′yəs] and beans.

Mayan cities also had large stone ball courts. In these courts, a very serious game was played by two teams. Players hit a large rubber ball with their elbows, hips, or knees and tried to get it through vertical stone or wooden rings about twenty feet (six meters) above the ground. Some scholars believe the ball represented the sun and that the two teams fought a symbolic struggle between the forces of light and darkness, or life and death. There is some evidence that the losing team was offered up as a sacrifice to the Mayan gods.

Maya women were skilled weavers. This terra cotta statue of a noblewoman was made between 600 and 800 A.D. One end of the loom is fastened around the woman's waist.

The Mayas excelled in many fields. In the field of the arts, Mayan architecture and sculpture were outstanding. The commonest type of building looked like a pyramid but had a flat top. The whole structure was faced with limestone. On top was a temple. All over the building were carved stone figures. Inside it were brightly colored murals.

The Mayas developed an *ideographic* system of writing in which symbols stood for ideas. Scholars have not yet learned to read it except for some of the symbols that stand for gods, stars, and dates. The Mayas produced paper from bark or tough fibers of the maguey [mag′wā] cactus and used it to make folding books. The Spanish conquerors destroyed all but three of these.

Perhaps the Mayas' greatest accomplishment was their calendar. Mayan astronomers discovered that the year was slightly less than 365¼ days long.

The Mayas were also skilled in mathematics. They worked out a system of numbers that included the idea of zero. The Mayan zeros looked like this: 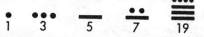 Numbers up to nineteen were made by adding ones and fives. For example:

The number system was based on the number 20. That is, zero at the end of a number meant twenty times the number before it.

section review 2

1. Where did the Mayan civilization develop?
2. During what years did the New Empire flourish?
3. Why did most of the people live on the outskirts of the cities?
4. What is an ideographic system of writing?

3 The Aztecs conquered much of central Mexico

North of the Mayas lived other Indian peoples. Some of them gradually extended their power and influence through military conquest. Among these were the early Toltecs, who laid a cultural foundation upon which the Aztecs later built a large empire.

The Toltecs preceded the Aztecs. At the time of the Mayan Old Empire, the Toltec Indians began to develop a culture of their own in central Mexico, near present-day Mexico City. They had come from the north about the 1st century A.D. By 700, the Toltecs were building great pyramids. Between 900 and 1200, the Toltecs were at the height of their development.

The Aztecs built a great city. In the 13th century, a warlike Indian people swept into central Mexico from the northwest. They called themselves Aztecs, which probably refers to their original name, Aztlan, meaning "White Land." Scholars think Aztlan may be what is now New Mexico or Arizona.

The Aztecs eventually conquered the Toltecs and many other neighboring tribes. Since the Aztecs also called themselves Mexica people, the lands they conquered eventually came to be known as Mexico. Aztec power reached its height during the 15th and early 16th centuries.

The center of the Aztec empire was their city of Tenochtitlan [tā nōch'tē tlän'], which was probably built about 1325. According to legend, the Aztecs decided to locate their capital where they saw a heaven-sent eagle, with a snake in its beak, sitting on a cactus growing from a rock in a lake. (This scene is pictured on the flag of modern-day Mexico, and Mexico City now stands on the ancient site of Tenochtitlan and the vanished lake.)

Tenochtitlan prospered and probably had a population of 400,000 by the early 15th century. The setting of this city was magnificent. It sat out in the water, on islands and land reclaimed from the shallow lake. There were canals between the islands. A visitor could enter the heart of the city either by canoe or by walking over one of the long stone causeways that connected the central city to the mainland.

Striking features of Tenochtitlan were the great temples and pyramids that stood in the city square. Near the temples were ball courts, where the Aztecs played a ball game of religious significance similar to that of the Mayas. Most of the people lived in adobe houses, which they painted white and then trimmed in bright colors.

There were several great marketplaces in Tenochtitlan. In one section fruits and vegetables were for sale, in other cloth and ready-to-wear clothing. There were also booths that sold delicate jewelry made of jade, shell, and turquoise. Customers either traded items by barter or paid for them with cacao [kə kā'ō] beans—the source of chocolate—which were used as a kind of money.

The Aztecs ruled an empire. The Aztecs did not destroy the tribes they conquered. Instead, they ruled over them and forced them to pay tribute. Payments were made in cacao beans, deer hides, conch shells, and bolts of cotton cloth. A kind of picture writing was used to record these payments. By 1500, the city of Tenochtitlan was the center of an empire that included at least 5 million people, most of whom made their livings by farming.

The head of the Aztec government was called the Chief of Men. At the time the Spanish arrived, the Aztec leader was Montezuma [mon'tə zü'mə]. Although the Chief of Men was looked upon almost as a god, many nobles, merchants, and leaders had nearly as much power.

ESKIMO

NORTH   AMERICA

PLAINS

INDIANS

Mesa
Verde

Rio   Grande

MEXICO

Tenochtitlan

YUCATAN   Chichen Itza

CENTRAL

AMERICA   Caribbean Sea

SOME EARLY PEOPLES
IN THE AMERICAS

ATLANTIC

OCEAN

TROPIC OF CANCER

45°

30°

15°

EQUATOR   0°

PACIFIC

OCEAN

North Pacific Coast Tribes,
1300s–1800s A.D.

Pueblos,
500s–1690 A.D.

Iroquois,
1000s–1600s A.D.

Aztecs,
1200s–1520 A.D.

Toltecs,
700s–1200 A.D.

Mayas,
500s B.C.–1200 A.D.

Incas,
1000s–1532 A.D.

SOUTH   AMERICA

ANDES MTS.

Machu Picchu
Cuzco
Lake
Titicaca   Tiahuanaco

15°

TROPIC OF CAPRICORN

ANDES MTS.

30°

0   250   500   1000 MILES

0   250 500   1000 KILOMETERS

120°   105°   90°   75°

60°

45°

45°

30°

30°

45°

■ MAP LESSON 14: SOME EARLY PEOPLES IN THE AMERICAS

During the time period covered by this map—roughly the last 2 thousand years—people lived throughout the American continents. This map indicates only a few of these groups. Because an area is not colored or labeled does not mean it was uninhabited.

1. The Mayan civilization centered on the Yucatan peninsula in what is now Mexico, Belize, and Guatemala. How many centuries did this civilization last?

2. The Toltec civilization existed at the same time as the later Mayan civilization. It was located in central Mexico, an area later part of the Aztec Empire. What date marks the approximate division between the Toltecs and the Aztecs?

3. Which culture occupied the region east of the Great Lakes in North America? Did these people live about the same time as the Incas?

4. Mesa Verde, Machu Picchu, and Chichen Itza are visited by many tourists each year. With what cultures is each of these places identified?

5. Lines of latitude measure distance in degrees north and south of the equator. These lines are often called parallels because they are all parallel to the equator, although they do not appear so on this map. Why do they not appear so here?

6. Which of the peoples identified on the map lived on the equator?

7. The Tropic of Cancer parallels the equator at 23.5°N latitude. What is the name of the comparable parallel in the Southern Hemisphere?

8. The region between 23.5°N and 23.5°S is sometimes called the tropics. Name four early American peoples who lived in the tropics.

Young people were strictly educated. At the age of 15, the sons of nobles and rich merchants began to study at the "house of youth." They trained to become warriors or priests, the two most important professions in Aztec life. At these schools, they learned how to use weapons, studied religious rites and duties, learned Aztec history, and were trained in arts and crafts. Aztec history was written on long strips of paper. These were folded like a fan to make a book called a *codex*. Priests also taught the boys Aztec rules of good conduct, such as "never tell lies" and "console the poor and unfortunate." Although barred from the top of society, even boys from poor Aztec families had a chance through education to become army officers, landholders, or government officials.

Some young women were trained to become priests and to take part in temple ceremonies. Others took charge of booths in the markets, watched over the production and sale of crops, or ran households. Aztec mothers taught their girls to be respectful daughters and faithful wives. One Aztec mother advised her daughter to "take care that your garments are decent and proper; and . . . do not adorn yourself with much finery, since this is a mark of vanity and folly."

Aztec girls married at 16 and the boys at 20. Parents arranged the marriage and at the time of the ceremony a feast was held. There were many presents and much drinking and dancing.

Religion and war dominated Aztec life. The Aztecs had many gods. Huitzilopochtli [wēt′zēl ō potch′tlē], the god of the sun and war was one. Another important one was Tlaloc [tlä′lok], the rain god. A third important god was Quetzalcoatl [ket′säl kō′ə tl], represented in the form of a feathered snake. The Aztecs believed the world had been created and destroyed four times. The fifth and

This map, made in the 1500s, shows Aztec lands. The eagle stands for Tenochtitlan. The figures around the outside symbolize the subject peoples of the area. All the figures have knives through their skulls except one whose tongue has been cut out.

section review 3

1. When was Tenochtitlan built? What city now stands there?

2. What was a codex?

3. What opportunities were available to Aztec boys from poor families?

4. Why did Aztecs believe it necessary to make continual human sacrifices?

4 The Incas controlled a vast empire in South America

Far to the south of the Mayas and Aztecs, various groups of Indians lived in the Andes Mountains and Pacific Coast regions of South America. Between 100 A.D. and 400 A.D., some of these people began to develop complex cultures.

The Tiahuanaco culture developed in the Andes Mountains. High in the Andes, near the shores of Lake Titicaca [tit′i kä′kä], lies a mass of gigantic stones—the ruins of Tiahuanaco [tē′ə wä nä′kō]. Like Mohenjo-Daro in India, the name of this site means "the place of the dead." Evidence indicates that this was a religious center.

Little is known about the people who lived in the Tiahuanaco region. But they were skillful builders. Some of the stone slabs they used at the Tiahuanaco site weigh 200 tons (180 megagrams or metric tons). These blocks were fitted together tightly without mortar.

Archaeologists do not know what caused the end of the Tiahuanaco culture. It apparently died out around 900 A.D. Some of its cultural achievements, however, were not forgotten and were evidently passed on to later peoples.

The Incas unified an extensive empire. A few centuries after the decline of Tiahuanaco, a people of the Peruvian mountains began to

present creation of the world was the result of Quetzalcoatl's sacrifice of his own blood. To keep the universe alive, then, the Aztecs believed that it was necessary to make continual human sacrifices.

The Aztecs needed large numbers of prisoners for these sacrifices. This was one reason they were almost always at war with other Indian tribes. There was deep bitterness among the subject peoples from whom the Aztecs constantly demanded victims to be sacrificed on the temple-pyramids of Tenochtitlan.

By the time a small band of Spaniards landed in Mexico in 1519 in search of gold, many conquered Indian tribes were ready to turn against their Aztec masters.

GEOGRAPHY
A Key to History

CLIMATE AND POPULATION IN SOUTH AMERICA

Before 1500 A.D., most of the people of South America lived in highland settlements. The climate in the hills and mountains was generally more attractive than that in the lowlands. The highlands favored the development of agriculture, which is necessary for civilization.

Much of South America lies between the Equator and the Tropic of Capricorn. In general, the lowlands in the tropics are always hot because they get a great deal of direct sunlight every day. In the highlands, however, the heat of the sun's rays is offset by the altitude. The higher the elevation, the cooler the air.

The most important highlands in South America are the Andes. These mountains parallel the Pacific Coast in an almost unbroken chain from north to south.

Among the mountain ranges of the Andes are valleys, basins, and plateaus. In some of these areas, the combination of sun, rain, and temperature is just right for the growing of staple crops. Therefore people have been able to inhabit these places for thousands of years. By contrast, the lowlands of South America were only lightly populated until about 300 years ago.

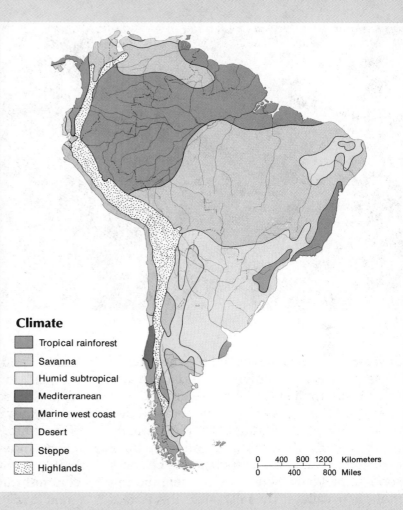

Climate
- Tropical rainforest
- Savanna
- Humid subtropical
- Mediterranean
- Marine west coast
- Desert
- Steppe
- Highlands

| 0 | 400 | 800 | 1200 | Kilometers |
| 0 | | 400 | 800 | Miles |

The muggy rain forests of the Amazon River Basin cover most of the northern third of the continent. Like the rain forests of Africa, those of the Amazon Basin are lush with plant growth. It is not easy to farm in these areas, however. They are too wet for crops such as corn to grow and clearing the land is a difficult task.

The people who first settled in the rain forest lived by hunting and gathering, not by farming. Tropical diseases and the limits of their food supply kept the population small.

It has been said that it is the small animals in the rain forest, not the large ones, that make life miserable. Mosquitoes and other insects are more than just pests. They carry diseases, such as malaria and yellow fever, that can greatly weaken or even kill humans. These insects are always present, since the tropical forest never has a frost that will kill them.

By contrast, the most heavily populated parts of the highlands have enough cold weather to keep down the insects. The highlands also have a long enough growing season for two crops a year.

269

Cotton and Alpaca wool were used by Tiahuanaco weavers to make beautiful clothing. This fragment of a shirt, now more than 1,000 years old, is proof of the technical and artistic skill of these early people.

develop a distinctive way of life. The ruler of these people was known as the *Inca*. It has since been applied to the entire group.

Around the 11th century, the Incas settled in a valley of the Andes. They eventually conquered the Indians there and set up a capital city called Cuzco [küs′kō]. The Incas soon expanded their rule to neighboring mountain valleys. By 1400—like the Aztecs far to the north—they were conquering distant regions. By the 1500s, the Incas were ruling an empire of more than 12 million people who spoke 20 different languages and belonged to more than 100 different ethnic groups.

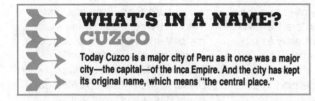

WHAT'S IN A NAME?
CUZCO

Today Cuzco is a major city of Peru as it once was a major city—the capital—of the Inca Empire. And the city has kept its original name, which means "the central place."

Unlike the Aztecs, the Incas absorbed those they conquered into their own culture. They brought the sons of conquered chiefs to Cuzco and educated them in the Inca schools. In addition, they sent colonies of loyal subjects to live in conquered areas, where they showed the new subjects the Inca way of life.

The Incas held the empire together with highly organized systems of government, communications, and transportation. One great Inca road ran from one end of the empire to the other along the Pacific Coast. Another ran along the crest of the Andes Mountains. Many sections of the roads were paved, and suspension bridges hung over gorges and rivers. These bridges were marvels of engineering for the age in which they were built. Over these roads and bridges, relays of Indian runners rushed messages from one part of the empire to another.

Inca life was carefully regulated. At the head of the Inca government was the emperor, or Inca. He claimed to be a descendant of the sun god and while he lived, he was worshiped. His rule was absolute. As the Inca ruler Atahualpa [ä′tə wäl′pä] said to the

Spanish conqueror Francisco Pizarro [pi zär'-ō], "In my kingdom no bird flies, no leaf quivers if I do not will it."

The Inca government owned and controlled all means of making and distributing goods. Land belonged to the state and not to those who lived on it. Government officials in Cuzco kept records of the number of people in every area of the empire. All persons were classified according to their age and ability to work. Most men had to serve in the army and to spend a certain amount of time working on government projects.

The government also regulated the private lives of individuals. If a young man were unmarried by a certain age, he had to choose a wife or take one selected by lot. Every so often, all engaged couples were married at huge state ceremonies held in the name of the Inca. Unlike the Mayas and Aztecs, the Incas had no written language. They kept records on knotted strings called quipus [kē'püz]. Using various kinds and colors of knots, they recorded crop production and other data needed by the Inca government. Only specially trained people could interpret

Daily Life

The Incas made outstanding statues and pottery vases. *Below left* are two vases decorated with warriors, axes, and shields. One of them has a double spout that made the vase easy to carry. Next to the two vases is a figure of a seated Inca god. *Below right* is a statue of a man with a cane. His hat and earrings are typical of Inca styles.

the quipus. Inca history and legends were learned by heart, and then passed down from generation to generation. Most of our information about the Incas comes from this memorized poetry, which was later written down in Spanish.

Incas worked at many occupations. Most Incas were farmers. In the mountainous landscape, they learned to raise crops on terraced hillside plots. Low stone walls kept the dirt from slipping. To water their crops, they built complex irrigation systems. As beasts of burden, the Inca farmers used the llama [lä'mə], a member of the camel family. The chief food crops were corn, white and sweet potatoes, and peanuts. For meat, they raised guinea pigs and ducks. Along the coast, fishing was important.

Some Incas were weavers who made fine cloth. Others made excellent pottery. Incas also worked as miners, digging for gold, silver, and copper. They smelted the ore and designed jewelry for priests and noble families. They also made decorations for temples. The Incas had specially trained surgeons who knew how to set broken bones, perform amputations, and even do brain surgery. For an anesthetic they probably gave the patients coca [kō'kə], a plant from which the drug cocaine is made.

The Incas had no formal schools. But they did train young men of the noble class in warfare and religion. Some were taught how to build. Like the people of Tiahuanaco, the Incas were great builders. Some of their temples still stand despite centuries of devastating earthquakes.

A small number of young women were selected to be Acllacuna [äk'lä kü'nä], "Chosen Women." They were especially trained in religion, weaving, and cooking. Some of them became wives of nobles and others served in the temples.

Like the Aztecs and various other peoples of the Americas, the Incas used human sacrifice. But they limited it to special occasions, for example, when a new emperor was installed or in times of great crisis such as plague or military defeat.

section review 4

1. What is known about the people of Tiahuanaco?
2. How did the Incas hold their empire together?
3. How has Inca history come down to us?
4. Who became Acllacuna? What role did they play?

5 Indians had distinctive customs

Out of the thousands of different customs practiced by the many groups of American Indians, some are of special interest. Indian religious beliefs, for example, reveal a great deal about the people who held them. Achievements in various fields indicate their cultural levels and help explain the nature and extent of the Indian contributions to Western civilization.

Religious practices were important. Religion was an important influence in the lives of most Indians, and among the Mayas, Aztecs, and Incas, the priests exercised great power. Many American Indians worshiped the sun. Several tribes had other gods that represented something in daily life, such as agriculture or an aspect of nature. Religious ceremonies took place constantly. They were an important part of everyday life.

One of the most important features of Indian religion was human sacrifice. This custom grew out of the widespread Indian belief that people must give something of great value to the gods in order to receive favors in return. As nothing was more valuable than human life itself, sacrifice took on a noble and holy quality.

Indians stressed group living. Indian life among most groups centered around the tribe or the clan and not around the individual. Often, the tribe owned all the land and individuals did not own land privately.

Among Indians who farmed for a living, the land was often given out to the people on a more or less equal basis. Upon marriage, every man usually received a plot of land. But this land could be redistributed at any time. For example, the land of an Aztec farmer might, and probably would, be worked by his son after the father's death. Neither the father nor son, however, had the right of private ownership. They could not prevent the village council from giving the land to someone else.

Indian achievements varied. In the field of writing and literature, the Mayas and Aztecs created a system of writing. All American Indian peoples had literature. It was passed on by word of mouth from generation to generation. Most of the literature took the form of poetry and often expressed religious ideas or tribal traditions. Indians also liked to tell myths and legends about animals and war.

In arts and crafts, Indians produced very beautiful basketry, weaving, embroidery, metalwork, painting, sculpture, and architecture. Sculpture decorated temples and palaces. Low-relief carvings adorned walls, illustrating historical events or religious ceremonies. Indians also made fine pottery, especially in what is now the southwestern United States and in Peru. Several of the Latin American tribes excelled in metalwork with gold, silver, and copper.

One serious obstacle to progress in such fields as science and technology was the lack of draft animals. Llamas could only carry light loads, and there were no horses or cattle in America before the coming of Europeans. As a result, Indians had to rely on human power for many difficult and time-consuming tasks. Probably because of the lack of draft animals, the early peoples of America did not develop the use of the wheel. We know that they knew about this important principle since ancient Indian toys with wheels have been found.

Indian contributions enriched world culture. Indian influences are seen in several aspects of American life. Indian names occur throughout the Western Hemisphere. They have been given to countries, provinces, states, towns, cities, rivers, and lakes throughout Canada, the United States, and Latin America. For example, Alaska, Mississippi, Illinois, and Wyoming are among states in the United States that have Indian names.

Some Indian words were adopted into English. For example, the English words of avocado, chocolate, tomato, chili, ocelot, and coyote were all originally Aztec words. Indians also are credited with many important inventions still in use today. They invented the snowshoe, toboggan, and canoe. In medicine, they first used quinine, cocaine, and the bulb syringe. They first discovered the properties of rubber, developed adobe for building, and invented the game of lacrosse. Indian ingenuity also provided such technical contributions as cochineal [koch'ə nēl'] dye, a red dye made from the dried bodies of an insect, and henequen [hen'ə kin], a fiber from the leaves of a desert plant used for making rope.

In most Indian groups, both men and women worked as farmers. Together, they planted, cared for, and harvested the crops.

The most important contributions of the early peoples of the Americas, however, were in the field of agriculture. Although most of the early Europeans who conquered the Indians had eyes only for the gold and silver they could carry home, it was the humble farm products they took back that made the most lasting impression on world civilization. The Indians were the first to grow corn, potatoes, tomatoes, squash, pumpkins, avocados, and several kinds of beans. From them other peoples of the world also learned about pineapples, strawberries, vanilla, cinnamon, tapioca, and chocolate. Indians were also the first to make maple sugar and to develop chicle [chik'əl], the main ingredient of chewing gum.

All these products greatly increased the quantity and variety of the food supply in Europe and Africa. In Ireland and much of northern Europe, for example, the white potato became a major food crop. And when Europeans began settling in the New World, it was these foods, as well as the farming techniques that the Indians taught them, that made it possible for the European colonists to survive and flourish.

section review 5

1. Which social group in Maya, Aztec, and Inca society was probably most important? Why?

2. In what way was the tribe more important than the individual in Indian life?

3. Name at least three or more agricultural contributions Indians made to world civilization.

4. What effect did Indian foods have in Europe and Africa?

Section Summaries

1. American Indian cultures developed over many centuries. The first peoples of North and South America probably came from Asia and spread gradually over two continents. There were many different Indian cultures. Each reflected the way Indians learned to live with their environment, and included Eskimos in the extreme north who were hunters and fishers, as well as Pueblo Indians in the southwestern United States who were farmers. After the Indians learned to grow corn, they established permanent settlements and developed new skills.

2. The Mayas achieved a most complex civilization. In the Mayan Old Empire, writing was developed, a system of numbers came into use, and a very accurate calendar was invented. Several cities were centers of learning. In the New Empire, city-states were ruled by priests. Toltec warriors conquered the Mayas.

3. The Aztecs conquered much of central Mexico. The Aztecs ruled a vast empire from their capital city of Tenochtitlan. Religion dominated Aztec life, and the Aztecs were frequently at war, capturing victims for their sacrifices.

4. The Incas controlled a vast empire in South America. Tiahuanaco culture developed in the Andes Mountains. The Inca was king, and a highly centralized government took care of all the people's needs.

5. Indians had distinctive customs. The various Indian cultures developed differently. But there are some customs that are similar among them. Religion was important in most cultures. Most Indians valued the group above the individual. And Indian achievements in the arts and handicrafts are among the most beautiful in the world. World culture has been enhanced by Indian contributions, especially in the areas of language and agriculture.

Who? What? When? Where?

1. Place these events in order from first to last:
   a. The Mayan New Empire flourished.
   b. Corn was developed in Central America.
   c. Spaniards landed in Mexico.
   d. The first Indians grew crops.
   e. Tenochtitlan was built.
   f. The Mayan Old Empire flourished.

2. Write sentences identifying each of these terms with the correct Indian culture:

   a. codex   f. potlatch
   b. feathered serpent g. pyramid
   c. Five Nations   h. quipus
   d. maguey   i. totem pole
   e. Mexica   j. warrior madness

3. Name the ruler who said, "In my kingdom no bird flies, no leaf quivers if I do not will it." What does this tell about the society this ruler controlled?

4. Tell which area each of the groups below lived in: North America, Central America, South America.

   a. Aztec   e. Maya
   b. Inca   f. Mohawk
   c. Eskimo   g. Oneida
   d. Hopi   h. Toltec

Questions for Critical Thinking

1. The Inca Empire expanded north and south along the coast of South America. What probably prevented eastward expansion?

2. What effect has environment had on the development of the cultures of the Eskimo, Maya, Aztec, and Inca peoples? What effect has environment had on your culture?

3. Which do you feel were the most important Indian achievements? Why?

4. Compare the Aztec and Inca methods of controlling their empires. How were the conquered peoples treated in each? What are some advantages and disadvantages of each system?

5. Why do you think the Spanish conquerors destroyed the Indian temples and books?

6. How was the Indian system of landholding different from others? What does the Indian system tell you about their attitude toward the tribe and toward the individual?

Skill Activities

1. Read *In the Trail of the Wind, American Indian Poems and Ritual Orations* by John Bierhorst to learn more about the cultures and beliefs of America's first settlers. (Farrar, Straus, and Giroux, 1971)

2. On a map of North America show the area controlled by the League of the Iroquois about 1700 A.D.

3. Prepare a chart listing four or more contributions of Indians to world culture. Illustrate it with pictures you find in magazines or draw yourself.

4. Write 37 using Mayan numerals. Try writing some others. Can you add or subtract using Mayan numerals? How might you write this equation: $23-3=20$?

5. Prepare a menu for a meal using only foods available to the American Indians before 1500.

6. On an outline map of the world, trace the spread of the use of different foods mentioned in this chapter.

7. Imagine you were an Aztec when the Spanish came. Write a diary account of the actions of the Spanish and the reactions of the Aztec people. Be sure to include your own personal reactions to the events.

chapter **14** *quiz*

Section 1

1. The first people to live in the Americas came from: a. Asia, b. Europe, c. Africa

2. True or false: Wheat was domesticated by peoples in the New World perhaps as early as 4000 B.C.

3. The heavily carved wooden pole used to identify the spirit belonging to a North Pacific Coast Indian family was called a: a. potlatch, b. wigwam, c. totem

Section 2

4. The Mayan city-states were centers of: a. warfare, b. religion, c. manufacturing

5. Although evidence is not complete, it is believed that the ball game played in Mayan cities was a: a. religious ceremony, b. national spectator sport, c. children's game

6. One thing not invented by the Mayas was: a. a calendar, b. the codex, c. zero

Section 3

7. Mexico City stands today where once stood: a. Teotihuacan, b. Cuzco, c. Tenochtitlan

8. The Aztecs made many human sacrifices because they: a. did not value human life, b. believed the gods demanded it, c. enjoyed killing

Section 4

9. True or false: *Tiahuanaco* means "White Land."

10. Inca records were kept by means of: a. a number system based on 20, b. picture writing, c. knotted ropes

Section 5

11. The group most important to Indians was the: a. family, b. village council, c. tribe

12. The Indian contribution that changed European life most was: a. foods, b. gold, c. guns

1. Match the cultural group with the statement that describes it: Aztec, Five Nations, Ghana, Inca, Kanem-Bornu, Mali, Maya, Pueblo, Songhai, Zimbabwe

   a. The Portuguese traded for gold with these people but were never allowed to enter their territory.

   b. They controlled the area from Lake Michigan to the Atlantic Ocean and from Canada to Tennessee.

   c. This empire was carefully regulated by the ruler who used runners to carry messages to any part of it.

   d. Italian city-states used "Guinea gold" from this empire for their coins.

   e. Experts from Egypt and the Ottoman Empire trained the army of this state to use guns.

   f. Although very well organized, this empire was destroyed by wars with Muslim armies that had guns.

   g. This empire's power came from its location near the "silent trade."

   h. These people fought only when necessary; their warriors had to be cleansed of their "madness."

   i. Among this group's accomplishments were the calendar and the number zero.

   j. A warlike people from the northwest, they built a beautiful city on a lake.

2. People trained to remember important historical events were: a. North Africans and Mayas, b. West Africans and Aztecs, c. West Africans and Incas, d. East Africans and Pueblos

3. Plows were not used for farming in African rain forests because: a. iron was not used in Africa, b. only the top layer of soil was fertile, c. plots of land were too small to be plowed, d. there were too many wars

4. American Indians did not use wagons to carry loads because: a. there were no animals to pull the wagons, b. they did not know what wheels were, c. their roads were too narrow

5. The Portuguese explorers who reached the east coast of Africa: a. found only primitive tribal groups, b. brought items needed by the Africans, c. destroyed a thriving trading culture

6. Match the letters on the time line with the events they stand for.

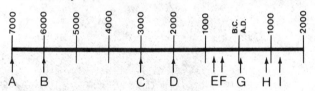

_____Ibn Batuta visited Timbuktu.

_____The Sahara became dry.

_____Kush conquered Egypt.

_____Indians first grew crops.

_____Ironworking became common in Egypt.

_____Sahara cave paintings were first made.

_____Corn developed in Central America.

_____Mayas had an accurate calendar and writing by this time.

_____Tiahuanaco culture died.

7. Match each letter on the map with the group that centered in that area:

_____Incas

_____North Pacific Coast Tribes

_____Aztecs

_____Mayas

_____Iroquois

UNIT FIVE
THE WORLD
OF ASIA

During early modern times, Asians did much to reach the promise of greatness foreshadowed in their early history. This unit looks at the history and culture of people in India, China, and Japan.

In India, Muslim rulers gave their Hindu subjects several centuries of generally good government. They were also great patrons of art and learning.

About the same time that Muslims pushed into India, nomadic northern people became a constant threat to China. From 906 to the late 1700s, four great dynasties governed: Sung, Mongol, Ming, and Manchu. Although two were foreign invaders, the Mongol and Manchu, Chinese civilization persisted. It produced great art and made important advances in science.

Off the Asian mainland was a group of islands whose people became known as the Japanese. Their legendary beginnings go back to the 7th century B.C. Feudalism shaped much of Japanese history. The Japanese developed a rich and distinctive civilization that included a strong love of nature. Great skill was also reached in poetry, drama, and painting.

All three of these Asian civilizations developed serious political weaknesses by the 18th century. In India and China, the weaknesses eventually led to European control.

The handscroll called Peach Blossom Spring uses the Chinese artistic style of painting the spirit of the subject rather than the exact image.

CHAPTER 15
INDIA UNDER MUSLIM RULE

● Muslims first invaded India

Mahmud of Ghazni first raided India ●

● Muslims began several kingdoms

CHAPTER 16
CHINA FROM THE SUNGS TO THE MANCHUS

● Arabs and Chinese clashed

● Tang dynasty ended

Wang An Shih became prime minister ●

● Sung dynasty began

CHAPTER 17
THE EMERGENCE OF JAPAN

● Capital city built at Nara

● Heian Era began

● Kyoto became capital

● *The Tale of Genji* written

● Prince Shotoku sent delegation to China

● Prince Shotoku died

● Japan sent last great embassy to China

600 650 700 750 800 850 900 950 1000 1050 1100 1150

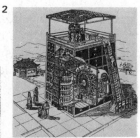

1. Japanese screen showing
Tale of Genji, detail,
2. Chinese observatory with
water-powered clock,
3. Japanese scroll, detail,
4. Chinese scroll, detail,
5. Tamerlane, 6. Akbar,
7. Dome of the Taj Mahal.

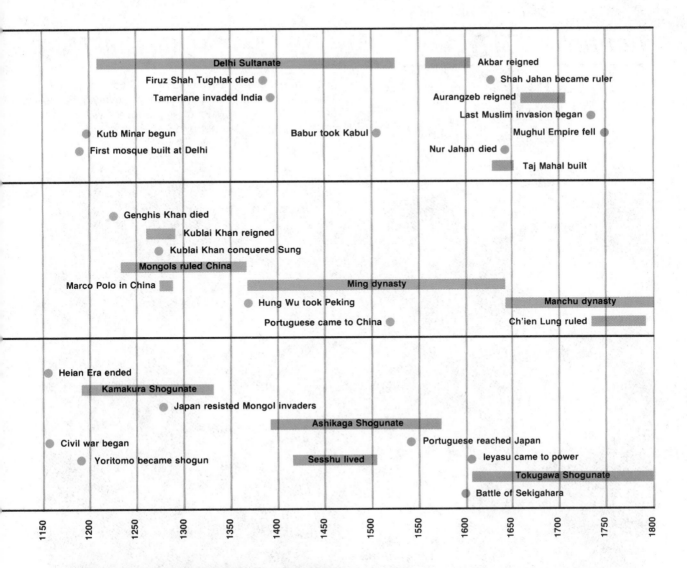

Delhi Sultanate

Firuz Shah Tughlak died

Tamerlane invaded India

Kutb Minar begun

First mosque built at Delhi

Babur took Kabul

Akbar reigned

Shah Jahan became ruler

Aurangzeb reigned

Last Muslim invasion began

Mughul Empire fell

Nur Jahan died

Taj Mahal built

Genghis Khan died

Kublai Khan reigned

Kublai Khan conquered Sung

Mongols ruled China

Marco Polo in China

Ming dynasty

Hung Wu took Peking

Portuguese came to China

Manchu dynasty

Ch'ien Lung ruled

Heian Era ended

Kamakura Shogunate

Japan resisted Mongol invaders

Ashikaga Shogunate

Portuguese reached Japan

Civil war began

Yoritomo became shogun

Sesshu lived

Ieyasu came to power

Tokugawa Shogunate

Battle of Sekigahara

1150 1200 1250 1300 1350 1400 1450 1500 1550 1600 1650 1700 1750 1800

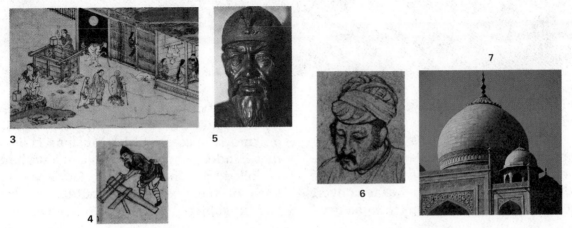

3

4

5

6

7

INDIA UNDER MUSLIM RULE

Painting, especially miniatures, flourished during Muslim rule. Much of the painting showed the everyday parts of court life. Here a Mughul emperor receives visitors while playing with his pet bird.

Beginning in the 13th century, Muslim rulers governed India for more than 600 years. One of their major problems was how to rule a large population in which Islam was the religion of only a minority. The Koran plainly stated that the duty of a ruler was to convert *infidels*, or unbelievers. Sultans in India used violence, social pressure, and missionaries to try to force the Hindus to convert, but without much success. Strict Muslims believed that Hindus who refused to convert should be killed. But the Muslim rulers knew that most of the taxes and tribute came from Hindu subjects; it would not have made good sense to kill all the Hindus. But how then, should India be governed? In the early 1300s, a sultan discussed this problem with a Muslim scholar. The scholar said,

> When the revenue officer demands silver from the Hindus, they should, without question and with all humility and respect, [give] gold. If the officer throws dirt into their mouths, they must without reluctance open their mouths wide to receive it. By doing so they show respect for the officer. . . . To keep the Hindus in abasement is especially a religious duty, because they are the most inveterate enemies of the Prophet, and because the Prophet has commanded us to slay them, plunder them, and make them captive.

Then the sultan said,

> Oh, doctor, thou art a learned man, but thou hast had no experience; I am an unlettered man, but I have seen a great deal; be assured then that the Hindus will never become submissive and obedient till they are reduced to poverty. I have, therefore, given orders that just [enough] shall be left to them from year to year, of corn, milk, and curds, but that they shall not be allowed to accumulate hoards and property.

Many sultans followed this harsh policy. They were able to do so because they had a strong military force. Even though the Hindus greatly outnumbered the Muslims, the Hindus were not united. India therefore was ruled by Muslims, but the small number of Muslims meant that Hindu life in the villages continued unchanged.

Not all Muslim rulers in India were cruel and brutal. Some governed with fairness and justice and were considered the greatest of all Muslim rulers. Others were strong supporters of art, literature, and architecture. During their reigns, masterpieces were produced that are among the finest the world has ever known. In this chapter, the following sections will describe how:

1. **Muslims controlled India for centuries.**

2. **Hindus lived and worked under Muslim rule.**

3. **The Mughuls united and ruled most of India.**

4. **The Mughul Empire declined quickly.**

1 Muslims controlled India for centuries

Arab Muslims invaded and established a foothold in the southern Indus Valley as early as the year 711 A.D., but rulers in India prevented them from expanding. Then, 300 years later, another Muslim force came to India. The Muslim sultanate of the city of Delhi [del′ē] became the most important power in India until 1526.

Muslim invaders came from the north. During the 11th and 12th centuries, warlike Muslim invaders came from the mountainous country of Afghanistan through the passes into northwest India. Some were Afghans and some were Turks from Turkestan in central Asia, but all of them believed in the religion of Islam, the faith of the Prophet Mohammad. They were firm believers in one God and looked down on the Hindus as heathen worshipers of many idols. In the Islamic religion, all followers were equal in the eyes of Allah; Muslims could not understand the inequalities of the Hindu caste system. They believed that India was to be conquered and plundered.

At first, the invaders came as robbers to

loot the gold and jewels of Indian cities and to destroy Hindu temples and shrines. Mahmud of Ghazni, who made his first raid on the India plains in 986, believed it was his duty to kill Hindus and his right to get a good profit of treasure from a holy war. He usually left his cool mountain country in the fall of the year, returning home with his plunder as the hot season began in India. In all, he made seventeen raids. Terrible battles were fought in which the Hindu forces were usually defeated. Cities were attacked and their populations massacred.

Several factors led to the invaders' victories. First, the Hindu fighting tactics were quite out of date. Second, although the Hindus had huge armies, the jealous commanders did not work well together to plan and carry out a consistent defense. Third, the many elephants used by the Hindus usually bolted in panic once the fighting began. Fourth, the Hindus used only one warrior caste for defense; in the Muslim forces every man was a soldier. Fifth, the invaders were physically bigger and stronger. And sixth, once the invaders had passed through the mountains there was no easy retreat. They had to win or die.

The Muslim leaders created kingdoms. Once it was clear how rich and weak India was, Muslim leaders began setting themselves up as kings and princes. Between the years 1000 and 1500 they established many *sultanates*, or independent Muslim kingdoms.

The Delhi Sultanate was the most powerful (1206 to 1526). The most important Muslim kingdom centered around the great city of Delhi. This kingdom lasted from 1206 to 1526. During this time, much of northern India and part of the Deccan region in southern India was governed from Delhi.

The history of the Delhi Sultanate is not a pleasant one. Its rulers were an amazing mixture of opposite qualities—cruelty, harshness, generosity, and often a keen interest in learning and art. One such sultan obtained his throne by murdering his father and getting rid of a number of close relatives whom he regarded as rivals. This ruler varied his actions from handsome gifts for those who had his favor to executions for those who earned his displeasure. It was said that at his door one could always see either some poor person on the way to wealth or on the way to execution.

Firuz Shah Tughlak [fē rüz' shä' təg lak'] was the best of the Delhi sultans. He stopped the torture of criminals and built towns, dams, bridges, and hospitals. He had little use for Hinduism and destroyed some of its temples, but he gave the country a prosperous reign.

Following Tughlak's death in 1388, civil war broke out. Taking advantage of the confusion, the Muslim conqueror Timur the Lame (Tamerlane) brought an army of 90 thousand horsemen into India in 1398. He came to find treasure and to kill as many infidel Hindus as possible. He met an Indian army outside the gates of Delhi. The defenders had 120 huge war elephants protected with armor. However, by skillful tactics, Tamerlane's army managed to stampede the elephants.

Delhi was captured and plundered. Most of its people fled or were massacred. It was said that "For two whole months not a bird moved a wing in the city." Tamerlane left India in 1399 as quickly as he had come. The Delhi sultanate slowly restored order, but its rulers had little authority. In 1526 the rulers, like their victims before them, were destroyed by an invasion from the north.

The Delhi sultans brought new ways of life to India. Until the time of the Muslim invasions, the Hindus had always been able to

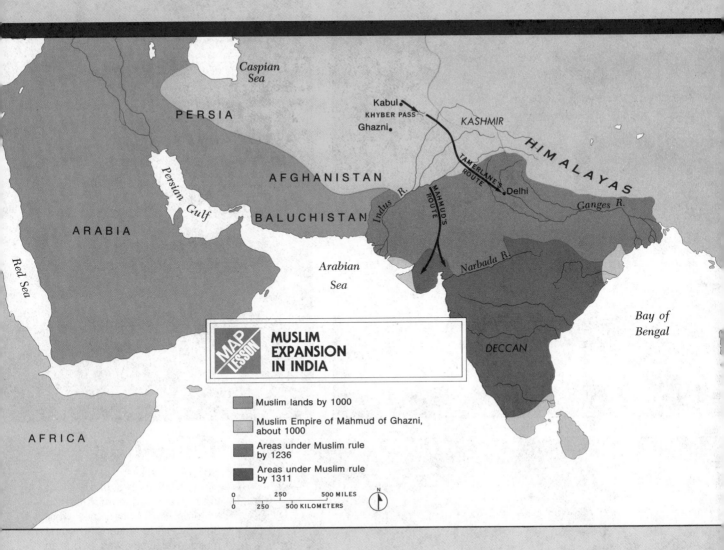

MAP
LESSON

MUSLIM EXPANSION IN INDIA

- ◼ Muslim lands by 1000
- ◻ Muslim Empire of Mahmud of Ghazni, about 1000
- ◼ Areas under Muslim rule by 1236
- ◼ Areas under Muslim rule by 1311

```
0        250        500 MILES
0    250      500 KILOMETERS
```

◼ MAP LESSON 15: MUSLIM EXPANSION IN INDIA

This is a relatively simple historical map. It provides a good opportunity to review basic map skills. Decide whether the following questions are true or false:

1. Although part of Africa is indicated on this map, most of the map shows Asia.

2. The entire Persian Gulf region became Muslim territory before 1000 A.D.

3. By 1311 A.D., Muslim territories included all of India and the nearby island of Sri Lanka.

4. The Empire of Mahmud of Ghazni extended from the mouth of the Ganges River to the Red Sea.

5. Kashmir is largely drained by the Indus River.

6. A person traveling from Kabul to the Caspian Sea would probably use the Khyber Pass.

7. Delhi became an important city in the Deccan.

8. The Himalayas did not form much of a barrier to the spread of Islam.

9. By 1311 A.D., Muslim lands reached from the Red Sea eastward to the Ganges Delta.

10. Baluchistan is located on the northern shore of the Arabian Sea.

11. The Bay of Bengal is mostly north of the Arabian Sea.

DailyLife

India became a land of many religions. Muslims brought Islam to India. The mosques had Islamic features, even when they were built by Hindu artisans. The first mosque at Delhi was begun in 1193. The ruins are shown at *top left*. The minaret is the Kutb Minar. It and the nearby arch are typical of Muslim architecture. The Hindus had been building fabulous temples for centuries. The Temple of Vishnu at Khajuraho, *left,* was built in 1003 and is typical of Hindu lavishness. Almost every inch is carved in floral and geometric designs. The Golden Temple of the Sikh religion is at Amritsar, *top right.* The Sikh religion was founded by Nanak to change what he saw as problems in Hinduism.

absorb invaders who took on Indian ways. However, this absorption did not happen during the Delhi Sultanate. There was very little mixing between the two peoples. The Muslims thought of themselves as a superior race. Muslim women were secluded in harems or veiled in public. The Muslims ate meat, which angered the Hindus. In addition, the Muslims created a great deal of bitterness by their brutal methods of conquest and the destruction of many Hindu temples.

However, there was some contact between the two peoples. Some Hindus were employed as officials in the Muslim government, and others were converted to Islam. Intermarriage of Muslim men and Hindu women, while not common, did take place. Various habits of living were exchanged. Some Hindus adopted the Muslim custom of *purdah* [pėr'də], the seclusion of women, and Muslim dress was also copied. Most of the Muslims lived in cities, and their rule had little effect on village life. The Hindu villagers continued the customs and ways developed over many centuries by their ancestors. Thus, the Muslims were a governing minority in a foreign land.

Muslim rulers, though often cruel, were great lovers of art. They put up many beautiful buildings and introduced a new style of architecture that blended both Indian and Islamic features. The arch, dome, and minaret (tower) were especially featured. Many fine examples, such as mosques, still stand in the modern city of Delhi. Most mosques had a minaret from which an official called Muslims to prayer several times a day. (Today, in large Muslim cities such as Cairo, Egypt, loudspeakers are used.) One of the most famous of these minarets at Delhi is the great tower of Kutb Minar [küb mə när']. It is 238 feet (71.4 meters) high, decorated with beautiful carving, and is unrivaled anywhere in the Muslim world.

section review 1

1. What were some reasons for the cruelty of the sultans?

2. Give at least five reasons for the victory of the Muslims over the Hindu armies. Which were Hindu weaknesses? Which were Muslim strengths?

3. Describe Firuz Shah Tughlak and the Delhi Sultanate.

4. Why weren't the Muslims absorbed into Hindu culture as other invaders had been?

2 Hindus lived and worked under Muslim rule

During the period of the Delhi Sultanate, the masses of Hindus had to bear heavy taxes and were made to feel that they were a conquered people. Village life, however, was little touched by Muslim government. The village was really a small self-governing unit, free to manage its own affairs.

Most Hindus were farmers. India has always been a farming country. The great majority of the people made their living on the land. Indian farmers grew crops such as wheat, barley, cotton, sugar cane, rice, and millet. The peasant in medieval India, like many today, had few and simple farming tools: plows, hoes, and water-lifts for irrigating. Oxen helped with the heavy work—pulling plows and carts and raising large buckets of water from wells.

Indian peasants were bound by ancient rules of landholding and taxes. There were always two parties: the ruler and the tenant farmer. The farmer worked the land and gave the ruler a share of what was produced.

DailyLife

Mughul rule was a busy time for India. Rulers, such as Akbar, organized great expeditions to hunt elephants, *top left*. The elephants were then trained for use in fighting wars. At the same time, the Mughuls were great art patrons. Akbar's tomb, *bottom left,* is a classic example of the elegance and symmetry of Mughul building. Throughout these years, religion continued to have great influence. At *top*, Hindus travel to a small temple of Siva.

The ruler, in turn, gave protection. While rulers might come and go, the role of farmer peasants changed very little as long as they paid their taxes. No matter who was the ruler, the peasants usually had very little left over after taxes.

The village was self-sufficient. Just as India's economic life depended on agriculture, so its social and family life centered around the village. In medieval times, nearly 90 percent of the people lived in the country. There was very little migration to other villages or to cities. People were born, lived, and died in their villages. The village was made up of various families who had lived there for centuries.

Villages were relatively isolated from one another, since roads were very poor. Each little community had to be responsible for its food and equipment. In the village, therefore, lived the artisans—the carpenters, ironworkers, potters, weavers, and leather workers—whose work produced what the community needed. The village people had no money, so they paid for supplies in produce or work.

Life in the village was busy. Barbers and washermen carried on their trades. The potter made jars, pitchers, cooking pots, and cups. The carpenter built chests, boxes, and bed frames. The blacksmith hammered out iron tips for plows and tools for the carpenter and the tailor.

Sometimes, entertainers came to the marketplace. They traveled from village to village, performing as jugglers, ropedancers, and acrobats. Snake charmers sat cross-legged on the ground. Each played a flute, thus seeming to cause a deadly cobra to swing and sway as it came out of a jar in front of him.

The houses in the village were small mud cottages with thatched roofs and dark, windowless rooms. These cottages were crowded together on narrow, dirty streets. A ditch in front of the houses served as the kitchen garbage pail: all the waste from the house was dumped out the door.

The family was the most important force in an Indian villager's life. Hindus had a joint-family system that has come down to the present. The joint family consisted of father and mother, their sons, grandsons, and the wives and daughters of all who were married. The joint family was controlled by the father while he was alive. After the father's death, the eldest son took charge. All males of the group were consulted on important matters. All land and income belonged to the group as a whole.

Within the family, Hindu women had inferior status. The most important event in a Hindu woman's life was marriage. Families arranged the marriages of their children, picking out prospective husbands and wives when they were very young. Dating, as it is known in the United States, did not exist. Wives treated their husbands with great respect. A wife called her husband, "My master, my lord." However, he often treated her with little politeness.

The role of a widow was special. She could not remarry and had to live with her dead husband's family. She could not attend family feasts and was expected to get by on one small meal a day. Often she had to shave her head.

If a widow did not obey these harsh rules, Hindus believed that she would have an unhappy rebirth in her next life. When the body of her dead husband was *cremated* [krē'māt əd], or burned, on a funeral pyre, it was considered most honorable for the wife to throw herself on the fire with her mate. This custom, called *suttee* [su'tē'], was not declared illegal until the early 1800s.

Hindu India was very religious. India was always a land of religion. Religious shrines and temples dotted the entire landscape. Indian villagers were Hindus who worshiped many gods and believed people were born into new lives after death (reincarnation). Many villages had several religious processions every year. The statue of a god was placed on a huge wooden cart and pulled through the streets.

Hindus were rigidly divided into castes, or classes, that strictly controlled all features of village life. A person's caste regulated what one's job could be, who one's friends could be, whom one could eat with, and whom one could marry. There were thousands of different castes. Some were considered to be very high while others were thought to be barely human. A person was born into his or her caste. Good behavior was rewarded in the next life, when it was believed a worthy person would be born into a higher caste. Caste is still very strong in rural India.

section review 2

1. How did Muslim rule affect Indian village life?

2. Why were the small villages so important to Indian society?

3. Who were the members of the joint family?

4. Describe the status of a married Hindu woman.

3 The Mughuls united and ruled most of India

By the early 1500s, the Delhi Sultanate had grown too weak to rule north India. New Muslim conquerors came through the mountain passes and established a rule, called Mughul [mú'gül] rule, in India. Mughul rulers expanded the territories under their control to include all but the southern tip of India.

Babur invades India. A young ruler named Babur [bä'bər] started his career as the ruler of a little kingdom in central Asia. He was an adventurer and a fighting man, a Muslim descendant of the dreaded Mongol conquerors Tamerlane and Genghis Khan. In 1504, Babur captured the important city of Kabul, in what is now Afghanistan.

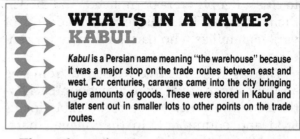

WHAT'S IN A NAME?
KABUL

Kabul is a Persian name meaning "the warehouse" because it was a major stop on the trade routes between east and west. For centuries, caravans came into the city bringing huge amounts of goods. These were stored in Kabul and later sent out in smaller lots to other points on the trade routes.

The riches of India aroused his ambition. He made several raids into the country. In 1526, he completely defeated the weak Muslim sultan at Delhi. A group of Hindu chiefs formed an army to try to regain control of northern India, but Babur defeated them too. The era of Mughul (from the Persian word for Mongol) rule now began.

Babur had little time to organize his new government. He died only five years after his conquest. However, he is regarded as one of India's great leaders. Not only a brave soldier and a wise statesman, he also was interested in the beauty of fine gardens, poetry, and art. His *Memoirs* are great literature.

Akbar became emperor. For about twenty years after Babur's death, rival groups weakened Mughul control. Then Babur's grandson, Akbar, became ruler at Delhi in 1556. Though only thirteen years old, he defeated a strong Hindu army. By 1576, he had extended his rule eastward by conquering

Bihar and Bengal. Ten years later, Kabul and Kashmir in the north were added. By 1595, when Baluchistan became a part of his empire, Akbar was the undisputed ruler of northern India.

Akbar created an excellent governmental system. His empire was divided into a dozen provinces and placed in the hands of well-paid and efficient civil servants. Well-educated men from various parts of central Asia came into his service. Seventy percent were from outside India, the rest were Hindu or Muslim Indians. These officials throughout the country formed a network that carried out the Mughul orders from Delhi. In addition, Akbar had many soldiers in the provinces and twelve thousand horsemen ready for any emergency.

Justice was administered uniformly. In each village, the headman was responsible for keeping law and order. In the cities, special officials decided law cases. Akbar himself often acted as judge; everyone under his rule had the right to appeal to him personally. He tried to outlaw the practice of suttee and allowed widows to remarry. Child marriages were also made illegal.

Akbar accepted all religions. Unlike the Delhi sultans, he was not hostile toward Hindus. He had been raised as a Muslim, but he had doubts about this faith and searched for a religion that all people in his empire could accept. Akbar enjoyed debates and discussions about religion. He invited several Catholic priests to visit him and explain the doctrine of Christianity. Finally, he created his own religion, called the Divine Faith, which borrowed from several religions. It did not, however, make many converts.

As emperor, Akbar's goal was to unite all Muslims and Hindus under a common loyalty to Mughul rule. He accepted Hindu chiefs into his government and also married several Hindu princesses, giving them an

International relations were important even during Mughul times. To cement their friendly relations, Emperor Jahangir of India and Shah Abbas of Persia had their portraits drawn in mutual embrace. They stand upon the lion and the lamb, symbols of peace, with part of a globe as the base. Jahangir probably selected the artist since he is drawn the larger.

Nur Jahan

A Persian, she was the wife of Emperor Jahangir. She wrote poetry, created a perfume, and once killed four tigers with just five arrows. She was smart, beautiful, well educated, filled with common sense, and very ambitious. In a time and place that kept wealthy women behind veils and walls, Nur Jahan ran an empire. Jahangir said all he needed was some wine and food; he had Nur Jahan to rule the kingdom.

She held royal audiences and carried on much of the daily administration of the kingdom. She made her father the chief minister of the government and gave other high posts to additional relatives, including her brother. Nobles saluted her as they did Jahangir. Her name appeared on coins. Twice she put down revolts. When Jahangir was once taken prisoner, Nur Jahan voluntarily joined him and then hatched a plot that brought their escape.

Jahangir died in October, 1627, a victim of his addiction to opium. His successor, Shah Jahan, exiled Nur Jahan to Lahore. There she spent the last 18 years of her life, once bitterly saying that being without power was like death itself.

honored place in the royal household. He tried to give all his subjects justice, religious freedom, and relief from unfair taxes.

Akbar was one of the greatest and most interesting rulers in history. He had many gifts. He enjoyed the sport of hunting and the excitement of battle and could ride for hours without tiring. He was also interested in architecture, painting, and good books. When he died in 1605, his empire was perhaps the best governed and most prosperous in the world.

Rulers after Akbar had serious faults. Akbar's successors, such as Jahangir and his wife Nur Jahan, continued the peace and prosperity that began during his rule. Generally, however, they did not have his wisdom. Bloody feuds often took place between contestants for the throne. Akbar's grandson, Shah Jahan [shä' jə hän'], became emperor in 1628 after a bitter quarrel in which most of his male relatives were murdered. His reign was the high point of Mughul power, a kind of golden age. The royal treasury is estimated to have had a value of more than one billion dollars. The emperor's court was famous for its luxury and splendor. Great palaces and forts were built; artists and musicians were supported.

But the people did not live as well as they had under Akbar. They were taxed too heavily. In addition, Shah Jahan began to end the religious freedom allowed by his grandfather. Hindu temples were destroyed, and Islam was restored as the official state religion.

The Mughuls were great builders. The Mughul emperors were very interested in the arts: painting, literature, music, and architecture.

Akbar was a great builder of forts, tombs, and palaces. His most famous work was the capital city of Fatehpur Sikri [fät'ə per si'-krē]. Within it there were many beautiful

Along the north bank of the Jumna River, at the town of Agra, stands the Taj Mahal. Nestled in a huge garden of trees and reflecting ponds, it is the tomb built by Shah Jahan for his wife Mumtaz Mahal. The queen's name means "jewel of the palace." And it is from her name that the tomb's name comes.

The number four and its multiples are repeated over and over in the buildings and gardens. The Taj itself is an eight-sided building topped by a bulbous dome. The white marble building sits on a raised square platform. At the four corners of the platform are matching minarets, or towers, also in white marble. At dusk, the sun's reflection turns the white into a soft pink.

The large garden is divided into four equal squares by the crossing of the two marble canals. One canal is lined with cypress trees, which stand for death. The other canal was lined with fruit trees, symbolizing life. The four squares are further divided into 16 flower beds. Each was planted with 400 flowers.

Inside the central eight-sided burial room are the monuments of Mumtaz Mahal and Shah Jahan. Surrounding the two monuments is an eight-sided marble screen that is carved in such a way that it looks like lace.

When at last the Taj Mahal was completed, Shah Jahan spread a blanket of pearls over the queen's monument. Around the coffin he placed a railing of solid gold. Gold lamps and silver candlesticks adorned the walls. Gates of solid silver guarded the entrances.

Legend says that as Mumtaz Mahal lay dying, she asked her husband to build for her a tomb of such perfect proportions and purity that no one could see it and not sense the power of love and its inevitable passing at death. Shah Jahan did just that.

At *left,* the quiet water of a marble canal acts as a mirror for the main building of the Taj Mahal. *Above,* the monument of Mumtaz Mahal stands in the center of the eight sided marble screen. Shah Jahan's monument is to the left.

buildings, such as a great mosque and a huge gateway made of delicate rose-colored sandstone which tourists visit today.

Under Shah Jahan, architecture reached its height. When his empress died, the sorrowing ruler built an exquisite tomb to her memory, the Taj Mahal [täj' mə häl']. It took more than twenty years, the labor of 20 thousand workers, and millions of dollars to build. With its decorated marble, minarets, formal gardens, and fountains, the Taj Mahal has been called "the miracle of miracles, the final wonder of the world."

At Delhi, Shah Jahan built fifty-two new palaces. One famous hall had ceilings of solid gold and silver. In it was the emperor's Peacock Throne, decorated with costly jewels.

Painting was not neglected by the Mughuls. Their artists developed an unusual style combining Persian, Hindu, and European methods. Literature also flourished, the official language being Persian. Valuable memoirs were written, and there were important poets and historians. The greatest historian of the age was Abul Fazl. He wrote a *Life of Akbar.*

section review 3

1. Why did Babur want to conquer India?

2. Describe the role of religion during Akbar's rule.

3. In what ways was Shah Jahan's rule a "golden age"?

4. How did the rule of Shah Jahan harm India?

4 The Mughul Empire declined quickly

When the aged Shah Jahan became ill and was unable to rule, rivalries broke out among his heirs. These ended in 1658, when one of his sons, Aurangzeb [ôr'əng zeb'], gained the throne after killing three of his brothers, as well as a son and a nephew. He also threw his father, Shah Jahan, into prison, where he died. Aurangzeb's rule was the beginning of the end of Mughul rule in India.

Aurangzeb tried to unite all of India. Once on the throne, Aurangzeb proved to be a stern and devout Muslim with a will of iron. He raised the taxes of Hindus, got rid of the Hindus in his government, and destroyed Hindu temples and schools. He came to think of himself as the ruler of a Muslim nation, not the ruler of all people of any faith. He was also opposed to most forms of recreation and the arts. Musicians and artists were dismissed from his service.

Aurangzeb's main ambition was to unite all India under Muslim rule, and this aim ended in disaster. He spent the last twenty-six years of his life trying to conquer the Hindu kingdoms in the Deccan and south

Aurangzeb

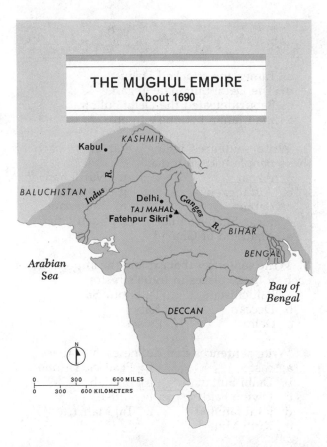

THE MUGHUL EMPIRE
About 1690

KASHMIR

Kabul.

BALUCHISTAN

Indus R.

Delhi.
TAJ MAHAL
Fatehpur Sikri.

Ganges R.

BIHAR

BENGAL

Arabian
Sea

Bay of
Bengal

DECCAN

N

0   300   600 MILES
0   300   600 KILOMETERS

India. Aurangzeb assembled great armies. In one huge tent city, 30 miles (48 kilometers) around, the army and servants totaled 500 thousand persons. In addition, there were 30 thousand elephants and 50 thousand camels.

By 1690, Aurangzeb claimed his authority extended from north India to its very tip in the far south. However, the conquest was never complete. Revolts continually broke out. Hindu forts, captured after hard fighting and several years of effort, were lost again to the Hindu armies.

Aurangzeb, tired and ill from directing his armies, left south India in 1705. He was now an old man. His pro-Islam policies and attempt to conquer all of India had failed. Despite the great amounts of money that had been spent, rebellions were taking place not only in the south but also in north India. The last of the great but misguided Mughul

emperors died in 1707, at the age of eighty-eight.

Conditions in India were miserable. During the next fifty years, law and order broke down in India. There were feuds between rival armies. Local governors set up independent kingdoms. The peasants were the victims of this lack of leadership; no law or power protected them from any prince or army in the area.

In 1739, a final Muslim invasion was led by the king of Persia. Delhi was captured and plundered. The crown jewels, the royal treasure, and the Peacock Throne were taken to Persia. The Mughuls never recovered from this blow.

Many reasons have been given for the fall of the Mughuls. For one, the old Mughul nobility, once so strong, had been wiped out in the bloody wars of succession. New nobles from central Asia were no longer recruited. Another reason was that the Mughuls were really an alien minority in a foreign land. Only Akbar's policies could have solved this weakness. There were also economic reasons, such as the corruption of officials who stole tax money, the oppression of the peasants, and the waste of money on wars.

By 1750, the Mughul Empire had split apart. The emperor still had his title but no power. India was now weak and open to new conquerors. This time they came not from across the mountains, but from across the seas, from Britain.

section review 4

1. In what ways did Aurangzeb's religious beliefs affect his rule?

2. What was Aurangzeb's main ambition?

3. When was the last Muslim invasion of India? What happened?

4. Give four or more reasons for the fall of the Mughuls.

Section Summaries

1. Muslims controlled India for centuries. The first Muslim invaders came into India in the 11th and 12th centuries. They set up kingdoms in north India. The most powerful of these was the Delhi Sultanate. The Delhi sultans were often cruel. However, they were lovers of art and architecture. Delhi rule was interrupted at the turn of the 15th century by Tamerlane. His fierce army captured Delhi and killed most of the population. The sultanate was rebuilt, but its rulers had little power, and in 1526, they were conquered by Babur.

2. Hindus lived and worked under Muslim rule. Muslim rule had very little effect on the vast majority of the Indian population, who were Hindu peasant farmers. Indian villages were small, isolated, and self-sufficient. Indian daily life was controlled by the joint-family system, the caste system, and the Hindu religion.

3. The Mughuls united and ruled most of India. After Babur's conquests, the first and greatest Mughul ruler was Akbar. He provided efficient government, uniform administration of justice, and religious toleration. He brought educated people into government service from within India and from central Asia. Akbar's grandson Shah Jahan is remembered for the luxury and magnificence of his reign. His buildings, such as the Taj Mahal, were fine pieces of architecture. He was a patron of the arts.

4. The Mughul Empire declined quickly. During Aurangzeb's reign, large amounts of money were spent on wars to bring all of the subcontinent under Muslim rule. Aurangzeb made enemies of his Hindu subjects. Revolts were frequent. After his death, India fell into chaos. In 1739, Persian invaders attacked the helpless empire. Delhi was captured, and its treasures were seized. By 1750, the Mughul Empire had fallen apart.

Who? What? When? Where?

1. Arrange these events in chronological order:
   a. Akbar became ruler at Delhi.
   b. Mahmud of Ghazni first raided India.
   c. Tamerlane attacked Delhi.
   d. The Delhi Sultanate began.
   e. Babur defeated the Delhi sultan.
   f. Shah Jahan became emperor.

2. Write sentences telling what effect each of these people had on India:
   a. Akbar   f. Nur Jahan
   b. Aurangzeb   g. Mumtaz
   c. Babur   h. Tamerlane
   d. Firuz Shah Tughlak   i. Shah Jahan
   e. Mahmud of Ghazni

3. Write sentences that explain the importance of each of these places in India's history:
   a. Baluchistan   d. Fatehpur Sikri
   b. Deccan   e. Kabul
   c. Delhi   f. Persia

4. Write sentences that define each of these:
   a. caste   f. Peacock Throne
   b. Delhi Sultanate   g. purdah
   c. Divine Faith   h. suttee
   d. joint family   i. Taj Mahal
   e. Kutb Minar

5. Write sentences that define these groups:
   a. Afghan   d. Mughul
   b. Hindu   e. Muslim
   c. Mongol   f. Turk

Questions for Critical Thinking

1. In your opinion, who was the greatest Muslim ruler of India? Explain your choice.

2. What internal problems did the Muslim governments in India have? What caused these problems? What might have been a solution?

3. What were the best and the worst aspects of Muslim rule in India?

4. In what ways did Muslim rule change Indian culture? What ways of life did not change? Why?

5. Why has it been difficult for Muslims and Hindus to live together peacefully in India? How could this problem be solved?

Skill Activities

1. Read *Historic India* by Lucille Shulberg to learn more about Akbar and Mughul rule in India. (Time-Life Books, 1968)

2. Draw a chart of all the members of a joint family. How many generations could be living at one time? How many different relationships could be included?

3. Class discussion: In what ways is India's joint family system like or unlike families in the United States?

4. Prepare a report on one of these: the Taj Mahal, the Peacock Throne, Muslim art, caste system in India today, or European contacts with India's Muslim rulers. If possible, show the class the books you used to write your report.

5. Trace the map in Chapter 3 called Ancient India. Draw arrows to show the directions from which the Indo-Aryans, Tamerlane, the Turks, and Mahmud of Ghazni came. Label the arrows. Also label the Deccan, Delhi, Kabul, Fatehpur Sikri, Ajanta, Mohenjo-Daro, Pataliputra, the Himalaya Mountains, the Hindu Kush Mountains, the Khyber Pass, the Arabian Sea, the Bay of Bengal, the Ganges River, and the Indus River. Use information from Chapter 3 as well as from this chapter to make the map.

chapter **15** quiz

Section 1

1. One thing that the Muslim invaders of India had in common was: a. race, b. religion, c. nationality

2. Elephants were not good for use in battle because: a. they often stampeded, b. they moved too slowly, c. they ate too much

3. True or false: The Muslim invaders made great changes at every level of Indian society.

Section 2

4. The most important part of India's economy has always been: a. trade, b. industry, c. farming

5. True or false: India's villages depended heavily on trade with each other.

6. The Indian custom of suttee is an example of: a. the high status of women in India, b. primitive farming methods, c. a male-dominated society

Section 3

7. Two things that Babur, Akbar, Shah Jahan, and Jahangir had in common were: a. they were all Mughul rulers and members of the same family, b. they all married Hindu women and were crowned on the Peacock Throne, c. they were all Mughul rulers and used Delhi as their capital

8. The Mughul ruler who built Fatehpur Sikri and brought large numbers of outsiders into government service was: a. Shah Jahan, b. Akbar, c. Jahangir

9. True or false: Shah Jahan tolerated all religions in his empire.

Section 4

10. A major problem of Muslim rule was: a. collecting taxes, b. choosing a new leader, c. finding artists to decorate buildings

11. One thing that did not contribute to the fall of the Mughuls was: a. corrupt officials angered the Hindu majority, b. invaders attacked from the north, c. Mughul nobles were weakened by rivalries

12. True or false: Aurangzeb ruled wisely and left the Mughul empire strong and peaceful at the end of his long reign.

CHINA FROM THE SUNGS THROUGH THE MANCHUS

This silk scroll was made during the Ming dynasty. It shows a noble family welcoming friends to a festival.

In Asia, Chinese civilization was the single greatest influence. From classical times, Chinese literature, philosophy, religion, and art affected the thinking of peoples throughout Asia. Chinese goods were traded widely in Asia and beyond.

A 13th-century European named Marco Polo returned to his home in Italy after nearly twenty years in China and wrote a travel book which gave a vivid picture of China. The things he described were so fantastic that Europeans refused to believe him. For example, he wrote of black stones that burn like logs. "These stones," he said, "keep a fire going better than wood." For writing such things, Marco Polo was called the "prince of liars" when he returned home.

The fact that coal was still not widely used in 13th-century Europe is only one example of how more advanced China was. For more than 1,000 years, no other nation in Asia could match the greatness of Chinese civilization. Even when the empire became politically or militarily weak and was invaded by foreigners, the invaders adopted Chinese culture and were absorbed into the Chinese population. China's way of life remained unchanged and continued to be the oldest civilization in the world. This chapter tells how:

1. Chinese civilization continued under the Sungs.

2. City life differed greatly from peasant life.

3. The Mongols ruled in China.

4. Mings and Manchus maintained Chinese culture.

1 Chinese civilization continued under the Sungs

In the years after the Tang dynasty, the Chinese Empire was not as big as it had been. Large areas were lost in wars, and the danger of invasion was always present. But scientific advances were made and great works of art and porcelain were completed. Scholars studied history and developed ideas that lasted to modern times.

The Chinese Empire lost much territory. At its height, Tang China included lands from Korea and Manchuria west through Tibet and central Asia to the Jaxartes River. (See map called China in Chapter 4.) Throughout this area, nobles and princes were vassals of the Chinese emperor. But the Chinese did not hold this territory long. In 751, Arabs intent on spreading Islam defeated the Chinese in central Asia. They took the province of Turkestan and converted the nomadic Turkic people living there.

The Tang dynasty came to an end in 906 after it was weakened by warfare on the borders and political corruption within the empire. Five weak dynasties followed the Tangs. Then, in 960, a strong new dynasty, the Sung, came to power. All through the years of Sung rule (960–1279), fierce nomadic tribes beyond the Great Wall were a constant danger.

Soon after the dynasty was established, a nomadic group from Manchuria began to fight its way into northern China. The Sung emperors believed they did not need to fight the nomads. They tried to appease them with bribes of money and silks. This only encouraged the nomads to ask for more. Then the Sungs tried to bribe one group of these barbarians to destroy another. This trick worked at first. But then the victors grew strong and turned against China. They captured the Chinese emperor and set up a Chin dynasty (not related to the earlier Ch'in) in northern China. The capital of the Chin Empire was Peking.

The Sung dynasty was not destroyed. The son of the captured emperor made a new capital at Hangchow in southern China. By 1127, there were two Chinese empires—the Chin in the north and the Sung in the south.

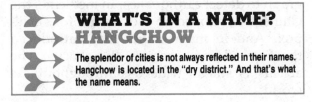

WHAT'S IN A NAME?
HANGCHOW

The splendor of cities is not always reflected in their names. Hangchow is located in the "dry district." And that's what the name means.

The fall of the Sungs in the north points up two themes in Chinese history. Chinese history can be seen as a succession of dynasties. Each, at its beginning was strong and prosperous. Then, rebellions and invasions troubled it, and corrupt and lazy officials further weakened it. At the end of each dynasty, it was overthrown. After a time, a new strong dynasty came to power. This process, called the *dynastic cycle*, is a major theme in Chinese history. The story of the Sungs illustrates it well.

A second theme of Chinese history is continuity. Empires were established and then disappeared. Even foreign invaders came to rule the land. But Chinese civilization went on. In spite of the nomadic conquest in the north, for example, Chinese speech, writing, civil service, and ways of life remained unchanged.

New inventions improved the way of life. Starting with the late Tang age and going into the Sung, Chinese artisans and scientists developed inventions that improved farming. Among these were the horse collar, stirrup, and moldboard (the curved plate on a plow that turns the earth over). The crossbow and, later, gunpowder were inventions that gave the Chinese improved military strength.

At first, gunpowder was used only in religious ceremonies for great fireworks displays at festivals. Giant firecrackers went off with tremendous bangs, and rockets burst into shapes and colors.

Other inventions included mechanical clocks, a magnetic compass, and a seismograph to detect earthquakes. In medicine, the Chinese developed an inoculation for smallpox. And in mathematics they introduced the first adding machine, the abacus. The abacus is still in wide use throughout the world.

Scholars made contributions to Chinese civilization. Learned men wrote on botany, chemistry, and geography. Map making techniques improved. And history was studied as a science.

No people in the world have prized history more than the Chinese. They believed that history was not just a record of the past but it served another purpose too. It could be a warning and a guide by which people could learn from past mistakes. Ever since the Han dynasty, it had been the custom to write an official history.

During the Sung age, many scholars wrote about history. Their writings told: (1) that history was important and why; (2) that it should be based on definite evidence, such as writings, government records, and biographies; and (3) that the historian should always be careful to be fair and not biased in his judgments. Many histories were written based on these rules. One such history covered events from 403 B.C. to 959 A.D. It took the author seventeen years to complete, and consisted of 294 written rolls.

Sung artists and craft workers created masterpieces. While the Tang age had been a time of great poets, the Sung period was one of great artists. Chinese painting reached a degree of perfection never again achieved.

The Chinese used a paintbrush in writing their language, and a distinctive style of painting grew from the special quality of lines made by the brush. The written characters are very complicated—some have twenty-five brush strokes. Certain writers were recognized as masters of the brush. They perfected their style by practicing brush strokes several hours a day. Because they wrote in ink on silk or special paper, artists had to be sure of every line they drew. They could not erase.

Chinese painting does not try to show

This ink drawing on silk shows the Chinese style of portraying the spirit of a picture. For example, the clouds completely blot out the mountains behind to show a calm, still feeling.

exactly what the eye sees, as a photograph does. Painters try to show the spirit of what they picture. So the Chinese painter believed that he or she had to spend days in thinking and looking at a scene until she or he understood its real meaning. Then he or she would paint it without looking at it. As one Chinese master told his students:

Understand the character of what you paint. Look at the pine tree; it is like a wise scholar, dignified and stern; it is strong and constant and lives a long time. The willow, on the other hand, is like a beautiful woman, all grace and gentleness. The bamboo combs the hair of the wind and sweeps the moon, it is so bold that its shoots can break the hard ground as they push their way up; it is so gentle that it sways before every breeze. It is like wisdom itself. Keep the character of these things in your mind as you paint them.

Another art in which the Sung Chinese excelled was the making of porcelain. This type of pottery was made from a special white clay that had been mixed with powdered rock and sand, moistened, and made into a smooth paste. The potter shaped this mixture and fired it in a kiln. The Chinese discovered unusual glazes and used them to give the surfaces of porcelain soft rich color. One piece of green-glazed porcelain was described as being "like curling disks of thinnest ice, filled with green clouds."

Many factories made porcelain plates, cups, bowls, candlesticks, and other objects. Later, when Europeans came to China, they set up shops that copied Chinese porcelain models. The Europeans exported the porcelain to Europe, and *china* has come to mean porcelain of an especially fine grade.

1. How did the Chinese lose the western part of the Tang Empire?

2. Name and describe briefly the two basic themes of Chinese history.

3. Why was history important in China?

4. What were the Chinese trying to show in their painting? How did they go about it?

2 City life differed greatly from peasant life

Sung China in the 12th century has been described as the most advanced country in the world. Economically, the empire was prosperous. Towns and cities were centers of artistic and scholarly activity. But the city riches of trade, ideas, and the arts touched lives of village peasants very little. However, in both town and country, the family unit was very important in people's lives.

Foreign trade supported a large population. The empire had a population of at least 100 million. The people were roughly divided into five main classes: (1) peasants, (2) merchants, (3) soldiers, (4) mechanics and artisans, and (5) scholars. The scholars were held in highest regard because they ran the government. Unlike medieval Europe, soldiers hardly counted in Sung China; they did not have high social standing.

Trade grew during the Sung period. In earlier centuries, foreign trade had consisted mainly of camel caravans traveling overland across central Asia with silk goods. In Sung times, the oceans became the highway of commerce. Many large ships, with crews of several hundred persons, carried cargoes to Korea, Japan, and South Asia. Chinese ships also sailed to Southeast Asia, the Persian Gulf, and the east coast of Africa. Exports included silks, art objects, and the highly prized porcelains.

As part of this business growth, paper money came into wide use and a kind of note similar to a modern check did away with the need to carry large amounts of money.

Cities were rich and comfortable. The prosperity of Sung life is best seen in its cities, especially the capital, Hangchow. It covered 8 square miles (20.8 square kilometers) and had a population of at least a million—much larger than the cities of Christendom.

One great central street led to the palace of the emperor. Scattered here and there were other fine buildings and palaces. The city also had many fine shops and restaurants. Most of the streets were paved, and a good garbage collection system kept Hangchow neat and clean.

Peasant life was poor. The luxury of the capital stopped at its walls. Beyond were the villages where peasants worked from dawn to dusk. The peasants' tiny fields produced barely enough food to support a family. Their homes were mud huts with windows made of oiled paper that resisted rain and allowed light to come through.

All farm work was done by hand by the members of the peasant family. Adults did the heavy work—digging, planting, hoeing, and harvesting. Children looked after the pigs and chickens, gathered firewood, and brought water from the well. During the year, a few feast days and festivals gave peasant families a little fun and relaxation.

There was very little contact between the peasants and the government. Officials collected taxes and picked several men from each village who were forced to repair dikes,

Farm methods started during Sung times continued for many centuries. Here an overseer is carrying an umbrella to keep off the hot sun while he supervises the rice harvest.

roads, and other public works. Peasants in their private lives were left alone. As one of their folk songs put it:

I begin to work when the sun rises;
I rest when the sun sets.
I dig a well for my drinking water;
I plow the field to provide my food.
Powerful as the emperors are,
What has that power to do with me?

The day-to-day life of the peasants in Sung China was not much different from that in feudal Christendom. But the Chinese farmers' lives remained almost unchanged down to the 20th century, while in Europe, farming life improved greatly over the centuries.

The family was the important unit of Chinese life. A family was made up of three or four generations. It was based on the authority of the older generations over younger ones and of males over females. While the grandfather, if alive, or the father had the final word in all family matters, the eldest son had authority over younger brothers and all sisters. The grandmother had authority over her daughters, daughters-in-law, and granddaughters.

The Chinese family, with its tight organization, took on duties that governments took care of in many other countries. When differences arose between members of a family or between members of different families, the problem was not taken to an official. The families involved tried to settle the problem themselves. In this way, families did many of the things that police or judges would do in other communities.

At a time when there were no government pension systems, insurance, or health-care programs, the family took care of any relatives that needed help. In case of famine in a village, the better-off farmers were expected to help their neighbors, even if they belonged to other families.

All marriages were arranged by heads of families. It could happen that a young couple had never seen each other until the marriage ceremony. The idea of romantic love was not absent from Chinese thought. There are great love stories in Chinese literature. But love had little to do with marriage.

Women had lower status than men. Like all people, the Chinese had a structure to their society. Some people had higher status than others. One famous philosopher described the order in Chinese society when he wrote, "I am happy because I am a human and not an animal; a male and not a female; a Chinese and not a barbarian." Women were considered to be of much less importance than men. Many customs developed from this belief.

In a dispute between a wife and her mother-in-law (with whom she lived), the husband was expected to support his mother. When a man appeared in public with his wife, she walked ten steps behind.

Among the wealthy upper classes, the practice of foot-binding illustrates the inferior place of women in China. It began when a girl was about four years old. Her feet were tightly wrapped and gradually bent until the arch was broken and the toes were pushed under. These upper-class women, therefore, had very tiny feet. Tiny feet were considered to be beautiful, but their owners were crippled permanently. In this way, wives became no more than ornaments in their husbands' homes.

The Sungs declined. The Sungs were never strong militarily. A little more than 150 years after they first came to power, other serious weaknesses developed in their government. Officials were more interested in their own comfort and wealth than in giving the people good government. Peasants were terribly burdened by very high interest rates on loans and by the forced labor they were required to give for public projects.

At this time, in 1069, the Sung emperor made a minor official named Wang An Shih [wäng' än shē'] his prime minister. Wang An Shih was a brilliant scholar who had studied the governments of the "ancient rulers." He made broad reforms, some of which were a return to ancient ways, while others brought China "up to date."

Daily Life

Life for women in the upper classes meant spending leisure time playing a popular board game called sixes, as at *bottom*. Sometimes, women prepared the fine silk fabrics that later became their clothing, as at *top*.

A MYSTERY IN HISTORY

THE PUZZLE OF THE BAN CHIENG POTS

Where did early people first learn to make bronze? This question is important because the use of bronze was a giant step forward in human development. Historians and archaeologists have for a long time believed that the first Bronze Age, and with it the rapid growth of civilization, began in Mesopotamia somewhere around 3000 B.C. Recently, a startling discovery was made in Thailand that may change many ideas about the early history of humans.

In 1966, Stephen Young, the son of a former U.S. ambassador to Thailand, was carrying on research near the remote village of Ban Chieng [ban chē eng']. One day while walking down a path that had been deeply rutted by heavy rains, he tripped over an exposed tree root. Trying to cushion his fall, he extended his arms. As he lay on the ground, his hands felt a number of round hard circles. They were the tops of clay pots, once deeply buried in graves.

An archaeological dig was soon begun. Many pot fragments were collected and sent to the University of Pennsylvania. A new method for dating pottery was being developed there.

This process, which is called thermoluminescence, heats pottery to a high temperature, at which point a faint ray of light is given off. By measuring its amount, scientists believe they can tell the age of the pottery. Tests at the university showed that the Ban Chieng pots were more than 6,000 years old.

Surprises came in 1973 when more funeral pots were unearthed with bronze tools. Bronze cannot be dated; but the pots with them were found to be from 3600 B.C. This was 600 years earlier than the Bronze Age in Mesopotamia.

Did the use of bronze originate in Southeast Asia? Was this knowledge carried to the Middle East? If so, it would solve one of the mysteries of archaeology. No source of tin has ever been found in the Middle East, and this metal, mixed with copper, is needed to make bronze. There are rich sources of tin in Southeast Asia.

Perhaps metallurgists from the Middle East in search of tin carried their skills to Southeast Asia. Or perhaps these skills developed in both places about the same time. Many scholars are coming to believe that such "independent inventions" are very common in the development of civilization. Either way, there is still much argument over the meaning of the Ban Chieng finds. These mysterious pots provide both new challenges and new clues to our understanding of human prehistory.

Wang An Shih's government temporarily stopped decline. Wang An Shih believed he could get good officials by improving three areas: (1) the training of officials, (2) the control of their income and expenses, and (3) the selection process.

He made the civil service examinations more practical and improved the universities. He adjusted officials' salaries and made rules about exactly how much officials of certain ranks could spend on weddings, funerals, and entertainment. He believed these rules would prevent officials from taking bribes or otherwise getting rich from their positions, because they would not be able to show off their wealth.

In addition, Wang An Shih began a *graduated income tax*, that is, a tax that requires wealthy people to pay a greater percentage of their income than poorer people pay. This tax money was used to hire workers for government projects. Thus, he got rid of the hated forced labor. He introduced measures to give loans to farmers at low interest rates, and he controlled inflation with rules about how much things could cost and how much people could be paid.

After the death of Wang An Shih in 1086, his reforms were scrapped and forgotten. The Sung Empire continued to decline until it met its end—the completion of this dynastic cycle—by foreign conquest in 1279.

section review 2

1. How did trade and business grow during Sung China times? Name at least two ways.

2. Describe the lives of peasants in Sung China.

3. Name at least three ways in which a Chinese family was like a government.

4. What were some of the methods Wang An Shih used to improve government?

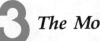

3 The Mongols ruled in China

Throughout Chinese history, nomadic groups from central Asia had been breaking through the Great Wall. In the 13th century, a group called the Mongols succeeded in completely taking over China. They ruled for 100 years.

Genghis Khan united nomadic peoples. The people who are known in history as "the Mongols" did not all come from Mongolia. In a series of tribal wars, the famous warrior Genghis Khan [jeng'gis kän'] united many of the nomadic peoples of central Asia. This group became known as the Mongols.

The civilized peoples had no chance against the cavalries of the nomads. Civilized peoples could not keep large cavalries because they used their land for farming. The nomads lived on the huge stretches of Asian *steppes*. They used these vast, treeless plains as pastures for their horses. They kept great numbers of horses and were skilled riders. When the mounted Mongol army, with swords flashing, galloped into a village or town, it simply cut down everyone in its path.

In the first decade of the 13th century, Genghis's armies repeatedly attacked the Chin dynasty in northern China. The Mongols swept west as well as east. In the 1220s, they defeated Muslim empires in the area around the Aral and Caspian seas. And in 1223, they moved into Russia. For twenty years, Genghis Khan terrified and conquered peoples from southern Russia to Korea. His armies killed more than 5 million people.

Kublai Khan became emperor of China. After Genghis Khan's death in 1227, the Mongols continued their conqests. In 1234,

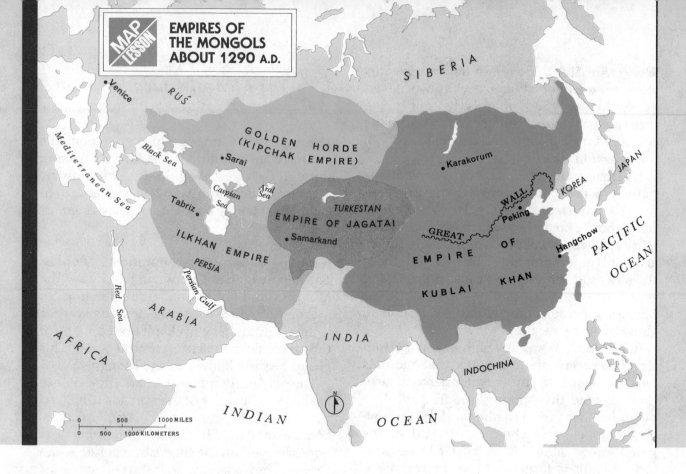

Genghis's successor brought the Chin dynasty to an end and established a Mongol dynasty in north China.

The greatest of Genghis's successors was his grandson Kublai Khan [kü′blī kän′]. He became Mongol emperor in 1260. He conquered the Sungs in southern China in 1279. From that year he ruled both north and south China until his death in 1294.

At the height of their power, the Mongols controlled China, Russia, Persia, and central Asia. In theory, Kublai Khan was the only Mongol ruler, but actually the Mongol conquests were divided into four empires. (See the map above.)

The Mongols showed great ability in governing the countries they conquered. Kublai Khan built roads, filled granaries with wheat for use in times of famine, and gave state aid to orphans and the sick. He also rebuilt the capital at Peking.

Marco Polo visited the Mongol court. A famous book, *The Travels of Marco Polo*, gives a great amount of information about Kublai Khan's empire. In 1271, when he was about seventeen years old, Marco Polo left his home town of Venice to travel with his father and uncle to the court of Kublai Khan.

The journey through central Asia and across the terrible Gobi took four years. Marco Polo became a favorite at the court of the Mongol emperor. He stayed in China for seventeen years, serving much of that time as an official of the government.

Marco Polo returned to Venice in 1295,

where he had trouble convincing his countrymen of the truth of what he had seen. They thought his stories exaggerated the size of the population and wealth of China, and they called him "Marco Millions." However, other Europeans—missionaries and merchants—followed his route to distant China and brought back the same reports.

Under the Mongol rulers, life in China went on much as before, and the influence of the Sung period remained strong. Kublai Khan encouraged his people to adopt Chinese ways. In time, the Mongols absorbed much of the Chinese way of life. In China, this process of *assimilation* [ə sim′ə lā′shən] took place again and again. There is a saying that "China is a sea that salts all rivers that flow into it."

4 Mings and Manchus maintained Chinese culture

In time, Mongol rule weakened, and the people began to revolt against their foreign masters. The Chinese continued to look on the Mongols as intruders, in spite of all the Mongol efforts to adapt themselves to Chinese life. Hung Wu, a leader of the discontented Chinese, gathered an army. He captured Peking in 1368 and drove out the Mongol rulers. China returned to the rule of the Ming, or "Brilliant" dynasty.

Ming China prospered. The Ming rulers tried to restore and strengthen all things Chinese. They cleared fields for farming and planted additional mulberry trees to provide food for silkworms. They increased trade with distant countries, and as a result, shipbuilding and navigation improved. Chinese ships sailed to the Philippines, India, and Africa.

The Ming emperors made the capital of Peking into one of the finest cities in the world. With many palaces, temples, and walls, it was really four cities in one. Each was surrounded by a wall. In the center of Peking was the Forbidden City, in which only members of the royal family could live.

Outside the Forbidden City was the Temple of Heaven, where the emperor prayed to the Supreme God for all of his people.

Ming rulers limited contact with the West.
After the downfall of the Mongols, Chinese contact with Europe stopped. Then, with the European exploration of the 15th century, it began again.

The Portuguese, eager for trade with the East, first sent representatives to Peking in 1520. This early contact did not work out well. The Portuguese plundered, kidnaped, and murdered, to the horror of the Chinese, who called them "ocean devils."

As a result, the government banned foreigners from China. However, it did allow the Portuguese to establish themselves at Macao [mə kou'], in southern China. Christian missionaries also came. But they, like the merchants, did not always respect the wishes of the Chinese government. Thus foreigners continued to be unwelcome in China.

China tried not only to keep foreigners out, but also to keep its own people from leaving the country. Although Ming emperors of the 15th century had encouraged trade with other nations, those of the 16th century believed in a policy of isolation. They forbade almost all contact with the outside world. In 1619, the Ming emperor wrote to the tsar of Russia: "O Tsar, I neither leave my own kingdom nor allow my ambassadors or merchants to do so."

The Manchus overran China.
Isolation, together with government corruption and high taxes, weakened the Ming Empire. And the early 1600s saw peasant uprisings.

Meanwhile, a nomadic tribe from Manchuria, the Manchus, started to expand their territory. They began breaking through the Great Wall and raiding the borders of Ming China. They conquered Korea in 1627.

Discontent grew within China, and bands of robbers roamed the countryside. One powerful robber chief seized much territory. In 1644, he threatened the capital at Peking. The Chinese asked the Manchus to help them put down this chief. They did so. But then the Manchus took Peking for themselves and made their own prince the emperor of China. The new Manchu dynasty ruled from the capital at Peking until 1912.

The Manchu Empire was huge. It included Mongolia, Manchuria, Korea, Indochina, Tibet, and eastern Turkestan, as well as China proper. The Manchus kept the Chinese system of government that had been set up by the Ch'ins. They divided the political jobs evenly between Chinese and Manchu nobles. The Chinese held most of the lesser offices.

Unlike the Mongols, the Manchus tried to keep their own customs and language. They forbade intermarriage with the Chinese. They made the Chinese wear *queues* [kyüz], or pigtails, as a sign of inferiority.

The first Manchu emperors were men of great ability. The first 150 years of their rule—to the end of the 18th century—was one of the most prosperous and peaceful in Chinese history. The rulers built roads and canals. They tried to stop famines and helped farmers clear new land.

Chinese glazed porcelains were among the most highly prized trade items in the world.

MING AND MANCHU CHINA

☐ Ming China, 1368-1644
☐ Areas added by Manchus, 1644-1912
☐ Provinces of Manchu China

SAKHALIN
MANCHURIA
MONGOLIA
SINKIANG
JAPAN
GREAT WALL
Peking
KOREA
TIBET
NEPAL
CHINA
TAIWAN
BURMA
Macao
Canton
Hong Kong
N
0   500   1000 MILES
0   500   1000 KILOMETERS
INDOCHINA
PHILIPPINES

lems was the Manchu policy of isolation that kept out of China good ideas developed in other countries.

China's rulers had little idea of the great advances in industry and science that were taking place in Europe. Chinese civilization was backward looking. It still saw itself as the Middle Kingdom, superior to all others.

For example, in the 1790s, a high-ranking Englishman traveled to Peking to try to get special trading privileges for English merchants. The Chinese emperor refused to grant the privileges. He explained why in his letter to the English king:

> The stores of goods in the Celestial Empire are extremely plentiful. There is nothing We do not possess, so that there is really no need for the products of the foreign barbarians in order to balance supply and demand.
>
> However, the tea, silk, and porcelain produced by the Celestial Empire are indispensable to the different states of Europe and to your kingdom. For this reason, We have, in Our grace and pity, established Our official trading companies. . . . It has been Our wish that all your daily needs be properly supplied and that everyone share in Our overly abundant riches.

While there was good reason for the Chinese to believe in the superiority of their culture—for more than 1,000 years no other nation in Asia could match them—this reply illustrates an unreal attitude toward the outside world. This failure was to cause China much grief and serious problems in the 19th century.

Ch'ien Lung (1736–1795) was the last of the great emperors. He was hardworking, sometimes reading government reports until well past midnight. His scholarly interests aided schools, and he was a supporter of the arts. In his ability to rule, he has been compared to the most outstanding rulers of his day: Catherine the Great of Russia and Frederick the Great of Prussia.

Isolation was a weakness of Chinese policy.
With Ch'ien Lung, the Manchu Empire reached its height. But the first signs of decline were present. The very peace and prosperity given by the Manchus led to a sharp increase in population. In 1710, it was 115 million and had doubled by 1793. This rapid increase had not been met by technical advances in agriculture and industry. By the end of the century, standards of living had begun to decline and there was growing unrest in the country. Added to these prob-

section review 4

1. How was Ming rule good for China?

2. What three factors weakened the Ming Empire?

3. How did the Manchus come to rule? What were the years of Manchu rule in China? What territories did they rule?

4. What effect did the Chinese isolation have?

Section Summaries

1. Chinese civilization continued under the Sungs. After the fall of the Tang rulers, China lost much territory and the empire became divided. A nomadic tribe, the Chin, ruled in the north. A Sung emperor set up a new capital in the south. The Sungs, while not militarily strong, gave their country prosperity. Advances in scholarship, art, and science took place.

The four different dynasties in this chapter all illustrate the dynastic cycle. Chinese empires run through a kind of life cycle: from early promise to great strength, then mortal weakness and downfall in each empire's old age.

2. City life differed greatly from peasant life. Sung China was a thriving empire. Exports brought great wealth to the cities, where life was elegant. But peasant life was little affected by the wealth and learning. Families provided much of the order and support in China; people relied on their families, not the government. Women had lower status than men.

A brilliant prime minister, Wang An Shih, stalled the decline of Sung rule with reforms. But with his death, corruption came back.

3. The Mongols ruled in China. Genghis Khan united the nomads of central Asia and conquered China. Mongol rule did not destroy Chinese civilization. In fact, the Mongols imitated and encouraged it. Marco Polo described Mongol China in a famous book.

4. Mings and Manchus maintained Chinese culture. As in the case of previous dynasties, the Mongols were ousted by a native Chinese government called the Ming. During Ming rule, Peking was rebuilt and trade flourished. But in less than 300 years, the Mings were overthrown by the invading Manchus. During the first 150 years of their rule, China had one of its most happy and prosperous periods. During the Ming and Manchu periods, anti-foreign feeling grew. European traders were not welcome, thus European inventions and ideas were kept out of China.

Who? What? When? Where?

1. Place these events in the correct order, beginning with the earliest:
  a. The Mongols conquered the Chin Empire.
  b. The Sung dynasty came to power.
  c. Kublai Khan conquered the Sung dynasty.
  d. The Tang dynasty fell.
  e. The Manchus took over China.
  f. A Chinese army drove out the Mongols.

2. Name the dynasties in which these events took place:
  a. Portuguese were called "ocean devils."
  b. Chinese men were forced to wear queues.
  c. Marco Polo visited China.
  d. Trade ships carried silks and porcelains to the Persian Gulf and Africa.
  e. The Forbidden City was built.
  f. Roads were built, grain stored for emergencies, and orphans helped by the government.
  g. Wang An Shih made reforms.
  h. The emperor of China rejected an offer to trade with England.
  i. Kublai Khan rebuilt Peking.
  j. The population of China was 230 million.
  k. Foreigners were banned from China because of Portuguese attacks.

3. Tell what these terms mean and why they are important in China's history:
  a. assimilation   d. "ocean devils"
  b. dynastic cycle   e. porcelain
  c. isolation   f. queues

4. Write a sentence for each of these men that tells the part he played in China's past:
  a. Chi'en Lung   d. Kublai Khan
  b. Genghis Khan   e. Marco Polo
  c. Hung Wu   f. Wang An Shih

5. Tell which of the following dynasties were Chinese and which were invaders:
  a. Chin   d. Sung
  b. Manchu   e. Tang
  c. Mongol

Questions for Critical Thinking

1. What is the meaning of the saying, "China is a sea that salts all rivers that flow into it"?

2. What factors explain the fall of the four dynasties in this chapter? What actions could have been taken to prevent their collapse?

3. What kinds of roles did the family fill in early China that are often filled by the government in America today?

Skill Activities

1. Read *Genghis Khan* by Harold Lamb to find out more about this famous ruler and his times. (Pinnacle Books, 1976)

2. Pretend you are Wang An Shih, and the President of the United States has just appointed you to improve the American government. What reforms would you propose?

3. Using the Chinese painters' way of looking at nature, choose a tree or flower to study. Write a paragraph about what you feel is the character or spirit of your subject.

4. Hold a class debate on: What were the advantages or disadvantages of China's voluntary isolation from the rest of the world?

5. Role-play a conversation between a Chinese emperor and a European visitor trying to set up trade relations between their two countries.

chapter **16** *quiz*

Section 1

1. The years of Sung rule were: a. 906 to 960, b. 960 to 1279, c. 403 to 906

2. Throughout history, the Chinese have always greatly prized: a. the dynastic cycle, b. history, c. new inventions

3. Chinese artists tried to: a. make their paintings as realistic as photographs, b. capture the spirit of their subject, c. imitate western European art forms

Section 2

4. True or false: In the Sung society, soldiers were highly respected because they helped keep out invaders.

5. Wang An Shih was a brilliant prime minister who: a. wrote many famous poems, b. hastened the end of the Sung dynasty, c. began a graduated income tax

6. Chinese families were run by: a. the oldest male, b. democratic methods, c. the mother and father

Section 3

7. The Mongol ruler Kublai Khan was: a. the grandfather of Genghis Khan, b. overthrown by Wang An Shih, c. a believer in assimilation.

8. One thing that did not happen when the Sungs fell was: a. culture was destroyed, b. life went on as before, c. the new rulers adopted Chinese ways

9. True or false: The Mongols originally lived on the steppes of central Asia.

Section 4

10. The Ming rulers tried to: a. restore and strengthen all things Chinese, b. encourage trade with the Russians and the English, c. move the capital city from Peking to Macao

11. The Manchu emperor who has been compared to other great rulers of his time is: a. Hung Wu, b. Kublai Khan, c. Ch'ien Lung

12. True or false: During Manchu rule, increased population and isolation from new ideas became serious problems.

THE EMERGENCE OF JAPAN

This screen was made in the 1500s and shows scenes from the book *Tale of Genji* by Lady Murasaki. The book, written in the 11th century, is a Japanese classic.

Yukio Mishima [yü kē′ō mē′shē mä] was one of Japan's most famous authors of the 20th century. His brilliant novels, plays, and short stories had given him an international reputation as a novelist and playwright. One of his works, *The Sound of Waves*, was a prize-winning story about life in a Japanese fishing village.

Mishima loved the old customs and traditions of Japan, especially the *samurai* [sam'ŭ-rī'], or warrior, way of life from feudal times. He thought that after World War II his country had been copying foreign, Western ways that were corrupting its people. He lamented the decay of family ties, the decline of simple country living, and the strange "un-Japanese" behavior of young people in modern-day Japan. To counter these changes, Mishima formed a patriotic group called the "Society of the Shield." Its members were taught unswerving loyalty to the emperor, respect for old ways, body-building, and the art of combat.

Determined to call attention to these ideas in a dramatic way, Mishima and a few of his followers broke into the quarters of the commanding general of the Tokyo garrison of the Japanese Self-Defense Force. They tied up the general, and then Mishima stepped out of his room onto a balcony to address the soldiers below. His plea to overthrow the government and to "return to the good old days" met with no response.

Feeling dishonored and a failure, Mishima acted in the manner of the samurai he admired. He plunged a dagger into his abdomen and gained the honorable death of sep-puku [sep'pŭ'kü] more commonly called hara-kiri [har'ə kir'ē]. Mishima said he sacrificed himself "for the old beautiful tradition of Japan."

It is difficult for people in the Western world to understand Mishima's act without some knowledge of this ancient Japanese samurai tradition. What Mishima did was curiously out of place in the commercial urban life of post-World War II Japan where the merchant and not the warrior commanded the greatest amount of respect from people. In the upcoming sections of this chapter you will read how:

1. **Japan's location influenced its history.**

2. **Early Japanese civilization borrowed from China.**

3. **Feudalism and a samurai warrior-class developed.**

4. **The Japanese created distinctive home and family customs.**

1 Japan's location influenced its history

Japan is a nation of islands. There are four large islands—called Hokkaido [hō kī' dō], Honshu [hon'shü], Kyushu [kyü'shü], and Shikoku [shi kō' kü]—and more than 3,000 small ones. In total land area, the country is about the same size as California.

WHAT'S IN A NAME?
JAPAN

The Chinese told Marco Polo of the island kingdom which they called *Zipangu*, meaning "sun-origin kingdom." This is how Europeans first learned it. Later, Zipangu became Japan.

The location of Japan has helped shape its people and history. About 100 miles (160 kilometers) of water separate it from Korea. It is 500 miles (800 kilometers) across the sea to mainland China. Japan has been far enough away from other countries to discourage invasion and to remain isolated when it chose to shut out the outside world. At the same time, the country has been near enough to the Asian mainland to be able to borrow from other civilizations, especially the Chinese, whenever the Japanese felt it desirable to do so.

MAP LESSON 17: JAPAN

1. Japan is a nation of islands. Green is used to show these islands on this map. The four major islands of Japan are labeled on this map. What are they?

2. Which of the four major islands is closest to Korea?

3. Which island is farthest north?

4. The Sea of Japan is to the west of Japan. What body of water is to the east?

5. What direction is the island of Kyushu from Shikoku?

6. What direction is Honshu from Shikoku?

7. This map shows several cities on the island of Honshu. What direction is Nara from Heian-Kyo?

8. What direction is Edo from Heian-Kyo?

9. What direction is Kamakura from Edo?

Japanese culture reflects a reverence for nature. Nature also has had a strong influence on Japanese life. Japan is a rugged, mountainous land noted for its picturesque scenery. One of the most impressive sights is Fujiyama (*yama* means "mountain"), a dormant volcano more than 12,000 feet (3,600 meters) high. In winter, Mt. Fuji is snow-capped. In spring, its lower slopes are covered with cherry blossoms. The Japanese have developed a zest and appreciation for such wonders of nature that is reflected in all aspects of their culture. Japan's native religion of Shintoism holds nature to be sacred, and Shinto shrines have been built in many beautiful places throughout the country. The Japanese love of simple, natural beauty is also seen in their arts—in their style of architecture, sculpture, painting, and literature.

The Japanese call their land Nippon [ni-pon'] or, especially in poetry, Yamato [yä'mä tō]. One of their poets wrote:

If one should ask you
  What is the heart
of Island Yamato—
It is the mountain cherry blossom
  Which shines brightly in the
morning sun.

section review 1

1. What are the names of the four large islands of Japan? About how many additional small islands are there?

2. About how far is Korea from Japan?

3. What is Fujiyama and what does its name mean?

4. What are two aspects of Japanese life that show a strong reverence for nature?

2 Early Japanese civilization borrowed from China

According to Japanese mythology, the islands were created and settled by a god and goddess. A divine grandson of the Sun Goddess was chosen as the ruler. In 660 B.C., one of his human descendants, Jimmu Tenno, was said to be the first Japanese emperor.

This belief in the divine origin of the emperor has played an important role in Japanese thinking. As one Japanese historian wrote:

> Great Yamato [Japan] is a divine country. It is only our land whose foundations were first laid by the Divine Ancestor. It alone has been transmitted by the Sun Goddess to a long line of her descendants. There is nothing of this kind in foreign countries.

Archaeology has revealed Japan's ancient past. Archaeological digging in the last thirty-five years has done much to fill in the gaps of knowledge about Japan's ancient history. People have lived in the Japanese islands for many thousands of years, probably from as early as 30,000 B.C. These early people hunted and fished and had a stone-age culture.

Around 250 B.C., a new people came to Japan, probably from eastern Asia. These people were farmers who knew how to grow rice in flooded fields, using a farming method common in south China. They also knew how to weave cloth and use metals. Today we know these facts because iron axes, knives, and hoes and bronze swords, spears, and mirrors have been found.

The first mention of Japan in writing appears in Chinese histories written at the beginning of the 1st century A.D. Japan is referred to as the "country of Wa," which is

The sun goddess and the sea god are creating the island of Japan in this 19th-century painting by Eitoku. As the goddess looks on, drops of water fall from the god's silver spear to form the islands.

divided into 100 "countries" (that is, tribal groups). In a 3rd-century record, the Chinese say that the 100 "countries" of Wa were now grouped into 30, all ruled by a queen named Himiko.

A chief becomes emperor. Japanese contact with the mainland, particularly Korea, was strong from the 3rd through the 6th centuries A.D. Large groups of immigrants bringing new skills and ideas continued to move into the country. Among these immigrants were people with a strong warrior-tradition. These warrior people were skilled at fighting on horseback, and they rapidly populated the islands.

By the 5th century A.D., one of these warrior chiefs, who ruled a small inland plain called Yamato, extended his rule over much of Japan and became recognized as emperor. The Yamato chief claimed descent from the Sun Goddess. His tokens of power—an iron sword, a curved jewel, and a bronze mirror representing the Sun Goddess—remain the symbols of the Japanese imperial family today.

As the Yamato chief and his descendants extended their rule, they spread the worship of the Sun Goddess. This faith, which later came to be called *Shinto* or "the way of the gods," held that nature had to be understood and reverenced. Many shrines were built during this early period in Japanese history to honor important features of nature, such as waterfalls, great groves of trees, and massive pieces of rock.

Japan learned from China. When the Yamato rulers became emperors, Japan had no written language and little architecture or art of any importance. The central government had little real power. China, however, had been developing a rich civilization for several centuries.

In the 6th century A.D., large numbers of Korean immigrants began crossing from the mainland. Educated Koreans brought with them the Chinese language with its character script possibly as early as the 5th century. Skilled workers brought their arts and crafts.

Under the guidance of a great statesman, Prince Shotoku (574–622), Chinese ways were systematically copied. Prince Shotoku [shō tō′ kü] ruled as regent for his aunt, Empress Suiko. In 600 A.D., he sent a large official delegation to China. In this delegation were a number of promising young men eager to study mainland civilization. They returned home as converts to Buddhism and champions of Chinese arts and institutions.

Prince Shotoku accepted Buddhism, as did the royal court. Buddhism gradually gained wide appeal. But Shintoism continued to be widely supported, and many Japanese practiced both faiths.

In addition to Buddhism, Japan borrowed other things from China including the calendar, ways of dress and cooking, and temple architecture. Chinese became the written language of the ruling class and scholars, who were then able to read the Chinese classics.

The Japanese tried to copy the efficient government of the Chinese. A law code similar to the Chinese one was drawn up, and strong efforts were made to extend the central government's power into the countryside as the Chinese had done. However, the Japanese rulers were never wholly successful in this extension of power. The Japanese rulers also made all land the property of the central government and established a taxing system.

Also following the Chinese example, the Japanese rulers decided to build a capital. Until this time, Japan had no important political center. In 710, however, a capital city was

GEOGRAPHY

A Key to History

EAST ASIA'S BRIDGELAND

While the Chinese influenced the Japanese, geographic features kept the two peoples separate. There is no major ocean current that conveniently flows between Japan and China. And, the Yellow Sea has many dangerous reefs and sandbars that hamper navigation. Also, the prevailing winds give little help to sea travelers. Thus, sea contact between China and Japan was difficult until modern times, when steam power made it possible for large ships to move against the current and the wind.

Korea served as a land bridge between China and Japan. And Korea's culture reflects that of both China and Japan. The Chinese first invaded Korea about 1122 B.C., settling near present-day Pyongyang. They introduced China's main crops, including rice and wheat. In later years, every major political change in China was felt in Korea. Chinese people who disagreed with the changes at home often fled to Korea.

During the Han dynasty, China sent troops to take over Korea. But these were pushed out by the Koreans about the end of the Han era.

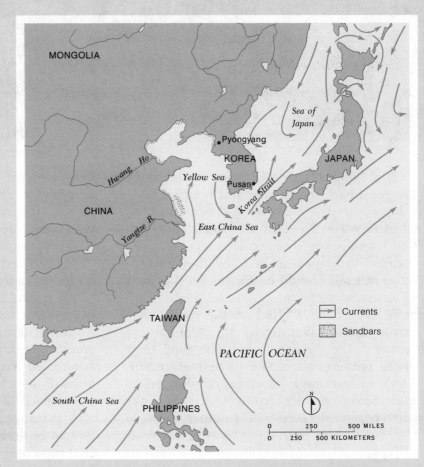

During the 1st century A.D., the Japanese invaded Korea, settling near present-day Pusan. They came across the Korea Strait in order to be near to Chinese culture. (Some anthropologists believe the people of southern Korea and Japan have the same ancestors who came by sea from Taiwan and the Philippines.)

For the past 2,000 years, the history of Korea has been marked by constant struggles between the Chinese and Japanese to control the country. And the cultural effects of this struggle can still be seen today.

This court building called Phoenix Hall was built in Kyoto in 1053. Like other court buildings, it shows the influence of Chinese architectural styles on Japanese architecture.

built at Nara. Like the Chinese capital of the Tangs, it had fine palaces and temples.

However, the Japanese did not adopt all Chinese ways. The Chinese examination system for selecting civil servants was not used because the Japanese believed that government officials should be chosen on the basis of birth and social rank. And unlike the Chinese, who believed that people could overthrow a bad ruler under the Mandate of Heaven, the Japanese thought that their divine emperor should never be overthrown. Thus, even though powerful families might gain actual political control, they always ruled behind the scenes. The emperor always remained honored in name as supreme ruler of Japan.

Japanese culture developed during the Heian Era (794–1192). In 784, Nara ceased to be the emperor's court and, after two moves, the capital was located in 794 at Heian-Kyo, which was later renamed Kyoto.

The founding of this new capital began what is known as the Heian [hā'än] period. During this time, Japan began to create its own kind of culture. It sent its last great embassy to Tang China in 838. By the early 900s, a distinct and new island civilization was being created in painting, architecture, and literature.

This flowering of cultural life was fostered by the emperor and his court in Heian-kyo. These nobles lived a sheltered life and hardly ever went out of the capital except to visit Buddhist temples and Shinto shrines. They spent their days in ceremonies and festivities connected with court life and in endless pursuits of taste and culture.

Some of Japan's earliest prose literature was produced at this time. It was written almost entirely by women. One reason was that men of the court were taught to write in Japanese by using the complicated and cumbersome characters of Chinese. For formal writing, educated Japanese men wrote only in Chinese (much like the scholars of medieval Europe who ignored their native languages and wrote only in Latin).

Japanese women, however, did not learn to write in Chinese. Instead, they wrote in their native language using *kana*. Kana was actually a kind of alphabetic representation of the 47 syllables of the Japanese language. Kana developed in the 9th century.

Using simple kana, court women wrote diaries, letters, essays, and novels in abundance. One of the most famous works of this period is the 11th-century *Tale of Genji* by Lady Murasaki. This novel—one of the first in any language—tells the story of Prince Genji, the "Shining Prince," and his many romances. It is a literary classic that is still read and studied today.

Another important and popular form of writing at this time was poetry. The form used was the *tanka*. It could only be five lines long and include a total of 31 syllables. The tanka was to remain the poetic model for more than 1,000 years. It is still a favorite form. Here are two early examples:

> When spring comes
> the melting snow
> leaves no trace
> Would that your heart too
> melted thus toward me.

and:

> I will think of you, love
> On evenings when the grey mist
> Rises above the rushes,
> And chill sounds the voice
> Of the wild ducks crying.

In a later period, the tanka became even more refined and compressed to three lines and 17 syllables. It was then called the *haiku* [hī'kü]. Here is an example:

> To the moon, a handle
> add—a good
> fan indeed.

While the aristocrats in Heian were living lives of ease and comfort, Japanese outside the capital had rough and hard lives. Most were serfs, who worked a bare existence out of the land and had to give a large share of their crops to their local warrior-landlords.

These landlords in turn had to pay heavy taxes to the tax collectors from the emperor's court to support the central government. The system gradually weakened when powerful court families and important local people got tax-free estates. As the taxing ability of the government declined, so did its power. By the middle of the 12th century, the emperor had authority in name only. He was in the hands of the warrior-landlords outside the capital who were fighting with each other for supremacy.

section review 2

1. How long ago do archaeologists think people first lived in Japan?

2. What are the beliefs of Shintoism based on?

3. What are some things the Japanese "borrowed" from the Chinese? In what two ways were Chinese and Japanese attitudes about government different?

4. What were two forms of poetry that developed during the Heian period?

3 Feudalism and a samurai warrior-class developed

In 1156, outright civil war burst out between two great provincial landowning families. Each had its own loyal following of warriors, called samurai. These followers pledged complete loyalty to their lord. This allegiance was similar to the lord-vassal system of feudalism that grew up in Europe following the fall of Rome.

The Kamakura Shogunate (1192–1333) began. During the fighting, palaces were burned and people massacred. A leader named Minamoto Yoritomo [mē nä mō'tō yō-rē tō'mō] won. As victor, he was completely ruthless. He had his rivals killed, including his own brother. Yoritomo became the undisputed ruler and in 1192 had the emperor name him the *shogun* [shō′gun] or supreme general of the entire country. This office became *hereditary*, that is, it passed down from father to son. Yoritomo's seat of government was Kamakura, a small coastal town. The emperor remained a mere figurehead in Kyoto.

Under Yoritomo, Japan entered its feudal age, which lasted nearly 700 years. The feudal age was divided into three major periods: the Kamakura [kä mä ku′rä] Shogunate, the Ashikaga [ä shē kä′gä] Shogunate, and the Tokugawa [tō ku gä′wä] Shogunate. The samurai warriors were the most important class of people during the feudal period.

The key to the military and governmental power of the shoguns was the loyalty of the samurai class. Unlike European feudalism, the loyalty of the samurai knights was not a legal, contractual obligation. Instead, it was a moral tie. The samurai developed a code of conduct that came to be called *Bushido* [bü′shē dō], "the way of the warrior." Bushido stressed unswerving loyalty and a kind of spartan spirit of indifference to pain and hardship. Suicide by means of seppuku, or hara-kiri, was preferred to dishonor or surrender. Much of this code has survived to modern times in Japan.

A samurai wore very light armor that weighed no more than 25 pounds, which made him very agile on the battlefield. His main weapon was a sword. Many stories are told about the perfection of these blades: swords that could split a hair floating in space or slice through a stack of coins without leaving a scratch on the blade.

The Chinese tried to invade Japan. The Kamakura shoguns created order in Japan with samurai rule. But their greatest test came from overseas. The Mongol ruler of

Minamoto Yoritomo made himself dictator of Japan in 1192. In this wooden sculpture he is wearing the crown and clothes of court.

China, Kublai Khan, sent two invasions to conquer his island neighbor. The final attempt was made in 1281 when 150,000 soldiers carried in a great fleet were sent to conquer Japan. The Mongols were able to force a landing, and the samurai fought desperately. When a great typhoon destroyed many of the Mongol supply ships, the invaders were forced to withdraw, thus losing many of their ships and soldiers. The Japanese gratefully called the typhoon the Kamikaze [kä'mē-kä'zē], "the Divine Wind."

The Kamakura victory over the Mongols was its last great effort. Much treasure and strength had been spent defending the country. By the end of the 13th century, the power of the Kamakura shoguns was rapidly declining. The country broke into various feudal groups. In 1333, Kamakura rule ended. A new military group soon seized power and established the Ashikaga Shogunate.

Nobles struggled for power during the Ashikaga Shogunate (1335–1573). In the Kamakura period of Japanese feudalism, the shoguns ruled through their vassals, the samurai knights. In this second period, the shoguns did not control their vassals. For one reason, there were too many vassals to make the old system work. The power of the shogun hardly extended outside the capital, now back at Kyoto. Instead, groups of samurai came to follow certain local nobles who were called *daimyo* [dī'myō], which meant "great name." The daimyo became absolute rulers on their lands. They had their own laws, which they could enforce over their followers. This system of regional rule was very similar to the type of feudal government that existed in Europe in the early Middle Ages.

During the period of the Ashikaga Shogunate, there was no effective central government in Japan. Daimyo struggled with each other for more power and territory. Local rivalries and wars raged over the countryside of Japan.

Warriors held the highest place in Japanese society and were admired for their skill and strength. This man was the standard-bearer for his group of samurai.

The arts flourished. Despite the turmoil, the country enjoyed one of its most productive eras in the arts. The Ashikaga period, like the Heian period long before it, was a golden age for Japanese culture. There were brilliant achievements in architecture, literature, and drama.

The *No* drama developed at this time. It was performed by two main characters and featured poetic passages chanted by a chorus. These ancient No plays are still performed today.

Another glory of this age was its painting. Beautiful landscapes, action-packed scenes of battle, and humorous drawings of people and animals were the chief subjects. The most famous artist of this time was a Buddhist monk named Sesshu (1420–1506).

During the Ashikaga era, the greatest form of art was landscape painting. In this style, the artist used bold brush strokes to bring out the essential parts of the drawing. Often people, buildings, and other human creations were blended into the painting to strengthen the feeling of nature. This detail, from a screen done in ink on paper by Sesshu, follows the Ashikaga style.

Many of his paintings have survived, including a magnificent landscape scroll that is 52 feet (about 15.6 meters) long.

The Ashikaga era is also important for its perfection of three typically Japanese arts. The first was flower arrangement. "Flower Experts" taught young women how to select and combine beautiful clusters for home decoration. The second art was the tea ceremony. This was held in a simple setting, in a room or tea house adjoining a garden. The tea was served with elaborate dignity amid quiet and thoughtful conversation. The third art was landscape gardening. Location was all-important for the garden, and the home had to form a single artistic unit. A well-developed garden usually had a little stream for a waterfall, then a bridge, and a small lake with its little island.

The Ashikaga period is also noted for another important event—the arrival of Europeans. In 1543, a group of Portuguese landed on a Japanese island. Within a few years,

ships made frequent stops. Soon after, the famous Jesuit Saint Francis Xavier began preaching Christianity in the islands. At first, the newcomers were welcomed. Foreign trade increased. There was also important economic growth as the handicraft industry advanced, farm production increased, and towns developed. There was a craze for all kinds of European gadgets, especially firearms. New plants, including tobacco and the potato, were introduced. Some Portuguese words—such as *pan* meaning "bread"— even found their way into the Japanese language.

During the end of the Ashikaga period in the late 1500s, fierce fighting continued between various noble groups. However, the larger and more powerful daimyo gradually began to win control over their weaker rivals. The field was finally dominated by two great rival groups. In 1600, the Battle of Sekigahara was fought between the two. The victor was Ieyasu [ē ye yä'sü], of the Tokugawas.

Samurai warriors were noted for their ferocity in battle.

Central government grew strong during the Tokugawa Era (1603–1868). In 1603, Ieyasu became shogun and master of a unified country (though the emperors still continued their unimportant existence in the old capital of Kyoto). The new shogun made all daimyo sign a written oath of loyalty to the central government. He exercised supreme military authority from his headquarters in Edo, a small coastal town, later known as Tokyo. The shogun made the daimyo live in Edo and spend every other year in the capital. Even when the daimyo left to go to their provincial homes, each had to leave his wife and his heir in Edo as hostages. The shogun also weakened the power of the daimyo in other ways. Thus, during this era, the central government grew strong again.

The second Tokugawa shogun began a policy of isolating his country from foreign influence. This policy was continued by his successors. No Japanese were permitted to leave their homeland and those who had gone to other countries were not permitted to return. All foreign missionaries were expelled from the country or killed. Thousands of Japanese who had become Christian converts were executed. By 1638, Christianity had become virtually extinct in Japan. Foreign trade was greatly restricted. Only a small number of Chinese and Dutch traders were permitted to reside at Nagasaki.

By these measures, the Tokugawa shogunate created a conservative system of rule that resulted in a peace that lasted for more than 250 years.

Changes came about in Japan. For a century, few important changes were noticeable in Tokugawa Japan. Japan remained a dominantly agricultural country. In the Tokugawa period, 8 out of 10 Japanese were farmer-serfs working on fiefs held by daimyo. But gradually, old feudal ways of life were challenged. During this period of peace, trade increased and cities grew in size. By the end of the 18th century, Tokyo's population had reached 1 million. As a result, the merchant and business classes became wealthy and influential. One of the leading families, the Mitsui, had a chain of stores in several cities by the 17th century. This chain became a leading company in modern Japan.

The wealth of the new business class helped it to support a new type of culture. Art and amusement were developed to please the city masses. The *Kabuki* [kä bü′kē] drama became popular. Unlike the dignified No plays, the Kabuki drama stressed violence, action, and melodrama. Its adventures of heroes and villains from stormy feudal times continue to be staged in modern times.

City people wanted art for their homes but could not afford costly paintings. To meet

Visitors to the theater often drank tea and ate rice cakes as they watched the plays. Sometimes, these plays lasted all day long.

this demand, woodblock prints were produced. These colorful, inexpensive prints pictured beautiful women, actors, and scenes of everyday life in the streets, eating houses, and markets. Woodblock art reached the height of its development in the 18th century. Woodblock prints have been called "the world's first art for the masses."

By the end of the 18th century, Japan was ripe for great changes. The samurai had become poorer and were out of place in the new commercial society. Young samurai became restless when they realized that the shogunate rule was out of date. Curious students obtained translations of books published in Europe and became eager to learn more about Western culture. The old feudal system was no longer able to meet the needs of the nation. It was swept away by the mid-19th century.

section review 3

1. How did Yoritomo rise to power? Who was stronger, the shogun or the emperor?

2. Who were the samurai? What did their code of conduct stress? How were they like the knights of feudal Christendom?

3. Describe five developments in the arts that took place during the Ashikaga Shogunate.

4. How did Ieyasu weaken the power of the daimyo? What other controls did the Tokugawa shoguns impose?

4 The Japanese created distinctive home and family customs

During their long history, the Japanese developed a unique way of life. In their homes and family lives, customs became quite different from those in other parts of the world.

Japanese houses were simple. Houses were made of wood, since there was a shortage of stone. The homes were usually one-story to withstand the earthquakes that frequently occurred in Japan. Sliding panels made of heavy paper on wooden frames separated the rooms. These panels could be moved easily to make a room larger or smaller or to open it to the garden. The idea of a sharp distinction between "outdoors" and "indoors" was not as strong as in the Western world.

The homes had very little furniture—no chairs, beds, or sofas. Usually, the only piece was a low table for serving food. Meals consisted mostly of rice, fish, and vegetables, with a little seaweed and fruit. Very little meat was eaten. People sat crosslegged on cushions around the table.

Floors were covered with straw mats. These were protected by the custom of taking off sandals and clogs before entering a house. Heat came from a large earthware pot, the *hibachi* [hi bä'chē], that burned charcoal. Mattresses and blankets were kept hidden in cupboards and were spread on the

This gold lacquered box was made during the 1300s. It may have been used by a noblewoman to hold her hairpins.

327

floor at night for sleeping. Most rooms had no decoration except for a nook or alcove in which flowers could be placed. On the wall of the alcove, there might be a single painting on paper or silk.

Houses had large tubs for very hot water. Whether rich or poor, everyone bathed daily. Before entering the tub, people washed thoroughly. The bath was mainly for relaxation.

This colored woodcut by Okmura Masanobu is called "A Pair of Young Lovers." It is an example of the style called ukiyo-e, or "picture of the passing scene."

The family in Japan, as in India and China, was the basic social unit. It was generally made up of a father and mother, their eldest son, his wife, and their children. The power of the father was unquestioned. Children were drilled in parental obedience. The head of the family represented it at all meetings and to some degree was responsible for the actions of its members.

The status of women changed. During the earliest period of Japanese history, some women enjoyed high political, social, and cultural status. In fact, from the end of the 6th century to the late 8th century, Japan had six empresses as rulers. At that time, women were the leaders in literary circles, and for one hundred years, all important authors were women. Laws protected the right of women to inherit and keep property. During Kamakura feudal days, samurai women were expected to have spartan virtues, and young girls were taught the use of weapons.

However, the trend was toward complete male supremacy. Women gradually lost their inheritance rights. By the Tokugawa period, they had become socially and legally inferior to men. Women were taught to serve men. Boys were valued more than girls. A wife did not share in her husband's social activities. This situation continued with little change well into the 20th century.

section review 4

1. What materials were Japanese homes made of? How were they furnished?

2. What is a hibachi?

3. What was the basic social unit? Who had the most power?

4. How did the role of women change in Japanese society?

Section Summaries

1. Japan's location influenced its history. The story of Japan has been greatly influenced by geography and climate. Beautiful rugged mountains, forested slopes, and varied landscapes created a strong love of nature among Japan's people. And the country's separation from the Asian mainland gave it protection from invasion.

2. Early Japanese civilization borrowed from China. In early stages of its history, Japan borrowed heavily from China. This was chiefly true in religion, government, and art. But by the 9th century when Japanese emperors had established their capital in Heian (Kyoto), Japan had begun to create its own special style of civilization. Poetic forms such as the tanka and haiku developed, and works of literature and painting were produced.

3. Feudalism and a samurai warrior-class developed. From the 12th through the mid-19th centuries, Japan's system of government was feudalism. There were three periods of feudal government—the Kamakura, Ashikaga, and Tokugawa—when the real ruler was the shogun. Emperors were mere figureheads but were respected because the Japanese thought them to be of divine descent.

During the early periods of feudal government, there was much discord and fighting between powerful noble families and their followers, the samurai. Finally, this civil war was ended by the advent of the Tokugawa Shogunate in 1603. The Tokugawa shoguns were able to control the unruly nobles and establish a strong central government. Japan was shut off from all contact with the outside world for more than 250 years. By the mid-19th century, a new merchant class had become powerful and influential in the cities. The old samurai class and feudal way of life seemed out of date. Japan was ready for sweeping changes.

4. The Japanese created distinctive home and family customs. During their long history, the Japanese people developed their own way of life.

Japanese homes and furnishings were simple, and family life revolved around the father. The place of women in society changed over the years. From the Tokugawa period on, women had a lower status than men.

Who? What? When? Where?

1. Place these periods from Japanese history in the correct order, beginning with the earliest:
- a. Ashikaga
- b. Heian
- c. Kamakura
- d. Nara
- e. Tokugawa
- f. Yamato

2. Match the items below with the correct period—Ashikaga, Heian, Kamakura, Tokugawa, or Yamato—from Japanese history:
- a. *The Tale of Genji* was written.
- b. Half of Japan's people became Buddhist.
- c. Christianity was destroyed in Japan.
- d. Yoritomo became the first shogun.
- e. Japanese culture became established.
- f. Portuguese traders came to Japan.
- g. Official Japanese delegations went to China and brought Chinese culture to Japan.
- h. A typhoon saved Japan from the Mongols.

3. Write a sentence for each of these terms that describes its meaning:
- a. Bushido
- b. daimyo
- c. Kamikaze
- d. Nippon
- e. samurai
- f. seppuku
- g. Shinto
- h. shogun

4. Write a sentence about each of these people that tells the role he or she played in the history of Japan:
- a. Jimmu Tenno
- b. Lady Murasaki
- c. Minamoto Yoritomo
- d. Prince Shotoku

5. Write a sentence for each of these that tells its meaning in Japanese literature or drama:
- a. haiku
- b. Kabuki
- c. kana
- d. No
- e. tanka

Questions for Critical Thinking

1. Why did the Japanese continue to support the emperor and his luxurious court after he had been reduced to a figurehead ruler?

2. What is the relationship between the art and life-style of the Japanese and the religious beliefs of Shintoism?

3. In what ways were the woodcut prints of Japan a form of "art for the masses"?

4. How was feudalism in Japan like feudalism in western Christendom? How was it different?

Skill Activities

1. Read *Ancient Japan* by J. Edward Kidder, Jr., to learn more about the archaeology, culture, history, and religion of Japan up to about 600 A.D. (John Day, 1965)

2. Write a tanka or haiku following the rules included in this chapter. Find examples of Japanese tanka or haiku in your library and choose more than one favorite. Tell why you like them.

3. Find out about Japanese holidays and special celebrations. What events are important to the Japanese people and how are they celebrated?

chapter **17** *quiz*

Section 1

1. Japan is: a. a group of islands, b. a high plateau, c. one large island

2. Japan has been protected from invaders by its: a. high mountains, b. large size, c. sea barrier

3. True or false: Japanese culture reflects a reverence for nature.

Section 2

4. True or false: People probably began to live in Japan about 300 B.C.

5. Some of Japan's earliest prose literature was written by: a. Buddhist monks, b. women at the Heian court, c. Chinese immigrants

6. The word Shinto means: a. way of the gods, b. Divine Ancestor, c. country of Wa

Section 3

7. The warriors of Japan's feudal families were called by the name: a. shoguns, b. samurai, c. daimyo

8. The first shogun was: a. seppuku, b. Yoritomo, c. Kamakura

9. The order, beginning with the earliest, of the three shogunates of feudal Japan is: a. Kamakura, Ashikaga, and Tokugawa, b. Ashikaga, Kamakura, and Tokugawa, c. Tokugawa, Kamakura, and Ashikaga

Section 4

10. The head of a Japanese family was the: a. mother, b. oldest son, c. father

11. True or false: At one time, women in Japan were trained to use weapons in the same ways as the samurai warriors.

12. Stone was not used for building because: a. there is a shortage of stone in Japan, b. the ground is too soft, c. there are many earthquakes

1. Show whether the events described below took place in India, China, Japan, or all three:

a. Women were considered less important than men.

b. Shah Jahan built a beautiful tomb to the memory of his dead wife.

c. The people thought of themselves as living in the Middle Kingdom, superior to all oth-other nations.

d. Families were run by the oldest male relative.

e. Water separates it on all sides from neighboring countries.

f. Marriages were arranged by heads of families.

g. The emperor was considered divine and could never be overthrown.

h. Civilization continued unchanged despite periodic invasions.

i. The people were divided into many castes.

j. Women wrote most of the early prose literature.

2. Match the letters on the time line with the events they stand for.

```
    900  1000  1100  1200  1300  1400  1500  1600  1700  1800
     |    |     |     |     |     |     |     |     |     |
     ↑    ↑↑   ↑↑  ↑        ↑ ↑  ↑↑  ↑
     A    B    CD  E        F G   H  I
```

____Ch'ien Lung ruled China.
____Minamoto Yoritomo became shogun.
____The Delhi Sultanate began.
____Tokugawa rule began.
____The Tang dynasty ended.
____Aurangzeb ruled the Mughul Empire.
____Akbar became ruler at Delhi.
____Kublai Khan conquered the Sungs.
____Wang An Shih made temporary reforms.

3. The Delhi Sultans ruled India during the time that: a. the Mongols and the Mings ruled China, b. the Japanese began to adopt Chinese customs, c. the Taj Mahal was built

4. The one who is remembered as a good ruler is: a. Aurangzeb, b. Tamerlane, c. Ch'ien Lung

5. Marco Polo visited: a. China, b. Japan, c. Korea

6. In the 16th century, the European nation that made contact with Asia was: a. Germany, b. Portugal, c. France

7. One who was not a Muslim ruler was: a. Mahmud of Ghazni, b. Prince Shotoku, c. Babur

8. One city that was not a capital was: Fatehpur Sikri, b. Macao, c. Kyoto

9. In writing literature, Japanese women used: a. suttee, b. purdah, c. kana

10. Match the letters on the map with the places described below:

____The most important Muslim kingdom in India centered around this great city.

____The Chinese first invaded this country in 1122 B.C., and the Japanese did so in the 1st century.

____Yamato rulers became the first emperors here about 500 A.D.

____This portion of India was not a part of the Mughul Empire.

____Ming rulers governed from this city.

UNIT SIX
THE RISE
OF THE WEST

If Martians had landed on Earth in the year 1200 and had looked for the most important civilization, they would not have picked Christendom. In 1200, the most advanced civilizations were in China, India, and the Middle East. Yet within 500 years, Christendom was transformed into modern Europe, the most powerful and influential civilization on Earth.

During the 500-year transition period, there were vast changes in government, philosophy, religion, art, weapons, and economic development. As Europeans established colonies and spread their culture overseas, an enlarged area of European civilization was created that came to be known as the West. The rise of the West, which no one could have predicted in 1200, was one of the remarkable happenings in human history.

How did the Europeans become so strong? An important part of the answer is that they organized themselves into large, rich, and powerful political units called *nations*. Kings of nations were able to do things that feudal nobles could not, such as pay for expensive overseas voyages, support large armies, conquer lands and set up colonies, and build great navies to protect them. This unit tells the story of how the Europeans changed their political organizations and carried their culture around the world.

Lorenzo Ghiberti labored for nineteen years to make the North Doors of the Baptistry at Florence, Italy. The gilded bronze doors are great evidence of the technical and artistic achievements of the West.

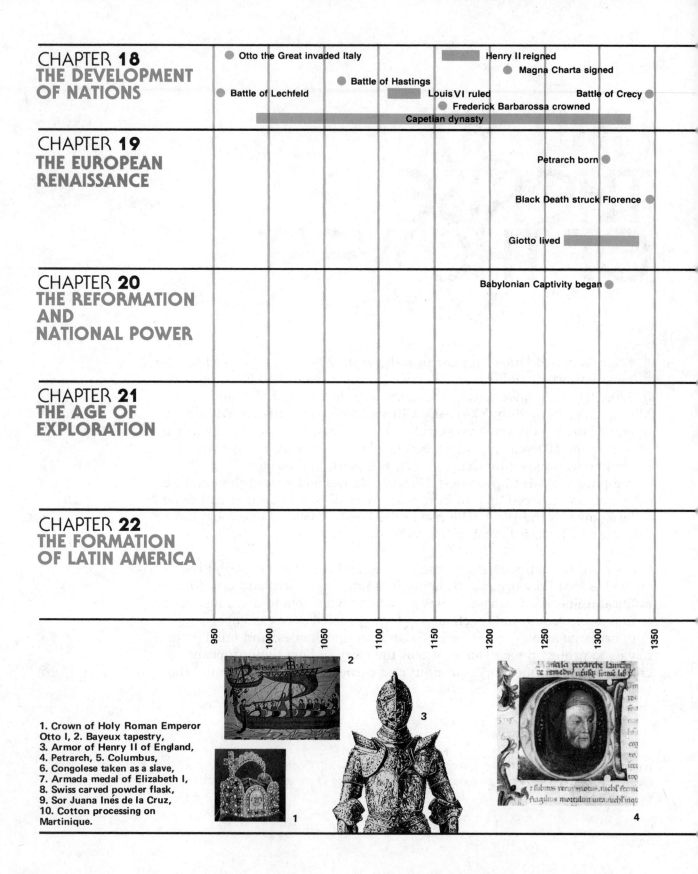

CHAPTER **18**
THE DEVELOPMENT OF NATIONS

● Otto the Great invaded Italy

● Battle of Lechfeld

● Battle of Hastings

Henry II reigned

● Magna Charta signed

Louis VI ruled

● Frederick Barbarossa crowned

Battle of Crecy ●

Capetian dynasty

CHAPTER **19**
THE EUROPEAN RENAISSANCE

Petrarch born ●

Black Death struck Florence ●

Giotto lived

CHAPTER **20**
THE REFORMATION AND NATIONAL POWER

Babylonian Captivity began ●

CHAPTER **21**
THE AGE OF EXPLORATION

CHAPTER **22**
THE FORMATION OF LATIN AMERICA

950 1000 1050 1100 1150 1200 1250 1300 1350

1. Crown of Holy Roman Emperor Otto I, 2. Bayeux tapestry, 3. Armor of Henry II of England, 4. Petrarch, 5. Columbus, 6. Congolese taken as a slave, 7. Armada medal of Elizabeth I, 8. Swiss carved powder flask, 9. Sor Juana Inés de la Cruz, 10. Cotton processing on Martinique.

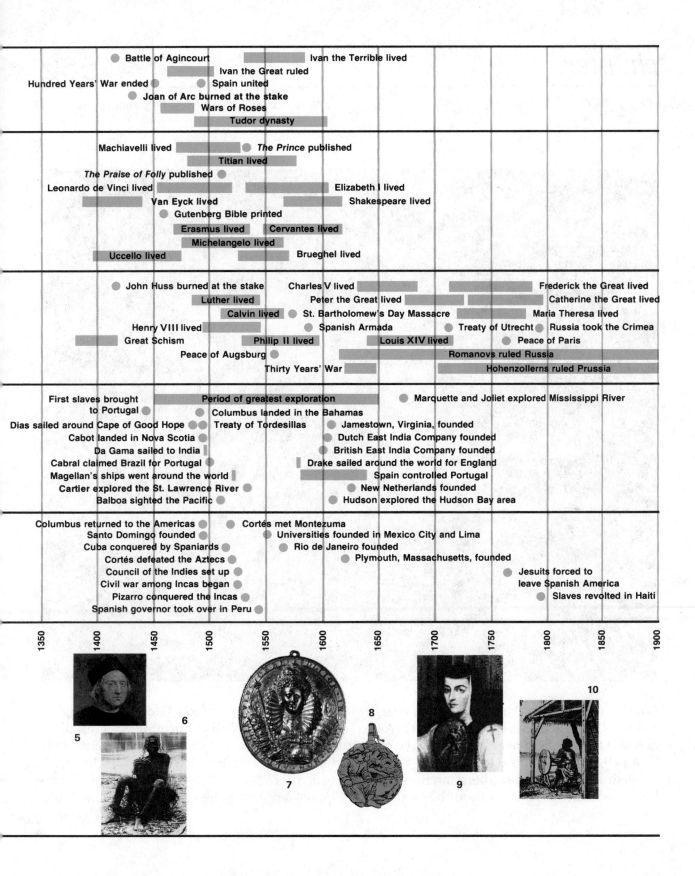

Battle of Agincourt • | Ivan the Terrible lived
Ivan the Great ruled
Hundred Years' War ended • | • Spain united
• Joan of Arc burned at the stake
Wars of Roses
Tudor dynasty

Machiavelli lived | • *The Prince* published
Titian lived
The Praise of Folly published •
Leonardo de Vinci lived | Elizabeth I lived
Van Eyck lived | Shakespeare lived
• Gutenberg Bible printed
Erasmus lived | Cervantes lived
Michelangelo lived
Uccello lived | Brueghel lived

• John Huss burned at the stake | Charles V lived | Frederick the Great lived
Luther lived | Peter the Great lived | Catherine the Great lived
Calvin lived | • St. Bartholomew's Day Massacre | Maria Theresa lived
Henry VIII lived | • Spanish Armada | • Treaty of Utrecht • Russia took the Crimea
Great Schism | Philip II lived | Louis XIV lived | • Peace of Paris
Peace of Augsburg • | Romanovs ruled Russia
Thirty Years' War | Hohenzollerns ruled Prussia

First slaves brought | Period of greatest exploration | • Marquette and Joliet explored Mississippi River
to Portugal • | • Columbus landed in the Bahamas
Dias sailed around Cape of Good Hope • • | Treaty of Tordesillas | • Jamestown, Virginia, founded
Cabot landed in Nova Scotia • | • Dutch East India Company founded
Da Gama sailed to India | • British East India Company founded
Cabral claimed Brazil for Portugal • | • Drake sailed around the world for England
Magellan's ships went around the world | Spain controlled Portugal
Cartier explored the St. Lawrence River • | • New Netherlands founded
Balboa sighted the Pacific • | • Hudson explored the Hudson Bay area

Columbus returned to the Americas • | • Cortés met Montezuma
Santo Domingo founded • | • Universities founded in Mexico City and Lima
Cuba conquered by Spaniards • | • Rio de Janeiro founded
Cortés defeated the Aztecs • | • Plymouth, Massachusetts, founded
Council of the Indies set up • | • Jesuits forced to
Civil war among Incas began • | leave Spanish America
Pizarro conquered the Incas • | • Slaves revolted in Haiti
Spanish governor took over in Peru •

1350 1400 1450 1500 1550 1600 1650 1700 1750 1800 1850 1900

5 6 7 8 9 10

THE DEVELOPMENT OF NATIONS

"Effects of Good Government" by Lorenzetti shows how Italian towns of the 1300s prospered.

On the afternoon of August 26, 1346, a large army of rain-soaked French knights rode across a muddy field near the village of Crécy [krā sē′], France. Before them stood a small English army of foot soldiers, archers with longbows, and knights without horses.

The showers ended. The French knights charged toward the outnumbered English. Suddenly, the English archers bent their longbows, and the arrows flew. One who was there said, "It was like snow." The heavy armor of the charging knights could not stop the deadly arrows. Many French fell, killed or wounded. But the army charged again and again. By midnight, more than a thousand French knights lay dead. The English had lost only about fifty men.

This battle was only one of many between the English and French in the Hundred Years' War (1337–1453). But it held many signs for the future. When the English bowmen defeated the French knights, the end of the whole feudal system began. Armor was almost no help against the longbow and cannon the English used. The battle at Crécy marked the first use of gunpowder in a field battle.

The future also showed in the victors' new feeling about themselves. They were becoming English, not merely people of a certain village or followers of a certain noble. In other words, they were becoming loyal to their country. With their love of the country, common language, customs, and growing central power, they were becoming a nation.

New weapons and a loyal people helped change the way lands and government were organized. The government of a national monarchy had more power. Its king ruled over more land and people than did the government of any local prince. The move toward strong national monarchies lasted into the 18th century. It started in western Europe. Later, it grew in eastern Europe. This chapter tells how:

1. Feudalism became
   old-fashioned.

2. England became one nation.

3. French kings built
   a national state.

4. Other European peoples
   made nations.

Feudalism became old-fashioned

During most of the Middle Ages in Europe, strong national governments were unknown. In France, at least 10 thousand separate pieces of land were in some way countries themselves. France had a king who in theory ruled over his nobles. But those nobles, who should have been loyal, often did just as they pleased.

Wider trade called for improved government. Times changed. By the year 1100, cities had begun to grow rather rapidly. Trade expanded, and the population grew.

The bourgeoisie disliked the lack of law and order that hurt business and threatened property. They were unhappy with feudal obligations. And the different legal systems upset them. The nobility had their own courts, as did the Church. Church courts tried not only churchmen, but also students, crusaders, and churchmen's servants.

Trade and commerce needed safer and better ways to move about. A feudal noble could decide alone whether a highway that passed through his fief should be kept in good repair. He often charged huge tolls for use of a road or river through his land. Worse, people had no able police force to protect them. The rocky, muddy roads were full of bandits who attacked travelers. The situation called for a change.

Strong kings extended their powers. Kings gained power at the expense of the Church and the nobles. Kings collected taxes from the growing merchant class and received their support against the nobles in exchange for protecting the merchants' property. This new source of wealth helped kings depend

Holy Roman
Empire

less on their nobles. Earlier, kings had relied on nobles who were their vassals to bring in men for the armies. With more tax money, kings could pay *mercenaries*—professional soldiers and officers. Husky peasants could become good soldiers of the king. Almost all countries that began central national governments during this time followed this pattern.

As kings gained power, they built up their governments. They hired civil servants, that is, government workers, to handle money matters, military affairs, and legal problems. Advisers were hired to help kings rule their countries. The kings freed people in towns from many feudal duties. And kings reduced the tolls merchants paid and protected them along the roads. Kings also began to bring all the people under one set of royal courts. These courts tried to make the law the same for everyone. In sum, kings were building bigger, stronger units called nations.

A nation has three important characteristics. First, its central government is strong enough to defend itself against enemies and keep order inside its borders. Second, a nation's people are set off from neighboring groups by language, religion, traditions, and

1. This map gives a simplified political picture of Europe as it was about 1000 A.D. Some borders on this map are shown by the use of red lines and dashes. Solid red lines are boundaries between kingdoms and other large states. Boundaries between dukedoms and smaller principalities within a larger political unit are shown by red dashes. Tell which are large states and which are smaller principalities or dukedoms:

    a. the area of Amsterdam
    b. Sweden
    c. the lands of the Bohemians
    d. Wallachia
    e. the area of Paris

2. Europe can be thought of as a series of peninsulas separating a series of seas. To help establish a sense of location, six of these seas are labeled on this map. Name the one which:

    a. has Danzig and Riga as sea ports
    b. is between England and Denmark
    c. forms much of Europe's southern boundary
    d. has the city of Venice at its head
    e. was dominated by the Byzantine Empire about 1000 A.D.
    f. would probably be crossed by travelers going from Moscow to Constantinople

way of life. Third, the people are loyal to and proud of their group. Their feeling is called *nationalism* or *patriotism*.

section review 1

1. Give three reasons the middle class disliked the feudal system.

2. How did merchants' taxes help kings free themselves from nobles?

3. Name three or more ways kings improved their governments as they gained power.

4. What are the characteristics of a nation?

2 England became one nation

England began to build a strong centralized government as early as the 1000s. When the king of England died in 1066, William, duke of Normandy, stated his right to be king. Although a Frenchman, William had distant ties to English kings. However, the throne was given to Harold, Earl of Wessex, instead. William then crossed the English Channel with an army whom he promised to reward with lands. In England, he defeated the new king, Harold, at the Battle of Hastings. William, who earned the name the Conqueror, became king of England.

William the Conqueror began a strong monarchy. As king, William the Conqueror was too strong to let his nobles challenge his power. He changed the feudal system so that it supported his own strong government. He made all nobles become his vassals, and he broke up the largest feudal holdings. He made all men of England bear arms for the king so that he did not have to rely on his nobles' armies.

William also added to his sources of money. He ordered a census of all the taxable wealth in his kingdom. These facts were gathered into the *Domesday Book*, which today gives an excellent picture of 11th-century England.

England was not one nation in 1066, and William did not make it one. But William did lay a firm base for a strong monarchy.

Henry II improved the legal system. William and the three kings who ruled after him are called the Norman kings. After them, England came under the rule of Henry II, a great-grandson of William's.

The reign of Henry II (1154–1189) was one

MAGNO: NAVIGIO:

The famous Bayeux Tapestry was made to celebrate William's invasion of England in 1066. Actually woolen embroidery on linen cloth, the tapestry was made during the late 11th century and is more than 230 feet (70 meters) long. This part shows the Norman troops sailing to England.

of the greatest in English history. Henry was determined to unite all of England under his rule. He wanted all the people to look to him and to their national government for justice and protection. Henry II made his royal law the law of the land. Because it was the same for everyone, it was fairer and better run than the many different kinds of law in use then. Over time, it came to be known as *common law*, because the whole country used it. It was based on custom and court decisions. Common law is used today in most of the United States and in nations and colonies that Great Britain began.

Henry II used an old custom of sending judges on regular tours all over the country. These traveling judges combined local legal customs with legal opinions from the king's court to form the common law. Judges who went from place to place were strangers in each district, so they were not open to bribes, threats, or feelings about friends. Each judge followed a *circuit*, or route. An important part of the English judicial system today, this practice also gave root to United States circuit courts.

The jury system also grew under Henry II.

The first juries were men who came before a royal judge to accuse someone of breaking a law. They did not decide whether the person was guilty. From this early jury came the *grand jury* of today. The grand jury decides whether evidence against the accused is enough to hold that person for trial. About a century after Henry's time, another kind of jury came into use. It heard a trial and decided on the guilt of the accused. This kind is called a *petit* (little), or trial, jury.

Henry II was an able, energetic man. He faced great problems that would have defeated others. The nobles—and even his sons—were against him.

The Church fought Henry's moves against its courts. Henry believed that Church courts were often too easy, and he wanted all his subjects under one system of justice. His stand led to a well-known quarrel with the Church. Thomas à Becket, archbishop of Canterbury, opposed Henry. So some of Henry's knights murdered Becket. Nobles and the Roman Church were greatly angered, and Henry's cause was hurt. His dream of equal justice for all was not realized until after the Middle Ages.

Magna Charta assured some rights. Henry's youngest son John became king in 1199. He was a cruel, unreasonable ruler. In 1215, King John's nobles rebelled against his unjust rule. They forced him to agree to the *Magna Charta* [mag'nə kär'tə], or Great Charter. This document limited John's power and protected nobles' feudal rights. The Magna Charta did not guarantee representative government. Taxation by the people's consent and trial by jury were not written in it. But these principles grew from the rights it did state.

The Magna Charta forced the king to make this promise: "To no one shall we sell, deny, or delay right or justice." He also promised to stop taking his vassals' property and forcing them to give him money.

The king could collect no money over that allowed by the old laws of feudalism except "by the common council of our kingdom." These words later grew to mean that the king could not raise any new taxes unless the people agreed through their representatives. American colonists used this principle in objecting to "taxation without representation."

Another clause of the Magna Charta declared:

No free man shall be seized, or imprisoned . . . nor shall we pass sentence on him except by the legal judgment of his peers or by the law of the land.

These words were later taken to mean that all freemen had a right to trial by jury. Most English people were still serfs. But as more people became free, they also gained the rights promised to freemen in 1215.

Parliament took shape under Edward I. Edward I (1239–1307) tried to bring the whole island under one rule. In 1284, he took over Wales. He also tried to take Scotland, but he could not defeat its freedom-loving people. These wars were costly, and Edward needed more money. So he collected extra taxes. The taxes were approved by the people's representatives in *Parliament* [pär'lə- mənt].

English kings had long had a group of advisers made up of churchmen and nobles. In 1295, Edward called these great nobles and churchmen to meet with him. He also ordered the *sheriffs* (local officers of the law) to hold elections in their counties. Freemen chose two knights from each county. From each chartered town, called a *borough*, they chose two *burgesses,* or citizens. This group is called the Model Parliament because later parliaments were modeled on it.

Probably the earliest view of Parliament, this picture shows the session called by Edward I in 1279. Lords and Church officials sat on the benches. Judges sat in the center on bags of wool. This reminded all present that wool was important to the economy.

341

On the north bank of the Thames River in southeast modern London stands an ancient fortress called the Tower of London. The fortress, including its gardens, covers 18 acres (7.2 hectares) and contains several buildings.

At the very center of the fortress is the White Tower. Some 90 feet (27 meters) high, it was built by William the Conqueror in 1078 to awe his newly acquired city. The White Tower's name comes from the white stone of its walls.

The White Tower is surrounded by an inner wall with 13 towers and an outer wall with six towers. The walls were built in the 1200s and 1300s. Beyond the outer wall is a moat that was originally fed by the Thames. The moat was drained in 1843 and planted with grass. It is now a parade ground.

The Tower of London has had many uses. Until the reign of James I (1603–1625), it was a royal residence. Over the centuries, it has also housed the mint, military weapons, and the public records. For six centuries, one part was the royal zoo. Today, the Tower is a museum that displays the dazzling collection of jewels, arms, and armor.

There is only one entrance to the Tower from the land side. Another entrance was built in the 1200s on the river side and is called the water gate. It is better known by its nickname, Traitors' Gate. It arose because so many prisoners accused of treason were brought through the gate to the Tower.

Many executions have taken place in the Tower. The most famous were during the Tudor period and included two of Henry VIII's wives, Anne Boleyn and Catherine Howard. In 1554, Mary I sent her young half-sister, Elizabeth, to the Tower. Brought by barge to the water gate, the future queen feared for her life. After two months, she was released from the Tower.

In 1485, the company of the Yeomen of the Guard was formed to watch over the Tower. To this day, they wear the Tudor uniform of stiff-skirted crimson coats and round black hats. Every evening at 10 they perform the Ceremony of the Keys. The Chief Yeoman Warder, carrying the Tower keys and a lantern, marches with an armed escort to the Tower gates. There he locks the gates, the present arms is given, and the Tower is closed until dawn. This custom has been unbroken for 500 years.

At *top left* is Queen Victoria's crown; *below left* is a Yeoman of the Guard. At *right* is the Tower of London from the parade ground.

In time, the Church withdrew from Parliament. Nobles made up what became the House of Lords. Elected knights and townsmen made up what became the House of Commons. This second group was a *representative body*. That is, each member spoke for many people and voted in their interests.

Early kings called Parliament mainly to get money. But Parliament began to have other ideas. Its members hit on the idea of refusing to grant money until a ruler corrected wrongs. This means was called *redress of grievances*. Parliament drew up statements of demands called *bills*. These bills became laws, called *acts* or *statutes*, after the ruler signed them. So Parliament became a lawmaking, or legislative, body. In many countries, the word *parliament* has come to mean the highest lawmaking body. Thus, England has earned the name "Mother of parliaments."

The Wars of the Roses brought a new line of strong kings. In 1455, two branches of the English royal family began to fight over the throne. Those wars between the House of York and the House of Lancaster lasted thirty years. They were called the Wars of the Roses because the York emblem was a white rose and the Lancaster, a red rose. During these wars, many noble families of England were destroyed. In 1485, Henry Tudor of the House of Lancaster won the throne. As Henry VII, he united the families by marrying a York heiress and began the Tudor dynasty. It ruled England until 1603.

WHAT'S IN A NAME?
YORK

Early people called this place *Eoforwic*, meaning "wildboar town." Later folks found this a bit clumsy and cut it down to *Jorvik*. Since then, Jorvik has been shortened again—to York.

The Tudor reign was a time of strong royal power. War had weakened the nobles. The king's judges carried out the common law.

And a well-run group of civil servants helped govern the kingdom. England under the Tudors gained as a leader in European affairs. Culture flowered.

By the end of the Tudor reign, the English nation had become strongly rooted. All the people lived under common law. A national government ruled in all parts of the land. People thought of themselves as English. They were as one people, proud of their ruler and their country.

section review 2

1. How did William the Conqueror make the English monarchy stronger?

2. Name three ways in which Henry II improved the legal system.

3. What was the purpose of the Magna Charta? Name two modern democratic principles that are based on it.

4. How did the rulers' needs for money change Parliament into a lawmaking body?

3 French kings built a national state

France was far behind England in moving toward a national government. Central power had ended after Charlemagne's death. A wholly feudal government had grown around strong local princes. In the late 900s, the name France meant only a small section around Paris. What was vaguely thought of as a kingdom was really just a group of feudal states. As a result, the French kings' task of uniting their nation was harder than that of their royal neighbors across the Channel.

In 987, the French nobles elected Hugh Capet [kā′pit], Count of Paris, as king. Many of his feudal nobles were much more powerful than he. But the Capetian [kə pē′shən]

343

DailyLife

These medieval book pages show what life was like in those times. An illuminated prayer book called *The Book of Hours* at *left* shows French peasants harvesting crops in what is now downtown Paris. Behind the peasants is the Louvre. At the time (1415), it was a king's palace and treasury. Today it is a famous museum. At *top* is a shop where paper was made.

family grew strong through wars and pacts with powerful nobles. The family ruled until 1328.

Kings strengthened the government. The Capetian kings first had to show that they were stronger than the nobles. The first king able to do that was Louis VI (Louis the Fat), who ruled from 1108 to 1137. He gained full control over his royal lands, called the Ile de France. His grandson, Philip II, won Normandy, Anjou, and other English holdings in France from King John. Year by year, the Capetian kings pushed out from their capital at Paris to make Ile de France larger and larger.

Like those in England, kings of France gave the people better government than had the feudal lords. Louis IX set up a system of royal courts. He also outlawed private wars and trial by combat. He told the people to ask his officials for help if nobles wronged them. In this way, he let all French people know that their government was important to their well-being. The French, however, did not develop a strong parliament. The king, for example, did not have to ask the French parliament for approval of new taxes.

Louis IX, who reigned from 1226 to 1270, was a true knightly king of the Middle Ages. He led his knights in the crusades. As a prisoner of the Muslims, he was brave and dignified. Peace and justice seemed to him far more important than military conquests. The

Church made him a saint some years after his death.

England threatened French freedom. French kings not only had worries at home but also often faced possible trouble with England. Some French lands still lay in English hands. Norman invaders under William the Conqueror had not given up their lands when they left France. So English rulers, such as Henry II whose holdings were large, were vassals of the French kings for land they held in France. The English, though, believed themselves equals of their French lords. From the mid-1100s to the mid-1400s, the English and French were often at war with each other.

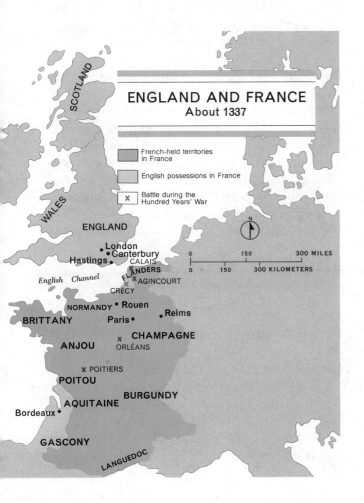

ENGLAND AND FRANCE
About 1337

French-held territories in France

English possessions in France

x Battle during the Hundred Years' War

SCOTLAND
WALES
ENGLAND
London
Canterbury
Hastings
CALAIS
English Channel
FLANDERS
AGINCOURT
CRÉCY
NORMANDY · Rouen
BRITTANY
Paris ·
· Reims
ANJOU
CHAMPAGNE
x ORLÉANS
x POITIERS
POITOU
BURGUNDY
AQUITAINE
Bordeaux ·
GASCONY
LANGUEDOC

0   150   300 MILES
0   150   300 KILOMETERS

In 1328, the last Capetian king died without a direct male heir. Edward III of England had blood ties to the Capets through his mother. Therefore, he claimed the throne of France, but the French refused to accept him. That dynastic quarrel was one reason Edward decided to take an army to France in 1337. Another was the attempt of the English to control Flanders, an important market for English wool and a center of wool cloth production. Edward's move began a number of wars that in all became known as the Hundred Years' War.

The fighting in all these wars took place in France, but the English often had the advantage of better generals and weapons. In 1346, Edward's troops, with longbows and cannons, crushed the French at Crécy. The next year they took Calais [ka lā']. In 1415, under King Henry V, English longbows helped defeat a large French army at Agincourt. With this battle, England took back Normandy.

Joan of Arc inspired patriotism. Joan of Arc's story shows the French people's growing love of country. By 1425, it seemed that England would conquer and rule France. Then an amazing story unfolded. A simple country girl, Joan of Arc, "knowing neither A nor B," as she said, had visions and believed that she heard the voices of saints calling on her to rid France of English soldiers.

In 1429, she went to Charles, the uncrowned king, and asked for an army to save the city of Orléans. She promised to defeat the English and save the throne for him. Charles and his court doubted her. However, they themselves could not stop the English. They gave her the soldiers she asked for.

In shining armor, mounted on a white horse, Joan appeared to the French soldiers as a heaven-sent leader. Filled with new hope, they attacked the English like a thun-

This picture of Joan of Arc, done after her death, shows her dressed for battle. Her banner has on it the three saints who spoke to her.

1. How did the Capetian kings grow strong?

2. How was French government improved by the Capetian kings?

3. Why did Edward III of England invade France in 1337?

4. Why were the French finally able to defeat the English?

derbolt. For a short time, Joan of Arc led her soldiers to victory after victory.

With her at his side, Charles was crowned king of France. Then Joan fell into the hands of the English. She was tried as a witch and burned at the stake in 1431.

The English could not destroy what Joan stood for. The French people treasured the memory of the simple peasant girl. Her love of country and her courage gave them a new sense of patriotism. Her loyal deeds helped a national spirit grow in France. People began to feel that France was united. No foreigner should be allowed to rule it. From this time on, the English fought a losing battle. By the end of the war in 1453, the English held only the city of Calais.

The French victory ended England's costly attempts to take France. Both nations now could turn to their own internal problems.

4 Other European peoples made nations

While England and France were growing stronger and more unified, nations were beginning in other parts of Europe.

Portugal and Spain became separate nations. A Germanic tribe, the Visigoths, had settled in the Iberian peninsula during the German invasions of the Roman Empire. Their kingdom lasted until early in the 700s. Then in 711, a group of Muslims known as Moors crossed the Strait of Gibraltar. They took most of the peninsula. A few Christians held out near the Pyrenees Mountains. Their groups were so small, though, that the Moors did not try very hard to defeat them.

The Moors built up a Muslim kingdom, the Caliphate of Cordova, that reached a high level of culture. In 1031, quarrels inside the kingdom caused it to break up into more than twenty small states. The breakup helped Christians in the north. They began a crusade to regain Spain for Christendom. Nobles from many parts of Europe came to help drive out the Moors.

Alphonso I of Portugal defeated the Moors in his country in 1139. He declared Portugal an independent kingdom in 1143. Gradually, the Christian kingdoms of the northern peninsula drove back the Moors. After a major victory at Las Navas de Tolosa in 1212, only Granada remained in Muslim hands.

In 1469, Ferdinand, the future king of Aragon [ar'ə gon], and Isabella, later queen of Castile [ka stēl'], were married. This joined the two leading Christian kingdoms of the area. The *Reconquista* (reconquest) to drive out the Moors began again. Finally in 1492, Ferdinand and Isabella took Granada. A united Spain was at last ready to become a strong nation.

Other Europeans began to build nations.
Nation making in medieval and early modern times fared best in western Europe, along the Atlantic coast. However, other national groups were forming elsewhere in Europe. In the north, Swedes, Norwegians, and Danes were becoming separate peoples. The Bohemians, a Slavic people, were united in the 11th century. One of their tribes, the Czechs, brought about that union. The Poles formed a strong group. Their lands became the Duchy of Poland. (A *duchy* is an area

ruled by a duke.) The Magyar tribes of Asia settled on rich lands along the Danube River. They formed the kingdom of Hungary.

Russian rulers became powerful. A strong central government also grew in Russia. Russian rulers' power over their subjects was greater than that of rulers in any other European country. There was no parliament or Magna Charta in Russia to limit the power of Russian rulers. The Russian nobles were weak and had no armies of their own. Towns had no special privileges. And the Orthodox church almost always favored the government. Very little, then, could stop ambitious leaders from becoming quite strong.

The beginnings of a Russian nation can be traced to two fierce but able rulers, both named Ivan. The first was Ivan III, sometimes called Ivan the Great. The second was his grandson Ivan IV, usually known as Ivan the Terrible.

Ivan the Great ruled from 1462 to 1505. He was a grand duke of Moscow. Slowly but surely he took over one small Russian feudal state after another. Finally, he ruled most of the Russian people.

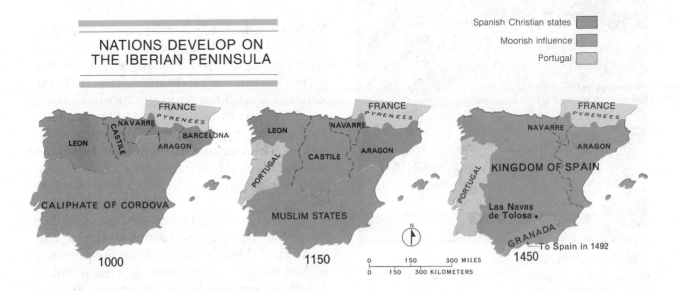

NATIONS DEVELOP ON THE IBERIAN PENINSULA

Spanish Christian states
Moorish influence
Portugal

FRANCE — PYRENEES — NAVARRE — CASTILE — LEON — BARCELONA — ARAGON — CALIPHATE OF CORDOVA — **1000**

FRANCE — PYRENEES — LEON — NAVARRE — PORTUGAL — CASTILE — ARAGON — MUSLIM STATES — **1150**

FRANCE — PYRENEES — NAVARRE — ARAGON — PORTUGAL — KINGDOM OF SPAIN — Las Navas de Tolosa — GRANADA — To Spain in 1492 — **1450**

0   150   300 MILES
0   150   300 KILOMETERS

Ivan also had to face foreign enemies. One, the Mongols, had conquered much of Russia in the 1200s. In 1480, Ivan stopped paying tribute to them. They then sent an army against him. For weeks, the two armies faced each other across a small river, but both decided to withdraw. Ivan's stand ended the two centuries of Mongol rule over Russia.

Next, Ivan III attacked the Polish-Lithuanian kingdom. It had taken over the western Russian regions while the Mongols held the country's middle and eastern lands. In two military campaigns, Ivan won back some border areas.

Under Ivan the Terrible (1533–1584), the Russians pushed into the eastern *steppes*, or plains. They defeated the nomadic tribes who lived there. Vast lands then came under

This woodcut print of Ivan the Terrible was made during his lifetime. Ivan's crown is typical of the ones worn by tsars in early Russia.

the rule of Moscow's grand duke. In 1552, Russian soldiers took Kazan on the eastern steppes. (See the map called Early Russia About 1000 A.D. in Chapter 9.) It was one of the chief cities of the Mongols.

The two Ivans moved Russia toward a united and a strong central government. They took the title *tsar* [zär], meaning caesar. And they called themselves the new Orthodox Christian emperors of the east. In uniting Russia, the tsars were becoming absolute rulers.

The Russian people paid a terrible price for the growing power of the Moscow rulers. The few towns that had governed themselves, such as Novgorod, lost freedom. Ivan the Terrible had thousands of Russian princes and landowners killed. Terror forced the *boyars*, Russian nobles, to obey Tsar Ivan's will. Loyal nobles were rewarded with lands. Heavier and heavier taxes and other duties forced Russian peasants into slavelike serfdom at the very time serfdom was ending in western Europe.

By the time Ivan the Terrible died in 1584, unrest was widespread. The country burst into an awful civil war. Russia then entered what is known as the Time of Troubles.

Nation making failed in Germany and Italy. By 850 A.D., the people of East Frankland were calling themselves Germans. Their language was becoming different from that spoken in West Frankland (France). German kings set out to bring their country under a strong central government. All went well for a time. The German tribes defeated Hungarian and Slav raiders from the east. Many German nobles promised to obey and serve their kings.

Shortly after 900, Henry the Fowler, a Saxon noble, became the German king of East Frankland. He was able to force his powerful nobles to be loyal to him. But each noble, master in his own lands, still raised his own army and joined with others to gain power.

Henry's son, Otto the Great, became one of the strongest kings of Germany. First, he defeated the Hungarians at the Battle of Lechfeld in 955. Then he began to move out eastward into the lands of the Slavs. (Through history, Germans often moved against these people. Possibly 60 percent of modern Germany once belonged to the Slavs.)

After his victory over the Hungarians, Otto was thought to be the strongest king in Europe, and his country, the most powerful. But Otto the Great made a mistake that had far-reaching effects. Instead of making himself supreme at home, he turned his attention toward Italy. In 962, Otto marched into the Italian peninsula and had the pope crown him as a new Roman emperor. From this time on, German emperors thought of themselves as rulers like the Roman caesars. The lands they ruled came to be called the Holy Roman Empire, although it was never really an empire.

Setting up the Holy Roman Empire was a sad mistake. German emperors wasted their time, money, and armies fighting to take all of Italy. At home, nobles regained power. Germany was only a collection of free cities and tiny feudal states. The emperor had little power. Seven of his feudal vassals became very important. They claimed the right to elect the ruler, and were called *Electors.*

Some of Germany's greatest kings were drawn to the idea of ruling an Italian empire. Frederick Barbarossa ("redbeard"), who began the Hohenstaufen dynasty, hoped to bring back the glory of Charlemagne. He wanted to unite Germany and Italy into one strong empire under his rule. He was crowned emperor at Rome in 1155. But he spent much of his reign, which lasted until 1190, in wasteful fighting. The liberty-loving Italian cities, supported by the papacy, completely defeated his efforts.

The grand ambitions of the German emperors destroyed more than the hope for a unified nation at home. Their desires also hurt Italy. German emperors were always interfering there. Instead of one nation, there were the Papal States, the kingdom of Naples and Sicily, and city-states—Venice, Milan, Florence, Genoa, and others. Each city-state controlled the land around it and had its own army and ambassadors. Because they disliked one another and were always warring, Italy could not become a nation. Neither Italy nor Germany became united kingdoms until the 1800s.

Frederick Barbarossa died on his way to the Third Crusade. In time, he became a folk hero, and people believed he would return someday to bring unity and strength to Germany.

section review 4

1. How did Spain and Portugal become nations? How was nation making there different from the French and English experiences?

2. List conditions in Russia that helped rulers grow very strong.

3. How did Ivan III and Ivan IV enlarge Russia?

4. How did the German kings' ambitions hurt nation making in both Germany and Italy?

Section Summaries

1. Feudalism became old-fashioned. Modern European nations began during the late Middle Ages. As the population grew, cities grew, and trade expanded. Feudalism no longer worked well as a form of government.

Kings gained more power over feudal nobles. New ways of warring also made mounted knights less important. As kings became stronger, they improved their national governments. Countries were better run, and court systems were fairer.

2. England became one nation. After the Norman conquest in 1066, England became a strong kingdom. William the Conqueror made his central government the supreme authority. Henry II helped advance common law and trial by jury. King John signed the Magna Charta, which guaranteed basic rights to freemen. Under Edward I, Parliament began to change, slowly but steadily, into a representative lawmaking body. As a result, England as a nation started to move toward representative government. After a confused time, the Tudors came to power. They began a great era.

3. French kings built a national state. In France, the Capetian kings took power from the nobles and improved government. In this way, the kings' holdings gradually grew. The Hundred Years' War began because of English claims to the French throne. England won several victories early in the war. Under Joan of Arc, France took back lost territory. The war helped both nations. The question of English claims in France was settled. Patriotism rose, and feudal ways of warring ended.

4. Other European peoples made nations. In Spain and Portugal, Christians fought for centuries to get rid of Moors. Portugal gained liberty in the 12th century. Over 300 years later, Spain's most important Christian kingdoms were joined when Isabella of Castile and Ferdinand of Aragon married. Under them, in 1492, the Christians finally pushed out the Moors. Spain became a unified nation.

Several regions of northern Europe had become nations by 1500. Under Ivan III and Ivan IV, Russia freed itself from Mongol rule. Strong German kings, especially Otto the Great, made a promising start in joining German states. However, the German kings made a mistake in setting up the Holy Roman Empire. They tried but could not rule Italy. Neither Germany nor Italy gained political unity.

Who? What? When? Where?

1. Put these events in the correct order, beginning with the earliest:

   a. Ivan the Terrible died.
   b. William of Normandy conquered England.
   c. Otto the Great was crowned emperor by the pope.
   d. Edward I formed the Model Parliament.
   e. King John signed the Magna Charta.

2. Write a sentence for each of these items that tells what happened at each of these places:

   a. Agincourt   e. Hastings
   b. Aragon   f. Kazan
   c. Crécy   g. Las Navas de Tolosa
   d. Danube River   h. Lechfeld

3. Write sentences that describe each of these:

   a. borough   f. Electors
   b. boyars   g. Magna Charta
   c. common law   h. Model Parliament
   d. *Domesday Book*   i. Parliament
   e. duchy   j. tsar

4. Write sentences that tell how each of these helped end fuedalism:

   a. bourgeoisie   d. mercenaries
   b. civil servants   e. new weapons
   c. kings   f. taxes

5. Write sentences that tell how each of these caused problems for people during the later Middle Ages.

   a. Church courts   d. lack of central
   b. feudal dues   government
   c. lack of police   e. transportation

Questions for Critical Thinking

1. Why did growing business and trade need strong central governments?

2. In what ways does the United States today have or not have the features of a nation as described in Section 1?

3. Compare the ways England and France or Spain and Russia became nations. What were the differences and similarities?

4. Why could an area not become a strong nation under the feudal system?

Skill Activities

1. Read *Girl in White Armor* by Albert Paine to find out more about the testimony given by witnesses at Joan of Arc's trial. (Macmillan, 1967)

2. If newspapers had existed at the time, they might have used headlines such as these. Write short news stories to fit these possibilities:
Bourgeoisie Growing in European Cities
King Recruits Mercenaries
Borough Election for Burgesses Held
Parliament Withholds Funds—Insists on Redress of Grievances
King Signs Magna Charta

3. Role-play a conversation between Otto the Great and the pope in which Otto convinces the pope to crown him emperor.

4. Write a *Domesday Book* entry on yourself. Include things such as records, clothes, books, jewelry, and bikes.

5. Use the development of England to describe the growth of centralized power as talked about in Section 1 of this chapter.

chapter 18 quiz

Section 1

1. One thing that was *not* a problem caused by feudalism was: a. many small independent areas, b. strong kings, c. rival nobles.

2. True or false: Mercenaries were government officials from royal families.

3. True or false: Mounted knights could be defeated by archers with longbows.

Section 2

4. The English began to bargain with their rulers through a representative body called the: a. Parliament, b. borough, c. grand jury

5. After the Wars of the Roses, English rulers were members of a branch of the House of Lancaster called the: a. Yorks, b. Normans, c. Tudors

6. Magna Charta: a. limited the power of English rulers, b. established Parliament, c. guaranteed representative government.

Section 3

7. True or false: All the people of France elected Hugh Capet, the most powerful feudal noble, as king of France.

8. True or false: Louis IX told the people to appeal to his officials when nobles wronged them.

9. Joan of Arc was a: a. leader of French armies, b. nun, c. peasant who became queen

Section 4

10. Mongol rule of Russia was ended by: a. Otto the Great, b. Ivan the Great, c. Ivan the Terrible

11. Alphonso I: a. married Isabella, b. declared Portugal an independent kingdom, c. was beaten by the Moors

12. The Holy Roman Empire was: a. a bad idea begun by Otto the Great, b. a strong, unified nation, c. strengthened by Frederick Barbarossa and the Electors.

THE EUROPEAN RENAISSANCE

Raphael's painting "The School of Athens" expresses the Renaissance awe of the ancient Greeks. The two main figures are Aristotle, in the center holding the book, and Plato, next to him.

March 25, 1436, was an exciting day for the people of Florence in northern Italy. They were dedicating a cathedral, begun in the late 1200s and just finished. Church officials, state leaders, artists, writers, musicians, and other well-known people of the time were there. They had journeyed to the proud city to see the cathedral christened Santa Maria del Fiore (Saint Mary of the Flower).

A long parade moved through the banner-lined streets. A person who was there wrote that a great band of musicians led the parade.

"[Each carried] his instrument in hand and [was dressed] in gorgeous cloth of gold garments." Following them were choirs. They "sang at times with such mighty harmonies that the songs seemed to the listeners to be coming from the angels themselves." Then came the pope, wearing white robes and a crown. Seven cardinals in bright red and thirty-seven bishops and archbishops in purple came next. Behind them walked city officials and heads of guilds.

The rich citizens of Florence filled the streets and crowded into the cathedral. Their eyes and thoughts were on its grand dome that crowned the cathedral and gave the city a brand-new skyline. Everyone felt that a new era had begun.

WHAT'S IN A NAME?
FLORENCE

Founders sometimes gave "good-luck names" to cities as the Romans did to a new colony in the northern Italian peninsula. Called *Florentia* in Latin, it meant "flowering," a metaphor for prosperous. Italians today know the city as Firenze, and English-speaking people call it Florence.

In many ways it had. As trade had improved, city life had grown rapidly in northern Italy. Florence and other rich urban centers dominated northern Italy in the 1400s. The wealth of these cities supported much creative activity. From it came some of the greatest art, architecture, and literature the world has known. A new questioning spirit led to a revival of learning.

These changes—a new birth of learning and a great creative flowering—are known as the *Renaissance* [ren'ə säns'], a French word that means "rebirth." The word also names the time during which these changes took place. The ideas and influence of the Renaissance spread from Italy to most European countries. The western world was moving from medieval to modern times. This chapter tells how:

1. The Renaissance began in Italy.

2. The Renaissance focused on the individual.

3. Italians created art masterpieces.

4. The Renaissance spread to other countries.

1 The Renaissance began in Italy

The Renaissance was mostly a *secular* movement, that is, its major interests lay outside the sphere of religion. Since the Renaissance began in Europe, Western Christendom was the first major civilization to be secularized.

During the Renaissance, people were interested in style and taste, government, education, proper behavior, and the development of personal character. The emphasis on *individualism* was an important characteristic of the Renaissance.

Renaissance ideas eventually spread through most of Europe. However, the center of the Renaissance, the place it lived longest, was northern Italy. It began there because the city-states of northern Italy were the first to gain from the revival of trade that took place in the later Middle Ages.

New wealth supported art and learning. Most of the trade routes from the East, whether by sea across the Indian Ocean or overland through Asia and the Middle East, met at the eastern end of the Mediterranean Sea. Italian merchants bought goods there and took them to ports in northern Italy. From there, the goods were carried across

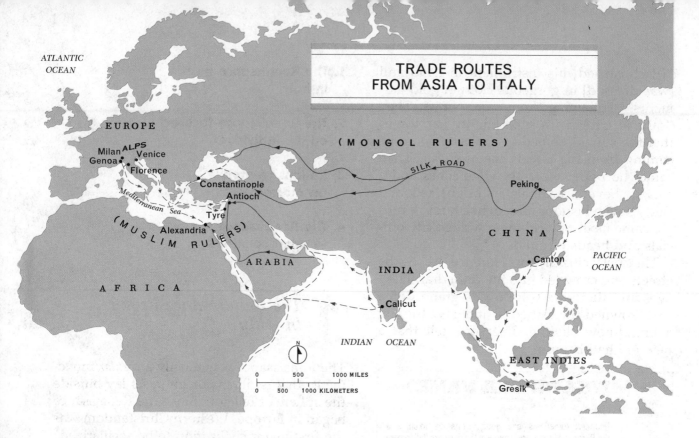

TRADE ROUTES FROM ASIA TO ITALY

the Alps into northern Europe. The main goods were pepper, ginger, cinnamon, clove, and jewels. These were easy to carry because they did not take up much space. And they were very valuable because they were available in small quantities only.

Northern Italy was divided into a number of city-states. In plan, they were like the city-states of ancient Greece. Each was made up of a city and an amount of land around it. Growing trade brought great riches to these cities. The most important were Venice, Florence, Milan, and Genoa. Venice, "Queen of the Adriatic," was built on 117 small islands. Its power and wealth came from the sea. As early as 1500, Venetian merchants had a fleet of 3,000 ships. Florence was known for its cloth industry with 30 thousand workers.

Italian bankers and merchants grew rich from trade. New wealth allowed them to enjoy free time. They could study and learn to understand the arts. They invited artists and philosophers to live and work in their palaces. Therefore, the Renaissance took place mostly among the rich because only they could financially support it.

Italian rulers also led in helping artists and writers. The reward was glory, not only for rulers' families but also for their cities. The Este family, rulers of Ferrara, supported such painters as Leonardo da Vinci, Raphael, and Titian. The Medici [med′ə chē] family of Florence were patrons of artists Donatello and Michelangelo, among others. The popes, too, played an important role. Leo X, himself a Medici, made Rome a great center of art and learning.

Political conditions helped individualism. German kings during the Middle Ages wanted to join Italy and Germany together as the Holy Roman Empire. The popes, however, were strongly against this idea. They did not want their power weakened. Both sides—Germans and popes—wanted the Italian city-states as allies. So both gave the city-states special privileges, such as electing their own officials, making their own laws, and raising taxes. As a result, a republican form of government arose in most cities.

Since there was no central government in Italy, each city became a law unto itself. Quarrels broke out between groups of wealthy merchants. Often, noble families joined in the feuds. Such fights were bad for business. Because people needed law and order, a class of despots arose in the 1300s. These daring men gained power by force and trickery, but most of them were interested in the people's well-being. Therefore, they gave their cities well-run government. Some despots, such as those of the Medici family of Florence, had been bankers and merchants. Others, such as the Sforzas of Milan, began as leaders of private bands of soldiers called *condottieri* [kon'dôt tye'rē].

Italian despots came to power because they were strong, clever, and able. Those who ruled after them had to equal these qualities. Otherwise, they soon lost power. Once on top, a ruler always watched out for plots to overturn him. Life in 14th-century Italy was dangerous. People were well trained in the use of daggers, poisoned drinks, and timely "accidents."

In such an atmosphere, the old medieval idea that the individual was not important turned upside down. In the Middle Ages, people lived in and depended upon groups. But new situations, such as the growth of trade, changed that. Now the individual was all-important. Old bars against freedom of thought and deed broke down. People began to express their own ideas about life and art. They started to speak out against long-held customs and beliefs. And they found new glory in their own strengths.

Machiavelli excused the use of force and tricks in politics. In the Middle Ages, writings on government were rare. Most of them only described the desired traits of a ruler. These guidebooks were well meaning and dull.

In 1532, five years after the author had died, a small book by Niccolò Machiavelli [mak'ē ə vel'ē] was published. It, too, gave advice on how to act as a ruler. But it was quite different from the medieval guides. It became one of the best-known works ever written.

Machiavelli was born in Florence in 1469. He served his city for many years as a diplomat and government officer. When he left public life, he wrote *The Prince*. The book is a set of rules. With them, a strong ruler could build a unified Italian government. He could fight off other newly powerful nations.

Machiavelli explained the political facts of life as he saw them. To get power and stay in power, a ruler had to forget ideals. Machiavelli had learned that by nature humans are not good, kind, loyal, or honest. So he advised:

> A wise ruler . . . cannot and should not observe faith when it is to his disadvantage and the causes that made him give his promise have vanished. If men were all good, this advice would not be good, but since men are wicked and do not keep their promises to you, you likewise do not have to keep yours to them.

Since it was published *The Prince* has been closely studied and hotly debated. For some, Machiavelli was a clever judge of why people behaved as they did. He saw what others missed. To others, he was immoral, since he seemed to pay no attention to religion.

Machiavelli believed that the state should be all-powerful. He said that every political act had only one means of measure—success. In *The Prince*, he seemed to approve the use of any possible means to get and keep power. Lying, cheating, and murder were acceptable if a ruler needed them to gain his ends. The rights of citizens were only those that the ruler allowed for the benefit of the state. In actual fact, Machiavelli did not approve of this behavior. He admitted it was bad, but insisted that this was the way successful rulers behaved. Machiavelli felt that the state must be stable at all costs. That thought became a blueprint for strong, united nations.

section review 1

1. How did geography help northern Italy become the home of the Renaissance?
2. Name some of the groups of people who were patrons of the arts. To what class did they belong?
3. In what ways did the Italian city-states gain from the political wranglings between the Holy Roman Emperors and the popes?
4. How was Machiavelli's *The Prince* different from earlier books on government?

2 The Renaissance focused on the individual

A new movement called *humanism* began in 14th-century Italy. The humanist way of looking at life is marked by an interest in people. The beauties and chances of life on Earth are important. Humanism taught people to live a full life and welcome new experiences. Humanists wanted people to have better lives in this world, rather than waiting for the next. This turned directly away from the medieval view that the only important part of life was working toward eternal salvation at death. All early art and thought were for the Church. The new movement was closely tied to a returning interest in classical learning. Humanists felt that the writings of Greece and Rome best told their ideas. It was for this renewed interest in ancient writings that the word *Renaissance* was first used.

Petrarch and Boccaccio were early humanists. Humanism owed much to the Italian writer, Francesco Petrarca, known as Petrarch [pē'trärk]. This writer, born in 1304, resented his father's desire to have him become a lawyer. For comfort, he began to read the Roman writers Cicero and Vergil. One story tells that Petrarch's father once threw the boy's books into the fire. The youth cried so much, though, that his father grabbed them back.

Petrarch gave his life to a study of classical writers. From his study came a new approach to life. He found that the Romans had believed this world was important. That was clear in their writings about love, nature, and everyday life.

Petrarch and later humanists tried to gather the actual writings of ancient authors. They studied Greek and Latin. And they spent much money and time trying to find old manuscripts. They tore apart ruins. They sent agents to Constantinople to buy what they could. Monasteries were searched for the prized pieces of parchment. Greek manuscripts became more plentiful after 1453, when the Turks took Constantinople and many Greek scholars escaped to Italy.

Petrarch wrote in Latin, imitating the works of Cicero and Vergil. But it was a group of sonnets written in Italian and inspired by his love for a woman named Laura that made him one of the greatest lyric poets of all time. Of his love for her he wrote:

If this should not be Love, O God, what shakes me?
If Love it is, what strange, what rich delight?

Another noted humanist was Giovanni Boccaccio [bō kä'chē ō], who wrote both poetry and prose. In 1348, the terrible plague known as the Black Death struck Florence, where Boccaccio lived. Thousands died from the awful disease. Boccaccio made this time

These drawings by John Dunstall show London during an epidemic of bubonic plague. Some 75,000 people in the city died.

the setting for the *Decameron*. In it, seven young women and three young men escaped the plague by living in a lonely country house. To pass the time, they tell the tales that make up the book. Many of the stories mirrored the spirit of the times by making fun of feudal customs.

Education aimed at "the complete man." In medieval times, education had two chief uses. It trained priests for preaching and scholars for debating with other scholars. During the Renaissance, people decided that education had more uses. Its goal, still aimed mostly at men, became that of making people well rounded.

The ideal Renaissance aristocrat was well-mannered and witty. He had learned enough to understand good literature, painting, and music. The so-called Renaissance man was well formed in body and good at sports. In the arts of war he was a brave and able sol-

dier. In *The Courtier*, Baldassare Castiglione [käs'tē lyô'ne] outlined this all-around person. Castiglione was himself a scholar, poet, and courtier (a person in service to a ruler).

To reach the goals of Renaissance education, Italian schools taught less theology and more literature, especially Latin and Greek. The humanists, who taught Greek and Latin language and literature, gained great respect. People journeyed far to hear their lectures. Rich men and rulers took humanists into their homes to teach their sons and daughters.

Earthly life was quite important to humanists, but most of them remained religious. Those who spoke against the Church believed in reform, not revolt. Humanist scholars carefully translated Greek and Hebrew sources of the Bible.

Renaissance people used many talents. Renaissance ideas about the individual gave people faith in their own powers. They were eager to search for new continents. They wanted to learn the secrets of nature. They questioned Church authority and showed their love of life in literature and art.

Rarely has the world seen so many people with so many talents. Not only could Renaissance people do many different things. They also could do them quite well.

Leonardo da Vinci [lē'ə när'dō də vin'chē] (1452–1519) was a genius who was an example of this many-sided person. He was one of the greatest painters of all time. He studied geology, chemistry, and anatomy and designed buildings, canals, and weapons.

Leonardo da Vinci left over 5,000 pages of notes and drawings. Besides human figures, he sketched cannons, engines, flying machines, and hundreds of other devices. Some were not made until centuries later. Leonardo left many tasks unfinished, but people marveled at his many skills. They admired him almost as if he were more than human.

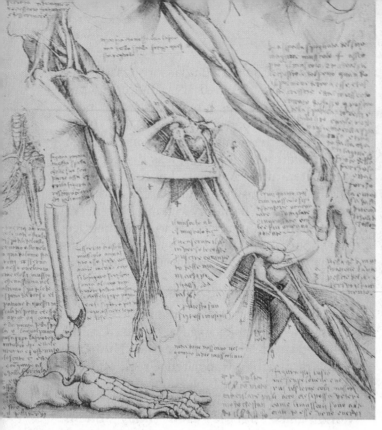

Da Vinci filled many notebooks with his drawings and descriptions of anatomy. The descriptions were written backwards to keep the thoughts and ideas private.

But da Vinci completed only a dozen paintings. Many more were left unfinished. Probably his most famous is "Mona Lisa." For centuries, people have wondered about the reason for her smile.

Some Renaissance people went too far in making the individual all-important. They turned away from the group. They cared not at all for laws or morals. Anything a person was able to get away with seemed to be all right.

Benvenuto Cellini [chə lē′nē] was an example of this type of person. He was a great artist in metalwork and sculpture, and he wrote well. But he was also a liar, braggart, and murderer. In his autobiography, he wrote honestly of his adventures, which reveal his cool ruthlessness.

section review 2

1. What is humanism's outlook on life? Why did humanists study Greek and Roman classics?
2. What did Petrarch learn from the works of ancient Romans?

3. How was education during the Renaissance different from that of medieval times?
4. Name three talents that made Leonardo da Vinci a Renaissance man.

3 Italians created art masterpieces

During the Middle Ages, religion had moved people to build beautiful churches. Artists and sculptors did not sign their works because it was the subject of the work, not the individual creator, that was most important. Artistic works showed Church teachings, human suffering, and the joys of life after death.

During the Renaissance, artists wanted to show how people and nature really were in life. Their new ways of painting and sculpt-

Painting of the Italian Renaissance was more realistic than that of the Middle Ages. In Giotto's "Lamentation over the Dead Christ" the figures have a solidity and roundness not found in medieval painting.

ing showed people as real individuals, often in nonreligious settings.

Florence led the way.   Changes in the art of painting began early in the 1300s. The man who started the new style was the Florentine Giotto di Bondone (1266–1336). He was the first European artist to make figures appear to move, to be alive. Giotto [jot'ō] decorated the walls of churches with *frescoes*—paintings on wet plaster. Most of these were scenes from the life of Jesus.

In the years after Giotto's death, Florence became the art center of Europe. Possibly only ancient Athens ever equaled it in numbers of artists in one place.

The Florentines learned to draw human figures accurately. They tried to make feelings and ideas show in the face and body. They used light and shadow to point up scenes. And they mixed new colors. Possibly most important, they figured out a way to make viewers feel as if they were looking into a painting instead of at it. Things appeared to be seen from a distance. This way of making a painting seem real is called *perspective*.

A Florentine artist well known for this kind of painting was Paolo Uccello [üt chel'lō] (1397–1475). His paintings were often crowded with people. But he placed them carefully and gave them different sizes for a pleasing sense of perspective.

Some of the most important figures in the history of Western art lived during the Italian Renaissance. Michelangelo [mī'kə lan'jə lō] was a great sculptor, painter, and architect. He was even a fair poet. He was born Michelangelo Buonarroti, near Florence in 1475. At thirteen, he became a helper to a painter and learned to make frescoes. For a number of years, Lorenzo de' Medici, ruler of Florence, helped Michelangelo carry on his studies.

Titian's "Portrait of a Man" *below* shows the Venetian love of color and texture of rich fabrics. Titian's portraits earned him his greatest fame. And Michelangelo's love of sculpture shows in such masterpieces as the "Pieta" *left*. Completed while Michelangelo was still in his twenties, the "Pieta" is Mary mourning over the body of Jesus.

Michelangelo liked sculpture better than painting. Many of his painted figures have the solid feeling of statues. He often said, "It is only well with me when I have a chisel in my hand." But people always wanted him to paint. Pope Julius II asked Michelangelo to paint frescoes on the walls and ceiling of the Sistine Chapel in the Vatican, the seat of Church government. He painted lying on his back on a scaffold most of the time. The huge task of picturing the Bible story of Genesis from the Creation to the Flood took four years. Michelangelo lived only for his art and had little interest in money or comfort. Those who knew him said he took no pleasure in eating or drinking. He was satisfied with a

little bread, a bit of cheese, a bed, and a workshop. He slept in his clothes to save time. Hard work made his sides and back misshapen.

Raphael [raf'ē əl], born in 1483, was most famous as a painter of religious subjects. Raphael was a great favorite of two popes. For Julius II, he painted several frescoes in the Vatican. Leo X appointed Raphael chief architect of St. Peter's Church.

Venice rivaled Florence as an art center. By the 1500s, Venetian painters had made their own traditions. They were most noted for their use of rich, glowing colors. Giovanni Bellini [be lē'nē], born about 1430, came from

To show Gattemelata dressed as a Roman statesman is a typical pose for the Renaissance.

a family of famous painters. His style was soft and gentle. Two of his pupils became well known. Giorgione [jôr jō′nā] painted many scenes from Greek and Roman mythology. Titian [tish′ən], born Tiziano Vecellio in 1477, painted scenes and people from the world around him. Another important Venetian was Tintoretto [tin′tə ret′ō]. His use of light and space made his paintings very dramatic.

Another important Italian artist was Sofonisba Anguisciola [sō′fō nēz′bä äng gwē′shō-lä] (1532–1625). Most famous for her work as a painter of portraits, she spent ten years in that work at the court of Philip II of Madrid.

Sculpture and architecture flourished. An outstanding sculptor of the early 1400s was the Florentine Donatello [don′ə tel′ō]. He was the first sculptor of this time to show that

he knew human anatomy. Possibly his best-known work is his grand statue of the Venetian general, Gattemelata. This statue was the first large-sized figure on horseback since Roman times. In the general's face, Donatello caught the spirit of the Italian despot— proud, powerful, and cruel.

In a class by himself was Michelangelo. Great as he was with brush and paint, he was even greater with chisel and stone. In his statue of the Biblical David, the sculptor showed how he saw the ideal young hero. David is shown with a fine head, classic features, and flowing body. Michelangelo also carved figures for the Medici chapel and for the tomb of Pope Julius.

Italian Renaissance architects used Greek and Roman models for their buildings. However, these uses of buildings and the needs of churches and palaces were different from those of classical times. So different treatments of Greek and Roman pillars and domes were needed. Therefore, Renaissance architects adapted their models to suit their own times. As a result, their work was new and had great beauty.

Several buildings were group efforts. Ten different architects worked on one of the greatest Renaissance buildings, the church of St. Peter in Rome. It is the largest Christian church in the world. Michelangelo designed most of the church.

section review 3

1. In what ways was Renaissance art different from art in the Middle Ages?

2. What role did Giotto play in the development of art?

3. What story did Michelangelo show in his frescoes on the Sistine Chapel?

4. For what kind of art did Raphael become known?

4 The Renaissance spread to other countries

From its beginnings in Italy, the Renaissance spread to many parts of Europe. Scholars and artists from the north journeyed southward to study with Italian masters. They took home new feelings and ideas. The Renaissance also spread through books printed by means of a new invention—movable type.

Printing helped spread the Renaissance. During the Middle Ages, people had written on *parchment* and on *vellum*. Parchment, made from sheepskin or goatskin, was expensive. One book might take the skins of twenty-five sheep. Vellum, made from calfskin, cost even more.

In the early 1100s, Europeans learned about paper from the Moors in Spain. The Moors knew about it through the Arabs. They, in turn, had learned of it from the Chinese.

Paper was less expensive than parchment or vellum. However, books were still expensive because they were written by hand. When the Medici family in Florence wanted 200 books for their library, forty-five skilled copyists worked two years to make them. Under such conditions, even large libraries had only a few hundred books. Many people never saw a book, much less owned one.

The use of printing to make copies of books or pictures did not appear in Europe until the late Middle Ages. The first printing in Europe, like that in China, was block printing. Letters, words, or pictures were carved into blocks of wood. Then the blocks were inked and pressed down on paper. In late medieval Europe, wooden blocks were often used for printing playing cards and saints' pictures.

The Chinese invented movable type. Whether it came directly to Europe from the Chinese is not known. Credit for the first use of movable type in Europe is generally given to a German, Johann Gutenberg [güt'n-bérg']. Possibly the first European book printed with movable type was the Gutenberg Bible, finished about 1456. By the end of the 1400s, eighteen countries had printing presses with movable type. European presses had printed 8 million books by the early 1500s.

The invention of movable type had important results. Books could be made rapidly and in great quantities. And the cost was much less than that of hand copying. The new books were far more accurate, too. Before printing, two exact copies of a book could not be made. Copyists always made mistakes. More important, printing made books available to more people.

■ MAP LESSON 19: RENAISSANCE EUROPE ABOUT 1490

1. The Renaissance began in Italy, mostly in the cities. In almost every case, these urban centers first experienced a great growth in trade. The profits from this trade were then used to support the arts and literature. This map shows how the Italian peninsula became divided into many small states, most of them centered around a city. Both the state and the leading city usually had the same name. Tell the Italian city-state that:

   a. was at the head of the Adriatic
   b. included the island of Corsica
   c. had no access to the sea
   d. was between Florence and the Papal States
   e. was immediately south of Bologna

2. The boundaries of the Holy Roman Empire are shown by heavy black lines on this map. Look at the map and decide which of the following states were part of the Holy Roman Empire and which were not:

   a. Bohemia
   b. Venice
   c. Ferrara
   d. the Swiss Confederation
   e. Denmark

MAP LESSON

RENAISSANCE EUROPE ABOUT 1490

Printing helped spread the Renaissance spirit. Italian books were sent all over Europe. The new movement in the rest of Europe was called the *Northern Renaissance*. It changed as each country added some ideas of its own.

Northern humanists looked at social and religious problems. Most humanists in northern Europe were more serious and interested in learning than were those in Italy. Italian humanists were interested in their own gains and expressions of self. Northern humanists cared about social problems. Religion and ethics, questions of right and wrong, were important.

Erasmus [i raz'məs], a Dutch scholar born about 1466, is often thought to be the greatest humanist. A priest, he spent much time studying Greek and Latin writings. He wrote many books, all in Latin. His satire *The Praise of Folly*, published in 1511, lashed out at the evils of the time. Erasmus attacked superstition, warlike princes, and false priests. He took to task scholars who wasted time with silly problems. Erasmus also used Greek sources for a Latin translation of the New Testament. He showed that the Bible used at the time had many errors.

All his life, Erasmus fought against ignorance, stupidity, and vice. He kept up a huge correspondence with learned people around

Europe. In that way, he helped spread humanistic ideals. When he died in 1536, he left behind a large number of writings that later thinkers could study.

A group of English scholars who studied medicine and Greek in Italy brought humanism to England. On their return, these English humanists gathered at Oxford University. There they became known as the *Oxford Reformers*. As teachers, preachers, and authors, they tried to bring the new learning to England. One of their students, Sir Thomas More, became a great humanist. He carried on a life-long correspondence with Erasmus. More became a lawyer and served in many government posts under King Henry VIII. His best-known book, *Utopia* (Nowhere), described a perfect society that was not real. However, people could compare it with their own society. This backdoor attack on society's evils later led to new laws that helped the poor.

Northern artists started different styles.
Painters in the Low Countries (now Belgium and the Netherlands) began early to break away from medieval ways. They started painting in new ways even before Italian Renaissance art reached northern Europe. Among the first was Jan van Eyck [van īk], born about 1380. He painted realistic landscapes and portraits. He very carefully showed trees, grass, and flowers as they appeared in nature. It was also Van Eyck who invented oil paints.

The skill of Italian painters impressed artists in northern Europe. Even more, they admired the Italians' use of perspective and mastery of anatomy. One of the earliest to study in Italy was the German Albrecht Dürer [dy'rər]. He first visited Italy about 1494. The artists' high social level there amazed him. He noted, "Here I am a lord, at home a parasite." Dürer's work put together medieval and Renaissance styles. He made a

Dürer was most famous for his engravings and woodcuts. This drawing, *top*, was completed about 1508. Over the years, Rembrandt painted many self-portraits. This one, *above*, was done about 1665. Many of his other self-portraits are done in much darker tones.

In "Peasant Wedding," Brueghel showed his interest in the universality of human customs.

great number of woodcuts and engravings to illustrate the new printed books.

German artist Hans Holbein [hōl′bīn] the Younger (1497–1543) was appointed court painter to King Henry VIII of England. He became known for his lifelike portraits of the royal family. He also painted portraits of the humanists Erasmus and Sir Thomas More. But Holbein was not the highest-paid painter at court. That honor went to Levina Teerlinc (1520–1576). A Flemish painter, Teerlinc was most famous for her miniatures.

Artist Pieter Brueghel [brœ′gəl] (1525–1569) was Flemish, that is, a native of Flanders. He spent his life painting country landscapes and hearty scenes of peasant life. The Low Countries also were home to two of the greatest 17th-century painters. Peter Paul Rubens was known for his large, dramatic canvases. Rembrandt van Rijn showed character so well that his works are thought of as among the best of all time.

Renaissance literature reached its height in Shakespeare and Cervantes. The English poet Chaucer is often thought of as the first writer of English Renaissance literature. He and the Oxford Reformers laid a base for English writers of the late 16th and early 17th centuries. On that base, they built a literature equal to any nation's written art.

Queen Elizabeth I, like many rulers of the time, helped and inspired writers. The greatest writer in the Elizabethan age—one of the greatest in world literature—was William Shakespeare (1564–1616).

Shakespeare's plays are part of the literary heritage of all English-speaking people. He

Someone You Should Know

Elizabeth I

When 25-year-old Elizabeth came to the English throne in 1558, England was a nation divided over religion and involved in a costly war with France. The new queen soon settled these two issues and set the tone for her 45-year reign.

The daughter of Henry VIII and Anne Boleyn, Elizabeth kept England from economic disaster. She even sold her own jewelry when the national treasury needed money. And yet, Elizabeth managed to build up the navy to make it the greatest in the world.

Elizabeth brought peace, prosperity, and national unity to England. Her grateful people called her Good Queen Bess. In her last address to Parliament in 1601, she honored her subjects and also summed up her own greatness. ". . . though you have had, and may have many wiser Princes sitting in this seat yet you never had or shall have any that will love you better."

had a deep understanding of human beings, and he expressed the whole range of human emotions in his plays. Some of the people he made so real are Hamlet, Lady Macbeth, Julius Caesar, Portia, and Falstaff. Hundreds of sayings have come from his rich writing into everyday English speech.

In France and Spain, humanists wrote about the evils of their day. An important author was the Spaniard Miguel de Cervantes [sər van'tēz]. He wrote the novel *Don Quixote.*

Toward the end of the 1500s, when Cervantes wrote *Don Quixote,* feudalism and knighthood were out of fashion. But the codes of chivalry still appealed to many people in Spain. Cervantes's hero, Don Quixote [kē hō'tē], was a poor but proud Spanish gentleman who loved to read knightly romances. At fifty, he made a suit of armor. Then he took his old horse and went to seek adventures. His servant Sancho Panza went with him. Cervantes's novel is a Renaissance work in two ways. First, it clearly shows Spanish life at the time. Second, it laughs at the ideals of knighthood and chivalry in the funny adventures of Don Quixote. His deeds were absurd, but Cervantes admired his hero's ideals of bravery and goodness. However, Cervantes seems to have felt that these ideals were no longer respected in the world as he knew it.

section review 4

1. What were two results of the invention of movable type?

2. How did northern European humanists differ from those in Italy?

3. For what were Van Eyck, Dürer, Brueghel, Teerlinc, and Rembrandt known?

4. In what ways were Shakespeare and Cervantes great Renaissance writers?

Section Summaries

1. The Renaissance began in Italy. Italian city-states were well placed on the trade routes between East and West. The new wealth that trade brought allowed merchants and rulers to help artists and writers. Out of this new wealth came the Renaissance.

2. The Renaissance focused on the individual. Italian humanists, such as Petrarch and Boccaccio, raised much interest in the classic writings of Greece and Rome. Renaissance humanism taught that the individual was important. People admired the many different talents of such humanists as Leonardo da Vinci.

3. Italians created art masterpieces. The greatest showing of the Renaissance spirit took place in art, especially painting. Well-known Italian artists of the time are Giotto, Raphael, Michelangelo, and Titian.

4. The Renaissance spread to other countries. People, together with books printed from movable type, spread the ideas of the Renaissance. The writings of Italian humanists influenced two great European scholars, Erasmus and Sir Thomas More. But northern writers were more interested in social problems than were Italians. Northern painting also gained from the Italian Renaissance. Among northern artists were Dürer, Holbein, Brueghel, Rubens, Teerlinc, and Rembrandt.

In England, the Renaissance blossomed in the Elizabethan Age. The greatest of the writers then was Shakespeare. Cervantes in Spain wrote *Don Quixote*. This memorable figure in fiction seems to show the end of the medieval era.

Who? What? When? Where?

1. Name one work by each of these writers:

a. Boccaccio   d. Erasmus
b. Castiglione   e. Machiavelli
c. Cervantes   f. More

2. Write sentences that describe the contribution made by each of these men to the Renaissance:

a. Boccaccio   e. Lorenzo de' Medici
b. Donatello   f. Machiavelli
c. Erasmus   g. Petrarch
d. Gutenberg   h. Shakespeare

3. Tell whether the following artists belonged to the Italian Renaissance or the Northern Renaissance:

a. Brueghel   e. Leonardo da Vinci
b. Dürer   f. Michelangelo
c. Jan van Eyck   g. Rembrandt
d. Giotto   h. Titian

4. With what city was the Medici family identified? The Este family? Name one or more artists that each family helped.

5. Write sentences that define each of these terms and tell why they were important to the Renaissance:

a. condottieri   e. Oxford Reformers
b. despots   f. patrons
c. frescoes   g. perspective
d. movable type   h. Renaissance man

6. Arrange the following events in chronological order:

a. *The Prince* was published.
b. The Black Death struck Florence.
c. Michelangelo was born.
d. The Gutenberg Bible was first printed.
e. *The Praise of Folly* was published.
f. Giotto was born.

Questions for Critical Thinking

1. What is your opinion of Machiavelli's advice to rulers during the Renaissance? What should be the standards of behavior for a government official? A business person? A high-school student?

2. Compare the purposes of education during medieval times, the Renaissance, and the present. Is the idea of a well-rounded person useful today? Explain.

3. In what ways was the Renaissance a break with the past? Are humanist ideals out of date today? Why or why not?

4. Why might Michelangelo be called a "Renaissance man"?

5. What are some explanations for the high degree of productivity during the Renaissance?

Skill Activities

1. Read *Lorenzo de' Medici and the Renaissance* by Charles L. Mee, Jr. and John Walker to find out more about Lorenzo the Magnificent and his role in this exciting era. (American Heritage, 1969)

2. Discuss what would happen if all printed matter were destroyed overnight. What changes would take place immediately? Over a long period of time?

3. Write a guidebook for United States Presidents. Have one person write on the board any and all ideas from the class—without discussion. After all ideas are on the board, discuss the value of each.

4. Use the pictures in this book to compare the artistic styles of different periods or areas. Some possible styles might be medieval, Indian, Greek, Roman, and Renaissance. What kind of subject matter did the artists choose? Why? What are the differences between the styles?

5. One of the Renaissance artists is a friend of yours. Write a description of that person, including your opinion and the opinions of others.

chapter **19** *quiz*

Section 1

1. Northern Italy was a key point in trade between Europe and: a. Asia, b. Africa, c. Russia

2. True or false: A strong central government in Italy held back the rise of city-states such as Florence and Milan for a long time.

3. Machiavelli's means of measuring the worth of political acts was: a. money, b. success, c. ethics

Section 2

4. Humanism as a basic philosophy stressed the role of: a. religion, b. discipline, c. the individual

5. True or false: Petrarch was a sculptor who was also remembered for his poetry.

6. A good example of the Renaissance man who went too far in making the individual all-important was: a. Petrarch, b. Leonardo da Vinci, c. Benvenuto Cellini

Section 3

7. True or false: Florentine artists used perspective to make scenes look real.

8. Michelangelo painted the Sistine Chapel and: a. had been a student of Giotto, b. made the statue of Venetian general Gattemelata, c. designed the dome of St. Peter's Church

9. Italian architects based their buildings on the styles of: a. Asante and Meroe, b. Greece and Rome, c. Japan and Mughul India

Section 4

10. One thing which did not help the spread of Renaissance ideas was: a. travel, b. parchment, c. movable type

11. True or false: Northern humanists were more interested in themselves than were the Italian humanists.

12. Peter Paul Rubens, Jan van Eyck, and Rembrandt van Rijn all came from: a. England, b. the Low Countries, c. Germany

THE REFORMATION AND NATIONAL POWER

Over Church objections, Henry VIII married Anne Boleyn in hopes that she might give him a male heir. Henry's act caused great problems for Cardinal Wolsey, who was England's lord chancellor.

Out of love for the faith and the desire to bring it to light, the following propositions will be discussed at Wittenberg under the chairmanship of the Reverend Father Martin Luther, Master of Arts and Sacred Theology . . . those who are unable to be present and debate orally . . . may do so by letter.

Thus Martin Luther, a German priest, began an important document. He nailed it to the door of the Castle Church of Wittenberg on October 31, 1517. It was a custom of the time for debates to be announced in this way. His document, written in Latin, attacked the sale of *papal indulgences,* which freed sinners from punishment after death. Luther and many others felt the Church of Rome abused this practice. His protest began the great movement called the Reformation.

The Reformation had two basic phases. One was the Protestant Reformation and the other was the Catholic, or Counter, Reformation. In both, leaders tried to bring Christian practices closer to Christian ideals. Roman Catholics believed that reforms had to take place within the Church. But they would not allow changes in church law. Protestants believed that there could be no reforms without major changes in church law. So they set up their own churches. They rejected the authority of the pope and his right to interpret the Bible for all Christians.

The events of the Reformation were closely tied to political and social conflict. Kings and princes used religious differences to gain political ends. As the power of nations grew, it seemed this might upset the balance of power in Europe. During the 1600s and 1700s, wars were fought to prevent any one nation from becoming too strong. This chapter tells how:

1. **The Catholic Church lost power.**

2. **The Reformation divided Europe.**

3. **Religious differences mixed with political conflicts.**

4. **France became Europe's leading power.**

5. **Strong rulers helped Russia grow.**

6. **Prussia became a powerful new state.**

1 The Catholic Church lost power

The medieval period had been truly an Age of Faith. The Catholic Church reached the height of its political power in the 1100s and 1200s. The Church began to lose its power after the reign of Pope Innocent III.

Reformers tried to improve the Church. In the later Middle Ages, weaknesses arose within the Church. Some of the clergy led immoral lives, forgetting their religious vows and duties. Many grew worldly. Some popes, for example, became involved in Italian politics. Furthermore, the growing wealth of the Church led to corruption. Men bought positions in the Church—a practice known as simony—so they could enjoy ease and luxury.

Many reformers tried to purify the Church. They wanted to return to its old ideals of poverty and service. Among the 13th-century reformers were the Franciscans and the Dominicans. In the 14th century, John Wycliffe, an Englishman, criticized Church ceremonies as formal and empty. He also translated the Bible from Latin into English so that common people could read it. Wycliffe's views influenced John Huss, who was burned at the stake in 1415 for heresy. He became a martyr, and his ideas did not die out.

The Renaissance spirit of free inquiry led to further questions about religion. Erasmus criticized religious hypocrisy and the worship of images. But he felt that the Church could reform itself from within.

New forces challenged the Church. Forces outside the Church also weakened it. Kings who were gaining more power did not want popes dictating to them. People did not like the rules and commands of foreign churchmen or the fact that most of the money they gave the Church went to Rome. Some people began to think it might be better to have a national church, run by their own country.

Another force that challenged the Church was the growth of business and commerce. The rising merchant class did not like the Church laws forbidding the lending of money at interest. Also, many of them welcomed any movement that could help them obtain the kind of wealth the Church had.

The Church was split. Several rulers defied the authority of the pope. Philip IV of France went further. In 1309, he forced the pope to leave Rome and live in Avignon [à vē nyôn′], France. This was called the Babylonian Captivity, and it lasted 65 years. It was named for the time when the ancient Hebrews were prisoners of the Babylonians.

In 1378, the Great Schism actually split the papacy. Italian cardinals elected an Italian pope, who ruled at Rome. French cardinals chose a French pope, who had his court at Avignon. Each pope claimed to be the only true head of the Church. Each enjoyed the support of several European rulers.

Finally, a majority of cardinals deposed both popes and elected a third in 1409. But neither of the deposed popes would leave, so the three became rivals. The dispute ended with the election of a fourth pope in 1417. By that time, however, the long conflict had greatly lowered the standing of the papacy.

section review 1

1. What were some of the weaknesses of the Catholic Church in the late Middle Ages?

2. Who tried to reform the Church in the 13th and 14th centuries? What did John Wycliffe do?

3. Why did kings, merchants, and others resent the power of the Church?

4. What were the Babylonian Captivity and the Great Schism? What effect did they have?

2 The Reformation divided Europe

Conditions in Germany were especially good for opposing the popes. Being so far away, the Church had difficulty keeping its control and collecting money from the hundreds of independent German states. All that was needed to bring about a revolution against the Church was a strong leader.

Luther objected to the sale of indulgences. Martin Luther was born of German peasant parents in 1483. His father hoped he would be a lawyer. But Luther became a monk and a professor of religion at the University of Wittenberg. There he studied the problem of salvation, or how to save one's soul from hell. Luther believed that salvation was a matter between an individual and God. Salvation was based on faith alone, an idea called *justification by faith*. He felt that it did not require the help of priests or good works—the showing of faith by doing the right things and taking part in Church ritual.

Luther's views brought him into direct conflict with the Church. This conflict came to center around the granting of indulgences. The Church granted indulgences to sinners on condition that they confess their sins, truly repent, and give a special donation. Gradually, the Church came to rely on the sale of indulgences when it was in need of money.

Luther objected strongly to these sales, especially when Pope Leo X sent an agent to Wittenberg to raise money for the completion of St. Peter's Church in Rome. Luther felt that indulgences had no value because sins could be forgiven only by faith in Christ's sacrifice. In 1517 Luther nailed up his list of statements against the sale of indulgences. These Ninety-five Theses, as they were called, caused a great stir.

Martin Luther and John Calvin

Luther started his own church and led the Reformation. Luther kept attacking the Church of Rome in his sermons and writings. In 1521, the pope excommunicated him and later Luther's life was endangered by others. German princes came to Luther's aid, however. He soon began to organize a new church. His writings were copied on the new printing presses and were widely read.

Luther taught that every individual had a direct relationship with God. People were able to interpret the Bible for themselves. In some ways, however, Luther disappointed the humanists. He did not listen to ideas different from his own. Once he had set up his own church, he felt that everyone else who broke with the Roman Catholic Church should accept his beliefs, which came to be called Lutheranism. He won many followers in Germany.

Civil war broke out. The Holy Roman Emperor, Charles V, and other Germans remained Catholic. Disputes between the two religious groups led to a civil war. When Catholic leaders tried to restrict Lutheran practices in Catholic areas, several Lutheran princes protested. This protest gave rise to the word *Protestant*.

Finally, an agreement called the Peace of Augsburg was reached in 1555. It said that each prince could choose between Catholicism and Lutheranism. His subjects would then follow his choice.

Luther's ideas spread to many other parts of Europe, particularly Scandinavia. There Protestantism gained the support of the governments of Denmark (which included Norway at that time) and Sweden.

Calvinism became important. Other Christian reformers also set up separate churches. John Calvin, born in 1509, was a French lawyer and scholar. He had had to flee from France because of his Protestant ideas. In 1536, he visited the city of Geneva (in present-day Switzerland). When the people there asked him to stay and organize a church, he did so.

Although Calvin had been inspired by

Luther, he disagreed with him on certain matters. One of Calvin's important ideas was that of *predestination*. This meant that God had already decided who was to be saved and who was to be damned. There was nothing a person could do to change this decision. Since nobody knew how God had decided in each case, a person's purpose in life, according to Calvin, was not to work out his salvation but to honor God. However, since anyone destined for salvation could be expected to behave righteously, correct behavior was a good clue as to who was among the chosen. Calvinists therefore strongly emphasized right behavior. Calvin set forth his ideas in a famous book, *The Institutes of the Christian Religion.*

At Geneva, Calvin set up a theocracy. It strictly controlled not only church affairs, but also politics, education, amusements, and family life. Calvinism taught that one's work was actually part of one's religious life. Hard work, moral living, and thrift were believed to be the Christian virtues. A moral life and wealth were looked upon as signs that a person was predestined to salvation. These ideas are still very much a part of the Protestant work ethic.

Other new churches were soon set up, based on the Calvinist model. The Swiss Reformed and Dutch Reformed churches were two examples. So was the Presbyterian Church, begun by John Knox in Scotland. In France, Calvinists were known as *Huguenots* [hü′gə notz].

England broke with Rome. Protestantism was also felt in England. But most of the English remained loyal to the Catholic Church. King Henry VIII even wrote a pamphlet in 1521 attacking Luther. For this the pope rewarded him with the title "Defender of the Faith."

Soon afterward, however, Henry quar-

Queen Mary of England

reled with the pope. He wanted the pope to dissolve his marriage to Catherine of Aragon because their only child was a daughter, Mary. When the pope refused, Henry chose a new archbishop of Canterbury. In 1533, the archbishop ruled that Catherine was not Henry's lawful wife. This left Henry free to marry Anne Boleyn, who he hoped would produce a male heir. But the marriage also produced only a daughter, Elizabeth.

In 1534, the king had Parliament issue the Act of Supremacy. This made Henry VIII head of the Church in England. Henry also abolished monasteries and took over much of the Catholic Church's property. He made few changes in the religion. But his son, Edward VI, adopted several Protestant reforms.

Edward VI was the son of Henry and one of his later wives, Jane Seymour. A sickly child, Edward died at age 16, and Henry's daughter Mary soon became queen in 1553. A loyal Catholic, she severely persecuted English Protestants. This led people to call her "Bloody Mary." Elizabeth I, who suc-

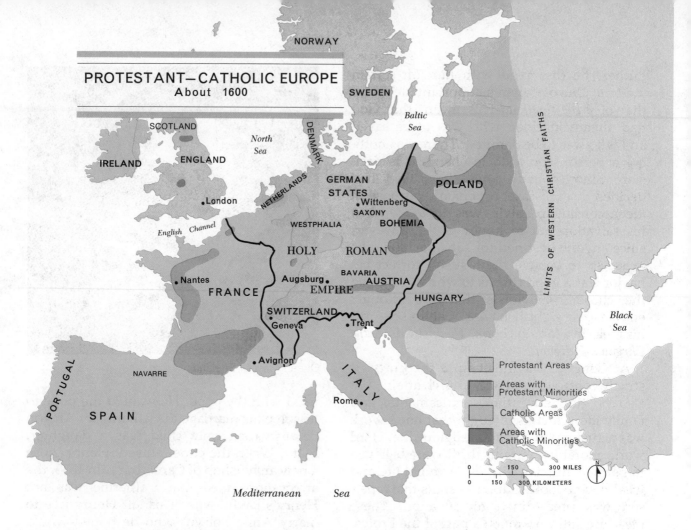

PROTESTANT—CATHOLIC EUROPE
About 1600

Protestant Areas

Areas with
Protestant Minorities

Catholic Areas

Areas with
Catholic Minorities

ceeded Mary, brought back moderate Protestantism. Parliament then passed laws that began a national church of England. The head of this *Anglican* Church, as it is often called, is the king or queen of England, not the pope.

Most English people were happy with the Anglican Church. But some objected because it still used certain Catholic sacraments. They wanted the Church of England to be so pure in its Protestantism that they were called Puritans. Unhappy in England, many of them left and took Puritanism to the colonies in America.

Roman Catholics began a Counter Reformation. After seeing the spread of Protes-

tantism, the Roman Catholic Church tried to win people back with the Counter Reformation. One part of the program was the founding of several new religious groups to help strengthen the Church. Most famous was the Jesuit order, which became known for excellent teaching and missionary work.

In 1542, Pope Paul III called the Council of Trent to deal with Church problems and suggest reforms. Delegates, meeting from 1545 to 1563, upheld all existing Roman Catholic doctrine. However, they ended such things as simony and the abuse of indulgences. They also improved church administration and education and reformed life in the monasteries.

The Counter Reformation, especially the

work of the Jesuits, was very successful. By the 17th century, the Roman Catholic Church had stopped the spread of Protestantism in France. It won back Hungary and Poland, and kept Catholicism strong in Bavaria, Austria, Ireland, and the southern Netherlands.

The effects of the Reformation were widespread. The Reformation strengthened new nations, kings, and the middle class. They gained from the limitation of papal power and from the Church wealth they seized.

The Reformation also helped the ideas of democracy and representative government to grow. The importance of lay people in church government increased, particularly among Calvinists. This idea of self-government carried over into political affairs. Calvinism also glorified work, thrift, and profits. Thus, the middle class gained new dignity and power.

In addition, the Reformation encouraged education, and in the long run, it aided religious toleration and freedom. But it had split the thousand-year-old unity of western Christendom. Protestants and Catholics were all Christians. But they no longer belonged to the same church organization. Northern Europe became mostly Protestant and southern Europe stayed mostly Catholic. The same division still exists.

section review 2

1. What ideas of Martin Luther's brought him into conflict with the Church?

2. What were the main beliefs of Calvinism? Name four countries to which it spread.

3. How did England become Protestant?

4. What were some of the effects of the Reformation?

3 Religious differences mixed with political conflicts

For a long time, Protestants and Catholics were bitter enemies. They fought a series of wars from 1550 to 1650. Often, religion got mixed up with politics in these wars.

Spanish power threatened Europe. King Charles, a member of the Hapsburg family of Austria, ruled Spain from 1516 to 1556. He was the strongest ruler of Europe. Through his mother and father Charles had inherited the Low Countries, southern Italy, and Austria. At the age of 19, he was elected Holy Roman Emperor Charles V. Thus by the year 1519, his control reached into central Europe as well.

The threatening power of Charles V led to the rise of a new idea in European politics. It was called the *balance of power*, which meant that no one country should have overwhelming power over other countries. Countries constantly shifted alliances to keep this balance.

In 1556, Charles abdicated. His health was failing and he was tired of trying to hold his vast empire together. Austria went to his brother Ferdinand I, who became Holy Roman Emperor in 1558. Spain and the rest of the lands went to his son Philip II.

England defeated Spain. Philip wanted to strengthen his own rule and defend Catholicism. He saw Protestant England as his chief enemy. The English queen, Elizabeth I, was hostile to Spain. She even allowed English pirating of Spanish treasure ships.

In 1588, Philip sent out the Spanish Armada, a fleet of over 130 ships. It was to attack England and to prepare the way for an invasion. But the ships of the English navy were smaller and faster. And they were

At *left* is Catherine de' Medici. At *right* is the St. Bartholomew's Day Massacre. Francois Dubois was an eyewitness to the event, and this engraving is based on a painting he did of it.

expertly sailed by such bold captains as Sir Francis Drake, John Hawkins, and Martin Frobisher. The Armada was defeated in the English Channel.

Elizabeth gained two important results from this battle. England remained free and Protestant, and it proved itself as a sea power. Under Elizabeth, England became an important naval power in Europe.

Civil war broke out in France. Meanwhile in France, Huguenots were fighting Roman Catholics. At issue was which group would control the throne. During most of this time,

France was ruled by weak kings. However, a regent, Catherine de' Medici, had great power. (A *regent* is a person who rules until the rightful ruler is able to.) Catherine's hatred of Protestantism was intense, and she planned to kill all Huguenots. In 1572, the bloody St. Bartholomew's Day Massacre took place. At least 10 thousand Huguenots were slain, but Protestantism was not stamped out.

In 1589, French King Henry III was assassinated. Henry of Navarre, leader of the Huguenot party, was heir to the throne. But French Catholics and Philip II of Spain denied his right to be king. With the aid of

Elizabeth I of England, Henry became king in 1594. But he had to become a Catholic before he could be crowned. He was the first of the Bourbon dynasty.

Although Henry IV became a Catholic, he did not forget the Huguenots. In 1598, he issued the Edict of Nantes. This edict protected the liberties of the Huguenots. Thus, France became the first large country to permit more than one form of Christianity.

Another war lasted thirty years. Of all the areas in Europe, the German states of the Holy Roman Empire were most sharply divided between Catholics and Protestants. These states fought each other and their neighbors between 1618 and 1648 in a bitter struggle known as the Thirty Years' War. The war lasted so long because power politics became mixed up with religious issues.

The fighting began when a Catholic Hapsburg prince was chosen king of Bohemia in 1618. Many Bohemians were Protestant. Afraid of Catholic rule, they started a civil war and got a Protestant elected ruler of Bohemia. In the meantime, the Catholic Hapsburg prince had become Holy Roman Emperor Ferdinand II. With the help of Catholic German princes and Catholic Hapsburg Spain, Ferdinand fought Bohemia and won it back to Catholicism.

It then looked as if Ferdinand II would try to defeat all the German Protestant states. His goal was to set up a powerful unified empire under Hapsburg rule. The nations bordering on the empire were afraid this would upset the balance of power. Protestant Denmark was the first to declare war. And Germany soon became a battleground.

When Ferdinand's armies defeated the Danes, Protestant Sweden became alarmed and entered the war. The Swedes got money from the French. Even though France was a Catholic country, it was more afraid of the growth of Hapsburg power than of Protestantism. The Swedes were led by their king, Gustavus Adolphus. He stopped the advance of the Hapsburgs, but was himself killed in battle.

As the war dragged on, the French too sent an army into German territory. After bloody fighting, the French and their allies won a major victory. The war ended in 1648 with the Peace of Westphalia. What began as a religious struggle in 1618 had ended as a war to stop the Hapsburgs from dominating Europe. In this sense, the Thirty Years' War was fought to maintain the balance of power in Europe.

The Thirty Years' War had many important results. First, Germany remained divided between Protestants in the north and Catholics in the south. Second, hundreds of small German states kept their independence. Thus, Germany remained politically disunited for more than two centuries. Third, the war meant the end of an old medieval dream—a united Holy Roman Empire under the Catholic Church. In its place would be a modern Europe made up of independent states, each jealous of its own power.

section review 3

1. How did Charles V come to rule so large an empire? What new idea did his great power lead to?

2. Why did Philip II send out his Armada in 1588? What two goals were gained by Elizabeth I when the Spanish Armada was defeated?

3. What caused the civil wars in 16th-century France? Why was the Edict of Nantes important?

4. In what ways was the Thirty Years' War a religious struggle as well as a political one? How was the balance of power maintained? What were three long-lasting results of this war?

4 *France became Europe's leading power*

The Thirty Years' War also led to the decline of Spain and the rise of France as the strongest nation in Europe. Ever since the time of Charles V in the mid-16th century, France had been surrounded by Hapsburg Spain and Hapsburg Austria. France had felt its security was in danger. Now that that danger was gone, the way was open for French power to grow.

Two cardinals helped make France strong. In 1610, Henry IV was assassinated. His wife became regent for their young son, but she mismanaged the country. Soon, an ambitious churchman named Richelieu [rish'ə lü] began to help her rule. In 1622, Richelieu was made a cardinal in the Catholic Church. Two years later, he became the chief minister of France. Even when Henry's son Louis XIII was old enough to reign, he found he could not get along without Richelieu. Louis allowed him almost absolute control over France.

Richelieu had two major aims. The first was to strengthen the power of the French king. The second was to make France supreme in Europe. To accomplish the first goal, he weakened others to make the king stronger. He issued orders that took away political rights from the Huguenots and power from the nobles. To reach the second goal, Richelieu took France into the Thirty Years' War. France came out the strongest nation in Europe.

Richelieu was harsh and made the common people pay heavy taxes. When he died in 1642 they rejoiced. Louis XIII died a year later. His son Louix XIV became king at the age of four. Richelieu had trained Jules Mazarin, an Italian-born cardinal, to be his successor. Until Louis XIV was 22 years old, Maza-

Louis XIV

rin actually ran the government. He followed Richelieu's policies, and France continued to grow strong.

Louis XIV was one of the most powerful French kings. Louis XIV ruled France from Mazarin's death in 1661 until 1715. He has been called the perfect example of an absolute ruler with unlimited power. His motto was "L'État, c'est moi" (The State, it is I). Louis believed in the divine right of kings. He enjoyed playing the part of God's agent on Earth.

Louis was intelligent and worked hard at being king. His capable economic adviser, Jean Colbert [kôl ber'], helped France become strong through overseas growth. Colbert set up rules to improve the quality of French goods so that more people would buy them. To compete with the powerful Dutch and British East India trading companies, the French East India Company was begun in 1664. Louis XIV also added to the powers of the *intendants*, appointed officials who carried out his orders in the country. Also, he reorganized the French army and strengthened the navy.

Some of Louis's policies were unwise. Louis was a strong believer in Catholicism. He felt that non-Catholics would not be loyal to the king and would weaken France. In 1685, he canceled the Edict of Nantes and took away freedom of worship from the Huguenots. Thousands fled to Prussia, England, and the British colonies in America. This hurt French trade and industry in which Huguenots were active.

In other areas, too, Louis's policies were unwise. "Le Roi Soleil" or Sun King, as Louis XIV was often called, demanded great luxury as well as power. He built a lavish palace at Versailles, a village about twelve miles (19 kilometers) outside Paris. There he surrounded himself with nobles who did nothing but serve and amuse him. Louis thus strengthened his power by making the nobles dependent on him. In this way, he kept them under his control.

The luxury and waste of Versailles cost the French taxpayers dearly. In addition, by moving from Paris to Versailles, Louis cut himself and his successors off from contact with the French people. Although this had serious results for the kings who came after him, Louis XIV gave France more unity and a stronger central government than ever before.

Louis's wars weakened France. Louis had the strongest army in Europe. His ambition, like Richelieu's, was to make France the most powerful state on the continent. Thus France fought with other European nations in four long wars that lasted nearly fifty years.

Louis had two specific goals: to gain more territory to the north and east of France and to have a French prince become king of Spain and control Spain's huge overseas empire. From 1667 to 1714, the other European states made alliances to fight Louis and prevent him from upsetting the balance of power.

In the first three wars, Louis won a few border territories, but only after heavy losses in men and money. The fourth war was the longest and most costly. It grew out of a conflict over who was to succeed to the throne of Spain. Called the War of the Spanish Succession, it lasted from 1701 to 1714. The Spanish king, a Hapsburg, had no heirs. Shortly before he died in 1700, he signed a will under French pressure. In it, he named Louis's grandson, Philip, as his successor to all Spanish territories in Europe and overseas.

The other European states had wanted to put a Hapsburg, Archduke Charles, on the Spanish throne. But in 1711, Charles inherited the Austrian throne and was in line to become the next Holy Roman Emperor. If he were made king of Spain as well, the Hapsburgs would control too much of Europe. The allies became divided on what to do. This led to a compromise peace with Louis.

The Treaty of Utrecht in 1713 ended the War of the Spanish Succession in Europe. Another treaty in 1714 ended the colonial conflict. Louis's grandson, Philip, stayed on the Spanish throne. But he and Louis had to promise that the same king would never rule both France and Spain. Spain kept its overseas empire. But land that the Spanish Hapsburgs controlled in Italy and in present-day Belgium went to the Austrian Hapsburgs. And Spain lost Gibraltar, which England had

EUROPE IN 1721

Glasgow • Edinburgh
North Sea
SCOTLAND
ULSTER
IRELAND
GREAT BRITAIN
WALES
ENGLAND
London •
DENMARK
SWEDEN
Stockholm •
Baltic Sea
Copenhagen •
Gulf of Finland
Narva • St. Petersburg
RUSSIA
PRUSSIA
HANOVER
UNITED NETHERLANDS
Amsterdam
Utrecht
BRANDENBURG
Berlin •
Warsaw •
POLAND
Kiev •
Poltava •
GERMAN STATES
SAXONY
Louvain •
AUSTRIAN NETHERLANDS
English Channel
HOLY ROMAN
Versailles • Paris •
LORRAINE
Blenheim •
Augsburg • BAVARIA
EMPIRE
AUSTRIA
Vienna •
Buda •
HUNGARY
Sea of Azov
ATLANTIC OCEAN
La Rochelle •
FRANCE
SWITZERLAND
MILAN
Venice •
VENICE
Black Sea
SAVOY
Genoa •
Avignon •
GENOA
Pisa •
TUSCANY
PAPAL STATES
Adriatic Sea
Istanbul •
OTTOMAN EMPIRE
CORSICA
Rome •
PORTUGAL
Lisbon •
Madrid •
SPAIN
BALEARIC ISLANDS
MINORCA
SARDINIA
Naples • NAPLES
N
0   150   300 MILES
0   150   300 KILOMETERS
Gibraltar •
Mediterranean
SICILY
Sea

captured during the war. England also took over some French colonies in Canada. In this way, France was stopped from dominating Europe, and the balance of power was kept.

Louis's wars and life of luxury left France with an empty treasury and a large debt. As he grew older, Louis doubted the wisdom of his many military adventures. On his deathbed in 1715, he warned his heir: "Try to preserve peace with your neighbors. I have been too fond of war."

section review 4

1. What were Richelieu's aims? What did he do to accomplish them?

2. In what ways did the style of life at Versailles strengthen Louis's absolutism, but weaken France?

3. What were the two specific goals that King Louis XIV had for France?

4. How did the peace treaties after the War of the Spanish Succession keep a balance of power in Europe?

5 Strong rulers helped Russia grow

At the end of the 16th century, Russia was swept by great unrest. It was called a Time of Troubles because all government had broken down. The old ruling family did not have a male heir, and the peasants rose up in rebellion. Armies from Poland and Sweden took advantage of Russia's weakness. For a short time, Poles ruled Moscow. But the Russians finally drove out the invaders and brought some order. The Time of Troubles ended in 1613 when a popular assembly chose a young nobleman named Mikhail Romanov as a compromise selection for tsar. The Romanovs built Russia into a great empire and ruled until 1917.

Peter the Great westernized Russia. Mikhail's grandson, Peter I—usually called Peter the Great—came to the throne in 1682. He was determined to make Russia a strong, modern state. To do this Peter decided to copy the European nations that lay to the west of Russia. He created a small navy and modernized the army. He brought to Russia many European scholars, craftsmen, and engineers. They introduced European fashions and customs to Russia's upper classes. More important, they helped Peter set up scientific institutions, reform the calendar and alphabet, and start new industries.

Peter the Great, like most other European rulers of the time, believed firmly in absolutism. He removed all traces of local self-government. And he put the Russian Orthodox Church completely under his control. Peter also made all Russians serve the state. This was hardest on the peasants who had to pay heavy taxes. Serfdom grew worse, and there were many peasant uprisings in Peter's time.

Peter the Great

Peter extended Russian boundaries. Peter the Great and later Russian rulers had a major goal in foreign affairs, to obtain "windows on the West." These were seaports on the Black Sea or Baltic Sea that would enable Russia to trade with western Europe by water. To gain such "windows," Peter waged war against the Swedes, who controlled much of the Baltic region. As a result, Russia was at war for most of the years that Peter ruled.

In these wars, Peter twice fought the Ottoman Turks, but without much lasting success. However, his Great Northern War against Sweden, for which he allied with Poland, Saxony, and Denmark, was successful. In 1703, Peter laid the foundations of St. Petersburg (now Leningrad), his new capital, on a region of the Baltic shore he had cap-

GEOGRAPHY

A Key to History

RUSSIA AND ICE-FREE PORTS

Throughout history, a nation with good seaports has had an advantage in carrying on trade and conducting wars. In general, trade by water has been easier, cheaper, and often faster than trade by land. Even today, water is the most efficient way to carry bulky goods, such as ore, fuel, and grain.

Russia has the longest seacoast of any country in the world, yet it has had few usable seaports. Waters along most of Russia's Arctic coast are frozen over for nine to ten months a year. Murmansk is the only Arctic port that is always ice-free. Its usefulness is limited because the seas tying it to the Atlantic Ocean are often stormy and treacherous.

The Russian desire for ice-free ports led to several wars. In particular, Russian leaders wanted ports on the Baltic Sea, because it offers an open route to the Atlantic Ocean and Western Europe.

One of the most important Baltic ports was Riga, near the mouth of the Western Dvina River. From 1557 to 1582, Tsar Ivan IV tried to conquer Riga and Narva, another Baltic port. He wanted to link Russia's internal trade routes with those of the Baltic Sea. After some initial successes, he was defeated by Polish and Swedish forces.

Peter the Great made further attempts to win control of Baltic ports. In 1703, hoping to open a new avenue to the West, he began building St. Petersburg on the Gulf of Finland. As a result of the Great Northern War (1707–1721), Peter became master of the eastern shores of the Baltic. When Russia acquired Finland in 1809, it gained still more outlets to the Baltic.

Russia's leaders have also looked south and east. Russia fought the Turks to gain access to the Black Sea. Then it tried to win control of the straits leading from the Black Sea to the Mediterranean. In the early 1900s, Russia fought Japan in its search for an ice-free port on the Pacific.

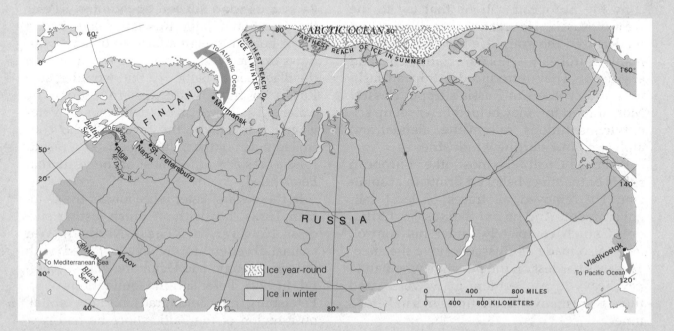

tured from Sweden. In 1709, the Russians won a smashing victory over the Swedes at Poltava in southern Russia. When the Great Northern War ended in 1721, Sweden had lost nearly all of its possessions along the eastern shore of the Baltic. Russia had gained its Baltic "window" and had also become the dominant power in northern Europe.

Catherine the Great continued Peter's policies. Several weak rulers followed Peter the Great. Finally in 1762, Catherine II, a German princess, seized the throne from her mentally unfit husband, Peter III. Catherine was gifted and well educated. She liked to think of herself as enlightened, but in reality she ruled as a despot. She continued Peter's westernization policy by improving schools and modernizing laws. But the condition of the peasantry actually became worse. Catherine made serfs of more than a million peasants who had been free. They lived in the newly conquered areas in the south of Russia.

Catherine goaded the Turks into war in 1768. By 1774, she had won back the part of Azov which had been lost by Peter the Great. She also won free access to the Black Sea and the right to protect Christians living within the Ottoman Empire. A few years later, Catherine seized the Crimea. This brought about a second war with the Turks in 1787. A treaty signed in 1792 gave Russia ownership of the Crimea and other Turkish lands north of the Black Sea. During the same period, Russia took over much Polish territory. It was for all these conquests that Catherine was called "the Great."

WHAT'S IN A NAME?
CRIMEA

The peninsula between the Black Sea and the Sea of Azov is known as the Crimea. The name comes from the Russian word *kremnoi*, which means "crags" or "rocky cliffs." This describes the area well.

Catherine the Great

section review 5

1. Why did Peter the Great try to westernize Russia? How did he strengthen Russian absolutism?

2. What were the goals of Peter's wars? How successful were they?

3. How did Catherine the Great view herself and how did she affect the westernization of Russia?

4. How did the rule of Catherine the Great affect the condition of the serfs? The growth of Russia?

6 *Prussia became a powerful new state*

During the late Middle Ages, a new state began to take shape in northeastern Europe. This state, later called Prussia, owed its rise to the Hohenzollern [hō′ən zol′ərn] family. The Hohenzollerns were capable rulers who obtained both land and power through clever diplomacy. By the end of the Thirty Years' War, they had become the most important Protestant rulers in the German states. By 1701, they were kings of Prussia.

Frederick William and his son brought about many changes. Frederick William I, the second king of Prussia, was an absolutist who ruled from 1713 to 1740. He made Prussia into a strong military state by tripling the size of its army. He also greatly improved the efficiency of both the army and the Prussian government.

His son, Frederick II, had many interests other than war. He enjoyed history, poetry, and music. He was also interested in the ideals of the Enlightenment. Frederick II abolished torture in criminal cases and reformed the civil courts. He granted religious toleration to all people in Prussia. He also worked hard to improve the government, industry, education, and living conditions of his people.

Frederick II made Prussia a great power. Frederick's major goal was to increase the power of Prussia. Shortly after he became king in 1740, Frederick invaded the Austrian territory of Silesia. This area was rich in farmland and industries. He thought he would succeed because Prussia had a stronger army than Austria.

At the time of Frederick's attack, the Austrian emperor had just died. Several heads of European states, including Frederick, had

■ MAP LESSON 20: THE DISAPPEARANCE OF POLAND, 1701–1795

1. Sometimes two or more maps are used together to show change over time. Maps such as these appear in chronological order, hence they are arranged just like sentences in a paragraph. The first map here shows the situation before any changes took place. The other three maps show the changes and the years in which they occurred. In what year does this sequence show the first changes as having taken place?

2. The disappearance of Poland was caused by the expansion of what three other countries?

3. Warsaw, the capital of Poland, eventually became part of what other country?

4. The expansion of Prussia between 1701 and 1742 occurred at the expense of Austria as well as Poland. What was the name of the Austrian province that became part of Prussia? According to these maps did Austria ever regain this territory?

5. The Russian city of Kiev was quite close to the Polish border for many years. In what year did Russian expansion change this?

6. Why would having a large city very close to the border cause difficulties for Russian defenses?

7. For a long time, the two major parts of Prussia were not connected to each other. What problems might this cause for Prussia?

8. In what year did Prussia acquire the area that connected its two parts?

9. What does Poland's disappearance probably indicate about its military might?

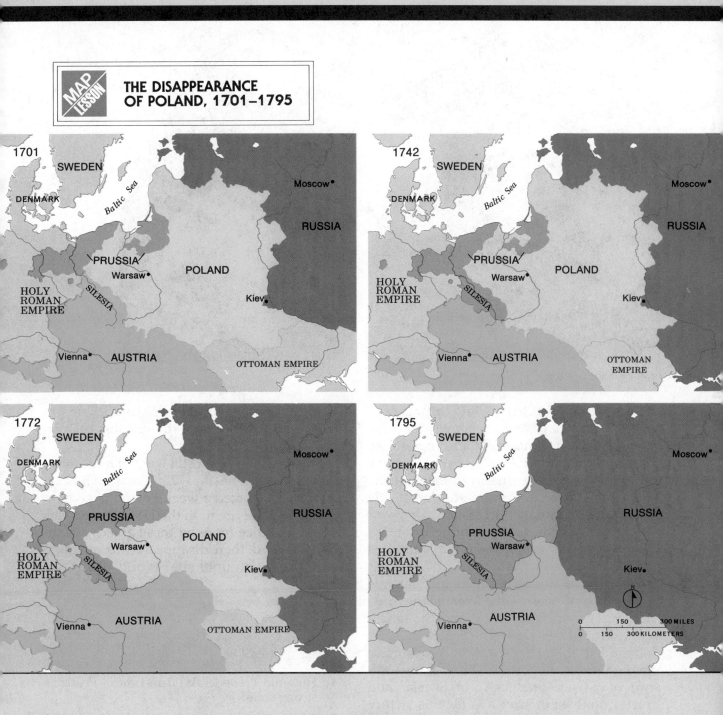

Frederick the Great and Maria Theresa

signed a pledge that they would respect Austrian boundaries and acknowledge the young Austrian princess, Maria Theresa, as the rightful heir to Austria. Frederick's attack broke the agreement. It also threatened the balance of power in Europe and led to the War of the Austrian Succession. This war became worldwide as the fighting extended to the overseas empires of the countries involved.

The general war that began in 1740 was fought in two phases, the War of the Austrian Succession, 1740–1748, and the Seven Years' War, 1756–1763. The Peace of Paris that ended it in 1763 was a compromise which allowed important shifts in the balance of power. Frederick got Silesia, and Prussia doubled in size. It is for this victory that Prussians called Frederick "the Great." Overseas, the English, who like other Europeans, had entered the war because of various alliances, had defeated France in North America. They gained Canada and all lands east of the Mississippi. England was also left

free to conquer India. England therefore came out of the war as the greatest colonial power in the world.

Frederick the Great still wanted more land. His chance came in 1772. Prussia, Russia, and Austria forced a weak Poland to give up land to each of them. In the 1790s Poland was sliced up twice more by these greedy neighbors. Poland then disappeared as an independent nation until after World War I.

section review 6

1. How did Frederick William I make Prussia a strong state?

2. From what does the name War of the Austrian Succession come? Who started the war?

3. How were North America and India involved in the War of the Austrian Succession?

4. What happened to Poland's status as an independent nation in the 1790s?

20 chapter review ✦ ✦ ✦

Section Summaries

1. The Catholic Church lost power. The Protestant Reformation that swept Europe in the 16th and 17th centuries greatly reduced the power of the Catholic Church. The Reformation had several causes. Corruption had weakened the Church from within, which led to criticism and attempts to cleanse the Church by many reformers. New events from outside also reduced Church authority. Europeans began to resent papal control. Merchants wanted to be free of religious restrictions on trade.

2. The Reformation divided Europe. The Reformation started in Germany in 1517 when Martin Luther criticized the sale of indulgences by the Church. In Geneva, John Calvin began a new sect of Protestantism. Calvinism inspired the French Huguenots, the English Puritans, the Scottish Presbyterians, and others. England broke with Rome after a quarrel between Henry VIII and the pope. And the English began the Anglican Church. As Protestantism grew, the Catholic Church began the Counter Reformation to regain lost ground. New religious orders and reforms helped do this. But the Reformation had shattered the religious unity of western Europe. It aided both royal power and the spirit of democracy in some countries.

3. Religious differences mixed with political conflicts. European countries were involved in several wars between 1550 and 1650. Under Charles V and Philip II, Spain enjoyed its greatest glory. Jealous nations tried to check Spain to keep a balance of power. That balance shifted when England defeated the Spanish Armada in 1588. Civil war between Protestants and Catholics weakened France. But the Edict of Nantes gave Protestants some religious freedom. Religious fighting reached its peak in the Thirty Years' War. France grew at the expense of the Hapsburgs.

4. France became Europe's leading power. Cardinals Richelieu and Mazarin started France on the path to greatness. Louis XIV, a "perfect" absolute ruler, unified France and made it the leader of Europe. But his excessive spending on luxuries and wars later weakened France.

5. Strong rulers helped Russia grow. Peter the Great used his absolute power to modernize Russia and expand its territory. He gained a "window" on the Baltic Sea and built St. Petersburg. Catherine the Great was an "enlightened" ruler who also adopted some Western ways. She too increased Russia's size and power by gaining access to the Black Sea and seizing the Crimea and parts of Poland.

6. Prussia became a powerful new state. Under Frederick William I and Frederick the Great, Prussia became a strong military state. Frederick the Great was enlightened, but he too wanted to increase Prussia's size. Prussia and other European powers became involved in the War of the Austrian Succession, which was also fought in overseas colonies. The Peace of Paris gave Silesia to Frederick. Later, he also took some of Poland. England emerged from the war as the greatest colonial power.

Who? What? When? Where?

1. Arrange these events in chronological order, beginning with the earliest:
   a. The St. Bartholomew's Day Massacre took place.
   b. Luther posted the Ninety-five Theses.
   c. Catherine the Great became Empress of Russia.
   d. Henry VIII had Parliament issue the Act of Supremacy.
   e. Richelieu became chief minister of France.

2. Write sentences that describe the influence each of these men had on the Reformation:
   a. John Calvin   d. Martin Luther
   b. Erasmus   e. Philip IV
   c. John Huss   f. John Wycliffe

3. Write sentences that describe the roles played by each of these women in the Protestant-Catholic conflicts;
   a. Anne Boleyn   d. Catherine de' Medici
   b. "Bloody Mary"   e. Elizabeth I
   c. Catherine of Aragon

4. Write sentences that name the nationality of each of these persons and tell an important contribution each made to the development of his or her nation:

    a. Cardinal Richelieu   d. Henry IV
    b. Catherine II   e. Henry VIII
    c. Frederick the Great   f. Peter the Great

5. Tell what these phrases mean:
    a. balance of power
    b. justification by faith
    c. predestination
    d. The State, it is I.

Questions for Critical Thinking

1. Why could the 1600s be called the "French century"?

2. After a lifetime spent gaining a great empire, why did Charles V choose to divide the empire at his abdication?

Skills Activities

1. Read *Peter the Revolutionary Tsar* by Peter B. Putnam to learn more about Peter the Great's European travels, personal life, and achievements and failures as a ruler. (Harper, 1973)

2. Write a report on one of these rulers and his palace:
    a. Henry VIII and Hampton Court
    b. Louis XIV and Versailles
    c. Peter the Great and the Great Palace at Petrodvorets

3. Role play one of the following ideas:
    a. Europeans of the 1700s discussing the effect of the Reformation on their lives
    b. Peter the Great "Westernizing" his people
    c. Mary Tudor and Elizabeth I discussing religion
    d. Maria Theresa discussing the War of the Austrian Succession

chapter **20** *quiz*

Section 1

1. The Babylonian Captivity was: a. the time when Philip IV forced the pope to leave Rome and live in Avignon, France, b. the years when popes were most heavily involved in Italian politics, c. another name for the Great Schism

2. True or false: Merchants favored Church laws forbidding the charging of interest on loans.

Section 2

3. Martin Luther developed the idea of: a. predestination, b. the Protestant work ethic, c. justification by faith

4. True or false: After the Peace of Augsburg, individuals could choose their own religion.

Section 3

5. The defeat of the Spanish Armada: a. led to the St. Bartholomew's Day Massacre, b. made England an important sea power, c. caused Philip II to abdicate

6. True or false: Henry IV was the first Protestant king of France.

Section 4

7. True or false: The Treaty of Utrecht put a French prince on the Spanish throne.

8. Louis XIV strengthened France by: a. building Versailles, b. strengthening the power of the *intendants*, c. waging many wars

Section 5

9. Peter the Great: a. increased religious freedom, b. got a "window" on the Baltic, c. lost much territory to Sweden

10. Catherine the Great fought: a. the British, b. the Swedes, c. the Turks

Section 6

11. After 1763, the world's greatest colonial power was: a. France, b. England, c. Prussia

12. True or false: Frederick the Great kept Prussia out of the War of the Austrian Succession.

THE AGE OF EXPLORATION

This map shows the route followed by Magellan's ships in the first voyage to ever go completely around the world.

After two months of sailing west across an unknown ocean, the crew was scared. They did not know where they were, the ocean seemed endless, and some wanted to turn back. But the admiral would not hear of it. Then finally, at 10 o'clock one night in October:

> the Admiral . . . being on the castle of the poop, saw a light, though it was so uncertain that he could not [be sure] it was land. He

called Pero Gutierrez . . . and said that there seemed to be a light, and that he should look at it. He did so, and saw it. . . . It seemed . . . to be an indication of land; but the Admiral [wanted to make] certain that land was close. . . . At two hours after midnight . . . land was sighted [by a sailor named Rodrigo de Triana] at a distance of two leagues [six miles] . . . . The vessels were hove to, waiting for daylight; and on Friday [October 12] they arrived at a small island. . . . Presently they saw naked people.

The admiral was Christopher Columbus. The words came from the journal of his first voyage in 1492. His landing on that island in the Bahamas marked the beginning of one of the most important periods in history. It opened the way for Europeans to discover a whole New World that they had never dreamed existed. It set off an Age of Exploration that led to the building of colonies and a great increase in world trade. That in turn helped bring about the rise of capitalism and major changes in the economic and cultural lives of Americans, Africans, and Asians as well as Europeans. Chapter 21 tells how all this came about:

1. **Europeans found lands unknown to them.**

2. **The world proved to be round.**

3. **Europeans built overseas empires.**

4. **The new discoveries brought many changes.**

1 Europeans found lands unknown to them

A European desire for new trade routes and better navigation tools led to a great period of exploration from 1450 to 1650. During this Age of Exploration, Europeans found many lands that had been unknown to them.

Europeans wanted new trade routes. In the late Middle Ages, there was a growth in trade between Europe and the East. European trade was particularly heavy with India, China, and the East Indies. All such trade used both sea and land routes. Goods passed through many hands. Of course, each handler wanted to make a profit. Italian merchants made the largest profits of all because they had almost complete control over the Mediterranean part of the journey. Because of this, Europeans outside of Italy paid well for spices, silks, and jewels from the East.

The upper classes of Europe were eager to buy imported goods. But they did not want to pay the high prices charged by the Italians. Merchants in other countries saw that there might be a way to change this. Costs would be much lower if goods could be shipped in a single sea voyage instead of in several stages across both land and sea. For these reasons, England, Portugal, France, Spain, and the Low Countries were interested in breaking the Italian monopoly. They wanted to trade directly with the East themselves. Thus they began to search for all-water routes to the East. They were aided in their search by better compasses (to tell direction), astrolabes (to show the ship's latitude), coastal maps, and improved sailing ships.

Prince Henry aided the Portuguese. One of the first nations to set out beyond the Mediterranean Sea was Portugal. It owes much to a member of its royal family, Prince Henry the Navigator. Henry wished to expand Portuguese control and spread the Christian faith. He did not travel himself, but used his wealth to pay for the work of others.

Prince Henry opened a naval school and hired the best captains and mapmakers he could find. Beginning about 1415, he sent ships out year after year. They discovered the so-called Gold Coast of Africa (now part of Ghana), the Azores, the Cape Verde Islands, and the Madeiras. In 1441, a Portuguese sea captain brought the first African slaves to Portugal, beginning a brutal slave trade that marked the Western world for 400 years.

WHAT'S IN A NAME?
THE AZORES

The Portuguese explorers named these islands *Ilhas dos Açores*, which means "Hawk Islands." They chose this name because many hawks frequent the area. The English name Azores comes from the Portuguese word Açores.

In 1460, Prince Henry died. He had given the Portuguese a good start in the field of discovery. Bartolomeu Dias picked up where Henry left off. In 1488, he sailed around the southern tip of Africa, giving it the name Cape of Storms. His voyage proved that a sea passage south of Africa did exist. This news pleased the king of Portugal so much that he renamed the point the Cape of Good Hope.

Proud of their nation's role in world exploration, the people of Portugal built this monument in Lisbon to honor Prince Henry the Navigator, *far right*, and those explorers whom he supported.

Columbus found the New World. Spain joined the search for an all-water route to India. Christopher Columbus was sure that he could reach the East by sailing west. Like many men of his time, he was certain that the world was round. But he believed the circumference of the earth to be much less than it actually is. Columbus thought, therefore, that a route westward to India would be shorter than an eastward route around Africa. Spain gave Columbus, an Italian, three ships for his exploration.

Columbus kept his ships pointed westward and landed on one of the Bahama Islands on October 12, 1492. Columbus went on to discover many other islands and even once reached the mainland of South America. Some historians say that Columbus always believed that he had found an outlying region of Asia rather than a New World. In their opinion, this is why Columbus called the islands the Indies and their inhabitants Indians.

The pope divided new lands between Spain and Portugal. Three papal decrees in the 1450s gave Portugal a monopoly on African exploration and trade. To confirm its rights to newly discovered lands and to prevent conflicts with Portugal, Spain asked Pope Alexander VI which areas of the world it might claim. In 1493, the pope drew an imaginary north-south line, called the *papal line of demarcation*. The line went through the Atlantic Ocean 100 leagues (about 250 miles or 400 kilometers) west of the Azores. All newly discovered lands west of the line were to go to Spain. However, Portugal would not agree to this. So envoys from both countries met in 1494 and drew up the Treaty of Tordesillas. This treaty moved the line of demarcation some 270 leagues farther to the west and gave Portugal the right to claim what later came to be known as Brazil.

A MYSTERY IN HISTORY

WHO REALLY DISCOVERED AMERICA?

The first discoverers of America were the ancestors of the American Indians—prehistoric people who crossed the Bering Strait between 10 and 30 thousand years ago. But the rest of the world did not know about the Americas until relatively recently.

Most of us believe that America was discovered by Christopher Columbus in 1492. But some scholars claim they have found evidence that long before Columbus, people from different parts of the world discovered the Americas. For example, there is evidence in Viking stories, called sagas, that Vikings, led by Leif Ericson, crossed the North Atlantic Ocean around 1000 A.D. and reached lands today called Newfoundland. Archeological discoveries support the sagas.

Other scholars say there is evidence that an Irish monk, Saint Brendan, came to Newfoundland in the 6th century to convert the Indians to Christianity. Some claim that a Welsh prince reached present-day Alabama in 1170, and they support their theory with similarities between certain Welsh words and Indian words.

The predecessor of Mansa Musa, the 14th-century king of the African state of Mali, set out to prove one could sail west around the world. He never returned. Two hundred years later, the Spanish conquistadores, though they had never heard this story, were certain they found descendants of Africans living in Central America.

And there are Chinese scholars who, because of similarities between Aztec and Chinese languages, myths, and coins, believe a Buddhist monk reached Mexico in 459 A.D. They also claim that Chinese-style anchor stones have been found in the Pacific Ocean near Los Angeles.

The most recent theory is that Phoenicians, who are known to have traveled to Spain and Britain in the 600s B.C., established a colony in North America. The evidence is a collection of 400 grave markers found near Philadelphia. A Harvard scholar, Barry Fell, has worked for 40 years to translate the inscriptions on them. He is sure the language is Iberian Punic.

Do all these theories mean Columbus is not important to history? No matter who reached America first, Columbus brought his discovery of land in the West to the attention of Europe. And he did it when Europeans were prepared to explore and establish colonies.

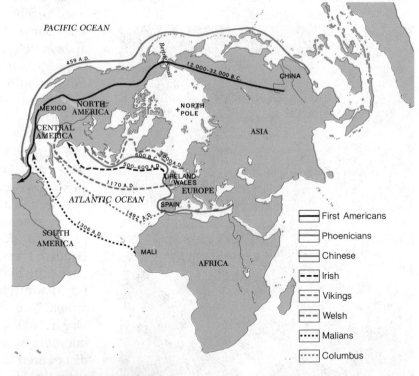

- First Americans
- Phoenicians
- Chinese
- --- Irish
- --- Vikings
- --- Welsh
- ····· Malians
- ····· Columbus

According to Dr. Fell, the name on this stone is *Qas,* meaning "Blondie."

Da Gama sailed to India. While the Spaniards were voyaging westward looking for India, the Portuguese kept up their search for a southern route around Africa. In 1497, Vasco da Gama rounded the Cape of Good Hope and sailed north along the east coast of Africa. His small fleet entered the Muslim-dominated Indian Ocean.

After some trouble with the Muslims of Mombasa, da Gama was able to hire an outstanding Arab guide. With this expert, he headed across the Indian Ocean and reached the city of Calicut, India, in May, 1498.

The Hindus at Calicut were friendly. But the Muslims there had a monopoly on the spice trade. They saw da Gama as a threat and plotted to have him killed. However, da Gama escaped with a small cargo of cinnamon and pepper to take home.

Da Gama was greeted wildly on his return to Lisbon in September, 1499. The goods he brought back sold for sixty times the cost of the trip. However, he had lost nearly two-thirds of his crew as a result of scurvy. Yet da Gama had found the first all-water route from western Europe to India. He had found a way to bypass the trade monopoly of the Italians.

section review 1

1. Explain why goods imported from the East cost so much in Europe. What could European countries do to change this?
2. How did Prince Henry help Portugal in the field of exploration? Why was Dias's voyage important?
3. In what way was Columbus's knowledge of geography wrong? What areas in the New World did he discover?
4. What part did the Catholic Church play in the Age of Exploration?

2 The world proved to be round

The voyages of Dias, Columbus, and da Gama excited many Europeans and led to other journeys. Eventually these journeys proved that the world was round. One could reach the East by sailing west.

America is found to be a new continent. One of the first to realize that the newly discovered lands to the west were not part of Asia was Amerigo Vespucci [ves pü'chē], an Italian. He made four voyages to the New World between 1497 and 1503. He believed that he was the first European to set foot on the South American mainland. Vespucci succeeded in spreading the idea that a new continent had been found. Thus, a German geographer named the new lands America after him. Some historians have doubts about Vespucci's claims, but the name, of course, has remained.

Meanwhile, in 1500 Pedro Cabral put forward the Portuguese claim to Brazil. And in 1510, Vasco de Balboa began the first Spanish settlement on the American mainland at the Isthmus of Panama. Three years later, Balboa became the first European to gaze out at what he called the South Sea. Magellan later gave this great ocean the name Pacific, from the Latin word meaning "peaceful."

Spaniards searched for gold. Other Spaniards continued to explore many parts of the Americas, mostly in search of gold. In 1513, Juan Ponce de León, while seeking a "Fountain of Youth," discovered Florida. Between 1539 and 1542, Hernando de Soto explored the southeastern part of the United States. He may have been the first European to sight the Mississippi River. In 1540, Francisco de Coronado traveled through the southwest-

European exploration was made possible in part by better ships and better tools. By the 1500s, navigators floated loadstones, or magnetic rocks, in water to make an early form of compass

ern United States. There he discovered the Grand Canyon and marveled at the buffalo herds roaming the plains.

Magellan circled the world. Ferdinand Magellan was Portuguese. But like Columbus, who was Italian, he got support from the king of Spain and set out in 1519 to reach India by sailing west. He had to stop several mutinies, and he lost many men and one of his five ships. Yet by 1520, Magellan rounded the southern tip of South America. His ships then had to edge their way through the narrow strait since called the Strait of Magellan. Because they were so close to the South Pole, ice formed on the sails and rigging. One ship turned back to Spain. However, Magellan forced the rest of his frightened sailors onward.

Once in the Pacific, food and water became scarce. The crew suffered terribly. Finally, in March, 1521, Magellan reached some islands, which he named the Philippines in honor of King Philip of Spain. There he and several crew members were killed in a battle with the natives.

Two other ships were later lost. But one, the *Victoria*, pushed on. Loaded with a rich cargo of spices, it crossed the Indian Ocean, rounded Africa, and anchored at Seville, Spain, in September, 1522. After three years and twelve days, with only 18 out of 243 sailors left, the first ship to go around the world had returned.

Many explorers looked for a Northwest Passage. Most people were still more interested in getting to the East than in exploring the Americas. The Spanish and Portuguese controlled the southern regions of the Americas. Thus northern European countries tried for years to find a route to the East by going around or through the continent of North America.

As early as 1497, John Cabot, an Italian, was sent out by King Henry VII of England. He landed on the coast of Nova Scotia, Canada, and claimed the area for the king. Cabot was the first European since the Norsemen to set foot on the mainland of North America. Most important, his discovery gave England a claim to the whole rich continent.

Jacques Cartier, sailing under the flag of France, made his way up the broad St. Lawrence River in 1534. He had hopes of reaching China. Instead, he claimed all of eastern North America, which he called New France. England also claimed the same territory for itself.

Other explorers continued searching for a Northwest Passage. One of the most famous English sea captains, Sir Francis Drake, combined exploration with piracy. In 1577, he sailed through the Strait of Magellan and north along the west coast of the Americas as far as California. On the way, he seized gold and silver from Spanish ships. He sailed northward, possibly as far as Vancouver Island. Not finding a western exit from the Northwest Passage, he headed back south. Then he journeyed home via the East Indies. He reached England in 1580, becoming the first Briton to sail around the world. His voyage brought a profit of 4,700 percent. It proved to many who had thought otherwise that the small English ships were well made. Henry Hudson also searched for a Northwest Passage. Working for the Dutch, he explored the Hudson River and the Hudson Bay area

in 1609. In 1610, he sailed for the English in search of a Northwest Passage. His mutinous crew made its way back to England, but Hudson was never seen again.

section review 2

1. Where did the name America come from?
2. What was important about the voyages of Cabral? Balboa? Magellan?
3. Why were the Europeans looking for new trade routes?
4. The voyages of Cabot and Cartier led England and France to claim what parts of the Americas?

3 Europeans built overseas empires

After their first discoveries, the Europeans began to take control over the areas they claimed. It was because they had superior weapons, such as cannons and guns, that so few Europeans could conquer so many natives. Once control was gained, the area was thought of as a colony belonging to the mother country. Europeans looked upon their colonies as a source of wealth. There was great competition among countries to get as many colonies as possible.

Portugal established a far-flung trade empire. The Portuguese overseas empire was based on trade. Portugal set up trading posts on the east and west coasts of Africa, in India, Java, Sumatra, the Spice Islands, and in southern China and also founded the colony of Angola. Except in Brazil, however, Portuguese merchants sent out only enough settlers to protect their commerce by controlling native rulers. Portugal was too small a country to spare the people. Besides, most of its territory lay in hot, humid lands with climates that Europeans disliked.

Spain took over Portugal and its overseas possessions in 1580. The Portuguese regained their independence in 1640. But in the meantime, the British and Dutch had seized much of the Portuguese empire. During the rest of the 1600s, Portugal's overseas power declined.

Most Spanish possessions lay in the New World. Except for the Philippines, most Spanish overseas possessions were in the Western Hemisphere. By 1575, the New World had about 200 Spanish settlements with about 160 thousand Spaniards living in them.

Because Spain was much stronger than Portugal, it could set up more colonies and could better develop the colonies' natural resources. Also, Spain's colonies were settled by people who planned to stay there. Thus European ways of living were more easily transplanted. For these reasons, Spain's colonial empire in America lasted much longer than did Portugal's in Asia.

England began to seek colonies. Two events encouraged the English also to look for colonies overseas. The first was Drake's voyage around the world. The second was the defeat of the Spanish Armada by the British in 1588. This victory proved that England had become a strong naval power.

The first successful English settlement on the American mainland was made in 1607 at Jamestown, Virginia. Plymouth, Massachusetts, was founded in 1620. Other colonies followed shortly. England also claimed a large area around Hudson Bay. There it set up posts to aid its fur traders. In addition, the English settled on islands in the West Indies and on the Bermudas. By 1640, about 60 thousand English people had moved to the New World. And England added to its possessions by taking Jamaica from Spain in 1655.

The English colonies in the New World grew strong. This was partly because England allowed religious minorities to settle there. These groups had a spirit and desire that made them ideal colonists. In addition, many English colonies were run by private companies. They allowed their settlers at least some self-government.

England became interested in the East, too, particularly as the power of Portugal declined. The British East India Company was set up in 1600. England later gained control of such wealthy trading posts as Bombay, Calcutta, and Madras.

France sent out traders and missionaries. The first permanent French settlement in North America was made at Quebec in 1608 by Samuel de Champlain. This armed post high above the St. Lawrence River became the capital of New France. Farther up the river, the French built another fort at Montreal.

Fur was to France what gold was to Spain. Fur trappers were among the first Europeans to explore the Great Lakes region. In 1673, Louis Joliet, a fur trader, and Jacques Marquette, a Jesuit missionary, came to believe that the Mississippi River flowed into the Gulf of Mexico. Robert de la Salle followed the Mississippi to its mouth in 1682. De la Salle claimed for France all the surrounding land and rivers. He called the territory Louisiana in honor of King Louis XIV. The French set up small outposts along the shores of the Great Lakes and the Mississippi. These included ones at Detroit, St. Louis, and New Orleans.

Few French people, however, were willing to settle in North America. The Huguenots were not allowed to go. This was because France, like Spain, excluded non-Catholics from its colonies. More French did settle in the warm Caribbean colonies of Martinique, Guadeloupe, Tortuga, and Haiti.

The Netherlands set up many colonies. The Netherlands, like Portugal, was a small country that built a large, wealthy empire. During their long fight for freedom from Spain, between 1567 and 1648, the Dutch built a strong navy. As Portugal came under Spanish control during this same period, the Dutch took over much of the Portuguese East Indian spice trade. The Dutch East India Company was founded in 1602. The Dutch made settlements on Java, Malacca, and at the Cape of Good Hope. They seized the Spice Islands (the Moluccas) in 1667.

In the New World, the Dutch settled Curaçao and other islands in the West Indies. They also set up Dutch Guiana on the coast of South America. They bought the island of Manhattan from the Indians in 1626 for about 25 dollars. They then began a colony, New Netherland, along the Hudson River. In 1664, the English seized this colony and renamed it New York.

section review **3**

1. On what was the Portuguese empire based? Why was Portugal unable to hold on to its overseas possessions?

2. In what ways was Spain's overseas empire different from Portugal's?

3. Why was the settlement at Jamestown, Virginia, significant to England?

4. How did relations between Spain and the Netherlands affect the Dutch empire? What areas belonged to the Dutch?

4 The new discoveries brought many changes

Through their discoveries, Europeans came into contact with lands and peoples different from their own. They learned about new foods, animals, and drugs, and about the true geography of the world. World trade grew rapidly. Large amounts of gold and silver were shipped back to Europe from the colonies. This led to a *Commercial Revolution* that brought great changes. These included new business methods, an increase in prices,

New Amsterdam in 1640 showed evidence, such as the windmill at *far left*, of its Dutch settlers. Also shown are the fort, *A*, the church, *B*, the jail, *C*, the governor's house, *D*, the town gallows, *E*, the pillory next to the gallows, *F*, the West India Company stores, *G*, and the city tavern, *H*.

MAP LESSON 21: MAJOR EMPIRES ABOUT 1700

1. Use the map key to determine which empire in 1700 controlled:

a. the African coast of the Mediterranean Sea
b. the western coast of Australia
c. the Great Lakes
d. the Malay Archipelago
e. Hudson Bay
f. the Pacific region of South America
g. Angola
h. the Philippine Islands
i. the Cape of Good Hope
j. Brazil

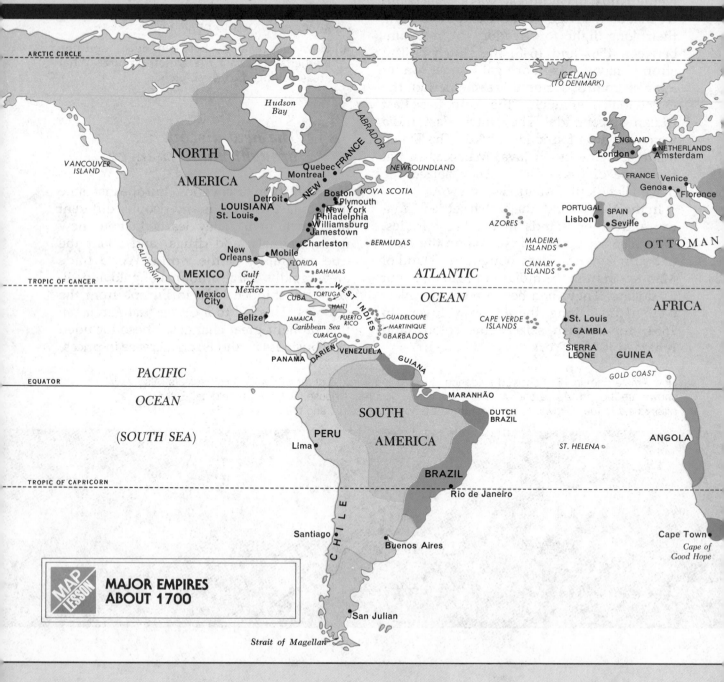

MAP
LESSON

MAJOR EMPIRES
ABOUT 1700

2. By 1700, European empires had established trading colonies in port cities of Mughul India and Manchu China. Which empire had interests in:
a. Bombay
b. Goa
c. Calcutta
d. Macao
e. Cochin

3. Study the map to determine
a. the group of islands in the Eastern Hemisphere that was controlled by Spain
b. the three empires that controlled the eastern coast of South America
c. the empire that controlled large parts of both the east and west coasts of Africa

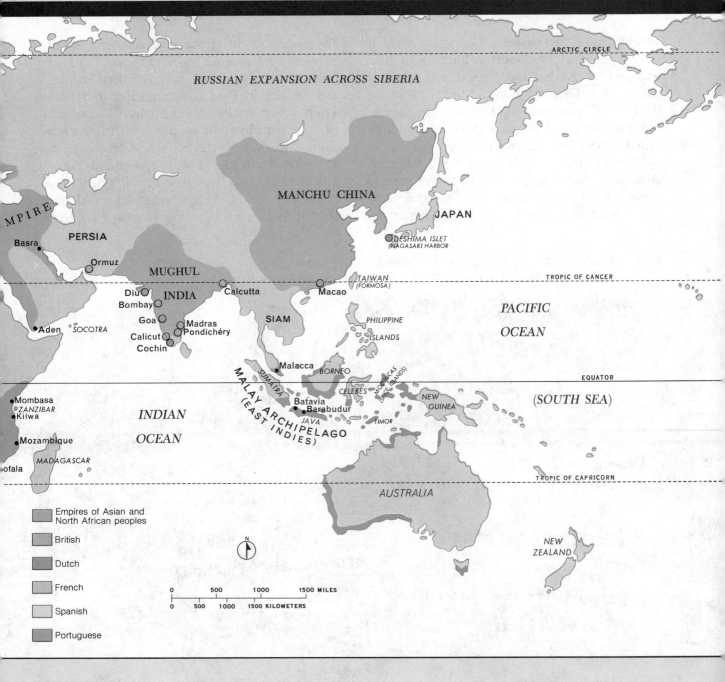

ARCTIC CIRCLE

RUSSIAN EXPANSION ACROSS SIBERIA

MANCHU CHINA

JAPAN

EMPIRE

PERSIA

Basra

Ormuz

MUGHUL

Diu

INDIA

Bombay

Calcutta

Macao

DESHIMA ISLET
(NAGASAKI HARBOR)

TAIWAN
(FORMOSA)

TROPIC OF CANCER

PACIFIC

OCEAN

Aden

SOCOTRA

Goa

Madras

Pondichéry

Calicut

Cochin

SIAM

PHILIPPINE

ISLANDS

Malacca

BORNEO

MOLUCCAS
(SPICE ISLANDS)

MALAY ARCHIPELAGO
(EAST INDIES)

SUMATRA

CELEBES

Batavia

Barabudur

JAVA

TIMOR

NEW
GUINEA

EQUATOR

(SOUTH SEA)

Mombasa

ZANZIBAR

Kilwa

INDIAN

OCEAN

Mozambique

MADAGASCAR

ofala

AUSTRALIA

TROPIC OF CAPRICORN

NEW
ZEALAND

Empires of Asian and North African peoples

British

Dutch

French

Spanish

Portuguese

N

0   500   1000   1500 MILES

0   500   1000   1500 KILOMETERS

and the growth of modern capitalism.

The expansion of European influence also spread Christianity and Western ideas to many parts of the world. Europeans interfered with the cultures of many native peoples. They tried to force these native peoples to become Christians and to adopt European ways. The most harmful effect was the growth of the slave trade.

World trade increased. The discovery of new trade routes ended the long monopoly enjoyed by the Italians. Proud and wealthy cities like Genoa, Venice, and Florence declined. Trade moved from the Mediterranean to the north Atlantic ports of London, Amsterdam, Bristol, and Antwerp.

The amount of trade grew rapidly. From Asia came larger shipments of spices, gems, paper, ivory, porcelain, textiles, and new items such as tea and coffee. The Americas shipped potatoes, tobacco, cocoa, and corn, which were also new to Europe. Canada exported furs and codfish. New England sent lye, ship timbers, pitch, and turpentine. From the West Indies came sugar, molasses, rum, and indigo. Africa sent hardwoods, ivory, gold, and ostrich feathers. All of these things were used to make finished goods in Europe.

The slave trade grew and became racist. Slavery had existed in Africa and Asia for centuries. Long before the coming of Europeans, Arabs in East Africa traded in slaves. There were slaves in the ancient Greek and Roman Empires. In medieval Christendom there were a few slaves, who were used as servants, barbers, or musicians. This ages-old slavery had nothing to do with race. Black people in Africa were captured and sold into slavery by other blacks. People of

English, French, Dutch, and Portuguese slave traders all maintained camps along the western coast of Africa. The rulers of this part of Africa would not let the Europeans move farther inland.

any race captured in war could be made slaves. For a ransom, they could sometimes be freed. A free person could often choose to become a slave to escape paying heavy taxes; he or she could buy back freedom later. However, after the Europeans entered the slave trade, the trade grew and attitudes toward slaves gradually changed.

With the European colonization of the Americas came large new markets for slaves. Altogether, about 20 million Africans were shipped to the Americas. Generally, they were rounded up by other Africans and sold to European slavers on the coast. The slaves traveled in filthy, crowded ships. Conditions on these slave ships were so bad that one fourth of the slaves died on the voyages. The survivors were forced to work in gold and diamond mines and on plantations that grew sugar, cacao, cotton, tobacco, and coffee.

Gradually many Europeans began to believe that blacks were born to be slaves. Both Catholics and Protestants tried to use the Bible to prove that black people were an inferior race and it was morally right to make them slaves. Slavery stopped being a temporary legal condition and became a permanent condition based on birth and African origin. For many Europeans, skin color became a sign of inferiority, and in this way slavery helped contribute to the growth of racial prejudice in the United States in later years.

Merchants learned new business methods. As European merchants grew rich, they looked for ways to protect, invest, and borrow money. Italians were the first European bankers. They had begun handling the money income of the popes as early as the 1100s. Banking did not become a big business until the 16th century, however. Checks, bank notes (a form of paper money), and bills of exchange (a receipt for payment of goods in one city that was exchanged for similar goods in another city), all came into widespread use.

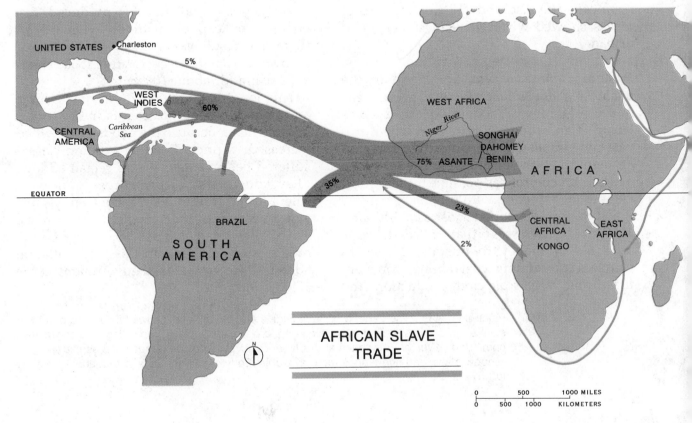

AFRICAN SLAVE TRADE

The growth in trade also led to the rise of insurance companies in the late 17th century. Merchants banded together and contributed to a common fund. Out of this, an owner would be paid for losses from fire, shipwreck, or piracy.

Another new idea was the joint-stock company. A person could gain part ownership in this type of company by buying one or more shares. If the company made a profit, each shareholder received part of the profit, called a *dividend*. If there were no profits, the value of the shares went down. Such companies made it possible to gather together much larger amounts of money than any single merchant could. Thus they were able to finance great fleets of trading ships. The Dutch East India Company and the British East India Company were both joint-stock companies.

Along with these companies came the growth of stock exchanges. There people could buy and sell their shares of stock. These exchanges also acted as barometers of business. The rise and fall in the price of stocks showed whether business was good or bad.

Modern capitalism was born. All of the business changes just described were signs of the beginning of modern *capitalism*. Capitalism is an economic system in which private individuals or companies, not the government, own the businesses. The goal is to make as much profit as possible by being efficient and competing with others.

Capitalism developed most strongly after 1500 in businesses that needed large amounts of money to operate. These included sugar refining, coal mining, iron manufacturing, large-scale cloth production, and especially, the outfitting of fleets for overseas trade. The people who worked in these businesses were wage earners. Unlike the members of medieval guilds, they did not own their materials or machines.

During the Middle Ages, people had dealt more in goods, services, and land than in money. The growing supply of gold and silver, however, allowed Europeans to coin more money. This made it easier to save or reinvest. Merchants and bankers could use the huge profits they made in trade to reinvest in joint-stock or other companies. Thus, this period became known as one of mercantile capitalism.

Prices rose in Europe. As we know, the Spaniards shipped great amounts of the gold and silver they found in Mexico and Peru back to Spain. There it was used to buy luxury goods and weapons from other European countries. In this way, Spanish gold and silver moved into the rest of Europe. It enabled people to buy more goods. However, goods could not be produced fast enough to keep up with the demand for them. The result was *inflation*, a rise in prices, all over Europe, especially after 1550. Prices kept rising for about 100 years.

This long-run inflation hurt some people and helped others. Merchants in the towns became richer because the goods they owned increased in price. But the working classes suffered because their wages remained low. They bought less as prices rose. European rulers found it more expensive to buy guns and uniforms for their new national armies. When they tried to raise taxes, the parliaments opposed them. In this way, inflation added to the problems of government in the 17th century.

Painted in 1449, "The Legend of Saint Eligius and Godeberta" shows Eligius, the patron saint of goldsmiths, selling a wedding ring to a bridal couple. The painting also shows the comfortable lives of Europeans at this time. Explorations made goods such as mirrors, window glass, and fine fabrics more available. Early capitalism gave Europeans the money to buy them.

European countries followed mercantilist policies. The economic policies followed by most European countries in this period were called *mercantilism*. A mercantilist country believed that it would be rich and strong if it exported more than it imported. That way, more gold and silver would flow into the country than out of it. This is known as a favorable balance of trade. To maintain it, each country tried to sell as much as it could to other countries and to buy as little as it could in return. A mercantilist government aided export and shipping companies with money. This reduced the cost of goods they sold abroad. A mercantilist government also helped set up many new industries to make products at home that had been bought from other countries in the past. Thus, a country did not have to depend on others for as many materials.

Colonies were very important to mercantilist nations for several reasons. First, they could supply raw materials and slaves. Second, they were used by the mother country as closed markets in which to sell its manufactured goods. Foreign traders were kept out. Colonies were not allowed to produce anything the mother country exported. Third, some colonies were good ports or controlled vital waterways.

Mercantilists looked upon business between nations as a kind of economic war. A business deal could not benefit both sides. One had to gain, the other lose. The system led to hard competition among nations, to struggles over colonies, and to war. Many of the conflicts in the period from 1650 to 1800 can be explained partly or completely in terms of the mercantile policy.

The daily life of Europeans changed. In the period between 1500 and 1750, ways of life in Europe changed more than they had in the preceding 1,000 years. A rising standard of living allowed more people, especially the merchant class, to live comfortably.

New kinds of timber, such as mahogany from the West Indies, meant better houses and furniture. For instance, chairs began to replace stools in many homes. Window glass, carpets, and wallpaper came into use. Feather beds, pillows, and mirrors also became more common. Textiles, particularly cotton and linen, became cheaper. People began to have more clothes, to wear underwear, and to use handkerchiefs. The use of forks, napkins, and delicate china improved table manners.

There was more variety in food. Europeans learned to eat potatoes, oranges, lemons, strawberries, pineapples, bananas, and peanuts. Sugar replaced honey as a sweetener. The growing popularity of coffee led to the development of coffeehouses. These became centers for literary and political discussions. Lloyd's of London, the insurance company, began as a coffeehouse. Tobacco also became popular among men and women. Like coffee and tea, tobacco was said to have healing powers.

A revolution in world ecology took place. The sailing ships of the Age of Exploration tied all parts of the world together for the first time in human history. They carried not only people, but also plants and animals from one part of the world to another. This brought about the greatest change in *ecology* (the distribution of plant and animal life) the world has ever known.

The coffee bean, which was native to the Middle East, was brought to Java in the east and to South America in the west. Today, South America produces more than four-fifths of the world coffee crop. From the Americas, the sweet potato was brought to Asia. Manioc (a plant with a large starchy root from which tapioca is made) was

Most of the early French settlers in North America made their livings by trapping or fishing. They exported to Europe many of the dried codfish and beaver pelts that they caught.

brought to Africa. These plants greatly increased the food supply on both continents. The potato and Indian corn (called maize) brought from America later did the same for Europe. Maize spread to other continents, especially Asia. Today it is the third largest food crop in the world, after wheat and rice.

But the greatest change took place in the New World. The Europeans brought wheat, rye, oats, and rice. All of these had been unknown in the Americas. Today the United States is the world's largest producer of wheat. Except for the llama, the peoples of the Americas had no beasts of burden or farm animals. The Europeans brought the horse, the donkey, and the mule to carry heavy loads. They brought cattle for meat and milk, the ox to pull the plow, as well as the pig, the goat, wool-bearing sheep, and barnyard chickens. From Asia, the Spanish brought sugar cane to the Caribbean. There it became the single most valuable crop. Cuba today is a leading producer of sugar. Unknowingly, the Europeans of the Age of Exploration started an ecological revolution that is still with us.

section review 4

1. How did the slave trade change the feelings of Europeans toward slavery and black people?

2. What is capitalism? How and when did it get started?

3. What was the main goal of mercantilism? How did colonies contribute to this goal?

4. How did world ecology and eating habits change as a result of the Age of Exploration?

Section Summaries

1. Europeans found lands unknown to them. The great era of European exploration began in the late 1400s. With the rise of overseas empires, it brought about a Commercial Revolution. At the beginning of this period, Europeans were mainly interested in finding new trade routes to the East. They hoped to break the Italian monopoly on east-west trade. Improvements in sailing aided their search. With the help of Prince Henry, Portuguese sea captains began to explore the coast of Africa trying to find a southeastern route to India. Although Columbus failed to reach India by going westward, he made the much more important discovery of a New World. Later da Gama reached India by sailing around Africa.

2. The world proved to be round. Meanwhile, Vespucci spread the idea that America was a new continent, not part of Asia. This was proved in 1521 when Magellan's ships reached the East by going west. The New World soon became important. Spaniards fanned out in search of gold. English, French, and Dutch explorers looked for a Northwest Passage. Each country staked out claims.

3. Europeans built overseas empires. The countries of Europe were quick to use their newly claimed territories. Portugal, France, and the Netherlands used them mainly for trade. The French built up a fur trade and the Dutch a spice trade. Spain and England also sent people to settle in their colonies, particularly in the New World. England allowed anyone to go, but Spain and France allowed only Catholics. Competition among Europeans for trade and colonies became intense. Portugal lost much of its empire to other nations.

4. The new discoveries brought many changes. The Age of Exploration led to a great increase in trade and in the supply of gold and silver. This caused important changes that became known as the Commercial Revolution. The changes included the development of banking, insurance, joint-stock companies, and stock exchanges. These led to modern capitalism. With it, there was a growth in industry, a rise in prices, and a higher standard of living for Europeans.

The policies of mercantilism and the exploitation of slaves and colonies helped make such changes possible. For the world as a whole, there was a great redistribution of ideas, people, plants, and animals. Native cultures broke down as Europeans imposed Christianity and Western ways. World ecology changed as new food plants and animals were introduced everywhere. Daily life changed for many peoples. It was better for some and worse for others, mainly the slaves. Both a cultural and an ecological revolution took place between the 15th and 17th centuries.

Who? What? When? Where?

1. Put these events in chronological order, beginning with the earliest:
   a. The Dutch bought Manhattan for $25.
   b. The first person sailed around the world.
   c. Columbus sighted land in the New World.
   d. The Portuguese first explored the African coast.

2. Look at the map called Major Empires About 1700 and list what European countries had colonies or trading posts in the following areas:
   a. The East Indies
   b. North America
   c. South America

3. Tell what flag each of these explorers sailed under:
   a. Cabot   f. Drake
   b. Cabral   g. da Gama
   c. Cartier   h. Marquette
   d. Columbus   i. Ponce de León
   e. Dias

4. Write a sentence for each of these terms that tells how it relates to the Age of Exploration:
   a. capitalism
   b. closed markets
   c. dividend
   d. favorable balance of trade
   e. joint-stock company
   f. mercantilism
   g. profit
   h. stock exchange

Questions for Critical Thinking

1. In the recent past, the United States and other nations have begun to explore our moon and the planets of the Solar System. In what ways does that make our time similar to the Age of Exploration?

2. Why was it possible for Europeans, who were few in number, to win control over large areas of the world?

3. What were the most important changes in people's lives brought about by the events of the Age of Exploration?

4. As overseas empires were built and capitalism took hold, why did the merchant class become more important in deciding government policies?

Skill Activities

1. Read *Christopher Columbus, Mariner* by Samuel Eliot Morison to learn more about this explorer and his voyages. (New American Library.)

2. Choose five people from this chapter and make up "quotes" for them. Read them to the class and see if the class can guess who made the statements.

3. Find the country of origin of your favorite foods or of everything you eat in one day.

chapter **21** *quiz*

Section 1

1. The people made rich by the early trade between the East and Europe were the: a. Spanish bourgeoisie, b. English and French kings, c. Italian merchants

2. True or false: European peasants demanded imported goods at lower prices so governments searched for all-water routes to America.

3. Early explorers were greatly aided by Prince Henry the Navigator of: a. England, b. Spain, c. Portugal

Section 2

4. The Spanish explorer who may have been the first European to see the Mississippi River was: a. Hernando de Soto, b. Francisco de Coronado, c. Juan Ponce de León

5. The first successful expedition to sail around the world was led by: a. Drake, b. Magellan, c. Cabot

6. The explorer who had America named for him was: a. Drake, b. Vespucci, c. Balboa

Section 3

7. True or false: Europeans greatly outnumbered the armies of the peoples in the areas they conquered.

8. The nation that did not have large numbers of people become settlers in its colonies was: a. Spain, b. Portugal, c. England

9. The nation that allowed religious minorities to settle in its colonies was: a. England, b. Spain, c. France

Section 4

10. True or false: One result of European exploration was the greatest change in ecology the world has ever known.

11. True or false: The development of colonies by Europeans led them to believe that all slavery was morally wrong.

12. One thing that was not part of the system that came to be known as mercantilism was: a. favorable balance of trade, b. control over colonies, c. aiding peasants.

THE FORMATION OF LATIN AMERICA

Aztec artists drew pictures of the arrival of Cortés in their land. At the front is Malinche, followed by the bearded Cortés. Slightly behind Cortés is his follower and servant, Estevanico, in the red pants.

On November 8, 1519, a Spanish soldier of fortune named Hernando Cortés became the first European ever to come face to face with the king of the Aztecs, Montezuma. The great meeting between Cortés and Montezuma was thus described by a Spanish member of Cortés's party who was an eyewitness to the event:

We proceeded by the grand causeway which is eight yards wide, and runs in a straight line to the city of Mexico. It was crowded with people, as were all the towers, temples, and causeways, in every part of the lake, attracted by curiosity to behold men, and animals, such as had never before been seen in these countries. . . . We were met by a great number of the lords of the court in their richest dress, sent [ahead by] the great Montezuma, to bid us welcome. After waiting . . . some time, . . . Montezuma . . . approached, carried in a most magnificent litter, which was supported by his principal nobility. . . . Montezuma [left] his litter, and was borne in the arms of the princes . . . under a canopy of the richest materials, ornamented with green feathers, gold, and precious stones that hung in the manner of a fringe; he was most richly dressed and adorned, and wore buskins [half-boots] of pure gold ornamented with jewels. . . .

When Cortés was told that the great Montezuma approached, he dismounted from his horse and advanced toward him with much respect; Montezuma bid him welcome, and Cortés replied with a compliment.

That first friendly meeting between Montezuma and Cortés turned out to be one of the most important events in the history of the Americas. It opened the way for Spain's conquest of Mexico, Central America, and the rich land of the Incas in Peru. Within a very short time, Spain ruled a huge colonial empire that stretched from Florida to Argentina. Portugal, meanwhile, took over Brazil.

The coming of Europeans to the Americas changed the course of history. Gold and silver from the Americas changed all of Europe, as did potatoes and corn. Even more important was the fact that Europeans came to the New World to settle permanently. The culture they brought with them blended with the culture of the Indians. There was a further blending as millions of Africans were brought over to work as slaves. During a period of three centuries, the mix gave rise to a new Latin American civilization. This chapter tells how:

1. Europeans conquered and colonized the Americas.

2. Spain controlled a large empire.

3. Indians and Africans were the main source of labor.

4. A Latin American civilization arose.

1 Europeans conquered and colonized the Americas

On his second voyage across the Atlantic in 1493, Columbus brought 1,500 Spaniards with him. It was the first step in the settlement and conquest of the Americas by Europeans. It laid the basis for the Latin America we know today.

Cortés searched for gold. More than 125 years before the Pilgrims landed at Plymouth Rock, the Spanish in 1494 founded the city of Santo Domingo. This city is the capital of today's Dominican Republic. By 1514, the Spanish had conquered the island of Cuba. Five years later, the Spanish governor of Cuba heard rumors of gold on the mainland. He chose 33-year-old Hernando Cortés [kôr-tez'], who had helped him conquer Cuba, to lead a daring expedition into Mexico.

Cortés was the son of well-to-do Spanish parents. He was one of the first, and greatest, of the conquistadores [kon kwis'tə dôr'-ēz] (conquerors) who came to the New World in search of adventure and gold. He was bold and ambitious, but also just and well liked as a leader. With 11 ships, 500 soldiers, 100 sailors, 16 horses, several small cannons, and gunpowder, he set sail for the coast of Mexico in 1519. Since the Mexican Indians had never seen cannons or horses before, Cortés had a great advantage when fighting them.

He also had good luck. Off the Mexican coast, he rescued a shipwrecked Spanish priest. This priest had been made the slave of a Mayan Indian chief. He had learned the Mayan language and now joined Cortés as an interpreter. The Mayan chiefs, frightened by the cannons and horses, gave Cortés a gift of 20 slaves. One of them was a young Aztec woman named Malinche [mä lēn'chä] who spoke Mayan and Nahuatl [nä'wä təl], the language of the Aztecs. The priest also taught her Spanish. Through her, Cortés spoke directly to Aztec and Mayan leaders. She acted as a diplomat and informant. Malinche even saved Cortés's life when she discovered an Indian plot to kill him.

Cortés sailed northward until he discovered a good harbor where he founded the town of Vera Cruz. He learned that the Aztecs ruled the tribes of eastern Mexico. The Aztecs forced these tribes to send them tribute and humans for sacrifices. The tribes hated this, but warned Cortés that the Aztec

Drawn in the 1500s, this Aztec manuscript shows the Spanish burning the main temple in Tenochtitlan.

king, Montezuma, was too powerful to be defeated. Some of Cortés's men wanted to return to Cuba to get more soldiers. But Cortés ordered all his ships burned. The men then had no choice but to march inland with him.

The Aztecs were defeated. The coastal Indians joined forces with Cortés. Others also joined Cortés as he moved inland and fought hard battles against independent tribes. Montezuma knew of Cortés's advance, but could not decide what to do. At first, he sent presents of gold to Cortés because he believed him to be an ancient Aztec god that was supposed to return one day.

Montezuma had thousands of armed Aztec warriors at his command. He could have ordered them to attack Cortés's 400 men. Instead, he decided to welcome the Spaniards to Tenochtitlan, the Aztec capital. Once inside the city, Cortés took Montezuma as a hostage. A short time later, one of Cortés's captains invited Aztec nobles to a feast and murdered them. The Aztecs rose up in anger against the Spaniards. Montezuma was killed, but the Spaniards lost more than half their men getting out of Tenochtitlan.

Cortés soon got fresh supplies, cannons, and gunpowder from Cuba. He was also able to get more Indian allies. Then he laid siege to Tenochtitlan for three months, cutting off the water supply. The Aztecs were further weakened by hundreds of deaths from smallpox. The Spaniards had unknowingly brought this disease with them. Finally in August, 1521, the Aztecs surrendered. Tenochtitlan was renamed Mexico City.

Pizarro conquered the Incas. Ten years after the fall of the Aztecs, another conquistador made his mark. His name was Francisco Pizarro [pi zär´ō]. He set out to find the rich Inca empire he had heard existed in Peru. Pizarro, the son of a soldier, wanted to be rich and important. Late in 1530, he set sail from Panama with his brothers, whom he had recruited, and some soldiers.

Like Cortés, Pizarro also had some good luck. In 1524, a civil war had broken out among the Incas. Two brothers were fighting each other to be ruler. Atahualpa [ä´tä-wäl´pä] won, but the fight weakened his empire. Pizarro met Atahualpa high in the Andes Mountains in 1531. He attacked with guns and cannons. Thousands of Incas were killed, and Atahualpa was taken prisoner. Not a single Spaniard was even badly wounded.

Atahualpa soon realized that the Spaniards wanted gold. He offered to buy his freedom by filling a large room with gold, then filling it twice more with silver. But after paying this ransom, Atahualpa was killed anyway. Pizarro and his men wanted to be masters of Peru.

Pizarro, his brothers, and about 150 Spanish soldiers divided up the treasure. But the men became greedy and began to fight among themselves. This kept Peru in chaos.

■ MAP LESSON 22: SPANISH AND PORTUGUESE COLONIES

1. This map shows the colonies of Spain in yellows and green. Which area belonged to Portugal?

2. What was the major city of Portugal's colony?

3. A viceroy was a person who ruled in the name of the king or queen in a colony. The area in which the viceroy ruled was called a viceroyalty. The major centers of Maya and Aztec civilization became part of which viceroyalty?

4. Lima, a major Inca city, became part of which viceroyalty?

5. What other city was also part of the viceroyalty that included Lima?

6. The Viceroyalty of New Spain included two island cities. What were they?

7. The Viceroyalty of New Granada included what three cities?

8. The Guarani inhabited the border area between Brazil and what viceroyalty?

9. What was the major city of this viceroyalty?

SPANISH AND PORTUGUESE COLONIES

Yet the rule of the Pizarro brothers lasted sixteen years. In 1547, a royal governor with Spanish troops took over.

Spanish rule reached other areas. Both Cortés and Pizarro later sent out small groups of Spanish troops to widen their control. Cortés's men pushed into Central America. Pizarro moved into present-day Ecuador and Chile. The Indians in Chile fought hard. But they were also weakened by smallpox, and were no match for the horses, muskets, and cannons.

Another of Pizarro's men led a group into a rich valley in present-day Colombia. It was ruled by an Indian king named Bogotá [bō′gə tä′]. There the Spaniards found houses decorated with gold and children playing "marbles" with what were actually uncut emeralds. Once again the Spaniards quickly took control as they had elsewhere.

In the mid-1530s, a rich Spanish noble led an expedition across the Atlantic at his own expense. He sent a dozen ships, 1,500 settlers, and several hundred cattle and horses. They landed at the mouth of the Plata River. There they founded a town named Buenos Aires [bwā′nəs er′ēz], now the capital of Argentina.

Portuguese settled on Brazil's coast. While the Spaniards rapidly took over a huge area from Mexico to Chile, the Portuguese did very little with their claim to Brazil. They were much more interested in the large profits they were making from the spice trade with Asia. By the 1530s, however, the king of Portugal feared that Spain might try to take over the coast of Brazil. To prevent this, he offered large grants of land to rich Portuguese nobles. In return, the nobles had to set up colonies at their own expense. By the mid-1500s, there were 15 armed towns along the Brazilian coast. The king of Portugal sent out a governor general. He also sent a thousand colonists and Jesuit missionaries to convert the Indians to Christianity. In 1565, the Portuguese founded the town of Rio de Janeiro [rē'ō dā zhə ner'ō].

WHAT'S IN A NAME?
BRAZIL

In Portuguese, "live coal" is *braza*. When Portuguese explorers landed on the eastern bulge of South America, they found a wood that produced a bright, red dye. So the wood was called brazil wood and the country that grew it, Brazil.

In general, the Portuguese settlement of Brazil was slow and peaceful. This was largely because there was no organized Indian state to fight against. By 1600, there were nearly 100 thousand people living in the Portuguese towns of Brazil. A fourth of these people were black slaves who had been brought over to work on the sugar plantations. Sugar became Brazil's major export.

section review 1

1. List two or more advantages that helped Cortés defeat the Aztecs.
2. Describe how Pizarro conquered Peru.
3. Why did Portugal finally begin to settle its lands in Brazil?
4. Why was Spain's colonization different from Portugal's?

2 Spain controlled a large empire

Spain's empire in America was different from most other empires in history. It lay far away, across the Atlantic. It included islands as well as a huge area on the mainland. Cities and towns were sometimes thousands of miles apart. They were separated by mountains, deserts, and tropical rain forests. Travel from place to place was very hard. Spain had to find a way to govern this empire that was many times larger than itself.

The king ruled through a Council and viceroys. In 1524, Charles I set up a Council of the Indies to help him govern the colonies. The Council met in Spain, but acted as a kind of legislature for the colonies. It drew up a code of laws to control colonial life for the benefit of the mother country. As time passed, new laws were added. By 1681, there was such confusion that all the laws had to be reorganized into a simpler code.

Viceroys were appointed for New Spain and Peru. These men ruled in the king's name. The viceroy of New Spain lived in Mexico City. He controlled all Spanish possessions in North and Central America and the Caribbean islands. The viceroy of Peru lived in Lima. He was in charge of all Spanish possessions in South America. In the 18th century, Spain divided Peru into two viceroyalties. There was New Granada, with its capital at Bogotá, and La Plata, with its capital at Buenos Aires.

Spanish nobles governed the colonies. The Council of the Indies chose nobles born in Spain to serve as officials in the colonies. Church leaders, such as bishops and archbishops, were also from Spain. Most of these officials were corrupt. They often returned to

The Catholic Church approved of marriages between Spaniards and Indian nobles. This picture is the announcement of such a wedding. The Inca bride and Spanish groom each wear their native dress.

D Beatris Cla
ra Coya Inga

Spain richer than when they had left.

All Spanish-born officials looked down on everyone else, even on very rich settlers who happened to have been born in the New World. The permanent settlers hated this high-and-mighty attitude of the *peninsulares* [pā nēn′sü lä′rās], as they called the officials born in Spain. They were angry at being denied important jobs in government. It made no sense to them since they all had a similar background. Spain permitted only Spanish Catholics to settle in the colonies. This was quite different from the policy followed in the English colonies of North America. There people of almost any religion and nationality were allowed to settle.

413

Creoles and mestizos had lower social standing. Children whose parents were Spanish but who were born in the colonies were called *creoles* [krē′ōlz]. They had a lower social rank than their parents, even if they were very rich. Creoles often copied the manners and dress of the peninsulares. They sometimes tried to pass themselves off as Spanish-born.

In the early years after the conquest, very few Spanish women came to Mexico or Peru. Many Spanish soldiers married Indian women. The children born of these marriages were called *mestizos* [mə stē′zōs]. They had even lower social standing than the creoles. And mestizos had a difficult time. Most of them did not own land. They worked either as farmers on rented land, or as shopkeepers, craftspeople, or soldiers. But, the mestizos were soon the largest group in colonial Latin America.

section review 2

1. Why was it hard for Spain to rule its new empire?

2. Who wrote laws for the colonies? Who ruled the colonies?

3. What religious requirements did Spain make on its colonial settlers?

4. Who were the creoles and mestizos?

3 Indians and Africans were the main source of labor

The greatest kind of wealth in the Spanish colonies was land. After the Aztecs and Incas were defeated, the conquistadores took away their land and divided it up among the Spanish soldiers. The creole children of these soldiers soon became the landed aristocracy. The Catholic Church also came to own very large amounts of land. But to make the land produce crops took a great deal of manual work. Finding that labor became the biggest problem facing the Spanish colonists.

Indians were forced to do heavy work. At first, the Spanish colonists had the Indians till the fields for them. The Indians also had to work in the rich silver mines that were discovered in Mexico and what is now Bolivia. Entire villages of Indians were assigned to a landowner. They not only had to work on his lands, but also had to pay tribute to him. For his part, the landowner was supposed to protect the Indians and convert them to Catholicism. In practice, he often treated them like slaves.

This system of forced labor was called the *encomienda* [en′kō mē en′də]. The Spanish government tried to reform the encomienda in the 1540s. But the viceroys and creole landowners ignored the reforms. Indians died by the thousands on the plantations and in the silver mines.

Not only did the Indians receive very cruel treatment, they also suffered terribly from European diseases such as smallpox. This led to perhaps the greatest population disaster in history. Before the Europeans came, there were about 15 to 25 million Indians in Latin America. Within a single century, the population shrank to about 4 million. This helps explain why lack of workers continued to be a major problem in the colonies.

The Church tried to protect the Indians. After Mexico and Peru had been conquered, many missionaries came to the New World to convert Indians to the Catholic faith. They also set up schools, founded hospitals, and explored frontier areas. Some missionaries tried to protect the Indians against creole owners, but they did not have much success.

The most famous defender of the Indians was Bartolomé de las Casas. He was a

The Catholic Church made many converts among the Indians. This detail of a wall painting shows Father Bartolomé de Olmedo baptizing Indians in what is now Mexico.

Spanish priest who spoke out against the cruel treatment of Indians by the Spaniards. Charles V chose him to be "Protector of the Indians." Charles also supported other missionaries who tried to help the Indians. The efforts of the Church at least stopped the creoles from working so many Indians to death.

Jesuits created missions in Paraguay. The most successful missionaries were the Jesuits. They set up mission villages among the Guarani [gwä′rä nē′] Indians in what is now the country of Paraguay. They taught the Guarani how to grow grapes, oranges, olives, sugar cane, and corn. They also showed them how to raise livestock. The Jesuits learned the Guarani language and taught the Indians how to write it. The Indians learned how to work printing presses and print books in their own language. Today, Guarani is still widely used in Paraguay.

However, Portuguese slave raiders from Brazil kept attacking the Jesuit missions. They kidnaped some 60 thousand Guarani and sold them into slavery. Meanwhile, the Spanish government became suspicious of the Jesuit mission system as a state within a state. This led the Spanish government to change its policy. In 1767, it ordered all Jesuits to leave Spanish America. The mission villages in Paraguay fell apart. Spanish land-owners then tried to use the Guarani for forced labor.

Many Indians were converted to Christianity.
Although the Jesuits were forced out, other missionary groups remained. In addition, the Catholic Church and its priests worked among the Indians. The priests also, of course, served the colonists.

Through these people, great numbers of Indians were baptized into the Catholic faith. Most, however, did not completely give up their old religions. They often blended their own rituals with Catholic customs and festivals. Sometimes, they simply gave Christian names to Indian gods. They built churches where old temples had once stood. In this way, Catholicism among the Indians of Spanish America developed an unusual form. Today in Peru, Ecuador, and Guatemala, Indians in Catholic churches use their own languages to say prayers that were used in the past for ancient gods.

African slaves were brought to Spanish America. As we have seen, there was a great loss of Indian population from European diseases and overwork. However, the large plantation owners in the West Indies and Brazil still needed thousands of field hands to do hot, back-breaking labor. The Spanish government therefore allowed them to import slaves from Africa. Altogether, over 11 million people were shipped across the Atlantic to Spanish colonies. About 2 million of them died on the way because of terrible conditions on the ships.

Slaves were used mostly in the Caribbean.
Most slaves worked on the sugar plantations of the Caribbean islands. By the mid-1600s, sugar cane had become the major crop of the islands. Slaves also worked on mainland plantations and on those where cacao, rice, cotton, and tobacco were grown. African slaves also did the heavy labor in mines. They worked on the docks in the port cities and were used as personal servants as well.

Slavery on the Caribbean sugar plantations was brutal. Owners were interested only in profits. They did not care how slaves were treated. They often worked slaves to death and then bought new ones. This was cheaper than treating them better so they would live longer. Men and women, young and old, slaved 18 hours a day during the sugar harvest. The work done by women was so heavy that very few of their babies were born alive. Those that did live seldom survived to become adults.

Brazilian slaves were treated differently.
African slaves also worked on the sugar plantations along the Brazilian coast. The Portuguese government also had allowed slaves to be imported. This was because they found that the Brazilian Indians were food gatherers and did not know much about plowing and planting.

Slaves in Brazil suffered just as those in the Caribbean islands did. But the Portuguese looked upon slaves as people with souls. They therefore converted the slaves to Christianity. Brazilian slaves attended church and took part in religious ceremonies.

Some Brazilian slaves became skilled workers and craftspeople. A few were able to buy their freedom. Some were freed when their masters died. Children of Portuguese masters and African mothers were often given their freedom at birth or when they grew up. Some slaves were taught to read and write and were even sent to study at universities in Portugal. Slaves in Brazil also had a legal right to earn money and inherit land.

Slaves on Caribbean islands such as Hispaniola worked under harsh conditions to turn sugar cane into sugar.

There were many slave rebellions. Although slaves were watched carefully, many rebellions broke out. Most rebellions were brutally put down. However, some slaves managed to escape to freedom. Runaway slaves in Cuba fled to the hills inland, where they lived for many generations. On the French-owned island of Haiti, slave conditions were particularly horrible. In the 1790s, Haitian slaves rose up in the largest and most successful slave revolt in the Americas. Haiti became the first independent black government in the Western Hemisphere.

section review 3

1. How did the Spanish colonists become wealthy?

2. What were the colonists and the Indians supposed to do for each other? Who benefited most? Why?

3. Why did many Indians die after the conquest?

4. Describe the differences between slavery on the Caribbean islands and the slavery found in Brazil.

4 A Latin American civilization arose

Spain and Portugal held on to their empires in the Americas for more than 300 years. During that period of colonial rule, three different peoples and cultures—Indian, African, and Spanish and Portuguese—blended together. The mixture gave rise to a new civilization called Latin American.

There was mixing of races. In spite of slavery and racial prejudice, whites, blacks, and Indians could mix and intermarry in the Spanish and Portuguese colonies. It was easier to mix in Latin America than it was in the English colonies of North America. Today, more than 50 million Latin Americans are descended from African slaves. In Mexico, much of the population is a mixture of Spanish and Indian.

The greatest amount of mixing took place in the towns of Brazil. On Brazilian plantations masters and slaves were still clearly divided. But black and white children played together and received religious training. Masters and slaves together took part in religious services. In Brazil, color lines became less sharp than anywhere else in the Americas.

Indian and African influences were strong. Both Indians and Africans played an important part in the growth of Latin American culture. They made major contributions in music, painting, literature, politics, and cooking. Even the Catholic faith was influenced by Indian and African religious ideas and customs.

Examples are easy to find. Sculptures and wall paintings in Spanish-American churches were often done by native artists. These artists usually showed Jesus as having Indian features. Latin American music was an interesting blend. It was made up of ancient Indian drums and pipes, new rhythms and dances brought by African slaves, and Spanish and Portuguese folk songs and religious chants from Europe. In this way, the traditions of three continents were blended together into a new Latin American music.

The dominant influence was European. Since Spain and Portugal were the conquerors, they forced their culture upon everyone else. Spanish and Portuguese replaced hundreds of Indian languages. Catholicism replaced many Indian beliefs. With only two major languages and one religion from Mexico to Argentina, Latin America gained cultural unity.

European settlers brought many different vegetables and animals to the Americas. They also introduced the plow, the potter's wheel, and the metal fishhook. They taught European methods of farming and weaving. Just as important, the European settlers brought with them their legal systems, their form of government, and their idea of private property.

Spanish aristocrats in the Americas lived mainly in the many new towns and cities that were founded. Most cities were copied after ones in Spain. The new towns had a central plaza in front of a large Catholic church. The streets were laid out in squares around the central plaza.

In 1620, when the Pilgrims were just landing at Plymouth Rock, there were already 4,000 stone houses in Lima, Peru. Spanish nobles lived in these great mansions, which had balconies that looked out over the streets. Rich Peruvians (creoles) dressed in the latest European fashions. They drove around Lima in fancy open carriages. The city had an aqueduct that carried melted snow down from the mountains. Poor people, though, still had a hard life. However, a

FOIRE DE PORTO BELLO.

DailyLife

The arrival of the Portuguese and Spanish in the Americas led to a mixing of three cultures: European, African, and Indian. The painted wooden bottle, *right,* from about 1650 shows the mix. Done in Inca style, it has three figures: an African drummer, a Spanish trumpeter, and an Indian official. Bottles such as this one were bought and sold at fairs as *above*. The picture shows Porto Bello, in what is now Panama. From 1561 to 1748, Porto Bello was one of the three main stops that Spanish ship convoys made. It was a small, disease-ridden town that came alive when the ships arrived. Then the 40-day fairs attracted merchants from as far away as Chile and Argentina.

Overcoming great pressures against scholarly lives for women, Sor Juana Inés de la Cruz devoted her life to study and writing. As a teenager, she astounded scholars with her knowledge. The viceroy said that she answered every question put to her "like a royal galleon beating off the attacks of a bunch of row boats." This portrait shows her in her library in the convent of San Jeronimo de Mexico.

visiting European scholar wrote that it was no worse than the life of poor peasants or city dwellers in Europe.

Schools and universities were set up. The Church controlled all levels of education in the colonies, just as it did in Spain and Portugal. Priests ran a few primary schools, but there were no high schools. Education was only for the upper classes. Only about 10 percent of the people could read and write.

In the 1550s, however, two universities were started. One was at Mexico City, and the other was at Lima. Today, they are the oldest universities in the New World. By the end of the 18th century, there were 25 colleges and universities in Spanish America.

The social status of women was low. Universities and colleges were attended mostly by young men. For the most part, Spaniards and Portuguese felt that women did not need higher education. A woman's main role was to have children. Poor women and slaves also had to do heavy work. Women whose husbands were landholders carried out the family's religious duties. A plantation owner respected his wife, but she was supposed to remain in the background. This attitude that gave women an important role in the home but a much lesser one in public life became part of Latin American culture. It has lasted into the 20th century. Sometimes, though, an extraordinary woman managed to break through this rigid pattern. One such notable exception was Sor Juana Inés de la Cruz (1651–1695), a Mexican nun who became the greatest lyric poet of the colonial period.

section review 4

1. In which colony did blacks and whites get along the best? Give examples.

2. Give specific examples to show how Latin American culture is a mixture of Indian, African, and European cultures.

3. Describe the lives and education of rich Spaniards in the cities.

4. In what ways were women in the colonies not considered to be equal to men? How long did this feeling toward women last?

Section Summaries

1. Europeans conquered and colonized the Americas. The formation of present-day Latin America began with the arrival of Spanish conquistadores in the early 1500s. Within a very short time, Spain took over all the territory from Mexico to Argentina. The only exception was Brazil which was claimed by Portugal.

One of the best-known conquistadores was Cortés, who defeated Montezuma and the Aztecs in 1521. Another was Pizarro, who conquered the Incas of Peru in 1531. Spain then owned the gold, silver, and other riches of the New World. Meanwhile, the Portuguese began to build rich sugar plantations in Brazil.

2. Spain controlled a large empire. To rule over its huge empire, Spain created a Council of the Indies at home. Viceroys were sent out to represent the king in the colonies. Spanish settlers born in the colonies, called creoles, hated the fact that high government positions were given only to nobles born in Spain, called peninsulares. Mestizos, people of mixed Indian and Spanish background, had even lower social standing.

3. Indians and Africans were the main source of labor. The colonies provided two major kinds of wealth. One was the plantations that grew sugar cane, especially in the West Indies. The other was the silver mines in Mexico and present-day Bolivia. At first, the plantation and mine owners used Indian forced labor to do the heavy work. The Church tried to protect the Indians. But the Indians died by the hundreds of thousands because of cruel treatment and disease.

Then many African slaves were shipped to the New World to work the mines and fields. Slavery was most brutal in the West Indies. It was a little less cruel in Brazil. There the Portuguese converted slaves to Christianity and gave them certain rights. From time to time, there were slave rebellions.

4. A Latin American civilization arose. During the 300 years that Spain and Portugal had their colonies in the Americas, there was a good deal of mixing between Indians, Africans, and Europeans. Their cultures blended and a new Latin American civilization grew up. Each of the three peoples made important contributions to life in the New World.

Who? What? When? Where?

1. List these events in chronological order beginning with the earliest:

    a. Rio de Janeiro was founded.
    b. Universities were started at Mexico City and Lima.
    c. Columbus made a second voyage.
    d. Pizarro arrived in Peru.
    e. Cortés was chosen to explore Mexico.
    f. The Jesuits left South America.

2. Write sentences that tell who these groups were and how each fit into Latin American society:

    a. conquistadores   d. mestizos
    b. creoles   e. peninsulares
    c. Jesuits   f. viceroys

3. Write sentences that tell the role played by Europeans in each of these:

    a. Buenos Aires   d. La Plata
    b. Cuba   e. New Spain
    c. Haiti   f. Santo Domingo

4. Write a sentence for each of these terms that tells how it affected the Indians or blacks of Latin America:

    a. baptism   e. intermarriage
    b. disease   f. missionaries
    c. education   g. silver and sugar
    d. encomienda   h. slavery

5. Write sentences that tell the role played by each of these people in the European conquest:

    a. Atahualpa
    b. Bartolomé de las Casas
    c. Cortés
    d. Malinche
    e. Montezuma
    f. Pizarro

Questions for Critical Thinking

1. What might have been the thoughts of Montezuma and Atahualpa toward the conquistadores? Why did Malinche help Cortés?

2. Why were the efforts of Catholic missionaries to protect the Indians not very successful?

3. How did the Indians keep their traditional religious beliefs alive?

4. What are some attitudes or feelings of Latin Americans today that began in colonial times?

5. In what ways were Spanish and Portuguese colonialism different from English colonialism in North America?

6. Why did the Spaniards and Portuguese think it was important to convert the Indians?

Skill Activities

1. Read *Captain Cortés Conquers Mexico* by William Johnson to learn more about this famous event. (Random House, 1960)

2. Debate or have a panel discussion on whether or not the Spanish conquest was a good thing for Latin America, using today's point of view.

3. In groups of four or five, act out scenes from the conquest and colonial times. Examples: Cortés's reaction to the first Indians he met in Mexico; Montezuma's decision to allow Cortés to enter Mexico.

chapter **22** quiz

Section 1

1. The first European settlers in the Americas were brought by: a. Cortés, b. Columbus, c. the English

2. True or false: Cortés was able to defeat the Aztecs because he had more soldiers than the Indians had.

3. Brazil's most important export by 1600 was: a. slaves, b. silver, c. sugar

Section 2

4. The Council of the Indies was: a. the lawmaking body for the colonies, b. an Aztec ceremony, c. a court located in Mexico

5. Colonial officials were chosen from: a. peninsulares, b. creoles, c. Jesuits

6. Children who were born in the colonies but whose parents had been born in Spain were called: a. mestizos, b. creoles, c. peninsulares

Section 3

7. True or false: Bartolomé de las Casas, a Spanish priest, was called "Protector of the Indians" by Charles V.

8. There was a shortage of workers in the colonies because: a. there had never been many Indians there, b. the Spanish government refused to allow the Indians to work, c. millions of Indians died from diseases brought in by the Spanish.

9. Slavery was especially cruel in: a. Brazil, b. the Caribbean islands, c. Mexico

Section 4

10. True or false: Pictures of Jesus in Latin American churches often have Indian features.

11. Education in the Spanish colonies was: a. controlled by the Catholic Church, b. open to all social classes, c. available to women

12. True or false: Women in Latin America generally had a higher social status than men.

1. Match the correct name with each phrase:
Atahualpa
Calvin
Catherine the Great
Catherine de' Medici
Bartholomeu Dias
Elizabeth I
Erasmus
Jan van Eyck
Gutenberg
Machiavelli
Malinche
Maria Theresa
Pizarro
Shakespeare
Leonardo da Vinci
William the Conqueror

  a. Spanish conqueror of Peru
  b. Great humanist
  c. French ruler who killed many Huguenots
  d. Movable type
  e. Doctrine of predestination
  f. English author of plays
  g. English king of French nationality
  h. Northern Renaissance artist
  i. Wrote *The Prince*
  j. German princess and Empress of Russia
  k. Cortés's interpreter and informant
  l. Found a sea passage south of Africa
  m. Tried to buy freedom with roomfuls of gold and silver
  n. A Renaissance genius
  o. Was the reason for the War of the Austrian Succession
  p. Ruler of England at the time of the Spanish Armada

2. Tell whether the statements are true or false:
  a. Magna Charta was one of Henry II's legal developments.
  b. Joan of Arc led France to victory during the Reconquista.
  c. The Renaissance began in Italy because of its good trade location.
  d. The first book printed on movable type in Europe was *Don Quixote*.
  e. Martin Luther objected to the sale of papal indulgences.
  f. The Peace of Augsburg allowed people to choose their religion.

3. Match the letters on the time line with the events they stand for.

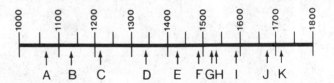

____Joan of Arc was burned at the stake.
____The Battle of Hastings was fought.
____The Black Death struck Florence.
____Louis XIV died.
____Martin Luther posted his 95 Theses.
____Alphonso I of Portugal defeated the Moors.
____Peter the Great became ruler of Russia.
____England defeated the Spanish Armada.
____The Magna Charta was signed.
____Cortés set sail for Mexico.
____Columbus sighted the Bahamas.

4. Match the letters on the map with the places described below:
____Spanish rulers established their first empire in the Americas here.
____Portugal's empire in the Americas centered in this area.
____In the 14th century, city-states here began a revival of art and learning.
____The fighting in the Hundred Years' War took place in this country.
____Portuguese seeking a passage to India explored the coast of this continent.

UNIT SEVEN REVOLUTIONARY CHANGES IN THE WEST

When people change their ways of life in a rather short time, we call that a *revolution*. Probably no other people have had so many changes in their lives as did those of the Western world between 1500 and 1900. A person living in Western Christendom in 1500 was not so different from one living there in 1100. But a person in 1900 was very different from one in 1500.

Every area of life changed, as did the ways people thought about themselves and the world they lived in. The organization of Western governments changed. Westerners invented new machines and found new sources of power—first steam, then electricity—to run them. People learned to grow new foods and more of their everyday foods. This led to a much larger population, and many people looked for work in industrial towns. By 1900, the age-old rural agricultural civilization of the West had become an urban, industrial one.

It is easy to say, now, that these changes were improvements. But these centuries were full of anger and violence as people searched for ways to live with all the changes. In 1900, the struggle was still going on. But between 1500 and 1900, life in the West changed so much that a new word was needed to describe this period. Historians call it the *modern era*. We in the 20th century are still living in the modern era.

In the 1600s, every country in Western Europe began an organization like the French Academy of Sciences. During the 1700s, these groups became an effective way of spreading new ideas. This drawing from the late 1600s shows King Louis XIV (with the cane) visiting the French Academy.

CHAPTER 23
SCIENCE AND THE AGE OF REASON

- Potato introduced in Europe
- *On the Fabric of the Human Body*
- *On the Revolutions of the Heavenly Bodies*
- Copernicus lived
- Galileo lived
- First microscope
- First telescope
- *An Anatomical Exercise on the Motion of the Heart and Blood in Animals*
- Molière lived
- Descartes died
- *The Skeptical Chemist*

CHAPTER 24
THE AGE OF DEMOCRATIC REVOLUTIONS

- James I lived
- Cromwell lived
- Charles I beheaded
- The Restoration began

CHAPTER 25
THE GROWTH OF LIBERALISM, NATIONALISM, AND DEMOCRACY

CHAPTER 26
THE INDUSTRIAL REVOLUTION

CHAPTER 27
SOCIAL PROTEST AND MASS SOCIETY

1500 1525 1550 1575 1600 1625 1650 1675

1

2

3

4

5

6

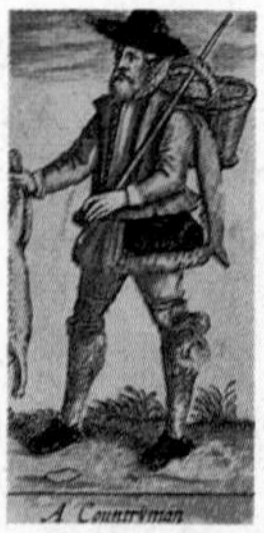

1. English countryman, 2. Mary, Queen of Scots, 3. Potato, 4. Galileo's telescope, 5. Early microscope, 6. Molière, 7. American colonial broom seller, 8. Beethoven, 9. Toussaint l'Ouverture, 10. Marie Antoinette, 11. Napoleon, 12. Maximilian, 13. Pankhurst.

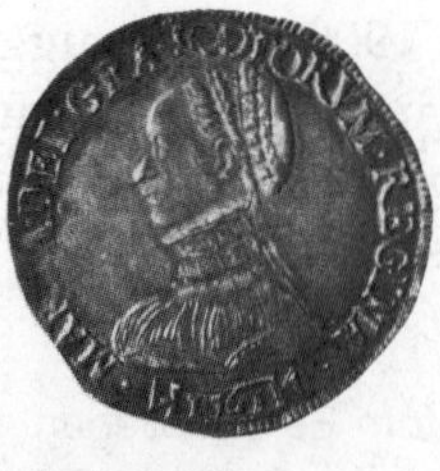

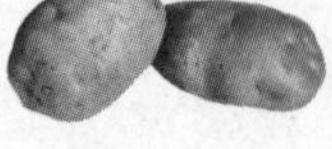

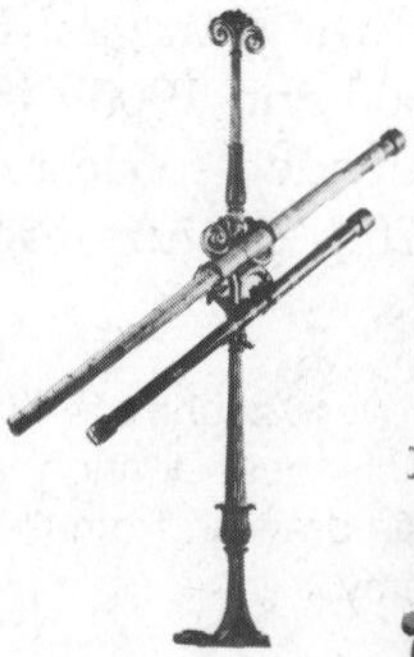

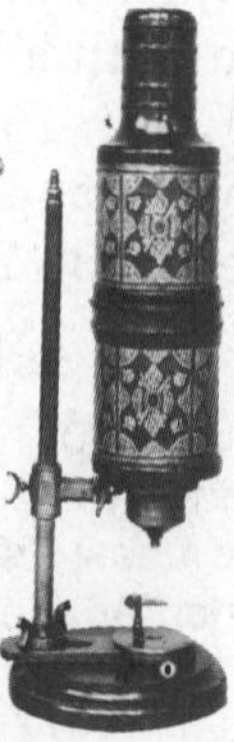

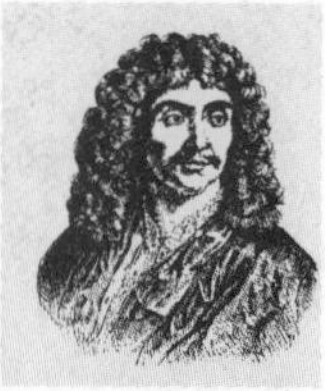

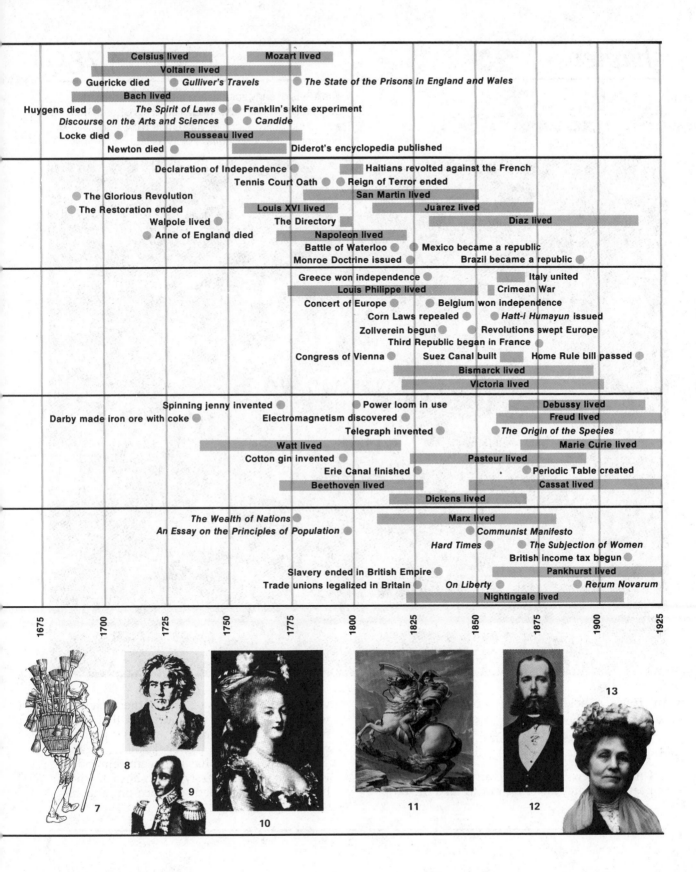

Celsius lived
Mozart lived
Voltaire lived
Guericke died — Gulliver's Travels — The State of the Prisons in England and Wales
Bach lived
Huygens died — The Spirit of Laws — Franklin's kite experiment
Discourse on the Arts and Sciences — Candide
Locke died — Rousseau lived
Newton died — Diderot's encyclopedia published

Declaration of Independence — Haitians revolted against the French
Tennis Court Oath — Reign of Terror ended
The Glorious Revolution — San Martin lived
The Restoration ended — Juárez lived
Louis XVI lived — Díaz lived
Walpole lived — The Directory
Anne of England died — Napoleon lived
Battle of Waterloo — Mexico became a republic
Monroe Doctrine issued — Brazil became a republic

Greece won independence — Italy united
Louis Philippe lived — Crimean War
Concert of Europe — Belgium won independence
Corn Laws repealed — Hatt-i Humayun issued
Zollverein begun — Revolutions swept Europe
Third Republic began in France
Congress of Vienna — Suez Canal built — Home Rule bill passed
Bismarck lived
Victoria lived

Spinning jenny invented — Power loom in use — Debussy lived
Darby made iron ore with coke — Freud lived
Electromagnetism discovered
Telegraph invented — The Origin of the Species
Watt lived — Marie Curie lived
Cotton gin invented — Pasteur lived
Erie Canal finished — Periodic Table created
Beethoven lived — Cassat lived
Dickens lived

The Wealth of Nations — Marx lived
An Essay on the Principles of Population — Communist Manifesto
Hard Times — The Subjection of Women
British income tax begun
Slavery ended in British Empire — Pankhurst lived
Trade unions legalized in Britain — On Liberty — Rerum Novarum
Nightingale lived

1675 1700 1725 1750 1775 1800 1825 1850 1875 1900 1925

7   8   9   10   11   12   13

SCIENCE AND THE AGE OF REASON

The ideas of early scientists often upset accepted beliefs. This picture shows Galileo at his Church trial. He was found guilty of disobeying Church law and presenting the heliocentric theory as fact.

In 1684, a scientist was working hard on what would become one of the best-known scientific books of all time. His secretary described how the scientist worked:

> I never knew him to take any recreation or pastime, either in riding out to take the air, walking, bowling, or any other exercise whatever, thinking all hours lost that were not spent in his studies. . . . He very rarely went to dine in the [college] hall . . . , and [when he did] if he has not been [re]minded would go very carelessly, with shoes down at heel, stockings untied, surplice on, and his

[hair] scarcely combed. [The few] times when he [decided] to dine in the hall, [he] would turn to the left [instead of to the right where the dining hall was] and [would find himself] out [in] the street. . . . When he found his mistake [he] would hastily turn back, and then sometimes instead of going into the hall, would return to his [room] again.

The man was Sir Isaac Newton, who discovered the laws of gravity and ended a scientific revolution that had been going on for 150 years.

Most important in history is an understanding of how people have changed their ideas about themselves and the world they live in. Perhaps nothing has done more to change those ideas than the advances in science—the study of nature—that began in the Western world toward the end of the 15th century. By 1800, educated people in the West were thinking about nature in a way far different from the way people thought in 1500. The steps to this new way of thinking made a *scientific revolution*.

The scientific revolution was a result of both new information about nature and a new way of gathering it, based on experiment and reasoning. Together, these factors entered into every area of thought and action—religion, government, literature, and social and economic life. Thus, the time of the scientific revolution was also an age of reason. This chapter tells how:

1. Scientists worked out new theories about the universe.

2. Several branches of science moved forward.

3. Medical knowledge grew.

4. The scientific method was used in many fields.

1 Scientists worked out new theories about the universe

The ancient Greeks had tried to explain nature by its appearance rather than by experimenting and carefully watching what happened. As a result, they were sometimes wrong. For example, the Greek astronomer Ptolemy believed that the earth did not move because it did not seem to move. He thought that the earth stood still at the center of the universe and that the sun, moon, stars, and planets moved around it. That was the way he saw it.

For more than a thousand years, most people in Christendom accepted Ptolemy's view of the universe, the *geocentric* (earth-centered) theory. The Church used Ptolemy's ideas because they fitted in so well with Christian teachings. People, the Church said, lived to serve God and were the center of God's attention. Since God had made the universe to serve people, certainly the home of people, Earth, also was at the center.

A scientific method began to develop. By the end of the Middle Ages, some thinkers began to doubt Ptolemy's theory because so many ideas had been added. They believed that God had simpler ways of explaining how nature worked. Others thought that a new way was needed to learn about nature. As early as the 15th century, Leonardo da Vinci wrote: "Those sciences are vain and full of errors which are not born of experiment, the mother of certainty. . . ."

In the 16th century, the English philosopher Sir Francis Bacon urged that all scientists experiment, carefully observe, and then write what happened in the experiment. Information gathered this way and used with reasoning led to explanations that could be tested by repeating the experiments.

Sir Francis Bacon

Today, this *scientific method* is the basis of all science. In the 16th and 17th centuries, it changed people's way of learning so much that it caused a revolution in their thinking.

Copernicus questioned an old belief. In the 16th century, Nicolaus Copernicus, a Pole, developed his own ideas about the way the sun and the planets move. In his view, the sun is the center of the solar system, and the earth and planets move around it. Then, too, the earth turns on its axis each day as it makes its yearly trip around the sun.

Copernicus set forth his *heliocentric* (sun-centered) theory in a book, *On the Revolutions of the Heavenly Bodies*. He did not publish it until 1543, twenty years after he wrote it, because he knew his ideas would upset people who accepted Ptolemy's view.

The Copernican theory really got little attention at first. Almost no one believed it. Even astronomers found it hard to accept. First, they had not seen the stars in different places at different times of the year, as Copernicus had said they would. Second, he did not explain some points very well. For example, why did things not fly off the earth if it was in motion? As answers to these questions were found, more people thought that the Copernican theory might be true.

Kepler improved the Copernican theory. The first professional astronomer to agree openly with Copernicus's views was the German Johannes Kepler. During the early 17th century, he formed three laws of planetary motion: (1) a planet moves, not in a circle, but in an oval path called an ellipse, while the sun stays in place; (2) a planet speeds up when it comes closer to the sun; and (3) the amount of time a planet takes to move around the sun depends on how far away it is from the sun.

One question that Kepler could not answer was why the planets remained fixed in their paths and did not fly off into space.

Galileo made important discoveries. The heliocentric theory received more help from the Italian astronomer Galileo. Born in Pisa, Italy, in 1564, Galileo later became a mathematics teacher at the university there.

In his laboratory, he rolled weights down an inclined plane to disprove Aristotle's theory that a body's weight decides how fast it will fall. Galileo showed that bodies of different weights fall at the same speed in the absence of air. (The story that he dropped the weights from the Leaning Tower of Pisa seems to be a legend.)

Galileo went from Pisa to the University of Padua, where he heard about the invention of the telescope in the Netherlands. He later built one and with it saw mountains on the

A MYSTERY IN HISTORY

DID THE POTATO CHANGE HISTORY?

For centuries, the population of Europe stayed at the same level. Then suddenly in the 1750s, it began to grow very fast, and by 1850 it had doubled. Such a fast increase changed the conditions of life not only in Europe but also in the whole world as millions of Europeans moved to other areas. Historians have called this sudden growth Europe's "population explosion."

Why did it happen? Historians are not sure. Many used to think it was because the death rate went down sharply in the 18th century. However, new research has shown that the death rate was not much lower in the 18th century than it had been before. Instead, the evidence shows that between 1750 and 1850 the birthrate rose among Europeans. Famine and disease still killed off many people because farming did not improve much, and advances in medicine were slow. Yet more people were born and stayed alive than ever.

How was this possible? To feed so many more people, much more food was needed, more than Europeans had ever had before. How did they get the extra food? That was the mystery.

Could it be that Europeans found new kinds of food? Some historians think so. They say Europeans learned to grow two new vegetables brought over from the New World—potatoes and corn. They are nutritious, easy to cultivate with hand tools (especially the potato), and can be grown in large amounts on only a small piece of land.

The Conquistadors had brought the potato to Europe from Peru in the 1530s. But not until the mid-18th century, did peasants in Europe get over their fear that the potato was poisonous. After that, it quickly became the main food of lower-class people, since a single acre of potatoes could feed a family of six, plus one farm animal, for nearly a whole year. As a result, more children lived to become adults and have children themselves. Thus, the population grew.

The potato may be the "missing link" to explain Europe's population explosion, and it may very well have changed history.

In "The Potato Eaters," Dutch painter Vincent Van Gogh showed great sympathy for the weary peasants who gathered together for their evening meal.

431

moon, stars of the Milky Way, and other wonders. Galileo became convinced that Copernicus's ideas were correct. One reason was Galileo's discovery of the moons that move around Jupiter. They proved that not all heavenly bodies move around the earth. So, Galileo reasoned, some planets might move around the sun.

Galileo did not say anything about his ideas because in 1616 the Church had told him not to teach or defend the heliocentric theory. But in 1632, in his *Dialogue on the Two Great Systems of the World*, he seemed to say that the Copernican theory was true. As he had feared, he was called before the courts of the Church in 1633 and closely questioned. Finally broken, Galileo, almost seventy years old, agreed to say that the earth does not move around the sun. (Legend says that after he publicly denied that the earth moves, he whispered to himself: "But it does move!")

Newton brought together scientific knowledge.   Born in England in 1642, the year that Galileo died, Isaac Newton became one of the greatest scientists the world has ever known. His work climaxed the movement that had begun with Copernicus.

Newton taught mathematics at Cambridge University. While still in his twenties, he worked out the system of advanced mathematical figuring called calculus.

Newton's most important work, however, was in discovering a mathematical formula that explained gravity. Every planet, he said, has a force called gravity that pulls things toward it. The strength of a planet's gravitational force depends on the planet's mass (its size and weight) and how far it is from another object. Since the earth has more mass than the moon, its gravity is stronger; things weigh more on the earth than they do on the moon. Gravity is the reason planets stay in orbit. The sun's gravity holds the earth near

it and keeps it from flying off in space. With this explanation, Newton was able to answer some of the unanswered questions about the heliocentric theory.

Newton called his formula the law of universal gravitation. In *Mathematical Principles of Natural Philosophy* (1687), he explained his ideas. It is one of the greatest scientific books ever written. Without Newton's discoveries, 20th-century scientists could not have sent astronauts to the moon.

section review **1**

1. Explain the geocentric theory. Why did the Church support it?

2. Describe the method Sir Francis Bacon urged all scientists to use.

3. What discoveries did Kepler and Galileo make that helped prove Copernicus correct? How did the Church react to Galileo's book?

4. Describe Newton's most important contribution to science. What did Newton's law explain?

2 Several branches of science moved forward

The 16th and 17th centuries saw great advances not only in astronomy but also in chemistry and physics. Physics is the study of matter and energy; chemistry is the study of substances.

Improved mathematics and new tools helped scientists.   Modern mathematics began in Christendom after 1100 A.D., when merchants and scholars started to use Arabic (really Indian) numerals. The decimal system was perfected, and math symbols, such as $+$, $\div$, $\times$, $=$, and $\overline{)}$, came into use.

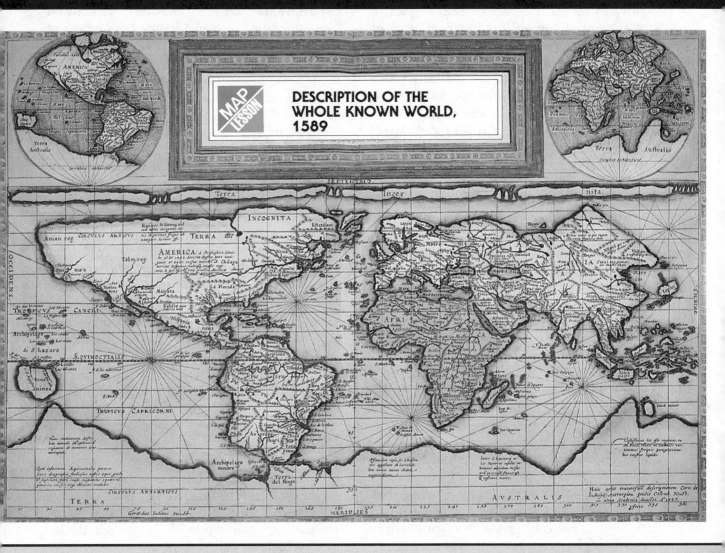

■ MAP LESSON 23: DESCRIPTION OF THE WHOLE KNOWN WORLD, 1589

1. Maps were one of the great achievements of the scientific approach that led to the Age of Reason. This map was engraved on a copper plate in the Netherlands in 1589, and it shows the world as it was known to Europeans of that time. Since this map was made in Europe, it was natural for the cartographer, or mapmaker, to put Europe in the center of the map, the position of most importance. If the map had been made in Japan, where would Japan probably be located?

2. Europeans knew little about the interior of North America at the time this map was made. Name two major bodies of water that are missing from this view of North America.

3. One basic problem with this map is that it greatly exaggerates the amount of the earth's surface that is covered by land. Because land was more important to people than oceans, early cartographers over-estimated the land area of the globe. In what way is the continent of South America exaggerated?

433

Early in the 17th century, John Napier, a Scot, invented logarithms, a short way of doing calculations with very large numbers. Because logarithms reduced the time needed to solve hard problems, Napier in a sense doubled the working lives of his fellow mathematicians. In France, mathematician and philosopher René Descartes [rə nā′ dā kärt′] developed analytic geometry.

By the 17th century, the work of science was becoming more exact because of new and more accurate tools for measuring and observing. In refracting telescopes, first made in the Netherlands about 1608, the image was focused by a lens. Because it was so long, the tool was hard to use. In 1668, Newton made a better one. The image in this telescope was focused by a mirror.

In 1645, Evangelista Torricelli [e vän′je lē′-stä tor′i chel′ē], a student of Galileo's, made the mercury barometer to measure air pressure. It is used in forecasting the weather.

Later, a German physicist, Gabriel Fahrenheit [far′ən hīt], made the first mercury thermometer. It showed freezing at 32° and boiling at 212°, higher than earlier alcohol thermometers that measured temperatures only to 173°F. A Swedish astronomer Anders Celsius [sel′sē əs] used another scale that read 0° at freezing and 100° at boiling when he invented the centigrade thermometer.

German physicist Otto von Guericke [gā′ri-kə] invented the first air pump capable of creating a vacuum. To show how strong atmospheric pressure is, Guericke pumped the air out of two hollow metal hemispheres. Only the pressure of the air on the outside held them together. To pull the hemispheres apart, sixteen horses were needed.

Galileo was one of the first to study the pendulum. His notes about its movements were used later in building clocks. In 1656, Dutch astronomer Christian Huygens [hī′-gənz] built the first useful pendulum clock. Using this, scientists could correctly measure small units of time.

Experiments began modern chemistry.
Long a mix of fact and magic, the study of chemistry had no scientific base until the middle of the 17th century. Medieval alchemists believed, as had the Greeks, that all matter was made of four elements—earth, fire, water, and air. Also, things that burned were thought to contain a strange substance, phlogiston [flō jis′tən], that made fire possible and was given off in burning.

The first person to use the scientific method in chemistry was Irishman Robert Boyle. In *The Sceptical Chemist* (1661), he attacked alchemists and the theory of the four elements. He proved that air could not be an element because it was a mixture of several gases. Boyle said that an *element* is a substance that cannot be broken down by chemical means. A century later, English scientist Henry Cavendish proved that water could not be an element because it was made up of hydrogen and oxygen.

Joseph Priestley, an English minister, identified several chemical substances, including ammonia and carbon monoxide. In 1774, he discovered an element he called "dephlogisticated air." Antoine Lavoisier [än twän′ lä vwä zyä′], who worked about the same time in France, proved that a burning substance does not give off phlogiston. Instead, it combines with "dephlogisticated air," which he called oxygen.

Physicists studied magnetism and electricity.
The first section of this chapter described some important works of Galileo and Newton in the branch of physics that is concerned with motion, sound, and light. Another branch of physics, the study of magnetism and electricity, owes much to William Gilbert, a doctor to Queen Elizabeth I of England. Gilbert's book *On the Magnet* (1600) explained how a compass needle acts by describing the earth itself as a large magnet.

Gilbert also studied static electricity. Ever

Benjamin Franklin

Electricity went through the rainsoaked string to a key tied to it. When Franklin put his hand near the key, he felt a shock. The experiment was dangerous, but it proved his idea and led to his invention of the lightning rod to protect buildings.

section review 2

1. How did the new discoveries of John Napier make mathematics easier?

2. How was the work of scientists helped by the inventions of Newton, Torricelli, Fahrenheit, Celsius, Guericke, and Huygens?

3. What discoveries of Boyle, Cavendish, Priestley, and Lavoisier proved that the alchemists of the Middle Ages were wrong?

4. What did Gilbert and Franklin contribute to the study of electricity?

3 Medical knowledge grew

since the time of the Greeks, thinkers had been puzzled by the power of amber, which when rubbed picked up bits of feathers or paper. Gilbert found that several other substances, such as sulfur and glass, behave in the same way. For them, he coined the word electric (from the Greek word elektron, which means "amber").

Scientists next made machines to produce the force that Gilbert had studied. One was a globe of sulfur mounted on a turning axis. When rubbed with a cloth, it gave off sound and light. With it, an electric current could be sent from one end of a thread to the other. Scientists also learned to store electricity in a Leyden [līd'n] jar, an early condenser.

The first important American scientist, Benjamin Franklin, believed that lightning was exactly like the static electricity in a Leyden jar. In 1752, he tested his idea by flying a wire-tipped kite during a thunderstorm.

Modern medicine began with Philippus Aureolus Paracelsus [par'ə sel'səs], a 16th-century Swiss doctor who joined chemistry with medicine. He told the alchemists that they should aim to make medicines, not gold. He threw out such remedies as powdered Egyptian mummy and crushed sow bugs. Instead, he asked for experiments with chemical drugs to test their effects.

Vesalius began the study of anatomy. Another important person in the history of medicine was Brussels-born Andreas Vesalius [və sā'lē əs]. When he studied medicine at Louvain and Paris, he became angry with his teachers. Instead of examining the human body themselves, they just read about it in the works of Galen, a 2nd-century Greek doctor. To learn anatomy on his own, Vesalius gathered dead bodies, sometimes

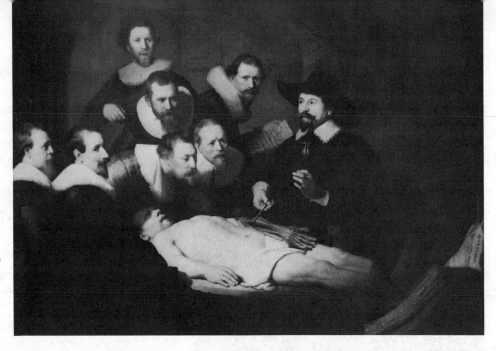

Scientists in the Age of Reason were thought of as people of wisdom, and artists paid honor to them. "The Anatomy of Dr. Tulp" by Rembrandt honors the study of anatomy as begun by Vesalius.

robbing the gallows. He got into trouble with the law for this but escaped to Padua. His work there helped to make that city the most important center for medicine in Europe.

WHAT'S IN A NAME?
BRUSSELS

Brussels is both the home of Andreas Vesalius and the capital of Belgium. The name Brussels comes from *brouch*, meaning marsh, and from *seli*, meaning house. Thus, Brussels means "house in the marsh."

In 1543, Vesalius published a book, *On the Fabric of the Human Body*. It was the first to correctly describe the anatomy of the human body. Fellow teachers, jealous of Vesalius, bitterly attacked his ideas. He left university life while still in his thirties and became the personal doctor of the Holy Roman Emperor, Charles V.

Harvey explained blood circulation. William Harvey, an English doctor, made great discoveries about how the human body works. He watched his patients closely and experimented with fish, frogs, and birds to find out how the heart works and whether the blood moves in a continuous stream. In 1628, he wrote *An Anatomical Exercise on the Motion of the Heart and Blood in Animals*. This thin book told for the first time how the heart pumps blood through the body.

Inventions aided diagnosis and treatment. Galileo may have helped invent the microscope, because he put lenses together to get large magnification. However, a Dutch eyeglass maker, Zacharias Janssen [zak'ə rī'əs yän'sən], built the first microscope about 1590.

In the 17th century, Anton van Leeuwenhoek [lā vən hük'], also Dutch, first saw bacteria. Leeuwenhoek made his own microscopes to see the wonders he described—red blood corpuscles, bacteria, yeast plants, and other tiny forms of life. But he never knew how important they are in human health.

section review 3

1. How did Paracelsus try to change the medical practices of his day?

2. How was Vesalius's way of studying anatomy different from that of his teachers?

3. What did Harvey discover about the human body?

4. How did Janssen and Leeuwenhoek help the study of medicine?

4 The scientific method was used in many fields

Scientists' discoveries showed that the physical universe was a well-ordered machine, working according to the laws of nature. Many thinkers reasoned that people also must be governed by some natural laws. They only needed to discover these laws. They could use the new scientific methods, just as astronomers had in discovering the laws that governed the heavens. These thinkers believed that they could use reason to discover how human societies worked. Then they could improve the ways that people live together. They had great hope for the future. Descartes declared:

> If we use the proper methods, we shall be able to outstrip our ancestors. The Golden Age is not behind us. Not only is progress possible, but there are no limits that can be assigned to it in advance.

This time of thought guided by scientific reasoning is called the Age of Reason. It lasted from 1628 to about 1789, or from the year Harvey announced his discovery of blood circulation to the French Revolution. It was an age in Europe when many thinkers looked at governments, religions, and the arts in relation to natural law. This whole effort to understand and improve society is called the Enlightenment.

The ideas of Locke and Montesquieu influenced government. The person who perhaps most influenced the Age of Reason was John Locke, an English philosopher born in 1632. Like many persons of his time, Locke believed that progress was certain if people would use their minds and follow reason.

In writing about government, Locke said that people had certain natural rights, chiefly to life, liberty, and property. When the people set up a government, he said, they gave it the power to protect these rights. He called this agreement between the people and the government a "social contract." If a government did not protect their rights, Locke said, the people could set up a new government.

Locke's social contract theory was eagerly studied in Europe and America. American revolutionaries used his ideas in their Declaration of Independence and later in the United States Constitution.

Another thinker who used reason in the study of government was a French noble and judge, the Baron de Montesquieu [mon'tə-skyü]. His most important work was *The Spirit of Laws* (1748). This 20-year project was a study of laws and constitutions from ancient times to his own. Because of the book, Montesquieu is called a founder of *political science*, the scientific study of government. One of his great doctrines was that to guard against royal absolutism, there must be a separation and balance of powers in government. He thought that a good example of this principle was the parliamentary system in England. Outside this, stood an independent judiciary. Montesquieu's ideas on government had wide influence and guided the people who drew up the United States Constitution.

Voltaire attacked intolerance. François Arouet, born in Paris in 1694, later gave himself the name Voltaire [vol tār'] because he thought it sounded more elegant than Arouet. A writer with a sharp and biting wit, Voltaire had no patience with fools.

Voltaire's attacks on what he saw as the follies of his time often got him into trouble. Once he was held for eleven months in the Bastille prison in Paris. Voltaire wrote several books and over fifty plays. His best-known work is the satire *Candide* [kän dēd'] (1759), which makes fun of the idea that this is "the best of all possible worlds."

Voltaire strongly influenced religious toleration. He accepted the teachings of a new religious movement, *deism* [dē'iz'əm]. The deists believed that God made the universe, set it up to work by natural laws, and then left it alone. The deists believed that God stayed out of people's daily lives and praying for help was useless. Therefore, rituals were not important, and religious differences were silly. Because Voltaire bitterly attacked the wrong acts he saw in organized religion, he was called an atheist [ā'thē ist], one who believes there is no God. But he saw a need for religious beliefs. He once said, "If there were no God, it would be necessary to invent one."

Voltaire hated intolerance. He directly entered into several cases of religious persecution to gain justice. He is thought to have said: "I do not agree with a word you say, but I will defend to the death your right to say it."

Rousseau praised freedom. Jean Jacques Rousseau's thinking about the new ideas of his time was emotional rather than reasoned. He was born in 1712 in Switzerland. His French mother died when he was a baby, and then relatives cared for him. Rousseau [rü sō'] was apprenticed to a lawyer and then to an engraver, and then he ran away. For twenty years, he led a hand-to-mouth life as servant, tutor, music teacher, and writer.

In 1750, an essay that won a contest suddenly made Rousseau well known. This *Discourse on the Arts and Sciences* stated that before people were civilized they had been pure and good. Social organization had spoiled them, and they could become pure and good again only by getting "back to nature." This idea of honor in the simple life became very popular in France. The queen had a peasant village built, where she and her ladies played at being milkmaids.

One of Rousseau's most important books was the *Social Contract* (1762). According to Rousseau, a community was based on an understanding among all the people. It went beyond Locke's idea of an agreement between a ruler and a people. In Rousseau's community, all members had a sense of belonging or feeling they were among people who shared common values and common attitudes. Rousseau named this feeling the "General Will." He said it expressed the true desires of a people and was the bond that held them together. Rousseau never fully explained how the General Will worked since

Many of the great philosophers were friends. This drawing shows Voltaire, with his arm raised, presiding over a dinner party. Diderot is seated on Voltaire's left.

Jean Jacques Rousseau and Wolfgang Amadeus Mozart

he was not interested in the mechanics of government. But, Rousseau's ideas influenced the growth of both democracy and nationalism.

Diderot's encyclopedia helped spread the new ideas. Denis Diderot [dē′də rō] of France took on a giant task when he decided to put all of the new learning and ideas of the Enlightenment into an encyclopedia. He wanted his books to speak for tolerance and against superstition and the unjust ways of the time, as well as to give facts about all branches of learning. Many important writers, such as Voltaire, Montesquieu, and Rousseau, sent articles to Diderot. He spent thirty years preparing the encyclopedia. The thirty-five large books, published between 1751 and 1772, greatly aided the spread of the new ideas of the Enlightenment. Thousands of sets were printed in France, and many editions appeared in other parts of Europe.

Reformers wanted to improve human well-being. The Age of Reason awakened concern for the well-being of all people. Religious liberty spread, and many improvements were made in public health and in the care of the sick and the insane.

Prisons also needed attention. Jails had always been dirty places governed by cruel laws. For example, in England, which had better prisons than did most countries, jailers got no salaries. They depended for their living on money that prisoners paid as "board." Some persons cleared of crimes could not leave jail until they had paid their bills.

Such conditions improved partly because of John Howard, a county sheriff who led a reform movement. His book, *The State of the Prisons in England and Wales* (1777), pointed out the need for better prison administration. Prisons, Howard wrote, should not be used for punishment alone. Rehabilitation or reform of the convicts should come first.

439

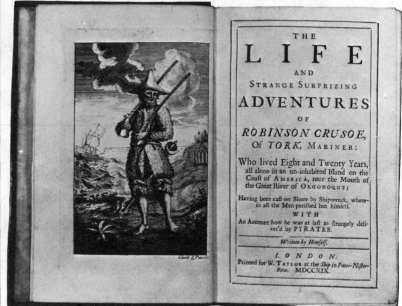

Artists in the Age of Reason had a view of life often criticized as sentimental. The German engraving of peasants in their simple cottage, *left*, shows the love of family members for each other. It ignores the realities of their harsh lives. *Robinson Crusoe, below,* was a romantic version of the real experiences of a British sailor.

Education also was reformed. The cruel discipline that was then common eased a little. And schools were opened for the lower classes.

Rousseau's ideas were important to education. He thought that children should be allowed to progress in their own ways and learn through observation and example. Above all, children should be educated to become good citizens.

The arts were refined. Reason ruled not only scientists and scholars but also writers, painters, and musicians. The artists of the 18th century were proud of their rational control and tried to follow certain rules in their works. Many admired and imitated the arts of Greece and Rome. Their work was called neoclassic.

The Age of Reason was noted for satire. The best-known poet of the time was Alexander Pope of England, whose elegant verses showed up the foolish ways of society. Jonathan Swift's book *Gulliver's Travels*, written in 1726, has the form of an adventure story. Children enjoy the tale. But to adults it is a bitter satire on the meanness of human quarrels, wars, and vices.

Other kinds of writing benefited from the emphasis on reason and clarity. An early work in the novel form was Daniel Defoe's adventure story, *Robinson Crusoe*. However, many people think the first novel was Samuel Richardson's *Pamela*, the romantic adventures of a servant girl. Today, it would be called soap opera. Another early novel was Henry Fielding's *Tom Jones*, a fascinating picture of 18th-century England. Important in the writing of history was Edward Gibbon's six-book study, *Decline and Fall of the Roman Empire*.

France had three dramatic writers. Pierre

Mount Vernon

Corneille [kôr nā'] and Jean Racine [ra sēn'] used stories from classical mythology in their tragedies. The witty comedies of Molière [mô lyer'] mocked false airs, mostly among doctors, lawyers, and the newly rich.

Music in the 18th century, like literature, was balanced, controlled, and refined. England and France were known for literature in the Age of Reason, but the greatest musicians then came from Germany and Austria. Religion was important in the works of Johann Sebastian Bach [bäk] and George Frederick Handel, who composed the *Messiah*. The Austrian musician Franz Joseph Haydn [hīd'n] wrote chamber music and started a new form of music, the symphony. His gifted pupil, Wolfgang Amadeus Mozart [mōt'särt], wrote more than 600 musical compositions, among them such operas as *Don Giovanni* and *The Marriage of Figaro*.

In architecture, the grand baroque form seen in Louis XIV's palace at Versailles gave way to a more delicate form called rococo [rō kō'kō]. Both of these forms lost favor after 1750. The quiet neoclassicism that followed can be seen in the stately mansion of Thomas Jefferson at Monticello and George Washington's home at Mount Vernon.

section review 4

1. How did scientists in the Age of Reason influence other thinkers?

2. In Locke's "social contract," what are the natural rights of people? What is the purpose of government? How were his ideas accepted in Europe and America?

3. What were Voltaire's objections to organized religion? How did he support the idea of freedom of speech?

4. What role did satire play in the Age of Reason?

Section Summaries

1. Scientists worked out new theories about the universe. A new era in Western thought began in the 16th century with the development of experimental science. One of its most important changes was a new view of the solar system. Some men of the Middle Ages had questioned Ptolemy's theory that the earth was at the center of the universe. Copernicus went further by proposing a new heliocentric theory. His ideas received little attention at first, but scientists later improved on them. Kepler's laws of planetary motion aided the heliocentric theory, and some of Galileo's discoveries helped, too. But the Church forced Galileo to renounce his views. The so-called Copernican revolution ended with Newton. He brought together earlier discoveries in the law of universal gravitation.

2. Several branches of science moved forward. New mathematical tools (logarithms, calculus, and analytic geometry) and means of measurement (clocks, barometers, and thermometers) aided scientists. Chemistry became a science with the work of Boyle, Priestley, and Lavoisier. Learning in physics owed much to the discoveries of Galileo, Newton, Gilbert, and Franklin.

3. Medical knowledge grew. Medical science, too, took great steps forward because of the work of Paracelsus, Vesalius, and Harvey. New tools, such as the microscope and thermometer, aided doctors.

4. The scientific method was used in many fields. Locke and Montesquieu applied the scientific method to government. Voltaire and Rousseau looked at morality, religion, and education. Diderot helped spread the new ideas with his encyclopedia. Reforms began in several fields. Reason also ruled in the arts, as seen in the satires of Pope, Swift, and Molière, the formal music of Haydn and Mozart, and the quiet balance of neoclassic architecture.

Who? What? When? Where?

1. Put these in the chronological order, beginning with the earliest:

a. Priestley discovered oxygen.
b. Janssen built the first microscope.
c. Franklin proved lightning was electricity.
d. Newton explained the law of gravity.
e. Copernicus developed the heliocentric theory.

2. Write a sentence for each of these men that tells how he tried to change the ideas of his time:

a. Bacon   e. Paracelsus
b. Diderot   f. Rousseau
c. Howard   g. Vesalius
d. Locke

3. Write a sentence for each of these men that tells what he added to our knowledge of the solar system:

a. Copernicus   c. Kepler
b. Galileo   d. Newton

4. Name the common interest shared by these:
a. Fahrenheit and Celsius
b. William Gilbert and Benjamin Franklin
c. Joseph Priestley and Antoine Lavoisier

5. Write a sentence for each of the following that describes his accomplishment:

a. Bach   e. Molière
b. Gibbon   f. Mozart
c. Harvey   g. Napier
d. Janssen

6. Write a sentence for each of the following that tells who wrote it and what it is about:
a. *Candide*
b. *Gulliver's Travels*
c. *Mathematical Principles of Natural Philosophy*
d. *On the Revolutions of the Heavenly Bodies*
e. *Pamela*
f. *The Sceptical Chemist*
g. *The Spirit of Laws*

7. Write a sentence for each of the following that tells what it means:
a. deism   d. heliocentric
b. element   e. neoclassic
c. geocentric   f. scientific revolution

Questions for Critical Thinking

1. What do you think is meant by the saying: "I do not agree with a word you say, but I will defend to the death your right to say it"? In what ways is this principle followed in our society?

2. In what ways do you agree or disagree with Rousseau's view that people were pure and good before civilization began but have been spoiled by social organization. Explain your answer.

3. How did the discoveries, inventions, or new ideas of the 17th and 18th centuries change the lives of people?

4. What is the importance of experimentation in testing new ideas?

Skill Activities

1. Read *Mozart* by Marcia Davenport to learn more about this famous composer. (Scribner, 1956.)

2. In groups of four or five, role-play a debate between supporters of the heliocentric theory and the geocentric as it would have been held in the 1500s.

3. Choose the person you feel made the most important contribution to the world during the Age of Reason and write a report on that person by researching biographies or encyclopedias. Your report should tell why you feel that person's contribution is most important.

4. Bring to class examples or pictures of some of the inventions discussed in this chapter, tell how they were invented, by whom, and what their uses are. Examples are a barometer, telescope, microscope, pendulum clock, thermometers (Celsius and Fahrenheit), or Leyden jar.

5. Listen to a recording of Handel's *Messiah*. Then write about your reactions to the music. Also tell why the audience often stands up during the "Halleluiah Chorus" section.

chapter **23** quiz

Section 1

1. The scientific method was developed by: a. Ptolemy, b. Bacon, c. Copernicus

2. The heliocentric theory was the work of: a. Copernicus, b. Galileo, c. Ptolemy

3. Newton's laws explained: a. the geocentric theory, b. magnetism, c. gravity

Section 2

4. In 1656, Dutch astronomer Christian Huygens: a. built the first useful pendulum clock, b. made the first mercury barometer, c. developed analytic geometry

5. True or false: On Celsius thermometers, 32° represents the freezing point.

6. True or false: The substance that Joseph Priestley discovered in 1774 and called "dephlogisticated air" was named "oxygen" by Antoine Lavoisier at about the same time.

Section 3

7. Alchemists tried to: a. cure diseases, b. make gold, c. dissect corpses

8. True or false: Anton van Leeuwenhoek did not understand the importance of his discoveries.

9. The first person to explain how the heart pumps blood through the body was: a. Harvey, b. Howard, c. Charles V

Section 4

10. True or false: Locke believed people had the right to change their government if it did not protect their rights.

11. The first encyclopedia contained articles by many important writers, but was put together by: a. Diderot, b. Montesquieu, c. Fielding

12. The symphony form of music was created by: a. Mozart, b. Handel, c. Haydn

THE AGE OF DEMOCRATIC REVOLUTIONS

The triumph of England's Parliament is vividly portrayed in this 1833 painting of the House of Commons. The men of the two parties, Tory and Whig, show calm assurance and determination on their faces. Clearly, they rule the nation.

In 1782, a twenty-year-old upper-class Hollander from Rotterdam visited the United States. He was not impressed. He did not believe the American system would last, and he did not think Europeans should do what the Americans had done. The Europeans paid little attention to him. Nearly ten years later, in 1791, he wrote:

Two great parties are forming in all nations . . . . For one, there is a right of government, to be exercised by one or several persons over the mass of people, of divine origin and to be supported by the church, which is protected by it. These principles are expressed in the formula, Church and State.

To this is opposed the new system, which admits no right of government except that arising from the free consent of those who submit to it, and which maintains that all persons who take part in government are accountable for their actions. These principles go under the formula, Sovereignty of the People, or Democracy.

The principles that the Hollander described formed over a long time. The ideas came from revolutions in England in the late 17th century, in North America and France in the late 18th century, and in Latin America in the early 19th century. Each revolution was different and had different causes. But all were fought for democratic ideas that changed the Western world. Thus some call this the "age of democratic revolutions."

During the age of democratic revolutions, these ideas spread through all of the Western world as first the English, and then North Americans, French, and Latin Americans tried to change their ways of government. This chapter tells how:

1. Parliament triumphed in Britain.

2. North American colonies fought for independence.

3. The French Revolution changed society and government.

4. Napoleon became ruler of France.

5. Latin American colonies became independent nations.

1 *Parliament triumphed in Britain*

The English kings never were as powerful as those on the European continent because Parliament was important in England. Without its consent, an English ruler could not make new laws, repeal old ones, or impose new taxes.

James I raised an important issue. Trouble began when Elizabeth I died in 1603, and James, king of Scotland, then became king of England also. He was the first Stuart king.

James I strongly believed in the divine right of kings. Therefore, he believed that no one could stop him from doing as he wanted. Since the English Parliament by tradition checked royal power, James's ideas were unwise. He was in constant need of money, and Parliament showed its anger by refusing to give him funds. This constant battle raised an important issue: did the king or Parliament have supreme power? In addition, two classes of people had become important in 16th-century England. One, the gentry, was made up of landowners who ranked just below the nobility. Merchants and manufacturers made up the other. Through their representatives in the House of Commons, both groups tried to gain more political power at the king's expense.

Religion made the problem worse. Roman Catholics still hoped to make England a Catholic country again. But Calvinist Protestants wanted a pure Anglican Church free of all remaining Catholic Church influence. Many of these Puritans were members of the gentry and middle class as well as being Parliament members who wanted more political power.

Charles I brought civil war. When James died in 1625, his son took the throne as

Charles I. Parliament, with many Puritan members, was just as suspicious of Charles as it had been of his father and refused to vote him the money he wanted. Charles tried to raise money by forcing his subjects to make payments to the government. Rich men who would not pay were put in prison, and poor men were sent into the army. When Parliament tried to stop such tactics, Charles dismissed it in 1629 and ruled alone for the next eleven years. Greatly in need of money to put down a Scottish rebellion, Charles finally recalled Parliament in 1640. Its members refused to vote any money unless Charles agreed that Parliament must meet at least once every three years and the king could not levy taxes without Parliament's consent.

Charles did not want to give up any of his power. In 1642, he led a band of soldiers into the House of Commons and arrested five of its leaders. Civil war began.

Charles's wartime supporters, called Cavaliers, included most of the nobles and large landowners. The men of Parliament and supporters of the Puritans were called Roundheads because they cut their hair short. Oliver Cromwell, a devout Puritan, became the leader of the Roundheads. After four years of fighting, Cromwell's army won, and the king surrendered. In 1649, Parliament had Charles I beheaded.

Parliament's power grew and political parties developed. Parliament then declared England to be a Commonwealth, and Cromwell eventually took control of the government. In 1653, he ended Parliament and became Lord Protector. Continuing arguments between the wartime factions forced Cromwell to rule as a strict Puritan and military dictator, although he believed in more freedom than the Puritans would allow.

When Cromwell died in 1658, no one was strong enough to replace him. By then, too,

Oliver Cromwell as Lord Protector of England

most English people were fed up with strict Puritanism. In 1660, Charles's son, an exile in France, became king by agreeing to share power with Parliament.

Charles II was a clever, fun-loving king. His subjects called him the Merry Monarch. His 25-year reign was known as the Restoration, for that is when the monarchy was restored. Since Charles had no legal heirs, his legitimate successor was his brother James, a strong Roman Catholic who believed in the divine right of kings.

A group in Parliament called Whigs tried to keep James off the throne. Whig supporters were the strongly Protestant middle class and merchants of London, as well as the upper nobility who saw a chance to become stronger under a weak king. Opposing the Whigs were the Tories (tôr'ēz). Tory supporters were lower nobility and gentry who did not trust the London merchants and were loyal to the king. When Charles died, James became king.

The Glorious Revolution confirmed the power of Parliament. James II wanted more authority for himself and for the Catholic Church. Thus, he soon angered almost everyone, including the Tories. In 1688, when the king's wife bore a son, Tories and Whigs, afraid of a long line of Catholic kings, offered the crown to James's older daughter Mary, wife of William III of Orange, the Dutch ruler and a strong Protestant. In November, 1688, William and Mary landed in England at the head of a large army. James escaped to France, and William and Mary became the new rulers of England and Scotland. This new show of parliamentary power is known as the Glorious Revolution.

Parliament passed several important measures, usually called the Revolution Settlement. One, the Bill of Rights of 1689, guaranteed freedom of speech in Parliament, which would meet more often. Further, the king could not interfere with the election of its members. The people gained the right to petition, that is, ask the help of, the government. Excessive bail was not allowed. And no army could be raised without Parliament's consent. Another part of the Revolution Settlement was the Toleration Act. It gave religious freedom to some Protestant groups. A third measure, the Act of Settlement of 1701, said that no Catholic could rule England.

In making the king subordinate to Parliament, the Glorious Revolution was a great victory for the principles of parliamentary government and the rule of law. But it was a limited victory. Since members of Commons received no pay, only landowners with large incomes could serve.

Cabinet government developed under a new royal line. The last of the reigning Stuarts, Anne, died in 1714, leaving no heirs. The Act of Settlement had said that the monarch's closest Protestant relative would take the throne. Thus, a German second cousin became George I of England and began the Hanoverian dynasty. He spoke no English and spent much time in Germany.

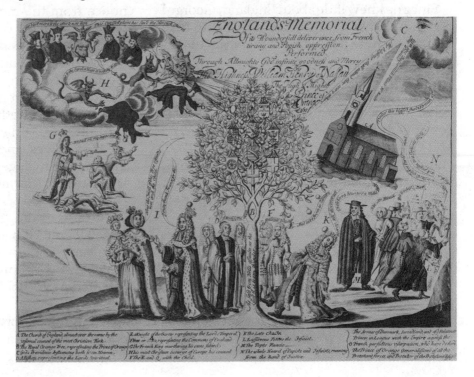

In this anti-Catholic cartoon about the Glorious Revolution, the orange tree stands for William of Orange, the new ruler. Fruit from the tree is knocking the crown off James II and is felling one of his officials.

Her devotion to church and state in a nation recently divided made Queen Anne very popular.

Since he knew little about England, George I depended on a group called a *cabinet* to help him rule. These people were members of Parliament, mostly ministers in charge of government departments. During George I's reign, the cabinet began to make policy.

For half a century after 1714, the Whigs controlled the House of Commons. George I and George II, who ruled from 1727 to 1760, chose their ministers from the Whig party. Robert Walpole, head of the party from 1721 to 1742, served as the principal minister—a position later called *prime minister*.

Walpole always chose his cabinet members from the Whig party to be sure his policies would be supported in the House of Commons. When he lost support in Commons in 1742, he resigned as prime minister. Since then, British prime ministers and cabinets have been drawn from the majority party in Parliament.

section review 1

1. What were two serious conflicts between James I and Charles I and their English subjects?

2. Why did the English bring back the monarchy after Oliver Cromwell died?

3. Why did Parliament force James II to give up his throne? How did the Glorious Revolution show Parliament's strength?

4. How did a German come to be king of England? What were the powers of the cabinet and prime minister?

2 North American colonies fought for independence

While England was dealing with its troubles at home, its colonies in North America were growing and prospering. For over a century after Jamestown was founded in 1607, the colonists went their own ways with little notice from the mother country.

The colonies and England grew apart. Many colonists had left Europe to escape religious persecution, debts, or to find jobs. Settlers came from England, Scotland, Germany, the Netherlands, France, and Ireland. In the colonies, people depended more on themselves and less on inherited social place and privileges. They were proud to be independent farmers, artisans, and merchants.

The American colonists also enjoyed a large degree of self-government. Every colony had its own representative assembly, which could put pressure on the governor by threatening to hold back money.

The English tightened their control. For many years, England did little to regulate the North American colonies. But in 1763, after

As the process of building a new nation continued, 39 delegates to the American Constitutional Convention signed the document on September 17, 1787, in Philadelphia.

England defeated France in a worldwide struggle for empire, the English government began a new policy.

The colonists in North America had done little in the war on their continent. It was won largely with British troops, ships, and taxes. British troops also protected the colonists against Indians. England reasoned that the colonists should share the costs. So England enforced old laws and passed new ones to raise money.

Between 1765 and 1774, the colonists strongly opposed every effort to make them pay more taxes. In 1774, to teach the colonists a lesson, the British Parliament passed the so-called Intolerable Acts. These acts closed Boston harbor to shipping, which meant economic ruin, and took back the charter of Massachusetts, which ended local self-government. The dispute had been about taxation; now it was about the right to self-government.

American colonists won their freedom. Fighting started in April, 1775. At first, only a few colonists wanted full independence. As fighting went on, however, feelings grew stronger because the British government seemed unwilling to give in at all. Finally, on July 4, 1776, representatives of the colonies signed the Declaration of Independence.

What had begun as an American fight for freedom soon became a worldwide conflict for empire among the European countries. France, Spain, and the Netherlands declared war against England to gain back territories lost in 1763 and earlier. The French fleet and 6,000 troops helped the American colonies win. In 1783, a peace treaty was signed, and England recognized the thirteen colonies as independent. England did not lose any other colonies, however. The English navy, in a striking comeback in the final year of the war, defeated the fleets of France and Spain.

The American Revolution had important results. Independence did not lead immediately to democratic government, but the seeds were well planted. The Revolution ended inherited titles and helped make people equal under the law.

The colonies eventually created a republic of a federal type, that is, a group of separate states, each giving up some governing rights to become united under a central government.

The Americans believed strongly in written constitutions and in limiting the powers of government. Besides the federal Constitution, all thirteen states had written constitutions that separated legislative, executive, and judicial powers, and included a bill of rights.

The American colonists' revolt became a symbol and source of inspiration to all peoples seeking freedom, especially in Latin America.

section review 2

1. Name three ways that life in the North American colonies was different from life in England.

2. Name three actions of the English government that caused the colonists to declare their independence.

3. How did the American struggle for independence become a European conflict for empire?

4. What were four results of the American Revolution? Describe the new kind of government set up by the Americans.

3 The French Revolution changed society and government

The success of the American Revolution encouraged French people who wanted far-reaching changes in their own nation. Discontent there had been growing for a long time.

Inequality bred discontent. French society was still divided along feudal lines. Every person belonged to one of three classes, or "estates." In the *First Estate* was the clergy, the *Second Estate* was the nobility, and the *Third Estate* included everyone else. Within this society, called the Old Regime, the estate decided a person's status, civil rights, and privileges. The clergy and the nobility were each less than one percent of the population. But the clergy owned ten percent of the land, and the nobility had all the best posts in the government and army.

The Third Estate was itself divided into three groups. On the top level were the bourgeoisie—lawyers, doctors, merchants, and business people. Below the bourgeoisie was a small group of city wage earners—skilled artisans, servants, and laborers. Some of them were near starving and could become a violent mob.

Over eighty percent of the French people were peasants, the largest part of the Third Estate. Although they owned forty percent of the land and serfdom had almost disappeared, they still had to pay certain feudal dues, which they saw as unfair.

Weak kings failed to reform taxes. The greatest single problem France faced was the unfair tax system. The First and Second Estates were excused from most taxes by law. The heaviest burden, then, fell on the peasants, who had the least money.

Louis XV, who ruled from 1715 to 1774, was not a strong leader. He knew about the unrest among the people, but comfortably settled at Versailles, he seemed not to care.

Louis XVI, who was only twenty when he became king in 1774, really wanted to govern well. However, he had neither a forceful personality nor will power, and was afraid to stand up to important people he dealt with.

France neared bankruptcy. During Louis XVI's reign, the French government soon neared bankruptcy. Three-fourths of the total budget was marked for military business and payments on the public debt.

Louis XIV's greatest creations were the Palace and park at Versailles, 12 miles (19 kilometers) southwest of Paris. After three centuries and four revolutions, Versailles is still a great wonder of the world.

Louis's purpose was to create the most splendid palace in Europe. To do this, he employed 36,000 workers for nearly 50 years. Finally, in 1682, some 21 years after construction had begun, Louis made Versailles his royal residence and thus the seat of French government.

The actual Palace of Versailles contains hundreds of rooms and is more than a half mile (0.8 kilometers) long. It is symmetrical in design and done in French Baroque style. Within the lavish central section are the royal apartments of the king and queen. These are separated by the Hall of Mirrors. It is decorated with marble, paintings, gilded statues, and 483 mirrors. The south wing of the palace contains the Hall of Battles with busts of more than 80 heroes who died for France. In the window openings are painted the names of ordinary soldiers who died for France and the battles in which they fell.

Among the most fabulous Versailles attractions are the fountains and waterworks of the parks. Because of the scarcity of water at Versailles, a system had to be devised to divert water from relatively distant rivers. Vast sums of money were spent and many lives were lost before a workable system was created. Extending westward from the Palace is a broad avenue of grass with trees on either side. The grass ends at the Grand Canal, which is a mile (1.6 kilometers) long and 200 feet (60 meters) wide. In Louis's day, it was covered with Venetian gondolas and other boats. The avenue leading northward from the Palace terrace has 22 groups of fountain statues. Each group has three children holding a marble basin from which a jet of water rises.

Beyond the present park, but within that of Louis XIV are two smaller palaces, the Grand Trianon and the Petit Trianon. Louis XIV used the Grand Trianon as a retreat, a place where he could get away from the strict court etiquette he imposed on Versailles. Today, this is a museum of state carriages. The Petit Trianon became a favorite spot for Marie Antoinette. She gave it a rustic aura and played there at being a shepherdess as was then in fashion.

Although most of the original Palace furniture has been lost, the glory of the buildings and parks of Versailles lives on. Today, they are all a national museum of France. Louis wanted to create a spot that would impress the world with its splendor. In this he succeeded.

The Fountain of Apollo, *near right,* is one of the most fabulous at Versailles. The Palace rises in the background. The fountain still works, but it uses more than a million gallons of water an hour, so today it is turned on only for special occasions. At *far right* is Napoleon's bedroom in the Grand Trianon. The patterns in the room were designed by the Empress Josephine.

In the late 1770s and in the 1780s, government officials tried to solve the money crisis by taxing the wealthy classes. They failed, however, because the nobility said new taxes could be approved only by the Estates-General. The Estates-General, made up of representatives from each of the three estates, had not met since 1614. Unable to collect taxes or borrow money, Louis agreed to have the Estates-General meet in 1789.

Conflicts between the Estates-General and the king led to revolution. The first meeting of the Estates-General in 175 years could not agree on a method of counting votes, the Third Estate wanting to be counted equally with the other two groups. After weeks of arguing, the Third Estate (bourgeoisie) declared itself a National Assembly. The members met on an indoor tennis court, where they swore to write a new constitution for France. Their "Tennis Court Oath" was the first act of revolution, for the Third Estate had no legal right to be a lawmaking body.

Meanwhile, the peasants and the workers suffered from bad harvests and depression. Food was scarce, prices were high, and unemployment was widespread. When the king threatened the Assembly, crowds in Paris started to look for weapons. On July 14, the crowd stormed the Bastille [ba stēl'], a prison that was a hated symbol of absolutism. Then they marched on the Town Hall, murdered the mayor of Paris, and set up a new city government. The king, who was then at Versailles, accepted the new government and ordered his troops to leave Paris.

In the countryside, the peasants thought the nobles would attack them. They refused to pay taxes, attacked the nobles' manor houses, destroyed the records of feudal dues, and burned manors to the ground.

The National Assembly set up a constitutional monarchy. The National Assembly was alarmed by the spreading disorder. On August 4, it boldly ended feudalism. The Assembly then started to create a new kind of government for France. For the next two years, it worked on a constitution that would include the principles of liberty, equality, and natural rights. The constitution favored the bourgeoisie. Only men who owned property could be elected to the new Legislative Assembly. The nobility lost all its privileges, and all people were said to be equal before the law. The king could delay new laws, but he could not veto them. The government took over Church lands, and also took control of the clergy. Louis XVI did not like the new constitution, but he had to accept it.

Foreign war led to a "second" revolution. When a Legislative Assembly was elected in October, 1791, France became a constitutional monarchy. This government lasted only eleven months, chiefly because of war with other countries. The revolution alarmed the monarchs of Europe, who feared that the principles of liberty, equality, and natural rights would weaken their own powers. Also, the émigrés, French nobles who had left in 1789, persuaded the kings of Austria and Prussia that it was their royal duty to restore the monarchy in France. The revolutionaries thought they would be attacked. In April, 1792, the Legislative Assembly declared war on Austria

As war fever rose in France, suspicion of the king mounted. In August, 1792, the Assembly suspended the monarchy, put the royal family in prison, and ended its powers. Paris was in panic. In September, a provisional government ordered more than 1,000 royalists executed.

The Legislative Assembly was set aside. A new National Constitutional Convention, elected on the basis of universal male suffrage, was to draw up a more democratic constitution. War hysteria and the people's dislike of the 1791 constitution had caused the uprising in August, 1792, and the September Massacre. Together, they were a "second" revolution.

France became a republic. Beginning in September, 1792, France was ruled by the National Constitutional Convention, usually called the Convention. It declared France a republic and stated that it would spread the ideas of "liberty, equality, and fraternity" over Europe. French armies swarmed over the Austrian Netherlands (Belgium) and the area south of the Rhine. By 1793, France was at war with almost all of Europe.

As the war went on, the revolution in France became more extreme. In January, 1793, Louis XVI went to the *guillotine* [gil'ə-tēn'], the dreadful machine that had beheaded so many people during the revolution.

The situation in 1793 was bad. Food was scarce, and prices were high. In the west, conservative peasants rebelled against the Convention. In June, 1793, a Parisian mob entered the Convention and seized the moderate leaders. Then the extreme radicals took over.

Radicals started a Reign of Terror. The Convention elected twelve members to be a Committee of Public Safety led by Maximilien de Robespierre [rōbz'pyer], a young lawyer. To stop any possible counterrevolution, the Committee started a Reign of Terror.

Between August, 1793, and July, 1794, more than 40 thousand persons were executed. The queen, Marie Antoinette, was among the first, and the moderates soon followed. Thousands of others, regardless of class, were put in prisons.

Meanwhile, the war had to be won. The Committee started a program of price controls and also began a national draft. These programs were the first attempt in modern times to bring together all the resources of a country for war. By the spring of 1794, France had the largest army in Europe.

The French Revolution turned the old order upside down. Louis XIV was executed in a public square in Paris on January 21, 1793. Marie Antoinette was similarly beheaded on October 16 of that same year.

Unlike others, it was a citizen army with a strong feeling for its country.

By summer 1794, this citizen army, whose leaders were young officers just up from the lower ranks, won several battles. Although the war lasted until 1797, the country was saved. The harsh rule of the Committee of Public Safety no longer had a purpose. In July, 1794, Robespierre and his followers went to the guillotine. The Reign of Terror ended.

Conservatives set up the Directory. The bourgeoisie were in power again, and they wanted to return to a moderate republic. In October, 1794, a new constitution ended the Convention, and set up a government known as the Directory. In the new government, a two-house legislature was responsible for electing a governing body of five men called directors. However, the Directory became corrupt and inefficient, and seemed unable to solve the country's problems. The time was ripe for a strong leader to seize power.

1. Describe the class structure of the Old Regime. What groups belonged to each estate, and what percentage of the total population made up each estate?

2. How was the National Assembly formed? Why was this an act of revolution?

3. What were the causes of the "second" French Revolution?

4. What was the purpose of the Reign of Terror? What did the Committee of Public Safety accomplish?

4 Napoleon became ruler of France

A strong leader appeared—Napoleon Bonaparte [nə pō′lē ən bō′nə pärt]—a lieutenant of artillery in Louis XVI's army. Because he belonged to the lesser nobility, Napoleon could not have hoped to rise much higher. But the revolution opened the door to fame and power.

By 1797, Napoleon was leading the French army in northern Italy. After several brilliant victories there, he crushed the Austrians. He was only twenty-eight years old and already a hero.

Napoleon's ambition had no limits. Well aware of the growing dislike for the Directory, he waited for an opportunity to seize power. Meanwhile, he thought of a bold plan to hurt England by taking Egypt and then striking at India. Napoleon landed in Egypt in 1798, but the English fleet destroyed his transport ships and cut off his army.

Napoleon returned to France and made his Egyptian defeat seem a great triumph. Many people saw him as France's savior. He and his followers moved quickly and overthrew the Directory by force on November 9, 1799.

Napoleon became a dictator. The new ruler of France had a sharp mind and a remarkable ability to understand problems and make quick decisions. Napoleon had read deeply in history and law as well as military science. People were dazzled by his qualities.

Although he rose from the revolution, Napoleon planned to rule as a dictator. The new constitution included a legislature and three consuls. But as First Consul, Napoleon had all the real power and claimed to represent the interests of the whole country. Napoleon then turned to military affairs. He forced Austria to make peace in 1801. And in 1802, England and France made peace.

In his first five years as ruler, Napoleon carried out several important reforms in France. He increased the power and efficiency of the national government. He offered a stable life and order in France to all willing to work for him—royalists and republicans alike.

In many ways, Napoleon finished the work of the revolution. No privileges were allowed, promotion in government or the army was based on proven ability, and the tax system was reformed. Probably Napoleon's best known work was in modernizing French law. The *Code Napoleon* firmly set forth the principle of equality before the law.

One of Napoleon's important acts was to end the Holy Roman Empire. Made up of hundreds of small and large states, it had no real power. Napoleon changed it to the Confederation of the Rhine. A group of only 38 states, it was under Napoleon's protection. The Confederation was the first step toward the making of a unified German nation. Napoleon savagely put down all opposition. But even without political liberty and true representative government, the people liked him because he could offer order, stability, and efficiency. In 1804, he had himself

On December 2, 1804, Napoleon, in imitation of Pepin, placed the crown of France on his own head. He then turned and crowned Josephine, his wife, as empress. The ceremony, at the Cathedral of Notre Dame in Paris, was consecrated by Pope Pius VII. Napoleon commissioned painter Louis David to portray the event.

crowned Napoleon I, Emperor of the French.

Napoleon made himself master of Europe. Napoleon ruled France for fifteen years— five years as First Consul and ten as emperor. Driven by his ambition to rule all of Europe, he spent fourteen of those years at war. By 1805, a group of countries including Britain, Austria, and Russia had allied against France. Napoleon defeated the Austrian and Russian armies with amazing speed.

Only England with its navy continued to fight the emperor. In 1805, Lord Horatio Nelson defeated the combined French and Spanish fleets in the Battle of Trafalgar. That victory proved British naval supremacy and protected England from invasion.

From 1806 to 1812, Napoleon controlled most of the continent. Since he could not defeat the British navy, he decided to wreck England in economic warfare. He declared all of Europe closed to British goods, and even Russia agreed to the plan. However, Napoleon's policy failed. The biggest reason was that the British found other markets, chiefly in Latin America.

To control ports on the Iberian peninsula, Napoleon invaded Portugal, placed his brother Joseph on the Spanish throne, and stationed a French army in Spain. The Spanish people fought back. The English

NAPOLEON'S EMPIRE, 1810

MAP LESSON

SWEDEN

NORWAY
AND
DENMARK

UNITED KINGDOM
OF GREAT BRITAIN
AND IRELAND

North Sea

Baltic Sea

MOSCOW ✕

R U S S I A N

E M P I R E

PRUSSIA

London •

KINGDOM
OF
WESTPHALIA

• Berlin

GRAND DUCHY
OF WARSAW

WATERLOO ✕

LEIPZIG ✕

ATLANTIC
OCEAN

Paris
Versailles • •

CONFEDERATION

OF THE

RHINE

AUSTRIAN

Vienna •

FRENCH

SWITZERLAND

EMPIRE

KINGDOM

EMPIRE

Oporto •

OF

ILLYRIAN
PROVINCES

LUCCA

ITALY

Black Sea

Lisbon •

Madrid •

KINGDOM
OF
SPAIN

CORSICA

ELBA

Rome •

O
T
T
O
M
A
N

• Istanbul

KINGDOM
OF
NAPLES

TRAFALGAR ✕

KINGDOM
OF
SARDINIA

Naples •

KINGDOM
OF
NAPLES

E M P I R E

Mediterranean

Sea

KINGDOM
OF SICILY

N

Napoleon's Empire

Subject to Napoleon

Allied to Napoleon

✕   Battles

0   200   400 MILES
0   200   400 KILOMETERS

■ MAP LESSON 24: NAPOLEON'S EMPIRE, 1810

1. This map uses colors to symbolize political alliances in Europe. What color indicates the area that made up Napoleon's Empire?

2. What major Mediterranean island is shown as being part of Napoleon's Empire?

3. What major city on the Italian peninsula was part of Napoleon's Empire?

4. Orange shows areas that were allied to Napoleon. What areas were these?

5. What color does this map use to stand for areas that were subject to Napoleon's control?

6. This map also shows the sites of some of Napoleon's important battles. What symbol is used to indicate these battles?

7. Different maps are made to show different kinds of information. Study this

map to determine what information it does show and what it does not. Then decide which of the following statements are true and which are false:

a. This map shows the area that was called the French Empire.

b. This map shows that Norway and Denmark became allied with Napoleon before Prussia did.

c. This map shows that the Kingdom of Spain and the Grand Duchy of Warsaw had similar relationships with Napoleon.

d. This map shows the years in which some important battles were fought.

e. This map shows that by 1810 Napoleon had some control over more than half of Europe.

f. This map shows that Napoleon had more control over the Illyrian Provinces than over Switzerland.

took advantage of this revolt, invaded Portugal and then Spain, and by 1813 had driven the French army back into France.

European powers joined forces to defeat Napoleon. People in the French-controlled nations were angered by Napoleon's demand that they give him money and soldiers. Also, Napoleon's economic blockade caused shortages of manufactured goods from Britain that French factories could not supply. Most important, patriotic feeling against the hated French arose in all the countries.

In 1812, Napoleon decided to crush Russia. The loss of trade with Britain had seriously hurt the Russian economy, and Tsar Alexander I had begun trade again in 1810. An angry Napoleon gathered a huge army of more than 500 thousand men and entered Russia in the summer of 1812. He won several battles, but he could not destroy the Russian army. In September, he reached Moscow, which the Russians had evacuated. Within a few days, fire broke out and destroyed most of the city. After five weeks,

On June 18, 1815, the Duke of Wellington defeated Napoleon at Waterloo. This red chalk sketch of Wellington as leader of the troops of the allies was done from life by Francisco Goya in 1812.

Napoleon ordered a retreat. Then the cruel Russian winter set in. Only 30 thousand of his army returned to France alive. The rest died in battles, blizzards, and snowdrifts.

This blow to Napoleon's power finished him. From all directions, enemies struck at the French tyrant—Russians, Prussians, Spaniards, English, Austrians, Italians. Napoleon's empire crumbled in 1814. He was sent to the island of Elba off the coast of Italy. But he escaped and for 100 days was emperor again.

Napoleon's return united the allies. They defeated him in a battle at the little Belgian village of Waterloo in 1815. Then they put him on the lonely south Atlantic island of St. Helena, where in 1821 he died.

French reform influenced other nations. Napoleon's soldiers and officials spread the ideas and reforms of the French Revolution throughout Europe. In all of the countries the French conquered, constitutions were drawn up. Feudalism, the manorial system, and medieval guilds were wiped out. The Napoleonic codes, which stressed equality before the law, directed the courts.

Church lands were seized, and the Church came under the state. Religious freedom for non-Catholics became the law. Taxes were reformed, and the metric system of weights and measures was used. Even after Napoleon was gone, most of these reforms remained.

section review 4

1. What reforms did Napoleon make in his first five years as ruler of France?

2. What was the purpose of the economic blockade of Britain? Why did it fail?

3. What events led to Napoleon's exile?

4. Name six reforms that the French made in European governments.

5 Latin American colonies became independent nations

The Age of Democratic Revolutions also affected the Latin American colonies. In the 300 years that Spain and Portugal had ruled Latin America, a new civilization had arisen. But many wrongs had grown along with it.

Discontent grew among the creoles. One wrong, the colonists thought, lay in the restrictions Spain placed on trade and manufactured goods. Another arose from Latin American society itself. Classes based on birth and background were very important.

At the top were the Spanish-born officials, the peninsulares [pā nēn′sü la′rās], who held all the important political and military posts. Below them, the colonial-born white aristocracy, the creoles [krē′ōlz], lived like feudal nobles on the income from their lands. At the bottom were millions of Indians, blacks, and mixed peoples—mestizos (white and Indian) and mulattoes (white and black). Most of them lived like serfs or slaves. They did all the hard labor, which to the aristocracy was degrading.

The creoles wanted to control their own affairs, but colonial rule placed all power in the hands of the peninsulares. Wealthy and well educated, many creoles knew the works of Locke, Voltaire, and Rousseau and the political ideas of the Enlightenment.

In the 1780s, encouraged by the North American example, colonists rebelled in Peru, Colombia, Ecuador, and Venezuela. One reason they failed was that unlike the North Americans whom France helped, Latin Americans fought alone. The only successful uprising in the 18th century was that on the western side of the island of Hispaniola. There, in 1794, Pierre Dominique Toussaint l'Ouverture [tü saɴ′ lü ver tʏr′], a freed black slave, led a rebellion against the

Pierre Dominique Toussaint l'Ouverture

French. Toussaint was captured, but his successor led the Haitians to independence in 1803.

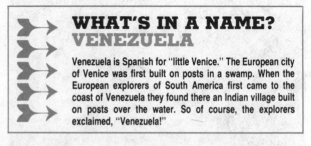

WHAT'S IN A NAME?
VENEZUELA

Venezuela is Spanish for "little Venice." The European city of Venice was first built on posts in a swamp. When the European explorers of South America first came to the coast of Venezuela they found there an Indian village built on posts over the water. So of course, the explorers exclaimed, "Venezuela!"

Successful revolts freed South America. When Napoleon took control of the Spanish government in 1808, the Spanish American colonists would not accept the new French regime. Revolts broke out all over the empire from Mexico to Argentina. The Spanish king returned to the throne in 1814 determined to bring back Spanish control, but the drive toward freedom had already gone too far.

The greatest leader was Simón Bolívar [bō lē'vär], called "the Liberator" and "the Washington of South America." Born in 1783, Bolívar fought for more than 20 years to win freedom for what became Venezuela, Colombia, Panama, Bolivia, and Ecuador.

Another hero, José de San Martín [sän' mär tēn'] was fighting in Spain against the French in 1811 when he learned that Buenos Aires had revolted. He went home and led armies against the Spanish in Argentina and Chile.

In 1821, San Martín entered Lima. There, he and Bolívar talked about how best to drive the Spanish from the rest of Peru. They disagreed, and San Martín unselfishly turned his army over to Bolívar and went to France. By 1826, Bolívar and others like him, inspired by the United States of North America, dreamed of a kind of united states for all of Spanish America. Their dream never came true.

Foreign powers held interests in Latin America. After Napoleon was defeated in 1814, the big powers of Europe began to worry about the Spanish American revolts. Most European nations wanted to either return the colonies to Spain or take over control themselves. But the United States and Great Britain opposed both ideas.

The British favored a joint declaration to warn Europeans to stay away from America. But United States President James Monroe acted alone and issued the Monroe Doctrine in 1823. Monroe warned that the United States would not allow any European country to enter the affairs of the Western Hemisphere. Europe accepted this warning, knowing the British navy would back it up.

Benito and Margarita Juarez

Mexico fought to win and keep its freedom. In Mexico in 1810, Father Miguel Hidalgo led Indians and mestizos in revolt against the Spanish. Although he soon died, his movement grew under a lieutenant, Father José Morelos. The group took several cities, and in 1813 Morelos called a congress that declared Mexico free. He was captured and shot, but in 1824 Mexico became a republic.

In the years that followed, many people fought to rule Mexico. In 1834, Antonio Lopez de Santa Anna made himself ruler. While he ruled, Mexico lost half its land to the United Sates in the Mexican War (1846–1848).

Mexicans who wanted reforms grew strong during the 1850s, and in 1861 their leader, Benito Juárez [hwär'es], an Indian, became president. He wanted the Church to give up some land and the army officers to give up some privileges. Many upper-class creoles became alarmed, and civil war broke out. To pay for the war, Mexico borrowed large sums of money in Europe, but it could not repay the debts. So in 1862, France sent troops to take over the country. The French ruled Mexico until 1867, when they were overthrown. Juárez again became president. Once more, he tried to carry out such reforms as democratic elections and free compulsory education, but lack of money held him back. He died in 1872. The next ruler was Porfirio Díaz, a mestizo army general, whose dictatorship lasted until 1911.

Brazil gained its freedom peacefully. When Napoleon's troops entered Portugal in 1807, the Portuguese royal family fled to Brazil, which became the seat of the Portuguese Empire. Soon afterward, the king made Brazil a self-governing dominion. When he went back to Portugal in 1821, his son Dom Pedro, who had stayed to rule Brazil, made the country an independent empire.

When the slaves were freed in 1888 without compensation to their owners, the Brazilians were angry. In 1889, they forced the emperor to step down and then set up a federal republic.

Internal problems slowed progress. The Creoles who led revolts in South America were more interested in power for themselves than in any real change in the social or political system. So the pattern of life did not change, especially for the lower classes.

Since Spain and Portugal had not allowed self-government in their colonies, the people had no political training. Very few Latin American republics were able to keep stable democratic governments. Many had corrupt dictatorships.

Sectional, racial, and class divisions made more government problems. At the time of independence, four-fifths of the people were poor, uneducated Indians, blacks, mestizos, and mulattoes. Many knew neither Spanish

LATIN AMERICAN NATIONS, 1830

nor Portuguese. And jealousy and distrust made cooperation among themselves and with the creoles and peninsulares almost impossible.

section review 5

1. What event gave the Latin Americans the chance to rebel against their governments?

2. What was the Monroe Doctrine?

3. Describe the different ways in which Mexico and Brazil each gained its independence.

4. Give three or more reasons Latin America did not set up stable democratic governments after independence.

Section Summaries

1. Parliament triumphed in Britain. In England, trouble began when the Stuarts came to the throne. Their challenge to the power of Parliament and Puritanism led to civil war. Oliver Cromwell brought victory to Parliamentary forces, and the king was executed in 1649. Cromwell became Lord Protector, but when he died the monarchy returned. Mistrust of the Stuart kings rose again, and in the Glorious Revolution of 1688 the crown was given to the Protestant William and Mary. Parliament made it clear that from then on the English ruler was the representative of a strictly limited monarchy. In the next fifty years, the development of a new kind of executive and the cabinet system were England's contribution to the concept of democratic government.

2. North American colonies fought for independence. Meanwhile, England's North American colonies refused to pay more taxes for their defense and wanted more home rule. Tempers rose, and fighting started in 1775. A year later, the colonists declared their independence, and with the help of France and other European countries, the Americans won their freedom. The Americans set up a constitutional republic that became an example for others.

3. The French Revolution changed society and government. One of the countries that followed America's lead was France. There, anger grew over the inequalities of the class system and the way of taxing, which was causing bankruptcy. When King Louis XVI called a meeting of the Estates-General in 1789, it made itself the National Assembly and drew up a new constitution for a limited monarchy. But foreign war led to a more radical government, the killing of the king, and a Reign of Terror in France.

4. Napoleon became ruler of France. France began to win the war, and the Terror ended. But the weak government allowed Napoleon Bonaparte to take power. Napoleon made himself dictator of France. He also brought together many of the revolutionary reforms in France. His military victories made a large European empire. But by 1814, the combined attacks of the other European powers had broken it. However, Napoleon's most important legacy was the spread of certain ideas of the French Revolution throughout Europe.

5. Latin American colonies became independent nations. The overseas empires of Spain and Portugal were the oldest and largest of any European country. Although Spain ruled strictly, its New World colonies revolted after Napoleon took Spain and finally won their freedom. Brazil, though, grew slowly and became independent only late in the 19th century. Many internal problems slowed progress in Latin America—unstable governments, class and racial divisions, illiteracy, and poverty.

Who? What? When? Where?

1. Put these events in chronological order, beginning with the earliest:

    a. Napoleon overthrew the Directory.
    b. The Monroe Doctrine was issued.
    c. A mob stormed the Bastille.
    d. England had the Glorious Revolution.
    e. Juárez became president of Mexico.
    f. Napoleon lost at Waterloo.

2. Write a sentence for each of the following people that tells what country each belonged to and what role he or she played in his or her country's revolution:

    a. Napoleon Bonaparte
    b. Oliver Cromwell
    c. Louis XVI
    d. San Martín
    e. Toussaint l'Ouverture
    f. Dom Pedro
    g. Robespierre
    h. William and Mary

3. Define each of these terms by describing its importance to the French Revolution:

    a. Bastille
    b. citizen army
    c. Committee of Public Safety
    d. Directory
    e. Reign of Terror
    f. Tennis Court Oath

Questions for Critical Thinking

1. In what ways can Napoleon Bonaparte be considered a "Son of the French Revolution"?

2. Why were the ideas of Locke, Voltaire, and Rousseau important in the independence movements of Latin America? How were they important in the French and American revolutions?

3. To what extent did the revolutions studied in this chapter succeed or fail in accomplishing what the revolutionaries set out to do?

4. Why did the colonists' success in winning the American Revolution have much to do with independence movements of other peoples?

Skill Activities

1. Read *Napoleon* by Herbert Butterfield to learn more about this famous ruler. (Macmillan, 1962)

2. Discuss the causes of the revolutions studied in this chapter. How might the rulers have prevented violence?

3. Revolutions inspire songs. "Yankee Doodle" came out of the American Revolution. The musical "1776" deals with the Declaration of Independence. The musical "Marat Sade" has many songs that express the anger of the French city mob before the French Revolution. Use the library to find other revolutionary songs from a revolution discussed in this chapter.

4. Based on this chapter, pretend you are a citizen of one of the countries that experienced a revolution. Prepare a political cartoon either for or against the revolution. Display all cartoons on the board and have class members cast ballots indicating (a) which country the revolution took place in and (b) whether the cartoonist was for or against the revolution.

chapter **24** *quiz*

Section 1

1. One thing that did not cause conflict between English rulers and their subjects was: a. religion, b. divine right, c. feudal dues

2. The Glorious Revolution took place when: a. Charles I was beheaded, b. Cromwell became ruler, c. William and Mary came to rule England

Section 2

3. True or false: For a long time, England allowed the American colonists to run their own affairs.

4. The American Revolution might have failed without the help of: a. Ireland, b. France, c. Russia.

Section 3

5. In the Old Regime, most of the people were: a. nobles, b. bourgeoisie, c. peasants and serfs

6. France was declared a republic by the: a. Directory, b. Convention, c. Estates-General

7. Robespierre led the: a. Legislative Assembly, b. Directory, c. Committee of Public Safety

Section 4

8. Napoleon was a member of the: a. lesser nobility, b. bourgeoisie, c. peasants

9. One thing that was not a reform made by Napoleon was: a. fair tax system, b. democratic government, c. improved laws

Section 5

10. The people that most wanted to change the government of Latin America were the: a. priests, b. peninsulares, c. creoles

11. True or false: The revolutions in Latin America established stable democratic governments that brought prosperity to their nations.

12. True or false: Brazil gained its independence through a bloody war that lasted many years and that continued the Portuguese monarchy there into the 20th century.

THE GROWTH OF LIBERALISM, NATIONALISM, AND DEMOCRACY

This engraving shows Europe's statesmen gathered at the Congress of Vienna. The Duke of Wellington is seen in profile at far left. Metternich is standing before an empty chair. The entire meeting in Vienna lasted some 10 months.

It was March, 1848. In an Austrian château not far from Vienna, an old man was alone with his host. Again and again on a violin he played the "Marseillaise," the revolutionary French national anthem. The old man was Prince Metternich, who until a few days before had been one of the most feared and hated men in Europe. Now, after more than

40 years in the role of the Austrian foreign minister, he had lost power because of a bloody uprising in the Austrian capitol of Vienna.

In many ways, the events of 1848 grew from the French revolutionary ideals of liberty, equality, and fraternity. They became known all over Europe and gave rise to three movements: (1) liberalism, which stressed progress and reform; (2) nationalism, which looked to give people of similar culture and traditions their own government; and (3) democracy, which moved toward giving a voice in government to more of the people than a small ruling class.

The political history of 19th-century Europe is mainly the story of how these three movements changed governments in Europe and around the world. It is a story full of struggle. Governments feared radical changes and looked upon liberals, nationalists, and democrats as dangerous radicals. Revolts occurred often. But there were few liberals, nationalists, and democrats in Europe in the early 1800s, and most of the revolts failed.

In the late 1800s, liberalism became strongly influenced by democracy. Democracy, though revolutionary in 1815 and radical in 1848, was by 1914 the most desired form of government. It gained ground fastest in western Europe and slowest in eastern Europe. But wherever people accepted it, political life changed.

The political map of Europe in 1914 was quite different from the map of 1815. Because of nationalism, two new great powers, Germany and Italy, were born. And in some way, liberalism and democracy had brought a role in politics to more people in most countries. This chapter shows how:

1. Governments resisted change.

2. Continental Europe was politically changed.

3. Democracy advanced in western Europe.

4. Reforms came slowly in southern and eastern Europe.

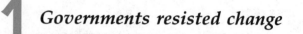

1 Governments resisted change

After Napoleon was defeated, the people of Europe, sick of war, wanted long-term peace and stable lives. To gain these ends, the allies who had won the war met in Vienna for peace talks.

The Congress of Vienna tried to bring stable life. The Congress of Vienna began in September, 1814. The Congress had two chief tasks. First, it had to strike a political balance among the powerful states of Europe. Second, it had to find a way to settle peacefully fights among the great powers. More than twenty years of revolution and war had led to great changes in the map of Europe. The statesmen who met to redraw it faced a very hard task.

There was, first of all, the matter of containing France, which was still considered the main threat to the peace of Europe. Small buffer states were created along its borders.

In Germany, Napoleon had set up the Confederation of the Rhine with thirty-eight states. The Congress turned this into a German confederation with some thirty-nine individual states of which Prussia was the largest.

The Vienna peacemakers knew that no treaty can make a perfectly sure peace. So they tried to find a way to settle disagreements between countries before war started.

In November, 1815, Austria, Russia, Prussia, and Britain set themselves up as a group called the Concert of Europe, which would meet at certain times to guard the Vienna settlement and keep peace. (In 1818, France joined the group.) The Concert of Europe was the first international group to try to deal with European affairs.

Boundary of German Confederation

■ MAP LESSON 25: EUROPE, 1815, AFTER THE CONGRESS OF VIENNA

1. This is a political map. To avoid obscuring the map with too much detail, rivers and mountains are not indicated and some minor states in the German Confederation are not named. How is the area of the German Confederation shown?

2. Europe divides into three general areas on this map. Western Europe is dominated by several kingdoms while Eastern Europe is divided among three large empires. Central Europe is a "shatter belt" of many small states. What three empires dominated Eastern Europe?

3. The United Kingdom in 1815 was really a union of several countries led by

England. Name the two that share the island of Great Britain with England.

4. The Russian Empire included two countries which are indicated separately on the map with the label "to Russia." What are these two countries?

5. In 1815, Belgium belonged to the Netherlands. A few years later, Belgium declared its independence. Note how this is indicated on the map. In which year did Belgium become a free and independent country?

6. A part of the Ottoman empire became independent in 1829. This is shown on the map in the same way as the independence of Belgium. What nation did this area become?

465

Discontent with the reign of Louis Philippe led to the 1848 revolutions in France. The revolutions produced some of the most bitter fighting France had ever seen. In this painting, government troops are storming the barricades in Paris during the bloody "June Days."

The Great Powers opposed liberalism and nationalism. After 1815, liberalism and nationalism became dangerous to the peace made at Vienna. Both movements grew most rapidly in the cities, where the growth of commercial, industrial, and professional classes was fastest. From these city middle classes came leaders and support for liberal programs and nationalistic movements in the 1800s.

Some liberals wanted a monarchy, some a republic. But all agreed on the need for parliaments that spoke for the people. Nineteenth-century liberals did not believe everyone should have a voice in government. However, by seeking to give a vote to every adult male who owned property, they aimed to broaden the base of government. Liberals believed that governments should protect the rights to speak, write, and gather freely for meetings. They believed that all persons should be treated as equals before the law.

Nationalists often favored liberal programs, but their main goal was self-rule. They said that all people who shared a language, customs, and culture had the right to decide their own form of government. To do that, they needed *self-determination*, or, freedom from foreign rule.

Nationalists felt that all true patriots should work for self-rule or for unification of a divided country. For example, nationalists in Hungary wanted freedom from Austrian rule, and German patriots did not like the disunity of the German Confederation.

The men who drew up the Vienna settlement almost completely ignored nationalistic feelings. The stand of the Great Powers was stated publicly by Metternich. He said that the Great Powers could rightly move to put down revolutions. In 1820 and 1821, Austrian troops crushed liberal revolts in Italy. In 1823, French troops ended a revolt in Spain.

Liberalism and nationalism made gains in the 1800s. In 1821, Greek nationalists rose against the Ottoman Turks. In 1827, England, France, and Russia joined the fight to gain Greek freedom from Turkish rule. Outnumbered by better and larger forces, the Turks lost. A peace treaty was signed in 1829, and the next year Greece became independent. The new country caused the first important change in the political map of Europe since the Congress of Vienna.

In France, the Bourbon monarchy had been restored by the victorious Allies in 1814. But feeling was turning against King Charles X because he opposed the constitution. In the general election of 1830, a large number of liberals won. Charles tried to put aside the elections, and revolution broke out. Charles X went into exile in England.

The wealthy middle classes then became leaders in the revolution. The crown was offered to Louis Philippe [lü'ē fə lēp'], Duke of Orleans, who promised to honor the constitution of 1814.

Louis Philippe's reign, called the July Monarchy, was a victory for the liberals. Censorship was ended, and trial by jury was guaranteed. More people were allowed to vote. However, voting was limited to men who owned large amounts of property. The king himself had been a successful businessman in his own right, and he protected private property and helped businesses. Merchants, bankers, and industrialists liked these policies, but radical democrats, who wanted to end property qualifications for voting, felt cheated. They became more and more unhappy with a government that seemed to work only for the wealthy classes.

Revolution also broke out in Belgium, under Dutch rule since 1815. Late in August, 1830, Belgian nationalists and middle-class liberals rose against the Dutch and declared Belgium a free country. The Belgians held national elections and drew up a constitution that was more liberal than any other in Europe at the time.

In 1831, all five Great Powers (Russia, Prussia, Austria, Britain, and France) signed the Treaty of London. It accepted Belgian independence and stated that Belgium must always remain neutral. The treaty was not fully in force until 1839, when the Dutch signed it.

Great Britain was the only major western European country to escape violent revolution in the 1830s. However, two important changes were made when Parliament passed the Reform Bill of 1832.

First, the amount of property a man needed in order to vote was lowered. Thus, the number of voters grew by over fifty percent. Second, the voting districts for the House of Commons were changed to give a voice to the new industrial towns. Political power no longer belonged only to the large landowners. From 1832 on, power was divided among members of the upper middle class—merchants, manufacturers, and business and professional people.

British reformers made some gains. In Britain, many working people remained unhappy. They felt cheated politically by the 1832 Reform Bill, which did not give them the right to vote. The factory owners kept

Demonstrations of this kind helped bring about repeal of the Corn Laws in 1846.

wages low, would not allow strikes, and tried to stop social legislation. Two movements drew much working-class support.

One, the Anti-Corn Law League, wanted to remove the protective tariffs on imported grain that kept the price of bread high. The League was well run and had money. Its cause was aided by failing businesses and crops in the mid-1840s.

Under pressure, Parliament ended the Corn Laws in 1846. This marked a turning point of political power in England. For the first time the middle and working classes won over the land-owning upper class.

Another reform movement, known as Chartism, took its name from the People's Charter (or petition) of 1838. It called for broad reforms. These included universal male suffrage, the secret ballot, and an end to the need to own property in order to hold seats in the House of Commons. Between 1838 and 1848, the chartists sent the House of Commons three petitions signed by millions. All three were turned down. But the movement was strong, and within fifty years, the reforms became law.

Revolutions shocked Europe in 1848. The rumblings of the 1830s furthered the liberal cause. However, only in western Europe, west of the Rhine River, did industrialism and liberalism grow rapidly. East of the river, feudalism and autocracy changed little. However, both sides of the imaginary line had many discontented groups.

In western Europe, especially in Britain and France, the bourgeoisie enjoyed a kind of golden age. The lower classes had no political power, and the middle-class governments would not pass laws to help them. To the east, the major unhappy groups were nationalists and liberals. The desire for unification grew stronger in Germany and Italy. In the huge Austrian Empire, Czechs, Magyars, and Croats all wanted freedom from

German control. Liberals, put down in 1820 and again in 1830, still wanted constitutional, representative government, civil liberties, and an end to serfdom.

In the mid-1840s, a business depression caused a great loss of jobs in the area from Britain to Silesia. Also, potatoes and wheat—those staple foods of the lower classes—were scarce, and prices were high. Potato blights swept across Europe from Poland to Ireland in 1845 and 1846. In 1846, the grain crops also failed, and famine was widespread. Economic distress, then, joined political discontent to cause a wave of revolutions in 1848.

The major powers in these revolts were France, Austria, Prussia, and the states of the German Confederation. In France, the king was removed, and a constitutional republic in which all adult males could vote was set up. Prince Louis Napoleon, nephew of Napoleon Bonaparte, was elected president in December, 1848. All other revolutions failed. Liberals and nationalists could not agree, and armies loyal to the monarchies put down the uprisings. The only gains were in the Austrian Empire, where liberals won an end to serfdom and in 1867 Hungarian nationals got self-government. From then on, the empire was called the Austro-Hungarian Empire.

section review 1

1. What steps did the Congress of Vienna take to protect the balance of power in Europe? How did the Concert of Europe hope to keep the peace?

2. What were the main goals of liberals and nationalists in the 19th century?

3. Describe the changes in government that took place in France, Belgium, and Britain in the 1830s.

4. What were two reasons that revolutions failed in 1848?

2 Continental Europe was politically changed

Although the 1848 revolutions tore almost all of Europe apart, the major countries did not war with one another. However, the revolutions brought forward a new kind of politician and state leader. These people were willing to use any way, even force, to push their national interests. This new spirit, known as *Realpolitik*, led to changes in Europe.

The Crimean War had important results. The new spirit of Realpolitik can be seen in the Crimean War. The first big armed clash in Europe after 1815, it pitted France and Britain against Russia. All three countries had interests in the Middle East and were seeking gains in the Ottoman Empire. The Crimean War began in 1854, when Britain and France, in order to stop any Russian moves into the Middle East, joined forces with the Turks.

Almost all of the fighting took place in the

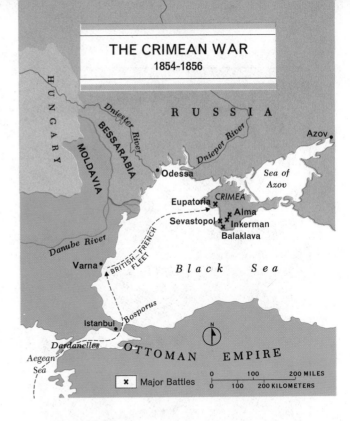

THE CRIMEAN WAR
1854-1856

X Major Battles

British troops sailed through the Atlantic and the Mediterranean to reach the Crimea. Then they set up camp, often near their ships. Here the troops are camped at Balaklava, the site of a later, major battle.

Crimea, a Russian peninsula that sticks out into the Black Sea. The war became a long siege with heavy losses. But in the British camp, Florence Nightingale eased some of the suffering. She introduced advanced nursing care through rigid standards and strong organization. And eventually, the British and French won in 1855.

In 1856, the warring countries gathered at Paris for a peace conference. The treaty hurt Russia in several ways. Worst of all was that no one could keep battleships on the Black Sea. Russia was hurt most by this, because it now had an undefended southern border. From then on, Russia's first aim was to change the Black Sea clauses. Russia could no longer be counted on to defend the existing balance of power, since this balance was not in its favor.

France became a dictatorship. After his election as president of the French Second Republic, Louis Napoleon worked to gain

Florence Nightingale

Florence Nightingale was born into a well-to-do English family. She had a good education, lived in two large country houses and a fashionable London apartment, went to parties and dances, and traveled in Europe. It was expected that one day she would marry an eligible gentleman and raise a family.

Florence had other ideas. In 1845, when she was 25, she told her parents that she wanted to become a nurse. Shocked and alarmed, her parents brushed aside the idea. In those days, a "nurse" was often a dirty, drunken old woman who could not be trusted.

But Florence did not give up. For the next several years, she visited hospitals and studied nursing. In 1854, she organized 38 nurses for an English hospital in the Crimean War. This effort displayed her genius for hospital administration and brought her great fame. Throughout her long life, her advice and counsel were sought by those who wanted to improve hospital care. And in 1907, a grateful nation made her the first woman to receive the coveted British Order of Merit.

more power for himself. In a *coup d'état* [kü′ dä tä′] he overturned the constitution. The next year, the people voted him Emperor Napoleon III.

Unlike his uncle, Louis Napoleon had no great ability in war or administration. But he was a clever politician. Although his methods were often unfair, he could turn the public's feelings in any direction. The parliament in France had no real power.

Napoleon III did help France economically. Railroad building was greatly expanded. Iron ships replaced wooden ones. And in 1859, a French company began the ten-year task of building the Suez Canal.

Baron Georges Haussman, a city planner, laid out a new Paris of broad streets, public parks, and great buildings. For the peasants, Napoleon III set up model farms. For the workers, he legalized strikes. Asylums and hospitals were built. Medicine was free to the poorest classes.

Had Napoleon stayed with problems at home, he might have remained on the throne a long time. Instead, he decided to make France a great power in world politics. By 1854, he had led France into the Crimean War. Other military adventures followed.

One of Napoleon's most disastrous projects was in Mexico. Mexico had borrowed heavily from outside investors. In 1861, it stopped paying its foreign debt. France, Spain, and Britain sent troops to force President Benito Juárez to pay. Spain and Britain soon left, seeing that Napoleon had ambitious plans.

Napoleon sent more troops to take Mexico City. Then in 1863, he made an Austrian archduke, Maximilian, emperor of Mexico. Maximilian meant well but depended on French troops to protect his government against the angry Mexicans.

The United States was then fighting its own civil war and could do nothing against the French. By 1866, the war was over, and the Americans told the French to leave. Napoleon, who needed his forces in Europe, deserted Maximilian. In 1867, Mexican soldiers captured and shot him.

Italy was unified. In 1859, Italy was still divided into several large and small states. Ever since the French Revolution, Italian nationalism had been growing. It showed in the writings of such patriots as Giuseppe Mazzini. More generally, it showed in the *Risorgimento* [rə sôr ji men'tō], or resurgence, a movement among middle-class liberals who wanted Italian unity.

The events of 1848 showed that brave men and high dreams were not enough. Without the power to remove Austria from northern Italy, the dream of unity could not come true. Count Camillo di Cavour [kä vŏŏr'] understood this fact better than did most Italians. In 1852, the count became prime minister of the Kingdom of Sardinia. He made Sardinia,

already politically and economically ahead of the other Italian states, a model of progress. It was the natural leader in unifying Italy.

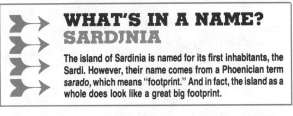

WHAT'S IN A NAME?
SARDINIA

The island of Sardinia is named for its first inhabitants, the Sardi. However, their name comes from a Phoenician term *sarado*, which means "footprint." And in fact, the island as a whole does look like a great big footprint.

Cavour was a clever man who knew that Italy could not gain unity without outside help. He won the aid of Napoleon III, who liked to think of himself as the champion of nationalism. In 1859, Cavour forced the Austrians into declaring war.

The French and Sardinian armies together easily defeated the Austrians. Revolutions broke out all over northern Italy. Napoleon III was afraid that the movement had gone too far. He angered Cavour by making peace with Austria.

After the French left Mexico, Maximilian tried to stay on as emperor. His young wife, Carlotta, returned to Europe in 1866 and unsuccessfully tried to get aid for him. Meanwhile Maximilian was captured. Edouard Manet's painting, *above*, shows his execution. Carlotta, *right*, lived on in Europe as an unhappy widow for some 60 years after his death.

THE UNIFICATION OF ITALY 1858-1870

FRANCE

SWITZERLAND

SAVOY

LOMBARDY 1859

PIEDMONT

NICE

to France 1860

CORSICA (FRENCH)

SARDINIA

AUSTRIAN EMPIRE

VENETIA

PARMA

MODENA

TUSCANY

PAPAL STATES

Rome

Tyrrhenian Sea

OTTOMAN EMPIRE

Adriatic Sea

KINGDOM

OF THE TWO

SICILIES

SICILY

Kingdom of Sardinia 1858
From Austria 1859
Added 1860
Added 1866
Added 1870

0   100   200 MILES
0 100 200 KILOMETERS

The revolutions did not stop. By 1860, all of northern Italy except Venetia had joined with Sardinia. Then Cavour made peace with Austria.

The Papal States and the Kingdom of the Two Sicilies remained outside the Italian union. At this point, a hot-tempered leader, Giuseppe Garibaldi [gar'ə bôl'dē], took matters into his own hands. In May, 1860, with an army of about 1,100 men, he took the Kingdom of the Two Sicilies. Cavour persuaded Garibaldi to allow the Two Sicilies to join Sardinia. In 1861, only a few months before Cavour died, the Kingdom of Italy became real. Victor Emmanuel of Sardinia became king. The final steps in forming modern Italy were taken in 1866 and 1870, when Venetia and Rome were added.

The German Empire was formed. Politically, the Germany of 1862 was not much different from the Germany of 1815, that is, a group of states inside the frame of the loose German Confederation. But socially and economically, important changes had taken place.

In 1834, the Prussians set up the *Zollverein* [tsôl'fer īn'], a union to deal with tariffs. Later, most of Germany (except Austria) joined it. To many German nationalists, greater economic unity pointed to political unity. They looked to Prussia to show the way.

Prussia, however, wanted to increase its own strength and importance within the Confederation, especially at the expense of Austria since Prussia and Austria were the strongest two in the group. This goal required a larger army, but the liberal Prussian parliament refused to allow new taxes that would pay for the army. At this point, in 1862, King William I of Prussia made Otto von Bismarck his prime minister, or chancellor.

It was a fateful move. Bismarck, a conservative landowner, had an iron will. He was a clever man who cared not at all about the public or its feelings. But he was deeply loyal to the Prussian monarchy.

As prime minister, Bismarck simply forgot about the liberal Prussian parliament and went ahead with the army. He ordered taxes collected without consent of parliament. The obedient people of Prussia did not revolt, and parliament's protests were ignored. Bismarck stated that the issues of the day would be decided not by speeches and votes, but "by blood and iron." Bismarck showed what he meant by quickly winning two wars. In these, he strengthened Prussia at the expense of Austria and Denmark.

Bismarck next turned his attention to southern Germany, where Prussia was disliked. He felt that only war with France would bring the southern states to the northern side—first as friends in war, and later as political partners.

THE UNIFICATION OF GERMANY 1865-1871

SWEDEN

Baltic Sea

DENMARK

North Sea

SCHLESWIG

HOLSTEIN

EAST PRUSSIA

WEST PRUSSIA

POMERANIA

MECKLENBURG SCHWERIN

MECKLENBURG STRELITZ

Hamburg

Bremen

OLDENBURG

KINGDOM OF HANOVER

BRANDENBURG

POSEN

• Berlin

RUSSIAN EMPIRE

NETHERLANDS

Rhine R.

WESTPHALIA

Ruhr R.

BRUNSWICK

HANOVER

ANHALT

SAXONY

KINGDOM OF SAXONY

SILESIA

RHINE PROV. OF PRUSSIA

HESSE-KASSEL

SAXON DUCHIES

BELGIUM

HESSE-DARMSTADT

NASSAU

LUXEM-BURG

DARMSTADT

Frankfort

AUSTRIAN EMPIRE

BAVARIAN PALATINATE

GRAND DUCHY OF BADEN

LORRAINE

KINGDOM OF WÜRTTEMBERG

KINGDOM OF BAVARIA

FRANCE

ALSACE

- ········· Boundary, German Confederation of 1815
- ☐ Kingdom of Prussia 1865
- ☐ Absorbed by Prussia 1866
- ☐ Became member of Federation 1867
- ☐ Became member of Empire 1871

SWITZERLAND

N

0   50   100 MILES
0   50   100 KILOMETERS

A chance for war came in 1870 when Spain needed a king and France would not agree to Bismarck's choice. The Franco-Prussian War lasted only six months. During that time, Napoleon III's government collapsed.

Paris was besieged for 130 days. When it fell, Prussian troops marched into Paris. In the peace treaty that followed, Prussia took the French border provinces of Alsace and Lorraine. The French never forgot their shame at the hands of the Germans.

On January 18, 1871, while Paris was still under siege, the German Empire was created with William of Prussia as its emperor. The new empire soon became the strongest power in continental Europe.

section review 2

1. How was the Crimean War an example of Realpolitik?

2. In what ways did Louis Napoleon improve France? How did he weaken France?

3. What acts of Cavour and Garibaldi helped form modern Italy?

4. How did Bismarck get the larger army that Prussia needed? How did he get the south German states to join Prussia?

3 *Democracy advanced in western Europe*

Between 1871 and 1914, the countries of western Europe grew socially, economically, and politically. The changes were very great, but important problems in these same areas remained.

Britain made many reforms. The economic, social, and political leader in these years was, again, Britain. For most of the time the reigning monarch was Queen Victoria. She became a symbol for an age of wide political power and great well-being. In the 1850s, the

Benjamin Disraeli

Whig and Tory parties became the Liberal and Conservative parties. William E. Gladstone led the Liberals, and Benjamin Disraeli [diz rā'lē], the Conservatives. The two alternated and competed for the job as prime minister from 1868 to 1880. After Disraeli died in 1881, Gladstone ruled politics until he retired in 1894.

Both parties put forward bills to extend voting rights. After 1884, most male adults had the right to vote. Under Gladstone and Disraeli, state-run public education was begun, the secret ballot became law, labor unions gained more freedom, and a workmen's compensation law was passed.

After 1900, important changes took place in British politics. The rise of the Labour party led the Liberals, who wanted to keep the workers' votes, to start social welfare legislation. The Liberals headed the government from 1905 to 1916. Led by Herbert Asquith and David Lloyd George, they passed laws that set up old-age pensions, unemployment insurance, and minimum wage laws.

Lloyd George's budget in 1909 was based on the idea that taxes on the incomes of rich people should be higher than those for poorer people. The House of Lords reluctantly agreed under pressure from the House of Commons and the king, Edward VII.

The so-called Irish Question was a difficult problem for England. The Roman Catholic Irish did not want to pay taxes to support the Anglican Church in Ireland. They also disliked England's political rule and a land system that kept the Irish poor. With the Disestablishment Act of 1869, Gladstone stopped Irish tax money from going to the Anglican Church in Ireland. He also made a start on land reform, giving peasants more rights over the land they farmed.

These economic measures helped the Irish. But at the same time, politics became

DailyLife

Victoria's name came to stand for an age of strong family ties, strict morals, and a comfortable economic level. The picture *above* shows Victoria and her husband, Prince Albert, with five of their nine children. But conditions were not so comfortable everywhere, even within Victoria's realm. In Ireland, *right*, economic conditions were severe. Many families were evicted from their rented farms when they fell behind in payments.

EJECTMENT OF IRISH TENANTRY.

the trouble point. The Irish had a strong leader in Charles Parnell. He favored Home Rule, that is, self-rule for Ireland.

Parliament finally passed the Home Rule bill in 1914. But the largely Presbyterian northern Irish population of Ulster objected. The problem was put aside during World War I. When the war ended, however, fighting broke out. In 1922, a compromise plan made southern Ireland (the Irish Free State) independent and allowed Ulster to stay in the United Kingdom. But friction between Protestants and Catholics in Ulster has repeatedly produced bloodshed.

France moved into a Third Republic. After the fall of the Second Empire and defeat in the Franco-Prussian War, the French elected a National Assembly to make peace with Germany and decide what form of government France would have. The Assembly in 1875 set up a republic. It had a president, premier, and cabinet responsible to a two-house legislature. The lower house (the Chamber of Deputies) was elected by universal male suffrage. The Third Republic lasted until 1940—longer than any other French government since 1789.

The Third Republic was often attacked by people who wanted to bring back the monarchy. The 1880s and 1890s were filled with crises, the climax being the Dreyfus case. Alfred Dreyfus, a Jew, was a French army officer. In 1894, a military court convicted him of treason. When evidence later showed that the real traitor was a Catholic aristocrat, public feeling divided sharply. Enemies of the Third Republic (the officer corps, monarchists, and

With Paris about to fall to the Prussian armies, King William of Prussia was proclaimed German emperor by his princes in the Hall of Mirrors at Versailles. This drawing shows Bismarck (in the white uniform) smiling with satisfaction.

the Church) were strongly against reopening the case. They said that to do so would weaken military authority. Pro-Republic forces finally won. When a civil court pardoned Dreyfus in 1906, the civil government was proven to be stronger than the army. The Dreyfus Affair became an example that any person of any race or creed could get justice in a democracy.

The Republic in 1914 still had enemies. But most French people favored it. However, many political parties existed. Public feelings about issues often were divided. Fifty government ministries rose and fell between 1871 and 1914. Other problems occurred as unhappy workers called for reforms.

Germany made some reforms. Between 1871 and 1890, Chancellor Bismarck led the German Empire. He built it as a union of monarchies in which Prussia had the strongest voice. The empire had a constitution and a lower house (Reichstag) elected by universal male suffrage. But real power lay with the chancellor and the aristocratic upper house (Bundesrat).

Bismarck's strong nationalism made him question other Germans who did not bow to the state. During the 1870s, he attacked the Roman Catholic Church in Germany and cut sharply into Catholic education and freedom of worship. After a few years, Bismarck ended these attacks. He felt that the Catholic Church was no longer a threat. Also, he wanted Catholic support for his drive against socialism.

German industry grew rapidly and so did the German working class. Many workers became interested in socialism. When the Social Democratic party was organized in 1875, Bismarck became alarmed. Beginning in 1878, Germany passed many laws against socialism, but was unable to destroy it.

In the 1880s, Bismarck tried to draw work-

This British cartoon shows young William II dismissing Bismarck from his command of the ship of state.

ers away from socialism with a sweeping program of social insurance. It was the most forward-looking program in Europe, but it did not destroy socialism. In 1890, Bismarck quarreled with the new emperor, William II, and was forced to retire.

William II was 29 when he became emperor in 1888. He reigned until 1918. An ambitious man with grand ideas about his own power, William II wanted to become a

477

world leader. Thus, he began an aggressive foreign policy. In Germany, he ended the antisocialist laws and furthered social insurance. However, he refused to allow greater political democracy. The Social Democrats grew stronger. By 1912, they were the largest single party in the Reichstag.

section review 3

1. List at least six social reforms begun in Britain.

2. What was the Irish Question? What solution was tried? Was it successful?

3. Who were the enemies of the Third Republic? Why was the Dreyfus Affair an important test for French government?

4. Why did Bismarck fight socialism?

4 Reforms came slowly in southern and eastern Europe

Outside the industrial center of western Europe were less economically advanced countries, such as Spain, Portugal, Italy, Austria-Hungary, the Balkans, and the Ottoman Empire. Their economies were chiefly agricultural. Unlike the industrial countries, they had few large cities, railroads, or factories and more poverty, illiteracy, and disease. The rich and poor classes were sharply divided, the middle class was small, and governments were not stable.

Spain and Portugal lacked stability. During the late 19th century, Spain had no effective government. A revolution in 1868 had

Isabella II ruled Spain for 25 years that were marked by frequent cabinet changes and party conflicts between moderates, progressives, and liberals. She was deposed in 1868.

478

deposed the corrupt queen, Isabella II. But opposing groups could not agree on the next step. Monarchists were split, and republicans did not want a monarchy at all. Both the army and the Roman Catholic Church often intervened in politics.

Finally, in 1876 Spain became a constitutional monarchy. The right to vote was given only to male property owners, however, and parliamentary rule had no meaning. The government remained corrupt and ineffective. The Spanish-American War against the United States reduced the size of the empire and emptied the treasury. In Spain, growing anger among peasants and workers led to radical social ideas. As the 20th century opened, Spain was faced with rising violence.

Violence in the neighboring monarchy of Portugal equaled that in Spain. Between 1853 and 1889, Portugal moved toward parliamentary government. But then the government returned to a monarchy that favored the established nobility. A revolution in 1910 overturned the hated monarchy, and Portugal became a republic. Stable government was impossible, however, as political parties fought for power.

Italy had great problems. Unification did not erase Italy's old problems. Sectional hatreds were strong. People were illiterate, and education was backward. The land system and tax structure were unfair. And the people had very little experience in parliamentary government.

Even though Italy was a constitutional monarchy, only men of education and property could vote. Out of 20 million people, only 150 thousand had voting rights. Politicians cared more about being elected than about making reforms.

Economic problems became so great in the 1890s that riots broke out in several Italian cities. In 1911, suffrage was given to all men over age thirty. This act, though, only led to larger extremist parties. To escape such conditions, thousands of young Italians moved to other countries.

Minority groups threatened Austria-Hungary. The greatest problem that Austria-Hungary had after 1870 was one of nationalities. The empire held so many different national groups that it was hard to find a policy that all would accept.

By the end of the century, the Magyars of Hungary began to push for full independence from Austria. Inside Hungary, the Magyars made up less than half the population. But they ran the government, and they were unfriendly toward the other nationalities in Hungary such as Romanians, Slovaks, and Serbs.

In Austria, Germans ruled the political, economic, and cultural life. The Czechs wanted to end German domination and have their own government. They were proud of their history and their cultural and economic advancement. The Emperor Francis Joseph tried to please all the nationalities and failed to please any. His failure finally led to the end of the empire.

The Ottoman Empire grew weaker. The Ottoman Empire had even more nationalities than Austria-Hungary. And it also had several religions. Most of its people were Muslims. But Jews and Christians, both Roman Catholic and Greek Orthodox, also lived there. Turks and other Muslims, the two most powerful groups, held all of the army and government posts.

The Ottoman Empire lagged far behind western Europe in economic and political development. For over two centuries, it had been ailing. Slowly, peoples on the borders of the empire broke away from Turkish rule. At the same time, in the late 18th and early 19th centuries, European states gained con-

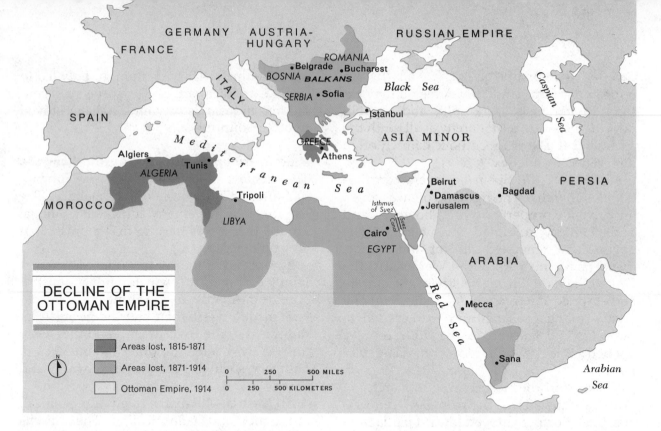

DECLINE OF THE OTTOMAN EMPIRE

- Areas lost, 1815-1871
- Areas lost, 1871-1914
- Ottoman Empire, 1914

0   250   500 MILES
0 250 500 KILOMETERS

trol over a number of outlying Turkish territories.

By the mid-19th century, the Turks had lost most of their power over southern Russia, the Crimea, Romania, Serbia, Greece, Egypt, and Algeria. Defeat in the Crimean War pointed up Turkish weaknesses and showed the need for reform.

In 1856, the Turkish government issued the Hatt-i Humayun [hat'i hǔ mä'yün], the most important Turkish reform of the 19th century. It promised that people would be equal before the law and that torture would end. A fairer tax system would be used. And the corruption in public office would end. A constitution in 1876 provided for parliamentary government.

These changes met powerful resistance. The ruling sultan from 1876 to 1909, Abdul Hamid II [ab'dǔl hä měd'], was strongly against reform. He dismissed parliament and began a reign of terror. He also drove into exile thousands of reformers known as the Young Turks.

In 1877, war broke out between Turkey and Russia. This time they fought over Turkish lands in the Balkans. The Turks were defeated and lost more Balkan land. Abdul Hamid's rule did not soften, and the nationalistic peoples of the Balkans went on fighting. A revolution in 1908 brought the reforming Young Turks, many of whom were no longer very young, to power. They restored parliament but could not stop the rise of nationalism in the Balkans.

section review 4

1. Name four problems that prevented Spain and Portugal from setting up democractic governments.

2. Why was it hard for parliamentary government to work well in Italy?

3. In what ways did the many national groups in Austria-Hungary cause problems in governing that empire?

4. What problems did the Ottoman Empire have? What reforms were tried?

Section Summaries

1. Governments resisted change. After Napoleon Bonaparte's defeat, European leaders met at the Congress of Vienna to restore the balance of power and make a new map of Europe. The Great Powers also tried to find a way to stop wars before they started. The Concert of Europe was formed to keep peace. After 1814, liberalism and nationalism led to fighting in Spain and Italy, but these revolts were quickly crushed. The Greeks, though, finally won their independence. In 1830, the French rose against the backward monarchy. The Belgians won their freedom from the Dutch Netherlands. Outbreaks in German and Italian states and in Poland were put down. Britain escaped revolution by making changes. In 1848, people rose all over Europe. The French again were first. After a bloody civil war, they wrote a new constitution. Other 1848 revolts in Europe failed. In the Austrian Empire, though, serfdom was ended and Hungary won self-rule.

2. Continental Europe was politically changed. In the second half of the 19th century, nationalism and the growth of democratic institutions brought many political changes in Europe. A new idea about power politics was known as Realpolitik. Emperor Louis Napoleon brought well-being to France. But he led his country into bad foreign adventures. Count Cavour, the Sardinian prime minister, led a drive that brought about the unification of Italy. Otto von Bismarck led Prussia through wars with Denmark, Austria, and France. From these wars came a new German Empire.

3. Democracy advanced in western Europe. Beginning about 1870, several forward-looking countries of western Europe made great social and economic gains. England, led by Gladstone, Disraeli, and Asquith, made many liberal and democratic changes. Troubled southern Ireland finally gained its freedom. France under the Third Republic was not politically stable, but its people were safe and at peace. And the government survived internal attacks. The German government lost its campaigns against the Roman Catholic Church and the socialists. The growing German working class gained social benefits.

4. Reforms came slowly in southern and eastern Europe. Bad governments stopped Spain and Portugal from equaling the forward steps of the countries to the north. Italy could not overcome hard economic and social problems. Austria-Hungary did little to please the unhappy nationalities inside its borders. In the failing Ottoman Empire, a weak government could not subdue the Balkans.

Who? What? When? Where?

1. Arrange these events in chronological order, beginning with the earliest:
  a. The Congress of Vienna took place.
  b. The Crimean War took place.
  c. Germany was unified.
  d. Greece won its freedom.
  e. Italy was unified.
  f. Serfdom was abolished in the Austrian Empire.
  g. The Treaty of London was signed.

2. Write a sentence for each of these terms that tells how it helped the growth of liberalism and democracy:
  a. Chartism
  b. constitutional monarchy
  c. Corn Laws repealed
  d. Hatt-i Humayun
  e. Home Rule
  f. Male suffrage
  g. Risorgimento

3. Write a sentence for each of the following that tells what country each of these people had power in and why each person was important:
  a. Abdul Hamid II
  b. Bismarck
  c. Cavour
  d. Disraeli
  e. Francis Joseph
  f. Gladstone
  g. Louis Napoleon
  h. Maximilian
  i. Metternich
  j. Parnell
  k. Queen Victoria
  l. Emperor William II

Questions for Critical Thinking

1. Would you be willing to live under a dictatorship if the ruler gave the people enough food, homes, and jobs?

2. Why did Bismarck and Louis Napoleon make many reforms even though they ruled as dictators?

3. Why did people in the countries that became industrialized achieve social reforms before people in the nonindustrialized countries sought similar reforms?

4. What were the biggest problems Italians and Germans faced in unifying their countries? Why did Germany become a Great Power while Italy did not?

5. Why was Britain so often the first country to make important social reforms?

Skill Activities

1. Read *Victoria and Albert at Home* by Tyler Whittle to learn more about the life and personality of the ruler who dominated her time. (Routledge and Kegan Paul, 1980)

2. Have a class discussion on whether the spirit of Realpolitik is still alive in the world today. Use current news reports for research.

3. Do outside research on the Crimean War. What mistakes did the governments make? Why were they fighting? What happened in "The Charge of the Light Brigade"?

4. Reformers in 19th-century Europe worked for prison reforms, improved health care, and improved working conditions. If you were a reformer today, what social changes would you work for? Write a petition to one of your government officials urging your changes.

chapter **25** *quiz*

Section 1

1. The purpose of the Congress of Vienna was to: a. unify Germany, b. strengthen France, c. keep a balance of power

2. True or false: The Great Powers of Europe in 1815 encouraged nationalism and liberalism.

3. In the early 1800s, the right to vote was meant for: a. all citizens, b. all men, c. men who owned property

Section 2

4. As a result of the Crimean War, the nation that lost power was: a. Russia, b. England, c. France

5. The movement to unify Italy was called: a. Realpolitik, b. Risorgimento, c. Zollverein

6. True or false: Bismarck wanted a war with France to create unity among the German states.

Section 3

7. A great Liberal leader in British government was: a. Gladstone, b. Dreyfus, c. Disraeli

8. Home Rule meant: a. the right to vote, b. freedom for Ireland, c. independence for Italy

9. True or false: Bismarck destroyed socialism in Germany by making many reforms.

Section 4

10. Problems were caused in Spain and Portugal by the: a. large industrialized cities, b. large middle class, c. conflicts between rich and poor

11. The country whose problems were caused by the many nationalities within its borders was: a. Portugal, b. Italy, c. Austria-Hungary

12. The country in which there were people of many different religions was: a. Spain, b. Italy, c. Turkey

THE INDUSTRIAL REVOLUTION

By 1888, the central telephone office in New York City was quite large. Women often worked as operators. Each call had to be connected with wires that the operators moved by hand.

A scientific revolution changed people's ideas about nature. Democratic revolutions changed their ideas about government. At the same time, a quiet revolution in business and industry was beginning to change the ways people lived and worked. Very few people then fully understood how new machines would change people's lives.

In November, 1774, a young inventor wrote to his father:

The business I am here about has turned out rather successful, that is to say, the fire engine I have invented is now going and answers much better than any other that has yet been made, and I expect that the invention will be beneficial to me.

The letter writer was James Watt, a Scottish instrument maker. His "fire engine" was a steam engine that would become known around the world. When James Watt wrote that letter, he could not have known that he would become one of the most important leaders in a huge industrial revolution.

In 1763, a fellow teacher at the University of Glasgow asked him to repair a model steam engine. Watt noticed that the engine wasted a great deal of fuel. He talked about the waste with several teachers at the university. No one could think of any useful solution. For months, Watt thought about the engine. He found an answer in 1765. For years after that, however, he worked on technical points. Finally, he took out a patent on his improved steam engine.

The use of steam power in industry helped change the world. The steam engine later reduced or replaced old energy sources—horses, oxen, water, and people.

By 1819 when James Watt died, steam-powered machines were replacing hand tools in British industry. Goods made in factories with machines shared markets with goods made in the home by hand. During the 1800s, industrialization spread to the rest of western Europe and across the seas to the United States and Japan.

Industrialization went along with progress in science and medicine. New discoveries in these fields brought better health and more comfort. They also changed people's ideas about human beginnings, development, and feelings about one another. Literature, art, music, and architecture also showed the great changes of the 1800s. This chapter tells how:

1. The Industrial Revolution changed the Western world.

2. Science and medicine progressed rapidly.

3. The arts showed great energy.

1 The Industrial Revolution changed the Western world

Historians once viewed the changes that began in the late 1700s as "the" Industrial Revolution. They decided that it was a "cataclysm followed by a catastrophe." That is, new machines suddenly appeared and began the factory system, which cruelly used men, women, and children. All these things were supposed to have happened in just a few decades.

It is now known that this picture was not a really true one. The most important point about the so-called Industrial Revolution is the way that power-driven machinery came to be used in place of hand tools in manufacturing. Thus, the Industrial Revolution had no certain beginning and has not yet ended.

Many new inventions appeared in the 18th and 19th centuries. They were based on hundreds of years of work and discovery in many countries. The search for new machines and new kinds of power to run them still goes on.

However, the idea of an Industrial Revolution is a useful one. It shows that in a rather short time—about 200 years—the Western economy grew very rapidly. This great speedup was first seen in England between about 1760 and 1830. It began in Germany in the 1860s, the United States in the 1870s, and Russia in the 1890s. Many parts of the world have not yet had an industrial revolution.

Several conditions in England favored industrialization. First, England had good natural resources. The land held rich deposits of coal and iron. From short, swift rivers came the water power to keep machines moving. Ships that carried finished goods around the world moved easily in and out of British harbors. Wool and cotton from the colonies were the raw materials for a growing English textile industry.

Second, England had a large labor force. In the 1700s, there was a great increase in food supply from the widespread use of the potato. This led to a huge growth in England's population. In addition, Parliament passed "enclosure acts." Wealthy landowners could then fence in open fields and common lands that for centuries had been used by poor small farmers. Most of these farmers became wage wherever there were jobs. ders in inventing m people to use them kers were more skille ere workers on the

Th ood labor force wer ess people who had buy the new ma w factories. For cer een building up cap work, and overse ness people and la companies even m efore, businesses h ment for a large n

 aiting for the fin-
 found markets at home. There, the greater numbers of people needed much more food, clothing, and housing. Colonies abroad also were markets. And the Napoleonic wars increased the need for homegrown food and iron and steel goods. Thus, trade grew rapidly.

Fifth, the government of 18th-century England helped industrialism grow. The English Parliament allowed great changes in the landholding system so that roads and canals could be built. And it gave patents to protect inventors' work. Taxes on profits were lowered, and businesses became freer. The British navy protected merchant sailors around the world. At home, a well-run legal system kept the roads free of robbers and promised justice for business people in the courts.

Finally, British society was rather mobile. That is, a poor person who worked hard and saved money might become wealthy. That person or a family member then could marry a landowner or a noble. Thus, business and industry grew because talented people could better themselves in it. The upper classes had long been in trade. The oldest son of a family took his father's noble title. The younger sons often turned to business. So work was not looked down upon.

Machines for the textile industry helped begin the factory system. Most goods before the late 1700s were made with hand tools in small shops or in people's homes. The *domestic system,* or cottage industry, was quite often used in textile manufacture. Managers handed out the raw materials. Workers spun the yarn and wove the cloth at home.

In the early 1700s, new city dwellers and markets abroad wanted so much cotton cloth that workers could not meet the need. In 1733, English weaver John Kay made a flying shuttle, which cut weaving time in half. Now the problem was that spinners could not supply enough yarn.

GEOGRAPHY
A Key to History

RESOURCES AND INDUSTRIAL DEVELOPMENT

Industrial development cannot take place just anywhere. It needs a place where raw materials and power can be easily obtained, where a large population is available to work in industry, where money is available to build machines and factories, and where the markets for goods can be reached easily. Conditions in 18th-century England met all of these requirements. And it was here that the Industrial Revolution began.

England's industrial development was greatly aided by the presence of mineral resources. England had rich, well-placed coal fields and iron ore deposits. Coal was used to convert iron ore into iron or steel and to provide steam power to run machines.

Both coal and iron ore are costly and bulky to ship. In England, shipping costs stayed low because business people built industrial centers near the coal and iron mines. Manchester, Sheffield, and Birmingham became great industrial cities.

Some raw materials and finished goods, however, had to be shipped between ocean ports or inland areas and the centers of industry. A low-cost system of transportation was needed. Canals and, later, railroads were built to link port cities with the industrial centers.

France and Germany also had deposits of coal and iron ore. These were linked by a network of rivers, canals, and railroads, and the two countries became the industrial leaders in continental Europe. The northeastern United States had similar advantages.

Some other places lacked the resources that favored industry. South America, Africa, and the Mediterranean region of Europe had little coal. South America did have iron ore, but much of it was hard to reach.

These circumstances help explain why some places did not industrialize at an early date. Since the 1930s, other resources have become increasingly important. Today, industrialization is taking place in areas that were once thought unsuitable.

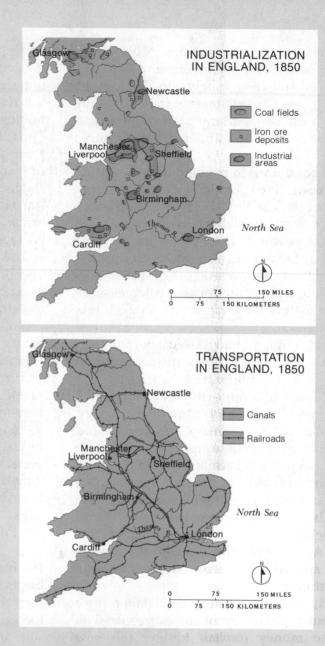

INDUSTRIALIZATION IN ENGLAND, 1850

Coal fields
Iron ore deposits
Industrial areas

Glasgow
Newcastle
Manchester
Liverpool
Sheffield
Birmingham
Thames R.
London
North Sea
Cardiff

0 75 150 MILES
0 75 150 KILOMETERS

TRANSPORTATION IN ENGLAND, 1850

Canals
Railroads

Glasgow
Newcastle
Manchester
Liverpool
Sheffield
Birmingham
Thames R.
London
North Sea
Cardiff

0 75 150 MILES
0 75 150 KILOMETERS

By 1769, two important inventions, the spinning jenny and the water-powered frame, provided yarn faster. Then in 1779, jenny-spinner Samuel Crompton found a way to use the best parts of the spinning jenny and the water frame together in one machine called a spinning mule. (By 1830, his water-driven spinning mule had advanced even further to become a steam-driven machine.)

The spinning jenny and the water frame ended the "famine in yarn." For a while, the weavers caused a jam. But by 1800, Edmund Cartwright's power loom was at work throughout England.

The new machines were used most in making cotton cloth. Raw cotton came into the market slowly because of the time needed to clean seeds from the cotton bolls. When New Englander Eli Whitney went to Georgia in 1793, he learned of the problem. In 10 days, he built a machine, the cotton gin, that could clean cotton as fast as 50 pairs of hands. By 1820, cotton led all exports from the southern United States. It was also Great Britain's chief import.

Manufacturers lowered costs by grouping machines together in factories close to sources of power. Both time and money were saved because workers no longer had materials brought to them. Instead, workers went to the factories. There they kept set hours and did not waste raw materials.

The so-called *factory system* allowed better control of quality and a steadier rate of production. Manufacturers could use such new techniques as mass production. That is, they could make many of the same sizes by having one type of machine rapidly do one small job, moving the product to another type of machine for another small job, and so on, until the product was finished.

Iron and steel manufacture was improved.
The many new machines called for larger

Making steel by the Bessemer process was often dangerous. Red-hot bits of molten metal and clouds of smoke filled the factories.

amounts of iron. Most early iron-making was done with charcoal, which was slow and costly. (Also, making charcoal was destroying English forests.) In 1735, Abraham Darby began to make iron ore with coke—purified coal. The iron industry then moved from forest areas to coal regions.

In the 1780s, Henry Cort, a contractor for the British navy, made two discoveries. By "puddling," or stirring, molten iron with long rods in a furnace, he could quickly burn off many impurities and make a large amount of wrought iron. Also, by passing hot iron through heavy rollers he could squeeze out further impurities and make iron sheets.

McCormick was [...] years old when his reaper had its first public display in July, 1831, in Virginia. Jo Anderson, a slave, raked the grain as McCormick strode behind his invention.

In 1856, Sir Henry Bessemer found a way to burn off impurities in molten iron to make steel, which was stronger and generally more useful. Ten years later, an Englishman, Sir William Siemens, and a Frenchman, Pierre Emile Martin, built an open-hearth furnace for making a greater range of steels.

Great steel centers grew up near large reserves of coal and iron ore in northern England, the Ruhr valley in Germany, and the Pittsburgh area of Pennsylvania. The many tons of iron and steel these centers turned out were then used to make bigger machines with more parts. Farmers in the western United States used machines instead of people to grow food on many acres of rich soil. Cyrus McCormick's horse-drawn grain reaper and Hiram and John Pitts's threshing and winnowing machine appeared in the 1830s. John Deere built an all-steel plow in 1847. In the 1880s, the reaper and thresher became one machine, the combine. Such machines helped open up the huge plains of North America and, later, of Europe.

Transportation became faster and cheaper.
Moving about in the early 1700s was little different from getting around during the Middle Ages. Roads were bad, and traveling on horseback was slow and uncomfortable.

The work of two Scottish engineers, Thomas Telford and John McAdam, greatly improved travel after 1770. Both worked for better drainage of roads and the use of layers of crushed rock. McAdam's money-saving plan, known as macadamizing, formed the base for all modern road building.

Waterways also changed. Rivers were made deeper to accept large ships. And in 1761, one of the first modern canals was dug. The Duke of Bridgewater built the seven-mile (4.2-kilometer) canal to link some of his coal mines with the city of Manchester. This watercourse worked so well that the price of coal in Manchester dropped by 80 percent. After that, canal-building began all over England. By 1830, the country had one of the best inland waterway systems in the Western world. In the United States, the Erie Canal was finished by 1825.

Meanwhile, the steam engine had appeared. Taking his ideas from work done in the 1600s, an Englishman, Thomas Newcomen, invented a steam engine. From about 1705 on, Newcomen engines were widely used for pumping water out of mines. It was

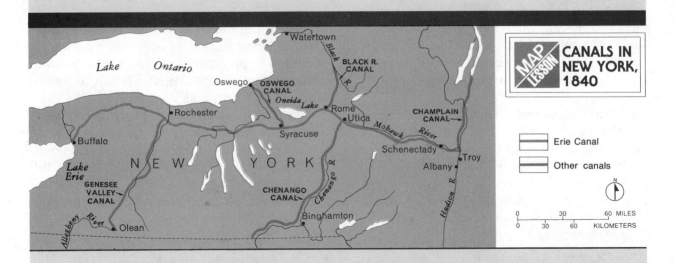

■ MAP LESSON 26: CANALS IN NEW YORK, 1840

1. The Erie Canal was one of the earliest, longest, and most celebrated canals in the United States. This map indicates the canal's route from the Hudson River in the east to Lake Erie in the west. It also shows several other canals. What are they?

2. This map shows that the Erie Canal was part of a whole system of canals and waterways in the state of New York. Thus, it was possible to travel by canal barge between other cities as well. Which canals and waterways were used to travel:

    a. from Binghamton to Oswego
    b. from Schenectady to Olean
    c. from Watertown to Albany
    d. from Rome to Utica

3. Canals often followed nearby rivers. Study the map to find the river followed by:

    a. the Chenango Canal
    b. the Erie Canal
    c. the Champlain Canal

---

a model of one of these engines that James Watt repaired in 1763. His new engine, patented in 1769, was much more efficient than Newcomen's. In 1781, Watt found a way to suit the engine to rotary motion. Then it could be used to run machines.

In the mid-1700s, donkeys pulled carts on iron rails around English coal mines. Richard Trevithick, an English mining engineer, thought that a steam engine on wheels would be better than animal power. Trevithick built two such engines in the early 1800s, but they were used only at mines.

In 1825, mining engineer George Stephenson built a locomotive that could do the work of 40 teams of horses. When a group of business people decided to build a railway between Liverpool and Manchester, they offered a prize for the best locomotive. Stephenson won the prize in 1829 with his Rocket. It pulled a train 31 miles (49.6 kilometers) at an average speed of 14 miles (22.4 kilometers) an hour.

Stephenson set off a railroad-building boom in England that reached its peak in the 1840s. By 1850, the most important routes were built, and freight trains ran steadily. Western Europe and the United States began building railroads in the mid-1800s.

Until about 1880, most ships still used wind and sail. A good supply of wood from the Americas and, after the 1830s, the use of iron hulls kept building costs low. Therefore, sailing vessels could offer very low rates.

In 1838, a British ship, the Sirius, crossed from Liverpool to New York under steam alone in 18 days. By 1850, fast ocean-going steamers ran at uniform times. They did a good business in mail and passenger traffic. But only after such inventions as the screw propeller did steamers begin to take the place of sailing vessels for carrying cargo.

Capitalism changed. During the Commercial Revolution, trade and commerce gave rise to mercantile capitalism. As industrialism grew in the 1700s, capitalism changed to suit new kinds of business. Called industrial capitalism, it was usually based on small companies that were managed directly by their owners.

Some industries, such as railroads and iron and steel companies, needed huge amounts of capital to buy machines and tools. No one person had so much capital. Therefore, some kind of joint firm was needed.

The joint-stock companies that had formed during the Commercial Revolution had generally been used for overseas trade and colonization. They were also closely limited by government charters. During the 1800s, a looser kind of group, the *corporation*, was born. It could own property, and bring and defend suits at law. And it continued

By standards of the times, this train and railway car on the Liverpool-Manchester line were quite fancy.

even though shareholders and directors changed.

By the end of the 1800s, many large businesses were corporations. They were managed not by their owners but by salaried people who used other persons' money. Banks and financiers became quite important because of the large amounts of capital needed. Therefore, in terms of economics, the time after 1850 is known as finance capitalism.

section review 1

1. What six conditions favored industrialization in England?

2. How was iron and steel manufacture improved? What effect did this have on agriculture?

3. What advances in transportation took place? What effect did they have?

4. What is the difference between a joint-stock company and a corporation?

2 Science and medicine progressed rapidly

Industrialism grew fast because people became more willing to work in new ways. That willing spirit also led to important discoveries in science and medicine. In the 1800s, most Europeans were sure that science was the key to unlocking nature's secrets. Then all the dreams of material progress would come true.

Chemists and physicists made important discoveries. Chemistry got a new base because of the work of John Dalton, an English schoolteacher in the early 1800s. Dalton believed that all matter is made of tiny pieces called *atoms.* He thought further that all atoms in any one chemical element are alike.

And he thought that each element's atoms have a weight different from any other's atoms. Dalton said that in chemical compounds, atoms join into units (now called molecules). He made up a kind of chemical formula to describe them.

During the next fifty years, chemists discovered more elements and improved the ways of joining them. In 1869, Russian Dmitri Mendeleev (men'dl ā'ef) drew up the Periodic Table. In it, he put into families by atomic weight all the known elements (sixty-two then). With this chart, he showed gaps where other elements might be and later were found.

Important discoveries in physics helped prove that electricity, magnetism, heat, and light were closely connected. In 1800, Alessandro Volta made one of the first batteries. Hans Christian Oersted [ėr'sted] of Denmark discovered electromagnetism in 1820. He found that electric current flowing through a wire would move a compass needle that lay next to it.

Further work on the connection between electricity and magnetism was done by English scientist Michael Faraday. In 1831, he showed that electric current could be made by moving a wire through the lines of force of a magnetic field. The electric generator and the electric motor are based upon the principles Faraday developed.

In the 1860s, Scottish scientist James Clerk Maxwell made up exact mathematical equations to explain Faraday's work. With Maxwell's equations, physicists showed that radiant heat and other invisible kinds of radiation were also electromagnetic waves.

In 1885, German Heinrich Hertz found and measured the speed of what were later called radio waves. Another German, Wilhelm Roentgen [rent'gən], in 1895 discovered rays that could pass through solids. He called them X rays. While looking for rays like these, Pierre and Marie Curie discovered the

Alexander Graham Bell's invention of the telephone brought him great fame.

element radium in 1898. Their discovery of this radioactive element was a high point in the new field of atomic physics.

New scientific discoveries led to inventions. In 1832, in the United States, Samuel Morse made the first electric telegraph. Another American, Alexander Graham Bell, patented the telephone in 1876. And American Thomas A. Edison made the first useful electric light in 1879. Italian Guglielmo Marconi's wireless telegraph began service across the English Channel in 1898. Three years later, messages crossed the Atlantic. All these inventions brought together the new world-wide economy and helped cities grow.

Many of the discoveries of pure science helped solve industry's problems. During the 1800s, chemists broke down nearly 70 thousand chemical compounds. From this work came portland cement, vulcanized rubber, synthetic dyes, and other products.

Building on the work of Faraday and others, inventors made electric generators that turned out steady amounts of electricity cheaply. Soon, electricity was used to power trolley cars, trains, and ships. Engineers quickly made electric motors to power machines in factories.

Rich natural resources were turned into power. Fuel gas had been known since ancient times. However, it was not commercially made and used until the late 1700s. Then English and French scientists made it useful for lighting. London, in 1807, became the first city to light streets with gas.

Petroleum gave rise to a new industry in the middle 1800s. The United States soon took the lead. At first, petroleum was used chiefly for lubrication and for making kerosene. Then in the 1860s and 1870s, scientists in France, Germany, and Austria began to build internal combustion engines. The more advanced of these used gasoline for fuel.

From then on, the by-product gasoline became petroleum's most important use. Gasoline engines were made lighter and finally could be made to power the automobile.

Another type of internal combustion machine, the diesel engine, was patented in 1892. It ran on fuel oils instead of gasoline. The engine was widely used in ships and locomotives. It was heavier than the gasoline engine, but it was cheaper to run.

Medical research helped people live longer. English physician Edward Jenner greatly advanced modern medicine when he used vaccination to protect against smallpox. For centuries, the often-deadly disease had been

492

feared. In 1796, he inoculated a boy with the virus of cowpox (a mild form of smallpox). When the boy was later inoculated with smallpox, he did not become ill.

Surgery gained from new discoveries in chemistry. Until the mid-1800s, operations were painful and patients were held down by force. In 1846, W. T. G. Morton, a Boston dentist, publicly showed the value of ether during an operation at Massachusetts General Hospital. News of his work helped an Englishman, Sir James Simpson, who taught medicine at the University of Edinburgh, to discover chloroform. Anesthetics made surgery painless and made medical research on living animals possible.

> ## WHAT'S IN A NAME?
> ### EDINBURGH
>
> Edinburgh was first Edwin's burg, or "fortress." The town is named for Edwin, an Anglo-Saxon king of Northumberland who sometimes lived there.

Operations became less feared. However, surgery was still very often fatal because of infection. Sterilization was unknown. Surgeons wore their operating coats for years before washing them. Most of them did not understand the cause of infection.

It was French scientist Louis Pasteur who finally proved that microscopic organisms called germs cause infectious diseases. In the 1850s, Pasteur began a study of fermentation. He found the cause to be certain bacteria. His heating process (later named pasteurization) slowed down fermentation. In other studies, Pasteur discovered several vaccines, including the one for rabies.

German scientist Robert Koch discovered each of the germs that cause eleven diseases, including tuberculosis and cholera.

Working with the new germ theory of disease, English surgeon Joseph Lister searched for a chemical antiseptic. He wanted to destroy bacteria and make surgery safe as well

Daily Life By 1883, magazines showed pictures of vaccinations in clinics as new medical practices came into wide acceptance.

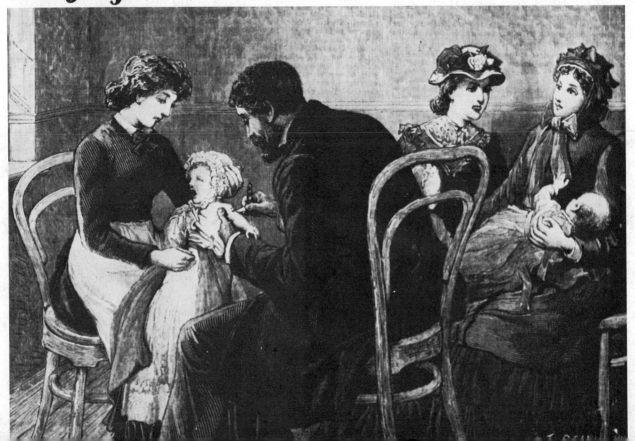

as painless. In the 1860s, he found that a mild carbolic acid solution was best for sterilizing hands, instruments, wounds, and dressings. Lister's discoveries are said to have saved more lives than were lost in all the wars of the 1800s.

Like the discoveries in modern agriculture and industry, discoveries in medicine helped people live longer. Because of these discoveries, cities could grow, and city dwellers could live healthy lives.

Biology changed ideas. Ever since the ancient Greeks, there were philosophers who believed that the earth and living things had evolved from simple to complex forms. In the 19th century, the English naturalist Charles Darwin developed a theory to explain why there was such a variety of plant and animal types and why some types had disappeared while others lived on. He suggested that, because animals multiply faster than their food supply, they are always fighting to live. Those that live must be in some way better fitted to live in their environment than are those that die. So the fittest live on to bring forth another generation that is adapted in the same way. Darwin called nature's way of choosing "the principle of natural selection."

These three ideas—the fight to live, the survival of the fittest, and natural selection—formed the base of Darwin's theory of evolution. For more than 20 years, he carefully gathered facts to support his theory. In 1859, his findings appeared in *The Origin of Species by Means of Natural Selection.*

Darwin's theory said that, in a way, all living things evolved from simpler forms over the ages of time. In *The Descent of Man* (1871), Darwin wrote that human beings and apes had the same ancestor.

Just as the 16th-century scientists had touched off a storm of protest when they said the earth was not the center of the universe, Darwin's ideas were the topic of arguments all over 19th-century Europe. The churches felt he went against the Bible's story of creation.

The defenders and enemies of Darwinism fought for half a century. Finally many persons, even church people, came to feel that science dealt with some parts of human life and religion with others. They decided that people could accept both Darwinism and Christianity.

What Darwin did not explain well was the way in which characteristics are passed on. Gregor Mendel, an Austrian monk, did pioneering work in that field. His careful work with plants led to the belief that passed-on characteristics are carried by tiny things now

Mary Shelley   Charles Dickens   George Eliot   Percy Bysshe Shelley

called *genes*. Mendel's laws of heredity did not become widely known when he first stated them in the 1860s. Later, they became the base of the science of genetics.

Psychology became a science. Modern *psychology*, the science of human behavior, grew from the work of doctors who studied people's conscious lives. They were quite interested in the ways the senses worked. In the 1890s, Russian Ivan Pavlov went much further. In his experiments, he gave food to a dog while he rang a bell. Food and bell became very closely joined in the dog's mind. Finally, the dog watered at the mouth when a bell was rung, even when no food was present.

Pavlov's work with dogs changed scientists' ideas about people. Many of them took the view that people often acted in response to stimuli.

Most important of all was the work of a Viennese doctor, Sigmund Freud. He believed that people often act because of unknown needs and desires. In the 1890s, he used psychoanalysis to bring out hidden motives. Freud's theory explained how these hidden motives worked. As a result, people began to learn about the impulses that direct their behavior. Freud's ideas gave understanding of human beings a new direction and provided new ways of treating mental illness.

section review 2

1. What chemical advances did John Dalton and Dmitri Mendeleev make?

2. How did discoveries about petroleum change transportation?

3. How did discoveries about antiseptics, vaccination, anesthetics, and fermentation change medical knowledge?

4. What was Darwin's theory of evolution?

3 The arts showed great energy

Literature and the fine arts in the 1800s were very much alive. Here, too, industrialism clearly was felt. Some writers and artists firmly turned their backs on their own fast-moving, mixed-up world. They favored a dream life, the strange, or the past. Others tried to understand and describe the forces that were changing society.

As the middle class grew in size and power, it became more important as a sound-

Edgar Allan Poe   Johannes Brahms   Peter Ilich Tchaikovsky   Giuseppe Verdi

ing board for creative works. In addition, the economic ability of the middle class to buy creative works meant that artists, writers, and musicians no longer depended on wealthy patrons. As a result, they were freer in using their own ideas in many different art forms.

Romanticism ruled the early 1800s. Toward the end of the 1700s, people began to turn against the firm hold of reason that had marked the Enlightenment. Several artists and thinkers took a different view, called *romanticism.*

Romanticists believed that people must pay attention to feelings they did not fully control. Feelings of love and the touch of beauty or religion, they said, could not be explained in rational terms alone. Romanticists believed above all that art must mirror the artist's self in the artist's own way. Romanticism was, in another sense, a turning away from the ugly and materialistic side of the new industrial society.

In literature, writers let their imaginations run freely. Liberty was an important theme. A German movement known as *Sturm und Drang* (Storm and Stress) developed the theme of youthful genius in defiance of accepted standards. Among its members was Johann Friedrich von Schiller. His drama *Wil-*

liam Tell dealt with the Swiss fight for freedom. Johann Wolfgang von Goethe in the early 1800s wrote the epic drama *Faust*. English poets Lord Byron and Percy Bysshe Shelley also showed a spirit of rebellion.

Romanticists believed that beauty should rule life, as English poet John Keats wrote in "Ode on a Grecian Urn."

"Beauty is truth, truth beauty,"—that is all
Ye know on earth, and all ye need to
know.

An important romantic theme was nature. However, nature was not orderly and mechanical, as 18th-century thinkers pictured it. Instead, it had a wild beauty.

The romanticists thought, as did the French social philosopher Jean Jacques Rousseau, that simple (primitive) people were noble and good because civilization had not spoiled them. So romanticists became quite interested in myths, fairy tales, and folk songs. Some collections of these stories and songs, such as the Grimm brothers' fairy tales, are treasures of the Romantic Movement.

Because reason was not enough, some romanticists took their ideas from unknown worlds, such as dreams. Examples are Englishman Samuel Taylor Coleridge's poem, "The Rime of the Ancient Mariner" and American Edgar Allan Poe's poetry.

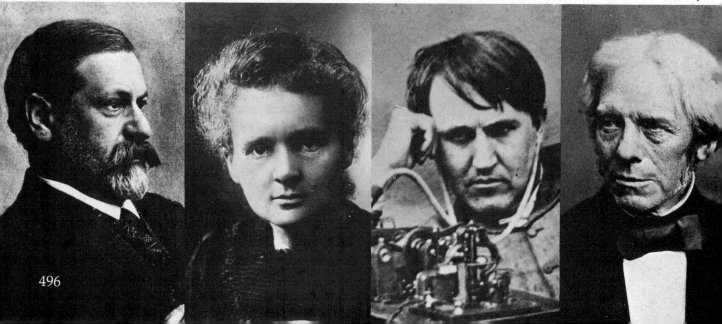

Sigmund Freud   Marie Curie   Thomas Edison   Michael Faraday

Interest in the strange led the romanticists back to the Middle Ages, which they saw as a golden time of brave and just deeds, romance, and adventure. Such feelings are written into the novels of the Scotsman Sir Walter Scott and the French author Victor Hugo.

Painting, like literature, mirrored romantic ideas. Frenchman Eugene Delacroix [də lä-krwä'], a master of color, painted strange scenes. Some of his subjects came from the revolts of the 1820s and 1830s. Painters in England, like poets, found subjects in nature. The works of John Constable and J. M. W. Turner were fresh and dramatic. Other landscape painters of the time thought these works revolutionary.

Romanticism in architecture was seen in a return to the Gothic style of the Middle Ages. In France and Germany, much work was done in repairing medieval buildings. In England, churches, houses, and public buildings were covered with pointed arches, flying buttresses, and turrets.

Romanticism in music, as in the other arts, meant a break with old forms. Composers added to 18th-century forms in order to say more with their music. For example, the symphony became much longer and had more parts. The orchestra grew in size, and many instruments were made easier to play. The piano, which allowed changes in tone, took the harpsichord's place. All of these changes appeared in the music of Ludwig van Beethoven. His grand symphonies and chamber music bridged classicism and romanticism.

The romanticists' music was quite emotional. Franz Schubert wrote hundreds of songs that covered a wide range of feelings. Romantic music was marked, too, by the use of subjects from folk music. And the solo performer became very important. Two composer-pianists who used folk subjects in their works were Frédéric Chopin [shō'pan] and Franz Liszt.

Later movements turned against romanticism. In the mid-1800s, some very sentimental romantic art caused people to turn against its ideals. Much of the art had become simply poured-out feelings.

In literature, *realism* became a popular form. Realists, like the romanticists, knew about the bad social conditions of their times. But as romanticists tried to run from life, realists tried to show it as it was. Possibly the best known of these was an Englishman, Charles Dickens. His pictures of poor and put-upon people called attention to needed reforms. *Oliver Twist* showed the hard lives of children in workhouses and slums. *Nicholas Nickleby* and *David Copperfield* pointed out wrongs in education. *Bleak House* dealt with the social evils of the legal system.

In France, Honoré de Balzac wrote more than 90 novels for a series, *The Human Comedy*. The stories presented a searching picture of lower- and middle-class French life. Many of his novels attacked greed and social climbing.

Humorist Mark Twain described American middle-western and frontier life. At the same time, his writings made clear the evils of slavery and other social wrongs.

A Norwegian, Henrik Ibsen, wrote realistic drama in a new way. Through it, he presented many problems that until then could not be talked about in public. In his well-known play *A Doll's House*, he attacked marriage without love as immoral.

Other realistic writers centered their works on the characters they drew so well. In *Madame Bovary*, author Gustave Flaubert [flō-bār'] described a weak woman whose boredom with her marriage led to her downfall. The works of two Russian novelists show deep understanding of the self. Feodor Dostoevski [dos'tə yef'skē] wrote *Crime and Punishment*. Leo Tolstoy wrote *War and Peace* and *Anna Karenina*. English authors William Makepeace Thackeray, George Eliot (Mary Ann Evans), and Robert Browning showed

498

Claude Monet said that light is the major person in the picture when he described the painting style called impressionism. Monet's "Water Lilies" *bottom left*, one of a series of paintings with the same title and subject, does make light the main idea. Like other impressionists, Monet used thick dabs of paint on the canvas. At close range, the painting is unintelligible. But viewed from a distance, objects appear on the canvas and shimmer with glowing light. American Mary Cassatt joined the impressionists in Paris and spent a long career as a painter. The theme of mother and child was a favorite of hers, as she showed in "The Bath" *bottom right*. Like Monet, Cassatt used dabs of paint to create the background pattern and made light the central subject, especially in the child's towel. Georges Seurat carried forward the ideas of impressionism. He worked out a system of painting entirely with tiny roundish dots of about the same size. These he applied with scientific precision from dot to dot. This very difficult procedure changed natural appearance into a mathematical plan of dots and space. Seurat was a master of this style, known as pointillism. His "Sunday Afternoon on the Island of Grand Jatte" *top* is a brilliant example of pointillism.

keen insight into personality and deep interest in their characters' lives.

Another group of writers, the naturalists, tried to describe life as scientists would. They thought that writers should tell their stories without comment or feeling. From 1871 to 1893, a Frenchman, Émile Zola, wrote about families in 20 novels that are almost like a doctor's case book of patients.

In painting, Gustave Courbet [kür bā'], son of a French peasant, spoke for realism. He believed in painting people and places as they were. He once stated that he did not paint angels because he had never seen one. Courbet stirred other painters to begin a movement known as *impressionism.*

The impressionists worked out new ways to put light and color into their paintings. They tried to present a single moment in time, before their own feelings changed it.

French painters in this style were Claude Monet, Edgar Degas, and August Renoir.

Other artists, though, turned away from impressionism. In France, Paul Cézanne [sā-zan'], led post-impressionists in the study of form and space. Dutch artist Vincent van Gogh used bright colors and bold outlines to show his feelings about people and places.

Architects in the time of realism left Gothic models in favor of more original styles. New building materials such as steel, reinforced concrete, and strong glass, helped in making the changes. In the United States, Louis Sullivan based his work on the idea that buildings must suit their functions. A modern bank, he said, should not look like a Greek temple. A warehouse was not a medieval castle. Sullivan was an early builder of skyscrapers, which put together new materials and new designs.

Music in the late 1800s showed several influences. German composer Johannes Brahms remained a romanticist in his symphonies. Italian Giuseppe Verdi, also a romanticist, composed such operas as *Rigoletto, La Traviata,* and *Aida.* Strong nationalist feeling is clear in the work of German Richard Wagner. His music dramas are based on German folk tales. Russians made up a school of nationalist composers. Peter Ilich Tchaikovsky and others drew on Russian folk music in their compositions. The French composer Claude Debussy, an impressionist, filled his music with bright, shimmering effects.

section review 3

1. What was romanticism?

2. How was realism different from romanticism?

3. Describe the style of painting known as impressionism.

4. How did architectural styles change during the time of realism?

26 *chapter review* ❖ ❖ ❖

Section Summaries

1. The Industrial Revolution changed the Western world. The Industrial Revolution began in England, where conditions were quite favorable. The rise of industrialism was aided by a doubling of population, which meant workers for the new factories. Economic life was changed by new inventions and methods. In the important textile industry in England, a rapid move from hand to machine work began the factory system. Especially important were changes in iron and steel manufacture and farming by machines. Improved transportation—better roads, canals, railroads, and steamships—knit regions more closely together. Capitalism itself changed to suit new conditions. Old ways of organizing business gave over to industrial and then finance capitalism.

2. Science and medicine progressed rapidly. Meanwhile, the scientific spirit spilled out an ever flowing stream of new discoveries to add to people's knowledge of the world. Dalton's work began a chain of discoveries in chemistry and physics that brought great changes in a few decades. Inventors such as Morse, Bell, Edison, and Marconi helped make a line of communications that would ring the world. Others found new power sources, such as gas and petroleum. In medicine, one of the greatest changes came with Pasteur's germ theory of disease. Because of it, age-old enemies, such as tuberculosis, were defeated. New chemicals helped make surgery painless as well as safer. The theories of Darwin, Mendel, and Freud opened up other fields for scientific study.

3. The arts showed great energy. The ongoing changes of the time were mirrored in literature and other arts. The ordered neoclassicism of the Age of Reason gave way to romanticism. Most of the arts felt its hold until the mid-1800s. From then on, a large number of forms and movements rose and fell. Among them were the literary realism of Dickens, Flaubert, and Zola; the impressionistic painting of Monet and Renoir; Sullivan's functional architecture; and Tchaikovsky's nationalistic music.

Who? What? When? Where?

1. Name the period—1751 to 1800, 1801 to 1850, or 1851 to 1900—when each of these books, discoveries, or inventions first appeared:
   a. Coleridge's "Rime of the Ancient Mariner"
   b. Darwin's *The Origin of Species by Means of Natural Selection*
   c. Deere's all-steel plow
   d. Dickens's *Oliver Twist*
   e. Edison's electric light
   f. Flaubert's *Madame Bovary*
   g. McAdam's road surface
   h. Morse's telegraph
   i. Pasteur's rabies vaccine
   j. Watt's steam engine

2. Write a sentence for each of these people that names a contribution made by her or him:
   a. Bessemer   h. Lister
   b. Cartwright   i. McCormick
   c. the Curies   j. Marconi
   d. Faraday   k. Mendel
   e. Freud   l. Mendeleev
   f. Jenner   m. Roentgen
   g. Koch   n. Whitney

3. Tell whether each of these writers was a realist, romanticist, or naturalist:
   a. Balzac   d. Ibsen
   b. Dickens   e. Scott
   c. Eliot   f. Twain

4. Tell whether each of these was a romanticist, realist, impressionist, or post-impressionist:
   a. Cézanne   d. Delacroix
   b. Constable e. Monet
   c. Courbet   f. Renoir

5. Tell what kind of musical form each of these composers is most famous for:
   a. Beethoven d. Liszt
   b. Brahms   e. Tchaikovsky
   c. Chopin   f. Verdi

500

Questions for Critical Thinking

1. Why did the Industrial Revolution begin in England and not in Germany or Russia?

2. Is the Industrial Revolution still going on today? If it is still going on, what are some of its latest developments?

Skill Activities

1. Read *Madame Curie* by Eve Curie to find out more about this famous scientist. Translated by Vincent Shean. (Pocket Books)

2. Report to the class on the life of the person you feel was the most important of this period. Include your ideas of why that person achieved what he or she did.

3. Write a diary of a 19th-century person. Include reactions to new developments and inventions and how these changed life.

4. Find pictures of paintings done in the different styles mentioned in this chapter. Write short paragraphs describing the differences in the paintings you have chosen.

5. Read passages to the class from one of the books named in this chapter. Read parts that show that the author was a romanticist, realist, or naturalist.

chapter **26** *quiz*

Section 1

1. True or false: By 1900, all nations had gone through an industrial revolution.

2. One thing that led to the Industrial Revolution in England was: a. a shortage of workers, b. good natural resources, c. a mild climate

3. John McAdam, James Watt, and George Stephenson all aided the development of: a. the textile industry, b. agriculture, c. transportation

4. Industrial capitalism was based on: a. small companies run by their owners, b. large corporations run by salaried managers, c. trade between weak nations

Section 2

5. One of the first batteries was made by: a. Watt, b. Roentgen, c. Volta

6. Morse's, Bell's, and Marconi's inventions improved: a. transportation, b. communication, c. agriculture.

7. True or false: Before 1850, surgeons did not wash their operating coats often because they did not know about germs.

8. The scientist who proved that germs cause diseases was: a. Pasteur, b. Lister, c. Koch

Section 3

9. Beethoven, Chopin, and Debussy were all musicians, while Renoir, van Gogh, and Delacroix were all: a. poets, b. painters, c. novelists

10. The artistic style that encouraged writers to express their own feelings was: a. realism, b. naturalism, c. romanticism

11. True or false: The novel *Oliver Twist* deals with the evils of slavery in France.

12. True or false: Louis Sullivan designed buildings to suit their functions, not to look like Greek temples or medieval castles.

SOCIAL PROTEST AND MASS SOCIETY

Käthe Kollwitz's lithograph of a workers' protest illustrates Marx's theory of class struggle.

It was a town of red brick, or of brick that would have been red if the smoke and ashes had allowed it; but as matters stood it was a town of unnatural red and black, like the painted face of a savage. . . . It had a black canal in it, and a river that ran purple with ill-smelling dye, and vast piles of buildings full of windows where there was a rattling and a trembling all day long, and where the piston of the steam-engine worked monotonously up and down, like the head of an elephant in a state of melancholy madness. It contained several large streets all very like one another, and many small streets still more like one another, inhabited by people equally like one another, who all went in and out at the same hours, with the same sound upon the same pavements, to do the same work, and to whom every day was the same as yesterday and tomorrow, and every year the counterpart of the last and the next.

This picture of a dirty, ugly industrial town and the deadly sameness of the lives of its people appeared in Charles Dickens's novel *Hard Times* (1854).

Dickens was one of several writers who managed to awaken the social conscience of the English people. Many others—social critics, church leaders, and well-doers—spoke out against the social evils of their time. This social protest movement covered Europe. Its roots were in the 1700s. Three great revolutions had centered attention on social problems.

The first was the intellectual movement known as the Enlightenment. It started the idea that social institutions must be studied to learn whether they did or did not help people in their natural right to seek life, liberty, and happiness.

The second was the French Revolution. It showed how the direct acts of the people could destroy the old feudal system and put in its place a republican government.

The third was the Industrial Revolution. In the long run, the steam engine, the factory, and the railroad changed society much more than had the French Revolution.

The rather swift change caused huge problems. For example, the new technology led to greater wealth. But many people thought that wealth was not fairly shared by everyone. Many stayed very poor, and others became very rich. The desire to share in the wealth brought bitter words and stronger social protest.

The three revolutions were all part of an even larger change. European society was turning into the first mass civilization. And it took several forms.

A mass market grew for manufactured goods. Millions of new voters changed small political parties into huge, nationwide groups. Workers built labor unions with millions of members. Compulsory public schools began to educate millions of children. Mass-circulation newspapers appeared for the first time. Mass public transportation systems were built in all large cities. Mass

spectator sports were born. In short, life as we know it today in the Western world—mass urban living—took shape in the late 1800s. This chapter tells how:

1. Urbanism and industrialism raised many problems.

2. Socialists asked for far-reaching changes.

3. An age of mass politics began.

4. An urban mass society grew.

1 Urbanism and industrialism raised many problems

The Industrial Revolution's strongest critics saw many evils. Those they marked as the seven deadly sins were: unhealthy, dangerous factories; impossibly long working hours; child labor; unjust use of women; low wages; slums; and repeated loss of jobs.

Growing cities had many different problems. In 1800, Europe was a giant farming community. No city anywhere held as many as a million people. By 1900, though, most western Europeans lived in great urban areas. Five cities held over a million people. London alone had more than 6.5 million.

Rapidly growing old cities and those newly built brought many problems. Streets often were unpaved. Lighting was poor. Water supplies were too small. London had no police force until 1829. In 1838, the industrial city of Birmingham still used pigs to get rid of garbage from its 170 thousand people. Tuberculosis and epidemics of typhoid fever and other diseases ended many lives.

In view of today's standards, living condi-

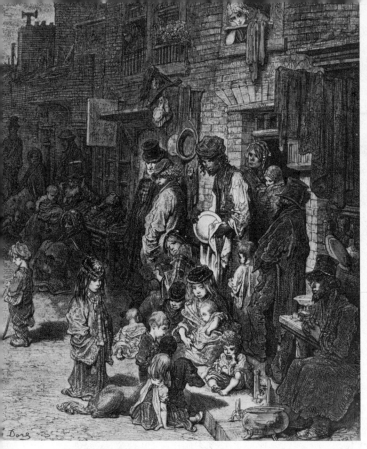

Gustave Doré drew these two views of London and the effects of growing cities. At *left* is a street scene showing a lane in a slum. *Above* is a more distant view of the crowded conditions of the time for London's poor.

tions in the great industrial towns of the mid-1800s certainly were terrible. But city living then was better than it had been in the mid-1700s. And English industrial towns in the mid-1800s were less crowded and no dirtier than the great nonindustrial towns of other countries. Part of the blame for the large amount of disease in cities can be laid on the laws of the time. Because people had to pay taxes on windows and bricks, few were used in buildings. The buildings of the day were dark, airless, and fire hazards. Taxes on tiles slowed the laying of drains and sewers.

Workers labored under hard conditions.
Working conditions in factories, mills, and mines were unhealthy and dangerous. With few safety devices on machines, there were many accidents. An injured worker almost never received compensation for loss of a leg or an arm.

Men, women, and children worked from 12 to 15 hours a day. In 1835, about a third of the factory workers in the cotton industry in England were young people. Half of them were less than 14 years old.

Industrialization should not be blamed for all the social problems of the 19th century. Women and children, for example, quite often worked on farms and in cottage industries. The most cruelly used workers were in country villages, not in the growing manufacturing towns. In the towns, the worst working conditions were in small shops in cellars or garrets, not in factories that used steam power.

Real wages, that is, what workers could actually buy with their earnings, remained low for unskilled factory workers. But for the large and growing number of skilled workers, real wages rose. Both their diet and clothing improved.

Suffering and poverty were still there. But the hard conditions were not new and were

504

not there simply because industrialism had arrived. What was new was an angry public awakened to the terrible conditions and a growing social consciousness that called for something to be done about them. This force was felt strongly first in England.

Business leaders favored the laissez-faire system. The Industrial Revolution made its own leaders. These bold middle-class men owned the railroads, mines, and factories that were so greatly changing the life of the times. They believed that government should not regulate business. And they favored the ideas of *laissez-faire* capitalism. (Laissez-faire [les′ā fār′] is French for "let

do." In business, the term came to mean "let them do as they please.")

Adam Smith, a Scottish teacher, was the first important person to write favorably about capitalism. In *The Wealth of Nations* (1776), Smith stated that nations could gain wealth by removing such trade restrictions as tariffs. Then supply and demand could govern the exchange of goods. If the demand for a product rose, producers would automatically increase the supply by increasing production. If demand fell, they would cut back on supply by reducing production.

Over twenty years later, Thomas Malthus, an English economist, made the laissez-faire idea much stronger with *An Essay on the Prin-*

Industry hired many children to work long hours for very little money. Children labored from 5:30 in the morning to 8 at night with only 40 minutes off for meals. Though they earned very little, their wages were needed by their families.

Daily Life

In some factories as at *left*, the children employed there were so small they had to climb onto the frames of the machines to reach their work. In England, the Children's Employment Commission of 1842 used the drawing *below* to show the abuse of child labor in coal mines. Children worked in the mines because adults were too big to fit in the narrow mine shafts.

ciples of Population (1798). Malthus placed the blame for poverty on the growing population. If it went on growing, it would be larger than its food supply. Malthus's answer was that people should marry later in life and have fewer children. He believed, too, that social reforms would not help. They would simply lead to a larger population.

Both Thomas Malthus and Adam Smith wrote at a time when English society was still largely agricultural. In the early 1800s, English banker and economist David Ricardo put together Smith's free-trade ideas and Malthus's population theories and applied them to the new industrial society.

It was useless to try to improve workers' wages, Ricardo said. Wages were governed by an "Iron Law." That is, when population grew, the labor supply would grow, too. As more workers competed for jobs, the jobs would go to those who would work for less. Workers would be poorer and so fewer of their children would survive to adulthood. The labor supply would then go down and wages would rise. Workers would have more children, and the labor market would again be too full. So, Ricardo reasoned, government efforts to improve the lot of factory workers were bad. Instead of interfering with the law of supply and demand, the government should practice laissez-faire.

Members of the new industrial capitalist class eagerly accepted and strongly supported laissez-faire. Supply and demand alone, they said, would control the production of goods and their selling prices. Consumers would have fair wages and prices and improved goods. And businesses could be sure of having good profits. Industrial capitalists cared little that laissez-faire did not always bring fair wages or just prices. For most of the 1800s these ideas were the accepted social philosophy of the growing middle class.

Many voices spoke out for reform. The most important piece of political legislation in 19th-century England was the Reform Bill of 1832. It gave seats in the House of Commons to the new industrial towns of the north. By extending the right to vote, it gave a share of political power to the new business class.

Those who spoke for business in the Reform Parliament then used their new power to end slavery in the British Empire (1833). They felt that slavery was morally wrong. In 1835, their power helped reduce the upper-class landowner's hold on city government and to gain a hold for the new industrialists.

These reforms helped the industrialist Whig party. So the Tory party, originally the party of the landowning class, took up the workers' cause. They set up parliamentary groups to look into conditions in the factories and mines. The awful state described in their reports caused public anger. Between 1833 and 1847, the Tories pushed through acts that regulated the use of children and stopped the use of women, girls, and young boys in mines. A 10-hour workday also was set.

The drive toward reform involved, besides Charles Dickens, philosophers Jeremy Bentham and John Stuart Mill. Bentham made known the phrase "the greatest happiness for the greatest number." He said that the true test of any institution was its usefulness to society.

Bentham's pupil, Mill, championed personal liberty. His essay *On Liberty* (1859) is a defense of individual freedom. He did not accept laissez-faire and thought that social laws were needed. Mill's ideas on liberty and his humane, practical ideas about problems have been used down to the present day.

section review 1

1. What were some of the problems caused by the quick growth of cities and factories?

2. In laissez-faire capitalism, what is the relationship of government to business? How did Smith, Malthus, and Ricardo help form the middle-class belief in laissez-faire?

3. What reforms did the Whigs and Tories make in England?

4. What conditions did people such as Dickens, Bentham, and Mill try to change?

2 Socialists asked for far-reaching changes

Throughout the 1800s, many plans were offered to help workers and society in general. Some thinkers believed that the workers should own, manage, and control all means of production. Others thought that the government should have that power. These systems of social organization came to be called *socialism*. The persons who believed in them were known as socialists.

Many kinds of socialism arose in the early 1800s. Each offered its own plan for making over society.

Early socialists hoped to build a better world. The first to deal with the problem of how to change society were a number of early 19th-century thinkers and writers in France and England who each had different ideas. In general, early socialists in England and France dreamed of a community based on the principles of cooperation and economic planning. They hoped that from their model communities all people would discover the good in socialism and would want the same kind of life. These early socialists wanted to bring about a good society through persuasion.

One of the best known of the early socialists was the Englishman Robert Owen. The textile mills he owned in New Lanark, Scotland, had 2,000 workers, 500 of whom were children.

Owen took charge of the mills in 1800. He wanted to improve the living and working conditions of his people. He raised wages, and built schools and new houses. No workers were less than 11 years old. As life improved, crime and disease were almost wiped out. And Owen's mills still made a profit.

Owen's ideas led to the founding of the Cooperative Movement. In 1844, a group of linen workers of Rochdale, England, gathered a sum equal to $140 and started a store. They were able to purchase goods at the store for fair prices and they shared the profits.

Other cooperative stores, or consumer co-ops, were formed elsewhere in Europe. Co-ops grew quite strong in England and in Scandinavia, where the co-ops owned and operated factories as well as retail stores. In the United States, storage and marketing co-ops became important among farmers and are still important today.

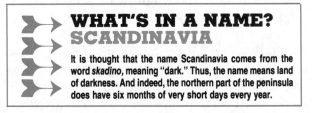

WHAT'S IN A NAME?
SCANDINAVIA

It is thought that the name Scandinavia comes from the word *skadino*, meaning "dark." Thus, the name means land of darkness. And indeed, the northern part of the peninsula does have six months of very short days every year.

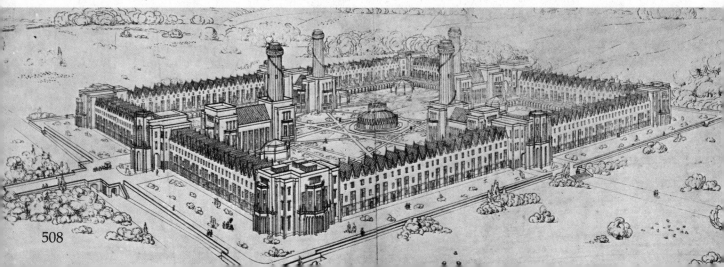

In New Harmony, Indiana, a community of 2,000 people tried to live by Robert Owen's principles.

Karl Marx brought a new kind of socialism.
Karl Marx thought the early socialists were just dreamers. He offered what he believed was the true solution to society's ills. The name he gave to his ideas was *scientific socialism*.

Marx was born in 1815. He attended school in Germany and then went to France as a journalist. There he met Friedrich Engels. They became friends for life.

In 1848, Marx and Engels wrote the *Communist Manifesto*. The pamphlet stated most of the ideas of Marxian socialism and set forth a whole plan for social revolution. The *Manifesto* drew little interest when it first appeared. But it would become one of the most important papers of modern history.

Also in 1848, Marx joined in the February revolution in Paris and the uprising in Germany. When these revolts failed, Marx escaped to London. There he began the first of three books that made up *Das Kapital*, his major work. The first book appeared in 1867. He died in 1883, before he could finish the third book. Engels completed the work for him.

Karl Marx was a revolutionary who believed that the capitalistic system was doomed. Capitalism would be destroyed, he believed, in a revolution. The workers—Marx called them the *proletariat* [prō′lə tar′ē-ət]—would tear control from the middle-class bourgeoisie. Too, Marx claimed that the socialist revolution must happen. He was sure of its coming because of the answers that he gave to two important questions: (1) Why do changes take place in history; and (2) How does the capitalist system work?

His answer to the first was that changes happen mostly because of changes in the economy. He stated that groups (he called them "classes") who decide the ways goods are made and distributed are the ones who control the society. So they decide its laws, government, religion, and culture.

When new groups find new ways of mak-

Karl Marx

ing or distributing goods, they become rich and strong. They begin to speak against the older ruling groups. Then a fight for control breaks out. That is when a revolution takes place. The new groups then take over control from the old ruling groups.

Marx called the process *class struggle*. He said that all important changes in history have come about through class struggle. The *Communist Manifesto* declared: "The history of all hitherto existing society is the history of class struggles."

Marx used the French Revolution to show how class struggle works. That, he said, was when the capitalist (bourgeois) class of merchants and bankers overturned the feudal regime of landowners. The bourgeoisie had been kept out of power. Now it ruled.

Industrialization, though, had begun to make a new lower class—the workers. So a new class struggle would begin. In the revolution, the workers would take control. The workers would destroy the capitalist system. They would control all the means of production and distribution themselves. Then no group would ever again be lower than another. A classless society would be born, and the class struggle would stop.

Marx based his belief in a coming workers' (socialist) revolution on his answer to the second question: How does the capitalist system work? In *Das Kapital* (German for "capital"), he made a very careful study of capitalism.

Marx began his work with his *labor theory of value.* He stated that the value of any product depends on the amount of work needed to make it. For example, making a piano might use 1,000 hours of labor. If the workers had been paid at the rate of $1.00 an hour, the real value of the piano would be $1,000. If the manufacturer sold it for $2,000, the extra $1,000 was surplus value. That really belonged to the workers, because they had made the real value of the product through their work. Instead, this surplus value was profit in the manufacturer's pocket.

Logically, in this system, Marx said, the poor would become poorer and the rich richer as wealth settled into a few hands. Meanwhile, goods would pile up because the workers would be too poor to buy them. Then businesses would fail, factories would close, and millions would lose their jobs. Finally, after several depressions, capitalism would fall. Then the workers would take control, destroy the capitalistic system, and set up a socialist society.

Marx's ideas were attacked. Marx's ideas about changes in history taught many people that economic forces are important. In the late 1800s and early 1900s, wealth did settle into a few hands. Industry did grow ever larger. And several depressions did hurt business and workers. Yet, the events have shown that Marx was a poor prophet.

In his own day, and long after, Marx's ideas have been widely attacked. Most historians believe that Marx's ideas about historical forces are too simple, that events do not happen because of economics alone. People also act for other reasons—patriotism, religion, political loyalties.

Class struggle as a theory of historical change has serious faults. Many events in history show that people in several classes fight together against a common enemy. The two world wars have shown that nationalism is a stronger force than class feelings.

Economists have shown that Marx's labor theory of value is not wholly correct. The cost of making a product is not just in the labor needed to make it. The manufacturer's costs in the factory, in materials, in workers' wages and benefits, and in storing, transporting, and advertising the product are also part of the cost. Then too, the general conditions of supply and demand help to decide the price of a product. For example, an oversupply of an item can send the selling price down. It may even fall below the cost of the work that went into it.

History did not bear out Marx's predictions. In the final years of the 1800s, conditions for the workers improved. Wages rose, and workers could buy the products made in the factories and mills. To be sure, some of the rich did become richer, but most of the poor did not become poorer. Instead, the general standard of living rose to heights never before reached in history.

section review 2

1. What kind of society did early socialists want to have? What successes did they have?

2. What was the Cooperative Movement?

3. What was Marx's "class struggle"? What was his labor theory of value?

4. What were some arguments used against Marx's ideas? In what ways were his predictions incorrect?

3 An age of mass politics began

In the years between 1870 and 1914, Western civilization was becoming a mass urban, industrialized society. No other like it had ever been seen before in all of human history. This great change came at the same time that the age of mass politics began. We are living in that age still.

Many countries began universal male suffrage. The most important political change in the half-century before World War I came in the new right of all men to vote. All property requirements were ended. Voting rights had become the chief symbol of democracy, and people fought long, bitter battles to get them. For a long time, property-owning classes turned away every effort to give men without property the right to vote.

France, in 1871, was the first country to allow all men to vote. Switzerland followed three years later. By 1884, Britain had allowed all male householders (homeowners) to vote. But not until 1918 could all Englishmen vote. In the 1890s, the Netherlands, Spain, and Norway removed property restrictions. Portugal, Sweden, and Denmark did so after 1900. Germany had granted the right by 1890, but Italy not until 1912.

The millions of new voters changed political parties into mass organizations. In the early 1800s, when only property owners could vote, political parties were small groups of upper-class men. Politicians did not ask for votes. In the late 1800s, though, more men had voting rights. Then a politician had to cover a whole district to meet people, make speeches, and win votes. Campaigns became costly. So politicians needed large parties with many dues-paying members to pay the bills. Today mass political

Susan B. Anthony and Emmeline Pankhurst

Elizabeth Cady Stanton and John Stuart Mill

parties and costly election campaigns are an expected part of political life in the West.

Women fought for legal rights. The general feeling toward women in the 1800s had two sides. Male-run society did not think highly of women's intelligence. But at the same time women were looked on as the base of the home and family. It was feared that if women had a part in public business they would not care for their families. Then the cornerstone of all civilized life, the home, would fall apart. In Britain and France, women were not allowed to own property. When a woman married, any property she had became her husband's. Women could not start divorce proceedings against their husbands, had no legal claim on their children, and could not vote in elections.

In the mid-1800s, reformers in Europe and the United States began to call for equal legal and political rights for women. Most of the leaders were intelligent, middle-class women, such as Susan B. Anthony, Elizabeth Cady Stanton, and Emmeline Pankhurst.

English philosopher John Stuart Mill helped the women's cause. In *The Subjection of Women* (1869), Mill stated that men taught women to believe from childhood that submission was a part of woman's nature. Then men could rule them more easily. As long as women had low legal and social status, he said, no one would ever know their true nature and abilities. He wrote:

What we now call the nature of women is an eminently artificial thing—the result of forced repression. . . . It may be asserted without scruple, that no other class of dependents have had their character so entirely distorted from its natural proportions by their relations with their masters.

But public feeling was hard to change and progress was slow. Gradually, women were able to find jobs outside the home. Florence Nightingale, an English nurse during the Crimean War (1854–1856), helped open nursing to women. Later, women entered some universities, especially in Italy and Switzerland. In the United States, where workers were needed, large numbers of women became factory workers, teachers, and secretaries.

By the end of the 1800s, women in most Western countries could by law own property. But the right to vote was still denied them.

The earliest voting rights for women were gained in the frontier areas. Women there were more nearly equal and had greater freedom. The first was New South Wales in Australia (1867). Wyoming in the United States followed (1869), and then New Zealand (1886). The first European country to allow women to vote was Norway (1907).

But the major countries held back. Only after World War I were women allowed to vote in Great Britain (1918). There, Emmeline Pankhurst and her two daughters led a long mass political fight to gain that right. The United States gave the right in 1920. Most other European countries followed after that.

Governments made social reforms. The kinds of reforms that western European governments made in the years after 1870 showed the influence of the new voters. The politics of all European states paid more attention to social problems. Big towns and mechanized industry meant more voters in the industrial wage-earning classes. These voters were the people who wanted their governments to become active in the social affairs of their nations.

The British government had already passed bills to regulate working conditions in factories, mines, and mills. So it began to work in new fields. In the 1870s, it passed laws to govern housing and public health. In 1902 the Education Act completed the work

American social worker Jane Addams established Hull House to service a slum neighborhood in Chicago.

of building a national system of primary and secondary education.

When the new Liberal party came to power in 1905, it made even stronger reforms. It granted legal holidays with pay and passed the National Insurance Act of 1911. That act required contributions from employers and workers, and gave the whole working population guaranteed income during absence from work due to sickness. And certain kinds of workers got unemployment insurance.

Britain had copied from Germany, which, in the 1880s, was the leader in social legislation. The German government hoped to weaken socialism by passing laws aimed at the three most common problems of urban industrial life—sickness, accident, and old age. Later, workers got free medical and hospital care. Factory codes and child labor laws came in 1914.

In France, where industrialization and

urbanization came more slowly, social legislation also was slower. Laws passed in the 1890s limited women to a 10-hour workday and provided in part for pensions and accident insurance. The 10-hour workday was made general in 1900. In 1906, a six-day work week was made legal.

Many other countries followed the leads of Britain, Germany, and France. By 1914, nearly every European country except Russia and the Balkan states had rather good factory codes and labor laws. Minimum standards for house and street building and the public preparation of food and drink also had been set.

Trade unions were formed. Modern *trade unions* are workers' groups that may legally bargain, one or more at a time, with employers for better wages and working conditions. Trade unions did not exist before the 1800s.

Business people and industrialists were bitterly against such workers' groups. They said they had the right to run their own businesses in their own ways. Trade unions would interfere with that right. Every European country in the early 1800s had laws against trade unions.

During most of the 1800s, workers fought a hard battle to make unions legal. The first country to act was Britain, in 1825. Countries on the continent held out much longer. In most countries, unions became legal only after 1860.

In the mid-1880s, trade unions changed. Until then, most unions were made up of skilled workers—mechanics, carpenters, printers. After that time, huge numbers of unskilled or semiskilled workers in whole industries, such as steel, banded together into country-wide unions.

These new unions came into being after a series of long and bitter strikes in the 1880s and 1890s in Belgium, England, France, and Germany. When a dock workers' strike in 1889 shut down the port of London, business people realized that they could not ignore workers' demands for better working conditions. The large industrial unions learned that they could get better results with strikes than with negotiations. As a result, in the years before World War I began in 1914, the whole union movement became more aggressive.

Socialists formed political parties. Workers also tried to improve their lot by forming political parties. The socialists chiefly took the lead. The first party was the German Social Democratic Party, founded in 1875. Soon after, socialist parties like it were formed in Britain, France, and most other countries of western Europe. Their ideas were Marxist, but not revolutionary. Wher-

William Booth founded the Salvation Army in England in 1865. A religious organization, the Salvation Army's main goals were the spiritual reclamation of people and the providing of food and shelter to the poor.

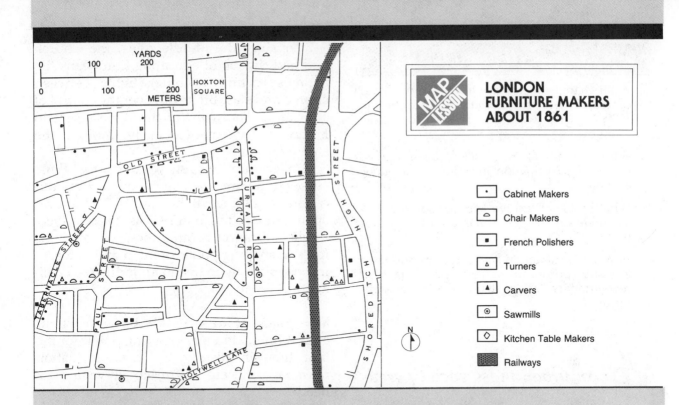

■ MAP LESSON 27: LONDON FURNITURE MAKERS ABOUT 1861

1. This map of part of London shows an area that specialized in furniture making midway through the Industrial Revolution. At that time, most furniture was made by hand, although some power tools were used. Later, furniture was mass produced in factories. But in 1861, the furniture-making industry was divided among several different crafts. Each did just one part of the manufacturing of an item. List the types of crafts found on the south side of Old Street.

2. Transportation systems have been important throughout history. From the map, what transportation system would you guess was the one most used by furniture makers in 1861? Why?

3. The railroad was a relatively new invention in 1861. Why are so few furniture makers found along its route?

4. How many turners are located east of the railway on this map?

5. What advantages did these turners have over the turner on Tabernacle Street?

6. Hoxton Square is the location of only three furniture makers. What are their crafts?

7. Is the sawmill on Tabernacle Street on the east or the west side of the street?

8. The square where Tabernacle Street meets Paul Street is the site of only one furniture maker. What is this person's craft?

9. How many sawmills are located on this map?

ever representative government and democracy were strong, workers used their parties to elect people who would work inside the system for reforms.

The countries of eastern Europe had no parliaments. Political parties and trade unions there were outlawed. Strikes were thought a crime against the state. Those countries had no orderly way to bring about reform. And it was there that Marxism remained strongly revolutionary. Russia was one of those countries.

515

1. What changes took place in the way political campaigns were run from the early to the late 1800s? What was the reason for these changes?

2. Why had a male-run society been against women's participation in politics and public activities?

3. What problems did workers have in organizing trade unions? What has been the goal of trade unions?

4. Why were the followers of Marxist socialism in eastern European countries more in favor of revolutionary tactics than those in western Europe?

4 · An urban mass society grew

The beginning of mass politics was only one sign of the growing mass civilization. Other signs were new social institutions and new ideas about government's role in society.

Public education was developed. Until about 1870, large numbers of Europeans could not read or write. Clearly, society needed people with at least a basic education to run modern factories and cities. So governments began to set up public school systems for children between the ages of 6 and 14.

Between 1871 and 1914 every Western country started a system of public education. On the lowest level, education was made compulsory and free. This was the only way to wipe out illiteracy. At the same time, higher-level schools grew in size and number. From them came engineers, doctors, teachers, technicians, and administrators to fill growing needs.

Ever since the Middle Ages, the Church had had the job of educating Europeans. So in most countries, bitter fights between church and state broke out over the control of education. The worst of these took place in France and Germany. Finally, though, the state won out.

Public education grew so rapidly that Prussia spent 30 times as much on primary education in 1901 as it had in 1871. England spent twice as much in 1914 as it had in 1900. Public education became the greatest single force in shaping public opinion and in teaching people how to live in an industrial civilization.

New kinds of newspapers began. Public education made a mass reading public for the first time in history. So mass-circulation newspapers were begun to serve a new need.

The reports in these newspapers were called yellow journalism (named for a cartoon, "The Yellow Kid," carried in a New York paper). Earlier newspapers had

This cartoon told its readers that ordinary men were too rowdy and ignorant to be trusted with important decisions.

Daily Life

Schools of the mid-19th century were quite different from schools of today. There were few books and no individual desks. Several classes often met in the same room. This drawing shows a school for poor boys in London in 1846.

reported mostly national and international news. Yellow journals reported murder, robbery, and scandal, in big, bold headlines. These stories, in a newspaper that cost only a penny, attracted large numbers of readers and advertisers. Begun in the United States in the 1880s, this type of newspaper quickly spread to other countries.

Another feature of the new yellow journals was sports news. During the late 1880s, mass spectator sports appeared. Games until then had been entertainment for the rich. But when paid public contests started, "games" became "sports."

In the 1870s, soccer became a spectator sport. To this day, it has remained the most popular sport in the world. Shortly after-

ward, boxing and baseball became spectator sports. By 1876, the United States had enough professional baseball teams to organize the National League.

Local government grew rapidly. While national governments were making social security systems for workers, local governments were finding ways to make crowded cities livable. Between 1870 and 1914 there were great changes in city living. Modern urban life was born in this time.

Forward-looking mayors of industrial cities led the way in adding new services. In England by 1900, nearly every large town owned its gas and water supplies. The cities built schools, libraries, hospitals, museums, parks, and art galleries. City-run police and fire departments protected the people. And the cities lighted the streets, collected the garbage, and disposed of the sewage. By 1914, most large cities on the continent had these services as well as city-owned public markets, laundries, slaughterhouses, and employment agencies.

Cities had to find a way for great numbers of people to move cheaply and quickly from one part of the city to another. Streetcars came into use in the 1860s. At first, horses pulled them. Later, in the 1880s electricity powered them.

In very large cities, underground railroads (subways) were built. London, in the 1860s, had the first subway. Boston built one in 1895, Paris in 1900, and New York in 1904. Many cities, especially in the United States, saved money by building elevated railroads. These, together with subways, made good, cheap public transportation.

The cost of government rose. The new national social security systems and city services cost a great deal of money. Taxing was the only way to get the large amounts needed. In 1870, no country in Europe had sales or income taxes. (Today, these two taxes are among the biggest sources of government income.) Money that governments needed came mostly from tariffs and from taxes on property.

As the costs of government rose, these taxes did not bring in enough money. Reformers said that new taxes were needed. They favored a *progressive income tax* (a higher tax on big incomes and a lower tax on small incomes). But many people, mostly in the middle and upper classes, were strongly against such a tax. The British government tried to push an income tax through Parliament in 1909. That move caused a constitutional crisis that lasted for two years. The tax

was finally passed in 1911. By 1914 most European countries and the United States had begun the income tax. France, however, did not have one until 1917.

Middle-class views changed. By 1914, a century of social and political change had brought about another important change. The strong laissez-faire feeling of the early 1800s was weakening. People still valued the freedom, dignity, and worth of the individual. But they came to believe that the state should look after the welfare of its people.

The Catholic Church supported this new feeling about government. In 1891, Pope Leo XIII issued a mass-circulated letter, *Rerum Novarum* (of modern things). It defended private property as a natural right. But it pointed out that capitalism had failed to give social justice to the working class. Poverty, insecurity, and degradation were called unjust and unchristian. Socialism, the document said, was Christian when it tried to remove these evils. Only in denying God was socialism unchristian. *Rerum Novarum* asked that Catholics form their own socialist parties and labor unions in order to seek a greater measure of social justice.

section review 4

1. When and why was public education developed?

2. What changes took place in newspapers and public games in the 1800s? What were the first popular spectator sports in Europe and America?

3. Name some of the ways in which city life changed between 1870 and 1914. How did city governments pay for the greater services they provided?

4. How had middle-class views of laissez-faire changed by 1914? In what way did the Catholic Church support this change?

Section Summaries

1. Urbanism and industrialism raised many problems. The rapid spread of industrialism upset many lives. Workers flocked from farms to cities. Crowded, unhealthy housing and poor water supply were problems of city dwellers. Conditions in factories and mines were bad: men, women, and children worked long hours for little pay. But still, the worker's lot in the 1800s was improved over the 1700s. Wages for skilled workers rose, and food and clothing were better. The middle class favored laissez-faire capitalism. Economists Smith, Malthus, and Ricardo supported the laissez-faire theory. Mill spoke for personal liberty. He wanted changes in laissez-faire policies and social laws.

2. Socialists asked for far-reaching changes. Some reformers wanted great social changes. Early socialists tried model communities based on cooperation and economic planning. Workers in the Cooperative Movement owned stores and factories, and shared the profits. Karl Marx began a different form of socialism. In the *Communist Manifesto,* he and Friedrich Engels said that the workers would revolt against the middle class and take over industry and government by force. The revolution, they said, must come because the capitalistic system was doomed. The worker's lot did not grow worse as Marx had predicted. Instead, after 1870 the general standard of living rose higher than ever before.

3. An age of mass politics began. Democracy took great strides forward with universal male suffrage and, later, legal and political rights for women. Labor unions became legal and gained members and power. Socialists worked with governments to reach their goals through reform laws. Only where democratic government was weak or did not exist, as in Russia, did revolutionary Marxism remain strong.

4. An urban mass society grew. In the years between 1870 and 1914, a mass urban civilization came into being. Countries began compulsory public education. Cities began new services for millions of people. Cheap newspapers reached a mass reading public. Political parties became huge organizations. As governments grew, costs rose. New kinds of taxes were invented to pay for them. Most important was the progressive income tax. Over time, middle-class views on government changed from a belief in laissez-faire to a belief in a social state.

Who? What? When? Where?

1. Place these events in chronological order, beginning with the earliest:

   a. The 10-hour workday was established in England.
   b. All English men were allowed to vote.
   c. Male suffrage began in Italy.
   d. Women were given the vote in Norway.
   e. Women were allowed to vote in the United States.
   f. Pope Leo XIII urged Catholics to seek social reform.

2. Write a sentence for each of these that names the author and the subject:

   a. *Rerum Novarum*
   b. *The Wealth of Nations*
   c. *An Essay on the Principles of Population*
   d. *Das Kapital*
   e. *The Subjection of Women*

3. Write a sentence for each of these that tells its main idea:

   a. laissez-faire capitalism
   b. Marxism
   c. early socialism

4. Write a sentence about each of these people that tells about the role she or he played in the growth of social protest:

   a. Susan B. Anthony
   b. Charles Dickens
   c. Emmeline Pankhurst
   d. Jeremy Bentham

Questions for Critical Thinking

1. Why did so many people move from rural areas to work in the unsafe and unhealthy conditions of early factories?

2. Do you agree with the arguments Malthus and Ricardo made for laissez-faire? Explain your thinking.

3. What are some forces in the United States today that unite people to work for certain goals? Which are based on class, ethnic, religious, or other interests?

4. To what extent do you feel Marx's analysis of history as "class struggle" is correct? Give examples of conflicts in the past and their causes.

5. Which of the reforms mentioned in this chapter made the most important changes in society? What reforms do you feel are still needed?

Skill Activities

1. Read *Charles Dickens, Eighteen Twelve to Eighteen Seventy* by Ivor Brown to learn more about the writer and the era in which he lived. (Viking Press, 1970)

2. Discuss the role of women in society today. Do research to find the numbers of women employed, salaries, life span, and so on. Are special laws needed to protect women today?

3. Find out the expense involved in making a particular product, perhaps by visiting a local manufacturer.

4. Collect news clippings about union activities or interview union members to determine the importance of unions today. Interview an employer to find out management's views on the need for unions.

chapter *27* quiz

Section 1

1. True or false: Early factory workers worked in worse conditions than anyone else in Europe.

2. Laissez-faire capitalism meant that: a. laws should be passed to regulate business practices, b. governments should let business owners run their businesses as they wished, c. workers should run the factories

3. An important reformer of the 1800s was: a. Malthus, b. Smith, c. Mill

Section 2

4. The people who believe that the means of production should be in the hands of the workers are called: a. socialists, b. trade unionists, c. capitalists

5. Marx believed that all conflicts are caused by: a. religion, b. nationalism, c. class struggles

6. True or false: Working conditions worsened in the late 1800s.

Section 3

7. The first nation to allow all of its male citizens to vote was: a. England, b. France, c. United States

8. True or false: Women were first given voting rights in the large industrialized nations.

9. Social reform laws were passed because they were wanted by: a. businessmen, b. communists, c. workers

Section 4

10. By 1914, education, transportation, and protection were being provided by: a. cooperatives, b. city governments, c. factory owners

11. True or false: A progressive income tax is one in which the tax rate for both the rich and the poor is the same amount.

12. In *Rerum Novarum* the Catholic Church supported: a. social reform, b. communism, c. laissez-faire capitalism

1. Match the letter on the time line with the event it refers to:

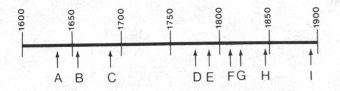

1600   1650   1700   1750   1800   1850   1900

A   B   C   D E   F G   H   I

____Adam Smith published *The Wealth of Nations*.
____Napoleon was defeated at Waterloo.
____Cromwell became Lord Protector.
____Marx and Engels wrote the *Communist Manifesto*.
____Newton published *Mathematical Principles of Natural Philosophy*.
____The Monroe Doctrine was issued.
____The National Assembly issued the "Tennis Court Oath."
____Galileo published *Dialogue on the Two Great Systems of the World*.
____Bismarck was forced to retire.

2. Tell whether each of these people was a leader in the arts, government, social philosophy and reform, or science:

a. Anthony
b. Beethoven
c. Copernicius
d. Degas
e. Díaz
f. Ibsen
g. Lavoisier
h. l'Ouverture
i. Metternich
j. Pankhurst
k. Robespierre
l. Tolstoy
m. Verdi

3. Match each term with its definition:

a. divine right
b. impressionists
c. laissez-faire
d. naturalists
e. scientific method
f. trade unions

____Groups of workers that may legally bargain with employers for better wages and working conditions.
____The belief that a king's power comes from God.

____A way of finding answers by experimentation and observation.
____Business term for "let them do as they please."
____Writers who tried to describe life as scientists would.
____Painters who worked out new ways to use light and color.

4. Match the letter on the map with the places described below:

____Conflict between the Estates-General and the king led to revolution here in the 18th century.
____Its powerful navy protected this country from invasion by Napoleon's army.
____Britain, France, and Russia helped this nation throw off Turkish rule in 1829.
____Otto von Bismarck helped William of Prussia build an empire here.
____Camillo di Cavour and Giuseppi Garibaldi helped to unify this country.

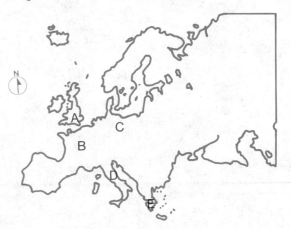

UNIT EIGHT
THE WORLD IN UPHEAVAL

By 1900, the countries of the West were the richest, most powerful, and technologically advanced in the world. Their empires, trade, and influence reached around the globe. No one would have believed that the world was facing fifty years of upheaval that would end Western dominance.

Why did this time have such turmoil? The answer lies in the rapid changes that took place everywhere. The speed of these changes made them hard to adjust to. In particular, national and economic rivalries led to the two world wars.

Wars often create more problems than they solve. In Europe, World War I opened the door to revolution and communism in Russia. War also opened the way for *totalitarianism* in Germany and Italy. The two governments had total control over their citizens. They were nationalistic dictatorships that used terror to protect the rule of a single party. When these countries tried to expand, tensions exploded into World War II.

Meanwhile, the idea of national independence spread in Asia, Africa, and the Middle East. In these areas, strong resentment was building up against *imperialism*, that is, the rule or authority of one country over other countries or colonies. Everywhere, nationalism became the single most powerful force of the 20th century. It, more than anything else, explains why the world has been in upheaval for so much of this century.

During World War II, Germany quickly overran France. Soon Nazi soldiers were parading past the Arc de Triomphe, in the very heart of Paris.

CHAPTER 28
THE BUILDING OF EMPIRES

● Monroe Doctrine issued
Opium War
Sepoy Rebellion began ●
Livingstone first visited Africa ●
● Perry sent to Japan
Meiji Era began ●
Suez Canal finished ●
Wilson born ●

CHAPTER 29
WORLD WAR I

International Red Cross founded ●
International Telegraph Union founded ●

CHAPTER 30
THE RISE OF COMMUNISM IN RUSSIA

● Alexander I died
● Decembrist Revolt
Russian serfs freed ●
Crimean War

Nicholas I lived

CHAPTER 31
THE GROWTH OF NATIONALISM AND DICTATORSHIP

CHAPTER 32
WORLD WAR II

| 1820 | 1830 | 1840 | 1850 | 1860 | 1870 |

1. Monroe, 2. Nicholas I, 3. Russian cossack, 4. Europeans in Yokohama, 5. Red Cross symbol, 6. Einstein, 7. Liliuokalani, 8. Tz'u Hsi, 9. Spanish-American War, 10. British Enfield rifle, 11. Churchill, 12. Trotsky, 13. Sherman tank.

1

2

3

4

5

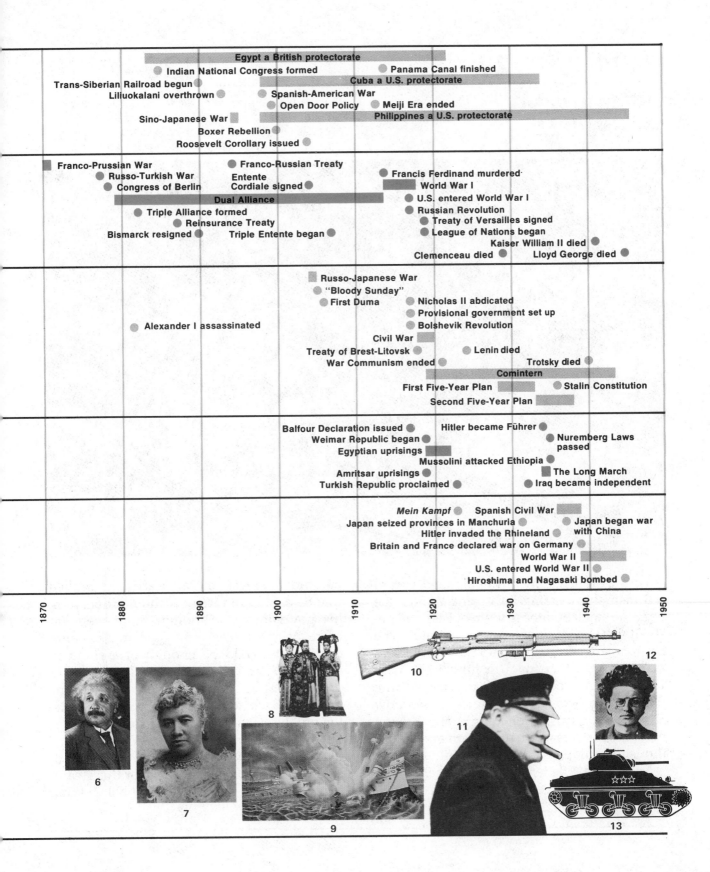

Egypt a British protectorate

Indian National Congress formed   Panama Canal finished

Trans-Siberian Railroad begun

Cuba a U.S. protectorate

Liliuokalani overthrown   Spanish-American War

Open Door Policy   Meiji Era ended

Sino-Japanese War

Philippines a U.S. protectorate

Boxer Rebellion

Roosevelt Corollary issued

Franco-Prussian War   Franco-Russian Treaty

Russo-Turkish War   Entente

Congress of Berlin   Cordiale signed   Francis Ferdinand murdered

Dual Alliance   World War I

    U.S. entered World War I

Triple Alliance formed   Russian Revolution

Reinsurance Treaty   Treaty of Versailles signed

Bismarck resigned   Triple Entente began   League of Nations began

Kaiser William II died

Clemenceau died   Lloyd George died

Russo-Japanese War

"Bloody Sunday"

First Duma   Nicholas II abdicated

Provisional government set up

Alexander I assassinated   Bolshevik Revolution

Civil War

Treaty of Brest-Litovsk   Lenin died

War Communism ended   Trotsky died

Comintern

First Five-Year Plan   Stalin Constitution

Second Five-Year Plan

Balfour Declaration issued   Hitler became Führer

Weimar Republic began   Nuremberg Laws passed

Egyptian uprisings

Mussolini attacked Ethiopia

Amritsar uprisings   The Long March

Turkish Republic proclaimed   Iraq became independent

Mein Kampf   Spanish Civil War

Japan seized provinces in Manchuria   Japan began war with China

Hitler invaded the Rhineland

Britain and France declared war on Germany

World War II

U.S. entered World War II

Hiroshima and Nagasaki bombed

1870   1880   1890   1900   1910   1920   1930   1940   1950

6   7   8   9   10   11   12   13

THE BUILDING OF EMPIRES

It was said that the sun never set on Britain's vast empire. Here Lord and Lady Curzon meet with His Highness the Nizam, or ruler, of Hyderabad, India, in 1900. Lord Curzon was the British viceroy.

A young French army officer stepped aboard a British ship waiting far up the White Nile near the small Sudanese town of Fashoda [fə-shō'də]. The situation was delicate. The Frenchman, Captain Jean Marchand, had marched into that town in July, 1898, with 120 African troops. He had hoisted the French flag over the fort there. It was now September. British General Horatio Kitchener had just steamed up the river with 25 thousand troops.

The White Nile territory, Kitchener said to Marchand, belonged to Egypt. The French had no business there. Marchand replied that he could not retreat without orders from his government. Although there were far more British forces than French, Kitchener decided it would be enough of a stand to raise the Egyptian and British flags south of the fort. Then, the two men referred the problem back to their home governments. Eventually, France backed down and ordered Marchand to remove his troops.

Why were two of the great powers of Europe willing to risk a war over this steaming little town on the White Nile? What brought them to Africa in the first place? The answers to these questions lie in imperialism, that is, control of weak countries by stronger ones through the use of military and political pressures. During the years from 1870 to 1914, several economic conditions made European nations become interested in colonies. (1) Rapid industrialism and a rising standard of living created the need for more raw materials. Many of these materials came from tropical areas. (2) Competition among industrial countries led each to raise its tariffs on imported goods and to look abroad for new export markets. (3) The less developed areas of the world offered not only markets for goods but also places for investment. Stock in railways in Africa and sugar plantations in the Caribbean might yield returns as high as 20 percent a year. To protect their investments, Westerners wanted their home governments to take over the foreign lands.

The growth of European empires was also helped by strong nationalistic rivalries among the Western countries. Two new European states—Germany and Italy—eagerly entered the race for colonies. Each felt it was in the interest of national security to see that certain areas did not fall into enemy hands. A nation's greatness came to be measured by its colonial possessions. Indeed, conflicts over imperialistic claims were a major cause of World War I.

Among Europeans, national pride was mixed with religious and humanitarian motives. Westerners often thought of their civilization as better than those of Asia and Africa. Missionaries, doctors, and colonial administrators believed they carried what the English poet Rudyard Kipling called the "white man's burden"—a duty to improve the natives' lives. This attitude led to certain reforms in some areas. Westerners helped end slavery, relieve famine, improve health and education, and advance justice. Too often, however, their superior attitude made enemies of the native peoples. And many Europeans who talked of noble purposes were more interested in profits and power. This chapter tells how:

1. India lost its independence.

2. Foreign powers exploited China.

3. Japan became a world power.

4. Many nations gained influence elsewhere in Asia and the Pacific.

5. Africa was carved into many colonies.

6. Intervention grew in Latin America.

1 India lost its independence

In the 17th century, Aurangzeb, the great-grandson of Akbar, had brought almost all of India under Mughul control. After his death in 1707, the empire was torn with unrest. Within forty years, it fell into chaos.

The British won control. By this time, England and France had strong trading interests in India. Mughul rulers had allowed the British East India Company to make several small settlements. These settlements, called factories, were rented to the English. They were armed, but used chiefly for storage and trading.

The French East India Company also set up trading posts along the east coast in the late 17th century. Competition between the two groups of traders grew stronger as

Mughul rule in India became increasingly weaker.

During the 18th century, when England and France were at war in Europe and North America, their quarrel spread to India. At first, the French were the winners. Then during the Seven Years' War (1756–1763), the English, led by the brilliant Robert Clive, defeated the French. The English were then masters of Bengal in northeastern India. This region became the cornerstone of the British Empire in India.

Company rule was limited. The British government decided that it did not want the East India Company to have political power. The India Act of 1784 gave power over the Company to a Board of Control whose president was a British cabinet member. The British government also chose the highest Company official in India, the governor general. In 1814, Parliament took away the Company's trade monopoly in India. In 1833, its China trade monopoly was also ended.

However, the East India Company remained active. As the Mughul Empire fell apart, the company extended British control over more and more territory. It sometimes did this by conquering lands directly through the use of the Company's own army. Or it arranged alliances with local rulers who accepted Company protection. By the mid-19th century, nearly all of India had come under British control.

Indian dissatisfaction grew. Indians resented British missionaries and policies. They were alarmed by the expansion activity of the Company in the mid-1800s. In 1857, a rumor spread among the native troops, or sepoys, serving the British. The rumor said that new rifle cartridges—the ends of which had to be bitten off—would be greased with beef and pork fat. Hindus thought cows to be sacred. Muslims considered pigs unclean. Both groups were very angry. They rose in

Robert Clive

mutiny and killed many Europeans. However, the Sepoy Rebellion did not have the support of the people. The British were able to end the rebellion by late 1858.

As a result of the Sepoy Rebellion, however, the British Parliament abolished the East India Company in 1858 and set up a new cabinet post, Secretary of State for India. A viceroy was chosen to rule within India. The British divided India into two parts, British India, which was ruled directly by the British, and Indian India, which was ruled by native princes who were in charge of their own internal affairs.

In British India, the viceroy had full power. By 1861, legislative and executive councils that included some Indians helped him. All the members were appointed rather than elected. An able Indian civil service developed. Although the British did hold all top positions, Indians slowly filled most of the middle and lower posts.

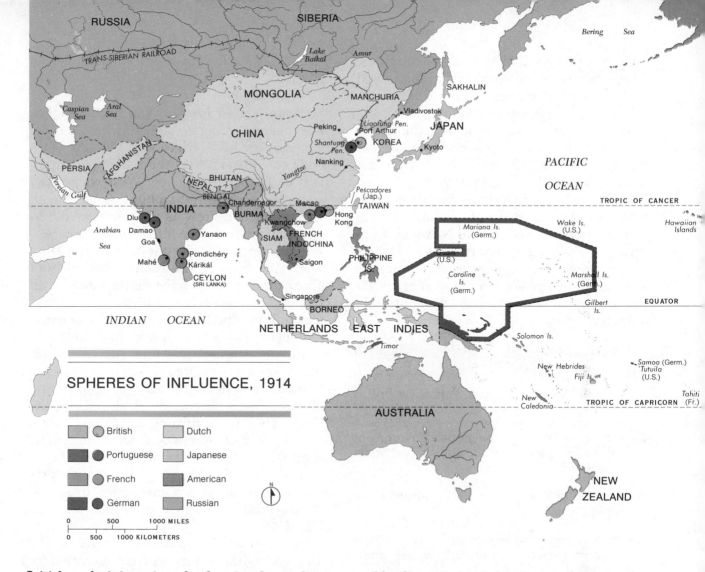

SPHERES OF INFLUENCE, 1914

British
Portuguese
French
German
Dutch
Japanese
American
Russian

0   500   1000 MILES

0   500   1000 KILOMETERS

British administration had mixed results.
Probably the most important thing that the
British did was to unify India. Now almost all
of the subcontinent had come under one
authority. The use of English as the official
language helped, since before this, there had
been no single language all educated Indians
could speak.

The British in India also stopped bands of
robbers, reduced the dangers of travel, and
protected life and property. They outlawed
suttee (the suicide of a widow on her husband's funeral pyre) and the killing of infant
girls. They also improved medical facilities,
added miles of railroad and telegraph lines,

and built extensive irrigation works throughout the countryside.

The picture had a dark side, too. Because
of such changes, the population grew rapidly
and food supplies could not keep up. Thus,
for many, the living standard became worse.
One bad harvest was enough to cause famine. Poverty was and still is a major problem.

Another heavy blow was the end of the
centuries-old handicraft system. With the
growth of British industry, India became a
market for cheap manufactured goods, especially cotton textiles. The Indians' handwo-
ven cloth could not sell as cheaply as imported cloth. And the Indians were not

allowed to sell their cloth to other countries. Thus, they were forced to depend more and more on agriculture for earning a living.

Yet, a small group of Indian intellectuals arose. Trained in British schools in the Indian cities, they learned English history as well as language. What they learned about the liberal traditions of 19th-century Europe brought out their own desire for self-government. In 1885, a group of primarily Hindu leaders formed the Indian National Congress. In 1906, a group of educated Muslims formed the Muslim League. Both groups wanted representative self-government for India. Indian nationalism grew steadily stronger.

section review 1

1. How did the Seven Years' War affect British and French interests in India?

2. Why and how did the British government reduce the powers of the British East India Company?

3. How did British rule in India change after the Sepoy Rebellion?

4. What changes did the British bring to India? What problems were caused by British rule?

2 Foreign powers exploited China

In the mid-17th century, the Manchus set up a new dynasty in China. For many years, they ruled a huge, rich empire. However, decline began about 1800. The population grew rapidly. Agriculture could not keep up. Not enough food and increasing poverty caused discontent. By the mid-19th century, Manchu leadership was in serious trouble. Rebellions broke out in many parts of the country.

Europeans used force to win trading rights. Europeans had begun some trade with Ming China in the mid-16th century. But the Manchus cut it back. With the rise of industrialism in Europe, however, Westerners tried again to increase the amount of trade with China. Friction grew as the two very different civilizations came into greater contact.

Open warfare broke out in 1839. Basically, war came because the Manchus would not allow the British to have regular trade with China. On the surface, however, the cause was opium. The British East India Company had been importing opium into China in return for Chinese tea and silk. Although there was a law against this importation, the Manchus had not enforced it for years. Many Chinese were becoming addicted to the drug. They were turning to robbery to get money to buy opium and were neglecting their farms. Chinese leaders were very concerned about this. One day, a Cantonese official seized a large amount of the drug and destroyed it. The British protested, but talks failed.

The Opium War lasted three years. The Chinese, without a navy, were no match for the British. The conflict ended with the Treaty of Nanking in 1842. The Chinese gave Hong Kong to the British. They paid damages for the opium they had destroyed. They also agreed to a fair tariff on trade. Most important, the Chinese were forced to open five port cities to trade. The Treaty of Nanking marked the real opening of China. Soon, other Western countries got similar trading rights.

Foreign traders, however, took advantage of the weakness of the Chinese government and often abused their trading rights. In 1856, war again broke out. This time, a combined English-French force attacked the Chi-

Before 1842, the Chinese allowed European and American merchants to live and travel only in small areas of China. This drawing shows the waterfront at Canton.

nese capital, Peking, and burned the beautiful summer palace. The treaties signed in 1858 and 1860 marked another defeat for the Chinese. The Manchus opened eleven more ports. They legalized the opium trade. They agreed to receive Western diplomats and to protect Christian missionaries. China also had to give foreigners the right of extraterritoriality. That is, foreigners were excused from trial in Chinese courts. They were subject only to the courts of their home country. Under Chinese law, a crime was the responsibility of a group and any group member could be punished. This was very different from Western ways.

The weakness of China was now clear to all. Foreign powers quickly moved in to carve up the "Chinese melon." They set up *spheres of influence.* In China, these were regions where the economic interests of another country were supreme. Within its sphere, a country had rights to specific tracts of land called concessions. It more or less controlled these concessions and enjoyed extraterritoriality there. Russia, Germany, Britain, and France had concessions.

The race to gain concessions from the Manchus caused the United States to state its Open Door Policy in 1899. The United States feared that China might be completely divided up into spheres that would shut out American trade. It therefore proposed that countries having such spheres should permit all nations to compete in them on equal terms. Several countries agreed to the American plan. This helped keep China together

During the Boxer Rebellion, many refugees fled to Tientsin. Here refugees have assembled on a boat landing at the river in the center of Tientsin.

territorially. It also assured Americans a chance to trade in China.

The Chinese deeply hated the exploitation and invasion of their country by foreigners. Their Manchu rulers held tightly to traditional Chinese customs and resisted change to Western ways. Many people joined the secret Society of Harmonious Fists (or "Boxers") which opposed all Westerners. In 1900, the Boxers took up arms. They destroyed railroads, burned bridges, and killed Europeans. The Boxer Rebellion was quickly put down by a combined force of Europeans, Americans, and Japanese. Afterwards, stricter controls were placed upon the Chinese government. However, there remained a group of Chinese who believed that change in their own government was needed in order to get rid of European control. They began a revolutionary movement that spread rapidly through the country.

section review **2**

1. What were the causes of the Opium War? How did the British profit from the Treaty of Nanking?

2. What did the foreign powers win from the Manchu government in the treaties of 1858 and 1860?

3. What were "spheres of influence" in China? What was the Open Door Policy of the United States?

4. How did some Chinese show their opposition to foreign imperialism?

3 Japan became a world power

In 1603, the Tokugawa [tō'kù gä'wä] clan won control of the shogunate in Japan. Their strong leadership unified Japan under a stable political system. Foreigners were expelled, and Christianity was outlawed. The country had little contact with outsiders.

The Tokugawas suppressed fighting among the great feudal lords, so that Japan enjoyed a long period of internal peace. Under these conditions, the warriors, the samurai, gradually turned into a landed aristocracy. They lived well by going deeply into debt and forcing their peasants to pay high rents. This led to peasant uprisings in the mid-18th century and to dissatisfaction among the aristocracy. Tokugawa rule became weaker.

The United States opened Japan to trade. Since the early 1800s, American whaling ships had sailed in the northern Pacific, and clipper ships trading with China sailed near Japan. American shippers were interested in Japan because they needed places where their ships could stop for food, fuel, and water. They also wanted protection for their sailors. Those who had been shipwrecked on Japanese shores had been badly treated.

In 1853, the American government sent Commodore Matthew Perry and four ships to Japan. Perry brought a message from President Millard Fillmore, requesting that the Japanese open their country to foreign trade. Then he left, promising to return the following spring for an answer.

In February, 1854, Perry returned with ten ships. He carried many presents for the Japanese officials. There were books, guns, clocks, perfume, sewing machines, and even a small locomotive. The Japanese were impressed by the gifts and by Perry's dignity and show of force. They agreed to the Treaty of Kanagawa. This treaty opened two Japanese ports to American ships, provided better treatment for shipwrecked sailors, and set up diplomatic relations between the two countries. In 1858, a second treaty opened more ports. It also granted extraterritoriality to Americans in Japan. Soon afterward, other Western nations worked out similar treaties. The door seemed to be open for large-scale foreign influence in Japan.

The Japanese adopted new ways. Japan, however, did not go the way of China. Unlike the Chinese rulers, the Japanese decided that their country could survive only by adopting some Western ways. One of the first changes was in the shogunate itself. The Treaty of Kanagawa had caused antiforeign demonstrations. The Tokugawas were blamed for these as well as for the poor conditions of the past hundred years. In 1867, strong leaders among the nobles forced the shogun to give up his powers. The next year, the emperor was restored to power. The capital was moved from Kyoto to Tokyo. Emperor Mutsuhito, aged fifteen, named his reign Meiji [mā'jē] meaning "enlightened rule."

During the forty-five years of the Meiji Era, Japan became a powerful, modern state, the first industrialized country in Asia. However, the great changes in political, social, and economic affairs were carefully controlled. Japanese leaders sent their own people to study all the major Western powers. The leaders then adopted only what they thought would be good for Japan.

In 1871, the emperor ended feudalism. In 1889, he set forth a constitution like that which Bismarck had written for the German Empire. Although it provided for a two-house legislature, the emperor remained supreme. Only the lower house was elected. And only about 1 percent of the people could vote although this number grew to about 20 percent within the next three decades.

The Japanese opened their ports to American and European merchants in the late 1800s. The picture shows Portuguese sailors in Japan. The Japanese thought that the Europeans wore funny clothes.

Military leaders had great power in the government. The army and navy were strengthened. The army was based on the German model and the navy on the British.

Other changes were made also. Compulsory education was introduced and illiteracy was almost wiped out. The government adopted new laws and a new judicial system, patterned after Western ones. All foreign rights of extraterritoriality were gone by 1899.

Perhaps even more surprising than the political changes were those in economic life. Japanese leaders knew that Western strength was based on industrial power. Thus, they pushed ahead with a major program to make Japan strong industrially. At the time of the Meiji Restoration (1868), there were almost no factory workers in Japan. By 1900, there were a half million.

Because money to invest was scarce, the government had to give loans to private business. The government also entered directly into the building of railroads, factories, shipyards, and telegraph and telephone systems. Japan developed a "mixed" system of private and governmental enterprise led by a few rich families that made up an economic ruling class.

Japanese ambitions led to foreign aggression. In becoming a modern industrial state, Japan also became imperialistic. A rapid rise in population resulted from better sanitation and medical services. In the Meiji Era alone, the population grew from about 30 to more than 50 million. The nation could not grow enough food for its people. It also lacked raw materials and markets for its manufactured goods. Japan saw the Asian mainland as a way to get around these troubles. As early as 1876, the Japanese had obtained trading privileges in Korea. This angered the Chinese and later led to the Sino-Japanese War of 1894–1895. By defeating China in this war, Japan made its first major gain of territory beyond its own borders.

The Treaty of Shimonoseki [shim'ō nō-se'ke] ended the war and gave Japan the islands of Taiwan and the Pescadores [pes'-kə dôr'ēz]. It also gave them the Liaotung [lyou'dùng'] peninsula of Manchuria. Meanwhile, the Russians were expanding into Manchuria, too. They had long wanted Liaotung because at its southern tip lay Port Arthur. This was one of the finest harbors in East Asia and could be used in all seasons. Backed by France and Germany, Russia forced Japan to return Liaotung to China.

534

Soon afterward, Russia leased the peninsula and harbor for itself through a treaty with China. This and other Russian moves in Korea angered Japan.

Talks between Japan and Russia over Korea and Manchuria broke down in 1904. Fighting began when Japan, without declaring war, attacked the Russian fleet at Port Arthur. Much to the surprise of the West, Japan won the Russo-Japanese War. This was the first time in modern history that an Asian country had defeated a European country. With the Treaty of Portsmouth (1905), Japan took back Liaotung and Port Arthur. Japan also got a sphere of influence in Korea, and won the southern half of the Russian island of Sakhalin. Five years later, Japan openly took over Korea. Almost overnight, Japan had become a major world power.

section review 3

1. What two problems weakened Tokugawa rule?

2. Why did the United States want to set up closer contacts with Japan? How did they accomplish this?

3. What Western ways were adopted by the Japanese?

4. Describe the causes and results of the Russo-Japanese War.

4 *Many nations gained influence elsewhere in Asia and the Pacific*

We have already seen how India and China became victims of European imperialism. Thus, it should not be surprising that smaller countries in Asia, as well as many islands in the Pacific, also came under Western rule. In the Pacific region, however, European imperialists found a new rival, the United States.

European powers expanded into several regions of Asia. For a long time, Russia had been building up its settlements in Siberia. When China became open to Western exploitation in the mid-19th century, the Russians also stepped in there. The Russians were always in search of warm-water ports. Thus, they moved to secure a large coastal area north of Korea where they founded the town of Vladivostok [vlad'ə vos'tok] in 1860.

In 1890, Russia began building the Trans-Siberian Railroad. China gave permission for the line to cross Manchuria and end at Port Arthur. The Russians, however, failed to keep possession of the Liaotung peninsula after the Russo-Japanese War. This was a major blow to their imperialistic plans in that area.

Meanwhile Russian imperialists were also moving into parts of Persia. This worried the British. They feared that Russia might reach the Persian Gulf and interfere with their shipping route to India and the East. The British were also upset that in central Asia the Russians had reached the borders of Afghanistan. Such a position threatened India. In 1907, Britain and Russia signed an agreement promising that neither country would take over Afghanistan. Persia was divided into spheres of influence, with Russia controlling the north and Britain controlling the south.

In Southeast Asia, Britain and France were the two chief rivals. The French first moved into the area in the late 18th century. By the mid-1800s, however, hostile Asian feelings led to attacks on French missionaries. A French fleet attacked and captured Saigon in 1860. During the next twenty years, France took control of Cochin-China, Cambodia, and Annam. These areas had always paid tributes to China. China tried but was not able to get rid of the French by force in the 1880s. In 1893, the French took over Laos [lä'os]. They grouped all these areas together to form the French colony of Indochina. It was nearly thirty percent larger in area than France itself. French rule in Indochina changed villagers into landless agricultural workers whose incomes came to depend on the rise and fall of world prices.

Burma meanwhile had come under British influence. Conflicts along the Indian border had touched off small wars. As the winner of these wars, Britain was able to take over more and more land. Burma was formally added to India in 1885. Other possessions of the British in this area were Ceylon (present-day Sri Lanka), Singapore, and northern Borneo.

One other important European power in this region was the Netherlands. It controlled the East Indies. As with the British in India, a private trading company (the Dutch East India Company) ruled for many years. Then in 1798, the home government took over. It made the territory a colony called the Netherlands East Indies. The Dutch made large profits from their colony. They shipped its spices, tobacco, sugar, coffee, and tea to Europe. They built schools, but made sure that the schools used native languages. This system preserved native cultures. More importantly, it delayed the spread of anticolonial ideas such as nationalism and democracy.

Pacific islands came under foreign rule. In the late 1800s, there was rapid development in ocean transportation. This was followed by a great increase in shipping. Naturally, many of the thousands of islands in the Pacific became important stops for ships.

Great Britain, the leading naval power, held Australia, New Zealand, and many Pacific islands. These included Fiji and the

Queen Liliuokalani

southern Solomons. Other nations followed this example. The Germans got the northern Solomons and bought some islands from Spain. Meanwhile, France secured Tahiti.

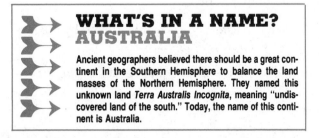

WHAT'S IN A NAME?
AUSTRALIA

Ancient geographers believed there should be a great continent in the Southern Hemisphere to balance the land masses of the Northern Hemisphere. They named this unknown land *Terra Australis Incognita*, meaning "undiscovered land of the south." Today, the name of this continent is Australia.

The United States, too, was interested in Pacific islands. During the 19th century, Americans and Europeans settled in the Hawaiian Islands. There they set up a thriving export trade in sugar. By the 1880s, Americans dominated the government, although Hawaii was still technically independent.

Hawaiian sugar planters wanted the islands to become part of the United States. When the Hawaiian queen, Liliuokalani, refused, she was overthrown. In 1898, Congress took over the Hawaiian Islands. In 1959, Hawaii became the 50th state.

Meanwhile, in the Spanish-American War of 1898, the United States acquired Guam and the Philippines, which had been Spanish possessions in the Pacific. When the war ended, the United States decided to keep the islands because of their economic and strategic value. The Filipinos fought for independence. However, after three years of hard fighting, they were finally defeated by the Americans. Military rule was set up. In 1902, the United States provided civilian rule and began to prepare the Philippines for self-government.

section review 4

1. Why did Russian advances in Persia cause conflicts with Britain?

2. Which areas in Southeast Asia came under British and French rule?

3. What role did the Dutch play in the East Indies?

4. Why did the islands of the Pacific become important in the late 19th century? How did the United States get control of Hawaii?

5 Africa was carved into many colonies

Nowhere did imperial powers move with such speed and nowhere were the effects as pronounced as in Africa. Only a tenth of its huge land area was under European control in 1875. Within twenty years, only a tenth was free of such control.

France and Britain gained control of North Africa. Africa north of the Sahara had been conquered by the Turks in the 15th century. It was made part of the Ottoman Empire. By the 19th century, however, Turkish power was declining. The nations of Europe then saw a chance to extend their influence.

One of the first important European moves into Africa was made by the French. They invaded Algeria in 1830, both for prestige and to stop Algerian pirates who attacked French ships. For many years, no other European state showed much interest in North Africa. Then in 1869, a French company finished building a canal across the Isthmus of Suez. The Middle East again became, as it had been in ancient times, a great crossroads of world trade.

In 1875, the British government bought a large bloc of shares in the Suez Canal Company. The canal was a vital link in Britain's

The Suez Canal opened on November 16, 1869. The next day, 68 European ships passed through.

lifeline to India, Australia, and New Zealand. When internal fighting broke out in Egypt in 1882, Britain sent in a military force. This force reduced the country to the status of a British *protectorate*, that is, a weaker country controlled and protected by a stronger one, particularly in foreign affairs.

The British next moved into the Sudan. They hoped eventually to control land from Cairo in the north to Cape Town in the south. But their immediate goal in the Sudan was to put down a native revolt. The first try ended in defeat when General Charles Gordon was killed by Sudanese forces at the seige of Khartoum [kär tüm'] in 1885. Thirteen years later, General Kitchener avenged Gordon's death by defeating the Sudanese at Omdurman. The following year, Britain and Egypt made the Sudan a *condominium*, that is, they made it an area they ruled jointly. In fact, Britain was the stronger power.

Meanwhile, France had been actively developing Algeria. French influence was also being felt in Tunisia [tü nē'zhə] and Morocco. The French had dreams of controlling the northern half of Africa, from Dakar on the west to French Somaliland [sə mä'lē land'] on the east coast. One step in carrying out this plan was Captain Marchand's expedition, which led to the Fashoda Incident described earlier in this chapter. The result was that the French were blocked by the British in the upper Nile region. But France continued to move into central and western Africa.

The rest of Africa was explored by Europeans. For centuries, only northern Africa and the coasts of the rest of the continent were familiar to Europeans. In the early 1800s, however, many Europeans began to explore the interior of Africa. One of the most famous was David Livingstone, a Scottish missionary. Between 1851 and 1873, he made several journeys. His writings increased interest in Africa and opposition to the slave trade.

Charles Gordon

Livingstone began his last journey in 1866. He was not heard from for several years, and many people feared that he was lost. In 1869, the New York *Herald* sent its best reporter, Henry M. Stanley, to Africa to "find Livingstone." He suffered great hardships in his search. Finally one day in 1871, he came into a village on Lake Tanganyika [tang'gə-nyē'kə]. There stood a lone white man. In Stanley's words:

As I advanced slowly toward him I noticed he was pale, looked wearied, had a grey beard, wore a bluish cap with a faded gold band around it, had on a red-sleeved waistcoat, and a pair of grey tweed trousers. I would have run to him, would have embraced him, only I did not know how he would receive me; so I walked deliberately to him, took off my hat, and said: "Dr. Livingstone, I presume?" "Yes," he said with a kind smile, lifting his cap slightly. "I thank God, Doctor, I have been permitted to see you."

Stanley tried to persuade Livingstone to give up his work as missionary and explorer and return to Europe. But Livingstone refused and died in Africa two years later.

Meanwhile, Stanley became an explorer in his own right. During his journeys, he learned that Africa offered vast possibilities for commerce. Stanley returned to Europe to seek financial backing. With money from King Leopold II of Belgium, he founded a private company called the International Congo Association.

Western powers divided Africa. The International Congo Association rapidly began to acquire the former African state of Kongo. In this region were many tribes who lived by farming or cattle raising. Stanley returned to the area in 1879. Within a few years, he made over 400 treaties with the native chiefs of these tribes. Stanley did not explain to the chiefs that by placing their marks on bits of paper in return for guns and cloth, they were giving their land to the Congo Association. Stanley gained huge tracts of land by these methods. Much of this area came to be known as the Belgian Congo.

Other explorers also used Stanley's methods and got huge areas of land for their countries. France took a vast area on the Congo River and important colonies in West Africa. Germany got slices of territory on the east and west coasts. The Italians made claims along the Red Sea. They were defeated soundly by the Abyssinians (later more often known as Ethiopians) in 1896 when the Italians tried to occupy their country.

The British, too, were active in all parts of Africa. Cecil Rhodes went to South Africa in 1870. He made a fortune there in the diamond and gold mines. He dreamed of British colonies stretching from the Cape of South Africa to Cairo in the north. Rhodes was also important in Britain's gaining Bechuanaland

In 1880, French explorer Pierre Savorgnan de Brazza met with Bateke chiefs in what later became known as Brazzaville.

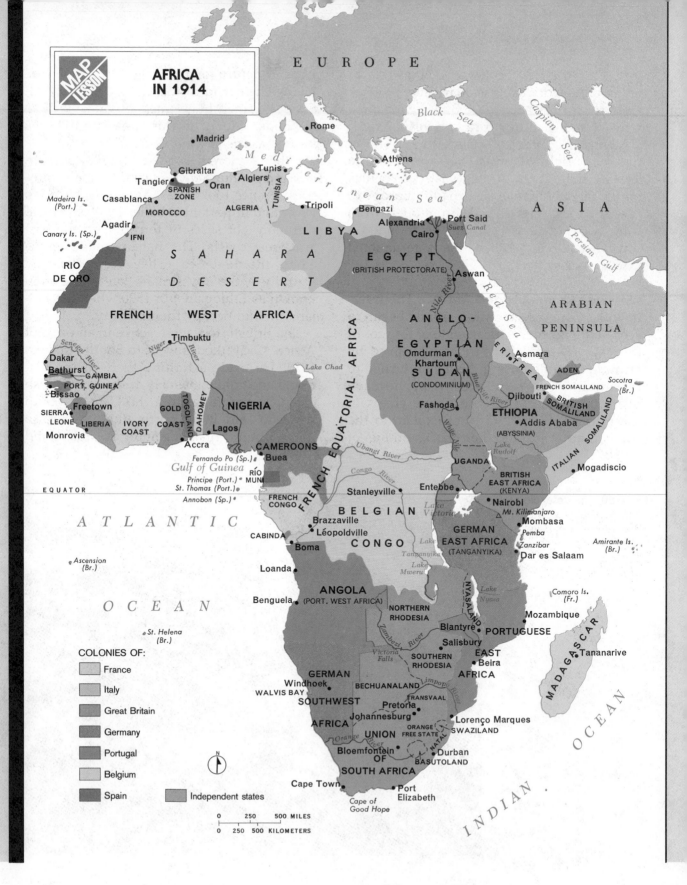

AFRICA
IN 1914

EUROPE

Black Sea

Caspian Sea

ASIA

Rome

Madrid

Mediterranean Sea

Tunis

Gibraltar

Tangier

Algiers

SPANISH ZONE

Oran

Athens

Madeira Is. (Port.)

Casablanca

MOROCCO

Agadir

Canary Is. (Sp.)

IFNI

RIO DE ORO

SPANISH ZONE

ALGERIA

TUNISIA

Tripoli

Bengazi

LIBYA

Alexandria

Port Said

Cairo

Suez Canal

Aswan

Persian Gulf

ARABIAN

PENINSULA

SAHARA DESERT

EGYPT
(BRITISH PROTECTORATE)

Nile River

Red Sea

FRENCH WEST AFRICA

ANGLO-

EGYPTIAN

SUDAN
(CONDOMINIUM)

Asmara

ERITREA

ADEN

Timbuktu

Senegal River

Niger River

Lake Chad

Omdurman

Khartoum

Blue Nile River

Socotra (Br.)

Djibouti

FRENCH SOMALILAND

BRITISH SOMALILAND

Dakar

Bathurst

GAMBIA

PORT. GUINEA

Bissao

Freetown

SIERRA LEONE

LIBERIA

Monrovia

IVORY COAST

GOLD COAST

TOGOLAND

DAHOMEY

NIGERIA

Lagos

Accra

CAMEROONS

Buea

FRENCH EQUATORIAL AFRICA

Fashoda

White Nile

ETHIOPIA

Addis Ababa

(ABYSSINIA)

Lake Rudolf

ITALIAN SOMALILAND

Mogadiscio

Fernando Po (Sp.)

Gulf of Guinea

Principe (Port.)

St. Thomas (Port.)

RIO MUNI

UGANDA

EQUATOR

Annobon (Sp.)

FRENCH CONGO

Stanleyville

Entebbe

BRITISH EAST AFRICA (KENYA)

Nairobi

Mt. Kilimanjaro

Mombasa

ATLANTIC

Ubangi River

Congo River

BELGIAN

Brazzaville

Léopoldville

Lake Victoria

GERMAN

EAST AFRICA
(TANGANYIKA)

Pemba

Zanzibar

Amirante Is. (Br.)

CABINDA

CONGO

Lake Tanganyika

Dar es Salaam

Ascension (Br.)

Boma

Loanda

Lake Mweru

OCEAN

ANGOLA
(PORT. WEST AFRICA)

NYASALAND

Lake Nyasa

Comoro Is. (Fr.)

Benguela

NORTHERN RHODESIA

Mozambique

St. Helena (Br.)

Zambezi River

Blantyre

PORTUGUESE

Salisbury

EAST

MADAGASCAR

Tananarive

Victoria Falls

SOUTHERN RHODESIA

Beira

AFRICA

COLONIES OF:

France

Italy

Great Britain

Germany

Portugal

Belgium

Spain

Independent states

GERMAN

Windhoek

WALVIS BAY

SOUTHWEST

AFRICA

BECHUANALAND

Limpopo River

TRANSVAAL

Pretoria

Johannesburg

ORANGE FREE STATE

UNION

Orange River

OF

Bloemfontein

SOUTH AFRICA

Lorenço Marques

SWAZILAND

NATAL

Durban

BASUTOLAND

N

Cape Town

Cape of Good Hope

Port Elizabeth

INDIAN

OCEAN

0   250   500 MILES

0   250   500 KILOMETERS

■ MAP LESSON 28: AFRICA IN 1914

1. The most striking feature about this map is the extent to which it shows how the huge continent of Africa was divided up by the imperial powers. Only two countries, shown in darker blue, were independent nations in 1914. What were these two?

2. The two leading imperial powers, France and Great Britain, both controlled extensive areas of Africa. France controlled French West Africa and French Equatorial Africa. What other two areas did France control?

3. French West Africa included both the source and the mouth of what major river?

4. The major northern section of Great Britain's African empire went from the mouth of the Nile River south to what lake?

5. The major southern section of Great Britain's African empire ran from the Cape of Good Hope north to what lakes?

6. Two major colonies separated the northern and southern sections of Great Britain's African empire. What were these colonies?

7. Which African country was a British protectorate?

8. Which of Great Britain's holdings in Africa was ruled jointly with Egypt?

9. The Belgian colony in Africa included most of the basin of which two rivers?

10. Which major rivers form much of the border between the Belgian African empire and an area controlled by the French?

11. The two major Portuguese colonies included both the source and the mouth of what major river?

12. Which European powers established colonies at the southeastern entrance to the Red Sea?

13. What three African colonies did Italy control?

14. Each of Italy's colonies bordered on a different sea or ocean. Which body of water formed the coastline for each colony?

15. Which country of Africa did not border on any sea or ocean?

[bech'ü ä'nə land'] and Rhodesia [rō dē'zhə]. Other British explorers and traders claimed parts of West and East Africa. Altogether, Britain ruled more than a dozen African colonial areas.

By 1914, most of Africa had been taken over by European powers. Only Liberia and Abyssinia remained independent. The coming of Europeans brought mixed results in Africa. On the one hand, they did away with slavery and tribal warfare in some areas. European help was also important in fighting disease and illiteracy and in building cities, roads, and industries.

On the other hand, Europeans wanted African labor most of all. Europeans used the Africans cruelly. Many were uprooted from their tribes and villages. Often their lands were taken over. They were made to pay heavy taxes and to supply forced labor. Some of the worst crimes took place in the Congo. There European overseers handed out brutal punishments in order to get greater rubber production. Execution, whipping, and torture were common.

Conditions slowly got better in the 20th century. A small Westernized class of Africans formed. These Africans formed the heart of a nationalistic movement that gathered strength as the years passed.

section review 5

1. How was North Africa affected by the decline of the Turks and the construction of the Suez Canal?

2. How did Britain gain control over Egypt and the Sudan?

3. What role did Rhodes play in the development of African colonies by European powers?

4. How did European imperialism affect the peoples of Africa?

6 Intervention grew in Latin America

The whole world was affected by imperialism, but not in the same way. In Africa and Asia imperialism meant colonization and control, mostly by European powers. In Latin America, however, it meant foreign intervention, mostly by the United States.

Foreign investments led to trouble. Latin America offered many important resources, including silver, gold, oil, rubber, platinum, tin, and copper. American and European investors were quick to make use of these resources. In the late 1800s, they spent billions of dollars to dig mines, sink oil wells, build railroads, and encourage public utilities. These developments improved conditions in the countries in which they were made, but they also caused major problems. Corrupt local officials often made dishonest deals with foreign investors. And the investors often made huge profits at the expense of the common people.

Another problem was that Latin-American governments tended to be very unstable. Revolutions often caused changes of rulers. The new governments sometimes took over foreign property without payment. When this happened, the foreigners called for help from their homelands.

The United States used the Monroe Doctrine to intervene. The idea of large-scale European interference to protect their investments in Latin America worried the United States. The Monroe Doctrine had long been used by Americans to protect the Americas from European intervention. In the 1890s, the United States used the Monroe Doctrine in other ways.

For one thing, the United States began to act as a negotiator in disputes between Latin-American countries and European powers.

More importantly, the United States now claimed that it had the right to intervene in Latin America itself to protect its own interests. The Spanish-American War of 1898 made this claim even clearer.

The Spanish-American War broke out. During the late 19th century, Cuba and Puerto Rico were swept by revolutions. These two colonies were all that remained of Spain's New World empire. Both islands now wanted their independence. The United States supported this desire and grew angry that the Cuban and Puerto Rican rebels were treated so harshly by the Spanish. These American feelings were backed up by other facts: (1) Americans had invested $50 million in Cuba, (2) Cuba was the largest supplier of American sugar, and (3) Cuba was strategically important because it controlled the entrance to the Gulf of Mexico.

It was clearly in the interest of the United States that Cuba be friendly and stable. To many Americans, this meant that Cuba should be free of Spanish rule. Thus, when the American battleship *Maine* was mysteriously sunk in Havana Harbor, those same Americans quickly blamed Spain and wanted to go to Cuba's aid. In 1898, the United States declared war and defeated Spain in less than five months.

As a result of the Spanish-American War, the United States took over Puerto Rico. (Puerto Ricans became United States citizens by birth in 1917.) The United States also got Guam and the Philippine Islands in the Pacific. The war was supposed to have been fought for Cuba's freedom. Although Cuba was allowed to set up an independent government, the United States placed several limits on the new government. America kept the right to intervene in the foreign and domestic affairs of Cuba. The United States could also build naval bases on the island. In effect, Cuba became an American protectorate.

After the battleship *Maine* sank, the debris was hung with flowers and garlands of mourning.

During the next twenty years, the United States actively intervened in Cuban affairs several times. Not until 1934 did the American government give up all such rights. Even then, the United States kept its naval base at Guantanamo [gwän tä′nə mō] Bay.

Dollar diplomacy characterized the early 20th century. In the thirty years after the Spanish-American War, American investments in Latin America reached new heights. The United States government worked closely with investors to get favorable terms for them. These joint efforts between government and business came to be referred to as the policy of "dollar diplomacy."

Theodore Roosevelt, President from 1901 to 1909, was a major spokesman for dollar diplomacy. He strongly favored the canal that the United States planned to build across the Isthmus of Panama. This area, however, belonged to Colombia. When revolution broke out there in 1903, President Roosevelt sent American marines to the scene. They kept Colombian troops from putting down the Panamanian rebels. Two weeks later, the United States formally recognized the new Republic of Panama. The United States then arranged a perpetual lease on a canal zone 10 miles (16 kilometers) wide. Panama, like

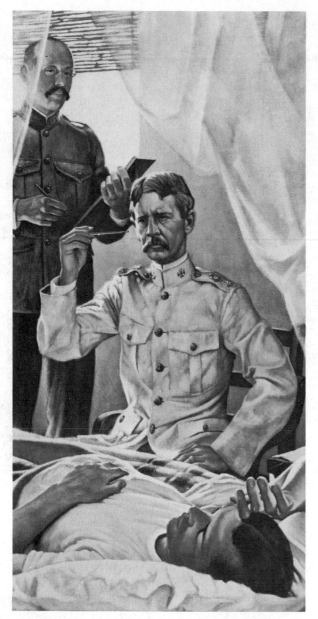

In 1900, a U.S. Army surgeon named Walter Reed proved that yellow fever, an often-fatal disease in tropical areas, was spread by mosquitos. This discovery made possible the eradication of the disease in Panama so that the Panama Canal could be built. This painting honors Reed's work.

Cuba, became an American protectorate. The Panama Canal, which had great strategic value for the United States, was finished in 1914.

Meanwhile, in 1904 Roosevelt stated his famous corollary to the Monroe Doctrine. The United States, he said, would be forced to take on the duties of international policeman in the Western Hemisphere.

During the era of dollar diplomacy, the *Roosevelt Corollary* was used to justify repeated American intervention in Central America and the Caribbean. In 1905, for example, the Dominican Republic went bankrupt. The United States took over the Dominican Republic's customs collections and made sure all its creditors were paid. The United States also stepped into Nicaragua [nik'ə rä'gwə] and Honduras [hon dùr'əs] to set finances in order and to protect American investments. In 1915, internal trouble broke out in Haiti. American marines were sent to restore order. They remained in that country for almost twenty years.

Many people in the United States did not favor these imperialistic moves. They knew of the growing Latin-American resentment toward the United States. Such feelings helped modify dollar diplomacy by the 1930s.

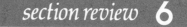

section review 6

1. What three conditions in Latin America invited imperialism?

2. How did the American government change the meaning of the Monroe Doctrine in the 1890s?

3. List three or more reasons why the United States went to war with Spain. How did the United States keep control over Cuba after the war?

4. What role did dollar diplomacy play in American foreign policy? What effect did the Roosevelt Corollary have?

SECTION SUMMARIES

1. India lost its independence. Up to 1914, many Western countries extended their rule over foreign areas. The greatest interest was in areas with many natural resources. This movement, known as imperialism, had several causes and took many different forms. As early as the 18th century, the British had defeated the French in India. The British were then able to take over more land at the expense of the weak Mughuls. Rule by the East India Company was replaced by British government control after the Sepoy Rebellion of 1857.

2. Foreign powers exploited China. China under the Manchus had grown poor and weak by the 19th century. After the Opium War in 1839, the British gained important trading rights. Later, other foreign powers began to divide China up into spheres of influence. Several defeats left China helpless at the hands of Britain, France, Germany, and Russia. The United States also tried to get a foot in through its Open Door Policy. China held together, but the Boxer Rebellion and revolutionary groups showed how much the people hated foreign control.

3. Japan became a world power. The Japanese were brought into closer contact with the outside world by the United States. Japan, however, did not give in to Western domination. Instead, the Japanese began a major modernization program. The feudal shogunate was ended. A constitution was put into effect. Reforms were brought about in education and law. Most far-reaching was the rapid change from an agricultural to an industrial economy. As a result, Japan became a major power and itself turned to imperialism.

4. Many nations gained influence elsewhere in Asia and the Pacific. Other parts of Asia also came under the influence of imperialism. Manchuria and Mongolia came under Russian influence. So did central and southwestern Asia. Indochina became a French protectorate. Burma was added to the British list. The Dutch ruled an island empire in the East Indies. Pacific islands were snapped up by Britain, Germany, France, and the United States.

5. Africa was carved into many colonies. Africa was quickly divided up after 1820. The French and the British each took parts of North Africa. Meanwhile, explorers moved into the interior south of the Sahara. By the end of the 19th century, all but two states of Africa had lost their independence. Britain and France controlled the most area. However, large portions went to Belgium, Germany, and Portugal. Italy also had some claims.

6. Intervention grew in Latin America. In Latin America, the United States played a dominant role, especially after the Spanish-American War. It took over Puerto Rico and turned Cuba into an American protectorate. The policy of dollar diplomacy also led to American intervention in Panama, Nicaragua, and Haiti.

Who? What? When? Where?

1. Place these events in chronological order, beginning with the earliest:
   a. The *Maine* exploded in Havana Harbor.
   b. The Opium War began.
   c. Work on the Suez Canal began.
   d. The Russo-Japanese War ended.
   e. The British East India Company was abolished.
   f. The United States acquired Guam.

2. Write a sentence for each of these men that describes his role in the development or takeover of Africa:
   a. Charles Gordon   d. Cecil Rhodes
   b. Horatio Kitchener   e. Henry Stanley
   c. Leopold II

3. Write a sentence for each of these movements that tells its causes:
   a. Indian National Congress
   b. Muslim League
   c. Sepoy Rebellion
   d. Society of Harmonious Fists

4. Write a sentence for each of these terms that gives its meaning:
   a. extraterritoriality   d. protectorate
   b. imperialism   e. Roosevelt Corollary
   c. Open Door Policy   f. spheres of influence

Questions for Critical Thinking

1. What were the motives of Britain, France, and Russia in taking over lands on the continents of Africa and Asia?

2. Why was Japan able to become an industrialized nation within fifty years?

3. Why was Japan's victory over Russia so surprising to the West?

4. Why did imperialism in Latin America mostly involve economic affairs, rather than political control?

Skill Activities

1. Read *Queen Victoria* by Lytton Strachey to learn about her influences on British imperialism and her era. (Harcourt Brace Jovanovich, 1966)

2. On a large wall map of the world, use colored string and pins to connect the imperialistic nations with the areas they ruled in 1914.

3. Prepare two maps of Africa, one showing the extent of foreign rule in 1875 and the other showing the extent of foreign rule in 1914.

4. Debate or discuss the harm and the good done by imperialistic rule.

chapter **28** *quiz*

Section 1

1. True or false: Indians were allowed to take part in the government of India under British rule.

2. During the Seven Years' War, Robert Clive defeated the: a. Japanese, b. French, c. Sepoys

Section 2

3. The Open Door Policy was begun by: a. the United States, b. Britain, c. China

4. True or false: The Boxer Rebellion was caused by Japanese sales of opium to the Chinese.

Section 3

5. True or false: The United States won the American-Japanese War, opening Japan to foreigners and ending the Meiji Era.

6. True or false: Japan won the Russo-Japanese War, much to the surprise of the West.

Section 4

7. Three European powers in Southeast Asia were Britain, France, and: a. Germany, b. the Netherlands, c. Italy

8. True or false: Liliuokalani gave the Hawaiian Islands to the United States.

Section 5

9. Three Europeans who were involved in the European colonization of Africa were: a. Rhodes, Livingstone, and Perry, b. Rhodes, Perry, and Stanley, c. Rhodes, Livingstone, and Kitchener

10. Under the rule of imperialism, tribal societies in Africa were: a. strengthened, b. weakened, c. untouched

Section 6

11. True or false: The Monroe Doctrine was used by the United States to justify its interference in Latin America.

12. As a result of the Spanish-American War, the United States gained control of: a. Mexico, b. the Philippines, c. Spain

WORLD WAR I

The area of the Somme River in northern France was the site of heavy fighting in World War I, especially in 1916 and 1917. Here weary British front line troops wait for the next onslaught by the opposing Germans.

A friend came to see me . . . he thinks it was on Monday, August 3 [1914]. We were standing at a window of my room in the Foreign Office. It was getting dusk, and the lamps were being lit in the space below on which we were looking. My friend recalls that I remarked on this [scene] with the words: "The lamps are going out all over Europe; we shall not see them lit again in our time."

These were the sad words of Sir Edward Grey, the foreign secretary of Great Britain. Europe was heading into a long and deadly war. This was the Great War that drew into it not only the major powers of Europe, but also those of America and Asia as well.

The Great War, or World War I as it was later known, lasted for more than four years.

Many think it was the single most important event of the 20th century. It was the beginning of Europe's decline as the center of world power and influence after 400 years of leadership. By the time the war ended, millions of people on both sides had been wiped out. Britain and France had been greatly weakened. The Hohenzollern, Hapsburg, and Romanov dynasties had fallen apart. Communists had taken over in Russia. Anti-colonialism had grown stronger in Asia, the Middle East, and Africa. Finally, the United States had come forth as the most powerful nation in the world.

Nobody in Europe in 1914 could have guessed these results. This turned out to be the first *total* war in history. It was fought by mass armies. It involved people at home as well as soldiers at the front. And for the first time, weapons of mass destruction were widely used. These included the machine gun, the tank, the airplane, and the submarine.

Why was the war fought at all? There is no simple answer. Basically, the European nations could not find a peaceful way to adjust to the great changes that had taken place since 1870. One of those changes was the rapid spread of industrialization, especially in countries such as Germany. This resulted in hard competition for trade, markets, and colonies. Another change was the growth of intense nationalism. This took place among both the old and new powers. When a new nation such as Germany, for example, tried to increase its power by building up a strong navy, an older nation such as Britain saw the new nation as a threat. An armaments race thus began. This came on top of the rivalries that already existed for colonies and for friendly allies. At the same time, the struggles of discontented peoples in the Balkans often broke out in fighting. Year by year, tensions built up in Europe. People began to feel that some day war would probably come. Thus we shall learn in this chapter how:

1. Disputes and alliances increased tensions.

2. Some forces promoted peace while others worked for war.

3. A Balkan crisis brought general war.

4. The world went to war.

5. The victors tried to build a lasting peace.

1 *Disputes and alliances increased tensions*

During the late 19th century, national rivalries in Europe became more and more dangerous to general peace. Each country looked for ways to provide itself with safety from enemy attack. One way was to form alliances against possible enemies. Another was to build up armaments. A third was to gain control of colonies because many people thought that colonies added to a country's strength.

Imperialism in Africa and Asia caused conflicts. In many places around the world, the imperialistic interests of different countries clashed. In Morocco, for example, Germany threatened French power. The first Moroccan crisis took place in 1905. It led to a diplomatic victory for France after a conference of European powers at Algeciras, Spain, in 1906. Six years later, the Germans again challenged the French. A German gunboat tried to enforce the kaiser's protest against French control in Morocco. This time, Britain's support of France forced Germany to yield.

Britain and France were not always allies, however. They came close to war in the 1898

The nations of Europe played a deadly game that led, in the end, to World War I. A Spanish cartoonist showed it as a game of billiards played by national leaders with rifles and swords for pool cues. The table is covered with a map of Europe, and bombs are stacked under it.

Fashoda Incident described in Chapter 28. Britain also clashed with Dutch settlers called Boers in South Africa. There, Britain came out the winner after the Boer War in 1902.

Britain was also involved with Russia in Asian rivalries. For centuries, the Russians had been trying to get a warm-water port. They needed an outlet to the sea that would be open all year; Russia's own coasts were blocked by ice most of the time. In 1877, Russia declared war on the Ottoman Empire in hopes of gaining control of the Dardanelles. The Russians said that they were just rescuing their fellow Slavs in the Balkan part of the Ottoman Empire from Turkish cruelties. After months of hard fighting, the Russians won this Russo-Turkish War. They were then in a position to get to the warm-water ports of the Mediterranean.

But Great Britain was alarmed at these Russian gains. They threatened British sea power in the Mediterranean and brought Russia close to the Suez Canal. The canal was the vital link in the sea route to India. To protect the canal, the British prime minister, Benjamin Disraeli, asked for the help of other European countries. In July, 1878, representatives of all the Great Powers met at the Congress of Berlin. The most important result of the Congress was to block Russia from further gains.

The actions taken at the Congress, however, did not halt Russia's drive for greater empire. Blocked in Europe and the Middle East, Russia in the 1890s turned to Manchuria. This move alarmed Japan since Russia had opposed Japanese control over Korea. And Manchuria belonged to China. But China was too weak to stand up for its rights. Thus, the rivalry led in 1904 to the Russo-Japanese War (Chapter 28) in which the Russians were defeated by Japan. Japan's victory had a great effect on the peoples of Asia. It led them to believe that they would one day be able to throw off Western imperialist rule entirely.

EUROPE IN 1914

Bismarck's alliances frightened Europe.

After France was defeated in the Franco-Prussian War of 1870–1871, the German prime minister, Bismarck, feared that the French might seek allies in a war of revenge. France, after all, had lost the valuable provinces of Alsace and Lorraine. He began to make alliances for Germany, mainly to isolate the French. Bismarck's most important alliance was with Austria in 1879. Called the Dual Alliance, it lasted until 1918. In 1882, Italy joined Germany and Austria, thus setting up the Triple Alliance. The members of the Triple Alliance promised that if any one of them should be attacked, all three would fight together.

Through very skillful diplomacy, Bismarck was also able to bring Germany and Russia together. This took the form of the so-called Reinsurance Treaty of 1887. Germany promised its support to Russia in certain Balkan matters. And Russia promised neutrality in the event of a French attack on Germany. These agreements served to carry out Bismarck's basic plan: the isolation of France. There was no major country left on the continent of Europe with whom France could make an alliance.

The kaiser changed German policy.

In 1890, young Kaiser William II dismissed Bismarck from office. Contrary to Bismarck's policy of friendship with Russia, the kaiser stopped making loans to the tsar. The treaty between Germany and Russia was allowed to die. And the kaiser joined Austria in a promise to defend their common interests in the Balkans against the Russians.

The Russians now had to look to other great powers for alliances and loans. France eagerly grabbed the chance to ally itself with Russia. Both countries feared Germany. France had made an amazing recovery from its defeat of 1871. It had built a strong army and was again prosperous. It loaned Russia millions of francs. Russia used this money to purchase arms and build the Trans-Siberian Railroad. In 1894, France and Russia signed a military alliance. Thus, Europe was split into two armed camps.

Great Britain began to seek allies and expand its navy. Great Britain was in neither camp. Protected by its great navy, Britain lived in what was called "splendid isolation." Its rich colonies circled the earth. Its strong navy brought a feeling of security to the home islands and colonies. Great Britain did not want to be tied down to alliances so long as no European nation threatened its interests.

By 1900, however, Great Britain decided that it needed allies. After all, Germany was building a merchant fleet and a navy to outstrip English sea power. In addition, Kaiser William's warlike speeches upset the British as much as his actions. Britain feared that an enemy blockade would put it in danger of starvation. This was because Britain imported most of its food. Thus, to keep control of the seas, Britain felt it had to build twice as many ships as Germany. At the same time, German industry rivaled that of Great Britain. The two nations competed in world markets.

Because of mutual distrust of Germany, Great Britain wanted to make an alliance with its old rival, France. In 1904, the British and French signed an agreement called the *Entente Cordiale* (French for "friendly understanding"). After this, France worked to bring Russia and Great Britain closer together. By 1907, Russia joined France and Britain in the second of the great European alliances, the Triple Entente.

section review 1

1. What were the three ways European nations tried to protect themselves from attack in the late 19th century?

2. Why did Bismarck try to isolate France after the Franco-Prussian War? What nations were allied with Germany by 1887?

3. What did Kaiser William II do that caused Russia and Britain to become allies of France?

4. What was the Entente Cordiale and who was involved in it?

2 Some forces promoted peace while others worked for war

We have seen some of the rivalries that were building national tensions. However, there was growing economic and political cooperation. These forces favored peace. Unfortunately, they could not stop the tide of war.

The world economy needed peace. By the early 20th century, the nations and peoples of the world had become economically interdependent. European capital and know-how had helped speed the economic growth of Asia, Africa, and the Americas. For example, money borrowed from Britain helped build the American railway system, as well as railroads in Argentina and eastern Europe.

Peace meant that raw materials could be bought and finished goods sold throughout the world. Large companies could set up offices, factories, and plantations in foreign countries. Telephones, telegraphs, and cables could be used for quick communication. Railroads and steamships could carry products anywhere without danger. Most important of all, the industrialized countries, while political rivals, were also each other's best customers for manufactured goods. Prosperity built on international trade would be destroyed by war. Because of this, many people in business and politics worked for world harmony.

International organizations were formed.
World organizations were another force favoring peace. In 1868, twenty nations set up the International Telegraph Union. In 1874, the General Postal Union was formed. International agreements also covered such matters as weights and measures, underwater cables, navigation of international rivers, and protection of wildlife. The Greek Olympic games were revived in 1896. This event, held every four years, brought together people from nearly every country of the world.

In the Western Hemisphere, the Pan-American movement encouraged cooperation among American nations. Trade was promoted, and an organization was set up which became known as the Pan American Union.

The International Red Cross was founded to help lessen the hardships of war. The Geneva Convention of 1864 was a set of agreements reached at the first meeting. It became a model for other international agreements covering victims of warfare at sea, prisoners of war, and civilians during wartime. National Red Cross societies also gave peacetime aid to disaster victims and others.

In spite of the growth of international organizations and trade, fear and suspicion

Baroness Bertha von Suttner was an Austrian writer who used her novels to further the cause of peace. Her best known novel, *Lay Down Your Arms*, was such a forceful indictment of war that it made her an international heroine and won for her the Nobel Peace Prize in 1905. Von Suttner was nicknamed the generalissimo of the peace movement.

spread among rival European countries between 1900 and 1914. Every Great Power, that is, Russia, Germany, Austria, Britain, and France, believed its own security depended on maintaining the alliance to which it belonged. That meant it had to support an ally if that ally got into a dispute with a rival. Allies of the rival would do the same. In this way, a local crisis anywhere in Europe could easily blow up into a general war among all the Great Powers.

1. How did international trade promote peace?

2. Give three examples of international cooperation before World War I began.

3. Why did the Great Powers feel that they had to support their allies?

4. How was it possible for a small local conflict to quickly become a widespread war?

3 A Balkan crisis brought general war

Just such a local crisis broke out in the Balkans in 1914. By then, relations between Serbia and Austria had reached a breaking point. Serbia, supported by Russia, wanted to unite with the Serbs living in the Austro-Hungarian Empire and create a Greater Serbia. Austria, supported by Germany, did not want to see that happen. Austria feared that if Serbia did unite, all the other minority Slavic groups living in the empire would also demand self-rule. The empire would then collapse. To save it, Austrian leaders felt they had to destroy Serbia as an independent nation.

The archduke of Austria was murdered. In June, 1914, Archduke Francis Ferdinand, heir to the Austrian throne, visited the Balkan city of Sarajevo [sär′ə yä′vō]. As Archduke Ferdinand rode through the streets in an open car, a young man sprang forward. He fired a gun and killed both the archduke and his wife.

Count Leopold von Berchtold, the Austrian foreign minister, suspected that the crime was of Serbian origin. At once, he took steps to stop Serbia from being a center for anti-Austrian propaganda. He sent a letter to Kai-

The photograph at *left* was taken on June 28, 1914. It shows Archduke Francis Ferdinand and his wife, Sophie, leaving the Senate House in Sarajevo, Bosnia. Five minutes later, they were both assassinated.

ser William II of Germany which was signed by the Austrian emperor, Francis Joseph I. In the letter, Berchtold asked for German help. The kaiser gladly agreed because he was eager to keep Austria as an ally. He also believed that the conflict could be kept within the Balkans. The kaiser's reply placed no limits on the amount of help Austria could expect from Germany. It became known as the "blank check."

With such strong support, Berchtold sent a message to Serbia on July 23, 1914. He warned that all anti-Austrian activities in Serbia must be stopped. He also said that Austro-Hungarian officials should be used to end such activities. Finally, all Serbian officials guilty of anti-Austrian propaganda should be dismissed.

Austria declared war on Serbia. Berchtold gave the Serbs forty-eight hours to reply to this ultimatum, as it was called. Should they refuse, he was sure that Austria could defeat Serbia in a local war. Furthermore, because

Germany was an ally of Austria, he believed other nations would be afraid to help Serbia.

The Serbs did agree to some of the Austrian demands. But they felt they would lose their independence if they agreed to all of them. Serbia called on Russia for help. The Russians pledged support. Thus, a local war was in danger of blowing up into a big war.

As tension mounted, Sir Edward Grey, the British foreign secretary, tried to arrange talks between Serbia and Austria. But meanwhile, Berchtold convinced the Austrian emperor that war was the only way to deal with the Serbs. He paid no attention to Grey's proposals for peace. German military leaders also encouraged Berchtold. On July 28, 1914, Austria declared war on Serbia.

Alliances brought other nations into the war. Even at that stage, more pressure from the German chancellor might have opened a path for a peaceful settlement. However, on July 30, mobilization of the Russian army began. This ended further tries at negotiation.

The Russians felt they should help their fellow Slavs, the Serbs. They also knew that a Serbian defeat would be a major blow to Russia's standing as a Great Power. When France assured Russia of support, Tsar Nicholas II gave in to the advice of his war-hungry generals.

News of Russian mobilization and French support caused alarm in the German capital. It looked as if Germany would have to fight on two fronts: France on the west and Russia on the east. Germany at once demanded that Russia halt war moves and that France stay neutral. These nations refused. On August 1, Germany declared war on France. The Germans demanded that their troops be allowed to cross Belgian frontiers on the way to the French front. Belgium refused and looked instead to Britain and France for help.

NATIONALITIES IN EASTERN EUROPE

GERMAN EMPIRE
Poles
RUSSIAN EMPIRE
SILESIA
Prague
Poles
Ukranians
Slovaks
Munich
Vienna
AUSTRO-HUNGARIAN
Budapest
TYROL
HUNGARY
Slovenes
EMPIRE
Belgrade
ROMANIA
Bucharest
Sarajevo
ITALY
N
SERBIA
BULGARIA
MONTENEGRO
Sofia
ALBANIA
GREECE

Czechs
Magyars
Croats
Austrians
Sudetens
Serbs
Other Slavs

0   100   200 MILES
0   100   200 KILOMETERS

Germany ignored the refusal and sent its troops across Belgium anyway.

Great Britain, as a member of the Triple Entente, was not bound to help France or Russia in a war. But in entering Belgium, Germany had broken a 75-year-old international treaty that guaranteed Belgium's neutrality. The violation angered Britain, which, like Germany, was a party to the treaty. It also made the British fearful because Germany might gain control of the North Sea coast and thus threaten the British Isles. Therefore, on August 4, 1914, Great Britain declared war on Germany.

section review 3

1. Why did the Austrian government feel threatened by Serbia before the death of the Archduke?

2. What demands did Austria make on Serbia after the murder of Francis Ferdinand? How much help did Germany promise Austria?

3. What steps were taken to prevent a war after Austria's message to Serbia?

4. Why did Germany declare war on France? Why did Great Britain declare war on Germany?

4 The world went to war

In August, 1914, at the start of the war, only six nations were fighting. On one side were the Allies—Great Britain, France, Russia, and Serbia. Opposing them were the Central Powers—Germany and Austria. The strength of the Central Powers grew when the Ottoman Empire joined them in October, 1914, and Bulgaria a year later.

Although Italy was an ally of Germany and Austria in the Triple Alliance, it felt no real friendship for Austria. When the war began, Italy declared it would stay *neutral*, meaning it would not choose one side or the other. For several months, the Allies and the Central Powers each tried to win Italy to their respective sides. In April, 1915, after promises of territory in Austria and Africa, Italy joined the Allies.

Japan had already joined the Allies in 1914. In 1917, China declared war against Germany and Austria. By the end, thirty-one countries had entered the war. It lasted more than four years and drew more than 61 million people into military service.

Because the kaiser had decided to make Germany the most powerful country in the world, many in the Allied nations felt that Germany was chiefly at fault for causing World War I. They felt that Germany had encouraged Austria's dispute with Serbia. Also, Germany had brought the other countries in by declaring war on France and by marching through neutral Belgium. Actually, each of the Allies had a reason for choosing war. All shared in the blame.

The Allies held firm. By striking fast through Belgium, Germany tried to deal France a quick blow. The highly trained German troops almost reached Paris before the French stopped them. The French were aided by a hasty Russian offensive on the Eastern Front. This made the Germans shift large numbers of troops from west to east. The French then forced the weakened Germans back at the Marne River. This ended German hopes for a quick victory.

From 1915 to 1917, bitter fighting on the Western Front raged back and forth. The Allies and the Germans built trenches. Separating the enemies was an area covered with barbed wire. It was called "no man's land." The war became a stalemate. Great battles were fought, and many were killed. But very little territory changed hands.

Allies	Australia	Guatemala	Nicaragua	**Central Powers**	Austria-Hungary
	Belgium	Haiti	Panama		Bulgaria
	Brazil	Honduras	Portugal		Germany
	Canada	India	Romania		Ottoman Empire
	China	Italy	Russia		
	Costa Rica	Japan	Serbia		
	Cuba	Liberia	South Africa		
	France	Montenegro	Thailand		
	Great Britain	New Zealand	United States		
	Greece				

𝔇aily𝔏ife

The years 1914 through 1918 brought new horrors of war that the world had never known before. Many of these horrors came from the advanced technology that developed during World War I. The British secretly developed the military tank in 1916. Although these steel monsters *above,* traveled at only a half mile per hour, German soldiers were terrified when the machines first appeared in battle. At the same time, many nations learned the uses of airplanes in war. At *right* is a "dogfight" between German and Allied planes. During all of this, the governments and peoples at home refused to make a compromise peace. This threw armies into battle again and again in search of victory. At *bottom left* are British and German soldiers walking back together after a battle at the Somme in July, 1916. At *top left* are British soldiers in November, 1916, at the Somme digging a position for a 16-inch howitzer, a short-barreled cannon for firing shells in a high curve. Many shells made in 1915 and 1916 failed to explode or exploded while still inside the cannon. The poster at *top right* expressed the view of many people about the wartime role of the Red Cross and nurses at the front. The war's most famous nurse was Edith Cavell of England. In October, 1915, Germany shocked the world by executing Cavell for having helped Allied soldiers escape to Holland from occupied Brussels, Belgium.

557

Technology gave both sides deadly weapons. Weapons had become more powerful than ever before in history. Battles were fought in the air and under the sea, as well as on land and on sea. Germany attacked British battleships with submarines. Early in the war, both Germany and the Allies used airplanes for spying. By 1917, both had developed fighter and bomber planes. Each side bombed targets hundreds of miles from their home air bases.

The British introduced tanks. Later, the Germans used them. Sea and land mines, torpedo boats, hand grenades, flamethrowers, machine guns, and many other weapons were created or improved by technological advances. Giant guns, such as the German "Big Bertha," fired shells more than 75 miles (120 kilometers).

The Central Powers won victories in the east. On the Eastern Front, the Russians kept a large part of the German army busy. The Russian invasion of East Prussia in 1914 drew German divisions from the Western Front. However, after the Germans made a successful counterattack there, the Russians drew back. Further defeats took away the Russian will to fight. Russian losses, mounting into the millions, were even greater than those of the French and British. They continued to resist the Germans and Austrians, but for the most part fought only a defensive war.

In 1915, the British and French tried to open the Dardanelles to send supplies to Russia. But these plans failed. Later in 1915, Austria and Bulgaria defeated Serbia and occupied it. This victory gave the Central Powers control of an unbroken line from Berlin to Istanbul.

Germany stepped up naval warfare. During the first months of the war, Allied shipping was heavily damaged by the German navy. Early in 1915, Germany stated that all the waters around the British Isles would be treated as a war zone. An enemy ship—even a merchant ship—found in this zone would be attacked. Britain fought back by ordering a blockade of Germany and seizing all goods headed for German ports.

By 1916, the British blockade caused a great shortage of food supplies in Germany. Later in the year, Germany added more submarines. With their help, German light cruisers were able to slip through the blockade to raid Atlantic shipping. Britain speeded up shipbuilding and developed depth bombs to use against submarines. But German naval warfare—especially submarine warfare—was very effective. By the early part of 1917, supplies of food in England were running low, and the country was close to starvation. In March, 1917, the people of Russia revolted against the tsar. They set up a new government that tried to carry on the war. But from that time on, Germany had little to fear from Russia.

The United States joined the Allies. One month after the Russian revolt, the United States entered the war. Since August, 1914, the United States had tried to stay neutral. As the war dragged on, however, German submarines attacked American ships carrying supplies to Britain and France. The Americans said that as neutrals, they had freedom of the seas and could go anywhere. The Germans felt that they could not let supplies reach their enemies. In 1915 and 1916, German submarine attacks caused the loss of hundreds of American lives. President Woodrow Wilson warned the Germans to stop the attacks. But the Germans felt they were in a life-and-death struggle and ignored the warning. Then on January 31, 1917, Germany announced "unrestricted submarine warfare." This meant that all ships headed toward Britain and France would be attacked without warning. In the next two months, several American ships were sunk.

Late in March, British agents got hold of a

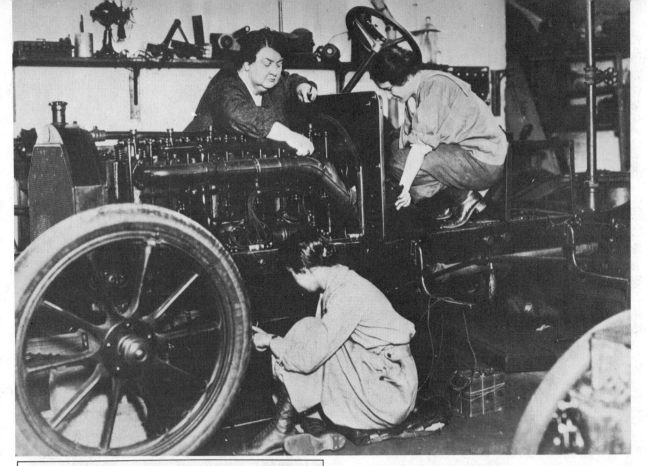

DailyLife

During the first two years of the war, many people on the home fronts were very enthusiastic. They rallied behind the war effort, made personal sacrifices, and changed life-styles so that money and materials could go to making weapons and sending more soldiers into battle. Women who had never worked outside their homes took jobs left by departing soldiers. *Above* are women in Newark, New Jersey, learning to be auto mechanics. At the same time, families learned to rely on themselves more for necessary goods, such as food. The poster at *left* urges Americans to grow their own fruits and vegetables as one way to "can the Kaiser."

EUROPE AFTER WORLD WAR I

telegram sent to Mexico by Alfred Zimmermann, the German foreign secretary. It asked Mexico to ally itself with Germany and help fight the United States. Besides financial aid, Zimmermann promised that Mexico would recover Texas, New Mexico, and Arizona when the Allies were defeated.

German submarine warfare and the Zimmermann telegram raised pro-war feelings in the United States to a feverish pitch. President Wilson gave up his efforts to end the war through negotiation. The United States entered the war on April 6, 1917.

Russia got out of the war. At the same time that Russian soldiers were fighting in the battlefields of World War I, the Russian people were fighting the tsar's forces in the capital. A revolution in November, 1917, left Russia under Bolshevik party leadership.

By this time, the Russians were sick of the war that had cost them so many lives and severe food and fuel shortages. The Bolshevik leader, Vladimir Ilyich Ulyanov [ül yä′nôf], better known as Lenin, offered to make peace with the leaders of Germany. On March 3, 1918, the Bolsheviks and the Germans signed the

1. One system for finding your way around Europe is to think of it as a series of peninsulas. The Scandinavian peninsula between the North Sea and the Baltic Sea is divided between two nations. What are they?

2. A small nation occupies the small peninsula jutting out from Germany also between the North Sea and the Baltic. What small nation is this?

3. The Iberian peninsula between the Atlantic Ocean and the Mediterranean Sea is divided between two nations also. What are these two?

4. The nation of Italy occupies the Italian peninsula. This peninsula extends between the Mediterranean Sea and what other sea?

5. Turkey is centered on the Anatolian peninsula. Traditionally, this area is considered to be a part of Asia, not Europe. Hence, it is often called Asia Minor. Turkey occupies a peninsula that borders what three seas?

6. The Balkan peninsula is more difficult to visualize than the other peninsulas discussed here. It is bordered by the Adriatic Sea, the Mediterranean Sea, the Aegean Sea, and the Black Sea. It is occupied by Greece, Turkey, Hungary, and four other nations. What are these four other nations?

Treaty of Brest-Litovsk. Through this treaty, Russia lost a third of its people, nine-tenths of its coal mines, and all of the great oil fields in the Caucasus to Germany. As a result, Germany greatly increased its power. Even more important, Germany no longer needed to fight on two fronts.

The tide turned for the Allies. While Russia was crumbling, the first troops from the United States landed in France. German leaders tried hard to win the war before the American army could get into action. Following the Brest-Litovsk treaty, they sent almost every German soldier to the Western Front. There they began a huge attack in the spring of 1918. But it failed as American, British, and French troops stopped the Germans. Later, American troops under General Pershing carried out brilliant offensives in France.

In the fall of 1918, German military leaders realized they could not win. One by one, Germany's allies quit. On November 3, German sailors mutinied at Kiel. Four days later, a revolution broke out in Germany. A republic was founded, and the kaiser fled to Holland. Thus ended Hohenzollern rule and the Second German Reich.

Leaders of the new German government agreed to an armistice. They asked that the peace settlement be based on the Fourteen Points that President Wilson had set forth in a speech to Congress on January 8, 1918. Some of the points were: an end to secret agreements, freedom of the seas in peace and war, reduction of armaments, the right of nationality groups to form their own nations, and an association of nations to keep the peace. In other speeches, Wilson called for a negotiated peace with reasonable demands on the losers. The Allies also agreed to model the peace settlement on the Fourteen Points. However, some felt that Wilson's terms would be too easy on Germany.

Early in the morning of November 11, 1918, the war was ended. In a railroad car in the Compiègne [koɴ'pyen'] Forest in northern France, two German delegates met Allied officials to sign the armistice.

section review 4

1. Why did Germany strike quickly through Belgium?

2. How did Germany step up the naval warfare around the British Isles in 1915?

3. What made the United States enter the war?

4. Why did the kaiser flee to Holland?

5 The victors tried to build a lasting peace

No previous war in the world's history had caused such widespread horror. More than 10 million were killed in battle. Twenty million more were wounded. And 13 million civilians died from war-related famine, disease, and injuries. The cost of the war was estimated at more than $350 billion.

Three leaders dominated the Paris Peace Conference. After the armistice had been signed, the Allied Nations met at Paris to discuss peace terms. Contrary to Wilson's wishes, the defeated countries were not allowed to send representatives to the peace conference. Thus the so-called Big Three dominated the meeting. They included President Wilson; David Lloyd George, prime minister of Great Britain; and Georges Clemenceau [klem'ən sō'], premier of France.

Woodrow Wilson was a great idealist. He stated the hopes of people everywhere when he said that the conflict had been fought "for . . . democracy. . . for the rights and liberties of small nations . . . for . . . free peoples . . . to make the world itself at last free." At the conference, Wilson upheld his Fourteen Points. Above all, he wanted to see a League of Nations set up to keep the peace. To get the others to agree to this, he had to compromise.

Lloyd George wanted Great Britain to take control of Germany's colonies. He also wanted the German navy destroyed.

Georges Clemenceau, known as the "Old Tiger," had led France during the darkest hours of the war. He wanted Germany to pay for war damages, since almost all the fighting in the West had been on French soil. Most of all, he insisted that France be made safe from attack by Germany. He wanted German power cut down and strong alliances created with Britain and the United States. Clemenceau placed little faith in a league of nations. However, when Wilson gave in on many details, Clemenceau and Lloyd George agreed to make the creation of the League of Nations part of the Versailles Treaty.

Germany lost territory and wealth. When the German delegation arrived to sign the Treaty of Versailles, they found its terms harsher than they had expected.

The Germans were very angry at a war-guilt clause, Article 231, which placed the entire blame for the war on Germany and its allies. In addition, they were unhappy that many of Wilson's Fourteen Points were missing or were weakened by changes. The first delegates from Germany refused to sign the treaty. To avoid occupation by Allied soldiers, however, a second delegation signed it on June 28, 1919.

In the treaty, France won back the provinces of Alsace and Lorraine. The German territory west of the Rhine, called the Rhineland, was to become a buffer zone between the two enemies. It was to be occupied by Allied troops for at least fifteen years. (In another agreement, Wilson and Lloyd George promised to protect France against possible future German attack.) France was also given the rich coal mines of the Saar. But the Saar was to be administered by the League of Nations. After fifteen years, the Saarlanders could vote to have their region go back to the German government or remain under the French. In 1935, they voted to become a part of Germany again.

In March, 1917, Poland had become independent of Russia. Through the Versailles Treaty, it won a broad stretch of land from Germany. This region became known as the Polish Corridor. It gave Poland an outlet to the Baltic Sea. The Polish Corridor also divided Germany, isolating its province of East Prussia.

The Versailles Treaty gave German colonies in Africa and in the Pacific to the League of Nations. The League in turn placed them under the control of the Allied Nations. These lands, known as *mandates,* were given mainly to Great Britain and France. (Mandates were lands given to nations by the League for those lands' administration and development.) Some also went to Japan, South Africa, Australia, and New Zealand.

In the treaty, the Allies required that Germany repay much of the cost of the war. They wanted an immediate payment of $5 billion in cash. Two years later, they billed Germany for $32 billion, plus interest.

The treaty reduced German military power and permitted Germany an army of no more than 100 thousand men. The navy was allowed only six warships and some other vessels and no submarines or military airplanes.

The Germans were not alone in thinking such peace terms unjust. Even David Lloyd George doubted the justice of the Versailles Treaty. President Wilson hoped that his dream, the League of Nations, could keep the peace. He thought the League could correct unjust treaty features later.

New independent nations were formed. Four empires had fallen apart in the course of World War I—the German, the Austro-Hungarian, the Ottoman, and the Russian empires. Based partly on secret agreements made during the war, the Allies drew up a series of peace treaties that broke up these empires. The Allies reorganized the land lost by Russia to Germany. From the western portion of the old Russian Empire came five new nations: Poland, Finland, Latvia, Lithuania, and Estonia.

The defeated Austro-Hungarian Empire was also broken up into several new countries. Austria and Hungary became two independent republics, as did Yugoslavia and Czechoslovakia. Some Austro-Hungarian land also went to Poland, Italy, and Romania.

The treaty ending World War I was signed in the Hall of Mirrors at Versailles. Seated center are Clemenceau (with mustache), Lloyd George (right), and Wilson (left).

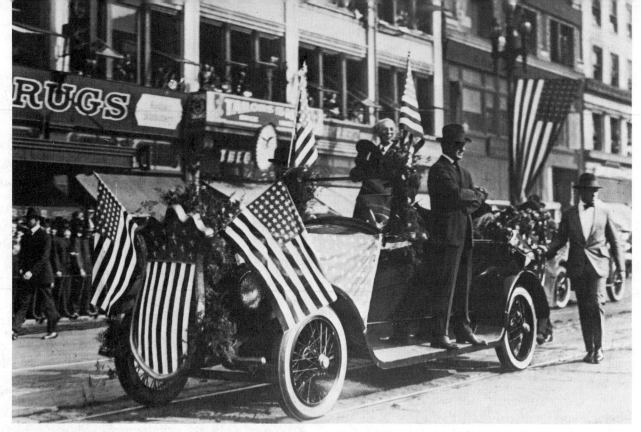

After he returned from Versailles, Woodrow Wilson toured the United States seeking support for the League of Nations. He is shown here in San Francisco.

WHAT'S IN A NAME?
ROMANIA

The people of Romania were originally colonists from Rome. Being very proud of their ancestry, they called themselves *Romani* or "Romans." They still speak a language similar to the old Latin of the early Romans.

The Ottoman Empire, too, was divided up. Syria, Iraq, Trans-Jordan, and Palestine became mandates. The first was ruled by France; the other three by Britain. These mandates were promised independence at a future time.

The creation of the new states helped fulfill one of Wilson's Fourteen Points. This was the right of *self-determination*, or the right of peoples to form their own nations. However, redrawing the map of Europe again brought some groups under foreign control. For example, Austrians living in the Tyrol came under the rule of Italy. Other German-speaking Austrians (the Sudetens) were placed under Czechoslovakian rule. Some Germans lived in the new Polish Corridor, and certain Hungarians came under Romanian control. Few of these peoples were happy about the changes made in their lives. Their discontent was a dangerous sign for the future of Europe.

section review 5

1. Who were the major participants at the Paris Peace Conference? What were the goals of each of the Big Three?

2. How did the League of Nations come to be part of the Treaty of Versailles?

3. Name at least three major terms that the treaty imposed on Germany.

4. What four empires fell apart during the war?

Section Summaries

1. Disputes and alliances increased tensions. In the late 19th century, there was growing economic cooperation among the Western nations. Progress and prosperity were made possible in part by peace. Yet a general mood for war began to take hold after 1900. National rivalries and colonial interests caused tensions. These led to an armaments race which added further fuel to the fire.

Nations tried to find security by joining various alliances. Under Bismarck, the German Empire set up the Triple Alliance with Austria-Hungary and Italy. To balance this, France, Russia, and Great Britain formed the Triple Entente. Such alliances meant that a local crisis could easily blow up into a general war.

2. Some forces promoted peace while others worked for war. Along with more economic interdependence, there was growing political cooperation. Several new international organizations were formed. But fears and insecurities caused the mood for war to grow stronger than the desire for peace.

3. A Balkan crisis brought general war. In 1914, the murder of Archduke Francis Ferdinand of Austria at Sarajevo led to war between Austria and Serbia. The war at once involved Russia, a friend of Serbia, and Germany, a partner of Austria. France and Great Britain joined Russia.

4. The world went to war. From 1914 to 1917, France and Britain fought bitterly against Germany on the Western Front. The British blockade in the North Sea prevented trade between Germany and neutral nations. This reduced food supplies in Germany. But German submarines sank so much Allied shipping that the British were also lacking food.

In 1917, the Bolsheviks gained control of Russia and made a separate peace with Germany. That same year, the United States declared war on the Central Powers. This was only after Germany began unrestricted submarine warfare and encouraged Mexico to attack the United States. In 1918, thousands of American soldiers joined the French and British in France. Together, the Allies pushed the Germans back and forced the Central Powers to ask for peace.

5. The victors tried to build a lasting peace. President Wilson's Fourteen Points set forth a basis for peace. But Wilson's points were not entirely acceptable to the other Allies. Agreement was reached, however, on the League of Nations.

The major part of the Versailles Treaty took away German territory, wealth, and military strength. Other treaties with the Central Powers set down the boundaries of new states. Some nationality groups gained independence. But others were unhappily placed under foreign control. The war had ended four major empires. It brought about the greatest change in the political map of Europe since 1815.

Who? What? When? Where?

1. Place these events in order, beginning with the earliest:
- a. The Treaty of Brest-Litovsk was signed.
- b. Archduke Francis Ferdinand was murdered.
- c. Russia mobilized for war.
- d. Germany promised a "blank check" to Austria.
- e. The World War I armistice was signed.
- f. England declared war on Germany.

2. Write a sentence about each of these men that describes the role he played in the 1914 crisis between Austria and Serbia:
- a. Leopold von Berchtold c. Edward Grey
- b. Francis Joseph I d. William II

3. Use each of these terms in a sentence describing events that happened in World War I:
- a. Brest-Litovsk e. neutral
- b. Central Powers f. Sarajevo
- c. Compiègne Forest g. Western Front
- d. Marne River h. Zimmermann telegram

4. Write a sentence for each of these terms that describes how it relates to the peace agreements of World War I:
- a. buffer zone d. mandates
- b. compromise e. self-determination
- c. Fourteen Points f. war-guilt clause

5. Write a sentence for each of these summarizing the role he played in World War I:
  - a. Clemenceau
  - b. Lenin
  - c. Lloyd George
  - d. Nicholas II
  - e. John J. Pershing
  - f. Wilson

Questions for Critical Thinking

1. Why were the great powers of Europe unable to stop the Serbian crisis from expanding into a world war?

2. Why did the Germans use unrestricted submarine warfare even though they knew it might bring the United States into the war?

3. How might World War I have been prevented?

4. World War I has sometimes been called a family squabble. What does this mean?

Skill Activities

1. Read *Versailles* by Christopher Hibbert to learn more about this famous palace and its history. (Newsweek Books, 1972)

2. Prepare a report on the new methods of warfare used in World War I. Tell how this war was different from previous wars.

3. Choose parts and role-play the debates at Versailles about the peace terms both before they were presented to the Germans and afterwards. Parts include: Wilson, Clemenceau, Lloyd George, and a German delegation led by the German foreign minister.

4. Draw a political cartoon for the editorial page of a British newspaper the day after Archduke Ferdinand was shot. Before you begin to draw, think carefully about the probable British reaction to the shooting.

chapter **29** quiz

Section 1

1. True or false: After the Franco-Prussian War, France joined Germany and Austria in the Triple Alliance.

2. The person who ended Germany's friendship with Russia was: a. Bismarck, b. William II, c. Nicholas II

3. True or false: Russia's defeat in the Russo-Japanese war was a great shock to Western nations.

Section 2

4. True or false: World economic interdependence was a strong force for peace in the early 1900s.

5. One factor that did not cause fear and distrust among the Great Powers before the war was: a. trade agreements, b. arms buildup, c. colonial rivalries

Section 3

6. In 1914, Serbia wanted to: a. become part of Russia, b. become free from Germany, c. unite all Serbs

7. The kaiser's blank check told: a. Austria it would get unlimited amounts of help from Germany, b. Tsar Nicholas to invade France, c. England that Germany planned to violate Belgium's neutrality

Section 4

8. The nation that changed sides from the Central Powers to the Allies was: a. Japan, b. Bulgaria, c. Italy

9. The nation that the Treaty of Versailles blamed for starting the war was: a. Austria, b. Germany, c. Serbia

Section 5

10. The Big Three were the United States, Britain, and the nation of: a. Germany, b. Russia, c. France

11. True or false: After World War I, new nations were created so that no national group was under foreign control.

12. True or false: The harsh terms of the Versailles Treaty made Germany give up the Rhineland, the Saar, Alsace and Lorraine, repay the cost of the war, and give up its colonies in Africa and the Pacific.

THE RISE OF COMMUNISM IN RUSSIA

The Bolshevik Revolution and Lenin's role in it are important events to people in the Soviet Union. This picture was made to honor that time. It shows Lenin addressing a crowd of revolutionaries. Behind him are Stalin and Trotsky.

Dear comrades, soldiers, sailors, and workers! I am happy to greet in your persons the victorious Russian revolution, and greet you as the vanguard of the worldwide proletarian army. . . . Any day now the whole of European capitalism may crash.

The speaker was Lenin, a bald, stocky man, who had led the Russian Bolsheviks for over ten years. The Bolsheviks were the radical Marxist group within the Social Democratic movement. Lenin, their leader, was in exile in Switzerland when revolution broke out in Russia. In 1917, he was secretly returned to Russia with the aid of the German High Command. The occasion for his speech was his arrival in Petrograd on April 16, 1917.

The Germans hoped that Lenin and his followers would undermine the Provisional Government of Russia. This had been set up in March, 1917, after Tsar Nicholas II was forced to give up his throne. The Germans got their wish, but in a way they never expected. Lenin and his followers seized power in November, 1917. They set up the first Communist state in history. To understand why and how this happened we must look into Russia's past.

Russia in the 19th century was unlike any other country in Europe. It was a huge empire, more than twice the size of the United States. It stretched from Germany to the Pacific Ocean. Within it lived 130 million people in 1900. But less than half of these people were Russians. There were other Slavs such as White Russians, Ukrainians, and Poles. There were also non-Slavs including Latvians, Lithuanians, Mongols, Turks, Estonians, Finns, Germans, Jews, and many others.

Ruling over this vast empire with its different nationalities, languages, and religions were the Romanov tsars. They were mostly autocrats who believed that only unlimited power could hold the empire together. After 1881, the tsars were generally opposed to major reforms.

The great majority of the peoples in the empire were peasants. They were poor and generally illiterate. Up until the mid-19th century most of them were serfs. Sometimes, the serfs would burst out in great fury against their landlords, the nobility. But tsarist troops always put down the outbursts with great brutality. The tsar felt he had to defend the nobles. He depended on them to help him rule the empire by serving as government and military officers.

Meanwhile, the ideas and economic changes that had been taking place in Europe since the end of the Middle Ages had hardly touched Russia. Revolution came in 1917 because the tsarist government had been unwilling or unable to find a way to modernize this huge backward empire and because Russians had no effective way to obtain reforms in a peaceful, orderly manner. After that, Communist leaders faced the very same problems of modernization. They were able to build a modern, industrial country but did so in such a way that it took a terrible cost in human lives. Chapter 30 traces the process by which Russia became a Communist state:

1. Autocratic rulers weakened Russia.

2. Bolsheviks took control of Russia.

3. Stalin created a totalitarian society.

4. The Soviet Union tried to protect its security.

1 Autocratic rulers weakened Russia

To Western Europeans and Americans of the time, the Russian Empire seemed distant, mysterious, and backward. The tsars had long ignored the deep desire of the Russian people for a better life. And the nobles continually objected to reforms that might weaken their power or limit their incomes.

Tsars opposed constitutional rule. After the death of Catherine the Great in 1796, her son, Paul I, became tsar. In 1801, he was assassinated.

Paul was succeeded by Alexander I, the most puzzling of all the Russian tsars. He said he hated despotism, but he did many cruel things. Growing dissatisfaction with Alexander led certain army officers to form secret societies. Many of these officers had come in contact with Western ideas during the Russian occupation of France after Napoleon's defeat. When Alexander died suddenly in December, 1825, these officers rebelled against the government. They had very little support from the people, and their uprising was easily put down. Yet the so-called Decembrist Revolt inspired later revolutionaries. It showed how ideas from the outside could spark a demand for reform.

After the revolt, Nicholas I became tsar. He felt that the only way to avoid future bloodshed was to be a strict autocrat. As one of his officials stated, "The tsar is a father, his subjects are his children, and children ought never to question their parents. . . ." Nicholas took personal control of everything. He censored the press and took away academic freedoms. He had police spies round up enemies and send them off to Siberia. However, Nicholas's bureaucracy was very corrupt and weak. As a result, the Russians suffered a terrible defeat in the Crimean War. Nicholas, a bitter man, died in 1855.

Alexander II brought about reforms. Alexander II was by nature as autocratic as his father. But the Russian defeat in the Crimean War led him to try reform. As he told a gathering of nobles in Moscow, "It is better to abolish serfdom from above than to wait until it begins to abolish itself from below." Thus in 1861, Alexander issued the Act on the Emancipation of the Peasants from Serfdom.

This act gave the serfs personal liberty and promised them some land of their own. The land was not given to them directly, however. Instead, it was placed under the rule of the local village or *mir* [mēr]. The landlords were allowed to keep about half of their old estates. The freed serfs had to pay a "redemption" tax to the landlords for the other half. The tax lasted forty-nine years. Though no longer in bondage, the former serfs found that they were often worse off than before. In many cases, the land they got was poor. The well-to-do peasants were able to buy or lease the more fertile land. The others had to work the rest as farm laborers at very low wages. Thus, peasant life remained hard.

Yet, freeing the serfs stands out as the single most important event in 19th-century Russia. It was the beginning of the end of power for the landed nobles. Emancipation brought free labor and industry, and a middle class arose.

There were other reforms in Russia in the 1860s and 1870s. Trial by jury was started. For the first time, law became a profession. More elementary schools were set up, and lower-class children were allowed to go to high schools. A form of local self-government known as a *zemstvo* [zemst'vō] was also set up in each district. The *zemstvo* had charge of schools, roads, health, and farming. But it was controlled mainly by the landowners.

These reforms raised hopes that Alexander II might even allow a constitutional government. But it soon became clear that he would not. Many educated people, particularly in the universities, then became bitter. They formed small revolutionary groups. These groups began to assassinate government leaders. In 1881, they killed Alexander himself. But the murder of the tsar did not change the tsarist system.

The tsarist system grew stricter. The last two tsars were Alexander III, who ruled until 1894, and Nicholas II, who was tsar until 1917. Neither of them made any effort at meaningful reform. In fact, both rulers tried to turn back the clock. They brought back repressive measures and did away with some of Alexander's reforms. Censorship again became severe. Religious persecution was allowed. Many Jews were either terrorized or killed in terrible mob attacks called *pogroms* [pō gromz′]. Secret agents of the tsar incited revolutionary groups to murder officials. The agents then exposed the rebels to the police. Things got worse when low wages, long hours, and poor working conditions led to a wave of strikes in the 1890s. Yet both strikes and labor unions remained illegal.

Russia lost a war with Japan. In 1904, Russian imperialism in East Asia brought a clash with Japan. By 1900, Russia had dominated Manchuria and was eager to add Korea. Because Japan was thought to be weak, Russia did not try to avoid a war. As one official put it, a "little victorious war to stem the tide of revolution" would be most welcome.

Japan, however, decided to strike first. In February, 1904, the Japanese fleet attacked Port Arthur. This was the Russian naval base on the tip of the southern Manchurian coast. As in the Crimean War, Russia was unprepared. Its army and navy suffered many defeats. The Russo-Japanese War ended with a peace treaty unfavorable to Russia that was signed in September, 1905.

The 1905 revolution warned the tsar. The Russo-Japanese War was very unpopular with the Russian people. This was partly because Russia lost the war and partly because the war effort prevented reform at home. During the war, a revolution broke out. It was touched off by "Bloody Sunday" on January 22, 1905. A large group of workers, carrying a petition to the tsar, was fired upon by troops in St. Petersburg. Several hundred unarmed workers were killed. News of this act aroused great anger against the government. Strikes shut down the railroads, the telegraph system, and government offices. Councils of workers called *soviets* sprang up in the cities to direct the rebellion. Crowds carried red banners and posters demanding reforms. (Red was the traditional color of revolutionary socialism.)

Shocked by this outcry, Nicholas finally allowed a constitution in October, 1905. Civil rights were protected, and a national parliament, known as the Duma, was set up. At last it seemed that Russia had become a constitutional monarchy. But the Duma was very limited in its powers. The first two Dumas, which met in 1906 and 1907, were dismissed by the tsar when they asked for reform. The third and fourth Dumas did pass some reforms. But these Dumas had members who represented wealthy people much more than poor people.

More industrial growth in Russia did help some workers and the middle class. But peasants and factory workers remained unhappy. Peasants were desperately short of land, and factory workers had low pay and miserable living conditions.

section review 1

1. How did Nicholas I view the Decembrist Revolt? How did he feel that Russia should be ruled?

2. Why did Alexander II end serfdom? What effects did this abolition have?

3. What were the pogroms?

4. How did the events of Bloody Sunday lead to a constitution and the Duma?

2 Bolsheviks took control of Russia

World War I caused the tsarist system great trouble. The shock of defeat in battles against the Germans and the shortages of food and other goods made the masses rebellious. Their mood was similar to that of 1905. In 1917, after more than 300 years of rule, the Romanov dynasty was swept from power.

The tsarist government fell. Russia had entered the war patriotically in 1914. But the people lost interest as the number of dead and wounded mounted. Food and fuel supplies fell, and prices went up. The tsar proved to be a poor leader. He refused to allow the Duma any share in running the country.

In March, 1917, food shortages led to street marches in Petrograd, the capital. (St. Petersburg had been patriotically renamed Petrograd in 1914 in a wave of anti-German feeling.) Police and soldiers fought the crowds. But within a few days, the armed forces mutinied and joined the people. The uprising had become a revolution. Tsar Nicholas, at his army headquarters near the front, was forced to abdicate his throne.

Duma members soon formed a cabinet of middle-class liberals and set up a Provisional Government. Meanwhile, workers and soldiers in the cities formed soviets, or councils, as had been done in the 1905 revolution. The soviets soon took over control of the local governments.

The Provisional Government in Petrograd restored civil rights and promised free elections. It also continued the war, even though by now most Russians wanted to end it. This lost the Provisional Government much support, as did its refusal to approve land reform for the peasants and its delay in holding free elections. Indeed, peasants had already begun to seize estates and divide the land among themselves.

In July, 1917, Alexander Kerensky, a moderate socialist, became prime minister. He tried hard, but failed to win the people's support because he refused to stop the war or carry out land reforms.

Alexander Kerensky

Russia's last royal family: Tsar Nicholas II, Empress Alexandra, their son, Tsarevich Alexis, and their daughters, Olga, Tatiana, Maria, and Anastasia.

DailyLife

Russia was a huge country of many contrasts where the differences between rich and poor were very great. The Imperial Easter Egg, *above,* is one example of the almost limitless use of money by the rich. Each year, Alexander III commissioned the court jeweler, Peter Carl Fabergé, to make an Easter egg for the empress. The cost was not to be considered, and the custom continued for some 35 years, right up to the time of the revolution. This egg contained a copy of the coach used for the tsars' coronations. The egg is enamel studded with diamonds. The coach is yellow gold, red enamel, and rose diamonds. The doors and wheels on the coach actually work.

This Easter egg was given to Empress Alexandra Feodorovna by her son, Nicholas II, in 1897. And this photograph shows the egg and coach at their actual size. At the same time, the poor peasants were very poor indeed. The technological revolution that changed the lives of people in Western Europe hardly affected Russia at all. At *top right* are men and women at work in an ore mine in Balask, a town in the Urals. And as industry developed slowly, so did business. At *far right bottom* is a dry-goods merchant in his shop in Samarkand. This part of Russia had a large Muslim population. At *near right bottom* is the weighing room at the Chakva Tea Plantation near Batum. The tea was weighed by hand before being wrapped in small paper containers.

The Bolsheviks took over the government.
Mounting unrest helped Lenin and his followers. They won a great deal of support by promising peace to the soldiers, land to the peasants, and bread to the workers. Seeing a chance to seize power, they planned their moves carefully.

The right moment came in the fall of 1917. The Bolsheviks were still a small party. But they were able to take over the Petrograd and Moscow soviets. They formed a workers' militia called the Red Guard. Then on November 6 and 7, the Red Guard, joined by pro-Bolshevik soldiers and sailors, seized the central government by force. They captured important buildings in the capital and stormed the Winter Palace, the site of the Kerensky government. All the ministers except Kerensky were arrested. He escaped and tried to fight against Lenin. But he failed and later fled the country.

Lenin's *coup d'état* was successful and daring. The Bolsheviks moved quickly to set up a party dictatorship and to adopt the name *Communist*.

The Communists faced many enemies. As the clear leader of the Communist party, Lenin became chief of state with unlimited power. He devoted his life to making Russia communistic. He began by applying Marxist principles to Russian society. In the early phase, known as "war communism," all private property went to the state. Industries, banks, railroads, and shipping were placed under government ownership. The landholdings of the Orthodox Church were taken away, and atheism was encouraged. To increase the food supply, however, the peasants were allowed to farm the land they had already taken over. But the peasants tried to hold back food from the cities because money was worthless and factory goods were not available. The Bolsheviks then sent soldiers and secret police to the villages to take the grain by force. The peasants again became angry and bitter.

In 1918, a furious civil war broke out against the Bolsheviks. It began after Lenin used armed sailors in January, 1918, to shut down the first freely elected Constituent

On November 7, 1917, the Red Guard stormed the Winter Palace, and an early photographer was there to record the event. The Winter Palace had been a home of the tsars. For a few short months, it became the home of the Provisional Government. Since the revolution, the Winter Palace has been turned into one of the world's greatest museums—the Hermitage.

A MYSTERY IN HISTORY

WAS LENIN A GERMAN AGENT?

The great hero of the Soviet Union is Vladimir Ilyich Lenin, creator of the Soviet Communist state. For Soviet citizens, Lenin is like a god who could do no wrong. In the eyes of the Soviet government, to attack Lenin's character is a terrible sin and must not be allowed. Yet ever since 1917, various people, some of them historians, have charged that Lenin was not the great revolutionary he seemed to be. He did what he did, they say, only because he was paid by the Germans and followed their orders. Whenever this accusation against Lenin is made, the Soviet government is outraged and angrily denounces the charge as an outright lie.

Is there any evidence that Lenin really was a paid German agent? When World War II ended, the archives of the German government were opened up to historians. There they found definite proof that during World War I the German government had secretly sent money to support Lenin and the Bolsheviks, in hopes of undermining the Russian war effort.

Did receiving money from the Germans make Lenin a German agent? Some historians say it did and argue that the Germans not only gave him money, but also told him what to do. Most historians, however, say that getting money

from the Germans is no proof that Lenin carried out German orders. They point out that the money came to Lenin from secret agents in Sweden and not directly from Germany. Therefore, Lenin may not even have known what the original source of the money was. Furthermore, they say, it is important to remember that Lenin was a fanatic revolutionary. It made little difference to him where he got the money to support his revolutionary activities. His goal always stayed the same, and he

always made all of his own decisions.

Although there is no way for historians to be absolutely certain, most of them have come to the conclusion that Lenin was not a German agent. But they have no doubt that German money helped Lenin carry out the most important revolution of the 20th century. And the fact that Lenin got money from the Germans is still a sensitive issue in the Soviet Union. To this day, no Soviet historian dares to write about it in a history textbook.

Assembly in Russian history, because the Bolsheviks did not have a majority and did not want to give up power. Lenin wanted to establish a Communist dictatorship. Many Russians, from socialists to monarchists, were opposed to his dictatorship and fought against Lenin. They were joined by many non-Russian nationalities—for example, Ukrainians, Poles, Finns, Estonians, Latvians, Lithuanians—who saw a chance to break away from Russian rule. Fighting soon spread to almost every part of the old Russian empire. This Civil War lasted until 1920. It was worse for Russia than World War I. Famine and disease killed hundreds of thousands, and casualties were in the millions. Both sides committed terrible atrocities. Among the casualties were the ex-tsar, his wife, and their five children. They were all shot by the Bolsheviks in 1918 at Ekaterinburg, a town along the route of the Trans-Siberian Railroad.

Meanwhile, Lenin took Russia out of World War I by signing the separate peace treaty of Brest-Litovsk with Germany in March, 1918. Britain and France, still desperately fighting to defeat Germany, wanted to bring Russia back into the war. They therefore sent troops and supplies to Russia to help the opposition overthrow Lenin. The United States also sent troops but they took no active part in the fighting. Japan, seeking to dominate eastern Siberia, occupied Vladivostok and other Pacific ports.

The Allies continued to take part in the civil war even after they signed an armistice with Germany in November, 1918. The Allies feared that communism would spread to the rest of Europe. Thus, they hoped to save Europe by destroying Lenin's regime. Faced with civil war and Allied intervention, the Communist government seemed likely to fall.

Yet the Communists finally defeated their enemies. The opposition armies were widely

The hardships of revolution and Civil War forced former bourgeoisie to sell their dresses in the streets of Leningrad. Bad droughts in 1920 and 1921 led to frightful famine. By 1926, the harvests were only a third of prewar levels.

scattered and uncoordinated. They were unable to win over many peasants because of the pro-landlord policy of the opposition generals. The Bolsheviks had also built up a superior army under Leon Trotsky, the Commissar for War. In addition, Allied intervention aroused Russian nationalism. All of these factors helped bring the Bolsheviks to victory. By late 1920, Communist rule was secure against internal enemies. But it enjoyed no great popularity.

Marxist principles were modified. To ease the strain of long years of war, the government in 1921 retreated from its policy of war

Leon Trotsky

sure that the Communist party controlled the government and the economy. They used force and terror to put down all enemies. They taught the people the ideas of Marx and Lenin. And they made everyone become a worker for the state. In 1922, the Communist party created the Union of Soviet Socialist Republics (the Soviet Union) to take the place of the old Russian Empire. It consisted of four republics; after World War II it included fifteen union republics.

Stalin got rid of Trotsky. The death of Lenin in 1924 brought a bitter fight for power between Leon Trotsky and Joseph Stalin. Trotsky, a brilliant writer and speaker, was as well known as Lenin. Most people expected him to become the new party leader. Stalin was not well known, but he was a shrewd politician. He used his post as party secretary to place his supporters in key jobs. The trend of the times also helped Stalin. The world revolution that Trotsky had talked about did not take place. Stalin, on the other hand, favored "building socialism in a single country." Russia should work by itself to become a "workers' paradise." Then perhaps communist ideas might spread to other countries.

Stalin's policy was accepted at the Fourteenth Party Congress in 1925. Trotsky was dismissed from the party in 1927. Two years later, he was exiled. In 1940, he was murdered in Mexico, by an agent of Stalin.

communism. It introduced instead the New Economic Policy (NEP). The state still owned basic industries. However, private enterprise in retail trade and small business was allowed. "Nepmen" (as small businessmen were called) did well under the new policy. The peasants were also happier. Except for a tax on surplus grain, they were free to grow and sell their produce as they wished.

Under Lenin, the Communists laid the base for a powerful dictatorship. They built a strong, well-organized party. They made

section review 2

1. What conditions led to the revolution in March, 1917?

2. Why did a civil war break out in Russia in 1918? Why did the Allies intervene?

3. What was the NEP?

4. How did Stalin defeat Trotsky after Lenin's death?

3 Stalin created a totalitarian society

By the late 1920s, Stalin was clearly in charge of the Communist party. Yet, until the mid-1930s, he was careful to consult others and to act modestly. Officially he was not the head of the government, but in practice he was. His only title until 1941 was general secretary of the Communist party. In 1941, he became premier as well as party secretary.

In 1928, the NEP came to an end. The economy had greatly improved. But the Marxist dream of a classless society had not come true; a full spectrum of economic classes still existed. Stalin felt that the Soviet Union would have to make some drastic changes if it was to catch up to the West economically. He explained:

> We were fifty to a hundred years behind the advanced countries. We must make up this lag in ten years. Either we do this or they will crush us.

Thus Stalin began a new policy, called the First Five-Year Plan. Its two major goals were rapid industrialization and the collectivization of agriculture. He believed that these goals could only be met by dictatorial controls. The huge amounts of money needed to build all the new plants and factories had to be squeezed out of the peasants. They would have to combine their small plots into large, collective farms. These farms would produce more by using tractors and other modern machines. The peasants would be forced to sell their crops at very low prices to the government. It would then export most of the crops to buy machines for the factories. Every effort was made to export Russian goods to obtain needed funds. In short, the peasants would have to pay the costs of industrialization. Their private land and other forms of private enterprise were again abolished.

Of course, most peasants strongly objected to giving up their land, tools, and animals. Instead, many burned their grain and killed their livestock. The government moved to crush this opposition. It shipped angry peasants to less fertile areas, where many of them starved to death. Other peasants were shot or sent to labor camps. Stalin called a halt to these brutal methods in 1930. From then on, propaganda and economic pressure were used instead. By 1936, about 90 percent of the peasants belonged to nearly 250 thousand collective farms that were scattered across the nation.

In 1933, the Second Five-Year Plan began. Waste, inefficiency, and a shortage of skilled workers held up the Plan. But in the short span of twelve years, the Soviet Union became a powerful industrial nation. The Third Five-Year Plan was cut short by World War II.

Life was "Stalinized." Under Stalin, ordinary citizens made some gains. The planned economy gave almost everyone jobs, and production increased. There was a drive to wipe out illiteracy and to enable many more people to receive free tuition and scholarships at universities. State medical care, old-age pensions, and illness and accident insurance were put into effect. Women also gained almost complete, although not total, equality with men. They were encouraged to enter the various professions, especially that of medicine.

These gains, however, did not hide the steady "Stalinization" of Soviet culture. In the early Stalin years, writers, artists, and scholars were able to work freely so long as they were not outspokenly anti-Communist. But by the mid-1930s, the party leaders decided that the intellectuals had a part to

Daily Life

Under Stalin, the schools became the mouthpiece of the government. Students were taught to conform, to love their country, and to believe that the leaders of the Soviet Union were always right. At the same time, adults were fed information about the glories of the communist system with newspapers and meetings.

play in building Communism. Thus, historians had to glorify Russian heroes of the national past. Novelists had to show all Communists as pure idealists. Composers had to write melodies that the common people could easily enjoy.

Marxist theory was also changed to fit the needs of the state. The Communist motto, "from each according to his ability; to each according to his needs," was scrapped. Training and skill were rewarded with higher salaries, bonuses, and more social prestige. Soviet patriotism was admired, while the unity of the world's working classes was played down. The family also gained new importance. Childbearing was encouraged, and divorce laws were tightened. Atheism remained the official position on religion. The government did not stop harassing the Orthodox Church and other religious groups.

Stalin became the absolute dictator. In 1936, the "Stalin Constitution" was adopted. Communists everywhere boasted that the Soviet Union was now the most democratic country in the world. In practice, however, the new constitution did not protect the basic freedoms of the individual. Those who hoped that there might be some loosening of totalitarianism were sadly mistaken. The Communist party still had all the political power. And behind the party stood Stalin. He was no longer willing to be first among equals. His drive for absolute power could not be stopped. His picture and his name appeared everywhere across the nation. He was always in the public eye as the "Great Marxist-Leninist."

Also, Stalin became suspicious of many of his old comrades. He had many, many party leaders arrested by the secret police on false charges of treason. After putting them through horrible tortures, he staged several public trials in Moscow from 1936 to 1938.

Most of the people confessed and were executed at once, although there was no evidence of their guilt.

The same things happened to many others. They included army officers, government officials, scientists, writers, artists, and ordinary citizens. Hundreds of thousands were shot. Millions of others were sent to forced labor camps, never to be heard from again. Stalin unleashed a reign of terror upon the Russian people. From his Kremlin office overlooking Red Square, he ruled as an absolute dictator. No one dared challenge him.

WHAT'S IN A NAME?
RED SQUARE

Red Square was built in the late 1400s next to the eastern wall of the Kremlin. The square's Russian name is *Krasnaia Ploshchad*. The word *krasnaia* means both "red" and "beautiful." And although the English translation is Red Square, it is certainly a beautiful place also.

section review **3**

1. What were the two major goals of the first Five-Year Plan?

2. How did the lives of ordinary citizens improve under Stalin?

3. Why was Marxist theory revised and creative work stifled during the 1930s?

4. How did Stalin become an absolute dictator?

4 The Soviet Union tried to protect its security

Relations between the Soviet Union and the West were not very friendly in the 1920s and 1930s. Soviet leaders were sure that the capitalists wanted to crush the Soviet Union. Many people in the democracies feared

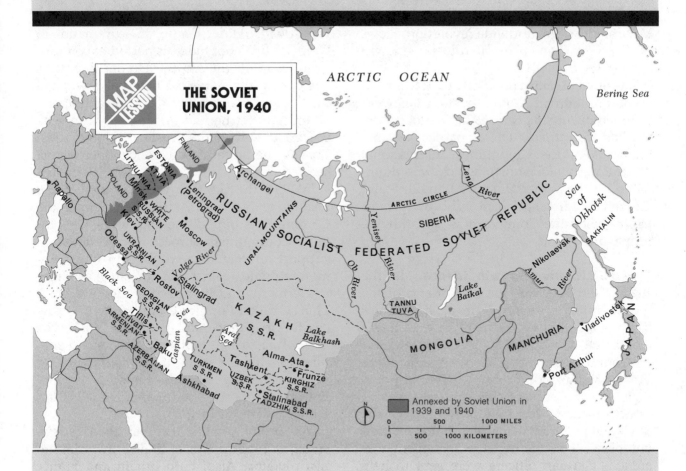

THE SOVIET UNION, 1940

ARCTIC OCEAN

Bering Sea

ARCTIC CIRCLE

SIBERIA

RUSSIAN SOCIALIST FEDERATED SOVIET REPUBLIC

FINLAND
ESTONIA
LATVIA
LITHUANIA
POLAND
Minsk
WHITE RUSSIAN S.S.R.
Kiev
UKRAINIAN S.S.R.
Odessa
Rapallo
Leningrad (Petrograd)
Archangel
Moscow
URAL MOUNTAINS
Ob River
Yenisei River
Lena River
Volga River
Rostov
Stalingrad
Black Sea
GEORGIAN S.S.R.
Tiflis
Erivan
ARMENIAN S.S.R.
Baku
AZERBAIJAN S.S.R.
Caspian Sea
Aral Sea
KAZAKH S.S.R.
Lake Balkhash
TURKMEN S.S.R.
Ashkhabad
UZBEK S.S.R.
Tashkent
Alma-Ata
Frunze
KIRGHIZ S.S.R.
Stalinabad
TADZHIK S.S.R.
TANNU TUVA
Lake Baikal
MONGOLIA
MANCHURIA
Amur River
Nikolaevsk
Vladivostok
Port Arthur
Sea of Okhotsk
SAKHALIN
JAPAN

Annexed by Soviet Union in 1939 and 1940

0   500   1000 MILES
0   500   1000 KILOMETERS

N

MAP LESSON 30: THE SOVIET UNION, 1940

1. The Soviet Union is composed of 15 union republics. The first of these, the Russian Soviet Federated Socialist Republic, was formed soon after the Bolsheviks came to power. It is by far the largest union republic in this very large nation. The last four union republics were not established until 1940 when the Soviet Union annexed Estonia, Latvia, Lithuania, and the part of Romania called Moldavia. Which republic reaches north of the arctic circle? Does this same republic extend more than 4,000 miles in an east-west direction?

2. About how many miles is Moscow from the Black Sea?

3. Is the Lena River more than 5,000 kilometers long?

4. About how many miles is the air route between Tashkent and Kiev?

5. About how many kilometers is it from Leningrad to Lake Balkhash?

6. What is the distance between Kiev and Stalingrad in kilometers?

7. Would an airplane flying from Archangel to a Caspian Sea resort have a trip of more than 2,000 kilometers?

8. Is it more than or less than 1,500 miles from Odessa to Baku?

9. Is Minsk more than 500 kilometers from Kiev?

10. Which republic do the following cities and geographical features belong to:
   a. Odessa
   b. Moscow
   c. Stalinabad
   d. Minsk
   e. Vladivostok
   f. Leningrad
   g. Baku
   h. Siberia
   i. Lake Balkhash
   j. Volga River

Marxist ideas of worldwide revolution. However, no government wanted to wage a war against the Soviet Union.

The Soviet Union constantly tried to stir up revolution abroad. Communist parties were founded during the early 1920s in most of the world's countries. These parties became members of the Communist International ("Comintern" for short), which was dominated by the Soviet Union. Although Stalin favored building socialism in his own country, he used the Comintern as a worldwide propaganda tool.

The U.S.S.R. tried to win friends. In the 1920s, Germany was the only friend of the Soviet Union in western Europe. Both countries were outcasts—Germany because it was a defeated power, the Soviet Union because of Communism. In 1922, they signed the Treaty of Rapallo. Under it, Germany formally recognized the Soviet Union and in return, received full trading rights with the Soviet Union. That same year, but at a different place, a secret military agreement was signed. German officers were sent to help train the Red Army. In exchange, Soviet factories supplied arms to Germany. This was a violation of the Versailles Treaty, which said that Germany could not rearm.

Later in the 1920s, most of the major powers set up diplomatic relations with the Soviet Union. Britain and France began such relations in 1924, but the United States waited until 1933.

In East Asia, the U.S.S.R. also tried to win friends. Beginning in 1923, the Soviet Union aided the Nationalist Peoples Party in its effort to unify China. In 1927, however, the Party, afraid of Communist control, rejected Soviet help. This dealt a sharp blow to Stalin's aim of revolutionizing China.

Stalin failed to get collective security. The 1930s saw a change in Soviet foreign policy. By 1934, the "Rapallo spirit" with Germany

was dead. Hitler, now in command in Germany, did not hide his hatred of communism and of the Soviet Union. Japanese designs on the Asian mainland also worried the Soviet Union. Faced with these dangers, Stalin felt that he had no choice but to seek the good will of the western democracies. That is, he advocated a policy of collective security.

In 1934, the U.S.S.R. was admitted to the League of Nations. At the same time, the Comintern stopped inciting world revolution. Communists abroad were ordered to support anyone who would join in a common struggle against dictators such as Hitler in Germany and Francisco Franco in Spain. This so-called Popular Front policy was successful in France in 1936 and 1937. The U.S.S.R. also sent military advisers and supplies to China in its fight against Japan during much of the 1930s. And it aided the anti-Franco forces in the Spanish Civil War, which broke out in 1936.

Yet Britain and France remained suspicious and distrustful of Stalin, the communist dictator. Also, both Britain and France wanted very much to avoid offending Hitler. Thus, Stalin was forced to change his foreign policy. The U.S.S.R. and Germany signed a pact of mutual neutrality in 1939. But only a few short days later, World War II began.

section review 4

1. What was the Comintern? How was it used by the Soviet Union?

2. What was the Treaty of Rapallo? How did each signer later violate the Versailles Treaty?

3. Why did Stalin come to favor "collective security"? How did he try to achieve it?

4. Why did Stalin agree to the 1939 pact with Hitler?

Section Summaries

1. Autocratic rulers weakened Russia. Although Russia was an important military and political force in 19th-century Europe, it remained an undeveloped country. The backward economy and government were in the hands of weak nobles and autocratic tsars. The majority of the people were poor, ill-treated peasants and serfs.

Major reform came in 1861 when Alexander II freed the serfs. Freedom, however, did little to help the peasants economically. In 1881, Alexander II was assassinated. Under succeeding autocrats, Alexander III and Nicholas II, Russia grew weaker. In 1905, it suffered a terrible military defeat by the Japanese. Some reforms were made after that, but they were not very effective.

2. Bolsheviks took control of Russia. Russian participation in World War I finally destroyed the tsarist system. In March, 1917, the tsar was forced to abdicate. A Provisional Government of middle-class liberals took over. But the Provisional Government lost support and by November, Lenin and the Bolsheviks had seized power. A bloody Civil War broke out in 1918 when Lenin tried to establish a Communist dictatorship. The Bolsheviks took Russia out of World War I by signing the Treaty of Brest-Litovsk with Germany.

Lenin began a strict Marxist program while faced with the Civil War and Allied intervention. In 1921, however, he made a temporary retreat from communism with the NEP. The government kept control of basic industries but allowed some private farming and small business. The Union of Soviet Socialist Republics was established in 1922.

3. Stalin created a totalitarian society. After Lenin's death in 1924, Trotsky and Stalin fought for leadership within the Communist party. The victor was Joseph Stalin who began his own type of despotism. In 1928, Stalin initiated the first of his famous Five-Year Plans. Factory workers were strictly controlled, and peasants were forced to work on collective farms. In the process of collectivization and rapid industrialization, millions of people lost their lives. By the mid-1930s, the Soviet Union had made important economic gains. Its people, however, had to live in a police state with all activities carefully regulated.

4. The Soviet Union tried to protect its security. In the 1930s, the U.S.S.R. began to take a more active role in world affairs. The Soviets gained diplomatic recognition from more western countries. With the rise of Hitler and others, the U.S.S.R. searched for allies. When Britain and France turned down his bid for a defensive alliance, Stalin signed a nonaggression pact with Hitler in 1939.

Who? What? When? Where?

1. Place these events in chronological order, beginning with the earliest:

   a. Lenin seized power.
   b. The Decembrist Revolt took place.
   c. Trotsky was expelled from the Communist Party.
   d. The "Bloody Sunday" massacre occurred.
   e. Kerensky became prime minister.
   f. The serfs were emancipated.
   g. Civil war began.

2. Write sentences to briefly explain the role each of these men played in changing tsarist Russia into the Soviet Union:

   a. Kerensky
   b. Lenin
   c. Trotsky

3. Write a sentence for each of these that tells the part it played in Russia's history:

   a. Bolsheviks
   b. Decembrist Revolt
   c. Duma
   d. pogroms
   e. soviets
   f. zemstvo

4. Name the person who:

   a. freed the serfs
   b. was the last tsar
   c. lost the power struggle with Stalin
   d. was a moderate socialist prime minister
   e. ruled during the Napoleonic wars
   f. began the first Five-Year Plan
   g. led the Bolsheviks

Questions for Critical Thinking

1. What might Kerensky have done differently that would have prevented the Bolshevik take-over?

2. Compare the power of the tsar before 1905 with Stalin's power in 1939. How were they alike? How were they different?

3. How might the U.S.S.R. of the 1930s have been different if the Allies had defeated the Bolsheviks in the civil war?

4. How was a mir in the time of Alexander II similar to a collective farm under Stalin?

Skill Activities

1. Read *Nicholas and Alexandra* by Robert K. Massie to learn more about the downfall of Russia's last tsar and his family. (Atheneum, 1967)

2. Write three or more news headlines that might have appeared in a Petrograd newspaper during 1917.

3. Role-play news conferences of Hitler and Stalin after the signing of their pact in 1939. Two class members should play Hitler and Stalin. The rest of the class should submit questions to be asked at the news conferences.

4. Write a letter from a Russian noble, worker, or peasant explaining the events of the revolution from that person's point of view.

5. Be a spokesperson for the serfs during the reign of Alexander I. Prepare your demands for change with reasons supporting them.

6. Make a time line of the rulers of Russia, beginning with Catherine the Great and ending with Stalin.

chapter **30** *quiz*

Section 1

1. Serfdom was abolished in Russia by: a. Nicholas II, b. Alexander I, c. Alexander II

2. In the 1905 revolution, workers organized into groups that were called: a. Dumas, b. pogroms, c. soviets

3. True or false: Reforms made by Tsar Nicholas II most benefited the peasants and factory workers.

Section 2

4. The Provisional Government was headed by: a. Trotsky, b. Kerensky, c. Lenin

5. True or false: War communism was replaced by the New Economic Policy.

6. True or false: In November, 1917, Lenin led the Bolsheviks to power in a coup d'état against the Provisional Government.

Section 3

7. A major goal of the first Five-Year Plan was to: a. bring the Romanovs back to power, b. collectivize agriculture, c. end NEP

8. One improvement made by Stalin was: a. full employment, b. artistic freedom, c. religious freedom

9. True or false: The "Stalin Constitution" made the Soviet Union in practice one of the most democratic governments in the world.

Section 4

10. Communist parties all over the world were members of the: a. Rapallo Treaty, b. NEP, c. Comintern

11. Germany and the U.S.S.R. signed a nonaggression treaty in: a. 1934, b. 1927, c. 1939

12. During the 1930s, Stalin sent military aid to China and: a. France, b. Spain, c. Italy

THE GROWTH OF NATIONALISM AND DICTATORSHIP

Hitler often used mass rallies to sway the feelings of the German people. In 1937, at Nuremberg, some 38 thousand "soldiers" of the German labor service paraded for two hours. Hitler took the salute from his car.

Nationalism was a European idea. But the building of empires (see Chapter 28) had helped spread the idea of nationalism to many areas outside of Europe. By the beginning of the twentieth century a demand for independence was growing among people in many Asian and Middle Eastern countries. In 1907, for example, one of the leaders of the Indian nationalist movement told the people of his country:

The point is to have the entire control in our hands. I want to have the key of my house, and not merely be a stranger turned out of it. Self-government is our goal. . . .

What the New Party wants you to do is realize . . . that your future rests entirely in your own hands. If you mean to be free, you can be free. . . .

Those words could just as easily have been spoken by a Chinese, African, or Arab nationalist. Each wanted to be free of outside control, in whatever form. In some areas nationalist revolutions broke out before World War I. But in all areas the war made the desire for independence stronger.

World War I also intensified the growth of nationalism in Europe. In its most extreme form European nationalism expressed itself in the rise of a dictatorial, militaristic movement known as fascism. This movement was the outgrowth of the unsettled conditions brought on by World War I. The European countries in which fascist regimes came to power were Italy, Germany, and Spain. On the other side of the world, a similar regime came to power in Japan. This chapter tells how:

1. **Chinese nationalists founded a republic.**

2. **Nationalists in India demanded independence.**

3. **Nationalists in the Middle East created new regimes.**

4. **Extreme nationalists in Europe and Japan established dictatorships.**

1 *Chinese nationalists founded a republic*

China was one of the oldest civilizations in Asia. It was never a European colony, but the ruling Manchu dynasty was weak. The rulers were forced to make many concessions to imperialist nations. These conditions led to the growth of a nationalist movement.

The last traditional ruler of China, Empress Tz'u Hsi firmly controlled China from 1862 until her death in 1908.

A revolution took place in China. During the late 1800s, China was forced to give up some territory to Japan. At the same time, European powers were establishing spheres of influence in China which gave them special political and economic privileges. Young Chinese who resented this foreign influence organized secret societies to fight it. Among these nationalists was Sun Yat-sen [sún' yät'-sen'].

Sun studied in Honolulu, Hawaii, for three years and later graduated from a medical college in the British colony of Hong Kong. Like other Chinese nationalists, Sun resented the Manchus for having made humiliating concessions to the imperialist powers. For many years, he made plans to overthrow the weak but tyrannical Manchu dynasty. His revolutionary activities forced him to flee China. For sixteen years, he worked among Chinese communities abroad to organize the Kuomintang [kwō′min tang′], or Nationalist People's Party.

In 1911, Chinese revolutionaries overthrew the government. Sun then returned to China and struggled against various regional leaders who wanted power for themselves. After a long conflict, Sun was elected president of China in 1921 and made plans to unify the country. He was not able to get aid from the Western powers, whom he had criticized for their imperialistic ambitions in China. So Sun turned to the Soviet Union for help. The Soviets sent him money, arms, and advisers.

Despite all Sun's efforts, he succeeded in establishing a government only in the south, at Canton. When Sun died in 1925, powerful regional leaders still controlled the rest of China, including the capital city of Peking in the north.

However, Sun was a source of inspiration to his followers. Sun's writings became guides for reform. One book, *Three Principles of the People*, became a guide for the Kuomintang. It called for nationalism and freedom from foreign control, government by the people and for the people, and economic security for all the Chinese.

Chiang Kai-shek came to power. Sun's place was taken by Chiang Kai-shek [chyang′ kī′shek′], a young military officer. In 1926, Chiang led his army northward from Canton toward Peking in hopes of uniting China. But soon Chiang became afraid that the communist wing of the Kuomintang was becoming too strong. In 1927, his forces launched a surprise attack against the Chinese Communists and killed many of them. A small group of

Chiang Kai-shek

Chinese Communists led by Mao Tse-tung [mou′ tse′túng′] survived. From that time on, the Nationalists and the Communists were bitter enemies.

In 1928, however, Chiang succeeded in taking Peking and united China. Chiang's government was recognized by the Western powers as the official government of China. But to increase his popular support, Chiang had to begin removing the special privileges that foreign countries had forced China to give them.

The new government faced many problems. One problem was growing dissatisfaction among the Chinese people over lack of reform. A second was Japanese aggression against China in 1931 and a full-scale invasion in 1937. A third was an unsuccessful attempt by the Communists in 1931 to set up a Chinese Soviet Republic in southeast China.

In 1934–1935, Mao, in defeat, led 90,000 Chinese Communists on the Long March. This 6,000-mile (9,600-kilometer) retreat

Sitting on a sandy plain in northeast China, modern-day Peking has been the site of various cities dating back as far as 1000 B.C. By 1274 A.D., it was famous as the capital city of Kublai Khan. That Venetian traveler, Marco Polo, described Kublai Khan's palace in the city as "the largest that ever was."

After the fall of the Mongols, the Mings came to power and in 1421 completed, on the site of the old, a new capital city which they named Peking. Its vast size, perfect symmetry, and magnificent buildings made Peking one of the greatest of all capitals.

The new Ming capital was actually a group of four cities. There was the Northern or Tartar City in the form of a square, bordered by walls nearly 15 miles (24 kilometers) long. Within it was the Imperial City, also a squared area, with walls 6.5 miles (10.4 kilometers) in extent. Inside this was the Forbidden City, also walled, with its galaxy of beautiful buildings. Here only the royal family and high nobles were permitted. Finally, there was the Southern or Chinese City enclosed by walls some 14 miles (22.4 kilometers) long.

The Forbidden City is a wonderful example of the unique qualities and beauty of Chinese architecture. Grouped around large courtyards, its palaces and temples have beautiful tile roofs that slope down to up-turned corners and are richly carved with dragons and other delights. The railings and terraces are carved from white marble. And everywhere is the splendor of color—blue, green, red, gold, and yellow—on the roof tiles, walls, and beams.

Each building in the Forbidden City had a special purpose and was given a special name. For example, the Dragon Pavement, a three-tiered, balustraded marble terrace, contained three great ceremonial throne rooms. The Hall of Honoring Ancestors had religious significance. To the school in the Forbidden City was attached the ominous title (for students) of the Hall of Industrious Energy.

Since 1644 when the Ming dynasty fell, Peking has seen civil wars, invasions, and the rise and fall of various governments. The Forbidden City, however, has survived and still retains much of its original beauty and glory.

At *top* is the Dragon Pavement as seen from the Supreme Imperial Gate of the Forbidden City. At *bottom left* are two of the fierce bronze lions that stand guard at the gates of the Forbidden City. The lion in the background has his paw on a pearl, the symbol of the imperial treasury. At *right bottom* is one of the three throne rooms in the Dragon Pavement.

Wars among themselves and war with Japan brought famine to the Chinese. This demonstration for more food was in Shanghai.

headed to Yenan, in north central China. Only half of those who started out survived the Long March. In Yenan, the Communists won the support of the peasants and continued to fight Chiang's armies.

When the Japanese invaded China in 1937, the Communists and Nationalists stopped their civil war and united against the Japanese. But the differences between the Communists and Nationalists were too deep to make the alliance last. When the Japanese were defeated, civil war broke out again.

section review 1

1. What did many young Chinese resent about their government in the late 19th and early 20th centuries?

2. Who was Sun Yat-sen?

3. What enemies did Sun Yat-sen fight in his struggles to unify China? What country sent him aid?

4. What group in the Kuomintang did Chiang try to eliminate? Who was its leader?

2 Nationalists in India demanded independence

In the mid-19th century, almost all of India came under British control. But within fifty years Indian intellectuals began seeking self-government for India. Then came World War I.

Gandhi led the Indian nationalists. During World War I, India loyally supported Britain. Almost a million Indian soldiers fought on the side of the British. Wealthy Indian princes made large financial contributions to the war effort. Indians hoped their loyalty and support would be rewarded by self-government. In 1917, Britain promised to give self-rule to India in several stages. At the end of the war, the Government of India Act of 1919 gave certain powers to provincial legislatures but reserved other, more important ones in the central government for Britain.

And thus, most Indians were disappointed by the act.

The widespread dissatisfaction found a spokesman in Mohandas K. Gandhi [gän'dē]. This remarkable nationalist leader had been educated in Britain as a lawyer. He then set up a successful practice in South Africa, helping the Indians who lived there. Gandhi returned to India during World War I. He became the champion of the oppressed and lowly. He led a very simple and self-sacrificing life, following the Hindu faith. Millions of Indians began to look up to him as a holy man, or *mahatma* [mə hät'mə].

Gandhi believed in nonviolent resistance. Gandhi strongly opposed the Government of India Act. Since he did not believe in violence, Gandhi led the people in a campaign of "nonviolent resistance" to force the British to give self-rule to India. Strikes, fasts, and protest marches were the "weapons" of Gandhi's campaign.

Not all Indian nationalists believed in non-

Margaret Bourke-White, one of the first photojournalists, took this famous picture of Mahatma Gandhi. He encouraged the people of India to rely on themselves. The spinning wheel in the foreground was one of Gandhi's symbols for this self-reliance.

violent resistance, however. In 1919, there was a wave of murder, looting, and arson. This violence reached its climax at the city of Amritsar when British soldiers fired on unarmed demonstrators. Nearly 400 innocent people, including women and children, were killed and some 1,200 were wounded. Gandhi and his followers in the Indian National Congress were shocked. They became determined to win complete freedom.

During the 1920s and 1930s, Gandhi launched several campaigns of nonviolent resistance against British authority. One of his methods was a boycott of British-made goods. The British arrested him several times and put him in jail.

While working for the independence of India, Gandhi tried to improve the lives of the "untouchables," those Indians who belonged to the lowest caste of Indian society. He also tried to bring about cooperation between Hindus and Muslims. Gandhi believed that injustice could be wiped out through love and patience.

During the 1930s, the British met with Indian leaders to gradually begin preparing India for self-government. In 1935, the British Parliament passed a law that gave the Indian provinces self-government. From New Delhi, the capital, Indian members of the legislature then controlled all matters except those relating to defense and foreign affairs. However, full independence for India was not granted until 1947.

section review 2

1. Why were Indian nationalists disappointed after World War I?

2. Who was Mohandas K. Gandhi? Why was he called *mahatma*?

3. What methods did Gandhi use in his effort to gain independence for India?

4. What progress was made toward Indian independence in the 1930s?

3 Nationalists in the Middle East created new regimes

Nationalist movements in North Africa and the Middle East developed among Arabs, Turks, Persians (Iranians), and Jews. Each group wanted its own independent country. Often the nationalist goal of independence went with a desire for modernization.

Arabs in North Africa and the Middle East sought independence. The majority of people living in the Middle East and North Africa are Arabs. Before World War I, none of them had total independence. They were controlled either by the French, the British, or the Ottoman Turks. World War I weakened the control of the British and French and ended that of the Ottomans. After the war, for example, several nonviolent underground movements challenged French rule in Tunisia, Algeria, and Morocco.

Nationalism first exploded into violence in Egypt. Egypt was a protectorate, that is, a weak country under the control of a strong one. Egypt was a protectorate of Britain.

After a delegation of Egyptian nationalists was denied permission to attend the Paris Peace Conference of 1919, Egypt rose up in revolt. Order was not restored until 1922, when the British agreed to end the protectorate. However, Britain kept the rights to have troops there, to direct Egyptian foreign affairs, and to defend the Suez Canal.

In the Middle East, Arab resentment against the corrupt rule of the Ottoman Turks had been building for a long time. When the Ottoman Empire entered World War I on the side of Germany, Britain tried to win over the Arabs under Ottoman rule to weaken Turkish power. In 1915 and 1916, Britain made promises of independence to the Arabs in hopes of sparking a rebellion against the Turks. In June, 1916, it worked.

Daily Life

Advances in science and technology during the early 20th century greatly changed the lives of people around the globe. President Franklin Roosevelt *below left* often used the radio to make speeches to the American public. Radio, as shown on this page, brought the first mass culture. For the first time in history, millions of people heard news, sports, and entertainment at the moment the events occurred. On May 21, 1927, Charles A. Lindbergh, *top center* thrilled the world with his non-stop New York to Paris flight. During the 1920s and 1930s, air travel became more and more common. The same two decades saw the tremendous growth

of a new form of entertainment—movies. *The Wizard of Oz, top right,* was made in 1939. By that year, millions of people, especially in Europe and the United States, went to the movies almost every week. *Below right* is the Golden Gate Bridge, one of the engineering marvels of the 1930s. Built between 1933 and 1937, the bridge is still in use today. Such engineering feats greatly advanced transportation. *Below center* is Alexander Fleming, the British research scientist who discovered penicillin. Penicillin revolutionized medical treatment for such diseases as gangrene, pneumonia, and meningitis.

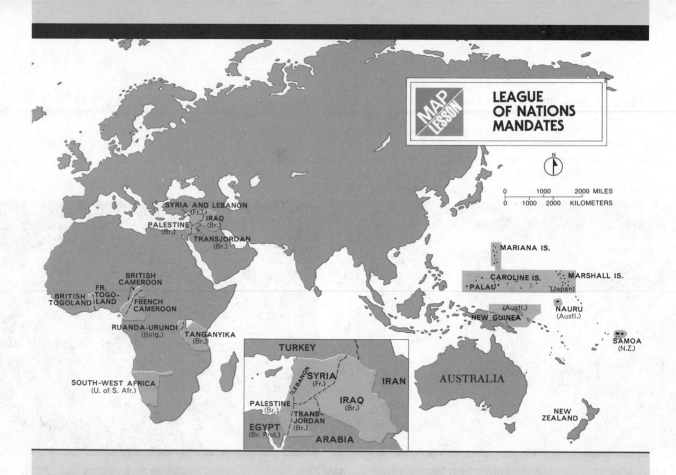

■ MAP LESSON 31: LEAGUE OF NATIONS MANDATES

1. After World War I, the League of Nations took control of the colonies of the defeated powers and placed them under the jurisdiction of various Allied nations. The Allies were to supervise the colonies until they were ready for self-government and independence. Three classes of mandates, based on geographic location and former ruler, were established. Class A mandates were former Turkish territories in the Middle East. Which nation took control of:

   a. Syria   b. Palestine   c. Transjordan

2. The inset map gives a larger view of the Class A mandates. Which mandate bordered Egypt? Which one bordered Iran?

3. Class B mandates were former German colonies in eastern and central Africa. Which nation or nations took control of:

   a. Ruanda-Urundi   c. Togoland
   b. Tanganyika   d. Cameroons

4. Class C mandates included other former German colonies in southern Arica and the Pacific. These areas were governed as part of the nation that was granted the mandate. Which nation governed:

   a. New Guinea
   b. South-West Africa
   c. Samoa

5. According to this map, which two Allied nations were given the most mandates?

When the war ended, Arab leaders claimed self-government as their reward. But it soon became clear that Arab independence would be a victim of European power politics. During the war, Britain and France had made a secret agreement to divide the Middle East between them. After the war, the newly formed League of Nations made Syria and Lebanon French mandates. Iraq, Palestine, and Transjordan were given to Britain as mandates. The Arabs felt that the mandates were poor substitutes for independence.

In the years that followed, Arab hostility toward European rule grew. The British recognized Transjordan as independent in 1928. Iraq became independent in 1932. But British military influence continued in both countries as protection for Britain's strategic interests there.

Meanwhile, the collapse of the Ottoman Empire in 1918 brought independence to several states in the Arabian peninsula. The most important was the newly created kingdom of the Hejaz [hē jaz']. Its ruler was Abdul-Aziz, commonly known as ibn-Saud [ib'ən sä üd']. Ibn-Saud conquered the warring Bedouin tribes and controlled nearly all of the peninsula by 1926. In 1932, ibn-Saud changed the name of his kingdom to Saudi Arabia. In that same year, rich oil reserves were discovered there that added greatly to his power and prestige.

A new leader arose in Turkey.   Since Turkey had been on the losing side in World War I, it had to accept great territorial losses as part of the peace settlement. Moreover, the forces of the Allies occupied various parts of Turkey, including Constantinople. However, the Turks put up strong resistance.

In the early 1920s, a powerful army officer named Mustafa Kemal [müs'tä fä kə mäl'] became the leader of Turkish national resistance. Under Kemal's leadership, the Turks drove out the Allied forces and regained control of Constantinople. They renamed the city Istanbul. For more security, they moved the capital to the interior city of Ankara.

ibn-Saud

WHAT'S IN A NAME?
ISTANBUL

The name Istanbul comes from two words: *islam*, meaning "true believing" and *bul*, meaning "copious." Thus, Istanbul means the city "abounding in the true faith," that is, the Muslim religion.

Kemal and his followers also carried out a successful revolution. They overthrew the sultan and in 1923 proclaimed the Turkish Republic. Kemal was elected Turkey's first president. The Turkish parliament gave him the name Ataturk [at'ətérk'], meaning "father of all the Turks."

The Turkish Republic was much smaller than the Ottoman Empire had been. The new republic consisted mainly of the Anatolian peninsula. The great majority of the people were Turks. A major non-Turkish group were the Greeks, a people who had been living in Anatolia since 1000 B.C. However, Turkish nationalists considered them "foreigners," and fighting broke out between the two groups. To settle the problem, 1.4 million Greeks were made to move to Greece and 400,000 Turks living in Greece were moved to Turkey. Uprooting so many people caused great hardship, but Turkey and Greece did have more homogeneous populations.

Kemal Ataturk transformed Turkey. Kemal's main goal was to modernize Turkey. Under his leadership, Turkey became the first traditional Islamic state in which church and state were separated. The new republic tolerated all religions. Instead of the law of the Koran, the government adopted a law code modeled on the Napoleonic code.

Kemal's modernization affected all people. Women gained the right to vote and to hold public office. The government encouraged them to become doctors, lawyers, and teachers. Illiteracy was reduced and use of the metric system began. The government also encouraged industrialization through the development of mines, railroads, and factories. By the time Kemal Ataturk died in 1938, Turkey had moved a long way toward becoming a modern nation.

Persia developed more slowly. In 1921, Reza Shah Pahlavi took over Persia. A Muslim but not an Arab land, Persia became known as Iran, or Land of the Aryans. The shah was a strong nationalist and fought any foreign influence in Iranian affairs. He also tried to modernize his country. He built schools, developed national resources, and supported the rights of women and other reforms. But the shah became a despot. In 1941, he abdicated and his son, Muhammad Reza Shah Pahlavi, became ruler.

Jews established a homeland in Palestine. Both Jews and Arabs had lived in Palestine ever since biblical times. In 1917, however, the British, in the Balfour Declaration, said that a national home for the Jews would be established in Palestine.

In 1920, when Palestine became a mandate, large-scale Jewish immigration began. Over the years, the immigrants started farms and industries and generally prospered.

Although the Arabs made up the larger part of the population in Palestine, they were

In June, 1934, Reza Shah Pahlavi visited Turkey. Here, on the terrace of the presidential palace, Ataturk, *left*, points out various improvements in the capital city of Ankara.

alarmed by these developments. They viewed the Jews as "intruders" and feared possible economic and political domination. As refugees fled from Nazi Germany in the 1930s and Jewish immigration increased, the Arabs began to use guerrilla warfare to stop immigration. The British tried but failed to bring peace to the area.

section review 3

1. Where did Arab nationalism first explode into violence? What consequences did it have?

2. Who was Kemal Ataturk? What was his main goal?

3. What was the goal of the Shah of Iran in the 1920s and 1930s?

4. What effects did the Balfour Declaration have on Palestine? Why did the Arabs in Palestine become alarmed?

4 Extreme nationalists in Europe and Japan established dictatorships

In some parts of Europe and in Japan, the aftermath of World War I brought deep discontent. Extremist groups in these nations took advantage of widespread fears and frustrations to gain support for themselves. They preached that national pride had to be restored and that the only way to do it was through the bold actions of strong leaders. The goal of these extremists was to establish dictatorships.

Dictatorships arose as a modern form of absolute government. A *dictator* is a person who seizes control of a government without claiming to rule through inheritance or free election. After World War I, several countries came under the rule of dictators. In Russia, the communist dictatorship centered on government ownership of property and capital. Another type of dictatorship, fascism, permitted private ownership of property and capital. But it placed strict government rules on the people. Fascism arose first in Italy and later appeared in Japan, Germany, and Spain. Both communism and fascism refused to allow opposing political parties. Each government used censorship, denied civil rights, and took complete control of people's lives. Communism and fascism became the strongest antidemocratic movements in the world.

Mussolini and the Fascists gained power in Italy. There was much unrest in Italy after World War I. Many Italians were angry that Italy had received so little territory in the peace settlement. Italy also faced the same problems of business slowdown, unemployment, and high prices that existed in other countries. By the end of 1920, the cost of living was eight times higher than it had been in 1914. Many people found it difficult even to buy bread. And the government, which was split into many different parties, had no strong leaders or programs.

As unrest grew, many Marxist workers in the factories of northern Italy went on strike. This scared middle-class people who were afraid of a communist revolution. These conditions caused many to swing their support to the Fascist party, headed by Benito Mussolini [mus'ə lē'nē].

In 1919, Mussolini had organized the Italian Fascist Party. He took the name fascist from the Latin word *fasces*. It meant the bundle of rods bound around an ax, which had been the symbol of authority during Roman times. The Fascist party was made up mainly of out-of-work men who had been soldiers in World War I. They wanted action in place of the do-nothing policy of the government. They were a super-patriotic group that had a great devotion to Italy and to *Il Duce* [ēl' dü'cha], "the leader," Mussolini.

The Fascists wore black shirts as uniforms. They used the old Roman salute of the raised arm and followed strict military discipline. They beat up, tortured, and sometimes killed political opponents.

At first, Mussolini tried to gain political power legally through elections. But the Fascists did not win many votes. In September, 1922, some 10 thousand armed Fascists marched on Rome. They wanted to take over the government. The king, afraid of a civil war, invited Mussolini to become prime minister. In the next nine years, Mussolini used every means, including terror, to make himself dictator of Italy. The Fascist party became the only legal party in the country. The secret police arrested anyone who dared to criticize the Fascists.

By 1930, the world depression had increased the problems within Italy. Although powerful, Mussolini felt that only

Military training in fascist countries began at an early age. These young Japanese boys, fully uniformed, raise their rifles in a salute.

some successful military move would enable him to keep his hold on Italy. Thus, in 1935, he attacked Ethiopia. It was the only major independent state left in Africa. And Ethiopia had defeated Italy in 1896 in Italy's attempt to enlarge Italian Somaliland. But in 1935, Italy quickly defeated Ethiopia. Mussolini was stronger than ever.

Military leaders won control in Japan. In the 1920s, democracy was making some progress in Japan. But the Japanese parliament had little power. It could not control the prime minister, who was responsible only to the emperor. Military leaders were nearly independent of the government, and they were eager for more power. They disliked democracy and disagreed with Japan's moderate policy toward China. In the 1930s, these militarists gained strength in parlia-

ment. They were supported by the peasants who blamed democracy for bad conditions.

By 1930, the effects of the depression were also being felt in Japan. Strikes gave the militarists a chance to seize more power. By late 1932, they were in control. Their main goal was to build up the most powerful army and navy in East Asia. They used murder to scare off political opposition. They justified their acts by glorifying Japan. They were supported by young men whose careers had been hurt by the depression. They also had the support of people with business interests in Manchuria who wanted a more aggressive policy toward China.

Hitler and the Nazi party rose to power in Germany. Germany began the postwar years with a new national assembly that met at the city of Weimar [vī'mär] in January,

1919. The Weimar constitution included many democratic features: freedom of speech and religion, compulsory education of children, and freedom of association that protected labor unions. However, the president of the Weimar Republic was given certain emergency powers. These made it possible for a dictator to take over the government by legal means.

The ruling group in the Weimar government was a coalition, or grouping, of socialist parties. Extremists on both the Right (fascists) and the Left (communists) threatened the ruling group. They blamed the coalition for accepting the hated Treaty of Versailles. They declared that the socialists were traitors to their country. As the German economy grew weaker, people in Germany began to listen to these charges. To make matters worse, the most stable element in the German population, the middle class, had been all but ruined by the terrible inflation of the postwar years.

In 1930, unemployment rose sharply, and the Weimar Republic seemed unable to help. The younger generation, disillusioned by this chaos, blamed the problems on the way their elders ran the country. Militarists blamed German defeat in World War I on liberals, pacifists, and Jews. There had long been deep-seated envy—and even hatred—of the Jews, who made up less than one percent of the population. Many Germans resented the fact that some Jews had achieved success as doctors, dentists, lawyers, authors, and musicians. It became popular to blame the Jews for Germany's troubles. Many Germans were willing to listen to anyone who made the Jews the scapegoats for all the nation's ills. Adolf Hitler did just that.

Hitler was born in an Austrian village in 1889. During World War I, he enlisted in the German army. While in a hospital recovering from war injuries, news of the armistice and the German defeat reached him. He felt great

Mussolini and Hitler

anger and shame for his adopted country. These feelings were mingled with frustrations in his personal life. He came to hate the new German government, Jews, and anyone associated with the Versailles Treaty.

After the war, Hitler joined a small political party. In 1920, it adopted the name of National Socialist German Workers' Party, or Nazi Party. Hitler helped draw up the program, which appealed to all discontented persons. He slowly began to build up the party through public speeches. Hitler was an extremely effective public speaker and had a moving effect on German audiences. But he was impatient for power. In 1923, he tried, but failed, to seize power in Bavaria. He was sent to prison for about a year. While in jail, he wrote the book *Mein Kampf* (My Struggle). The book was based on racist ideas. It presented a plan for aggression against other peoples and countries.

As economic conditions became worse, more and more people began to vote for Nazi representatives in the Reichstag [rīнs'täk'],

Daily Life

Art of the first half of the 20th century was greatly different from art of earlier years. Henri Matisse was a leader of the type of painting known as fauvism, which comes from a derogatory name given the group in 1905: *les fauves,* meaning "the beasts." Matisse was interested in surface richness and the use of subtle color changes to suggest depth. His "Apples," *above near right,* was done in 1916. At about the same time, Wassily Kandinsky was a leader of the school called non-objectivism. Kandinsky's paintings do not show specific objects and are meant to convey certain moods instead. His "Improvisation with Green Center," *below near right,* was done in 1913. Joán Miró was a leader of the school called surrealism. His paintings are a spontaneous expression of his thoughts. Even Miró cannot always explain the meanings of his pictures. His "Woman and Birds of Sun" is at *center.* The sculpture of Henry Moore is charged with a feeling of mass on a grand scale. Mountains of mass alternate with valleys of empty space. Often, Moore's starting point is the human figure. His "Recumbent Figure" is at *bottom far right.* Georgia O'Keefe's painting "Summer Days" is at *top far right.* It was done in 1936. O'Keefe paints images of the deserts of the American southwest. The paintings of Edward Hopper are strong views of city crowds, backyards, old houses, shops—everything that is common to American life. His "Nighthawks" is at *far right center.* It was done in 1942.

the German parliament. By 1932, the Nazis were the largest political party in Germany. In 1933, Hitler became chancellor (prime minister) of Germany. His government was known as the Third Reich [rīH]. (The First Reich, or empire, was begun by Charlemagne in 800 and was ended by Napoleon in 1806. The Second Reich began in 1871 with the unification of Germany and continued until 1918, when Germany was defeated in World War I.) In 1934, Hitler stripped the Reichstag of all power. He also got rid of all political parties except the Nazis, outlawed trade unions, set up labor camps, and got rid of laws he did not like. On August 2, 1934, Hitler became Führer [fʏ'rər], or leader, of Germany.

The Nazis preached the idea of a "super race." According to the Führer, Germans were Aryans and were the "master race" or "super race." All other peoples, particularly Jews and Slavs, were inferior. Jews were to be killed, and Slavs were to be made into slaves. The Nazis began a carefully planned program to eliminate Jews from German national life. In 1935, the infamous Nuremburg Laws were passed. These took citizenship rights away from Jews. The laws forbade the intermarriage of Jews and gentiles (non-Jews). The government encouraged other Germans to boycott Jewish businesses and services. By 1938, the Nazis had put tens of thousands of Jews into concentration camps. Jewish children were not allowed to attend German schools. And in 1939, the regime eliminated all Jews from the economic life of Germany and forced them to live in ghettoes [get'ōs], sections of cities restricted to Jews.

Hitler's ideas of the German "super race" gave a sense of prestige to many Germans. They felt that Hitler was replacing weakness, defeat, and depression with strength, importance, and prosperity. Most Germans gladly accepted Hitler as their leader.

The Third Reich got ready for war. As they did in Italy and Japan, fascists in Germany tried to mold the minds of their citizens through a program that glorified war. Textbooks were rewritten, and the press and radio were censored to carry out that program. Hitler said that Germany must have "living space," that is, more territory for the German people. He began huge preparations for German expansion. Strict food-rationing laws were put into effect to make Germany self-sufficient in case of war. A highway system called the autobahn was built so that troops could move rapidly. A huge stockpile of arms was also created.

German business leaders who in 1932 thought they could control Hitler found out too late that they could not. He had changed Germany into a police state. The government had total control over every area of life—the economy, schools, labor unions, newspapers, radio, and films. Such a system of total control is called *totalitarianism* [tō tal'ə ter'ē ə- niz'əm].

Many people outside Germany also believed that their countries could deal with Hitler. They felt that he only wanted to return Germany to its rightful place among nations. Some people in democratic countries even admired Naziism for its discipline and its hostility to communism. Some, especially in England, saw Hitler as a barrier against the spread of communism.

section review 4

1. Name the two forms of dictatorship described in this section. How were they similar? How were they different?

2. How did Mussolini come to power? What groups supported him? Why?

3. What group took over in Japan in the 1930s? How and with whose support was this accomplished?

4. What was Hitler's idea of "super race"? Why did many Germans accept this idea?

Section Summaries

1. Chinese nationalists founded a republic. Nationalists in China resented the weak and corrupt Manchu dynasty which granted special privileges to foreign powers. In 1912, the nationalists overthrew the Manchus and established a republic. The leading nationalist was Sun Yat-sen. He was succeeded in 1925 by Chiang Kai-shek, who tried to unify the country. After 1927, he and the Chinese Communists, who were led by Mao Tse-tung, became bitter enemies. The two sides fought a civil war. It stopped temporarily after 1937 when they united to fight against the Japanese invaders.

2. Nationalists in India demanded independence. India was a British colony in the 19th century. A strong nationalist movement developed late in the century. During World War I, Mohandas Gandhi became the leader of the Indian nationalists. Gandhi wanted full independence for India. He used boycotts and other forms of nonviolent resistance against British rule. During the 1930s, Britain granted India a limited amount of self-government.

3. Nationalists in the Middle East created new regimes. After World War I, nationalist movements in the Middle East arose among Arab Muslims, non-Arab Muslims, and Jewish Zionists. Egypt gained independence in 1922 and was followed by three other Arab countries—Saudi Arabia, Transjordan, and Iraq—in the 1920s and 1930s. Turkey, a non-Arab country, became a republic in 1923. Its leader, Mustafa Kemal, began an intensive program of modernization. Persia, another non-Arab Muslim country, changed its name to Iran and also started a program of modernization. Zionists wanted to create a national homeland for Jews in Palestine. Large-scale Jewish immigration began in the 1920s and 1930s. The Arabs in Palestine became alarmed.

4. Extremist nationalists in Europe and Japan established dictatorships. Unsettled conditions in Europe and Japan after World War I helped the rise of extremist nationalist movements. By 1922, Italy had become a Fascist dictatorship under Benito Mussolini. By 1933 the world depression helped Adolf Hitler become the Nazi dictator of Germany. Militarists took control in Japan. Mussolini and Hitler both set up police states. They outlawed all political parties except their own. They built totalitarian systems in which the state controlled everything. Citizens had no rights—only the duty to obey. The real aim of dictators such as Mussolini and Hitler was not to improve living conditions, but to expand their own power and that of the state.

Who? What? When? Where?

1. Arrange the following events in chronological order:

    a. Hitler became Führer of Germany.
    b. Revolutionaries overthrew the Manchu government.
    c. Mussolini became prime minister of Italy.
    d. The Long March reached Yenan.
    e. Japanese militarists took control of Japan.
    f. Britain promised self-rule to India.

2. Name the nation led by each of these men and tell one important change each made in his country:

    a. Chiang Kai-shek
    b. ibn-Saud
    c. Adolf Hitler
    d. Benito Mussolini
    e. Reza Shah Pahlavi
    f. Mao Tse-tung

3. Write sentences that tell the role each of these played in the growth of nationalism or dictatorship:

    a. the Balfour Declaration
    b. the Government of India Act
    c. fascism
    d. Kuomintang
    e. the Long March
    f. mandates
    g. nonviolent resistance
    h. Nuremberg Laws

4. Name the authors, subjects, and purposes of *Mein Kampf* and *Three Principles of the People.*

Questions for Critical Thinking

1. Which of the leaders in this chapter would you consider to be heroes? Explain your answer by listing the personal qualities of that person or persons.

2. Why were many people willing to accept dictators as national rulers when their countries suffered hardships?

3. Would nonviolent resistance always be an effective method of protest? Why or why not might this always be so?

Skill Activities

1. Pretend you are a national leader wanting more power. Give a speech persuading citizens to give it to you.

2. Pretend that it is 1936 and all the class members live on the same block in Berlin. One day, a family on the block is arrested, but none of the neighbors seems to know why. Divide the class into two groups—one group of neighbors who would try to help the family and one group who would not. Hold a block meeting to decide what to do.

3. Hold a debate in which students representing the nationalist leaders of China, India, and the Middle East meet with representatives of the colonial powers to discuss the views of each side on the subject of self-government.

4. Choose one of the areas discussed here, Japan, India, China, the Middle East, or Europe, and make a time line of the important events from this chapter.

chapter **31** *quiz*

Section 1

1. The 90,000 Communists on the Long March were led by: a. Sun Yat-sen, b. Chiang Kai-shek, c. Mao Tse-tung

2. True or false: China's Nationalist Party began to fight for freedom from British colonial rule in 1926.

3. The Chinese civil war was fought between Chiang Kai-shek's government and the: a. Manchus, b. Communists, c. Japanese

Section 2

4. During the years of World War I, India: a. stayed neutral, b. rebelled against Britain, c. supported Britain

5. True or false: The Government of India Act of 1919 that was passed by Britain disappointed many Indian leaders.

6. The system used by Gandhi against British rule is called: a. terrorism, b. nonviolent resistance, c. nationalism

Section 3

7. In 1932, Abdul-Aziz changed the name of his kingdom from Hejaz to: a. Transjordan, b. Saudi Arabia, c. Iraq

8. Under Kemal's rule in Turkey: a. women gained the right to vote, b. Koranic law was strengthened, c. illiteracy increased

9. The British encouraged a Jewish homeland by: a. issuing the Balfour Declaration, b. removing the Greeks from Anatolia, c. granting independence to Transjordan

Section 4

10. True or false: Hitler became known as the Führer of Germany while Mussolini was sometimes called Il Duce.

11. In Japan, the group that came to power in 1930: a. wanted a strong military, b. were communists, c. wanted more democratic reforms

12. Among those that were not blamed for Germany's postwar problems were the: a. Jews, b. socialists, c. Nazis

WORLD DEPRESSION AND WAR

On D-Day, thousands of Allied troops, under the command of General Dwight D. Eisenhower, crossed the English Channel and landed on the French coast at Normandy.

Twenty years after the end of World War I, many nations of the world plunged into World War II. World war again came when many of the nations of Europe saw Germany's aggressions as a threat to their own security. World War I had left Germany temporarily weakened, but still united. Then Adolf Hitler gained control of the country. In a book called *Mein Kampf* (My Struggle), Hitler wrote:

> If men wish to live, then they are forced to kill others . . . we National Socialists . . . aim . . . to secure for the German people the land and soil to which they are entitled on this earth. . . . Only the might of a victorious sword . . . will win soil for us. . . .

These words show Hitler's extreme nationalism and violence, along with his drive for expansion. Such forces helped push the nations of Europe into World War II in 1939.

However, Adolf Hitler did not bring on World War II all by himself. There were other causes for the war. After World War I, the nations of Europe faced major problems in trying to return to peacetime economies. Partly because of these problems, Britain and France could not agree on a common policy toward Germany. As a result, the restrictions against Germany in the Treaty of Versailles were not well enforced. Hitler was quick to take advantage of Anglo-French disagreements to build up German power and follow an aggressive foreign policy. Mussolini sought to do the same for Italy. At a time when the world was already in the grip of the worst economic depression in history, both dictators created more crises. Tensions mounted.

The world depression affected all nations, including Japan. As the depression deepened, Japan's export trade shrank and unemployment rose. Japanese militarists decided that Japan could survive as a great power only by conquering a vast empire in Asia. When the United States opposed this policy of expansion, Japan decided to use force. In this way, the problems of Germany in Europe and Japan in Asia were linked together in causing the second great war of the 20th century.

The League of Nations was unable to prevent the coming of World War II. From the very beginning the League was weak and ineffective as a peace-keeping organization. In part, this was because the United States never became a member. A more important reason for the League's weakness was that it could not enforce its decisions. Thus no nation would obey the League when that nation's interests were not well served.

World War II involved more than 30 nations, was fought in Europe, Asia, and Africa, and lasted six years. When it ended, the victorious allies divided Germany and deprived Japan of all of its overseas empire. This chapter tells how:

1. The world economy broke down.

2. Aggression destroyed peaceful relations.

3. Total war engulfed the world.

4. The Allies were victorious.

1 *The world economy broke down*

By the 20th century, no nation possessed all the raw materials it needed, and none could produce all the manufactured goods its people wanted. Thus, through international trade a world economy came into existence. The prosperity of nations that sold goods depended on the ability of other nations to buy them. In 1929, that system broke down. However, there were major weaknesses in the world economy even before this time.

Agricultural prices fell during the 1920s. One of the major economic weaknesses was in agriculture. After the war, the high wartime demand for wheat fell. At the same time, the use of more advanced equipment and techniques led to a huge expansion of wheat production. As a result of the larger supply and lower demand, the world price of wheat dropped sharply. By 1930, a bushel of wheat cost less than it had in 400 years. Wheat growers all over the world were facing ruin.

The growers of other crops were also troubled by overproduction. World prices for cotton, corn, coffee, cocoa, and sugar fell. Planters in Brazil, Africa, and the East Indies had to sell their crops at heavy losses. Farmers everywhere had less money to spend on manufactured goods. The farmers' problem became even worse when depression struck industry. City people then had less to spend for food.

Industrial recovery depended on loans. A second major weakness in the world economy was that much of the industrial expansion of the late 1920s was paid for with borrowed money. Running a business with borrowed money is known as *credit financing.* The system develops serious problems if the lender demands repayment and the borrower can't pay. Many European countries had received large private loans from the United States. This was especially true of Germany. If American lenders suddenly recalled their loans, industrial borrowers would not have enough money to buy raw materials and needed machinery to keep their factories going. Factories would close, industrial production would go down, and many people would be thrown out of work. Thus, the prosperity of Germany and the other European countries who had borrowed from the United States was insecure. It depended on the stability of the American financial system.

A financial crisis started a world depression. In October, 1929, prices on the New York Stock Exchange began to drop very quickly. Stock prices had been far above their normal levels because many people had bought stocks in hopes of making quick fortunes.

This picture shows the somber crowds that gathered in front of the New York Stock Exchange when the market collapse was reported. Although not the only cause of the Depression, the events on Wall Street in October, 1929, had much to do with the worldwide panic and fear that soon came. "In Wall Street, every wall is wet by tears," said one newspaper.

Suddenly these people began to fear that their gambles might not pay off. As they rushed to sell their stocks, prices fell.

The falling prices caused fear and panic in the business world. Banks called in their loans, and industries stopped expanding. American lenders recalled their loans from Europe. Businesses everywhere began to go bankrupt. Banks failed, and prices dropped all over the world. Between 1929 and 1932, world manufacturing production fell by 38 percent. International trade shrank by more than 65 percent. Unemployment went up everywhere. By 1932, one of every four Britons and two of every five Germans were out of work. It was the worst depression the world had ever known.

The world depression had important results.
Every country in the world felt the effects of the depression. Each thought it could help itself by being less dependent on the world market and by protecting home industries. Every country thus began raising its tariffs, or taxes, on imported goods. The United States, the richest market in the world, passed the highest tariff in its history in 1930. High tariffs further reduced international trade, since foreign borrowers could not get cash by selling in American markets. Without this cash, foreign borrowers found it almost impossible to pay off their loans.

The world depression also led to the growth of big government. The problems of mass unemployment were so great that people looked to their governments for help. Many governments began to take a much more active role in solving economic and social problems. In countries such as Italy and Germany, the world depression encouraged dictatorship. Moreover, because other countries were involved in their own problems, they were less willing to oppose acts of aggression by these fascist states.

section review 1

1. What were the major weaknesses in the world economy after World War I?
2. Why did the price of wheat fall sharply after World War I? What were the effects of this fall?
3. Why did the price of stocks begin to fall in October, 1929? What effects did this have on the United States and Europe?
4. Why did the depression cause countries to raise tariffs?

2 Aggression destroyed peaceful relations

When the dictators of the fascist states began to rearm their countries and make demands for additional territory, tension began to build up among the great powers. For a while, no effective action was taken against the moves of the dictators, for fear that it would start another war. But continued fascist aggression finally destroyed the shaky peace and brought on a second world war.

Japan attacked China. Japanese militarists were set on controlling China. In September, 1931, Japan seized several provinces in Manchuria. The Japanese then made Manchuria a puppet state called Manchukuo [man'chü'kwō']. They said they would not give up this territory, which was very rich in natural resources. The Chinese retaliated by boycotting Japanese goods. They cut imports from Japan by 94 percent.

In 1937, Japan began full-scale war against China. Shanghai, Nanking, and other large cities fell to the Japanese. But the Chinese would not surrender. Instead, 50 million of them fled to the western part of China. They took machinery, farm equipment, and furniture in carts or on their backs. In 1938, they set up a new capital for China at Chungking.

The League of Nations condemned the Japanese aggression. Its members—as well as the United States—spoke out against Japanese actions. But they were unwilling to use military force against Japan. Most countries were still suffering from the depression. They did not want to lose their trade with Japan. And countries such as Britain and France that had huge numbers of casualties in World War I had a deep aversion to war.

A woman and boy stare numbly at the wreckage of their home in Chungking after a Japanese bombing attack.

Hitler and Mussolini caused tension in Europe. In 1935, Hitler openly stated that he was rearming Germany. Later that same year, Mussolini attacked and conquered Ethiopia. In 1936, Hitler sent German troops into the Rhineland area northeast of France.

Hitler's moves were direct violations of the Versailles Treaty. Mussolini's aggression was a challenge to the League of Nations. As with Japan, however, no effective action was taken against either dictator. Neither France nor Britain, the two strongest neighbors, wanted to get into another war. Public opinion in both countries was strongly against war. But failure to act only encouraged the two dictators, especially Hitler. Both felt they could make more aggressive moves without being stopped by the western democracies.

Fascism also gained control in Spain. Meanwhile, in 1931 the Spaniards had overthrown their monarch and set up a republic. The new government tried to deal with the problems of poverty, illiteracy, and social unrest. But it failed to control a strong fascist group that blocked the attempts to improve conditions. Led by General Francisco Franco, military chiefs revolted against the republic in 1936. The Spanish Civil War had begun. Franco's forces were joined by the fascists and extreme nationalists.

Thousands of people, known as Loyalists, rushed to the defense of the republic. They were aided by a communist group who felt their best interests would be served by fighting fascism. Volunteers from other countries also helped the Loyalists. For a while they were successful, but they lacked arms.

As in the Rhineland crisis, Britain, France, and the other European states wanted to keep out of a war. Therefore, they followed a policy of strict neutrality, as did the United States. Such policies stopped the democra-

Pablo Picasso painted this view of the Spanish Civil War. Called "Guernica," after a village that was destroyed in the war, it expresses the horrors Picasso saw in his homeland.

cies from helping the Loyalists. The Soviet Union was the only non-fascist country to send aid.

Mussolini and Hitler, however, sent large amounts of arms and troops to help Franco. In March, 1939, the capital city, Madrid, was taken by Franco. This ended the republic. Many people feel that the neutral policy of the democratic states was largely to blame for the rise of yet another fascist dictatorship in Europe.

Meanwhile, the Spanish Civil War brought Mussolini and Hitler closer together. In 1936, shortly after the war began, the two dictators worked out an agreement which they called the Rome-Berlin Axis. They hoped the world would turn around this axis. In less than two years, Germany and Japan formed a diplomatic alliance, which Italy also joined. Having allies, each of the three felt it could push its demands more aggressively.

Hitler took over Austria and Czechoslovakia.
Hitler's goal was to expand the power of Germany until he controlled all of Europe. British and French leaders, however, did not know that. They believed they could work out compromises to appease, or satisfy, Hitler. In this way they hoped to avoid war. But this policy of appeasement only proved to Hitler that he could take whatever land he wanted.

In March, 1938, Hitler invaded Austria and annexed, or added, the area of that country to Germany. Hitler gained $100 million in gold, 7 million more citizens, and rich timber resources. Neither the British nor the French did anything more than protest this aggressive act.

Hitler's next target was Czechoslovakia. He claimed that the 3 million Germans living in the Sudeten Mountains in Czechoslovakia were being oppressed by the Czechs. In the

GEOGRAPHY
A Key to History

GEOPOLITICS AND NAZI POWER

Adolf Hitler's quest for power was aided by a geographic theory known as geopolitics. In one form, the theory was developed by Karl Haushofer, a retired general who taught geography at the University of Munich. Haushofer distorted the teachings of political geography to serve military purposes.

Haushofer's works on geopolitics described a nation as a living organism that has a life, a death, and a past from which it evolved. In order to live, he said, it must conquer other nations to gain needed Lebensraum [lā′bens-roum′], or "living space." Through a series of conquests, Germany had evolved from a group of small states to a great empire. It would continue to thrive if it continued to conquer, he said.

Haushofer taught that control of the land areas of east Europe and central Asia was the key to world conquest. He explained that whoever controlled the Heartland (an area extending from the southeastern Soviet Union to Mongolia) controlled the World Island (Europe, Asia, and Africa) and thereby controlled the world. Haushofer backed up this idea with statistics that showed that the Heartland had the potential to be

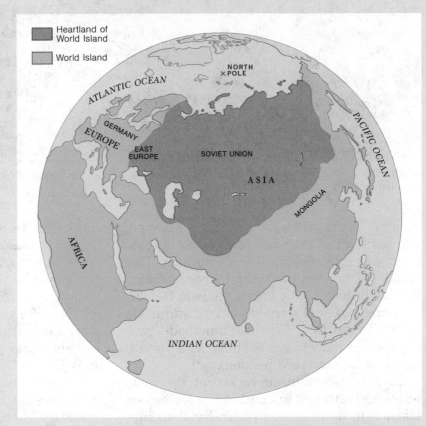

the greatest agricultural and industrial region in the world. The Heartland, he said, provided space for withdrawal of vital industries beyond range of possible attack. It was also a base from which armies could attack any country on the rim of the Heartland. He urged Germans to conquer all of eastern Europe and the Soviet Union.

Haushofer had great influence during the Hitler regime. His theories were taught in the schools and popularized in the press. They justified Nazi expansion as "natural" and necessary growth.

Some geographers opposed his theories, pointing out that a nation is not an organism and that geography can only influence, not determine, human behavior. But these were unhealthy views to hold in Nazi Germany.

By the war's end, the study of geopolitics had fallen into disrepute because of Haushofer's distortions. He cast a shadow over the legitimate questions that political geographers ask, such as: What is the relationship between a country's strength and its climate, access to the sea, and soil quality?

Chamberlain, Daladier, Hitler, and Mussolini posed for a group picture at their Munich meeting in 1938.

summer of 1938, he said that the Sudeten Germans must have self-rule. Hitler threatened war if his demands were not met. The Czechs turned to Britain and France for help. But the British, led by Prime Minister Neville Chamberlain, still wanted to avoid war at all costs. To do this, Chamberlain made two trips to Germany to talk to Hitler. The second time, Hitler increased his demands.

Chamberlain refused to accept the new terms and returned to London. He seemed to take a firm stand against Hitler. But then Hitler announced, "This is the last territorial claim I shall make in Europe." He asked Chamberlain and French Premier Edouard Daladier [da la dyā'] to meet with him and Mussolini in Munich on September 29, 1938. They agreed. No one from Czechoslovakia or Russia (which had promised to protect Czechoslovakia) was invited to the meeting.

During the Munich Conference, Chamberlain and Daladier decided to let Hitler take over the Sudetenland. In return, Hitler promised he would take no more Czech territory. The Czechs had no choice but to give in. Six months later, however, Hitler took over the rest of Czechoslovakia.

This brutal action finally convinced Chamberlain and Daladier that Hitler could not be appeased. They realized that his real aim was to dominate all of Europe. They therefore gave up their policy of appeasement and decided to oppose any further German demands.

Hitler attacked Poland. Hitler's next move was against Poland. The Treaty of Versailles had given Poland a corridor of land through Prussia. This gave Poland an outlet to the Baltic Sea at the port of Danzig. Danzig was declared a free or independent city under the protection of the League of Nations. About 90 percent of the corridor's population was Polish, but most of the people in Danzig were German.

In March, 1939, Hitler demanded that Danzig be given to Germany. He also said that the Nazis must be allowed to occupy a nar-

WHAT'S IN A NAME?
MUNICH

Some places are known by the people who were its first settlers. Munich comes from the Latin word *monachus*, meaning "a monk." The name fits because monks at one time owned the land that the city now stands on.

AXIS ACQUISITIONS
March, 1936–April, 1939

NORWAY
SWEDEN
FINLAND
ESTONIA
LATVIA
LITHUANIA
DENMARK
North Sea
Baltic Sea
GREAT BRITAIN
THE NETHERLANDS
BELGIUM
EAST PRUSSIA GERMANY
Danzig
PRUSSIA
POLISH CORRIDOR
GERMANY
POLAND
SOVIET UNION
THE RHINE-LAND
Maginot Line
SUDETENLAND
CZECHOSLOVAKIA
ATLANTIC OCEAN
FRANCE
Munich
Vienna
AUSTRIA
HUNGARY
ROMANIA
SWITZERLAND
PORTUGAL
SPAIN
ITALY
YUGOSLAVIA
BULGARIA
ALBANIA 1939
GREECE
TURKEY
LIBYA (It.)
AFRICA
ETHIOPIA 1936
DODECANESE IS. (It.)

Annexed by Germany, March, 1936
Annexed by Germany, March, 1938
Annexed by Germany, September, 1938
Annexed by Germany, March, 1939
Annexed by Italy, 1936–1939

N

0   150   300 MILES
0   150   300 KILOMETERS

row strip of the corridor connecting Germany with East Prussia. Poland refused, and this time both Britain and France warned Hitler they would come to Poland's aid if he attacked it.

The major question now was what the Soviet Union would do. Britain and France knew that Poland could not be defended without Russian help. Hitler, however, wanted to avoid fighting a two-front war. Hitler could do this by having the Soviets remain neutral. Stalin was mainly interested in protecting his western frontiers. Thus, he asked Britain and France for control over the

countries in eastern Europe that bordered on the Soviet Union. For Britain and France, that was too high a price to pay for Soviet cooperation. But Hitler was willing to pay such a price because he expected to conquer all that territory at a later time.

At the end of August, 1939, the world was shocked to learn that Germany and the Soviet Union had signed a pact agreeing not to go to war with each other. Hitler was now free to strike at Poland. On September 1, 1939, he did. Two days later, Britain and France declared war on Germany. World War II had begun.

1. Why did Japan seize Manchuria? Why didn't the League of Nations try to stop it?

2. What actions were taken by the leaders of Germany and Italy in 1935 and 1936? Why was nothing done to stop them?

3. What groups wanted to overthrow the Spanish Republic? What groups supported it? Why did the Republic not survive?

4. What areas did Hitler take over in 1938 and 1939? What efforts were made to stop him? Why were they unsuccessful?

3 Total war engulfed the world

When war broke out, it was mainly a European war. For more than two years, most of the fighting took place in Europe and the Atlantic Ocean. But the war became worldwide when Japan attacked the United States. From that time on, there was heavy fighting in the Pacific, as well as in Asia and Africa. Thus, World War II was much more truly a world war than World War I had been.

Eastern Europe was the first battlefield. In attacking Poland, Hitler struck very quickly. He used planes, tanks, and mechanized units. He called this a *blitzkrieg* [blitz′krēg′], a German word meaning "lightning warfare." The Poles were not prepared for that kind of warfare. In three weeks, they were totally crushed by the Germans.

As part of their agreement with Hitler, Soviet forces moved into eastern Poland, Latvia, Lithuania, and Estonia. The Soviet Union then ordered Finland to give up some of its land near Leningrad. When Finland refused, the Soviet Union attacked it in November, 1939. By March, 1940, Finland was defeated. It was forced to surrender the land that the Soviet Union wanted for better protection of Leningrad.

The Germans conquered western Europe. After defeating Poland, Hitler made plans to crush France and Britain. First, he invaded and conquered Denmark and Norway in April, 1940. In May, he turned south and overran the Netherlands and Belgium. By conquering Belgium, Hitler had bypassed France's major defenses along the Maginot [mazh′ə nō] Line. The French army was cut to pieces. In June, 1940, France surrendered. That same month, Mussolini brought Italy into the war on the German side. Hitler was now in control of almost all of western Europe.

After the summer of 1940, Britain was left to stand alone against Germany. Hitler thought the British would be willing to make a compromise peace. But Winston Churchill, who had become prime minister in May, refused. Hitler then decided to attack Britain by sea. However, Hermann Goering [gœ′ring], commander of the German air force, convinced Hitler that the British could be bombed into surrender. Mass bombings of Britain began in August, 1940. The British fought back. For the next ten months, a terrible air battle raged in the skies over Britain. The Germans lost more than twice as many planes as the British. By May, 1941, Hitler knew that he had lost the Battle of Britain.

Hitler attacked the Soviet Union. In spite of his pact with the Soviet Union, Hitler decided as early as December, 1940, to invade it. He wanted to conquer the Soviet Union because of its rich grain fields and its large supplies of oil, coal, and iron ore. Then he planned to turn back against Britain. Before moving into the Soviet Union, however, Hitler took control of the Balkans. He made alliances with Hungary, Romania, and Bulgaria. He also overran Greece and Yugoslavia early in 1941.

During the Battle of Britain, St. Paul's Cathedral, in the heart of London, became a symbol of resistance to the British people. Here the dome of St. Paul's is illuminated by the burning buildings nearby on the night of December 29, 1940. St. Paul's dome survived the Battle of Britain untouched.

In June, 1941, German forces swept into the Soviet Union. By December, Germany had conquered 600 thousand square miles (1.55 million square kilometers) of territory. More than 3.5 million Soviet soldiers were killed or captured, and the Soviet Union lost almost its entire air force. The Germans were close to Moscow and had surrounded Leningrad. For 900 days Leningrad held out against constant bombardment. Nearly 1 million people died of starvation and disease.

Stalin did not believe that Hitler would break their 1939 treaty and so was not fully prepared for war. But despite terrible losses, the Soviet army was not destroyed. They still had huge reserves of manpower. Early in December, 1941, the Russians launched a counterattack to drive the Germans back from Moscow. The Germans were not prepared for fighting in the severe winter weather. They had no antifreeze in their tanks and wore only their summer uniforms. Many Germans froze to death in the $-30°F.$ ($-34.5°C.$) weather. The Russians, well prepared for winter fighting, halted the German army and forced it back from Moscow.

The battleship *West Virginia* went up in flames at Pearl Harbor on December 7, 1941. The *West Virginia* and seven other American battleships were sunk or severely damaged that day.

Japan bombed Pearl Harbor. On the morning of December 7, 1941, without warning or declaration of war, Japan attacked the American naval base at Pearl Harbor in Hawaii. The Japanese also attacked the Philippines, British Malaya, and other places in Asia. The Japanese planned to build a great empire in Southeast Asia. Such an empire could supply Japan with oil, rubber, tin, and rice. It could also become a market for Japanese factory goods. Only the United States could stop Japan, because the European countries that had colonies in Asia were too busy fighting in Europe.

The Japanese attacks destroyed much of the American Pacific fleet. They also brought the United States into the war. The United States declared war on Japan; then Germany and Italy declared war on the United States. By January 1, 1942, the United States, the Soviet Union, Britain, and twenty-three other nations had become allied to fight against Germany, Italy, Japan, and their allies. The war between the Axis and the Allies was now worldwide.

section review 3

1. What was the first country Hitler attacked in World War II? Why was he able to conquer it so quickly?

2. What countries did the Germans conquer in western Europe between April and June, 1940? What was the Battle of Britain? Who won it?

3. Why did Hitler want to conquer the Soviet Union? What stopped the German advance there?

4. Describe the steps by which Asia, America, and Europe became linked in World War II. What were the reasons behind Japan's attack on Pearl Harbor?

4 *The Allies were victorious*

The power of the fascist states reached its greatest extent by May, 1942. The Japanese had created an empire that included Burma, Malaya, French Indochina, the Dutch East Indies, Thailand, the Philippines, Hong Kong, the coast of China, and various islands in the South Pacific. Hitler controlled Europe from Norway to Northern Africa and from the Atlantic coast to deep inside the Soviet Union. But 1942 was also the year the tide of battle began to turn against the Axis powers.

Hitler created a brutal New Order. Both Japan and Germany forced their conquered peoples to work for them. Hitler began to reorganize Europe for the benefit of the "master race." He called his scheme the "New Order." It was a plan to make all of Europe serve Germany. Huge amounts of French food, Soviet grain, Czech weapons, and Romanian oil were shipped to Germany. Seven million foreign workers were brought to Germany as slaves.

In the conquered lands, the Nazis used ruthless terror to control the local people. The horrors of Nazi rule were most brutal against Poles, Russians, Czechs, Yugoslavs, and Gypsies. These groups were all considered to be "inferior" peoples. More than 3 million people from the Soviet Union alone died in German prison camps.

Worst of all was the Nazi program of genocide, the murder of an entire people. This was carried out against the Jews of Europe. In the early years of the war, special Nazi execution squads shot hundreds of thousands of Jewish men, women, and children in Poland and the Soviet Union. Then, to speed up the slaughter, the Nazis built special death camps equipped with poison gas chambers and cremating ovens. Millions of

Nazis rounded up whole families of Jews and sent them to concentration camps. These people were taken from Warsaw in 1939.

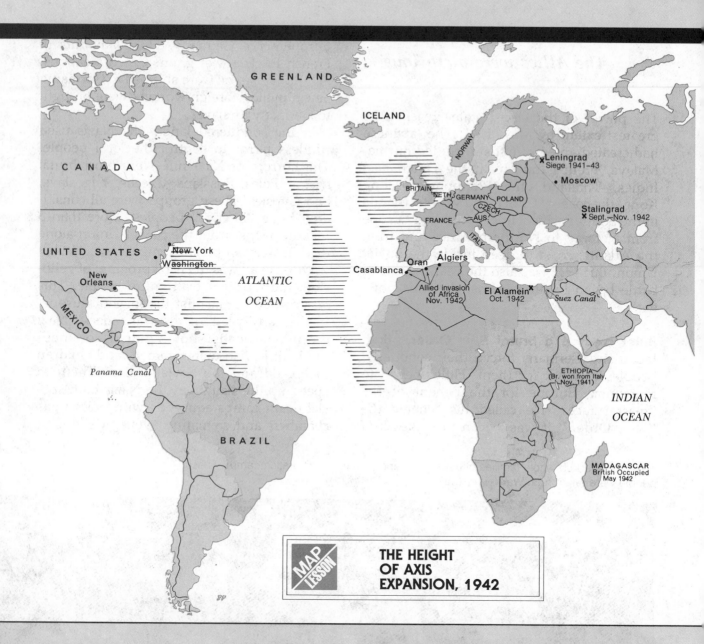

The Height of Axis Expansion, 1942 map showing:

GREENLAND

ICELAND

CANADA

NORWAY

Leningrad
Siege 1941–43

• Moscow

BRITAIN

NETH GERMANY POLAND
CZECH
FRANCE AUS

Stalingrad
✕ Sept.–Nov. 1942

ITALY

UNITED STATES

New York
Washington

New
Orleans

ATLANTIC
OCEAN

Casablanca
Oran
Algiers

Allied invasion
of Africa
Nov. 1942

El Alamein ✕
Oct. 1942

Suez Canal

MEXICO

Panama Canal

BRAZIL

ETHIOPIA
(Br. won from Italy,
Nov. 1941)

INDIAN
OCEAN

MADAGASCAR
British Occupied
May 1942

MAP
LESSON

THE HEIGHT
OF AXIS
EXPANSION, 1942

■ MAP LESSON 32: THE HEIGHT OF AXIS EXPANSION, 1942

1. This type of map is often used in history books, newspapers, and magazines. It is a political map of the world with only a few nations, cities, and geographic features labeled. Most of these areas are of particular interest to the topic, but others are included for general reference. Why then, are more labels included for Europe than for South America?

2. This map shows several things. Its major purpose is to show the areas under the control of the Allies and under the control of the Axis powers in later

1942 at the height of Axis expansion. In addition, the map shows with gray tints, the areas that did not participate in the war. It also locates some of the major battles in the war even though they took place before or after 1942. How does this map show areas of German submarine concentration?

3. The map shows land areas of the Pacific controlled by Axis powers by using solid green tints over these areas. How are water areas of control shown?

4. Study the map and decide which of the following statements are true and which are false:

S O V I E T   U N I O N
(Did not fight in the Pacific until Aug., 1945)

ALASKA

MANCHURIA

CHINA

KOREA

JAPAN
• Tokyo

Nagasaki • • Hiroshima
• Shanghai

San Francisco •

INDIA

BURMA

OKINAWA   IWO JIMA

FRENCH
INDOCHINA

PHILIPPINE IS.

WAKE I.

GUAM

• MIDWAY IS.
   X
June 1942

Pearl Harbor X • HAWAIIAN IS.
Dec. 1941

ATTU
KISKA ALEUTIAN IS.

Singapore •

DUTCH EAST INDIES

CAROLINE IS.

NEW GUINEA

Rabaul •
   SOLOMON IS.
   X GUADALCANAL
     May 1942

MARSHALL IS.

PACIFIC
OCEAN

INDIAN
OCEAN

AUSTRALIA

Coral Sea
   X
May 1942

NEW CALEDONIA
(Fr.)

• AMERICAN SAMOA

NEW
ZEALAND

0   750   1500 MILES
0   750   1500 KILOMETERS

Allies

Territory controlled by
Axis powers, late 1942

Nonbelligerents

Areas of German
submarine concentration

X Battle

a. German submarines did not hinder shipping around Great Britain very much.

b. Most of World War II was fought in the Eastern Hemisphere.

c. Axis control was centered in two great areas of the world that are widely separated from each other.

d. Most of the important sea battles were fought in the Pacific rather than the Atlantic.

e. Axis advances in the Soviet Union were stopped at a line running from Stalingrad north to Leningrad.

f. Many German submarines patrolled the Mediterranean Sea.

g. No major battles in World War II were fought in Africa.

h. France was controlled by the Axis powers in late 1942.

i. By late 1942, the Philippine Islands and Burma were under Axis control.

j. The Allies controlled most of the nations of Europe in late 1942.

k. Major battles were fought at Guadalcanal, Midway Island, and El Alamein.

Someone You Should Know

Anne Frank

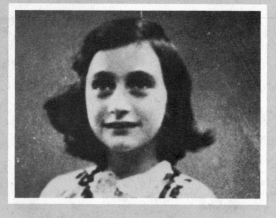

On August 4, 1944, the Nazis broke into a secret apartment at the back of an office building in Amsterdam, the Netherlands. For more than two years, a small group of Jews had been hiding there. They were arrested and sent to concentration camps. The youngest in the group, Anne Frank, just fifteen years old, went to the Belsen camp. Eight months later, she died there of typhus.

Left behind on the floor of the apartment was a diary that Anne had kept. In it she told about her family and their life in the Netherlands during the German occupation. In July, just a month after Anne began her diary, the Franks and four other people hastily moved to their hiding place.

Anne missed the outside world; but she studied and wrote in her diary. She was tormented with thoughts that people were suffering. Though Anne died, her diary lives on. It has become a symbol of courage to many people around the world.

Franz Hoessler, commander of the notorious Auschwitz and Belsen death camps, posed with a truckload of his victims.

Jews were rounded up all over Europe. They were crammed into sealed cattle cars and shipped to the death camps. By the end of the war, the Nazis had murdered nearly 6 million Jews. Jewish community life in Europe, which had existed for centuries, was almost totally destroyed. This destruction and slaughter is often called the Holocaust.

The tide of battle turned. In June, 1942, a great sea and air battle took place between the Japanese and the Americans at Midway Island in the South Pacific. When the battle ended, the Japanese had lost four large aircraft carriers and many airplanes and trained pilots. The United States was able to restore the naval balance it had lost at Pearl Harbor. The tide of war had now begun to shift in favor of the Allies. Several months later, the Americans began to push the Japanese out of the South Pacific.

One month after the Battle of Midway, the Germans started another offensive in the southern Soviet Union, which became a sec-

The British defeated Axis troops at El Alamein, Egypt. It was a decisive battle of the North Africa Campaign.

ond turning point of the war. The German goal was to reach the Caucasus Mountains and cut off the food and oil supplies to the central Soviet Union. By September, 1942, the Germans had reached the important city of Stalingrad on the Volga River. The Germans pounded the city and killed 40 thousand civilians. But the Soviets fought ferociously and held on. Although the German commander knew he could not win, Hitler refused to let him retreat and save the army. The Soviets brought up fresh reserves, surrounded the Germans, and crushed them. In January, 1943, the Germans at Stalingrad surrendered. It was their worst defeat of the war. They had lost an army of more than 350 thousand men. From that time on, the Soviet Union took the offensive in eastern Europe, and Germany steadily retreated.

A third important turning point of the war came in North Africa. The aim of the German and Italian troops was to march east across northern Africa to the Suez Canal and the rich oil fields of the Middle East. By October,

1942, they had come to within 70 miles (113 kilometers) of Alexandria, Egypt. But the British began a counterattack and by January, 1943, had driven the Italians and Germans back 1,400 miles (2,258 kilometers) to the west. Meanwhile, in November, 1942, American and British troops landed in French Morocco and Algeria and pushed eastward. Squeezed from both sides, over 250 thousand German and Italian troops surrendered in May, 1943.

Italy declared war on Germany. After the North African victory, the path to Europe was open and the Allies invaded Sicily in July, 1943. Within two weeks, Mussolini was forced out of office and put in jail. A new government signed an armistice on September 8. They surrendered unconditionally to the Allies on the day before the Allies invaded Italy.

However, the new Italian government had very little real control. The Allied invasion met with stiff resistance from German forces

Daily Life

For the soldiers of World War II, daily life meant seemingly endless battles. *Below* Allied troops inch their way up the beach at Normandy. The large steel crosses had been put up by the Nazis to hinder the landing of tanks, jeeps, and trucks. *Below right* sailors on the USS *Bunker Hill* hurry to put out the fires on board on May 11, 1945. Two Japanese kamikaze, or suicide, planes hit the ship that day within thirty minutes. At right *inset* is the famous photograph of American soldiers raising their flag on Mount Suribachi on the island of Iwo Jima. Only two of these men survived the war. At *far right top* sailors help a Marine on board their ship after a two-day battle on the island of Eniwetok in the Marshall Islands. At *near right top* British soldiers in Egypt in 1941 stand in a dinner line. Every army faced the enormous task of feeding its soldiers while they were on the move, in the midst of jungles and deserts, and during great battles.

The Allies

Argentina	Cuba	Greece	Mexico	Poland
Australia	Czechoslovakia	Guatemala	Mongolian	Russia
Belgium	Dominican	Haiti	People's	San Marino
Bolivia	Republic	Honduras	Republic	Saudi Arabia
Brazil	Ecuador	India	Netherlands	South Africa
Canada	Egypt	Iran	New Zealand	Syria
Chile	El Salvador	Iraq	Nicaragua	Turkey
China	Ethiopia	Lebanon	Norway	United States
Colombia	France	Liberia	Panama	Uruguay
Costa Rica	Great Britain	Luxembourg	Paraguay	Venezuela
			Peru	Yugoslavia

The Axis

Albania	Finland	Hungary	Japan	Thailand
Bulgaria	Germany	Italy	Romania	

Smashed guns, branchless trees, and dead animals give mute testimony to the fierceness of fighting in a small Russian town before the Russians drove out the Nazi invaders.

and Italian supporters of Mussolini. On October 13, the new government declared war on Germany. In June, 1944, the Allies fought their way into Rome, but the Germans held northern Italy until early 1945.

A second front was opened. The Allied leaders felt that a direct attack on Germany from the west was the quickest way to end the war. Stalin had been arguing for the opening of this second front ever since 1942. For nearly three years, since the Nazi invasion of June, 1941, the Russians fought alone against Hitler's forces on the continent of Europe. Russian losses were horrendous. In the battle for Stalingrad alone, for example, the Russians lost more men than the United States lost in combat during all of World War II.

Stalin was convinced that only a ground invasion by Allied forces in the west would relieve the terrible pressure against the Russians on the eastern front. From his point of view, Allied actions in North Africa and Italy did not help the Russians. The longer it took to open a second front, the more suspicious Stalin became of the motives of Roosevelt and Churchill. As he saw it, they were leaders of capitalist countries and were deliberately delaying the opening of a second front to keep Nazi forces concentrated against

Communist Russia. These suspicions stayed with him even though, all through 1943, the United States sent to the Soviet Union enormous quantities of American planes, guns, trucks, jeeps, clothing, food, and machinery for Soviet arms plants. These supplies made an invaluable contribution to the Soviet war effort.

The real reason for the delay in opening the second front was that it took time to assemble all the necessary equipment and train all the troops for what would be the largest amphibious invasion in history. Plans had to be worked out very carefully. By 1944, some 1.5 million trained troops were ready in Britain. Ships and landing craft were waiting at British ports. The Nazis did not expect the Allies to invade the Normandy coast. This part of the French coast lacked natural ports and had extreme tides. It was also defended by Hitler's "Atlantic Wall," which was many miles of underwater obstacles and cement bunkers along the shore.

"Operation Overlord," under the command of General Dwight D. Eisenhower, moved across the English Channel on June 6, 1944. After a week of fierce fighting, the invasion army held a 60 mile (96 kilometer) strip of the Normandy beach. In July, the Allied armored divisions broke through the German lines. By August, Paris was liberated.

Churchill, Roosevelt, and Stalin posed for photographers at Yalta.

A major conference was held at Yalta. By February, 1945, victory in Europe was in sight for the Allies. Roosevelt, Churchill, and Stalin met at Yalta, a seacoast resort in the southern Soviet Union, to discuss peace terms. They decided that Germany would be divided into four occupation zones controlled by each of the Allies, including France.

The most difficult problem for the Allies was control of eastern Europe. By the time of the Yalta Conference, Soviet armies had fought to within 40 miles (64 kilometers) of Berlin and were in control of almost all of eastern and central Europe. Roosevelt and Churchill were fearful that Stalin would impose communist dictatorships on the east European nations. They insisted that Stalin give assurances that this would not happen. Stalin promised that free elections would be held and independent governments would be set up in all the east European countries.

Shortly after Yalta it became clear that Stalin did not intend to honor his promise. You will read about this in Chapter 33.

Throughout the war the Soviet Union had been neutral in the fight against Japan. But in early 1945, Roosevelt believed that Soviet help was needed to end the war in East Asia quickly. At Yalta, Stalin promised to enter the war against Japan within ninety days after the war against Germany ended. He made this promise in return for territorial concessions in East Asia, at the expense of China.

Looking toward the postwar world, Roosevelt was convinced that big power cooperation within an international organization was the best way to preserve future peace and security. He proposed the creation of a United Nations organization and urged that the Soviet Union become a member. Stalin agreed. The three leaders then pledged that when the war was over, a group to be called the United Nations would be established.

Daily Life

The lives of people on the home front were greatly affected by the war. At *near right* is British flyer Amy Johnson who was the idol of a generation of British schoolgirls as she set flying records around the world during the 1930s. "Amy, wonderful Amy" was killed in January, 1941, as she was ferrying a war plane from its factory to the front. While relatively few women worked as pilots, millions of women took jobs that were left by departing soldiers. And governments encouraged women to take the jobs. The American poster *below* is one such example. For people whose homes were in battle zones, life was especially tough. At *top center* a London bomb disposal team carefully removes a huge, 2,750-pound, unexploded bomb from the heart of the city. At *bottom center* people in Leningrad are getting their drinking water from an open sewer since the water system was smashed. Food was so scarce that people took wallpaper off their walls and cooked it with water to make soup. At *far right top* is an American grocery-store meat counter. Each person was allowed to buy only so much of rationed items, no matter how much money the person was willing to pay. Many countries needed more money to fight the war so they sold government bonds to their citizens to raise money. The picture *far right bottom* shows American singer Kate Smith selling $10 bonds.

"THE GIRL HE LEFT BEHIND" IS STILL BEHIND HIM
She's a WOW
WOMAN ORDNANCE WORKER

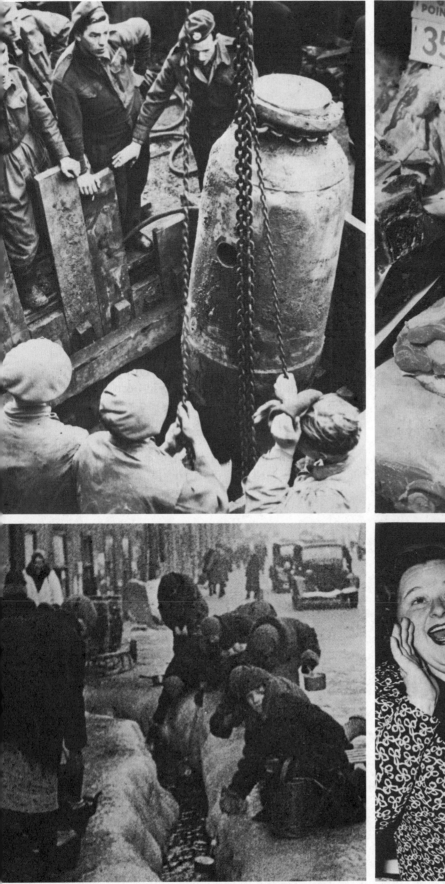

Germany and Japan surrendered. A few weeks after Yalta, Soviet troops entered Berlin. German forces in Italy gave way to the Allies late in April. The final surrender of Germany took place on May 8, 1945.

A few days earlier, Hitler had committed suicide. Mussolini had already been captured and shot by Italians. The Allied nations, too, had lost a leader. President Roosevelt had died on April 12, 1945. He was succeeded by Vice-President Harry S. Truman.

While the war in Europe was over, the war in East Asia continued. The United States wanted to avoid an invasion of Japan that would have meant the loss of hundreds of thousands of American soldiers. Instead, President Truman ordered that an atomic bomb be dropped.

In 1905, Albert Einstein had published a scientific paper that related matter to energy in a famous formula: $E = mc^2$ (energy equals mass times the velocity of light squared). This means that mass and energy are equivalent, and a small amount of matter can be transformed into a huge amount of energy. Then other scientists exploring the structure and behavior of atoms succeeded in splitting the uranium atom. Building on these discoveries and on Einstein's formula, scientists in the United States were able to build an atomic bomb.

On August 6, 1945, the destructive force of 20 thousand tons of dynamite destroyed most of the Japanese city of Hiroshima [hir′ ō shē′mə]. This single atomic bomb wounded or killed over 160 thousand persons.

On August 9, an atomic bomb was dropped on Nagasaki [nä′gə sä′kē], Japan. On the same day, Soviet troops declared war on Japan and invaded the Japanese-held areas of Korea and Manchuria. On September 2, 1945, the Japanese signed a formal surrender. The Soviet action did not affect Japan's decision to surrender. But it would have far-reaching implications, as you will see, in the years to come.

A rumor of impending German surrender brought thousands of New Yorkers to Wall Street on May 7, 1945.

section review 4

1. How was Hitler's "New Order" put into practice? What was the result of the Nazi program of genocide against the Jews?

2. How did the battles at Midway, Stalingrad, and in North Africa change the course of the war?

3. What major decisions were made at the Yalta Conference?

4. Why did the United States want to avoid an invasion of Japan? How were the Japanese forced to surrender?

Section Summaries

1. The world economy broke down. A world depression began in 1929 and became the worst in history. Partly this was because of weaknesses in the world economy after World War I, especially agriculture. The world prices of wheat and other crops dropped, and many farmers faced ruin. When the New York stock market crashed, American lenders began to recall European loans. Businesses failed, and people were thrown out of work. All countries raised their tariffs, and international trade fell sharply.

2. Aggression destroyed peaceful relations. In the 1930s, the leaders of Nazi Germany, fascist Italy, and militaristic Japan made aggressive moves. They broke treaties and bullied other countries. Japan attacked China. Hitler sent troops into the Rhineland. Mussolini conquered Ethiopia. A fascist government came to power in Spain. In 1938 and 1939, Hitler gobbled up Austria and Czechoslovakia, breaking the promise he made at the Munich Conference. After Hitler signed a nonaggression pact with the Soviet Union in August, 1939, he attacked Poland on September 1, 1939. Britain and France then declared war on Germany.

3. Total war engulfed the world. By June, 1941, Hitler controlled almost all of central and western Europe, except Britain and had Italy as an ally. He then attacked the Soviet Union. On December 7, 1941, Japan made a surprise attack on the American naval base at Pearl Harbor. The United States declared war on Japan, and Germany and Italy soon declared war on the United States. Japan's plan was to cripple American naval power in the Pacific. Then the United States could not oppose Japanese expansion. By early 1942, Japan had conquered a huge empire in Southeast Asia.

4. The Allies were victorious. Hitler set up a brutal "New Order" in Europe and began a policy of genocide. The tide of battle turned against Japan, Germany, and Italy in 1942–43, after battles at Midway Island, Stalingrad, and in North Africa. Then in June, 1944, the Allies invaded Normandy. In February, 1945, Roosevelt, Churchill, and Stalin met at Yalta to make deci-sions about the postwar world. Germany surrendered in May, 1945, and Japan surrendered in September, 1945, after the United States dropped atomic bombs on Hiroshima and Nagasaki.

Who? What? When? Where?

1. Arrange these events in chronological order:
   a. The U.S. won the battle of Midway Island.
   b. An atomic bomb was dropped on Hiroshima.
   c. Daladier, Chamberlain, and Hitler met at Munich.
   d. The Battle of Britain began.
   e. Prices fell on the New York Stock Exchange.
   f. Japanese bombers attacked Pearl Harbor.
   g. Britain and France declared war on Germany.
   h. Japan seized Manchuria.

2. Write sentences that describe the ways these events caused problems for industrialized nations after World War I:
   a. credit financing by the United States
   b. decline in foreign trade
   c. high tariffs
   d. increased crop production
   e. unemployment

3. Write sentences telling about World War II events associated with each of these leaders:
   a. Chamberlain   f. Mussolini
   b. Churchill   g. Roosevelt
   c. Daladier   h. Stalin
   d. Eisenhower   i. Truman
   e. Hitler

4. Write sentences that tell what each of these terms means:
   a. Allies   e. blitzkrieg
   b. appeasement   f. genocide
   c. Atlantic Wall   g. Maginot Line
   d. Axis Powers   h. New Order

Questions for Critical Thinking

1. How did the economic problems of the depression bring about political changes in the major countries of the world?

2. How might World War II have been prevented?

3. Why is it important for students today to learn about what happened to the Jewish people in Nazi Germany?

4. If the Japanese had not bombed Pearl Harbor, do you think the United States would have entered the war? Explain your answer.

Skill Activities

1. Read *Anne Frank: The Diary of a Young Girl* by Anne Frank to find out more about this teenager's life under Nazi rule. (Doubleday, 1967, rev. ed.)

2. Find out what it was like to live during the depression. Ask older relatives or others to tell you what they remember. Or read firsthand accounts such as those in *Hard Times* by Studs Terkel. One or two of these accounts might be acted out for the class by a few students.

3. Using the World Almanac, graph the losses of human life by the Soviet Union, Britain, Germany, France, Japan, and the United States in World War II. Graph the total male population in each of these countries before and after the war.

4. Prepare "battle plans" and maps for one of the battles described in this chapter. Use library sources to find information on the names of military commanders, troop movements, dates of engagements, etc.

chapter **32** *quiz*

Section 1

1. True or false: By the 20th century, no nation possessed all the raw materials it needed.

2. In the 1920s, many European nations borrowed money to build and run their factories from: a. Japan, b. the Soviet Union, c. the United States

3. One thing that did not result from the depression was: a. worldwide revolutions, b. unemployment, c. high tariffs

Section 2

4. One thing that did not lead to Japan's attack on China in 1937 was: a. Japan's need for natural resources; b. China's boycott of Japanese products; c. League of Nations actions against Japan

5. During the Spanish Civil War, the Loyalists were helped by: a. the United States, b. France, c. the Soviet Union

6. At the Munich Conference, it was agreed that Hitler could take over: a. Czechoslovakia, b. Poland, c. the Sudetenland

Section 3

7. Hitler's method of warfare used in taking Poland was the: a. New Order, b. blitzkrieg, c. Atlantic Wall

8. In 1940, the man who was Britain's prime minister was: a. Churchill, b. Chamberlain, c. Daladier

9. True or false: Japan attacked Pearl Harbor in November, 1939.

Section 4

10. True or false: Hitler's plan in Europe was to form a "New Order" in which all national groups would become German.

11. True or false: The Allied invasion of Normandy was led by General Dwight D. Eisenhower.

12. True or false: In 1945, the Nazis finally captured the major Soviet cities of Leningrad and Stalingrad.

1. Match each of these people with the description listed below:

Chamberlain
Gandhi
Hitler
Lenin
Lilioukalani
Mao
Mussolini
Mutsuhito
Nicholas II
Truman
Wilson

a. Was deposed as queen of Hawaii
b. Favored a negotiated peace after World War I
c. Favored nonviolent resistance
d. Was the last tsar of Russia
e. Tried to unite Europe under German rule
f. Led followers on the Long March
g. Used Marxist ideas to run the Russian government
h. Organized the Italian Fascist Party
i. Made the Meiji Restoration
j. Ordered that an atomic bomb be dropped on Japan
k. Tried to avoid war by sacrificing Czechoslovakia

2. Match the letters on the time line with these events described below:

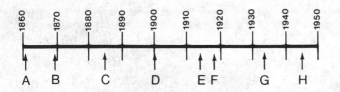

____The Boxer Rebellion occurred.
____The Indian National Congress was formed.
____The Bolshevik Revolution began.
____World War II ended.
____The Long March began.
____The Suez Canal was finished.
____World War I began.
____The serfs were freed in Russia.

3. Match the letters on the map with the places described below:

____European powers divided up most of this continent in the 19th century.
____A canal in this area had great importance for the United States.
____Beginning in the 1930s, this nation began to acquire a large empire in Asia.
____A canal in this area linked Britain with several important colonies.
____World War I brought the end to tsarist rule in this nation.

4. A direct cause of World War I was: a. the Bolshevik Revolution in Russia, b. the assassination of Francis Ferdinand, c. the seizure of Manchuria by Japan

5. One thing that was not a problem after World War I was: a. fear of German power, b. a communist takeover in France, c. Indian unhappiness with the Government of India Act

6. One reason for the rise of communism in Russia was: a. the failure of Nicholas II to end serfdom, b. the hardships caused by World War I, c. the pogroms

7. One cause of World War II was: a. the death of Lenin, b. the Zimmermann telegram, c. the bombing of Pearl Harbor

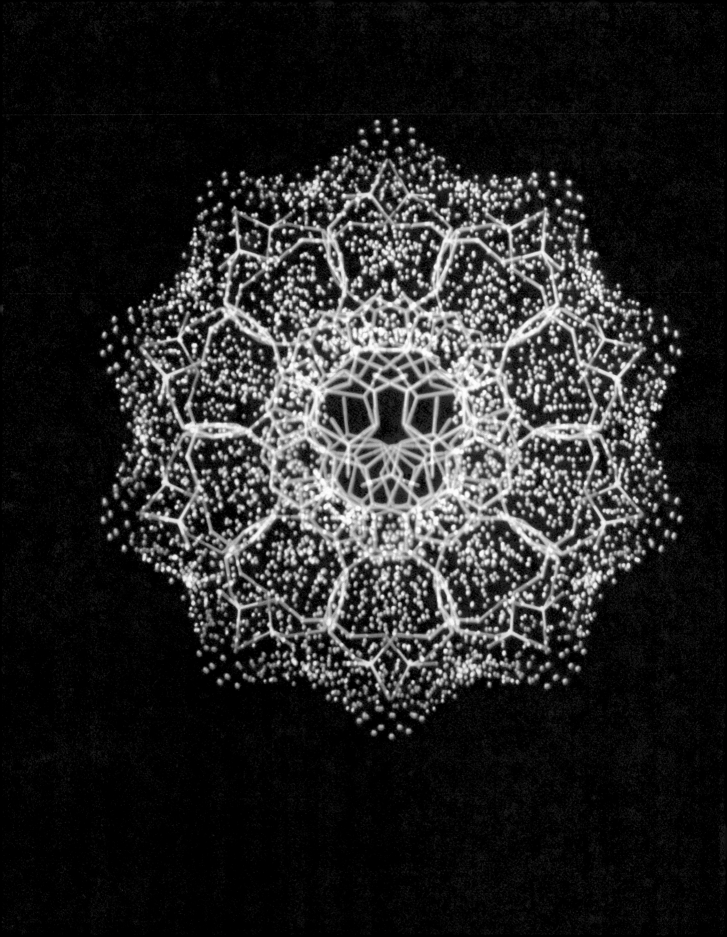

UNIT NINE THE CONTEMPORARY WORLD

The contemporary world is the world of everyone living today. It is the most recent phase in history. It began after World War II, when the world became much different from what it had been.

For the first time in history people live with the possibility that all human existence could be ended by nuclear war. For the first time, too, people have begun to understand that Earth's resources are limited and that pollution can seriously damage the quality of life.

More people are alive today than ever before, and the demand for food and resources has never been greater. But the differences between rich and poor nations are greater than ever. Our contemporary era is quite different politically, too. For much of the period the United States and the Soviet Union have dominated international relations. But more independent nations now exist than ever before. This era is the first in which people have traveled beyond Earth itself and have seen Mars, Saturn, and Jupiter at close range.

And all this change has occurred rapidly, which makes the present era especially hard to understand. This unit describes many of the new developments and the problems that rapid change has created. But because our era, like every other, contains a mixture of the old and new, the unit also discusses the important older issues that are still with us.

DNA, the molecule that forms genes, is now being used in new ways to produce new kinds of microorganisms for medical and industrial uses. This picture of a DNA molecule was made by a computer.

CHAPTER 33
THE AFTERMATH OF WORLD WAR II

- Yalta Conference
- UN Charter signed
- People's Republic of China formed
- NATO set up
- Chinese Civil War
- Korean War
- French fought in Vietnam
- Warsaw Pact set up
- Truman Doctrine enacted
- Marshall Plan started
- India and Pakistan became independent
- Gandhi died
- Soviets launched Sputnik
- Cold War started
- Stalin died
- Berlin airlift
- Hungarian uprising crushed

CHAPTER 34
THE FORGING OF NATIONS IN THE MIDDLE EAST AND AFRICA

- Israel formed
- Egypt nationalized Suez Canal
- South Africa began apartheid
- Ghana became independent

CHAPTER 35
THE STRUGGLE FOR NATIONAL DEVELOPMENT IN LATIN AMERICA AND SOUTHERN ASIA

- Women gained the vote in Argentina
- Women gained the vote in Mexico
- Vargas died
- Eva Peron died
- U.S. first involved in Vietnam

CHAPTER 36
A NEW SYSTEM OF WORLD RELATIONSHIPS

- Labour Party came to power in England
- Adenaur became chancellor
- United States exploded H-bomb
- Soviet Union exploded H-bomb
- Great Britain exploded A-bomb
- Common Market formed

1944 1946 1948 1950 1952 1954 1956 1958

1. UN symbol, 2. H-bomb, 3. Elizabeth II,
4. Sputnik, 5. Flag of Ghana, 6. De Gaulle,
7. The Beatles, 8. Khrushchev, 9. Astronaut
on the moon, 10. Allende, 11. Meir,
12. Mao Tse-tung, 13. Olympic symbol,
14. Space shuttle.

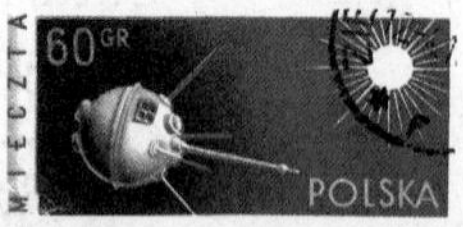

60 GR
POLSKA

1
2
3
4
5

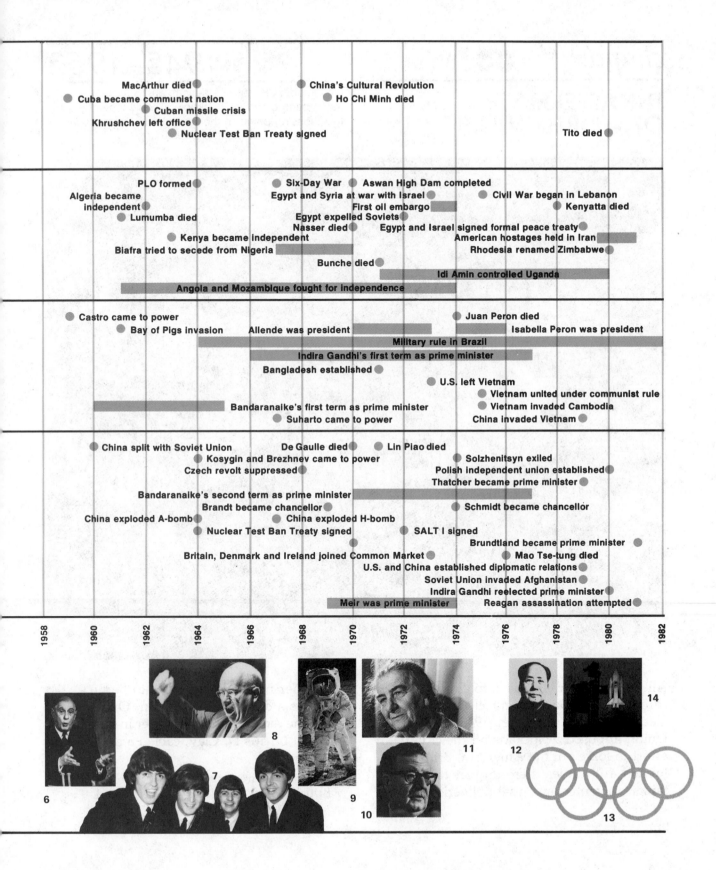

MacArthur died
Cuba became communist nation
Cuban missile crisis
Khrushchev left office
Nuclear Test Ban Treaty signed
China's Cultural Revolution
Ho Chi Minh died
Tito died

PLO formed
Algeria became independent
Lumumba died
Kenya became independent
Biafra tried to secede from Nigeria
Six-Day War
Egypt and Syria at war with Israel
First oil embargo
Egypt expelled Soviets
Nasser died
Bunche died
Angola and Mozambique fought for independence
Aswan High Dam completed
Civil War began in Lebanon
Kenyatta died
Egypt and Israel signed formal peace treaty
American hostages held in Iran
Rhodesia renamed Zimbabwe
Idi Amin controlled Uganda

Castro came to power
Bay of Pigs invasion
Allende was president
Military rule in Brazil
Indira Gandhi's first term as prime minister
Bangladesh established
Bandaranaike's first term as prime minister
Suharto came to power
Juan Peron died
Isabella Peron was president
U.S. left Vietnam
Vietnam united under communist rule
Vietnam invaded Cambodia
China invaded Vietnam

China split with Soviet Union
Kosygin and Brezhnev came to power
Czech revolt suppressed
Bandaranaike's second term as prime minister
Brandt became chancellor
China exploded A-bomb
China exploded H-bomb
Nuclear Test Ban Treaty signed
Britain, Denmark and Ireland joined Common Market
Meir was prime minister
De Gaulle died
Lin Piao died
Solzhenitsyn exiled
Polish independent union established
Thatcher became prime minister
Schmidt became chancellor
SALT I signed
Brundtland became prime minister
Mao Tse-tung died
U.S. and China established diplomatic relations
Soviet Union invaded Afghanistan
Indira Gandhi reelected prime minister
Reagan assassination attempted

1958 1960 1962 1964 1966 1968 1970 1972 1974 1976 1978 1980 1982

6 7 8 9 10 11 12 13 14

THE AFTERMATH OF WORLD WAR II

On October 28, 1961, American and Soviet tanks faced each other at Checkpoint Charlie, one of the few crossing points in the Berlin Wall. The tanks faced off for 16 tense hours in a crisis there.

All roads and railroads into Berlin passed through the Soviet-controlled section of Germany. And in June, 1948, the Soviet Union imposed a blockade on the city, in an effort to force out the American, British, and French authorities there. Soviet troops and tanks prevented essential deliveries of food and other necessary supplies to Berlin.

It was a dangerous situation. On June 25, 1948, the American commander in Germany, General Lucius D. Clay, cabled a message to Washington:

> Conditions are tense. . . . Our troops and British are in hand and can be trusted. . . .

Every [non-communist] German leader . . . and thousands of Germans have courageously expressed their opposition to Communism. We must not destroy their confidence by any indication of departure from Berlin.

The Western Allies held firm. They airlifted food, clothing, and supplies into Berlin all through the winter. Finally, in May, 1949, the Soviet government ended the blockade. The Berlin crisis was over. But the crisis showed how far from alliance the Allies had moved since the end of World War II in 1945. Antipathy had developed between the Allies, especially the United States and the Soviet Union. This state of affairs came to be called Cold War. The Cold War, which began over issues in Europe, dominated international relations in the post-World War II period.

The aftermath of World War II brought dramatic changes in other parts of the world. In the short period of fifteen years, from 1947 to 1962, the British, French, Dutch, and Belgian empires in Asia and Africa almost completely disappeared. At the same time, a communist regime came to power in China. These were among the most important and long-lasting effects that grew out of World War II.

This chapter tells how:

1. Two superpowers dominated world relations.

2. A Cold War began in Europe.

3. The Soviets dominated Eastern Europe.

4. Empires crumbled in Asia.

5. Communists came to power in China.

1 Two superpowers dominated world relations

Before 1945, no one used the word "superpower" to describe an especially strong nation. World War II radically changed that situation.

Two superpowers emerged after 1945. When World War II ended, most of the strong nations of the prewar period had either been defeated or seriously weakened. These included Germany, Italy, Japan, France, Great Britain, and China. But two nations survived the war with such strength that no other nation could match them. The United States and the Soviet Union came to be known as superpowers. Each of the two superpowers was a land giant that stretched across a continent. Each had a large population, possessed huge natural resources, and had great military strength.

In addition to its own territory, the Soviet Union at the end of World War II controlled a vast area in Europe that included Germany's second greatest industrial region. In East Asia, Soviet forces occupied Manchuria, northern Korea, and Mongolia.

The United States had military forces in Western Europe and naval and air bases on the continents of Asia and Europe. Unlike other nations, the United States had not been damaged by enemy attacks during the war, and it had emerged as the greatest industrial power in the world. It was also the only nation that possessed the atomic bomb.

The presence of two superpowers served to polarize international relations in the years after World War II. Each superpower tended to look at the other as a rival, at times a dangerous enemy. When one of the superpowers sought to strengthen its security, the other saw that as a threat. When one gained

At UN headquarters, *above left*, in New York City, members of the General Assembly meet to seek peaceful solutions to international problems. And the UN does much through agencies such as the World Health Organization to help solve world health and food problems. *Above right* a medical team works in Tokoindzi, Togo, in a program to stamp out malaria.

influence in some country, the other superpower saw that as a loss. This kind of relationship between the United States and the Soviet Union has existed ever since the end of World War II. It spilled over into the United Nations which was created in 1945 to keep world peace.

Superpower rivalry affected the United Nations. After World War II, the victorious Allies replaced the old League of Nations with a new world organization. Representatives of fifty nations signed the United Nations charter in San Francisco in June, 1945, and by October of that year the organization had been established.

Two major UN bodies were created, the General Assembly and the Security Council.

Every member country had a representative in the General Assembly. The Security Council originally had eleven members, which was increased to fifteen in 1965. Five nations—the United States, the Soviet Union, France, Great Britain, and China—were to be permanent members. The others would be elected for two-year terms by the General Assembly. The chief responsibility of the Security Council was to keep peace in the world. An elected Secretary General and his staff, called the Secretariat, administered the UN and carried out its decisions.

Any one of the permanent members of the Security Council could veto any decision. Thus, if the permanent members disagreed, as the United States and the Soviet Union often did, the Security Council could not work effectively as a peacekeeping agency. The Soviet Union used the veto in the Security Council so much that by 1950 the council was paralyzed. The General Assembly then began to play a larger role. It gained the power to authorize emergency action on its own if the Security Council was blocked by a veto.

In the postwar years, the UN showed it could play a significant peacekeeping role in places like Cyprus, the Sinai peninsula, and Korea. But the rivalry between the two superpowers made it difficult for the UN to agree on international actions to promote peace and weapons control. Even small nations at times refused to obey the United Nations.

As it turned out, the major value of the United Nations was that it became a forum for discussion and a channel for international aid and research. The spread of worldwide communications created a new world public. Member UN states, large and small, came to feel they had to explain—and justify—their actions before the General Assembly. And the world public expected them to explain. Also, UN agencies such as the World Health Organization, UNICEF (United Nations Children's Fund), and the World Bank were set up to coordinate efforts for improving life around the globe.

section review 1

1. How many nations can truly be called superpowers? Why only those nations?

2. How did the existence of superpowers after World War II make international relations different?

3. How did the Soviet Union paralyze the Security Council? What effect did this have on the General Assembly?

4. What became the UN's most important function?

2 A Cold War began in Europe

The term *Cold War* was first used by American journalists in 1948 to describe the increasingly hostile relations between the Soviet Union and the United States. The hostility at first grew out of Stalin's rejection of attempts at big power cooperation in the postwar world. It later influenced other international issues.

Wartime unity began to crack. Serious differences among the Allies first appeared at the most important wartime conference—the meeting of Franklin D. Roosevelt, Winston Churchill, and Joseph Stalin at Yalta in the U.S.S.R. in February, 1945. There, the three agreed that the countries of Eastern Europe, especially Poland, should hold free elections to establish new governments after the war. It soon became clear that the Soviet Union would support only communist governments in areas the Soviet army then occupied. From the Russian point of view, the Soviet Union could be secure only by having friendly, communist countries on its western border. By 1948 Romania, Bulgaria, Poland, Hungary, and Czechoslovakia were under communist rule.

The Allies' differences concerning Germany were even greater. Stalin wanted a peace treaty so harsh that Germany would be turned back into an agricultural country. In his view, Germany must never again be strong enough, industrially and militarily, to threaten the Soviet Union. Roosevelt and Churchill thought that so severe a treaty would cause a revolution in Germany and rejected Stalin's proposal. Western leaders were also coming to believe that a strong Germany would be necessary to prevent an

BERLIN OCCUPATION ZONES

FRENCH ZONE

SOVIET ZONE

SOVIET ZONE

WEST BERLIN

BRITISH ZONE

Brandenburg Gate

EAST BERLIN

Grosser Wannsee

Tempelhof

AMERICAN ZONE

Potsdam

Teltow Canal

Seddinsee

E A S T   G E R M A N Y

0   2   4 MILES
0   2   4 KILOMETERS

MAP LESSON 33: OCCUPATION ZONES OF BERLIN

1. This map shows how the city of Berlin was divided among four of the Allies for occupation zones at the end of World War II. What four Allies had occupation zones?

2. The Brandenburg Gate, built in 1791, is Berlin's most famous landmark. It is located in which occupation zone?

3. In which zone is Berlin's major airport located? What is its name?

4. The Olympiastadion, built for the 1936 Berlin Olympics, is located almost due west of the Brandenburg Gate and just north of the Grosser Wannsee. Thus, it is in which zone?

5. Berlin is surrounded by many small lakes, two of which are named on the map. One is partly in the British zone. What is its name? The other lake is southeast of the American zone. What is its name?

6. Berlin also has several canals. One major canal runs through the American zone. What is its name?

expansion of Soviet influence in Europe. The three leaders agreed to a temporary plan. Germany was divided into four zones. Britain, the United States, the Soviet Union, and France each occupied and governed a zone. The capital city, Berlin, was located within the Soviet zone of Germany, but the city was occupied and administered jointly by the four powers. This "temporary" arrangement became, after the war, the basis of the "German problem."

The distrust between the two sides grew deeper as they tried to solve the problem. The Soviet Union wanted heavy reparations, or payments, from Germany to rebuild its own country. It also wanted to make its occupation zone in Germany a satellite. (*Satellite* is a word used to describe the technically independent nations that came under Soviet control in the years after World War II.) British and American leaders, on the other hand, thought that Germany, with its rich industrial resources, should be allowed to grow strong again. Europe's economy depended on that of Germany, they believed. But the Soviets had suffered much from their German neighbor and they did not wish to see Germany again grow strong. The "temporary" division of Germany took on a more permanent character. In 1949, West Germany (the American, British, and French zones) became, officially, the Federal Republic of Germany. East Germany (the Soviet zone) became the German Democratic Republic, under a communist government.

The rivalry between the United States and the Soviet Union increased. The differences over Germany and Eastern Europe intensified the suspicion and mistrust between the two superpowers. Their rivalry spread to other parts of Europe as each side tried to prevent the other side from increasing its influence.

In 1947, a civil war broke out in Greece, in

Daily Life

The Marshall Plan was named for George Catlett Marshall who was U.S. Secretary of State from 1947 to 1949. Through the Marshall Plan, the United States sent steel to England and farm machinery to Turkey.

which Greek communists, among other groups, tried by force to prevent the restoration of the monarchy that had ruled that country before the war. At the same time, the Soviet Union exerted strong pressure on Turkey to share control of two important straits, the Bosporus and the Dardanelles.

The United States, under President Harry S. Truman, responded by supplying $400 million in military aid to Greece and Turkey. The Truman Doctrine, as it was called, became the basis of a new American policy of "containment," that is, preventing the spread of communism beyond its already established borders. Truman Doctrine aid helped Turkey resist Russian pressure. It also helped defeat anti-monarchical forces in Greece.

Further to contain communism and to help rebuild war-torn Europe, the United States launched the Marshall Plan in 1947. This was a broad program of economic aid originally offered to all European nations, including communist countries. Stalin saw it as an anticommunist move. He refused to let the satellite countries and the Soviet Union participate. Therefore, only Western European countries received Marshall Plan aid. It helped them recover economically and preserve their democratic institutions. It also deepened the division between Eastern and Western Europe.

The most dangerous incident in the Cold War was the Berlin blockade in 1948. The Soviet Union's acts broke Russian pledges, and the Western Allies responded strongly.

The peaceful ending of the Berlin blockade showed that both the Soviet Union and the United States wanted to avoid a third world war and nuclear holocaust. But that did not reduce fears that Stalin planned to conquer Western Europe. These fears stimulated the

CHANGES IN EUROPE AFTER WORLD WAR II

Added to Soviet Union

Added to Poland

Added to Yugoslavia

Added to Bulgaria

.... Boundary of Allied occupation forces, withdrawn 1955

0   100   200   300 MILES
0 100 200 300 KILOMETERS

N

NORWAY

SWEDEN

FINLAND

North Sea

Baltic Sea

DENMARK

ESTONIA

LATVIA

LITHUANIA

SOVIET

UNION

American Enclave

NETHERLANDS

British Zone

Danzig

EAST PRUSSIA

WHITE

RUSSIA

EAST Soviet Zone Berlin (Joint Occupancy)

BELG.

WEST GERMANY

French Zone

LUX.

GERMANY

FRANCE

American Zone

French Zone

SWITZERLAND

French Zone

POLAND

CZECHOSLOVAKIA

Vienna (Joint Occ.)

Soviet Zone

Amer. Zone

AUSTRIA

British Zone

To Czech.

RUTHENIA

BUCOVINA

BESSARABIA

HUNGARY

ROMANIA

(To France)

Trieste (Free City)

Zadar

YUGOSLAVIA

BULGARIA

ITALY

PELAGOSA IS. (To Yugoslavia)

SAZAN I. (To Albania)

ALBANIA

GREECE

DODECANESE IS. (To Greece)

Mediterranean Sea

development of the North Atlantic Treaty Organization (NATO) in 1949, made up of nine European nations plus Iceland, Canada, and the United States. Those nations agreed to defend each other if attacked, and they set up a NATO military force. Russia established its own military alliance, called the Warsaw Pact. It included the Soviet Union and all the communist countries of Eastern Europe under Russian control.

section review 2

1. What is meant by the term Cold War? Where did it begin?

2. Name two major issues on which the World War II Allies disagreed.

3. What were the purposes of the Truman Doctrine, Marshall Plan, and NATO?

4. What was the purpose of the Warsaw Pact?

3 The Soviets dominated Eastern Europe

The Soviet Union emerged from World War II having suffered enormous destruction. Despite this, the Soviet Union was still a superpower that had the most powerful army in Europe, control over most of Eastern Europe, and growing influence in world affairs.

The Soviet Union faced staggering problems in rebuilding itself. No country suffered more from World War II than the Soviet Union. In addition to the 20 million lives lost and the millions of homeless people, one-quarter of Soviet wealth in industries, schools, libraries, and other buildings had been wiped out.

The most important task facing the government was to rebuild the country and its economy. The Soviet government issued a new Five-Year Plan. Stalin wanted to overcome all the wartime damage in only five years, between 1946 and 1950. In the next Five-Year Plan, 1951 to 1955, he wanted to expand production beyond prewar levels.

These goals were only partly reached. By 1953, the Soviet output of steel, coal, and electricity had nearly doubled over that of 1940. But consumer goods were scarcer than they had been in the 1920s, a time of great scarcity.

Agriculture was in even worse shape. By 1953, farm production was only 10 percent higher than it had been in 1914, before the Russian revolution. Meanwhile, the population had grown by more than 20 percent.

The Soviets encouraged and supported communist governments in Eastern Europe. The Soviet government had political as well as economic goals. It wanted to secure the country's western borders by strengthening Soviet influence over Eastern Europe. This is why Bulgaria, Czechoslovakia, Hungary, Poland, and Romania were brought under Soviet control after World War II. The Soviet Union also took over Estonia, Latvia, and Lithuania and established strong influence over Finland.

WHAT'S IN A NAME?
CZECHOSLOVAKIA

The name Czechoslovakia means "land of the first slavs." The word *czech* means "beginners."

The one important exception to Soviet dominance in Eastern Europe was Yugoslavia. Led by Josip Broz, who called himself Tito [tē'tō], the Yugoslav Communist party set up a communist government without Soviet help. Tito had gained fame as a wartime leader against the Nazis. Yugoslavs

Tito posed for this picture in the Cabinet Room of the Yugoslav government in Belgrade. The painting behind him was one of his favorites. It shows a 16th-century rebellion by peasants against their feudal overlords in the part of the country where Tito was born.

united behind him to resist German invasion and occupation.

Tito's independence angered Stalin. Determined to destroy Tito, Stalin in 1948 shut off Yugoslavia from the rest of the communist world and ended all Soviet economic aid.

Tito, however, kept Yugoslavia independent and turned to Western countries for economic and military aid. Gradually, he relaxed some totalitarian government controls. He allowed private farming again. Tito also established workers' councils in industry and granted some civil rights to the people. Yugoslavia stayed a communist country, but it remained free of Soviet control and followed a moderate type of communism. Yugoslavia continued on its independent way after Tito's death in 1980.

If there is one place that symbolizes Russia to all the world, it is the Kremlin. For centuries, it has been the fortress where Russia's rulers have lived and worked.

The Kremlin covers 90 acres (36 hectares) in the center of Moscow. Started in the 1200s, it is shaped like a triangle and enclosed by red brick walls. The original wooden walls were replaced by brick ones in the late 1400s.

The Kremlin walls have an exotic look. They are notched at the top and are up to 70 feet (21 meters) high and 20 feet (6 meters) wide. The walls also contain 20 watchtowers and five gates, all of individual design.

The most famous of the Kremlin towers and gates is the Spaskaia, or Savior, gate which faces Red Square. The name Savior comes from the picture of Jesus that was painted over the entrance during tsarist times. In the early 1600s, a huge clock was installed, and a century later, Peter the Great added chimes. Today, every hour on the hour, the tower chimes play the "Soviet Hymn."

Inside the Kremlin walls are golden-domed cathedrals and brightly colored palaces. Three cathedrals are especially renowned. In the Cathedral of the Assumption the tsars were crowned. In the Cathedral of the Annunciation they were married. And in the Cathedral of the Archangel Michael, some 47 of the tsars were buried, too.

One of the most famous palaces is the Palace of Facets. It contains the lavishly decorated throne room and a great banquet hall. A second palace, the Armory, is now a museum. It holds the crown of Peter the Great and the wedding dress of Catherine the Great. A third, the Grand Palace, is where the tsars sometimes lived. Today it houses the Supreme Soviet of the U.S.S.R.

As it was in tsarist times, the Kremlin is still the main center of government for the country. But it is now also a national museum. With its magnificent buildings and breathtaking treasures of centuries past, the Kremlin is one of the spectacular sights of the world.

This view of the Kremlin shows the side that faces the Moscow River with the Grand Kremlin Palace, the Cathedrals of the Annunciation and Archangel Michael, and the Belfry of Ivan the Great. The tops of many buildings have gilded domes as *above left.* Inside the churches are many icons as *above right.*

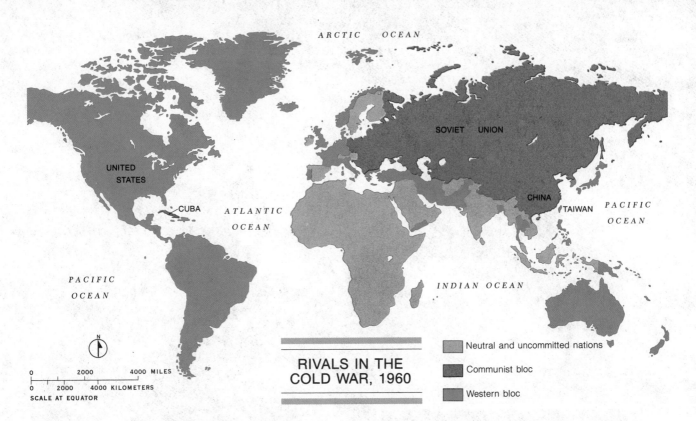

SOVIET UNION

UNITED STATES

CUBA

ATLANTIC OCEAN

PACIFIC OCEAN

CHINA

TAIWAN

PACIFIC OCEAN

INDIAN OCEAN

PACIFIC OCEAN

N

0   2000   4000 MILES

0   2000   4000 KILOMETERS

SCALE AT EQUATOR

RIVALS IN THE
COLD WAR, 1960

Neutral and uncommitted nations

Communist bloc

Western bloc

Stalin's death led to important changes in the Soviet Union. Stalin's death in 1953 touched off a struggle for power among the remaining leaders of the Soviet Communist party. In 1956, Nikita S. Khrushchev [krüsh-chôf'] won the struggle.

In February, 1956, Khrushchev rocked the communist world with a speech that blamed Stalin for many crimes against the Soviet people. De-Stalinization—playing down the greatness of Stalin—became official policy. This new policy brought other changes. Several forced-labor camps, begun in the 1930s, were closed. The secret police became somewhat less vital to the regime's success. Writers, artists, and composers enjoyed a little more freedom of expression. Cultural exchanges were begun with the West, and tourists from abroad were welcomed.

Khrushchev's policies reflected a changed Soviet society. The Five-Year Plans from 1945 through 1955 had stressed the manufacture of farm and factory equipment and other products of heavy industry. But few consumer goods—cars, TV sets, refrigerators, and clothes—were produced. Shortages of such goods became critical. The growing number of urban workers as well as the rising middle class of managers and professional people wanted a more comfortable life.

In the late 1950s and early 1960s, clothing and television sets became more available in the Soviet Union. A building program increased the numbers of housing units. Khrushchev also tried to raise farm production, but it barely kept up with population growth.

While increasing the supply of consumer goods, Khrushchev and other Soviet leaders continued to emphasize heavy industry, weapons, and space technology. In 1949, the Soviets exploded an atom bomb, and they had the hydrogen bomb by 1953. They launched the first satellite in orbit around the earth in 1957. In 1961, they put the first human into space.

645

Daily Life The decades after World War II saw the dawn of the space age. In the 1960s, American astronauts walked on the moon, and they left their space capsules and "walked" in space as *above left*. America's Landsat program made possible—and economical—the mapping of the whole globe for the first time. The Landsat view *inset*

above left shows the Nile River delta. The red area is inhabited, the light brown part is not. *Above right* is the space shuttle *Columbia* before its successful first launch in April, 1981. It brought the possibility of the industrial development of space. *Inset above right* is a model of the tiny Soviet *Sputnik* that began the space era.

Relations with countries of Eastern Europe became less rigid. In 1955, Khrushchev improved relations with Yugoslavia. In early 1956, Khrushchev said that communism could be achieved through ways other than those followed by the Soviet Union. These words had a dramatic impact on the Soviet satellite countries. Many of their people resented Soviet control and some now saw a chance to end Soviet domination.

In October, 1956, an armed rebellion began in Hungary against the ruling communist Soviet-supported government. Savage fighting swept the Hungarian capital. A new communist regime took over and renounced ties with the Soviet bloc. Khrushchev and other Soviet leaders proved unwilling to give up control, however. Soviet troops poured into Hungary, crushed the rebellion, and restored communist power under Soviet dominance. Thousands of people died, and 200,000 escaped to the West. The Hungarian uprising led the Soviet Union to increase political pressure on its satellite countries.

In 1959, Cuba became a communist nation and received Soviet aid and support. The aid included missile bases, which the United States discovered in 1962. In a tense showdown, President John F. Kennedy made it clear that the United States would not let the missiles remain. Khrushchev finally withdrew the missiles in exchange for a pledge that the United States would not invade Cuba.

Adding to the tension of the Cold War was the Soviet erection of the Berlin Wall in 1961. After the Berlin airlift of 1948, things quieted down in this divided city. By 1960, West Germany had become an economically strong country. Communist East Germany, on the other hand, was not as prosperous and suffered under an oppressive government. Consequently, many East Germans fled to West Germany by way of West Berlin. In 1960, 4,000 East Germans fled each week.

Budapest, the capital of Hungary, was the site of much bitter fighting during the Hungarian uprising.

The Soviet Union wanted this migration to stop. In 1961, a giant wall was built to stop East Germans from reaching West Berlin. The Berlin Wall has proved a sturdy obstacle. Nonetheless, some have found ways to dodge the armed East German guards and scale the wall to freedom.

The crises of the early 1960s fueled talk about the possibility of nuclear war between the superpowers. Since neither side claimed to want such a confrontation, in 1961 the nations set up an emergency hot line between Washington and Moscow. Such a line, it was thought, would help prevent "accidental" war. In the same year, the superpowers signed a nuclear test ban treaty. It forbade nuclear tests in the atmosphere, in outer space, and under water.

section review 3

1. How did World War II affect the Soviet Union? In what ways did the new Five-Year Plans succeed? In what ways did they fail?

2. What changes took place in the Soviet Union after Nikita Khrushchev became leader?

3. How did the Soviets react to the uprising in Hungary? How did relations between the Soviet Union and its satellites change after the uprising?

4. What was the missile crisis of 1962? How was it resolved?

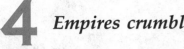

4 Empires crumbled in Asia

As the Cold War developed in Europe, political change took place in Asia. One of the most important changes was the crumbling of the European and Japanese empires. The old European colonies in Asia demanded independence. At the same time, the European colonial powers were exhausted by World War II and were no longer able to control their former colonies.

India and Pakistan became independent countries. India, the "jewel of the British Empire" for nearly 200 years, was the first major European colony to gain independence after World War II. The British hoped the huge Indian subcontinent would stay politically united under one government, but that proved impossible.

India's population of about 400 million people spoke more than fourteen different languages. Indians were also divided by deep religious differences. Muslims made up 25 percent of the population. As a minority, Muslims feared that the vastly larger number of Hindus might follow a policy of persecution toward them. So the Muslims demanded an independent state of their own.

Because of this and other serious divisions, the British eventually established two countries. One, India, was mostly Hindu, while the other, Pakistan, was mostly Muslim.

The creation of India and Pakistan did not bring peace. Religious fanatics on both sides rioted, and in 1947, at least 500 thousand people died. When Mohandas K. Gandhi, the leader of the Indian independence movement, tried to make peace between the Hindus and Muslims in 1948, he was killed by a religious fanatic. Following Gandhi's assassination, rioting died out. However, the issue of control of the area called Kashmir continued to cause conflict between the two new nations.

India chose a democratic form of government. Of the two new states, India was the larger, with an area one-third the size of the United States. Most of the people of India lived in poverty. Food shortages, even famine, were constant threats. And the population was growing at the rate of about 10 million per year.

The government introduced measures for family planning to slow down population growth. It also started a program of land reform to increase food production and an industrialization program to diversify the economy and provide more jobs.

Indians chose to solve their problems under a democratic government. Led by Jawaharlal Nehru [nā'rü], the first prime minister, the government practiced state planning. But it also fostered free enterprise and a multiparty political system. The Indian government's goal was a semi-socialist state and gradual economic development.

Nehru remained prime minister until his death in 1964. During his term of office, important gains were made in food production and industrialization, and democracy flourished. But the living standard of most people remained practically unchanged because of the continued increase in population.

Military dictatorship developed in Pakistan. Unlike India, Pakistan suffered from political instability after independence. In 1958, however, a military leader, General Mohammad Ayub Khan [ä yüb kän'], seized control of the government. Politics in Pakistan became more stable under his dictatorial rule.

Like India, Pakistan was a poor country. It had few railroads or roads and little industry. Some 80 percent of the people were farmers who barely made a living from their extremely tiny plots of usable farm land.

In the 1960s, Pakistan enjoyed some economic progress. A land-reform program began. Other reforms in education and transportation followed. And a new constitution was written.

Democracy, however, did not flourish in Pakistan. Heads of government, whether military or civilian, tended to be dictatorial.

Countries of Southeast Asia demanded independence. Southeast Asia lies east of India. Before World War II, most of this complex region was divided among four empires—the British, the French, the Dutch, and the American.

During World War II, all of Southeast Asia was conquered by Japan and became part of the Japanese empire. Japanese rule lasted only three years, but in that period, the Japanese allowed local leaders to take over important government posts. Near the end of the war, Japan trained local troops and officers to fight the Allies. After the Japanese surrendered and before the European colonial powers could reestablish control, many of these popular local leaders proclaimed their countries to be independent. When

In emerging India, old farming methods are used along side more modern ones.

European powers brought in troops to reestablish their control, conflict resulted.

In some cases, however, independence came peacefully. The United States, faithful to a prewar promise, gave independence to the Philippines in 1948. Britain gave independence to Burma, Malaya, part of Borneo, and Singapore over a period of years.

In other areas of Southeast Asia, however, independence came only after bitter fighting. The longest colonial wars were fought in Indonesia (formerly the Dutch East Indies) against the Dutch and in Indochina against the French.

Indonesia won its freedom. In Indonesia, the Dutch fought local nationalists for four years. Then in 1949, the Dutch finally granted independence to Indonesia.

Following independence, Indonesia had many difficulties. Food supply did not keep up with population growth. Exports dropped, inflation increased, and rebellions against the government broke out. Indonesia's president, Sukarno [sü kär′nō], came to believe that democracy could not solve these problems quickly enough. In 1963, supported by the army, Sukarno became absolute ruler for life. All opposition political parties were banned.

Sukarno became increasingly procommunist. The army feared a communist takeover. As a result, in 1965 hundreds of thousands of Indonesians suspected of being communist were killed. A military regime led by General Suharto eventually took over the government in 1967.

Vietnamese fought a long war. After Japan was defeated in World War II, France tried to reclaim control in Indochina. In 1946, however, it was forced to grant some self-rule to Laos and Cambodia. The status of Vietnam, the third political unit in French Indochina, remained unsettled. There, the most effective anti-colonial group was the Viet Minh

Many nations who followed neither the American nor Soviet line came to be known as nonaligned nations. In 1961, Sukarno of Indonesia and Nehru of India met in Yugoslavia at a conference for heads of nonaligned countries.

French troops in Vietnam fought continual battles to return the area to colonial status.

[vē yet′ män′] led by Ho Chi Minh, a communist who had proclaimed independence for the Democratic Republic of Vietnam.

The French refused to recognize Ho Chi Minh's government, and fighting began in 1946. The war lasted until 1954, ending with French defeat. Later that year, agreements were signed at Geneva, Switzerland, that gave full independence to Laos and Cambodia and called for free elections in Vietnam. A temporary line was drawn at the 17th parallel dividing Vietnam into north and south.

Elections were never held. Ho's communist government controlled the north, and an anticommunist government ruled the south. In 1957, rebellion against the South Vietnamese government began, and North Vietnam eventually aided it. The Soviet Union supported North Vietnam. The United States backed the government of South Vietnam, believing that by doing so it could prevent the spread of communism into other areas of Southeast Asia. This was in keeping with the American policy of the containment of communism.

Japan lost an empire and became a democracy. The aftermath of World War II brought an end to the European empires in Asia. But defeat in the war also destroyed the Japanese empire. Japan now controlled only its original home islands. Many Japanese were hungry and ill-clothed. Cities, factories, and railroads had been bombed, and the economy had collapsed.

Allied troops, almost entirely from the United States, occupied the country. Japan was given a new constitution in 1946 and soon developed into the leading democratic country in East Asia.

In 1951, the United States and forty-seven other countries (not including the Soviet Union) signed a peace treaty with Japan that restored Japanese independence and ended the American occupation. The treaty also committed the United States to defend Japan.

Throughout the 1950s and 1960s, Japan's new democratic system became firmly established, and remarkable economic growth took place. By 1962, economic output had more than doubled. Foreign trade expanded greatly, and the standard of living of the Japanese people increased greatly, too.

section review 4

1. Why did the British divide India into two countries? Were the two countries able to maintain peaceful relations? Why?

2. Who was India's first prime minister? What program did he follow?

3. What kind of government did Pakistan have?

4. How did Japan become a democracy?

5 Communists came to power in China

As we saw in Chapter 31, a struggle for control of China had been going on between Nationalists and Communists since the 1930s. The two sides temporarily stopped their civil war in 1937 after Japan attacked China. The temporary truce lasted until the end of World War II and the defeat of the Japanese in 1945.

A Communist revolution triumphed in China. Late in 1945, civil war broke out again between the Nationalist government in China, led by Chiang Kai-shek [chyäng' kī'shek], and the Chinese Communists, led by Mao Tse-tung [mä'ō dzŭ'dŭng']. Mao had the support of the peasant masses. And while the United States supported Chiang and the Nationalist government, it tried to bring the two sides together. The suggestion of a coalition—or cooperative—government, however, was turned down.

By 1949 the Communists had conquered most of China. In October of that year, they proclaimed the birth of the People's Republic of China. It was the most populous communist state in the world.

Chiang and his remaining forces fled to the island of Taiwan. There they set up the Nationalist Chinese government in exile. Chiang died on Taiwan in 1975, and his son took over the government.

After 1949, the United States continued to support the Nationalist regime on Taiwan as the only legitimate Chinese government. It refused to recognize Mao's government and used its influence to prevent the UN from admitting the People's Republic as a member. The United States also set up the Southeast Asia Treaty Organization, aimed at containing communism in China.

China and the United States clashed in Korea. Korea, like Germany, had been "temporarily" divided at the end of World War II, with the 38th parallel of latitude as the boundary line. The Soviet Union controlled the northern part of the country. The United States controlled the southern part. The Soviets set up a communist government in the north. They refused a United States proposal to create a unified nation by holding elections in all of Korea under UN supervision. Soviet and American occupation forces later withdrew from Korea.

In June, 1950, in an effort to unify the country by force, North Korea invaded South Korea. The United Nations called the invasion an "act of aggression." During a Soviet boycott of the UN Security Council, the United States got that body to take military action. Altogether, sixteen UN members sent troops to Korea, although by far the largest number of troops came from the United States.

UN troops pushed North Korean forces back north of the 38th parallel and toward the Yalu River, which separated Korea from China. Thus, in November, 1950, to protect its border and to help the North Koreans

During the brutal battles in Korea in 1951, UN and communist troops became deadlocked, winning and losing the same gray, muddy hills near the 38th parallel.

KOREA, 1953

China poured 200 thousand troops into Korea. They drove UN forces back south to the 38th parallel.

The conflict continued until July, 1953. At that time, an armistice (temporary peace agreement) was signed. The armistice left Korea divided in the same way it had been before the conflict began.

Chinese society changed greatly. The People's Republic of China, with some 600 million people, in 1950 was the largest nation in the world. Like other communist countries, its government was a totalitarian dictatorship. All power was concentrated in the Communist Party's Central Committee, which was led by Chairman Mao Tse-tung. Thousands of people who resisted the establishment of the communist regime were executed or imprisoned.

Mao was determined to transform China into a Marxist nation, communist in every respect. He destroyed the landlord class and reformed land ownership. He lowered rents

Daily Life

Everyday life in China changed greatly after the Communists came to power. Communist rule brought study groups of Mao's writings. This posed view of farmworkers, *right,* shows them among hand-stacked haystacks. Communist rule also brought women into the army for the first time. By 1958 they marched beside the men in parades such as the one, *lower right,* in Ulan Bator, Mongolia, to celebrate Independence Day. And the arts were also used to promote communist ideas. The ballet, *lower left,* called "Red Detachment of Women," tells of an early uprising against the Nationalist government.

and built schools. The Communists also tried to build up Chinese industrial and military strength as quickly as possible.

In 1957, Mao launched the "Great Leap Forward," aimed at increasing food and industrial production at the same time. To increase the amount of food produced, Communist leaders established *agricultural collectives* of several hundred farm families. Other collectives mobilized people for road building and irrigation.

The next step was the establishment of *communes*. At first, these were made up of 4,000 to 5,000 farm or industrial families. Each commune was directed by political leaders who answered to the government. But the communes were too large, inefficient, and impersonal. In addition, bad weather and floods damaged crops and resulted in food shortages in 1959. The "Great Leap Forward" failed.

Faced with these setbacks, Chinese leaders greatly reduced the size of the communes in the early 1960s. They also slowed down the pace of industrial growth and put more resources into agricultural improvement.

Following communist victory in China, the Soviet Union helped that nation with military, industrial, and technical aid. By the end of the 1950s, though, a split had developed. There were disputes about borders, quarrels over which nation was following true communist doctrine, and arguments over which nation deserved the role of leader of the communist world. In the early 1960s, Soviet advisers in China were sent home.

Mao revived the revolutionary spirit. By the mid-1960s, though life was still hard, most Chinese had somewhat better living conditions. Food was rationed, but few people starved. Health conditions had improved. The average Chinese could buy small consumer goods, such as a bicycle and a sewing machine.

Mao began to fear that the Chinese people were losing their revolutionary spirit and becoming too concerned with the "easy life." He feared that the Chinese might become "bourgeois," that is, attached to middle-class values.

In 1966, Mao began the "Great Proletarian Cultural Revolution." This involved a purge of intellectuals whom he felt were lukewarm in their devotion to true communism. Later that year, schools were closed. University students and teachers were sent into the countryside to do farm work alongside the peasants. Hundreds of thousands of teenagers were organized into groups called the Red Guards. They were told they were crusaders for a better China. The young people attacked teachers, party officials, and others who held to "old ideas, old culture, old customs, and old habits."

As the great purge shook the nation, violent uprisings broke out in some cities. Peasants and Red Guards clashed in the countryside. Some regional army commanders refused to obey orders from the central government. Ironically, the order and unity that had been so painfully imposed by the Communists were breaking down.

Late in 1968, Mao realized that the Cultural Revolution was out of control. He stopped it by using the army to restore order. The Red Guards were disbanded. He reopened schools and revived industry. The year 1969 was one of national recuperation.

section review 5

1. Why were the Chinese Communists able to win control of China?

2. Why did America and China clash in Korea?

3. What was the "Great Leap Forward"? What changes were made in agriculture? Were they successful?

4. What was the "Great Proletarian Cultural Revolution"? What were some of its results?

Section Summaries

1. Two superpowers dominated world relations. The word "superpower" came into use after World War II to describe the United States and the Soviet Union. The existence of only two superpowers in the world affected international relations in the postwar world. A new international organization, the United Nations, was created to keep the peace. Its powers were limited but the UN became an important forum for discussion.

2. A Cold War began in Europe. After World War II, sharp differences developed between the former wartime Allies over policies toward Germany and Eastern Europe. These differences led to a rivalry called the Cold War. In 1949, the United States formed NATO, a military alliance of other Western countries to guard against the danger of communist aggression in Western Europe. On its side, the Soviet Union formed the Warsaw Pact.

3. The Soviets dominated Eastern Europe. Economically, the Soviet Union suffered greatly from World War II and recovered very slowly. But politically and militarily, the U.S.S.R. was one of the two strongest nations of the world in 1945. To secure its western borders and to spread communism, it encouraged and supported Soviet-style governments in Eastern Europe and eventually controlled all of Eastern Europe. Only Yugoslavia managed some degree of independence. When Hungary tried to shake Soviet control, the revolt was crushed.

4. Empires crumbled in Asia. With independence, the former British colony of India split apart into two unfriendly states: India, mainly Hindu, and Pakistan, mainly Muslim. Both countries were poor and underdeveloped. In addition, Pakistan was politically unstable. Independence also came to Indonesia, Malaysia, and Burma. After a long war Vietnam gained freedom from France. Under American guidance, Japan became a democratic nation.

5. Communists came to power in China. When World War II ended, civil war broke out again in China between the Nationalists and Communists. The Communists won in 1949. Mao Tse-tung then transformed China into a Marxist nation. Special efforts were made to push the development of industry and agriculture. In the late 1960s, Mao tried to revive the revolutionary spirit through a series of purges called the "Great Proletarian Cultural Revolution."

Who? What? When? Where?

1. Place these events in chronological order, beginning with the earliest:
   a. Soviet soldiers crushed the Hungarian uprising.
   b. The United Nations charter was signed.
   c. The French were defeated in Indochina.
   d. North Korea invaded South Korea.
   e. The Soviet Union began the Berlin blockade.
   f. Mao began the Great Proletarian Cultural Revolution.
   g. Communists came to power in Cuba.
   h. The Cuban missile crisis took place.

2. Write sentences that give the meanings of each of these terms:
   a. Cold War   d. de-Stalinization
   b. communes   e. Five-Year Plan
   c. containment   f. hot line
                        g. superpowers

3. What were the purposes of the Truman Doctrine, NATO, and the Marshall Plan?

4. What kind of special relationship did Tito and Yugoslavia create with the Soviet Union?

5. Name the country led by each of these men:
   a. Ho Chi Minh
   b. Mohammad Ayub Khan
   c. Nikita Khrushchev
   d. Mao Tse-tung
   e. Jawaharlal Nehru
   f. Tito
   g. Harry Truman

Questions for Critical Thinking

1. Why did Khrushchev change the Soviet policy that all communist countries must follow Moscow's rule?

2. Why did journalists call the era of conflicts between the United States and the Soviet Union a cold war?

3. Why did the United States formulate the Truman Doctrine and the Marshall Plan to help Europe recover from World War II?

4. What caused the collapse of the old colonial empires after World War II?

Skill Activities

1. Read *Jawaharlal Nehru: The Brahman from Kashmir* by Emil Lengyel to learn more about one of India's first leaders. (Watts, 1968)

2. In groups of three, pretend to be a representative from the United States, a representative from the Soviet Union, and a farmer from a poor country. The two representatives should try to convince the farmer which country has the best plan for a better life. Then all the "farmers" in the class should vote to decide whether the poor country will have a communist government or a democratic one.

3. Make a chart of the accomplishments of the United States and the Soviet Union in the field of space exploration. The chart should show what the achievement is, what year it took place in, and which nation was involved.

4. Write a report on the United Nations. Include a list of all of the men who have served in the role of Secretary General. Use an almanac to find out how many member nations there are this year and which nations are serving on the Security Council. Also describe two or more projects that are now being done by the UN.

chapter **33** *quiz*

Section 1

1. True or false: At the end of World War II, France, the Soviet Union, China, and the United States emerged as superpowers.

2. All members of the United Nations are represented in the: a. General Assembly, b. the Security Council, c. the General Council

Section 2

3. True or false: After World War II, Berlin was occupied jointly by France, Britain, the Soviet Union, and the United States.

4. The countries that received aid from the United States through the Marshall Plan were: a. the Soviet satellites, b. only Greece and Japan, c. the nations of Western Europe

Section 3

5. After Stalin's death, the man who emerged as leader of the Soviet Union was: a. Kennedy, b. Tito, c. Khrushchev

6. In 1956, open rebellion against Soviet domination broke out in: a. Cuba, b. Germany, c. Hungary

Section 4

7. Colonial India was divided into two nations because of problems of: a. politics, b. language, c. religion

8. Ho Chi Minh was the leader of: a. North Vietnam, b. Indonesia, c. Pakistan

9. During occupation by Allied troops, Japan became a: a. democracy, b. colony, c. dictatorship

Section 5

10. True or false: The armistice of 1953 divided Korea as it had been before the conflict.

11. True or false: China and the Soviet Union quarreled over which nation should act as leader of the communist world.

12. True or false: Mao's Great Leap Forward was a failure.

THE FORGING OF NATIONS IN THE MIDDLE EAST AND AFRICA

The coming of independence to former colonies was a cause for great celebration. This Independence Day celebration was in Nigeria.

A change in status from colony to nationhood characterized the Middle East and Africa as well as parts of Asia in the postwar period. In addition, a new nation, Israel, arose in the Middle East.

In Africa and the Middle East, the determination to throw off European control became overpowering. Peter Abrahams, an African writer, dramatically expressed this feeling in his novel, *A Wreath for Udomo:*

Mother Africa! Oh, Mother Africa, make me strong for the work I must do! Don't forget me in the many you nurse. I would make you great. I would have the world respect you and your children. I would have the sun of freedom shine over you once more.

As it turned out, the development of nations in Africa and the Middle East proved to be much more difficult than gaining independence. Problems of widespread illiteracy, poverty, tribal rivalries, and conflicts with neighbors often led to political instability, frequent changes in government, and military dictatorships.

This chapter tells how:

1. Arab Muslims and Jewish Zionists began nations.

2. The Middle East was troubled by conflict and instability.

3. Africans created a variety of governments.

4. The struggle for black rule reached southern Africa.

1 Arab Muslims and Jewish Zionists began nations

World War II greatly changed the Middle East. It stimulated nationalism and speeded up the movement to throw off the last remains of European control. After the war, two new factors were added. One was the creation of Israel. The other was the rivalry of the United States and the Soviet Union for influence in the Middle East.

Arab Muslims ended colonialism. Among the Arab Muslim states, only Egypt, Iraq, Saudi Arabia, and Yemen had independence—at least in name—before World War II. Between 1944 and 1956, Syria, Jordan, Libya, Tunisia, Morocco, and Sudan all gained full independence from European powers.

In Algeria, the situation was especially complicated. France considered Algeria to be a part of France, not a colony. The area contained some 10 million Algerians. One million of these were of European descent, mostly French. They owned nearly all of the best land and most of the businesses. The rest of the Algerian population, some 9 million, were mostly Arabs. They had little wealth. Over the years, an Algerian nationalist movement developed, demanding independence. And in 1954, civil war broke out between the Arabs and French. Both sides used terrorism and torture. After seven years of fighting, the French president, Charles de Gaulle, made peace with nationalist leaders. Algeria then was given its independence in 1962.

In Egypt, the army overthrew the corrupt rule of King Farouk in 1952. Colonel Gamal Abdel Nasser was one of the leaders of the plot. He officially became president in 1956. To help Egypt's poor, Nasser sought a more equal distribution of wealth. He promoted land reforms, increased the pace of industrialization, and developed natural resources.

One of Nasser's chief projects was a huge dam and electrical power station on the Nile River near Aswan. The United States and Britain withdrew their offer to finance the dam in 1956 because Nasser bought military equipment from Czechoslovakia, a communist nation. Nasser retaliated by *nationalizing*, that is, by taking over, the Suez Canal. This act brought an attack on Egypt by Britain, France, and the new nation of Israel in 1956. For a time, the world teetered on the brink of a major war. But quick action by the UN, supported by Russia and the United States, forced a cease-fire. Egypt kept control of the canal and the Soviets financed the Aswan High Dam, which was completed in 1970.

Jews founded the state of Israel. In 1945, Britain still controlled all of Palestine as a mandate under the League of Nations. Large numbers of Jewish refugees from Europe began to pour into Palestine at the end of World War II. Many of them were homeless survivors of the Nazi Holocaust. They looked to Palestine as their ancient homeland, a place where they would no longer suffer from the persecution they had endured for so long in Europe. But the Arabs living in Palestine became fearful as they saw the Jewish minority grow from only about a tenth of the population to nearly a third of the total population of the area.

To calm the fears of the Arabs, Britain tried to limit Jewish immigration which angered the Jews. In an effort to find a solution, Britain proposed that Palestine be partitioned between Arabs and Jews, but the Arabs denounced partition. As a result, beginning in 1945 both Jewish and Arab organizations in Palestine engaged in terrorism and guerrilla warfare against the British and against each other. When the British took the matter to the United Nations, it too recommended partition.

In 1947, the British announced their withdrawal from Palestine. On the day they withdrew in 1948, the Jews proclaimed the state of Israel. Almost at once seven Arab countries attacked Israel, but the new nation proved to be surprisingly strong. In 1949, UN mediator Ralph Bunche helped bring about an armistice.

The Israelis developed modern industry and converted huge areas of desert into fertile lands on which they grew citrus and other crops. They enacted a democratic constitution and built up powerful military forces.

Palestinian Arabs became refugees. Israel now controlled the larger part of what had been Palestine, including part of Jerusalem.

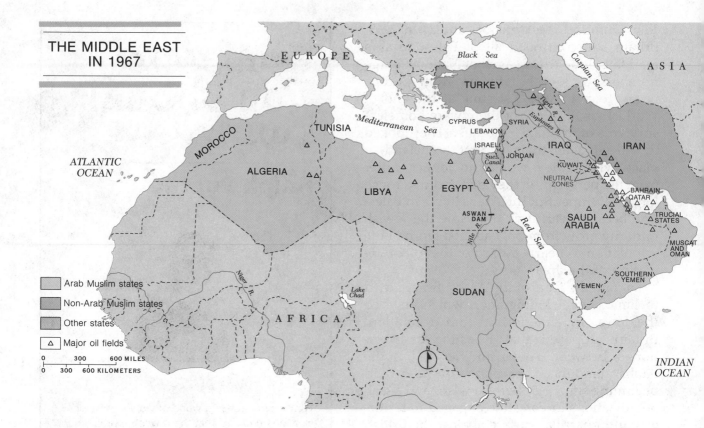

EUROPE

Black Sea

Caspian Sea

ASIA

TURKEY

Mediterranean Sea

CYPRUS

Tigris R.

Euphrates R.

SYRIA

LEBANON

ISRAEL

IRAQ

IRAN

TUNISIA

MOROCCO

ATLANTIC
OCEAN

ALGERIA

LIBYA

EGYPT

Suez
Canal

JORDAN

KUWAIT

NEUTRAL
ZONES

BAHRAIN
QATAR

TRUCIAL
STATES

ASWAN
DAM

Nile R.

Red Sea

SAUDI
ARABIA

MUSCAT
AND
OMAN

SOUTHERN
YEMEN

YEMEN

SUDAN

Niger R.

Lake
Chad

AFRICA

INDIAN
OCEAN

Arab Muslim states

Non-Arab Muslim states

Other states

△ Major oil fields

0   300   600 MILES

0   300   600 KILOMETERS

During the 1947–48 war, more than 700 thousand Palestinian Arabs fled their homes. These refugees were housed in makeshift camps run by the UN in nearby Arab lands.

The misery of the Palestinian refugees developed into an explosive force in the Middle East. The Palestinians became more militant. In 1964, the refugees created the Palestine Liberation Organization. The PLO said it was a government in exile and spoke for 2.5 million Palestinians. It refused to recognize the existence of Israel.

Arabs and Israelis went to war again. In June, 1967, thinking that Egypt, Syria, and Jordan were planning an attack, Israel struck first. In a six-day war, the Israelis destroyed the Egyptian air force and defeated the armies of all three Arab states. The Israelis

took possession of Arab territories, including the West Bank of the Jordan River, the Jordanian sector of the city of Jerusalem, and the entire Sinai peninsula. More than a million more Arabs now lived under Israeli occupation. After 1967, the main objective of the Arab states was to oust Israel from the newly occupied territories.

In the next few years, no progress was made toward a lasting peace. Egypt's new leader, Anwar Sadat [än wär' sà dat'], who came to power after Nasser's death in 1970, insisted that Israel withdraw from all lands it had taken in 1967. Only then would Egypt agree to negotiate a peace treaty. Israel refused to withdraw until a peace treaty was made in which the Arab states finally recognized Israel's legal existence. And the PLO demanded that an independent Palestinian state be established on the West Bank of the

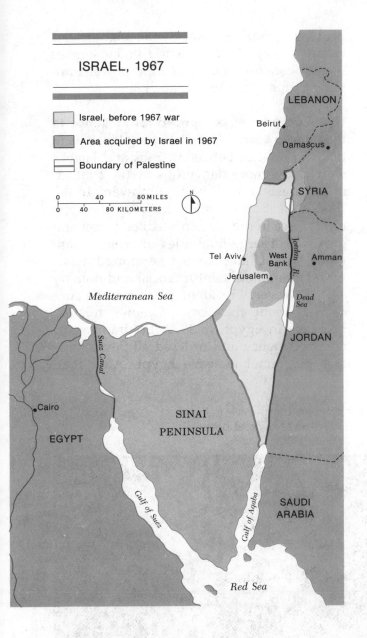

ISRAEL, 1967

Israel, before 1967 war

Area acquired by Israel in 1967

Boundary of Palestine

0   40   80 MILES
0   40   80 KILOMETERS

N

LEBANON

Beirut

Damascus

SYRIA

Tel Aviv

West Bank

Amman

Jerusalem

Jordan R.

Dead Sea

JORDAN

Mediterranean Sea

Suez Canal

Cairo

EGYPT

SINAI PENINSULA

Gulf of Suez

Gulf of Aqaba

SAUDI ARABIA

Red Sea

All the oil-producing Arab countries, which had grown greatly in power since 1945, now came to the aid of Egypt and Syria with a new strategic weapon. They imposed an embargo on the shipment of oil. They hoped this would pressure the United States and Western European nations into demanding Israeli withdrawal from the occupied territories. The embargo was lifted early in 1974, but producing nations now quadrupled the price of oil. The embargo, the cutback in production, and the sudden rise in oil prices deeply affected both industrialized and developing nations.

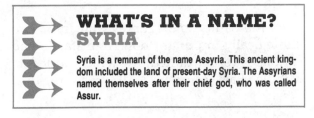

WHAT'S IN A NAME?
SYRIA

Syria is a remnant of the name Assyria. This ancient kingdom included the land of present-day Syria. The Assyrians named themselves after their chief god, who was called Assur.

Meanwhile, guided by the United States, Egypt and Israel agreed to a truce, and the fighting ended. The Suez Canal was reopened, and Israel gave up some occupied territory in the Sinai and on the Syrian border. At the same time, the PLO continued to push for an independent state and engaged in terrorist activities against the Israelis. The Israelis retaliated with ground and air attacks on PLO camps.

Jordan River. The Arab states supported the PLO, as did the Soviet Union, and later, the UN.

In 1973, Egypt and Syria again attacked Israel. The Israelis were driven back from the Suez Canal. But they won strategically important territory from the Syrians and then launched a counterattack against Egypt by crossing the Suez Canal.

section review 1

1. How did Algeria gain its independence?

2. What major political changes took place in Egypt in 1952? Who was the new leader? What was his program?

3. How and when was the state of Israel created? Why did the Arabs oppose it?

4. What is the PLO? When did it come into being? What are its goals?

2 The Middle East was troubled by conflict and instability

The hostility between Israel and the Arab states was the single most important cause of tension in the Middle East. It was not, however, the only one. Continuing rifts among the Arab states themselves also led to problems. Border clashes occurred periodically between Egypt and Libya, between Iraq and Kuwait, and between Syria and Jordan. In 1975, a civil war between Christians and Muslims broke out in Lebanon, eventually bringing intervention by Syria and the PLO.

At the same time, Turkey and Iran, two strategically important non-Arab states, had serious internal difficulties which added to Middle East tensions. All these regional problems took on worldwide significance because so much of the world's oil resources were there and because of superpower competition for influence in the area.

The superpowers competed for influence in the Middle East. The deepening tensions in the Middle East between Arabs and Israelis were made more dangerous by the conflicting interests of the two superpowers. In the 1960s, the Soviet Union built up a strong naval force in the eastern Mediterranean and gave Egypt large quantities of arms. Meanwhile, the United States supported Israel with large amounts of financial and military aid. However, President Sadat became concerned about the Soviet Union's military presence in Egypt. In 1972, he dramatically reversed policy and ordered all Soviet military personnel to leave Egypt. After that,

The Lebanese civil war brought great destruction to the countryside and especially to the capital, Beirut. Once known as the "Paris of the Middle East" because of its great beauty, much of Beirut now lies in ruin.

Egypt drew closer to the United States. Some other Arab states, however, continued to rely on the Soviet Union.

Egypt and Israel made peace. President Sadat boldly flew to Jerusalem in 1977 and personally pleaded for peace before the Israeli parliament. After lengthy discussions in the United States between President Carter, President Sadat, and Israeli Prime Minister Begin, Egypt and Israel signed a formal peace treaty in March, 1979. Egypt thus became the first Arab country to recognize the legal existence of Israel. Israel agreed to return all of the Sinai to Egypt, and both nations pledged to work toward a solution of the Palestinian problem. Two years later, fanatics assassinated President Sadat in Cairo, the capital of Egypt. Saddened Egyptian voters then elected Hosni Mubarak to be the new president of Egypt.

Israel invaded Lebanon. PLO and Syrian forces had occupied Lebanon since the 1975-1976 civil war. To Israel, they posed a serious threat. In 1982, Israel invaded Lebanon and expelled the PLO and Syrian fighters from Beirut. Still unresolved was the status of the Gaza and West Bank Palestinians.

Turkey and Iran were strategically important. Two Muslim states in the Middle East were non-Arab. They were Turkey and Iran, whose populations were predominantly Turkish and Persian. Both countries were of great strategic importance. Turkey had a common border with the Soviet Union and also controlled the straits between the Black Sea and the Mediterranean. As a member of the North Atlantic Treaty Organization, Tur-

In a colorful ceremony on the White House lawn, Jimmy Carter presided over the signing by Anwar Sadat and Menachem Begin of the Egyptian-Israeli treaty.

Daily Life

After World War II, Western culture spread around the globe. American clothing, especially blue jeans, became a part of life everywhere. The mother and son on Tokyo's Ginza Street, *top right,* show how Western clothing changed the styles in Japan. The Japanese also adopted the American game of baseball, *center.* It became as popular in Japan as it was in the United States. Western medical discoveries changed world health standards, too. Jonas Salk, *below right,* created a vaccine for polio. Within a few years, this terrible disease was almost eliminated worldwide. At the same time, the once-mighty colonial empires, especially of the Europeans, gave way to independent nations in Africa and Asia. Elizabeth II, *far right,* was crowned in London's Westminster Abbey in 1952. But the British Empire that became hers was not nearly so large and grand as the one that had been ruled by her ancestors. However, many former colonies began Western-style governments once they achieved independence. And Western music, especially rock, was heard everywhere. Britain's rock group called the Beatles, *top far right,* shot to fame during the 1960s. They became perhaps the most popular musicians of all times.

key was a vital link in Western defenses.

Iran had strategic importance because of its large oil resources and its location on the Persian Gulf, where the world's greatest concentration of oil reserves were found. Iran also shared a border with the Soviet Union.

Turkey faced internal instability. Turkey and Iran experienced rapid modernization. The majority of the population in each country was rural, traditionally Muslim, and conservative. In the 1920s and 1930s, leaders in both countries began programs of modernization, which continued after World War II. However, democracy in Turkey was weak, and there were frequent changes in government. Internal stability was threatened by serious economic problems.

In the years after World War II, modernization made the average Turk literate and politically aware. His or her individual expectations rose, but the economy could not keep pace. Frustration resulted, and Turkey suffered from constant political and social turmoil, with great loss of life and property. In 1980, the military seized power and tried to restore order.

A revolution took place in Iran. In Iran, the man most responsible for modernization was Muhammad Reza Pahlavi, who became shah in 1941. Investing money from large oil profits, the shah in 1960 began a program of reform and industrial development. He built factories, schools, and superhighways. He also emancipated women from some traditional Muslim restrictions. An economic boom began, but the new wealth was distributed unequally.

The shah used dictatorial methods to promote modernization. Those who opposed or criticized him were arrested and often tortured by the secret police. Many of these were members of the new and educated middle class that the shah's own modernization

Ayatollah Khomeini

had created. In the 1960s and 1970s, the shah sent thousands of Iranian students to Western universities where, among other things, they learned democratic ways. Upon returning to Iran, many joined the opposition to the shah's dictatorship. In the mid-1970s, the shah also began a program of enormous military expenditures to make Iran the strongest power in the Persian Gulf. High inflation set in, and unrest began to mount.

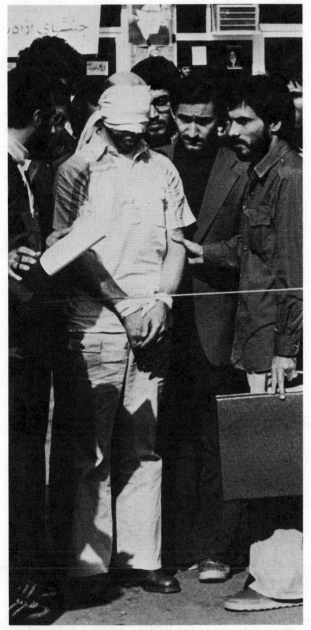

The Iranian militants who seized the American embassy in Teheran quickly learned how to use the 53 hostages to get attention. Here a blindfolded hostage is brought to the gates of the embassy where he can be photographed easily by newspeople.

The strongest opposition came from Muslim religious leaders. You will recall that in Islam religious rulers were also political rulers. In Iran, the religious leaders saw their authority being undermined by civil courts, which had replaced those run by the Muslim clergy. The religious leaders felt the shah's programs of national modernization and emancipation for women threatened traditional religious values. The religious leaders also resented the shah's land reform program, which took land from them to be redistributed among peasants.

Early in 1979, violent demonstrations forced the shah to leave Iran. The monarchy was ended, and a revolutionary government was established.

Under the Ayatollah Ruhollah Khomeini, a 79-year-old extremist religious leader, efforts were made to create an Islamic republic. But central governmental authority broke down. In November, 1979, militants seized the American embassy in the capital city of Teheran and took more than fifty Americans hostage. After prolonged negotiation, the hostages were freed in January, 1981.

As Iran struggled to regain internal stability, her weakness led Iraq, a hostile Arab neighbor, to launch war in September, 1980. The aim of Iraq was to become the dominant power in the Persian Gulf. But that aim was frustrated by the fierce resistance of Iran.

section review 2

1. How did the two superpowers compete in the Middle East?

2. Which Arab nation made peace with Israel? What problems stood in the way of peace between Israel and the other Arab nations?

3. What internal problems did Turkey face?

4. Why was the shah of Iran overthrown? What problems did the new regime face?

3 Africans created a variety of governments

Before World War II, almost all of Africa south of the Sahara, populated mainly by black people, was controlled by four European nations. They were Britain, France, Belgium, and Portugal. After World War II, independence movements swept through black Africa with amazing speed. In 1950, only four states on the entire African continent were free. By 1980, some 50 independent African states represented a third of the total membership of the United Nations.

Black Africans faced many difficulties. The rush into independence created many difficulties. Under colonial rule, peoples in black African countries were allowed to participate in government mainly on local levels only, so most new nations were not prepared for national self-government. None of the new African states had any strong traditions of political unity. Most had no common language other than their colonial language, usually French or English. Most citizens could not read or write. And only a few people had been able to get university educations during the years of European rule.

During the 19th century, European colonialists who created the political systems paid little attention to African ways of life. Various tribal groups, who had nothing in common, were ruled under one colonial unit because this seemed a practical means to Europeans. When colonialism ended, these artificial units gained independence. Over the years, many Africans had begun to identify themselves with these units, for instance as Kenyans, Ugandans, or Nigerians. But many still regarded themselves primarily as tribal members, such as Hausa, or as members of a particular religious group, such as Muslim. These loyalties often led to hostilities, feuds, and even civil wars.

Rebellion troubled Zaïre. Lack of education and political experience, tribal rivalries, and superpower competition all led to tragic results in Zaïre [zä ir'], the former Belgian Congo. In 1960, the Belgians suddenly announced they were giving up their colony. Almost no one was prepared to run the new government. Independence was soon followed by mutiny in the army, tribal feuds, attacks on whites, riots, and looting. The rich mining province of Katanga [kə täng'gə], encouraged and supported by western business interests, seceded. United Nations troops, made up mostly of Africans, restored order after two and a half years. During that time, many people, including Dag Hammarskjöld, the UN Secretary-General, and Patrice Lumumba, Zaïre's first prime minister, lost their lives. When the UN withdrew, violence broke out again in Katanga. Finally, an army officer named Joseph D. Mobutu came to power in 1965, ended the rebellion, and set up a personal dictatorship.

One of Mobutu's policies was Africanization. In part, this meant replacing European technicians with Africans and changing European names to more authentically African ones. Joseph D. Mobutu became Mobutu Sese Seko, and Katanga province became Shaba province. The names of the country and the river were changed from Congo to Zaïre.

Mobutu also planned economic development. Zaïre, one of the largest countries in Africa, had vast mineral deposits, especially cobalt and copper. But its cities were widely separated, and its transportation system was poor. Economic progress depended on developing natural resources and providing better communications and transportation systems. In 1977 and 1978, economic development was interrupted when Soviet-backed rebels in the mineral-rich province of Shaba once again tried to bring about secession. With Western support, Mobutu defeated the

GEOGRAPHY

A Key to History

ECONOMIC INDEPENDENCE AND RESOURCES

Many nations have found that political independence does not bring economic independence with it. The mineral and water resources of the world are unevenly distributed, the lion's share being in Western Europe and North America. Many new nations face big economic problems because they lack mineral resources.

The nations of Africa are a good example. The map shows the location of major mineral resources and economic activity. Compare this map with the political map of Africa in the atlas to see which nations have what resources.

Compared with the rest of the world, Africa has few deposits of iron ore. Moreover, most of its iron ore is located far from its few sources of coal, and coal is needed to get iron from iron ore. The ironworkers of ancient Africa burned charcoal to smelt iron from the ore. But this takes too much charcoal to be profitable in producing large quantities of iron.

Electric power is also needed for industrial development, and some parts of Africa have tremendous potential water power to generate hydro-electric power. However, the attempts to harness water power by building dams have brought problems as well as progress.

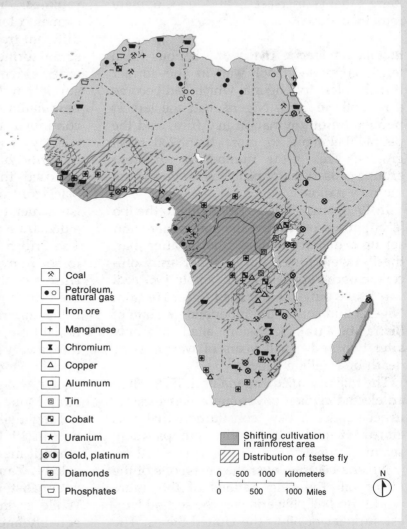

Where once streams flowed rapidly, now stagnant lakes form in back of dams—perfect breeding grounds for the mosquitoes and snails that carry debilitating diseases.

The African continent has some minerals that industrialized countries want. But it is more profitable for an industry to buy ore and ship it to its refineries elsewhere than to ship coal to Africa to refine the ore there.

Much of the economic activity in Africa is extractive. The Africans extract minerals from the soil, hardwood trees from the forests, and palm-oil fruit from trees. Many of these raw materials are shipped elsewhere to be processed or refined.

Some African countries are investing the money from their raw materials in refineries or other facilities that will bring more business into their country. For other African countries, such a course is impossible. They have few raw materials to sell and so have little money to invest.

rebels, but the economic cost was high. Zaïre's debts increased, and development remained slow.

Nigeria survived a civil war. Serious tribal tensions caused civil war in the former British colony of Nigeria, which had become a republic in 1963. Nigeria had the largest population of any nation in Africa, and the people belonged to more than 200 tribal groups. This great number of different groups caused many problems in governing the new nation.

In 1966, army officers belonging to the Ibo [ē'bō] group overthrew the government and set up a military regime. Shortly after that, the Ibo were forced out by other army officers. Bloody reprisals began, and in 1967 civil war broke out. The Ibo tried to secede from Nigeria and set up the independent state of Biafra [bē ä'frə]. Secession failed, but only after two and a half years of war and the death of a million people.

The military ruled Nigeria until 1979. Then an elected civilian government was reestablished under a new constitution that was aimed at making minority groups more secure.

Nigeria became, over the years, one of the major oil-producing nations of the entire world. By 1980, Nigeria was the second largest supplier of oil to the United States. The enormous income produced by all this oil made Nigeria the wealthiest nation in all of black Africa.

During the years of military rule, the money from oil sales was used to make improvements in roads, communications, and ports. But inflation got out of hand, and agriculture was largely neglected. The goals of the new civilian government were to control inflation, make the country self-sufficient in agricultural needs, and promote the growth of various types of industries.

Some African countries developed stable regimes. The experiences of some other former colonies of Britain and France were different from the experiences of Nigeria. In some former colonies, the leaders of the independence movements had wide popular support and became strong presidents of the new nations. But parliamentary institutions continued, too.

Kenya had the most difficult problem. A minority of white settlers there strongly opposed the creation of an independent, black-controlled government. Black nationalists struck back with terrorism and violence, aided by a secret society called Mau Mau. The British arrested the leading nationalist, Jomo Kenyatta, and put him in prison. Unrest continued from 1953 to 1963, when the British granted independence to Kenya. Kenyatta, released from prison and a national hero, was elected president. He ruled Kenya very firmly but maintained a constitutional system. Kenyatta, who died in 1978 at age 81, was succeeded as president by Daniel Arap Moi.

Tanganyika became an independent nation in 1961 and became Tanzania in 1964 when it merged with another former British colony, Zanzibar. Julius Nyerere, the black nationalist leader, was elected president. While trying to pursue socialist goals of equality and communal ownership of property, Nyerere still followed forms of constitutional government.

In Senegal the poet and patriot Leopold Senghor became president, while in Ivory Coast the nationalist and labor leader Houphouet-Boigny became president. Both men were strong rulers, holding their offices for life, but permitting parliamentary institutions to function. Like many former French colonies, Senegal and Ivory Coast maintained strong ties with France, which aided their economic development.

Daily Life

As in many new nations in Africa, everyday life in Kenya is a blend of old and new. At *top* trade union members and Kikuyu women in traditional dress march in a May Day parade. At *center* two Luo tribesmen ride their modern bicycles to Kisumu, Kenya, to perform a traditional dance. *Below* modern skyscrapers rise up behind Uhuru Park in downtown Nairobi.

Many new African nations faced similar problems and sought to share possible solutions. Here Nyerere of Tanganyika, Obote of Uganda, and Kenyatta of Kenya greet the crowds before attending the East African Heads of Government Conference in Nairobi, Kenya, in 1964.

Dictators came to power in Ghana and Uganda. Nearly all the newly independent African states had constitutions patterned after Western models. Successful "government of the people," however, usually needed educated citizens with experience in self-government and a stable economy. These did not exist in some African societies.

In many countries of black Africa, the outward forms of democratic, representative government were kept. But a "strong man" with popular appeal became the actual ruler with all power concentrated in his hands. In a number of cases, the leader became a dictator. Kwame Nkrumah [kwä′mē nə krü′mə], the first prime minister of Ghana, was such a leader. In 1957, he led Ghana through a peaceful transition from colonialism to independence. But it soon became clear that Nkrumah's radical development plans were not suitable for Ghana's economy. As criticism grew, Nkrumah gagged the press and jailed opponents. In 1966, army officers took control of the government. The military dictatorship tried to stabilize political and eco-

To encourage stable self-government, Ghana sought to educate its citizens.

nomic affairs, but failed. The people demanded and won civilian parliamentary rule in 1979.

One of the most brutal dictators in black Africa was General Idi Amin. In 1971, he seized control of Uganda and ruled through terror for eight years. Eventually Amin was ousted, but an occupying army from neighboring Tanzania was the only force maintaining order. At the same time, a general level of social upheaval continued while rival Ugandan leaders competed for political control of the nation.

section review 3

1. How did colonial rule cause problems for the newly independent African states?

2. List four economic or social problems that led to difficulties in Zaïre.

3. Why was there a civil war in Nigeria? How was it resolved?

4. Name three or more countries that were able to avoid dictatorships.

4 The struggle for black rule reached southern Africa

The growth of black nationalism also affected the southernmost part of the African continent. This area included the Portuguese colonies of Angola and Mozambique, the British colony of Rhodesia, and the independent Republic of South Africa.

Angola and Mozambique, the oldest European colonies in Africa, both gained independence in 1974. In Rhodesia, the white minority agreed to a black-dominated government only after a fierce guerrilla war. The white minority in South Africa, on the other hand, completely controlled the government and the economy, following a policy of separation of whites and blacks. South Africa remained the only African country where a white minority government ruled a population with a black majority.

Angola and Mozambique fought for independence. In 1961, nationalist rebellions began in Portugal's two large African colonies—Angola on the west coast and Mozambique on the east coast. Bloody fighting lasted for more than a decade. Then in 1974 army officers and soldiers overthrew the dic-

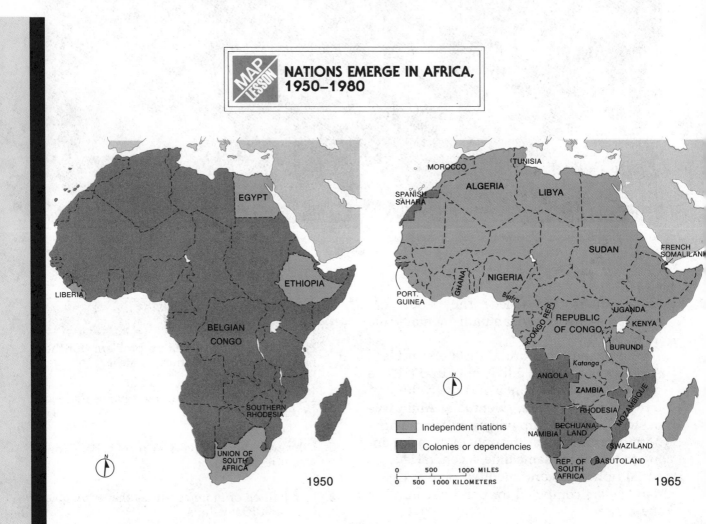

MAP LESSON

NATIONS EMERGE IN AFRICA, 1950–1980

1950

1965

Independent nations

Colonies or dependencies

0   500   1000 MILES
0   500   1000 KILOMETERS

tatorial regime in Portugal. The new revolutionary government granted independence to Angola and Mozambique.

Three different nationalist groups immediately began to fight for control of Angola. Each of the three received support from different outside powers. The Marxist group got support from the Soviet Union, and Soviet-armed Cuban soldiers were sent to Angola. The other two nationalist groups were backed in various ways by the United States, South Africa, China, and Zaïre. Angola became an area of rivalry between the two superpowers. The Soviet- and Cuban-supported group won the military struggle and

came to power in 1976. Agostinho Neto, a poet and medical doctor, became Angola's first president.

Angola faced the usual problems of economic development, made worse by years of war. Neto, who died of cancer in 1979, tried to improve relations with the United States and Portugal to bolster the economy. But as the 1980s began, Angola was still heavily dependent on Soviet and Cuban aid.

Independent Mozambique experienced problems, too. Samora Machel, a Marxist, became head of the government in 1974. He aimed to install a communist system, nationalizing private plantations and establishing

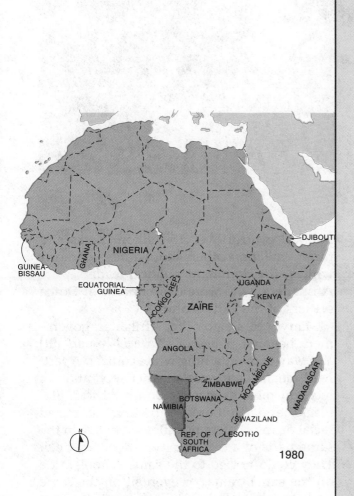

1980

■ MAP LESSON 34: NATIONS EMERGE IN AFRICA, 1950–1980

This sequence of three maps shows change over time. It clearly shows that most European colonies in Africa became independent states within a thirty-year period.

1. Was the Belgian Congo independent in 1950? Did it achieve independence by 1965? What was its name in 1965? What was its name in 1980?

2. The 1965 map locates Katanga as a province of the Republic of Congo. Some leaders in Katanga tried to break away and found an independent nation. How does this map sequence show that the revolt failed?

3. The 1965 map shows that what other nation had a province that revolted during this period? What was the name of the province? Was this revolt successful?

4. With independence, many nations dropped their old colonial names and took new ones. What were the names of Rhodesia and Bechuanaland in 1980?

5. Locate Ghana. Do these maps tell the exact year it gained independence?

6. Based on these maps, most African nations became independent in what time period?

state farms. Continuing economic problems forced Machel also to appeal to the West for aid.

Whites and blacks fought for control in Rhodesia.

In the British colony of Rhodesia, a white minority of about 270 thousand governed a black majority of 6 million. In 1965, white leaders demanded independence from Britain. The British would not agree until political rights were first granted to blacks. Rhodesia's white prime minister, Ian Smith, refused and proclaimed Rhodesia to be independent. The British then imposed a *trade embargo*, that is, the government made trade with Rhodesia illegal for British citizens. The United States joined the trade embargo. The embargo hurt Rhodesia's economy but it did not topple Smith's government.

In 1972, black Rhodesian nationalists began a guerrilla war to overthrow the white-dominated Rhodesian government. After seven years of fighting and the loss of 20 thousand lives, a cease-fire was arranged. Elections were held in early 1980 for a 100-member Executive National Assembly. Robert Mugabe, one of the black nationalist guerrilla leaders, became prime minister. The British then granted independence to Rhodesia. Mugabe's government, which included whites, proclaimed the new independent state of Zimbabwe. The name recalled the powerful 15th-century African state that had existed in the area.

A white minority ruled South Africa.

South Africa was the most powerful African state both economically and militarily. Its natural resources included diamonds and gold, and it was highly industrialized. Once a British colony, the country declared its complete separation from Britain in 1961 and took a new name, the Republic of South Africa.

Since its founding, South Africa had been ruled by a white minority. In the years after World War II, about 4 million whites held

political control over 15 million blacks and three million other nonwhites. Among whites, the dominant political leaders were Afrikaners, who were descendants of Dutch settlers of the 17th century.

Many years ago, the Afrikaner government began a policy of *apartheid* [ə pärt' hīt] as a way of maintaining white control. Apartheid means apartness or strict separation of races in most aspects of South African life. Blacks and "coloureds" (people of mixed racial descent) were not allowed to live in the same parts of a community as white people. They could not go to the same schools, ride on the same trains, or even sit on the same park benches. They could not vote or own

property except in some small areas called "homelands." To go from one area of the country to another, they had to carry "passes" and identification cards and follow strict regulations. They could work only at jobs no white people wanted.

A few restrictions were lifted in 1979. Blacks were allowed into previously off-limits restaurants, and most sports were integrated. But the basic principles of "separate development" remained unchanged. The law still prevented blacks from participating in politics and from living where whites lived.

Many political and religious leaders throughout the world have protested these harsh racist laws. But their protests have had little practical effect on South African racial policy.

section review 4

1. Which two European colonies in Africa were the last to gain independence? How did that struggle lead to a revolution in the former colonial power?

2. What kind of government came to power in Angola? How was that made possible?

3. How did the British colony of Rhodesia achieve black majority rule as Zimbabwe?

4. What is the policy of apartheid? Where is it practiced?

Section Summaries

1. Arab Muslims and Jewish Zionists began nations. After World War II, numerous Arab political units joined Egypt, Iraq, Saudi Arabia, and Yemen as independent states. A new government took power in Egypt in 1952. It sought to modernize the country and ease poverty. In 1947 Jews proclaimed the new state of Israel. This created a Palestinian refugee problem and led to three wars between Israel and Arab nations. The Palestine Liberation Organization was formed to work for an independent Palestinian state in the area.

2. The Middle East was troubled by conflict and instability. While the superpowers competed for influence in the Middle East, Egypt made peace with Israel in 1979. PLO and Syrian forces were expelled from Beirut by the Israelis in 1982. Turkey, after modernization, had political and economic problems. Opposition to the Shah of Iran for his modernization program and dictatorial methods led to his downfall in 1979. In the early 1980s, Iraq and Iran went to war over control of the Persian Gulf.

3. Africans created a variety of governments. Many new independent black African states had come into being by 1980. Among them, Zaïre and Nigeria experienced civil war. Bloodshed also marked Kenya's move toward nationhood, but that nation eventually achieved stability. Ghana and Uganda experienced dictatorial rule. The change from colony to nation was most peaceful in Tanzania, Senegal, and Ivory Coast.

4. The struggle for black rule reached southern Africa. The Portuguese colonies of Angola and Mozambique won independence in the 1970s. Marxist governments were established in both countries. In Rhodesia, the white minority finally agreed to black majority rule in 1979 and the nation became Zimbabwe. In South Africa, white rule over millions of blacks continued under a policy of race separation.

Who? What? When? Where?

1. Put the events listed below in chronological order, beginning with the earliest:
 a. South Africa declared its independence.
 b. The shah was forced to leave Iran.
 c. King Farouk was overthrown in Egypt.
 d. Britain granted independence to Rhodesia.
 e. Nigeria became a republic.
 f. Israel won the six-day war.
 g. Ghana became independent.
 h. Sadat appeared before the Knesset.

2. Name the nation associated with each of the following leaders:
 a. Kenyatta
 b. Khomeini
 c. Mobutu
 d. Mugabe
 e. Nasser
 f. Neto
 g. Nyerere
 h. Sadat

3. Write sentences that define each term listed below:
 a. Afrikaners
 b. Aswan High Dam
 c. PLO
 d. six-day war
 e. trade embargo
 f. West Bank

Questions for Critical Thinking

1. What do you think are the major problems that face the countries of black Africa?

2. Why is the Middle East of such importance to the rest of the world?

3. What conditions are necessary for successful democratic government?

4. How might the shah have stayed in power in Iran?

5. Why are nationalism and self-determination so much sought after by the peoples of the world?

Skill Activities

1. Read *The Arabs: Their History, Aims, and Challenge to the Industrialized World* by Thomas Kiernan to find out more about the Arab-Israeli dispute. (Little Brown, 1975)

2. Do research in this book and in the school library to find out more about the historical basis for the problems in Palestine today. Then hold a debate on whether or not Palestine should be part of Israel or should be independent.

3. Divide the class into committees of four or five students each. Then have each committee make lists of reforms that might be needed in a newly independent country. Now compare the list of each committee with those made by the others. Make one list of reforms that the whole class agrees are needed.

4. Use reference books to make charts or maps showing the natural resources of the nations of Africa and the Middle East. *Aldine's University Atlas* (Scott, Foresman) and *Goode's World Atlas* are both good sources for this information.

5. Using the information from Activity 4, hold a class discussion on the potential for successful economic development of the countries involved. Some of the questions you might try to answer are these: Where are the natural resources located in relation to each other? In relation to population centers? What places have iron ore but lack coal? Do political boundaries separate sources of natural resources from each other? How do these factors affect a nation's chances of becoming industrialized?

chapter **34** *quiz*

Section 1

1. True or false: American and Egyptian relations became strong when the United States financed the Aswan High Dam.

2. The new nation of Israel was created in: a. 1948, b. 1967, c. 1973

3. At one time, there was a large European population in: a. Saudi Arabia, b. Syria, c. Algeria

Section 2

4. True or false: Egypt was the first Arab country to recognize the legal existence of Israel.

5. In 1979, American citizens were taken hostage in the United States embassy in: a. Iraq, b. Israel, c. Iran

6. In 1972, Anwar Sadat ordered the withdrawal from Egypt of all military personnel from: a. the United States, b. the Soviet Union, c. France

Section 3

7. Nationalism was threatened in Africa by people's loyalties to their: a. village, b. family, c. tribe

8. True or false: The Nigerian civil war gave Biafra its independence.

9. True or false: In many countries of black Africa, a strong man with popular appeal became the actual ruler.

Section 4

10. In the 1970s, a Marxist government was established in: a. Angola, b. South Africa, c. Rhodesia

11. True or false: Britain granted independence to Rhodesia after black majority rule was established.

12. The Republic of South Africa was controlled by its: a. white majority, b. black majority, c. white minority

NATIONAL DEVELOPMENT IN LATIN AMERICA AND SOUTHERN ASIA

The struggle for national development means a blending of old and new. Here farmers in Asia grow rice in the traditional way as modern ships are built nearby.

The time was 1964. A Chilean economist was speaking urgently about a great economic problem in Latin America:

> If the economy of Latin America continues to grow at the rate of 1% a year, it would take us 70 years to double the present per capita income. . . . To achieve the present per capita income of the United States, we would have to wait almost 200 years. . . . Latin America must accelerate its rate of development, for the needs of our peoples are so pressing that their satisfaction cannot wait the passage of several generations.

As in south Asian countries, the desire for a better life has been a powerful force in Latin America since the end of World War II.

Latin America and southern Asia have been among the economically underdeveloped regions of the world. Both areas had large peasant populations and widespread poverty. For many years, most of the countries in both regions produced mainly raw materials for export. This put them at the mercy of sharp swings in world prices. In both areas there was a strong urge to break the heavy dependence on these exports. This meant pushing for a more varied economic development and a more equal distribution of wealth. Rapid modernization and economic development were seen as the only hope for improving living conditions. In southern Asia, the problems were further complicated by the struggle for political independence, which became entangled in the Cold War.

This chapter tells how:

1. **Two revolutions shook Latin America.**

2. **Latin Americans worked to become self-sufficient.**

3. **South Asian countries struggled with problems of development.**

4. **War ravaged Vietnam and Cambodia.**

1 *Two revolutions shook Latin America*

Latin America in the 20th century has had a turbulent history, filled with economic crises, political rebellions, and social unrest. The basic source of this instability has been the need to create a more just economic and social system. Although great differences exist among Latin American nations, the goal of building a just and stable society has been common to all of them.

Extremes of wealth and poverty existed for a long time. Since colonial times, Latin America has had great extremes of wealth. At the top of society was a small, wealthy landowning class. Almost everyone else was without land or property and very poor.

Peasants worked on the estates of the rich. Throughout the 19th and early 20th centuries, the economic condition, educational opportunities, and health of most of these people did not improve much. Few learned to read and write. Most suffered from disease and malnutrition.

One reason for the poverty was that Latin American nations did not industrialize. Most had agricultural economies based on the export of a major product. Others relied on the mining and export of mineral resources.

In Colombia, coffee was the chief export crop. In Cuba it was sugar, in Nicaragua bananas, in Uruguay wool, in Chile copper, in Bolivia tin, and in Venezuela oil. The trouble with having only one main product to export is that when the price of that product falls, the entire country suffers. Having several major exports would have meant less dependence on any one. Also, bad weather could ruin a crop and thus destroy the major national source of income for a year. Without a reliable source of foreign income, most Latin American nations were unable to modernize farming methods or develop industry that would provide income and jobs. Moreover, most of Latin America's natural resources were developed by foreign companies. Though Latin Americans needed the foreign capital, they deeply resented the foreign control over their economies.

From the early days of political independence, landowners had held political control in Latin America. They were supported by the Roman Catholic Church and by the military. There were frequent changes in government, often violent, but these upheavals did not really change the lives of most people. They remained poor.

The Mexican Revolution brought important changes. The first major change came through the Mexican Revolution, beginning in 1911. Rebel leaders overthrew a long-time

As part of its development program, the Mexican government has built huge oil refineries to process the nation's vast oil reserves.

dictator, Porfirio Diaz, wrote a new constitution, and established a more democratic government.

The Institutional Revolutionary Party has held firm power in Mexico since 1929. The government eventually broke up many of the large estates, distributed land to peasants, and improved living conditions. In 1938, the government took control of the foreign-owned oil fields in Mexico. Since then a government agency called Pemex has operated the Mexican oil industry.

National development became a major goal. Mexico promoted national development in numerous ways. After World War II, for example, it placed about 2.5 million acres (1 million hectares) of land under irrigation. This land, along with advanced farming technology, helped Mexico for the first time produce enough food to feed its people. Mexico also began to export large quantities of sugar, beef, and coffee.

In the mid-1950s, Mexico began a program of industrial development. Within ten years, it was producing its own iron, steel, chemicals, and electrical goods. Government development of a large tourist industry also strengthened the economy.

At the same time, the government improved social conditions. Public health programs cut down the incidence of disease. Low-cost housing programs provided homes for thousands of new city dwellers. Other programs brought pure drinking water to villages for the first time. And the government built new schools across the country. In 1958, women gained the right to vote in presidential elections.

By the mid-1970s, Mexico had the fastest-growing economy in the Americas. More than a fourth of the Mexican people were now in the middle class. Mexico also had one of the most stable governments in all of Latin America. In the late 1970s, huge new oil discoveries promised even greater economic possibilities.

However, the people who benefited most from industrial development were the upper and middle classes. For large numbers of peasants, life improved very little. Many of the millions who flocked to cities found no jobs. They were forced to live in sprawling slums. To make matters worse, the population continued to grow at a high rate. Mexico began to make huge loans abroad. By 1982, as the world's largest debtor nation, Mexico came close to bankruptcy.

Revolution made Cuba a socialist state.
Another country where revolution brought real change was Cuba. It was transformed from a corrupt dictatorship under Fulgencio Batista [bä tēs′tä] to a communist dictatorship led by Fidel Castro.

After the revolution in 1959, Castro prom-ised free elections, democratic government, and far-reaching social and economic reforms. At first, Castro had the support of the United States. However, he lost this support when free elections were not held, properties belonging to people in the United States were taken over without payment, criticism of the government was not allowed, and people opposing Castro were executed or jailed. Thousands of refugees, mostly professionals and other members of the middle class, fled to the United States and to Latin American countries. Some of these refugees, with the help of the United States government, organized an armed force to try to invade Cuba and remove Castro from power. However, their landing at the Bay of Pigs in Cuba in 1961 failed miserably. The invasion further strained relations between the United States and Cuba.

Shortly afterward, Castro declared Cuba to

Castro, surrounded by his bearded bodyguards, made a triumphal entrance into Havana in January, 1959.

Artists after World War II broke old patterns. Jackson Pollack, whose "Greyed Rainbow, 1953" is at *near right,* used house paint rather than artists' paint on his canvasses. "Evening, 9:10, 461 Lexington Ave." *below* is by Romare Bearden. He cut out magazine pictures and pasted them together in a different order to make his art. Roy Lichtenstein took the tough, crude world of the comic strip and blew it up to outsize proportions. "Torpedo Los," *center,* is a serious painting. Robert Smithson tried to move away from the idea that art could be exhibited, bought, sold, and collected. He created his greatest work, "Spiral Jetty," *far right,* in Utah's Great Salt Lake. Sculptor Louise Nevelson stacked wood in architectural forms. Her "American Dawn" is a *right bottom.*

be a socialist state. He then began to receive economic aid from the Soviet Union. In 1962, the Cuban missile crisis, discussed earlier, soured relations with the United States even more.

Castro also supported *guerrillas*, that is, fighters who harass the enemy and are not part of a regular army, and *terrorist* groups in Latin American countries. These groups posed a threat to many governments and to the business interests of the United States there. Cuban troops were also sent to aid Marxists in Angola and Ethiopia.

One of Castro's major goals was to make Cuba an industrial nation. But Cuba did not have adequate resources or sufficient numbers of trained people to develop industry. In 1963, Castro put aside rapid industrialization and returned to a program of producing as much sugar as possible. But sugar harvests constantly fell short of Castro's production goals. In the more than twenty years of Castro's regime, Cuba has suffered repeated economic setbacks.

In transforming Cuba into a socialist state, Castro's government took control of all factories, mines, and banks. It also confiscated all large and many medium-size farms. These were made into state farms, occupying some 70 percent of the land. Very little land was distributed to small farmers. In fact, small farmers were forced to sell their crops to the government at low prices.

The achievements of Castro's revolution were in public housing, health, and education. Cuba's people, especially workers and rural people, had better housing, more schools, and better medical care than before the revolution. Although most Cuban citizens had enough to eat, there were shortages of certain foods and manufactured goods. Many products have been rationed since the 1960s. Cuba continued to face serious economic problems. Conditions became so bad that in 1980 Castro allowed 120,000 refugees to flee to the United States.

section review 1

1. Why didn't most Latin American countries produce great wealth from their natural resources and agriculture?

2. What groups controlled Latin American governments? Why did the frequent revolutions not bring about lasting changes?

3. What is Mexico's greatest problem today?

4. What kind of government did Castro set up in Cuba? How has his government helped Cuba? Hurt Cuba?

2 Latin Americans worked to become self-sufficient

Unlike Cuba and Mexico, other Latin American countries did not experience radical change. But they did seek economic self-sufficiency by promoting industrialization. When these programs did not work out well, unrest became widespread and military dictatorships took control.

Unrest and upheaval troubled Argentina. In 1943, a group of army officers seized power in Argentina. Among them was a colonel named Juan Peron. By settling strikes and making friends with labor leaders, Peron built up his power and made himself a dictator. He was elected president in 1946 with the overwhelming support of the workers in Argentine towns and cities. Peron rewarded the workers with laws that provided higher wages, paid holidays, pensions, and health benefits.

Peron was also helped by his wife, Eva, whom he appointed Minister of Social Welfare. Largely through her efforts, women were given the right to vote in 1947. She distributed government funds for education and relief. She also collected money from

In August, 1951, Eva and Juan Peron greeted Argentinian workers during a rally during Juan Peron's reelection campaign that year.

labor and business which was used to help orphans, the aged, and other needy persons. People called her Evita (little Eva), as a sign of their affection. She died of cancer in July, 1952.

Peron started to industrialize Argentina, but there was not enough money to pay for his grandiose program. Meanwhile, Peron neglected agriculture. This hurt Argentina, which was one of the world's leading exporters of beef and grain. When the world price of beef fell, Argentina's income declined even more. Inflation set in and wiped out the gains workers had made. As unrest grew, Peron's dictatorship became harsher. He attacked the Catholic church and suppressed newspapers. The police responded to dissent with torture, imprisonment, and exile. But opposition continued to build up. In 1955, Peron was forced out of office, and he fled to Spain.

From 1955 to 1973, one military dictatorship after another tried to solve the problems of high inflation and rising unemployment. None succeeded. In June, 1973, Peron, then 78 years old, returned to Argentina and again was elected president. But he died the following year.

Peron's new wife, Isabella, who had been elected vice-president, took over as president. She was the first woman in Latin America to hold such high office. But in 1976 the military forced Isabella to resign and established a dictatorship.

Military dictatorship continued as violence by extremist groups on the right and left increased in Buenos Aires and other cities. The economic situation grew worse. In 1977, the inflation rate reached 160 percent. In 1982, Argentina attempted to seize the British-held Falkland Islands, just west of its southern border, but failed to do so.

WHAT'S IN A NAME?
ARGENTINA

Argentina comes from the Latin word *argentum*, meaning "silver." Early Europeans mistakenly believed that the area had a lot of silver. They saw Indians bringing silver down river and believed it came from a nearby place. In fact, the silver came from the mountains of Bolivia, far to the north.

Chile had serious economic and social problems. In Chile, agriculture played a smaller role in the economy than in most Latin American countries. Chile is rich in minerals, and mining is the most important industry. Chile is one of the world's leading producers of copper, which provides more than half of the nation's foreign income.

For most of the 20th century, land and industry were concentrated in the hands of a small number of wealthy landowners and powerful business groups. Chile suffered from rural poverty, labor unrest, and inflation. These conditions became worse whenever the world price of copper fell and reduced Chile's income.

The first serious effort to reform the land system came under President Eduardo Frei [frā], who was elected in 1964. He began a program of distributing land to small farmers. Frei also increased government control of large mines and other industries. But inflation, rising taxes, and shortages of consumer goods led to widespread discontent.

In 1970, Salvador Allende [ä yän'dä], a Marxist, was elected president. Allende's government nationalized many large industries and all the copper mines, many of them owned by companies in the United States. It also took over the large landed estates and organized them into state farms. These programs created resentment among the middle and upper classes. In 1973, with approval of and aid from the United States, the army seized control. During the takeover, Allende was killed.

Since 1973 Chile has been ruled by a military dictatorship headed by General Augusto Pinochet [pē nō chä']. Thousands of Chileans were jailed, tortured, or put to death. Concentration camps were set up. The national congress was dissolved, and civil liberties were abolished. General Pinochet announced that he planned to remain in

Among the copper mines that Allende nationalized was this one. The largest underground copper mine in the world, El Teniente had been 49 percent owned by companies in the United States.

power until the end of the decade of the 1980s at least.

Pinochet canceled the economic policies of Allende and brought back a system of free-market capitalism. Inflation fell from an annual rate of more than 600 percent in 1973 to 30 percent in 1980. But unemployment ran to 15 percent or more, wealth was increasingly concentrated in the hands of a small elite, and political oppression continued.

Brazil moved toward rapid modernization.
Brazil is the fifth largest country in the world in area. It covers almost half of South America's land and contains more than half of South America's people. With millions of square miles (hectares) of unused fertile land, the world's greatest reserves of iron ore and the 10th most productive economy, Brazil has the potential to become a powerful nation. The realization of that potential through modernization and industrialization has been the central theme of Brazil's history since the end of World War II.

For many years, Brazil's economy depended on the export of coffee, and the government was dominated by powerful coffee growers. In 1930, a politician and rancher named Getulio Vargas seized power with the help of the army. Vargas made himself a dictator and ruled Brazil for most of the next quarter-century. He began the push toward industrialization and also encouraged the growing of crops other than coffee.

Vargas improved working conditions for laborers, promoted elementary education, and restricted child labor. By the time Vargas died in 1954, Brazil was well started on an industrial revolution, with large new factories to produce iron, steel, automobiles, and textiles.

In the decade after 1954, Brazil had a series of civilian presidents who were determined to continue modernization. Industry grew at a high rate. It was during this period that the new capital city of Brasilia was built in just three years. Brasilia was deliberately located away from the settled coastal region to encourage Brazilians to move into and develop the interior of the country.

Much of this modernization depended on huge foreign investment and loans. The country went deeply into debt. Prices rose quickly. Dishonesty and corruption in government became a serious problem. In 1964, Brazilian army officers overthrew the civilian government and then set up a military dictatorship.

Since 1964, various military leaders have governed Brazil. These military leaders have given higher priority to economic and social development than to democratic government. They have permitted a small amount of democracy by allowing the parliament to meet. But they also suppressed dissent, imposed censorship, and terrorized many of their opponents.

By the end of the 1970s, Brazil's economy still depended mainly on the export of a few agricultural products such as coffee and sugar. But the country had become the most industrialized nation in Latin America and had even begun to develop nuclear energy as a power source.

As the 1980s opened, Brazil was a land of great contrasts. The upper and middle classes who lived in the cities benefited most from Brazil's rapid modernization. On the outskirts of those cities lived millions of other Brazilians. They were crowded into shanty-towns with no running water, no sewage system, no electricity, and no schools. They had fled even worse rural poverty. They hoped to find work in the new factories, but they streamed into the cities faster than jobs could be created. Modern cities like Rio de Janeiro, São Paulo, and Brasilia found themselves surrounded by slums. Brazil, which had made astounding progress in modernization, faced the immense challenge of finding ways to distribute the benefits more evenly among its millions of deprived.

section review 2

1. Who was Juan Peron? What were his policies? How did his wife Eva help him?

2. How did Chile's great copper reserves make it different from most underdeveloped countries?

3. Who was Salvador Allende? What were his policies? Were they successful?

4. What has been the main theme of Brazil's history since the end of World War II? What have been Brazil's major achievements since 1945? What are its most serious problems?

3 South Asian countries struggled with problems of development

In Chapter 33 we read how the impact of World War II led to the crumbling of empires in Asia. Within ten years after the end of the war, Indonesia, India, and Pakistan all became independent nations. After independence, each of these nations had to grapple with the difficulties of exploding populations and widespread poverty. In each country there was an urgent need for economic development, but this was often complicated by political problems.

Economic and social progress was slow in Indonesia. Indonesia had enormous natural resources. In addition to large reserves of oil, natural gas, nickel, zinc, copper, tin, and other minerals, it had large timber and rubber resources. But under the military regime of General Suharto [sü'här'tō'], who came to power in 1967, only a privileged minority benefited from these riches. Almost half the people lived in poverty. For example, only 6 percent of the population had safe drinking water, and half of all the deaths in the country were among preschool children.

■ MAP LESSON 35: ASIA: POPULATION DENSITY

Use the map at right and the map on page 727 to answer the following questions:

1. Most of the world's people live in Asia. Nearly six out of every ten human beings alive today are Asians. Yet the population density for much of the continent is very low. The result is the concentration of many, many people in a few areas of Asia. What are the two largest areas of population density?

2. The population density increases along many rivers. This is especially true in the Ganges Valley of northern India. What large city is located on the delta of the Ganges?

3. Name the large city that is located:
   a. on the island of Sri Lanka
   b. between the Caspian Sea and China
   c. in the Philippines
   d. on India's west coast
   e. east of Nanking on China's coast

4. Which region has the greater population density:
   a. The Philippines or New Guinea
   b. the Malay peninsula or Japan
   c. the Arabian peninsula or Korea
   d. India or Thailand
   e. eastern China or western China

Many people in Indonesia blamed the military rule of General Suharto for government corruption and mismanagement of the economy. They resented the failure to relieve poverty, the social injustice, and the authoritarian political system. But General Suharto and the army continued to dominate every phase of Indonesian life.

Indira Gandhi became the leader of India. In 1966, the ruling Congress party chose Indira Gandhi as prime minister of India. She was the daughter of Jawaharlal Nehru, India's first prime minister. With the slogan "Banish Poverty," Indira Gandhi won the national election in 1967. Her government followed a policy of more equal distribution

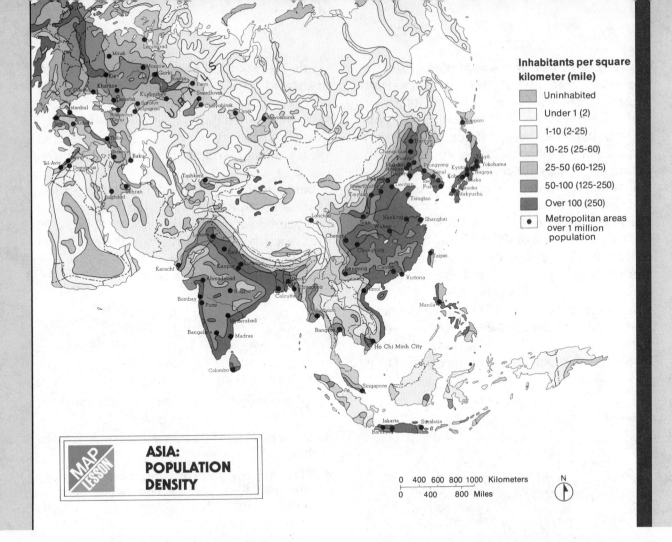

Inhabitants per square kilometer (mile)

- Uninhabited
- Under 1 (2)
- 1-10 (2-25)
- 10-25 (25-60)
- 25-50 (60-125)
- 50-100 (125-250)
- Over 100 (250)
- • Metropolitan areas over 1 million population

ASIA:
POPULATION
DENSITY

0 400 600 800 1000 Kilometers
0   400   800 Miles

N

of wealth by moderate socialism. However, her programs were not very successful, and opposition to her government grew. Gandhi tried to silence her political opponents by having them arrested. She established strict censorship of the press and allowed no criticism of her policies. Although she was voted out of office in 1977, she was overwhelmingly reelected in 1980.

India's greatest success in recent years has been in agriculture. Historically, India has had to import much of its food. Food production was never high enough to support India's millions. But with the help of no-interest loans from the World Bank's International Development Association, Indian agricultural output has greatly increased.

The military controlled Pakistan. In 1958, the government of Pakistan came under the control of a military dictator named General Mohammad Ayub Khan. After 1965, Ayub grew unpopular as corruption flourished. In 1969, rioting occurred and Ayub was forced out of office. Later, a civilian was elected president.

In 1977, the military again seized power, and General Mohammed Zia [mō ham'id zē'a], became president. He set up a strict regime of martial, or military, law. But corruption in the government continued, industrial development slowed down, and the government debt became increasingly heavy. Most of the people of the nation continued to live lives of great poverty.

East Pakistan became Bangladesh. In the late 1960s, the eastern region of Pakistan became increasingly resentful of its union with the western region. Although both regions had the same religion, Islam, they were different in most other ways, especially in language and culture. Moreover, the West Pakistanis controlled the economy, the army, and the government.

These conditions led East Pakistani leaders to demand control of their region's taxes and economy. The powers of the central government, they argued, should be limited to defense and foreign affairs.

In effect, these demands would have made East Pakistan almost self-governing. West Pakistan refused. In 1971, West Pakistan attacked the rebellious eastern region. Thousands were killed, and much property was destroyed. The East Pakistanis declared their independence. India supported East Pakistan, now called Bangladesh, and sent troops there. Within two weeks, India defeated West Pakistan, and Bangladesh became independent.

Bangladesh faced an uncertain future. Most of its capital city and other major towns had been destroyed in the war. With few natural resources and a large population, it had to import millions of tons of rice and wheat yearly to feed its people.

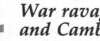

section review 3

1. Name at least two factors that help explain Indonesia's slow economic progress.

2. Who is Indira Gandhi? Why was she voted out of office? Why was she reelected?

3. What conditions created political instability in Pakistan?

4. How did the state of Bangladesh come into existence? Why did the new nation have an uncertain future?

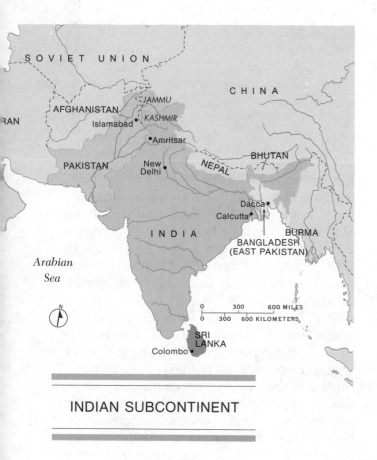

INDIAN SUBCONTINENT

4 War ravaged Vietnam and Cambodia

Less than ten years after the end of World War II, the old French colony of Indochina ceased to exist. By 1954, Laos and Cambodia had become independent, and Vietnam had been divided into a communist North and a non-communist South. A few years later, North Vietnam began a campaign to bring all of Vietnam under communist rule. The United States actively intervened to prevent that from happening.

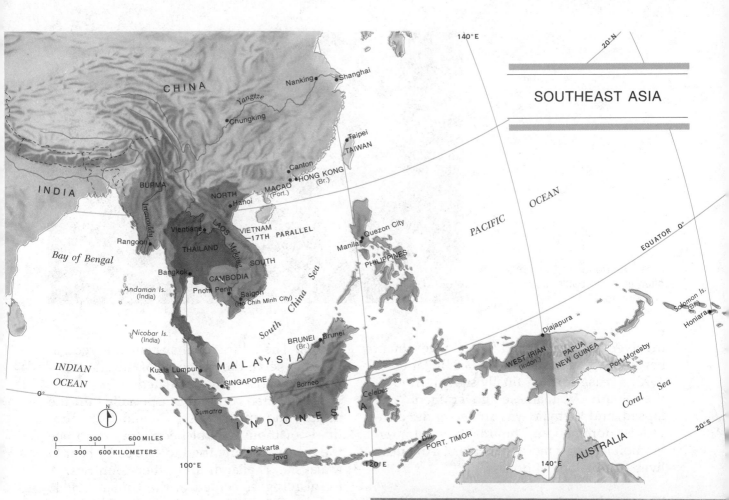

SOUTHEAST ASIA

The United States sent military forces to Vietnam. In the late 1950s, the United States began sending money and arms to South Vietnam. This was to help that government maintain its influence in the countryside and repel invasion from the communist North. The American aid was based on the policy of containment to prevent the spread of communism. This was as it had been in Korea. American troops began to arrive in South Vietnam in the early 1960s. By 1968, more than half a million Americans were fighting in Vietnam. But the war seemed to go on forever without decisive results.

In the United States, there was much criticism of American involvement in the war. As a result of growing public pressure to end

The United States spent more than $2 billion a month to support its troops, such as these Marines near Danang, in the Vietnamese war effort.

American troops in Vietnam often flew into battle areas in helicopters.

involvement, the United States government began peace negotiations in 1968. In January, 1973, a cease-fire was finally signed. In 1975, the South Vietnamese government collapsed, and Vietnam was unified under communist domination. The unsuccessful intervention had cost more than 55,000 American lives and billions of dollars.

Vietnam became a communist state. Both parts of Vietnam were unified under the North Vietnamese communists. Hanoi became the capital of the Socialist Republic of Vietnam. But after 30 years of continuous wars, Vietnam had suffered great destruction. More than 2 million men, women, and children had been killed. Much of the countryside had been laid waste. The nation faced an enormous job of rebuilding.

As the Socialist Republic of Vietnam, the country became one of the most populous communist nations in the world. All political parties except the Communist party were outlawed. Hundreds of thousands of South Vietnamese were sent to special re-education camps to be taught communism. Many were made to go to remote camps as forced laborers. Thousands of others were sent to prison camps. The educational system was reorganized to serve the purposes of the state. Private enterprise was eliminated.

These harsh conditions especially hurt the middle and upper classes. In mid-1978, hundreds of thousands of people began to flee the country. Many tried to escape by boat to Malaysia, Thailand, and other countries. A lot of refugees settled in the United States, France, Germany, and Australia. But many others remained in refugee camps in Thailand and Malaysia.

Vietnam became an imperialist power. In 1975, a border war began between Cambodia and Vietnam. Backed by China, Cambodia was ruled by a tyrannical communist dictatorship that practiced genocide and murdered some 2 million of its people. The Soviet Union supported Vietnam.

Although Vietnam and Cambodia were both communist countries, they were ancient enemies, too. The Cambodians launched raids across the Vietnamese border and seized villages they claimed were rightfully theirs historically. The Vietnamese made counter-raids against Cambodia. The war expanded, and late in 1978, the Vietnamese

Only one of many such dramas, the freighter *Huey Fong* rescued 2,700 Vietnamese refugees adrift in the South China Sea. In early 1979, Hong Kong gave temporary asylum to this group of refugees.

conquered Cambodia. They installed a puppet government in January, 1979, and proclaimed Cambodia to be the People's Republic of Kampuchea.

To punish the Vietnamese for destroying the Chinese-supported regime in Cambodia, China invaded Vietnam in February, 1979. The Chinese inflicted heavy damage and *casualties*, that is, human losses through death, wounds, and capture, in Vietnam and then withdrew. But Vietnam had already emerged as the new imperialist power in Southeast Asia.

section review 4

1. Why did the United States send military forces to Vietnam?

2. What damage did Vietnam suffer as a result of the war?

3. How did the new Socialist Republic of Vietnam rank in size among communist nations? What political party controlled the new state?

4. How did Vietnam become the new imperialist power in Southeast Asia?

Section Summaries

1. Two revolutions shook Latin America. Latin America was an economically underdeveloped area where extremes of wealth and poverty had existed for a long time. This started to change in the 20th century. The Mexican Revolution of 1911 began a long period of social and economic reform. Mexico made great economic progress, especially after World War II. In Cuba, a revolution in 1959 brought Fidel Castro to power. He transformed Cuba into a socialist state. There were advances in health, housing, and education, but Cuba faced serious economic problems.

2. Latin Americans worked to become self-sufficient. After World War II, the major goal of Latin American governments was to encourage faster national development, especially industrialization. In Argentina, this began under the dictatorship of Juan Peron. In Chile, a Marxist president, Salvador Allende, was overthrown when his programs created great opposition. In Brazil, a program of development transformed that country into the leading industrial nation in Latin America. But all three countries were ruled by military dictatorships. Everywhere in Latin America, the great inequities of wealth remained a serious problem.

3. South Asian countries struggled with problems of development. After gaining independence, Indonesia, India, and Pakistan had an urgent need for economic development. Political problems created additional difficulties. Indonesia was ruled by a military dictatorship. Although the country was wealthy in natural resources, economic and social progress was slow. In India, Indira Gandhi's social programs were not very successful. While Indians rejected her attempt at authoritarian rule, they also disliked indecisive leadership and voted her back into office. A military dictatorship governed Pakistan, but it remained an unstable nation because of internal economic and social underdevelopment. Bangladesh broke away from Pakistan and became independent in 1971. However, it had one of the poorest populations in the world.

4. War ravaged Vietnam and Cambodia. Even after independence and partition in 1954, war continued in Vietnam between communist and anti-communist forces. The United States entered the war, hoping to stop the spread of communism. It withdrew in 1973 and two years later the South Vietnamese government collapsed. North and South Vietnam were united and became the Socialist Republic of Vietnam, one of the most populous communist nations in the world. By 1979, Vietnam had conquered Cambodia and set up a puppet government. Vietnam became the new imperialist power in Southeast Asia.

Who? What? When? Where?

1. Match the correct time period with each of the events listed below: before 1960, 1961–1965, 1966–1970, 1971–1975, since 1976
   a. Military rule was begun in Brazil.
   b. War began between Vietnam and Cambodia.
   c. Ayub was forced out of power in Pakistan.
   d. The Mexican Revolution began.
   e. Batista was overthrown in Cuba.
   f. Frei was elected president in Chile.
   g. Gandhi was reelected in India.
   h. The Bay of Pigs invasion failed.
   i. The United States signed a cease-fire in Vietnam.
   j. Huge new oil reserves were discovered in Mexico.
   k. Allende became president of Chile.
   l. Bangladesh became an independent nation.
   m. Women in Mexico gained the vote.

2. Identify each of these leaders by nationality:
   a. Allende   e. Peron
   b. Castro   f. Pinochet
   c. Frei   g. Vargas
   d. Gandhi

3. Write a sentence for each of these terms that gives its definition:
   a. Bangladesh   e. Kampuchea
   b. Banish Poverty f. land reform
   c. Bay of Pigs   g. Pemex
   d. Brasilia

Questions for Critical Thinking

1. Why is it not in a nation's best interests to have foreign-based companies controlling resources and industries?

2. What are some reasons that wars start? Give examples from this chapter.

3. In what ways was the American experience in Vietnam similar to that in Korea? In what ways was it different?

4. Why do dictators so often come from the ranks of a country's military establishment?

Skill Activities

1. Read *The Land and People of Chile* by J. David Bowen to find out about this nation and its future prospects. (Lippincott, 1976)

2. Use the *Readers' Guide to Periodical Literature* to find additional information on the plight of the Vietnamese boat people and which countries have taken them as immigrants.

3. Write a short biography of a person discussed in this chapter. Then read your biography to the rest of the class.

4. Make a chart of three or more countries of Central or South America. On the chart show populations, average per person incomes, gross national products, natural resources, exports, imports, and types of government. One place to find this information is in an almanac in the school library. Make a short presentation to the rest of the class on what the chart shows.

5. After the presentation of the chart from the activity above, have a class discussion on the advantages and disadvantages each country has in dealing with the problems of today.

chapter **35** *quiz*

Section 1

1. True or false: A major reason for poverty in Latin America was the lack of industrialization.

2. The Bay of Pigs invasion and the Cuban missile crisis involved Cuba and: a. Brazil, b. the United States, c. Mexico

3. True or false: By the mid-1970s, Mexico had the fastest growing economy in the Americas.

Section 2

4. The first nation in Latin America to elect a Marxist as president was: a. Cuba, b. Brazil, c. Chile

5. An important leader in the recent history of Argentina was: a. Eduardo Frei, b. Juan Peron, c. Getulio Vargas

6. A frequent event in the political history of many nations in Latin America was: a. the rise of military dictatorships, b. a move away from the nationalization of major industries and resources, c. the elections of many leaders who are sensitive to the needs of the poor

Section 3

7. True or false: Indonesia's great poverty is due in large part to its lack of natural resources.

8. In 1977, Indira Gandhi was voted out of office because: a. many Indians did not like her authoritarian rule, b. the military seized power, c. she involved India in a war with East Pakistan

9. East Pakistan sought independence from West Pakistan because: a. the East Pakistanis resented being controlled by the West, b. East Pakistan wanted to unite with India, c. East Pakistan was denying religious freedom to West Pakistan

Section 4

10. True or false: Public opinion caused the United States to end its involvement in Vietnam.

11. After Vietnam was united under North Vietnamese communists, the nation was called the Socialist Republic of Vietnam and the capital was: a. Saigon, b. Bangkok, c. Hanoi

12. In 1975, a border war erupted between Vietnam and: a. Laos, b. Japan, c. Cambodia

A NEW SYSTEM OF WORLD RELATIONSHIPS

One of the facts of contemporary life is the growing scarcity of oil. Here, the Organization of Petroleum Exporting Countries (OPEC) is having one of its regular meetings to decide how much oil to produce and how much to charge for it.

The date was December, 1979. A crisis in Iran had led to a drastic reduction in that country's oil production. An American reporter interviewed Japanese officials about the effect of that on Japan's economy. The Japanese were very blunt:

Our problem is oil, we cannot survive without it. If we don't get oil, our gross national product collapses. Really, it's that simple.

Those words illustrate how much world conditions had changed. They could have been spoken by an official of almost any industrialized country. No longer were the European-based issues of the Cold War the center of international attention. No longer were world affairs dominated exclusively by two superpowers. No longer could either of the superpowers expect their leadership to be accepted without question by respective allies.

By the 1970s, the world was much different from what it had been in the 1950s and 1960s. The United States and the Soviet Union were still the only superpowers and were still each other's greatest rival. But both had discovered there were limits to their power. The United States did not achieve its goals in Vietnam. The Soviet Union could not dictate to China. Other nations—Britain, France, India, and China—had developed nuclear weapons. Oil had become a major new factor in the world economy and in world diplomacy. Third World countries had gained greater influence in world affairs. International relations had become much more complicated.

The following sections in this final chapter of the book will tell how:

1. The communist world fragmented.

2. Western Europe and Japan became economic giants.

3. Superpower rivalry entered a new stage.

4. Third World countries gained a greater voice in world affairs.

5. The world faced many challenges.

1 The communist world fragmented

At the beginning of the Cold War in the late 1940s, the world was polarized into two camps, each led by one of the superpowers. By the end of the 1960s, that was no longer true. In the communist camp, the Soviet Union faced increasing hostility from the People's Republic of China and growing restiveness among some of its satellite countries in Eastern Europe.

Disputes split the communist camp. A new move to loosen ties to the Soviet Union among Eastern European countries began in the early 1960s. Romania announced that it would follow its own program of industrialization. It also gave diplomatic recognition to West Germany. The Soviet Union chose to do nothing about Romania's actions.

Distrusting Russia, in 1960 Mao Tse-tung began to move China away from close association with the Soviet Union. Ideological arguments arose about which of the two countries practiced "pure" communism. It signaled yet another crack in what had been regarded as a worldwide communist monolith. Furthermore, communist Albania chose to follow the Chinese, not the Russian, lead.

Within the Soviet Union, Nikita Khrushchev lost power, mainly because of failed agricultural plans and the Cuban missile crisis of 1962. In October, 1964, he was removed from office.

Kosygin and Brezhnev became the new Soviet leaders. Aleksei N. Kosygin [kə sē'gin] succeeded Khrushchev as premier. Leonid I. Brezhnev [brezh'nef] became Communist party secretary. The Kosygin-Brezhnev leadership continued to promote a policy of coexistence with the West. But internally, the new regime for the most part continued a policy of suppressing freedom of expression. Kosygin died in early 1981. After that, Brezhnev ruled alone although he was in poor health and quite elderly.

The Soviets suppressed internal and external dissent. A new generation of young intellectuals began to express open dissatisfaction with some parts of the Soviet system. Although strongly patriotic, they insisted on greater freedom of expression in literature and other arts. Because of their worldwide reputations, such poets as Yevgeny Yevtushenko [yef gyā′nyi yef′tü shen′kō] and Andrei Voznesensky [voz′nə sens′kē] were not punished for their critical outbursts. Some writers who were not as well known, however, were put on trial, convicted, and sent to prison. The Communist party let it be known that freedom of expression was still severely limited.

The Soviet government also tried to silence writer Alexander Solzhenitsyn [sōl′zhə-nē′tsən], who had become world famous for his criticism of labor camps and Soviet oppression in general. Scientist Andrei Sakharov [sä′kä rof], foremost developer of the Soviet H-bomb, also spoke out for civil rights. In 1974, Solzhenitsyn was expelled from the Soviet Union. Six years later, Sakharov was banished from Moscow to a rural area to prevent him from communicating with Western newspeople.

Meanwhile, Soviet production problems persisted, as goals in agriculture and industry were not met. By the 1970s, the Soviet Union had to buy large amounts of grain from the United States and others to meet its food needs.

In Soviet-dominated Eastern Europe, some nations tried to change the communist system. Czechoslovakia sought to make its communist regime more democratic in 1968. The Soviet Union saw the change as a dangerous

After being sent into exile, Alexander Solzhenitsyn, *above left*, and his family moved to Zurich, Switzerland. Eventually they moved to the United States. The same Soviet government that sent Solzhenitsyn into exile also sent Warsaw Pact troops into Czechoslovakia. Many young people, such as those *above right*, participated in the 1968 uprisings in Czechoslovakia.

threat to Soviet-style communism. It sent Warsaw Pact troops into Czechoslovakia and restored hard-line communism. In Poland, workers formed the independent trade union Solidarity in 1980 and demanded reforms. The regime, under Soviet pressure, declared martial law in 1981 and suspended the union.

section review 1

1. How did Romania defy the Soviet Union? Was it successful? Why?

2. What caused the split between the Soviet Union and China?

3. Why was Khrushchev removed from power? Who were his successors?

4. Why did the Soviet Union invade Czechoslovakia in 1968?

2 Western Europe and Japan became economic giants

Despite a decline in political influence after World War II, Western Europe was still an important economic region. It had a wealth of raw materials, a skilled and educated population, and one of the best-developed industrial systems in the world. With Marshall Plan aid, Western Europe recovered economically from World War II in about ten years.

Japan, also with United States aid, recovered her economic strength after World War II. As Western Europe and Japan became major centers of industrial power, they once again took an active role in world affairs.

Britain became a welfare state. After World War II, Britain's economy became a mixture of free enterprise and socialism. A Labour party government was elected in 1945. During the next six years, that government placed the Bank of England, coal mines, iron and steel works, communications and transportation systems, and electric and gas utilities under public ownership. Four-fifths of the economy, however, remained in private hands.

The Labour government also started broad social programs that made major changes in British society. It greatly expanded welfare services by extending unemployment and old age insurance. It launched a comprehensive free medical and health service for the entire population. Income and inheritance taxes were also increased in order to redistribute wealth.

In 1951, the Conservative party was voted back into office and remained there until 1964. Although party leaders criticized the idea of a welfare state, they did not change the basic features of the social security and health insurance programs. The Conservative government accepted the mixed economy and welfare democracy Labour had put into practice. Between 1964 and 1979 the two parties alternated. In 1979, the Conservatives again won. Margaret Thatcher, the leader of the Conservative party, became the first female prime minister in British history.

During the 1960s and 1970s, the British educational system was made more democratic, slum clearance programs were promoted, and much public housing was constructed. By 1980, Britain had more public housing than any other country in Western Europe, serving 35 to 40 percent of the nation's population.

Both the Labour and the Conservative parties had to deal with serious economic problems. World War II had weakened Britain's economy. Recovery was slow, but by the 1960s British citizens enjoyed the highest standard of living in their history. Problems of low productivity, high amounts of im-

Daily Life

The roles of women changed greatly in the 1960s and 1970s. For the first time in history, women in many nations rose to positions of leadership, both in politics and in other areas. Indira Gandhi (1) twice held the office of prime minister of India. Jehan Sadat (2), as the wife of the president of Egypt, did much to further the status of women throughout the Middle East. Gro Brundtland (3), a Harvard-educated medical doctor, became prime minister of her homeland, Norway, in 1981. Golda Meir (4) moved to Israel in her youth and rose to be prime minister of that young nation. Meir led Israel during its 1973 war with its Arab neighbors. In the United States, Ella Grasso (5) was elected governor of the state of Connecticut in 1976 and reelected in 1980. In 1976, another woman, Dixy Lee Ray, was also elected governor of the state of Washington. Also in the mid-1970s, Margaret Thatcher (6) became prime minister of England, thus becoming the first woman to be head of a European nation. In France, Francoise Giroud (7) in 1974 became Secretary of State for the Status of Women. In Ireland, Betty Williams and Mairead Corrigan (8) rose to international prominence in a way other than politics. In 1976, they won the Nobel Peace Prize for their worldwide campaign to end the violence between Catholics and Protestants in Northern Ireland. The two women started their campaign after Williams saw three children killed in Belfast. Corrigan was the children's aunt.

1

ports, and inflation continued, however. Economic problems became worse in the 1970s, when Britain had the highest rate of inflation of all industrialized nations, as well as a high level of unemployment.

Britain also had to cope with troubles in Northern Ireland, a self-governing part of the United Kingdom since 1922. In 1969, violence broke out between the Protestant majority and the Catholic minority there. The Catholics insisted that they were victims of discrimination and demanded that Northern Ireland be annexed to the Republic of Ireland, where Catholics dominated. An extremist Catholic group called the Irish Republican Army launched a campaign of terrorism, and that in turn led to Protestant terrorism. Thousands of persons were killed. The bloody fighting continued into the 1980s, with no solution in sight.

France became a modern industrial democracy. France suffered from political instability in the early postwar years. Still, the French economy began to improve in the mid-1950s, and foundations for a modern industrial economy were established. Like the British, the French developed a mixed economy. Industrial production grew rapidly, and French living standards rose.

But the French became bitterly divided over their government's struggle to preserve the old French empire in Indochina and Algeria. General Charles de Gaulle's election as president in 1958 headed off civil war in France.

A stable government, a new constitution that strengthened the presidency, and economic prosperity allowed France to play an active role in world affairs. President de Gaulle refused to follow the American lead and developed an independent foreign policy in Europe, Asia, and the Middle East.

However, de Gaulle paid little attention to social reform at home. In 1968, workers and students paralyzed France with strikes.

France was close to revolution. The strikes ended when reforms were promised.

De Gaulle left office in 1969 but his successors continued his independent policy in foreign affairs. However, like other industrial nations in the 1970s, France suffered from inflation, industrial slowdown, and unemployment. These led to the election of Francois Mitterrand, a socialist, as president in 1981. Thus ended more than 20 years of rule by de Gaulle and his followers.

West Germany became Europe's most prosperous country. Defeated and devasted in 1945, West Germany emerged during the 1950s as the most prosperous country in Europe. Strong, stable, democratic government was begun under Chancellor Konrad Adenauer [ad'n ou'ər].

In 1969, Willy Brandt [vil'ē bränt] became chancellor. He moved to improve relations with Eastern Europe and the Soviet Union. In 1970, West Germany signed a treaty with the Soviet Union in which both sides renounced the use of force. Brandt also signed a treaty with Poland in which both countries accepted the postwar German-Polish border.

These treaties laid the groundwork for a four-power agreement in 1971 between the United States, the Soviet Union, Britain, and France. The agreement left the city of Berlin divided and recognized East Germany as a nation. The division of Germany, which had been a reality since the end of World War II, now became legal. Brandt accepted this as the price for better relations with the Soviet Union and the countries of Eastern Europe.

In 1974, a spy scandal forced Brandt out of office, and Helmut Schmidt became chancellor. By then West Germany was the strongest economic power in Western Europe. It ranked fourth in the entire world in the production of goods and services. In the 1970s West Germany suffered from economic recession, as did all other industrialized

Willy Brandt and Helmut Schmidt

countries. But it appeared to be the most successful European nation in coping with inflation, industrial slowdown, and unemployment.

The European Common Market was formed.
In 1958, the European Economic Community (Common Market) was formed by Belgium, France, Italy, Luxembourg, the Netherlands, and West Germany. The goal of this organization was to create a common market in which goods would flow tariff-free across the various borders. By 1962, the European Common Market was the largest single trading bloc in the world. It produced almost as much coal and steel as the United States and more than the Soviet Union.

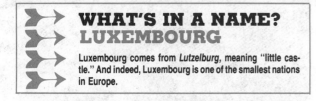

WHAT'S IN A NAME?
LUXEMBOURG

Luxembourg comes from *Lutzelburg*, meaning "little castle." And indeed, Luxembourg is one of the smallest nations in Europe.

Throughout the 1960s, Britain made several efforts to join the Common Market. Each time, France blocked its application. Finally, after long negotiations, Britain entered the Common Market in 1973, as did Ireland and Denmark. By then, the Common Market was

a center of world trade, with one-fourth of all world exports and one-third of all imports.

Japan became a world leader again. By 1980, the Japanese population had reached 115 million. Tokyo was the largest city in the world. Japan was second in world industrial production, just behind the United States. It led the world in shipbuilding and ranked high in the production of cars and computers. Japan had achieved what some people called an economic miracle.

Several factors contributed to Japan's economic growth. First, Japan's work force was highly skilled. Second, money and effort were concentrated on economic development rather than on weapons and armies. And third, government policy favored tariffs on imports and aid to industry.

However, Japan paid a price for its industrial growth, particularly with respect to the environment. Industrial and automotive smog made Tokyo's air some of the most polluted in the world. In addition, water pollution seriously affected the Japanese fishing industry. In 1970, the Japanese government finally enacted strong laws against pollution.

As to foreign affairs, Japan's prime minister paid an official visit in 1972 to China to promote friendly trade relations with that nation. Relations between Japan and the United States also changed. The United States bowed to Japanese pressure and in 1972 returned to Japanese authority the Ryukyu Islands, which the United States had taken during World War II. But the United States retained its military bases on the islands.

At the same time, tensions developed between the United States and Japan over trade relations. High Japanese tariffs kept many American products from entering Japan. Yet Japanese exports of such goods as TV sets and automobiles to the United States increased. And Japan captured a large share of the American market for many items. The unequal flow of goods caused manufacturers in the United States, especially automobile makers, to call for restrictions on Japanese goods coming into the country. During the 1980s, the United States government negotiated with Japan and tried to reach an agreement on limiting Japanese exports to America.

section review 2

1. How did new economic and social policies introduced after World War II change Britain?

2. How did the German economy fare after World War II?

3. How important was the Common Market for Europe?

4. How did Japan's rise to the rank of a world power after World War II affect its relations with China and with the United States?

Superpower rivalry entered a new phase

As cracks appeared in the communist world and the Western Europeans and the Japanese became more independent in international affairs, the rivalry between the two superpowers continued. But the rivalry entered a new phase as some older issues were settled and different ones arose to command world attention. In addition, the rivalry now existed under conditions different from those of the two decades of the Cold War.

More nations developed nuclear weapons. One of the new conditions was the cracking of the superpowers' monopoly on nuclear weapons. Great Britain exploded an atomic bomb in 1952, the same year the United

The United States tested its hydrogen bomb on the South Pacific island of Mururoa. As with earlier bombs, it made the familiar mushroom cloud of smoke.

States tested an even more powerful hydrogen bomb. (The Soviet Union tested one in 1953.) France exploded an atomic bomb in 1960, followed by China in 1964. In 1967, China also successfully tested a hydrogen bomb. India tested a nuclear bomb in 1974. Many experts believed that Israel, Pakistan, and South Africa developed nuclear weapons during the 1970s, too.

The continued testing of nuclear weapons threatened to poison the earth's atmosphere. Early on, in 1963, to avoid such poisoning, the United States, the Soviet Union, and Great Britain signed a treaty that banned nuclear testing in the atmosphere, in outer space, and under water. But France, China, and India refused to sign.

Oil became a major factor in world affairs. A second new world condition was the growth in the importance of oil. In the 1950s, vast new reserves of oil were discovered, particularly in the Middle East. At the same time, the consumption of oil began to increase rapidly in Western Europe, Japan, and the United States. By 1980, the Middle East supplied Western Europe with 70 percent of its oil imports, Japan with 90 percent, and the United States with 30 percent.

Such dependence on Middle Eastern oil had serious consequences. Those were dramatically revealed during the 1973–74 Arab-Israeli war, when the Arab oil-producing states cut back supplies and quadrupled the price of oil. These actions seriously affected many economies. Inflation rose sharply. By the mid-1970s, the Western industrialized countries and Japan were suffering from the worst economic recession in more than 40 years. At the same time, the oil money pouring into Arab states created the greatest single redistribution of wealth in the history of the world.

The oil crisis also led to disputes between the United States and its Western European and Japanese allies over the best way to meet the Arab challenge. As oil prices continued to rise in the 1980s, the disagreements became sharper. The problem was aggravated by the Iran crisis of 1979 and the sudden drop in Iranian oil production that resulted.

To reduce dependence on oil produced in the Middle East, the Western European nations arranged to buy natural gas from the Soviet Union. The contracts involved building a 3,600-mile pipeline from Siberia to Western Europe, using Western credits and technology. President Reagan's efforts to block pipeline construction in 1982 threatened a dangerous split in the Atlantic alliance.

China embarked on the "Four Modernizations." A third new condition was China's determination to become a thoroughly modernized country. By the time Mao Tse-tung and Chou En-lai died in 1976, China had made progress in recovering from the disastrous effects of the Great Cultural Revolution of 1966–1969. (See Chapter 33.) The new Chinese leaders wanted to make their country the world's third superpower by the year 2000. To reach this goal they planned to modernize China's agriculture, industry, military forces, and science and technology. They called their program the "Four Modernizations."

Agriculture was given top priority. In the late 1970s, the government had to spend large sums to import grain from Western countries. In 1980, at least three-quarters of China's people were farmers who still used preindustrial farming methods. They could not produce enough food to feed the nation. The aim of modernization was to increase food production through more efficient farming and thus eliminate expensive food imports.

In industry China planned to spend the enormous sum of $600 billion between 1979 and 1985 on new technology. About a third was to be used for the purchase of new plants, equipment, and services from Japan,

WHAT HAPPENED TO LIN PIAO?

In 1969, Lin Piao [lĭn′ byou′] seemed likely to become the leader of China some day. A hero of the revolution, Lin controlled all of China's armed forces and had just been named as Mao Tse-tung's successor.

Two years later, Lin Piao was dead. After his death, Lin was charged with plotting to kill Mao. To this day, both this charge and the story of Lin Piao's death remain a confusing puzzle to everyone except a few Chinese government officials.

Lin Piao met Mao Tse-tung in 1928 when Mao was building his peasant army in a mountain hideout. From that time on, Lin was one of Mao's closest comrades. In 1959, Mao made Lin minister of defense, giving him control of the army. After Mao started the Cultural Revolution in 1966, Lin and his army helped carry out the program. When the Cultural Revolution ended, Lin Piao appeared to be one of the most powerful people in the country.

Then, in September, 1971, word leaked out of China that a Chinese Air Force jet had crashed about 250 miles (400 kilometers) beyond the Chinese border. All aboard were killed. No announcement was made by the Chinese government, however. Later, people noticed that Lin Piao had dropped from sight.

Ten months passed. Finally, in July, 1972, the Chinese government gave an explanation. It said that Lin had taken part in a plot to assassinate Mao. When the plot failed, Lin, his wife, his son, and other conspirators tried to flee to the Soviet Union on a jet plane. But the plane crashed, and all on board were killed.

In August, 1973, Lin's name was removed from the official documents that named him as Mao's successor, and Lin was called a traitor. In 1980, some nine years after his death, Lin was tried and convicted of plotting against Mao.

Are the charges true? It is possible that Lin and Mao did differ over some important matters. Mao may also have come to fear Lin's power. However, some people doubt that Lin would ever have plotted to kill Mao. And the Chinese government has never released much evidence that the plot existed or that Lin played a role in the plot. Unfortunately, Lin's side of the story may be lost forever. So until the Chinese government tells the full story of Lin Piao's downfall, it will remain a mystery to most of the world.

Lin Piao attended many rallies, such as this one in Peking, during the Cultural Revolution. The rallies were meant as encouragement for the Red Guard and others to work harder for the revolutionary cause.

the United States, and Western Europe. Altogether the modernization program included 120 large-scale projects. Among them were ten iron and steel complexes, six new trunk railways, and five new harbors. But to make the program succeed, China had to overcome a shortage of skilled workers, technicians, and managers.

China had one of the largest armies in the world but its weapons were outdated. Military confrontation with the Soviet Union was an ever present danger. The two communist giants shared a 1,900-mile- (3,040-kilometer)-long border, along which the Soviets stationed a million troops with the most up-to-date weapons. Chinese leaders wanted to build modern armaments factories to produce new weapons. Their aim was to develop the capability to meet successfully any Soviet challenge.

To achieve all these goals, China had to improve greatly its level of science and technology. China's leaders made plans to send thousands of students to America, Europe, and Japan for technical training.

Along with plans for the "Four Modernizations" in the 1970s, an important change took place in China's foreign policy. If rapid modernization was to be successful, China needed the cooperation of the Western powers and Japan. China had already pulled away from close association with the Soviet Union. Now it moved closer to the West. In 1971, the People's Republic replaced Taiwan in the UN. Relations between China and the United States improved when President Richard M. Nixon visited China in 1972. In 1979, both countries established full diplomatic relations and exchanged ambassadors. That same year, the senior deputy prime

The United States staged lavish ceremonies, including this one at the White House with President Jimmy Carter, for Deng Xiaoping when he visited America.

minister of China, Deng Xiaoping [dung' shyou'pēng'], visited the United States on a goodwill mission.

The policy of détente encountered obstacles. A fourth new condition came in the late 1960s when tensions between the two superpowers eased somewhat. After 1969 this came to be called "détente," a relaxing of tension between nations. Discussions on a Strategic Arms Limitation Treaty (SALT) began, and preliminary agreements (SALT I) on nuclear arms limitations were signed in Moscow in 1972. Three years later, 35 nations met at Helsinki, Finland, and agreed to the European territorial boundaries between West Germany and Poland that had been set up after World War II. The agreement recognized Eastern Europe as a sphere of Soviet influence. All 35 countries, including the United States and the Soviet Union, pledged to work for peaceful cooperation in Europe and to respect human rights. The Soviet Union did not live up to the human rights agreement, however.

The policy of détente reduced the direct threat of war between the two superpowers, but it did not end their rivalry. The United States and the Soviet Union supported opposing sides in the Arab-Israeli wars. The United States condemned Soviet intervention in Angola. The Soviet Union built up a powerful navy and placed warships in the major oceans of the world. It increased the size of its army until it was larger and better equipped than that of the United States.

In 1978, the Soviets sent $1 billion in arms, 20 thousand Cuban troops, and 1,500 Soviet military advisers and technicians to Ethiopia to aid the Marxist government there.

In December, 1979, the Soviets invaded Afghanistan to bring that country under their complete control. The UN and the United States condemned the invasion. Soviet forces in Afghanistan were only 250 miles (400 kilometers) from the Persian Gulf.

The Soviet invasion of Afghanistan caused the United States Senate to stop consideration of a second nuclear arms limitation agreement, SALT II. In addition, the United States refused to participate in the summer Olympics, held in Moscow in 1980. In 1981, President Ronald Reagan further stiffened the policies against the Soviet Union. He declared that good relations with the United States depended on an end to interventionism by the Soviet Union. Meanwhile, he got Congress to approve a major buildup of American military strength.

The Soviet Union's actions in Poland also angered United States leaders. In 1981, in response to nationwide strikes called by Poland's Solidarity union, the Kremlin directed its puppet government in Warsaw to declare martial law. The Solidarity union, led by Lech Walesa, had moved for political reforms such as a national vote on the future of the communist government.

Under martial law, thousands, including Walesa, were imprisoned. Travel was curtailed and nightime curfews imposed. Economic conditions gradually worsened. Demonstrations against martial law and the imprisonment of Walesa and his followers were supressed with fire hoses and tear gas. Non-communist nations strongly protested these actions and President Reagan imposed economic sanctions against Poland and the Soviet Union.

In late 1982, Walesa and other union members were set free. But their freedom was in name only. Walesa had to promise not to engage in union activities. Restrictions on his movements and constant surveillance made him a prisoner in his own home.

In November, 1982, Soviet leader Leonid Brezhnev died. His successor as general secretary of the Communist Party's Central Committee, the most powerful position in the Soviet hierarchy, was Yuri V. Andropov. Andropov pledged to continue the Leninist policies of Brezhnev.

1. What nations besides the superpowers got nuclear weapons?

2. How did the oil crisis of 1973–74 affect the industrialized nations of the noncommunist world?

3. How did the Four Modernizations affect China's foreign policy?

4. What events affected détente?

4 Third World countries gained a greater voice in world affairs

In the years after World War II, the term *Third World* came into use to refer to the developing countries of Asia, Africa, and Latin America. Third World nations were extremely poor economically, but they played an important role in world affairs.

The Third World suffered from widespread poverty. Three-quarters of the earth's people lived in Third World countries, but they shared only one-fifth of the world's income. Income per person in these countries averaged less than $300 a year. This low income provided such a limited tax base that there was little money available for schools, road building, public health services, and other community needs.

In most Third World countries, farming was the main means of earning a living. But the simple, traditional methods that the peasants used produced barely enough food to feed their families. Many peasants had only small plots of land to till. Most had no technical training and no knowledge of modern farming methods.

The most critical problem facing Third World countries was the threat of hunger. Every day during the 1970s, about 10 thousand persons died from malnutrition. Each year more than 30 million children under the age of 5 died of starvation. When drought struck large areas along the southern edge of the Sahara in the mid-1970s, hundreds of thousands of Africans died for lack of food. In 1980, the UN estimated that people in 26

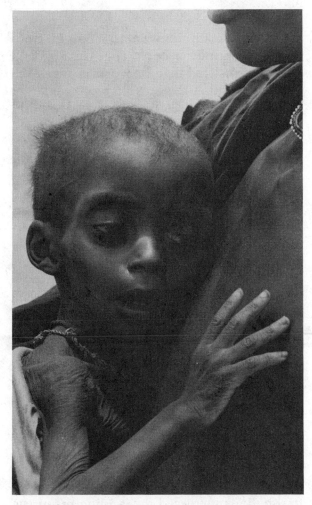

Children seemed to suffer the most from the sub-Saharan drought. This 1973 picture vividly shows the effects of starvation on a baby that is thus close to death.

nations—some 17 of them in Africa—faced the threat of famine.

The gap between rich and poor countries widened. In the 1960s and 1970s, the industrial nations supported economic development programs in many Third World countries. But these did not overcome extreme poverty. Some Third World countries were worse off in 1980 than they had been in 1970. As the wealthy countries grew richer at an increasingly faster pace, the gap between them and the Third World widened.

Third World countries wanted a new international economic order. The Third World countries insisted that the world economy be reshaped so that they would receive a larger share of the world's resources and wealth. They pointed out that they had benefited very little from the remarkable economic advances made in industrial countries after World War II. Among the nations of the North Atlantic community, for example, the standard of living rose more between 1945 and 1980 than it did between the French Revolution in 1789 and 1945.

There were about 120 Third World nations in 1980, and they made up more than two-thirds of the UN's 154 members. In the 1970s, the UN became the major platform from which Third World countries expressed their hopes and frustrations and where they mobilized world opinion. It was there that Third World nations asked for a doubling or tripling of foreign aid, more trade concessions, and more assurance of market stability. They also insisted on fairer prices for their commodities and a larger voice in such international financial agencies as the World Bank. In the early 1980s, the leading industrial nations increased the lending resources of the International Monetary Fund.

section review 4

1. What is meant by "Third World" countries? Where are they located?

2. What was the most critical problem facing Third World countries?

3. Why did the gap between rich and poor countries grow wider?

4. Why was the UN important to Third World countries?

5 The world faced many challenges

As the 1980s opened, many nations of the world faced tough problems. Some of the major problems were tremendous increases in population, environmental pollution, and control of nuclear energy.

World population increased enormously. Early in 1980, the world's population reached 4.5 billion. Almost 2 million years were needed for the world's population to reach its first billion, about 1850. The fourth billion was added in just 16 years, between 1960 and 1976.

The most rapid increase in population took place in Third World countries. Improved health and sanitation led to a sharp fall in death rates, while birth rates remained high. The death rate in India in 1976 was half what it had been in 1950. Population grew faster than food supply in India and in other Third World countries. This helped make poverty and malnutrition a way of life for millions.

With varying success, some underdeveloped nations tried to limit population growth. But to farm families in poor countries, children were the major source of labor.

714

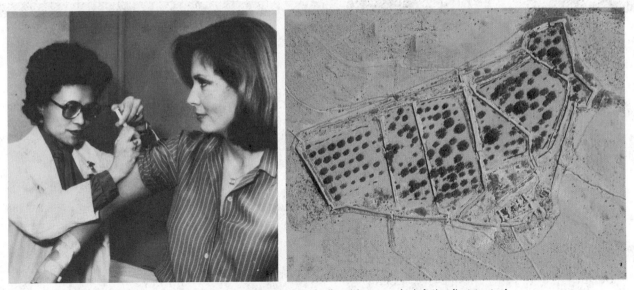

The wonders of modern medicine meant that more people lived longer. At *left* the first test of artificial interferon, a cancer treatment, in 1981 in Texas. But modern medicine also contributed, in part, to the world food shortage. At *right* Israeli farmers use extensive irrigation to grow crops in the Negev desert.

Moreover, in countries where there was no such thing as social security, children were relied on to support elderly parents.

These nations also sought to increase food production as a way to deal with the population problems. As most of the world's fertile land was already in use, the best way to do this was through the increased use of fertilizer. But that, too, presented problems. The use of fertilizer, though, depended on having the money to buy the product or to build the factories to make it. Poor countries did not have the money.

Pollution was an unpleasant result of technology. In the 1960s and 1970s, people in industrialized countries became aware of air, water, and soil pollution and its dangers. Many of the things that made these countries rich also gave them pollution. Automobiles, airplanes, factories, and furnaces all contributed to air pollution.

Careless dumping and faulty storage of toxic chemical wastes from industry brought severe problems of soil as well as water pollution. This affected underground water supplies and food. By 1980, for example, the United States faced problems of chemical spills in various regions. And citizens could not agree on a method for disposing of chemical wastes safely.

The problem of environmental pollution stemmed mainly from industrialization, and as industrialization spread in developing nations, they too felt its effects. In 1980, for example, it was reported that a group of peasants working in a suburb of Peking, China, built a fire to warm themselves against the winter cold. When one of them threw some of the smoldering brushwood into a nearby river, the stream caught fire. An investigation revealed that the surface of the water had been coated with oil discharged upstream by several factories.

Pollution was an inter-regional and, in some respects, an international problem. Some industrial wastes from factories in the American Middle West, for example, rose

715

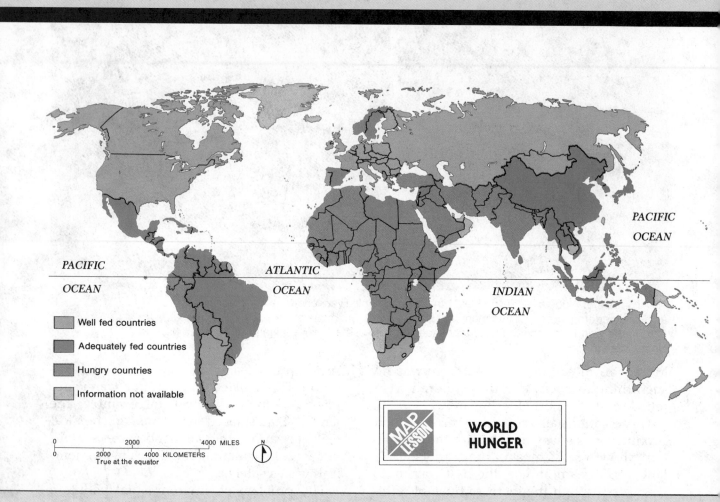

PACIFIC
OCEAN

PACIFIC

OCEAN

ATLANTIC

OCEAN

INDIAN
OCEAN

Well fed countries

Adequately fed countries

Hungry countries

Information not available

0   2000   4000 MILES
0   2000   4000 KILOMETERS
True at the equator

N

MAP
LESSON

WORLD
HUNGER

■ MAP LESSON 36:
WORLD HUNGER

1. This type of map is found in newspapers and news magazines. It divides the nations of the world into several categories and uses a different color for each classification. To simplify matters, the nations are not named. Only national boundaries are shown. It is assumed that the reader will recognize the major nations of the world by their shapes and locations. What two major nations of North America are classified as well fed?

2. What continent in the southern hemisphere is the most well fed?

3. What continent on the map has the largest number of hungry nations?

4. According to this map, which nation has the more adequate food supply:
   a. China or India
   b. Brazil or Argentina
   c. Spain or the Soviet Union
   d. Egypt or Canada
   e. Norway or Iran
   f. Libya or Nigeria

The problems of nuclear energy led some people to look for other forms of energy. This power plant in France is one of the most advanced in the world in use of solar energy.

into the atmosphere. There they combined with water droplets. These later fell as *acid rain* in the eastern United States, bringing soil and water pollution. On a larger scale, when China tested a nuclear device, westerly winds brought nuclear fallout to the United States and Canada.

Nuclear energy was the threat and the promise of the future. Nuclear fallout was one thing, the continued development of nuclear weapons another. The United States and the Soviet Union discussed nuclear arms limitation and signed treaties. Real control, however, remained out of reach. While the possibility of nuclear war between the superpowers remained, the capability of producing nuclear weapons increased in other countries. In addition, there was the possibility that a terrorist group might somehow obtain a nuclear weapon with which to threaten an entire nation. As terrorism grew around the world, this possibility grew also.

The use of nuclear energy for such peaceful purposes as generating electricity gave great hope for the future in a world running short of other supplies, especially oil. But nuclear energy also created its own set of possible disasters through accidents such as the one at Three Mile Island, in the state of Pennsylvania.

Technology, the product of human ingenuity, produced comforts of which people of earlier ages had never dreamed. But it also created serious new problems for people to solve.

section review 5

1. How long did it take the world's population to grow from 3 billion to 4 billion?

2. How is technology linked to pollution?

3. What is acid rain?

4. How was nuclear power both the threat and the hope of the future?

Section Summaries

1. The communist world fragmented. Cracks appeared in the communist monolith as unfriendly relations developed between China and the Soviet Union. The Soviets sent troops into Czechoslovakia when that nation tried to change its Soviet-style communist system. Poland imposed martial law and suspended the independent labor union Solidarity.

2. Western Europe and Japan became economic giants. Under a Labour government, Britain became a welfare state. France moved toward a mixed economy and finally achieved stable government. West Germany recovered from the war to become a leading industrial nation. The development of the Common Market marked a move toward European economic cooperation. Japan became an industrial giant, and its growing exports to the United States caused trade problems between the two nations.

3. Superpower rivalry entered a new stage. As more nations developed nuclear weapons, and as oil became a vital factor in international relations, aspects of superpower rivalry changed. The policies of oil-producing nations of the Middle East became keystones in industrialized nations' economies. Increases in oil prices caused severe problems in those nations. Under new leadership, China began a program of modernization. China also drew closer to the West, establishing diplomatic and trade relations with the United States. The Soviet Union and the United States pursued a policy of détente. Yet continued rivalry in Africa and the Soviet invasion of Afghanistan in 1979 cast serious doubts on that policy's endurance.

4. Third World countries gained a greater voice in world affairs. Poverty characterized Third World countries, and many people in them experienced continual hunger. The Third World countries sought increased aid, trade concessions, and better prices from industrialized nations, but with little success.

5. The world faced many challenges. High rates of population growth, especially in developing nations, was one challenge. Some nations tried to curb population growth and increase food production. Environmental pollution, which became a world problem, was another challenge. A third challenge was the continued development of nuclear weapons and the possible hope of nuclear power in an energy-short world.

Who? What? When? Where?

1. Put the following events in chronological order, beginning with the earliest:
   a. SALT I was signed.
   b. Khrushchev was removed from office.
   c. Britain, Ireland, and Denmark joined the Common Market.
   d. China tested its first hydrogen bomb.
   e. Violence began in Northern Ireland.
   f. Warsaw Pact troops invaded Czechoslovakia.
   g. Chou En-lai and Mao Tse-tung died.
   h. The Soviets invaded Afghanistan.
   i. A spy scandal forced Willy Brandt out of office.

2. Name the nation led by each of these persons:
   a. Brandt   e. Mao
   b. Brezhnev   f. Nixon
   c. Carter   g. Schmidt
   d. de Gaulle   h. Thatcher

3. Write short sentences that define each of these terms:
   a. acid rain
   b. Common Market
   c. Four Modernizations
   d. pollution
   e. Third World

Questions for Critical Thinking

1. Why might the Soviet Union fear closer relations between the United States and China?

2. Why did the Soviet Union view as dangerous the attempts at liberalization in Czechoslovakia?

3. How might improved health and sanitation conditions be said to be a factor in increasing starvation?

4. In what ways is it in the interests of rich countries to come to the aid of poor countries?

5. How is air and water pollution an international rather than just a national problem?

6. Why is it so difficult for an underdeveloped nation to provide goods and services for its citizens?

Skill Activities

1. Read *How Will We Feed the Hungry Billions: Food for Tomorrow's World* by Nigel Hey to learn more about the worldwide problems of adequate food supplies. (Messner, 1971)

2. Choose one of the Soviet intellectuals discussed in Section 1 of the chapter and report to the class on that man's present situation.

3. Choose two of the following groups and prepare an oral report on how they help people in Third World nations achieve a better way of life:

a. A.I.D.	d. Foster Parents Plan
b. CARE	e. UNICEF
c. FAO	f. WHO

4. Use the school library to find out more about solar energy, nuclear energy, and other possible energy sources that are now being studied. Some of these sources are winds, tidal action, and thermal energy.

chapter **36** *quiz*

Section 1

1. The country that became the Soviet Union's rival for power in the communist world was: a. East Germany, b. China, c. Albania

2. Nikita Khrushchev was replaced by the leadership team of: a. Kosygin and Brezhnev, b. Sakharov and Yevtushenko, b. Solzhenitsyn and Kosygin

Section 2

3. True or false: Britain's Labour party began programs that put important industries under public ownership.

4. After World War II, the nation that became Europe's most prosperous was: a. Britain, b. France, c. West Germany

5. By 1962, the largest single trading bloc in the world was: a. Japan, b. the United States, c. the Common Market

Section 3

6. True or false: In 1963, the Soviet Union refused to sign a treaty to ban nuclear testing in the atmosphere.

7. A critical new factor in world affairs in the 1970s was: a. the end of the Great Cultural Revolution, b. maintaining an uninterrupted supply of oil, c. the death of Chou En-lai

8. True or false: China's needs for modern technology brought it closer to the Soviet Union.

Section 4

9. During the 1960s and 1970s, the gap between rich and poor countries: a. decreased, b. increased, c. stayed the same

10. True or false: In the 1980s, Third World nations made up more than two-thirds of the membership of the United Nations.

Section 5

11. Between 1960 and 1976, the greatest population increase was in: a. the industrialized nations, b. the Third World countries, c. the Soviet satellites

12. True or false: By 1980, two major world problems were control of nuclear arms and environmental pollution.

1. Match the letters on the time line with the events they stand for:

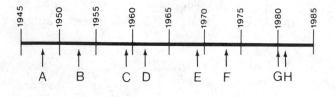

____ The Cuban missile crisis occurred.

____ Iran released its American hostages.

____ The state of Israel began.

____ The United States landed astronauts on the moon.

____ The French left Algeria.

____ Rhodesia became Zimbabwe.

____ The United States left Vietnam.

____ The Korean War ended.

2. Match these people with the correct statements below:

Castro   Sadat

Krushchev Solzhenitsyn

Mao   Thatcher

Mugabe

a. Declared Cuba to be a socialist state.

b. Was the first Arab leader to make peace with Israel.

c. Was expelled from the Soviet Union for criticizing the Soviet system.

d. Was the first woman prime minister of Britain.

e. Was the first leader of Zimbabwe.

f. Started a policy of de-Stalinization in the Soviet Union.

g. Led China through the Great Proletarian Cultural Revolution.

3. Match these nations with the correct statements below:

Angola   Korea

Bangladesh   Mexico

Chile   South Africa

Hungary   Vietnam

Japan   West Germany

a. Although it suffered great damage in World War II, it became the greatest industrial power in Asia.

b. Its 1956 rebellion was forcibly put down by the Soviet Union.

c. After World War II, it became the leading industrial power in Europe.

d. With India's help, it broke away from West Pakistan and became a separate nation.

e. In 1973, its Marxist president was overthrown by a right wing coup.

f. In the late 1970s, it became the leading imperialist power in Southeast Asia.

g. It continued its policy of apartheid.

h. Its economic possibilities were greatly expanded by the discovery of huge oil reserves in the late 1970s.

i. It became independent of Portugal in the mid-1970s.

j. UN troops were used here to stop communist aggression in the early 1950s.

4. Match the letters on the map with the places described below:

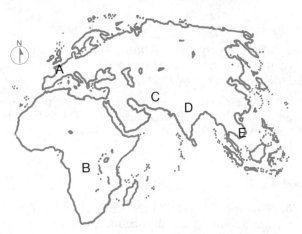

____ A Soviet invasion in this area in 1979 added to the tensions between the two superpowers.

____ This former British colony became two independent nations, one Hindu and one Muslim.

____ Once a French colony, this nation was united under communist control after more than 30 years of warfare.

____ Once a Belgian colony, this nation became independent and then suffered a civil war as the province called Katanga tried to secede.

____ Countries in this area received Marshall Plan aid after World War II.

ATLAS OF THE CONTEMPORARY WORLD

THE WORLD

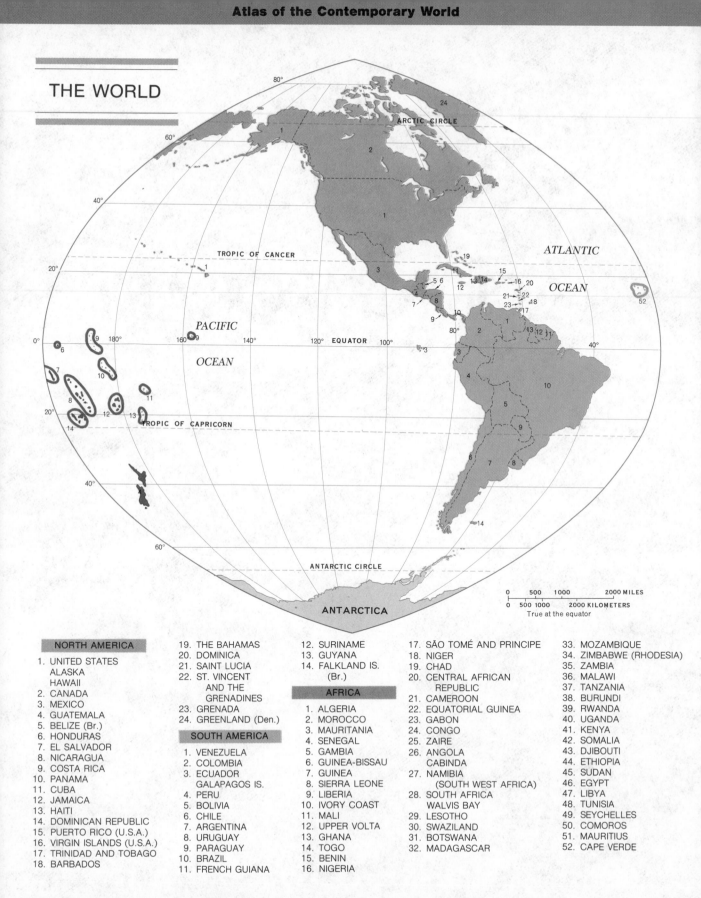

ATLANTIC OCEAN

PACIFIC OCEAN

ANTARCTICA

```
0    500  1000        2000 MILES
0  500 1000      2000 KILOMETERS
True at the equator
```

NORTH AMERICA

1. UNITED STATES
   ALASKA
   HAWAII
2. CANADA
3. MEXICO
4. GUATEMALA
5. BELIZE (Br.)
6. HONDURAS
7. EL SALVADOR
8. NICARAGUA
9. COSTA RICA
10. PANAMA
11. CUBA
12. JAMAICA
13. HAITI
14. DOMINICAN REPUBLIC
15. PUERTO RICO (U.S.A.)
16. VIRGIN ISLANDS (U.S.A.)
17. TRINIDAD AND TOBAGO
18. BARBADOS
19. THE BAHAMAS
20. DOMINICA
21. SAINT LUCIA
22. ST. VINCENT
    AND THE
    GRENADINES
23. GRENADA
24. GREENLAND (Den.)

SOUTH AMERICA

1. VENEZUELA
2. COLOMBIA
3. ECUADOR
   GALAPAGOS IS.
4. PERU
5. BOLIVIA
6. CHILE
7. ARGENTINA
8. URUGUAY
9. PARAGUAY
10. BRAZIL
11. FRENCH GUIANA
12. SURINAME
13. GUYANA
14. FALKLAND IS.
    (Br.)

AFRICA

1. ALGERIA
2. MOROCCO
3. MAURITANIA
4. SENEGAL
5. GAMBIA
6. GUINEA-BISSAU
7. GUINEA
8. SIERRA LEONE
9. LIBERIA
10. IVORY COAST
11. MALI
12. UPPER VOLTA
13. GHANA
14. TOGO
15. BENIN
16. NIGERIA
17. SÃO TOMÉ AND PRINCIPE
18. NIGER
19. CHAD
20. CENTRAL AFRICAN
    REPUBLIC
21. CAMEROON
22. EQUATORIAL GUINEA
23. GABON
24. CONGO
25. ZAIRE
26. ANGOLA
    CABINDA
27. NAMIBIA
    (SOUTH WEST AFRICA)
28. SOUTH AFRICA
    WALVIS BAY
29. LESOTHO
30. SWAZILAND
31. BOTSWANA
32. MADAGASCAR
33. MOZAMBIQUE
34. ZIMBABWE (RHODESIA)
35. ZAMBIA
36. MALAWI
37. TANZANIA
38. BURUNDI
39. RWANDA
40. UGANDA
41. KENYA
42. SOMALIA
43. DJIBOUTI
44. ETHIOPIA
45. SUDAN
46. EGYPT
47. LIBYA
48. TUNISIA
49. SEYCHELLES
50. COMOROS
51. MAURITIUS
52. CAPE VERDE

722

Map based on information available March 1, 1981

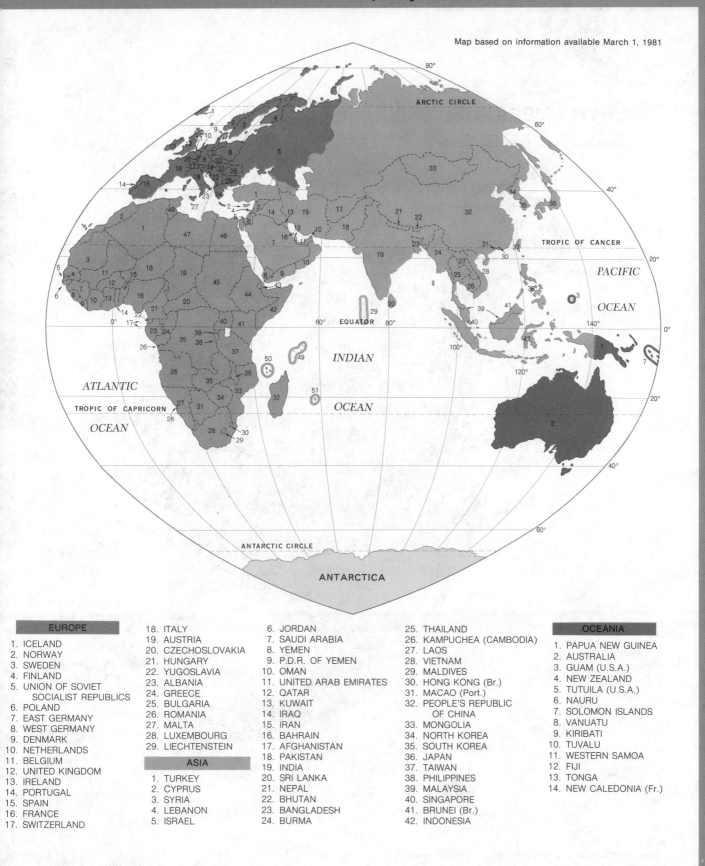

EUROPE		
1. ICELAND		
2. NORWAY		
3. SWEDEN		
4. FINLAND		
5. UNION OF SOVIET SOCIALIST REPUBLICS		
6. POLAND		
7. EAST GERMANY		
8. WEST GERMANY		
9. DENMARK		
10. NETHERLANDS		
11. BELGIUM		
12. UNITED KINGDOM		
13. IRELAND		
14. PORTUGAL		
15. SPAIN		
16. FRANCE		
17. SWITZERLAND		

18. ITALY
19. AUSTRIA
20. CZECHOSLOVAKIA
21. HUNGARY
22. YUGOSLAVIA
23. ALBANIA
24. GREECE
25. BULGARIA
26. ROMANIA
27. MALTA
28. LUXEMBOURG
29. LIECHTENSTEIN

ASIA

1. TURKEY
2. CYPRUS
3. SYRIA
4. LEBANON
5. ISRAEL

6. JORDAN
7. SAUDI ARABIA
8. YEMEN
9. P.D.R. OF YEMEN
10. OMAN
11. UNITED ARAB EMIRATES
12. QATAR
13. KUWAIT
14. IRAQ
15. IRAN
16. BAHRAIN
17. AFGHANISTAN
18. PAKISTAN
19. INDIA
20. SRI LANKA
21. NEPAL
22. BHUTAN
23. BANGLADESH
24. BURMA

25. THAILAND
26. KAMPUCHEA (CAMBODIA)
27. LAOS
28. VIETNAM
29. MALDIVES
30. HONG KONG (Br.)
31. MACAO (Port.)
32. PEOPLE'S REPUBLIC OF CHINA
33. MONGOLIA
34. NORTH KOREA
35. SOUTH KOREA
36. JAPAN
37. TAIWAN
38. PHILIPPINES
39. MALAYSIA
40. SINGAPORE
41. BRUNEI (Br.)
42. INDONESIA

OCEANIA

1. PAPUA NEW GUINEA
2. AUSTRALIA
3. GUAM (U.S.A.)
4. NEW ZEALAND
5. TUTUILA (U.S.A.)
6. NAURU
7. SOLOMON ISLANDS
8. VANUATU
9. KIRIBATI
10. TUVALU
11. WESTERN SAMOA
12. FIJI
13. TONGA
14. NEW CALEDONIA (Fr.)

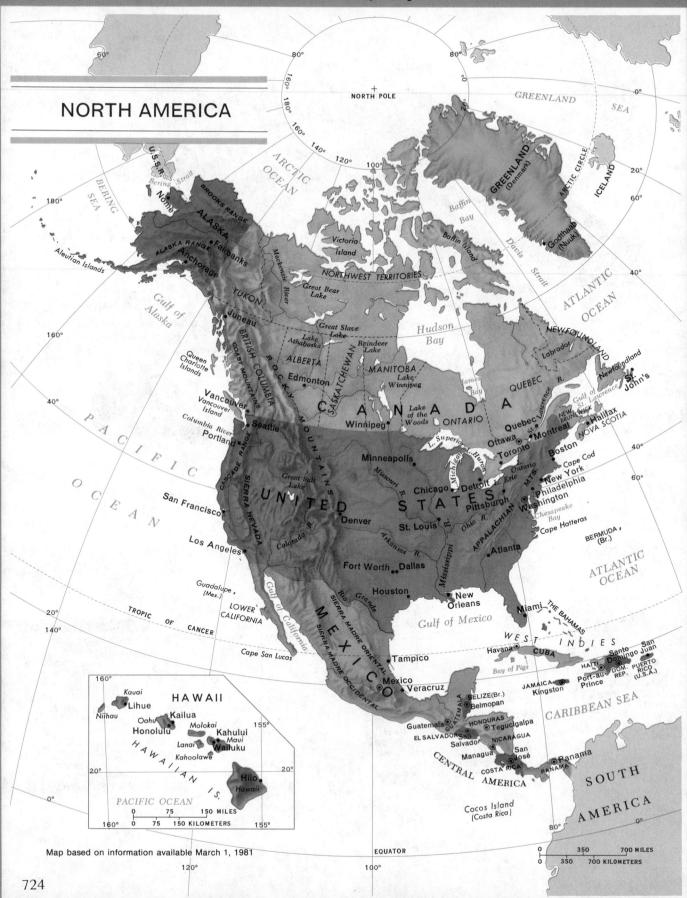

NORTH AMERICA

NORTH POLE

GREENLAND SEA

ARCTIC OCEAN

GREENLAND (Denmark)

ARCTIC CIRCLE

ICELAND

U.S.S.R.

Bering Strait

Nome

BROOKS RANGE

ALASKA

Fairbanks

ALASKA RANGE

Anchorage

Aleutian Islands

BERING SEA

Baffin Bay

Baffin Island

Victoria Island

NORTHWEST TERRITORIES

Mackenzie River

Great Bear Lake

YUKON

Juneau

Gulf of Alaska

Queen Charlotte Islands

COAST MOUNTAINS

BRITISH COLUMBIA

Great Slave Lake

Lake Athabasca

Reindeer Lake

Godthaab (Nuuk)

Davis Strait

Hudson Bay

NEWFOUNDLAND

Labrador

ATLANTIC OCEAN

Vancouver
Vancouver Island

ROCKY MOUNTAINS

Edmonton

ALBERTA

SASKATCHEWAN

MANITOBA

Lake Winnipeg

James Bay

QUEBEC

Newfoundland

St. John's

Columbia River

Seattle

Portland

CASCADE RANGE

Winnipeg

Lake of the Woods

ONTARIO

C A N A D A

Ottawa

St. Lawrence R.

Gulf of St. Lawrence

NEW BRUNSWICK

Quebec

Montreal

NOVA SCOTIA

Halifax

PACIFIC OCEAN

SIERRA NEVADA

Great Salt Lake

San Francisco

UNITED STATES

Minneapolis

L. Superior

Missouri R.

Chicago

L. Michigan

L. Huron

Detroit

L. Erie

L. Ontario

Toronto

Boston

Cape Cod

New York

Philadelphia

APPALACHIAN MTS.

Pittsburgh

Washington

Chesapeake Bay

Los Angeles

Denver

Colorado R.

St. Louis

Ohio R.

Arkansas R.

Mississippi R.

Cape Hatteras

BERMUDA (Br.)

Guadalupe (Mex.)

LOWER CALIFORNIA

TROPIC OF CANCER

Cape San Lucas

Fort Worth

Dallas

Houston

Atlanta

New Orleans

Miami

THE BAHAMAS

ATLANTIC OCEAN

Rio Grande

SIERRA MADRE ORIENTAL

SIERRA MADRE OCCIDENTAL

Gulf of California

M E X I C O

Gulf of Mexico

W E S T   I N D I E S

Havana

CUBA

Bay of Pigs

HAITI

Port-au-Prince

DOM. REP.

Santo Domingo

San Juan

PUERTO RICO (U.S.A.)

CARIBBEAN SEA

Tampico

Mexico

Veracruz

JAMAICA

Kingston

BELIZE (Br.)

Belmopan

GUATEMALA

Guatemala

HONDURAS

Tegucigalpa

EL SALVADOR

San Salvador

NICARAGUA

Managua

San José

COSTA RICA

Panama

PANAMA

SOUTH AMERICA

CENTRAL AMERICA

Cocos Island (Costa Rica)

HAWAII

Kauai

Lihue

Niihau

Oahu

Honolulu

Kailua

Molokai

Lanai

Maui

Kahului

Wailuku

Kahoolawe

HAWAIIAN IS.

Hilo

Hawaii

PACIFIC OCEAN

0   75   150 MILES

0   75   150 KILOMETERS

Map based on information available March 1, 1981

EQUATOR

0   350   700 MILES

0   350   700 KILOMETERS

West Indies

CENTRAL AMERICA

CARIBBEAN SEA

Guadeloupe (Fr.)   DOMINICA
Martinique (Fr.)   ST. LUCIA
Curaçao (Neth.)   BARBADOS
GRENADA   ST. VINCENT AND THE GRENADINES
TRINIDAD AND TOBAGO

SOUTH AMERICA

Barranquilla
Colón   Balboa
Lake Maracaibo
Caracas
VENEZUELA
Georgetown
Paramaribo
Cayenne
Bogotá
GUYANA
SURINAME   FRENCH GUIANA
Buenaventura
COLOMBIA
Magdalena R.
Orinoco R.

Quito
ECUADOR
Galápagos Islands (Ecuador)
Guayaquil
Iquitos
Napo R.
Ucayali R.
EQUATOR   0°
Rio Negro
Amazon   River
Manaus
Belém

P E R U
A N D E S
Lima
Arequipa
Madeira R.
B R A Z I L
Tocantins R.
Recife
São Francisco R.
Salvador

Lake Titicaca
La Paz
BOLIVIA
Sucre
MATO GROSSO
Brasília
Belo Horizonte
Paraná R.

GRAN CHACO
PARAGUAY
Antofagasta
Asunción
São Paulo
Rio de Janeiro
Santos

TROPIC OF CAPRICORN
Tucumán
A R G E N T I N A
C H I L E
A N D E S
Córdoba
Santa Fé
URUGUAY
Paraguay R.
Valparaíso
Mendoza
Rosario
Montevideo
Santiago
Salado R.
Buenos Aires
Rio de la Plata
Valdivia
Colorado R.
Bahía Blanca

PACIFIC OCEAN
ATLANTIC OCEAN

Chubut R.
PATAGONIA

Falkland Is. (Br.)
West Falkland
East Falkland
Punta Arenas
TIERRA DEL FUEGO
Cape Horn

0   300   600 MILES
0   300   600 KILOMETERS

Map based on information available March 1, 1981

105°   90°   75°   60°   45°   30°   15°   0°

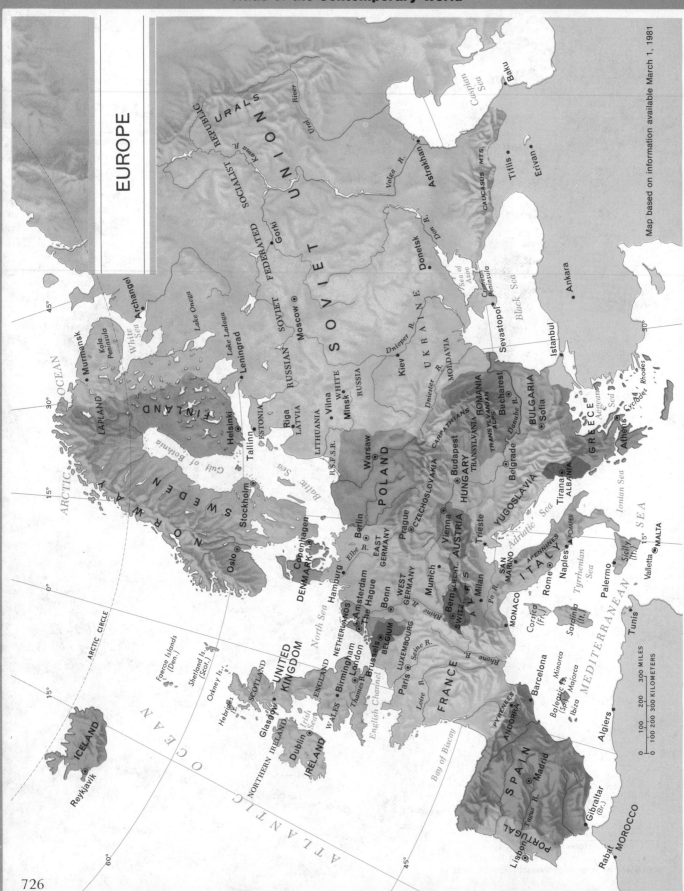

EUROPE

Map based on information available March 1, 1981

ARCTIC OCEAN

Murmansk
Kola Peninsula
LAPLAND
Archangel
White Sea
Lake Onega
Lake Ladoga

FINLAND
Helsinki
Leningrad
Moscow
Gorki
RUSSIAN SOVIET FEDERATED SOCIALIST REPUBLIC
URALS
Kama R.
Ural R.
Volga R.
Kama R.
Astrakhan
Caspian Sea
Baku

NORWAY
SWEDEN
Oslo
Stockholm
Gulf of Bothnia
Baltic Sea
Tallinn
ESTONIA
Riga
LATVIA
LITHUANIA
Vilna
Minsk
WHITE RUSSIA
R.S.F.S.R.

Copenhagen
DENMARK
Warsaw
POLAND
Berlin
EAST GERMANY
Elbe R.
Prague
CZECHOSLOVAKIA

Dnieper R.
Kiev
UKRAINE
Dniester R.
MOLDAVIA
Sevastopol
Black Sea
Sea of Azov
Crimean Peninsula
Donetsk
Don R.
CAUCASUS MTS.
Tiflis
Erivan
Ankara

Istanbul
BULGARIA
Sofia
ROMANIA
Bucharest
Danube R.
TRANSYLVANIAN ALPS
TRANSYLVANIA
CARPATHIANS
HUNGARY
Budapest
Vienna
AUSTRIA
Belgrade
YUGOSLAVIA
Tirana
ALBANIA
GREECE
Athens
Aegean Sea
Rhodes
Cyclades
Scit
Ionian Sea

Hamburg
Amsterdam
NETHERLANDS
The Hague
WEST GERMANY
Bonn
Munich
Bern
SWITZ.
Liecht.
ALPS
Milan
Po R.
Trieste
SAN MARINO
APENNINES
ITALY
Rome
Naples
POMPEII
Tyrrhenian Sea
Sicily (It.)
Palermo
MALTA
Valletta
Rhine R.

UNITED KINGDOM
SCOTLAND
Glasgow
Shetland Is. (Scot.)
Orkney Is.
Hebrides
NORTHERN IRELAND
Irish Sea
Dublin
IRELAND
WALES
Birmingham
ENGLAND
London
Thames R.
English Channel
North Sea
Brussels
BELGIUM
LUXEMBOURG
Paris
Seine R.
Loire R.
FRANCE
Rhône R.
Bay of Biscay
MONACO
Corsica (Fr.)
Sardinia (It.)

Barcelona
Minorca
Balearic Is. (Sp.)
Majorca
Ibiza
PYRENEES
ANDORRA
SPAIN
Madrid
Tagus R.
PORTUGAL
Lisbon
Gibraltar (Br.)
MOROCCO
Rabat
Algiers
Tunis
MEDITERRANEAN SEA
MOROCCO

Foeroe Islands (Den.)
ICELAND
Reykjavik
ATLANTIC OCEAN
ARCTIC CIRCLE

SOVIET UNION

300 MILES
300 KILOMETERS
0 100 200 300
0 100 200 300

45°
30°
15°
0°
15°
60°
45°

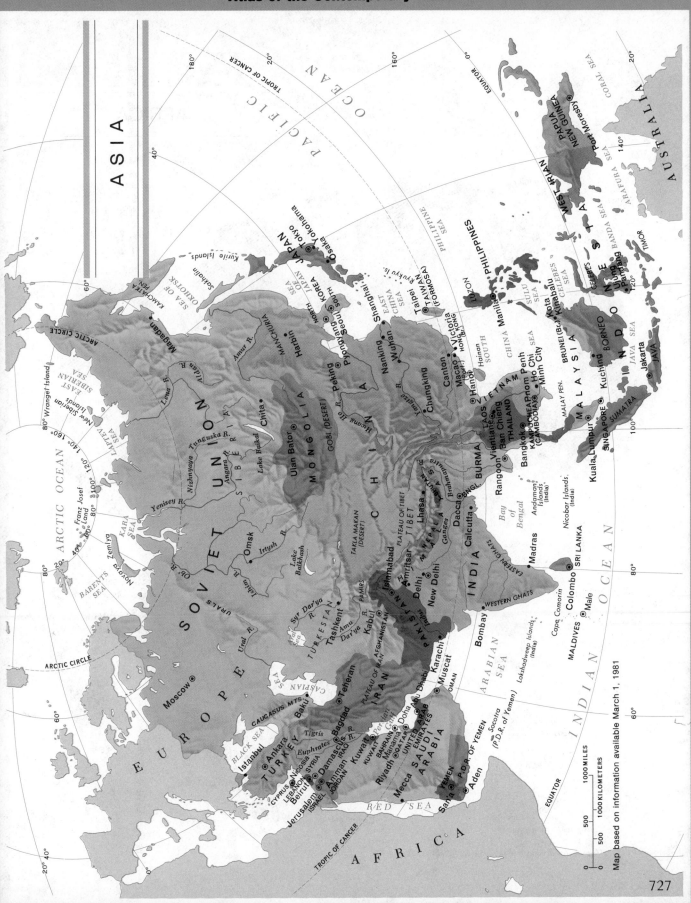

ASIA

PACIFIC OCEAN

TROPIC OF CANCER

CORAL SEA

AUSTRALIA

WEST IRIAN

PAPUA NEW GUINEA
Port Moresby

ARAFURA SEA
BANDA SEA
TIMOR
Ujung Pandang
CELEBES SEA
CELEBES

PHILIPPINE SEA

PHILIPPINES
LUZON
Manila

SULU SEA
Kota Kinabalu
BRUNEI (Br.)
BORNEO
Kuching
MALAYSIA
Kuala Lumpur
SINGAPORE
SUMATRA
JAVA SEA
Jakarta
JAVA

INDONESIA

SOUTH CHINA SEA
Hainan
HONG KONG (Br.)
Macao (Port.)
Canton
Hanoi
VIETNAM
LAOS
Phnom Penh
KAMPUCHEA (CAMBODIA)
Ho Chi Minh City
Vientiane
Ban Chieng
THAILAND
Bangkok
BURMA
Rangoon
MALAY PEN.

Andaman Islands (India)
Nicobar Islands (India)

Bay of Bengal

BANGL.
Dacca
Calcutta
EASTERN GHATS
Madras
SRI LANKA
Colombo
Cape Comorin
WESTERN GHATS
MALDIVES
Male
Lokshadweep Islands (India)

INDIAN OCEAN

JAPAN
Tokyo
Yokohama
Osaka

Kurile Islands
Sakhalin
SEA OF OKHOTSK
KAMCHATKA PEN.
Magadan
ARCTIC CIRCLE
Wrangel Island
New Siberian Islands
EAST SIBERIAN SEA
LAPTEV SEA

SEA OF JAPAN
NORTH KOREA
Pyongyang
SOUTH KOREA
Seoul
Shanghai
EAST CHINA SEA
RYUKYU Is.
TAIWAN (FORMOSA)
Taipei

MANCHURIA
Harbin
Amur R.

Nanking
Wuhan
Chungking
CHINA
Peking
Huang Ho R.
Yangtze R.

SIBERIA
Lena R.
Vilyui R.
Chita
Lake Baikal
Nizhnyaya Tunguska R.
Angara R.
Yenisey R.
Franz Josef Land
Novaya Zemlya
KARA SEA
BARENTS SEA

MONGOLIA
Ulan Bator
GOBI (DESERT)

SOVIET UNION
Omsk
Irtysh R.
Lake Balkhash
Ob' R.
Ishim R.
URALS
Moscow

TAKLA MAKAN (DESERT)
PLATEAU OF TIBET
TIBET
Lhasa
HIMALAYA
Brahmaputra
NEPAL
Ganges
New Delhi
Delhi
Amritsar
Islamabad
PAKISTAN
INDIA
Bombay
Karachi
ARABIAN SEA

PAMIRS
Syr Dar'ya
Amu Dar'ya
TURKESTAN
Tashkent
Aral Sea
Kabul
AFGHANISTAN
PLATEAU OF AFGHANISTAN
Tehran
IRAN
PLATEAU OF IRAN
Baku
CASPIAN SEA
CAUCASUS MTS.

ARCTIC OCEAN
ARCTIC CIRCLE

EUROPE

BLACK SEA
Istanbul
Ankara
TURKEY
CYPRUS
Nicosia
LEBANON
Beirut
Jerusalem
ISRAEL
Damascus
SYRIA
Amman
JORDAN
Tigris
Euphrates
IRAQ
Bagdad
KUWAIT
Kuwait
SAUDI ARABIA
Riyadh
Mecca
Medina
BAHRAIN
Manama
QATAR
Doha
Abu Dhabi
UNITED ARAB EMIRATES
Persian Gulf
Muscat
OMAN
YEMEN
San'a
P.D.R. OF YEMEN
Aden
Socotra (P.D.R. of Yemen)

RED SEA
TROPIC OF CANCER

AFRICA

EQUATOR

Map based on information available March 1, 1981

1000 MILES
1000 KILOMETERS
500
500
0

727

AFRICA

EUROPE

ATLANTIC OCEAN

MEDITERRANEAN SEA

ASIA

Lisbon
Rome
Athens
Tangier
Rabat
Algiers
Tunis
TUNISIA
Tripoli
Bengasi
Alexandria
Cairo
Luxor
Sinai Pen.
MOROCCO
Madeira Is. (Port.)
Sidi Ifni
Canary Is. (Sp.)

ALGERIA
LIBYA
LIBYAN DESERT
EGYPT

ATLAS MOUNTAINS

S A H A R A
TROPIC OF CANCER
Mecca
ARABIAN PENINSULA
Lake Nasser
RED SEA

MAURITANIA
MALI
NIGER
TIBESTI MASSIF
CHAD
S U D A N
Omdurman
Khartoum
ERITREA
Nouakchott
Timbuktu
Gao
Niamey
Lake Chad
N'Djamena
KORDOFAN PLATEAU
Lake Tana
Djibouti DJIBOUTI
Gulf of Aden

Sénégal R.
Dakar
SENEGAL
Banjul
GAMBIA
Bissau
GUINEA-BISSAU
Gambia R.
Bamako
Niger R.
UPPER VOLTA
Ouagadougou
NIGERIA
Volta R.
Niger River
AMHARA PLATEAU
Addis Ababa
ETHIOPIA
Blue Nile
White Nile

Conakry
GUINEA
Freetown
SIERRA LEONE
LIBERIA
Monrovia
IVORY COAST
GHANA
TOGO
BENIN
Lomé
Accra
Lagos
Porto-Novo
CAMEROON
Yaoundé
CENTRAL AFRICAN REPUBLIC
Bangui
Ubangi
CONGO BASIN
UGANDA
SOMALIA
Mogadishu
Lake Rudolf
Kampala
KENYA
Nairobi

Abidjan
EQUATOR
Macias Nguema Bigoyo
Malabo
EQUATORIAL GUINEA
Gulf of Guinea
SÃO TOMÉ AND PRINCIPE
RIO MUNI
São Tomé
Libreville
GABON
Pagalu
Congo River
Lake Mai-Ndombe
RWANDA
Kigali
BURUNDI
Bujumbura
Lake Victoria

Brazzaville
CABINDA (Ang.)
Kinshasa
ZAÏRE
Lake Tanganyika
TANZANIA
Dar es Salaam
Zanzibar Is.
Aldabra Is. (Br.)

ATLANTIC OCEAN
Ascension (St. Helena–Br.)
Luanda

ANGOLA
MALAWI
Lake Nyasa
Moroni
COMOROS

ZAMBIA
Lusaka
Zambezi River
Liongwe
MOZAMBIQUE

St. Helena (Br.)
Victoria Falls
Kariba Lake
Salisbury
ZIMBABWE (RHODESIA)
Antananarivo
MADAGASCAR
Mozambique Channel

NAMIBIA (SOUTH WEST AFRICA)
Okovanggo Swamp
Windhoek
BOTSWANA
TROPIC OF CAPRICORN
Walvis Bay (S. Africa)
Gaborone
KALAHARI DESERT
Mafeking
Pretoria
Maputo
Mbabane
SWAZILAND

SOUTH AFRICA
Maseru
LESOTHO

INDIAN OCEAN

Cape Town
Cape of Good Hope

0   300   600 MILES
0   300   600 KILOMETERS

Map based on information available March 1, 1981

OCEANIA

120°   130°   140°   150°   160°

10°

EQUATOR   0°

INDONESIA

WEST IRIAN

NEW GUINEA

BISMARCK ARCH.

New Ireland

Rabaul

Papua New Guinea

New Britain

Lae

Salamaua

Port Moresby

NAURU ⊙ Yaren   EQUATOR   0°

Bougainville

Kieta   SOLOMON ISLANDS

Honiara ⊙ Guadalcanal

ARAFURA SEA

Torres Strait

Cape York

Gulf of Carpentaria

Great Barrier Reef

CORAL SEA

10°

TIMOR SEA

Darwin

ARNHEM LAND

Wyndham

Broome

GREAT SANDY DESERT

NORTHERN TERRITORY

Normanton

Townsville

VANUATU

Port-Vila ⊙

Roebourne

WESTERN AUSTRALIA

HAMMERSLEY PLATEAU

MACDONNELL RANGES

AUSTRALIA

GIBSON DESERT

Alice Springs

MUSGRAVE RANGES

ARUNTA DESERT

QUEENSLAND

GREAT DIVIDING RANGE

Rockhampton

Charleville

New Caledonia (Fr.)

Nouméa

20°

TROPIC OF CAPRICORN

GREAT VICTORIA DESERT

Lake Eyre

SOUTH AUSTRALIA

FLINDERS RANGE

Broken Hill

Darling R.

NEW SOUTH WALES

Brisbane

PACIFIC OCEAN

Perth

Fremantle

NULLARBOR PLAIN

Great Australian Bight

Port Lincoln

Spencer Gulf

Adelaide

Murray R.

VICTORIA

Canberra

AUSTRALIAN CAPITAL TERRITORY

Newcastle

Sydney

TASMAN SEA

30°

Albany

Melbourne

Bass Strait

INDIAN OCEAN

TASMANIA

Launceston

Hobart

North Cape

Auckland

North Island

NEW ZEALAND

Cook Strait

Wellington

40°

0   250   500 MILES

0   250   500 KILOMETERS

South Island

Christchurch

Dunedin

Map based on information available March 1, 1981

50°

110°   120°   130°   140°   150°   160°   170°   180°

GLOSSARY

Pronunciation Key

hat, āge, fär; let, ēqual, tėrm; it, īce; hot, ōpen, ôrder; oil, out; cup, pút, rüle; ə represents *a* in about, *e* in taken, *i* in pencil, *o* in lemon, *u* in circus.

A

acid rain industrial wastes in the atmosphere that combine with water droplets and fall to the ground.

act (akt), *n.* decision of a legislature; law; statute.

administrator (ad min′ə strā′tər), *n.* person who directs the work of a group or business; manager.

agricultural collectives in communist countries, large farms in which most of the land is worked cooperatively by many families.

alabaster (al′ə bas′tər), *n.* a white, marblelike stone.

Allah (al′ə), *n.* the Muslim name for God.

ally (al′ī), *n.* nation that supports the policies and actions of another nation

alphabet (al′fə bet), *n.* set of letters or characters representing sounds, used in writing a language.

Amir (ə mir′), *n.* title of honor, meaning leader, that was given to the descendants of Mohammad.

Anglican (ang′glə kən), *adj.* of or having to do with the Church of England.

anthropologist (an′thrə pol′ə jist), *n.* a scientist who studies the origin, races, and customs of people, both ancient and modern.

apartheid (ə pärt′hīt) *n.* policy of South Africa of the strict separation of the races.

aqueduct (ak′wə dukt), *n.* bridgelike structure that holds pipes for bringing water from a distance.

archaeologist (är′kē ol′ə jist), *n.* a scientist who studies the remains of ancient cultures by excavating and classifying material.

assimilation (ə sim′ə lā′shən), *n.* the process of becoming like the people of a nation in customs, viewpoint, character, and ways of living.

atom (at′əm), *n.* the smallest particle of a chemical element that can take part in a chemical reaction without being permanently changed.

Australopithecines (ô′strə lō pith′ə-sēns), *n.* a name scientists have given to an early group of beings who lived before *Homo sapiens.* Their fossil remains were first found in South Africa and later in other parts of the world.

B

bailiff (bā′lif), *n.* in the feudal system, a person who supervised the work of the peasants and the farming of the land. He also checked the financial accounts and the collection of rents, dues, and fines.

balance of power a term meaning that no one country should have overwhelming power over other countries.

baptism (bap′tiz′əm), *n.* rite or sacrament by which a person is admitted into the Christian church.

bill (bil), *n.* a proposed law presented to a lawmaking body for its approval.

blitzkrieg (blits′krēg′), *n.* a German word meaning "lightning warfare."

block printing early Chinese printing done during the Tang era. The printer carved raised characters on a block of wood, wet the surface of the characters with ink, and pressed sheets of paper against them.

borough (bėr′ō), *n.* a chartered town.

bourgeoisie (bùr′zhwä zē′), *n.* the social class that arose during the Middle Ages; the middle class, made up of skilled workers and merchants; in Marxist theory, the capitalist class.

boyar (bō yär′), *n.* Russian noble.

Brahma (brä′mə), *n.* in Hinduism, the pervading soul of the universe, the god of creation.

Brahman (brä′mən), *n.* member of the priestly caste, the highest caste in India.

brotherhood (bruth′ər hùd), *n.* association of people with some common aim, characteristic, belief, profession; bond between brothers.

burgess (bėr′jis), *n.* in England, a citizen of a borough.

burgher (bėr′gər), *n.* a member of the bourgeoisie.

Bushido (bü′shē dō), *n.* moral code of the knights and warriors of feudal Japan.

buttress (but′ris), *n.* support built against a wall or building to strengthen it.

Byzantine (biz′n tēn′), *adj.* of or like the Byzantine Empire or Byzantium; of or like a style of architecture developed by the Byzantine Empire, characterized by a circular dome over a square space, and the use of mosaics and frescoes.

C

cabinet (kab′ə nit), *n.* group of advisers chosen by the head of a government to aid in administration.

caliph (kā′lif), *n.* the former title of religious and political heads of some Muslim states; a successor of Mohammad.

capital (kap′ə təl), *n.* in economics, the money, goods, and property that a company or a person uses in carrying on a business.

capitalism (kap′ə tə liz′əm), *n.* an economic system in which private individuals or companies own the businesses and compete with each other in a free market.

caravan (kar′ə van), *n.* a group of people traveling together for safety through difficult or dangerous country.

caste system social classes into which the people of India were divided. By tradition, a person was born into the caste of his or her father and could not rise above it.

casualty (kazh′ü əl tē), *n. pl.* **ties.** soldier who is wounded, killed, or captured during a war.

cavalry (kav′əl rē), *n., pl.* **-ries.** soldiers mounted on horseback.

china (chī′nə), *n.* porcelain of an especially fine grade, developed by a process first used in China.

circuit (sėr′kit), *n.* route over which a journey is made and repeated at certain times.

citadel (sit′ə dəl), *n.* a fortress guarding a city.

city-state an independent state consisting of a city and the territories surrounding it.

civilization (siv′ə lə zā′shən), *n.* the advanced stage of human life in which people have cities and organized governments.

civil service employees of a government, except for elected officials and those in the military, naval, legislative, or judicial branches.

clan (klan), *n.* group of related families that are descended from a common ancestor.

classical (klas′ə kəl), *adj.* something thought of as a kind of standard or ideal; being the original or traditional form of something.

classical culture that blend of Greek and Roman culture that became the basis for Western civilization.

class struggle according to Marx, a situation that occurs when new groups find new ways of making or distributing goods which give them power against the older, ruling groups. This power results in a fight for control that leads to revolution.

Code Napoleon in Napoleon's modernization of French law, a series of codes that established the principle of equality before the law.

codex (ko'deks), *n., pl.* **codices.** an ancient manuscript of the Scriptures or of a classical author; a book used by the Aztecs in the 15th century to record their history. It was written on long strips of paper and folded like a fan.

codify (kod'ə fī), *v.* **-fied, -fying.** organize into a system that can be more easily used.

Cold War a term first used by American journalists to describe hostile relations between the Soviet Union and the United States. It has come to mean conflict between nations for national advantage conducted by political, economic, and psychological means rather than by direct military action.

commerce (kom'ərs), *n.* trade; buying and selling, especially in large amounts between different places.

Commercial Revolution changes in the business life in Europe, brought about by increased trade with the European empires overseas. It resulted in the introduction of new business methods, an increase in prices, and the growth of modern capitalism.

common law law based on custom and court decisions.

commune (kom'yün), *n.* formerly, a political division made up of groups of collective farms.

Communist (kom'yə nist), *n.* member of a Communist Party; **communist,** a person who favors and supports the principles of communism.

company (kum'pə nē), *n., pl.* **-nies.** a group of people joined together for some purpose; a military group. The early Roman legions were divided into groups of 120 men called *companies.*

compound (kom'pound), *n.* something made by combining parts; many little buildings connected by a wall or fence with a center courtyard.

condominium (kon'də min'ē əm), *n.* country whose government is controlled jointly by two or more other countries.

condottieri (kon'dôt tye'rē), *n.* soldiers in 14th-century Italy.

confirmation (kon'fər mā'shən), *n.* in religion, the ceremony of admitting a person to full membership in a church or synagogue.

Confucianism (kən fyü'shə niz'əm), *n.* the moral teachings of Confucius and his followers.

consul (kon'səl), *n.* in ancient Rome, either of the two chief magistrates who together with the senate governed the republic.

corporation (kôr'pə rā'shən), *n.* a group of persons who obtain a charter that gives them as a group certain legal rights and privileges distinct from those of the individual members of the group, such as the right to buy, sell, and own property and the right to limit their financial responsibility for the business.

county (koun'tē), *n., pl.* **-ties.** one of the districts into which a state or country is divided for administrative, judicial, and political purposes. During his reign, Charlemagne divided his empire into counties.

coup d'état (kü' dā tä'), *n.* a sudden, decisive act in politics, usually bringing about a change of government unlawfully or by force.

credit financing a system of running a business with borrowed money.

cremate (krē'māt), *v.* **-mated, -mating.** burn a dead body to ashes instead of burying it.

creole (krē'ōl), *n.* a child born in Latin America whose parents had been born in Spain.

crusade (krü sād'), *n.* one of a series of military campaigns mounted by the medieval Christian church for the purpose of recovering the Holy Land from the Muslims.

crusader (krü sā'dər), *n.* person who took part in any of the crusades to recover the Holy Land.

culture (kul'chər), *n.* the way in which people live and work to satisfy their basic needs.

cuneiform (kyü nē'ə fôrm), *n.* the wedge-shaped characters used in the written languages of ancient Babylonia, Assyria, Persia, etc.

Cyrillic (si ril'ik), *adj.* of or having to do with a modified form of the Greek alphabet that is used in Russian, Bulgarian, Serbian, and other languages.

D

daimyo (dī'myō), *n., pl.* **-myo** or **-myos.** one of the feudal nobles of Japan; member of the highest social class.

deism (dē'is'əm), *n.* belief that God made the universe, set it up to work by natural laws, and then left it alone. Deists accept no particular religion.

democracy (di mok'rə sē), *n., pl.* **-cies.** government that is run by the people who live under it. In a democracy, power is in the hands not of a few but of the whole people.

despot (des'pət), *n.* monarch or other ruler having unlimited power; an absolute ruler.

despotism (des'pə tiz'əm), *n.* government by a ruler with unlimited power, usually equated with tyranny or oppression.

Diaspora (dī as'pər ə), *n.* the scattering of the Jews to countries outside of Palestine following the Roman destruction of Jerusalem in 66 A.D.

dictator (dik'tā tər), *n.* person exercising absolute authority, especially a person who, without having any claim through inheritance or free popular election, seizes control of a government; in Roman history, an official given absolute authority over the state in times of emergency.

dividend (div'ə dend), *n.* money earned as a profit by a company and divided among the owners or shareholders of the company.

domesticate (də mes′tə kāt), *v.* change from a wild to a tame or cultivated state.

domestic system a system used in Europe before the industrial revolution in which goods were made by workers in their homes; also referred to as "cottage industry."

dowry (dou′rē), *n., pl.* **-ries.** money or property that a woman brings to her husband when she marries him.

duchy (duch′ē), *n.* an area ruled by a duke or a duchess.

dynastic cycle a cyclical process that dynasties followed in places such as China. At the beginning, a dynasty was strong and prosperous. Then came periods of rebellions, invasions, and corruption, and finally downfall. After a time, a strong new dynasty arose.

dynasty (dī′nə stē), *n.* succession of rulers belonging to the same family; period of time during which such a group rules.

E

Eastern (Orthodox) Church group of Christian churches in eastern Europe, western Asia, and Egypt that consider the patriarch of Constantinople as head of the church.

ecology (ē kol′ə jē), *n.* the distribution of plant and animal life around the world.

Eightfold Path one of the Four Noble Truths formulated by the Buddha. The Eightfold Path is the way to stop longing and thus to end pain.

Elector (i lek′tər), *n.* in the time of the Holy Roman Empire, one of the princes who had the right to elect the emperor.

electric (i lek′trik), *adj.* of or having to do with electricity, a form of energy which can produce light, heat, magnetism, and chemical changes, from the Greek word *electron,* meaning "amber."

element (el′ə mənt), *n.* a substance composed of atoms that are chemically alike and cannot be broken down by chemical means.

empire (em′pīr), *n.* group of countries or states under one ruler or government.

encomienda (en′kō mē en′də), *n.* a system of forced labor used in the Spanish colonies in Latin America.

Entente Cordiale an agreement or alliance signed by the British and French in 1904. The words mean "friendly understanding."

Epic Age a 400-year-long period in India beginning in 900 B.C. during which the Indo-Aryan civilization made many advances. Knowledge of this time comes from the epics written during the period.

epistle (i pis′əl), *n.* letter; any of the letters written by the Apostles to various churches and individuals.

excommunication (ek′skə myü-nə kā′shən), *n.* a formal cutting off from membership in the church.

extreme unction sacrament of the church given by a priest to a dying person or one in danger of death.

F

Fabian policy a policy of watchful waiting, named for the Roman dictator Fabius Maximus, a cautious leader who refused to risk an all-out battle.

factory system system in which machines were grouped together in factories and workers came to the factories, instead of working in their homes. Through this system, items could be mass produced at lower costs and with more standard quality.

fasces (fas′ēz′), *n.* the symbol of authority during Roman times, which consisted of a bundle of rods bound around an ax. The name *fascist* comes from *fasces.*

feud (fyüd), *n.* in the feudal system, the land received by a vassal from a lord; also called a *fief.*

feudal (fyü′dl), *adj.* having to do with a system in which land was given by a lord in return for military and other service.

feudalism (fyü′dl iz′əm), *n.* a system of land ownership and personal service. Under this system, vassals gave military and other services to their lord in return for his protection and use of the land.

fief (fēf), *n.* land received from a lord by a vassal; also called a *feud.*

First Estate one of the three classes of French society that existed before the French Revolution in 1789. The *First Estate* was the clergy.

flax (flaks), *n.* a plant from which linen is made. The long stalk fibers are spun into thread and then woven into cloth.

forum (fōr′əm), *n.* in ancient Rome, a central, open-air meeting place.

fossil (fos′əl), *n.* hardened remains of an animal or plant that have been preserved in the earth's strata.

fresco (fres′kō), *n., pl.* **-coes** or **-cos.** picture or design painted on plaster walls.

funeral oration a speech given in honor of the dead.

G

geocentric (jē′ō sen′trik), *adj.* viewed or measured from the earth's center.

glacier (glā′shər), *n.* giant mass of ice formed over many years.

Gothic (goth′ik), *n.* style of architecture using pointed arches, flying buttresses, and high, steep roofs, developed in western Europe during the Middle Ages.

graduated income tax a tax that requires people of higher incomes to pay a greater percentage of their income than people of lower incomes.

grand jury a jury that decides whether evidence against an accused is enough to hold that person for trial.

guerilla (gə ril′ə) *n.* member of a band of fighters who are not part of a regular army and who harass the enemy.

guild (gild), *n.* in the Middle Ages, an association of merchants, or of persons in a particular trade or craft, formed to keep standards high, promote business interests, and regulate economic life.

guillotine (gil′ə tēn′), *n.* machine for beheading people by means of a heavy blade that slides down between two grooved posts.

guinea (gin′ē), *n.* a gold coin made originally of gold from Guinea. Guinea is an old word for West Africa.

H

haiku (hī′kü), *n.* a Japanese verse form consisting of three lines and containing only 17 syllables.

Hajj (haj), *n.* a pilgrimage to Mecca, a desired goal of every Muslim at least once in his or her life.

Han one of the most outstanding dynasties in Chinese history. The Hans ruled for more than 400 years during which China grew and prospered.

headman (hed′mən), *n.* in early Indian village life, the village leader was the headman.

heir (er), *n.* person who receives or has the right to someone else's property or title after that one dies.

heliocentric (hē′lē ō sen′trik), *adj.* viewed or measured from the center of the sun.

Hellenic period the era in Greece from about 750 B.C. to 338 B.C. It followed the time of transition when the basis of Greek civilization was established.

Hellenistic Age the two centuries following the death of Alexander the Great in 323 B.C., during which time the three kingdoms of his divided empire flourished.

Hellenistic world the kingdoms of Macedonia, Egypt, and Syria and Persia, the three parts into which Alexander the Great's empire was divided after his death.

helot (hel′ət), *n.* member of a class of slaves or serfs in ancient Sparta.

hereditary (hə red′ə ter′ē), *adj.* passing by inheritance from generation to generation.

heretic (her′ə tik), *n.* person whose beliefs differ from the established of accepted beliefs, especially from the accepted teachings of a church.

hibachi (hi bä′chē), *n., pl.* **-chi** or **-chis.** a small, portable, potlike container used for burning charcoal for cooking or heating.

hieroglyphics (hī′ər ə glif′iks), *n.* a type of picture writing developed by the Egyptians between 4000 B.C. and 3000 B.C.

Hijra (hi′jər ə), *n.* name given to Mohammad's flight from Mecca to Medina in 622 A.D.

history (his′tər ē), *n., pl.* **-tor ies.** a recording and explaining of past events.

Holy Eucharist sacrament of the reenactment of Jesus' Last Supper, in which people receive consecrated bread and wine.

holy orders the rite or sacrament of ordination in which a person becomes a priest.

Homo erectus (hō′mō ə rek′təs), *n.* a name scientists have given to creatures who lived at the same time as some of the later Australopithecines but who were more like modern humans. They walked upright.

Homo sapiens (hō′mō sā′pē enz), *n.* modern human beings, including all existing races of people alive today.

Huguenot (hyü′gə not), *n.* a French Protestant of the Calvinist group in the 1500s and 1600s.

humanism (hyü′mə niz′əm), *n.* a system of thought or action concerned with human interests and values. Humanism spread throughout Europe in the Middle Ages when scholars began to study Latin and Greek culture.

I

icon (ī′kon), *n.* image, usually painted, of a sacred figure.

ideographic system a system of writing in which symbols stand for ideas.

Il Duce (ēl′ dü′chā), *n.* title, meaning "the leader," given to Benito Mussolini as head of the Italian Fascist Party in the early 1900s.

illuminate (i lü′mə nāt), *v.* **-nat ed, -nat ing.** light up; make bright; illustrate with decorative designs done in gold and brilliant colors.

Imam (i mäm′), *n.* leader of the Islamic prayer ritual; leader of the Muslim community.

imperator (im′pə rä′tər), *n.* supreme leader of the army in ancient Rome.

imperialism (im pir′ē ə liz′əm), *n.* policy of extending the rule or authority of one country over other countries and colonies.

impressionism (im presh′ə niz′əm), *n.* in art, a style of painting developed by French artists in the late 1800s characterized by the use of bright colors applied in dabs to convey impressions rather than exact representations.

Inca (ing′kə), *n., pl.* **-cas** or **-ca.** ruler of a group of people who lived in the Peruvian mountains before the Spanish conquest. The term later was applied to the entire group.

individualism (in′də vij′ü ə liz′əm), *n.* the pursuit of a person's own ideas as a mode of life.

Indo-European (in′dō yùr′ə pē′ən), *adj.* of or having to do with a group of related languages spoken in India, western Asia, and Europe. Aryan, English, German, Latin, Greek, Persian, and Sanskrit are Indo-European languages.

infantry (in′fən trē), *n., pl.* **-tries.** soldiers trained to fight on foot.

infidel (in′fə dəl), *n.* a person who does not accept a particular religion.

inflation (in flā′shən), *n.* a sharp increase in prices.

intendant (in ten′dənt), *n.* an appointed official in France during the 1600s and 1700s who carried out the orders of the king.

irrigate (ir′ə gāt), *v.* to supply land with water by using ditches from a water source, such as a lake, river, or stream.

Islam (is′ləm), *n.* the Muslim religion, based on the teachings of Mohammad.

J

jade (jād), *n.* a semiprecious stone that is usually whitish or pale green in color. The most prized stones are emerald green or pure white.

Janissary corps during the Ottoman Empire, a government organization of slaves, recruited from the non-Muslim peoples of the empire, who were then educated, converted to Islam, and trained to become military and governmental leaders.

jihad (jə häd), *n.* a holy war.

Judaism (jü′de iz′əm), *n.* religion of the Jews, based on the teachings of the Old Testament and belief in one God.

junk (jungk), *n.* a Chinese sailing ship.

justification by faith Martin Luther's idea that salvation was based on faith alone, was a matter between an individual and God, and did not require the help of priests or good works.

K

Kaaba (kä′bə), *n.* the cube-shaped building containing a black stone in the courtyard of the Sacred Mosque in Mecca.

Kabuki (kä bü′kē), *n.* a form of Japanese drama with song and dance and a flamboyant style of acting which stresses violence, action, and melodrama and is rich in decor and costuming.

kana (kä′nä), *n.* a kind of alphabetic representation developed in the 9th century of the 47 syllables of the Japanese language.

keep (kēp), *n.* the strongest part of a castle or fort, such as a great stone tower.

Koran (kô rän′), *n.* the sacred book of the Muslims.

L

labor theory of value according to Marx, the theory that the value of any product depends on the amount of work needed to make it.

labyrinth (lab′ə rinth), *n.* an intricate and bewildering series of passageways.

lady (lā′dē), *n., pl.* **-dies.** woman who has the rights or authority of a lord; noblewoman.

laissez faire (les′ā fār′). economic principle of letting people do as they please.

legal interpretations decisions in law of different magistrates.

levee (lev′ē), *n.* bank built to keep a river from overflowing; dike.

lineage (lin′ē ij), *n.* several generations of people who are all descended from the same person.

lord (lord), *n.* one who has power over others or to whom service and obedience are due; title used in writing or speaking about noblemen of certain ranks.

lost-wax process a method of bronze casting developed about 1100 A.D. by sculptors in the kingdom of Ife, in present-day Nigeria.

M

Magna Charta the Great Charter that King John of England was forced to sign in 1215. It limited his power and provided the basis for later principles of taxation by the people's consent and trial by jury.

mahatma (mə hät′mə), *n.* a wise and holy person.

mandate (man′dāt), *n.* order authorizing a nation to administer the government and affairs of a territory

Mandate of Heaven Chinese theory that all rulers were expected to govern justly and to look after the well-being of the people. If a monarch did not do this, he or she would no longer have the favor of the gods and could be overthrown by the people.

manorial system the economic system of the Middle Ages.

mansa (män′sə), *n.* in ancient Ghana, the king was called *mansa*.

matrimony (mat′rə mō′nē), *n., pl.* **-nies.** rite or ceremony of marriage.

mercantilism (mėr′kən ti liz′əm), *n.* the economic system of Europe in the 1500s and 1600s that favored a balance of exports of commodities over imports. Nations regulated their agriculture, industry, and trade with that balance as a goal.

mercenary (mėr′sə ner′ē), *n., pl.* **-nar ies.** a professional soldier.

Mesolithic (mes′ə lith′ik), *adj.* of or having to do with the Middle Stone Age, a period which lasted from about 8000 B.C. to 6000 B.C.

mestizo (mə stē′zō), *n., pl.* **-zos** or **-zoes.** person of mixed descent, especially the child of a Spaniard and an American Indian.

millet (mil′it), *n.* a cereal grass bearing a large crop of very small, nutritious seeds. It is eaten today by a third of the world's population.

Minoan (mi nō′ən), *adj.* of or having to do with the civilization, named for King Minos, that developed on Crete. Crete became a power in the ancient world between 1600 B.C. and 1400 B.C.

mir (mir), *n.* a type of agricultural community created by the state in Russia. The mir owned the farmland, rather than the individual peasants in the community.

missi dominici agents called "messengers of the lord" through whom Charlemagne kept law and order in the counties.

modern era the period from 1500 to the present time.

monastery (mon′ə ster′ē), *n., pl.* **-ter ies.** place where groups of monks live apart from the world.

monk (mungk), *n.* a holy man who lives apart from society.

monotheism (mon′ə thē′iz′əm), *n.* belief in only one God.

monsoon (mon sün′), *n.* a seasonal wind that blows from the Arabian Sea and the Indian Ocean. The summer monsoons carry the moisture upon which India is so dependent.

morality plays in the Middle Ages, plays with a religious character.

mosaic (mō zā′ik), *n.* decoration made of small pieces of stone, glass, wood, or other material inlaid to form a pattern, picture, or design.

mosque (mosk), *n.* a Muslim place of worship.

Muslim (muz′ləm), *n.* believer in the religion, called Islam, that was founded by Mohammad.

N

nation (nā′shən), *n.* people occupying the same country, under the same government, and usually speaking the same language.

nationalism (nash′ə nə liz′əm), *n.* patriotic feelings or efforts.

nationalize (nash′ən l īz) *v.,* **-ized, -izing.** bring land, industries, or other property under the control or ownership of a nation.

Neolithic (nē′ə lith′ik), *adj.* of or having to do with the last part of the Stone Age, a period which lasted from about 6000 B.C. to 3000 B.C.

neutral (nü′trəl), *adj.* on neither side in a quarrel or war.

nirvana (nir vä′nə), *n.* according to Buddhist belief, the end of all earthly desires at which time the soul finds perfect peace.

No (nō), *n.* a type of drama developed in feudal Japan that was performed by two main characters and featured poetic passages chanted by a chorus.

nomad (nō′mad), *n.* member of a group of people who move from place to place to have food or pasture for their animals.

Northern Renaissance the spread of the spirit of the Renaissance, the great revival of art and learning that began in Italy, to the rest of Europe.

O

oasis (ō ā′sis), *n., pl.* **-ses.** a fertile spot in the desert where there is water and some vegetation.

Oba (ō bə), *n.* a king in the state of Benin, located in what is now southern Nigeria. The reigns of the Obas were recorded on bronze plaques that hung on the palace walls. Many have been preserved and give details about Benin's past.

Old Kingdom a period of unification in Egypt, which began when King Menes united Upper Egypt and Lower Egypt and made Memphis the capital city.

oligarchy (ol′ə gär′kē), *n., pl.* **-chies.** a form of government in which a few people have the ruling power.

ostracism (os′trə siz′əm), *n.* in ancient Greece, a system that gave the citizens a yearly chance to banish officials they thought were dangerous to the Athenian state.

Oxford Reformers group of English scholars who studied medicine and Greek in Italy and brought humanism to England. On their return from Italy, they gathered at Oxford University and became teachers, preachers, and authors of the new learning.

P

paddy (pad′ē), *n., pl.* **-dies.** flooded field where rice is grown.

Paleolithic (pā′lē ə lith′ik), *adj.* of or having to do with the earliest period of the Stone Age, a period which lasted until about 8000 B.C.

paleontologist (pā′lē on tol′ə jist), *n.* a scientist who studies fossils, the hardened remains of life forms, which existed in prehistoric times.

pan (pan) *n.* Portuguese word meaning "bread" that was adopted by the Japanese.

papacy (pā′pə sē), *n., pl.* **-cies.** the office and government of a pope.

papal indulgence the freeing of a sinner from punishment after death.

papal line of demarcation an imaginary north-south line drawn by Pope Alexander VI in 1493 that went through the Atlantic Ocean 100 leagues (about 250 miles or 400 kilometers) west of the Azores. All the Europeans' newly discovered lands west of the line were to go to Spain; those to the east were to go to Portugal. The Treaty of Tordesillas in 1494 moved the line 270 leagues farther west.

papyrus (pə pī′rəs), *n., pl.* **-ri.** a type of paper made by ancient Egyptians from the pith of the papyrus plant.

parchment (pärch′mənt), *n.* the skin of sheep or goats prepared for use as writing paper.

pariah (pə rī′ə), *n.* person generally despised; outcast; also called *untouchable.*

Parliament (pär′lə mənt), *n.* the highest lawmaking body of England and many other nations.

pass (pas), *n.* referring to mountains, a narrow road, path, way, or opening providing access to regions beyond.

pastoral (pas′tər əl), *adj.* of herding and raising animals; country life.

patriarch (pā′trē ärk), *n.* the highest church official in the early Christian church.

patrician (pə trish′ən), *n.* member of the nobility of ancient Rome, which was composed of the families descended from the original body of Roman citizens.

patriotism (pā′trē ə tiz′əm), *n.* love for and loyal support of one's country.

patron (pā′trən), *n.* person who gives approval and support to some other person, art, cause, or undertaking.

Pax Romana a period from 27 B.C. to 180 A.D. The words mean "Roman Peace," which the Romans maintained during this time throughout their domain.

penance (pen′əns), *n.* in religion, a sacrament that includes repentance, intention to amend, full confession of sin, and absolution.

peninsulares (pā nēn sü lä′räs), *n.* Spanish-born nobles who served as government officials in the Spanish colonies.

perspective (pər spek′tiv), *n.* art of picturing objects on a flat surface so as to give the appearance of distance or depth.

petit (pet′ē), *adj.* little; petty. A petit jury is one that hears a trial and decides on the guilt of the accused.

pharaoh (fer′ō), *n.* in ancient Egypt, the king was called *pharaoh.*

plebeian (pli bē′ən), *n.* small farmer or trader of ancient Rome; a person who was not a noble.

pogrom (pō grom′), *n.* organized massacre, especially of Jews.

polis (pō′lis), *n.* in early Greek society, a settlement established by a clan and ruled by a king or tribal chief, where people were safe from attack.

political science the scientific study of government.

polytheism (pol′ē thē′is′əm), *n.* belief in, or worship of, many gods.

pope (pōp), *n.* the head of the Roman Catholic Church.

Post-Classic period a period, also called the *New Empire,* in which the Mayas began a new civilization that flourished in the northern tip of the Yucatan peninsula from 900 A.D. to 1200 A.D.

potlatch (pot′lach′), *n.* a ceremonial festival among certain American Indians of the northern Pacific Coast. On important occasions, noble families gave a great feast at which their most prized and beautiful possession was given away.

potter's wheel a small, flat wheel set on top of a vertical axis, called a spindle. As the wheel turns, clay placed on the wheel can be molded into a uniform shape by hand.

predestination (prē des tə nā′shən), *n.* John Calvin's idea that God had already decided which souls will be saved and which will be damned.

prehistoric (prē′hi stôr′ik), *adj.* of or belonging to a period before writing was invented and history was recorded.

prevailing winds winds that blow in a predictable pattern.

prime minister the chief minister in certain governments; premier. The *prime minister* is the head of the cabinet.

progressive income tax a system of putting a higher tax on big incomes and a lower tax on small incomes.

proletariat (prō′lə ter′ē ət), *n.* the poorest class of working people; in Marxist theory, the class of modern wage earners who lack their own means of production.

propaganda (prop′ə gan′də), *n.* systematic effort to spread ideas or beliefs.

protectorate (prə tek′tər it), *n.* a weak country under the protection and partial control of a strong country. Many parts of Africa were once European protectorates.

Protestant (prot′ə stənt), *n.* member or follower of any of the Christian churches that refused to accept papal authority. The protests of Lutheran princes to Catholic leaders during the Reformation gave rise to the word *Protestant*.

psychology (sī kol′ə jē), *n., pl.* **-gies.** science of human behavior.

Punici Latin word for Phoenicians.

Pyrrhic victory a costly victory, named after Pyrrhus, a Greek military leader who defeated the Romans in battle but at too great a cost.

purdah (pėr′də), *n.* a curtain serving to screen women from the sight of men or strangers; the Muslim system of keeping women hidden from men or strangers.

pure or direct democracy a system of government which allows each citizen a vote in all political decisions. *See* representative democracy.

Q

queue (kyu), *n.* in China, a braid of hair hanging down from the back of the head.

R

rajah (rä′jə), *n.* ruler or chief in India, Java, Borneo, etc.

Ramadan (ram′ə dän′), *n.* the ninth month of the Muslim year, during which a Muslim must fast from dawn until sunset.

ratify (rat′ə fī), *v.,* **-fied, -fy ing.** to confirm formally as valid; give approval.

realism (rē′ə liz′əm), *n.* in art and literature, the picturing of life as it really is.

Realpolitik (rä äl′pō li tēk′), *n.* a new kind of politics that emerged in Europe after the 1848 revolutions, characterized by politicians and state leaders who were willing to use any way, even force, to push their national interests.

Reconquista a series of campaigns to drive the Moors out of Spain and Portugal, ending in 1492.

redress of grievances refusal by Parliament to grant money until the ruler has corrected wrongs.

reeve (rēv), *n.* in the feudal system, a person who helped the bailiff supervise farm work.

regent (rē′gənt), *n.* a person who rules until the rightful ruler is able to do so.

reincarnation (rē′in kär nā′shən), *n.* belief that after death the soul will be reborn in a new body.

religious toleration government policy permitting freedom of religion.

Renaissance (ren′ə säns′), *n.* the great revival of art and learning in Europe during the 1300s, 1400s, and 1500s.

representative body a group in which each member speaks for many people and votes in their interests.

representative democracy or republic a system of government in which the citizens elect representatives to act for them in political decision-making.

republic (ri pub′lik), *n.* a state in which the citizens elect representatives to run the government.

Rerum Novarum a letter by Pope Leo XIII in 1891 that asked Catholics to form their own socialist parties and labor unions in order to seek a greater measure of social justice.

revolution (rev′ə lu′shən), *n.* a complete change; a complete overthrow of an established government, political system, or way of doing things.

Risorgimento (rə sôr ji men′tō), *n.* in Italy, the spirit of nationalism among middle-class liberals who wanted Italian unity.

Roman Catholic Church the Christian church that recognizes the pope as the supreme head.

Romance languages French, Italian, Spanish, Portuguese, Romanian, Provençal, and other languages that came from Latin.

Romanesque (rō′mə nesk′), *n.* style of architecture using round arches and vaults that developed in Europe during the Middle Ages.

romanticism (rō man′tə siz′əm), *n.* style of literature, art, and music, especially widespread in the 1800s, that allows freedom of form and stresses strong feeling, imagination, love of nature, and often, the unusual and supernatural.

Roosevelt Corollary the corollary to the Monroe Doctrine issued by Theodore Roosevelt in 1904 which said the United States would be forced to take on the duties of an international police force in the Western Hemisphere.

S

sacrament (sak′rə mənt), *n.* any of certain religious ceremonies of the Christian church considered to be especially sacred, such as baptism.

samurai (sam′ủ rī′), *n., pl.* **-rai.** the military class in feudal Japan; member of this class.

sanctuary (sangk′chü er′ē), *n., pl.* **-ar ies.** place of refuge or protection; sacred place.

Sanskrit (san′skrit), *n.* the ancient sacred and literary language of India. It was developed by the Indo-Aryans in India over a period of a thousand years as a written language which had its own alphabet. Later, spoken Sanskrit became different from the written forms used by the poets and priests.

satellite (sat′l īt), *n.* a country technically independent but actually controlled by a more powerful country, especially a country under the control of the Soviet Union.

savanna (sə van′ə), *n.* grassland with scattered trees between the equatorial forests and the hot deserts in either hemisphere.

scientific method an orderly method used in scientific research, generally consisting of identifying a problem, gathering all the pertinent data, formulating a hypothesis, performing experiments, interpreting the results, and drawing a conclusion.

scientific revolution advances in science that changed the way people thought about nature, religion, government, literature, and social and economic life.

scientific socialism a type of socialism, supported by people such as Marx and Engels, that uses direct and aggressive methods for transforming society; communism.

scribe (skrīb), *n.* person who wrote letters and documents for others who did not know how to write.

Second Estate one of the three classes of French society before 1789. The *Second Estate* was the nobility.

secular (sek′yə lər), *adj.* not religious or sacred; worldly.

self-determination (self′di tėr′mə nā′shən), *n.* the deciding by the people of a nation as to what form of government they shall have, without reference to the wishes of any other nation; freedom from outside rule.

senate (sen′it), *n.* in ancient Rome, the highest council of state. It was first established by the Etruscans in the 7th century B.C., when the king chose a group of nobles known as the *senate* to advise him.

serf (sèrf), *n.* in the feudal system, a slave who could not be sold off the land but passed from one owner to another with the land.

sheriff (sher′if), *n.* the most important law-enforcing officer of a county.

Shinto (shin′tō), *n., pl.* **-tos.** meaning "the way of the Gods," it is the native religion of Japan, primarily the worship of nature deities and ancestral heroes.

shogun (shō′gun), *n.* the former hereditary commander in chief of the Japanese army. The shoguns were the real rulers of Japan for hundreds of years.

socialism (sō′shə liz′əm), *n.* system of social organization by which the major means of production and distribution are owned, managed, or controlled by the government, by associations of workers, or by the community as a whole. Socialism seeks to establish itself by peaceful means as contrasted with communism, which uses revolution to gain its end.

Son of Heaven name the Chinese called their king, beginning with the Chou period.

soviet (sō′vē et), *n.* an elected assembly concerned with local government, especially in Russia.

spartan (spärt′n), *adj.* sternly disciplined, as were the people of the city-state of Sparta.

spheres of influence in the mid-1800s, regions especially in China set up by foreign powers where the economic interests of another country were supreme.

statute (stach′üt), *n.* law enacted by a legislative body.

steppe (step), *n.* one of the vast, treeless plains in southeastern Europe and in Asia.

steward (stü′ərd), *n.* in the system of feudalism, a legal adviser to the lord. He also ran the manor court and traveled from one manor to another, checking on conditions.

stoa (stō′ə), *n.* in ancient Greece, a portico, usually long and detached, used as a promenade or meeting place. Because the followers of Zeno's philosophy often met on a *stoa,* they were called *Stoics,* and his philosophy became known as *Stoicism.*

Stoic (stō′ik), *n.* a follower of a philosophy known as Stoicism, which taught that true happiness, or inner peace, can be reached by people when they find their proper place in nature.

strait (strāt), *n.* a narrow channel connecting two major bodies of water.

Sturm and Drang a German movement in the 1800s that developed the theme of youthful genius in defiance of accepted standards. The German phrase means "storm and stress."

stylus (stī′ləs), *n., pl.* **-lus es, -li.** a pointed instrument used to make impressions. In early civilizations, the stylus was a pointed stick, used for writing on soft clay bricks or tablets.

subcontinent (sub kon′tə nənt), *n.* a large, self-contained land mass that is part of a continent.

sultan (sult′n), *n.* ruler of a Muslim country.

sultanate (sult′n āt), *n.* Muslim kingdom, ruled over by a sultan; the period of rule of a sultan.

suttee (su′tē′), *n.* a Hindu custom in which the widow threw herself on the burning funeral pyre of her husband.

Swahili culture a way of life followed by the African, Indian, and Arab traders who settled in the port cities of East Africa between the 7th and 14th centuries.

T

Tamils (tam′əls), *n.* in the 1st century A.D., people of south India, who were descendants of the Dravidians and noted for their well-equipped ports.

tanka (tän′kä), *n.* a form of poetry developed in Japan in the 9th century. It could be only five lines long and include a total of 31 syllables. It remained the poetic model for more than 1,000 years.

Taoism (dou′iz′əm), *n.* a Chinese religion founded by Lao-tse that says the best way to live is according to nature. It teaches that natural simplicity and humility are a way to peace and harmony in life.

terrorist (ter′ər ist), *n.* person who uses deliberate violence against other persons or groups.

theocracy (thē ok′rə sē), *n., pl.* **-cies.** any government headed by religious authorities.

theology (thē ol′ə jē), *n., pl.* **-gies.** doctrines concerning God and His relations to people and the universe.

Third Estate one of the three classes of society in France before 1789. The *Third Estate* included everyone except the nobility and the clergy.

Third World the developing countries of Asia, Africa, and Latin America. The term came into use after World War II.

ting vase slender, rectangular vase which stood on four legs and was used by the Chinese for honoring ancestors.

tithe (tīth), *n.* the one tenth of a person's income that is paid to the church or charity.

totalitarianism (tō tal′ə ter′ē-ə niz′əm), *n.* rule by a government controlled by one political group which suppresses all opposition, often by force, and which controls many aspects of its citizens' lives.

total war war in which all the resources of a nation are used and in which attack is made not only on the armed forces of the opponent, but also on its civilian people and property.

totem pole wooden pole, often put up in front of a home and carved with figures of natural objects such as animals and plants that are the emblems of the family or group.

trade embargo government order prohibiting the purchase, sale, or exchange of goods.

trade unions workers' groups that may legally bargain, one or more at a time, with employers for better wages and working conditions.

tribe (trīb), *n.* a large group of people united by common ancestry and customs.

tribune (trib′yün), *n.* in ancient Rome, an official chosen by the plebeians to protect their rights and interests from injustices by the patricians.

tribute (trib′yüt), *n.* any forced payment; tax.

tyrant (tī′rənt), *n.* leader who has seized power unlawfully.

tsar (zär), *n.* title meaning "caesar," used for the monarchs of Russia.

U

ulema (ü′lə mä), *n.* in the Muslim world, a learned teacher who explains the religious doctrine of Islam.

university (yü′nə vėr′sə tē), *n., pl.* **-ties.** institution of learning of the highest grade.

untouchable (un tuch′ə bəl), *n.* in India, a term formerly applied to those lowest in the Hindu social order, whose touch was thought to defile Hindus of higher caste.

V

vassal (vas′əl), *n.* in the feudal system, a person who received land from a lord.

vault (vôlt), *n.* in architecture, an arched roof or ceiling.

Vedic Age the first Indo-Aryan civilization which lasted about 600 years. During this time Sanskrit writing became well developed, and religious writings were produced.

vellum (vel′əm), *n.* the finest grade of parchment, prepared from the skins of calves and lambs for use as writing paper

vernacular (vər nak′yə lər), *n.* a simplified, spoken language used in people's everyday dealings with each other.

veto (vē′tō), *n.* in ancient Rome, a phrase of protest meaning "I forbid" that was uttered by the tribunes during senate discussions. Since tribunes could not take part in the debates or vote, the veto expressed their dissent.

viceroy (vīs′roi), *n.* a person who governs a country or a province as the monarch's representative.

Y

yama (yä′mə), *n.* Japanese word meaning "mountain."

yoke (yōk), *n.* a frame or crossbar that holds two work animals together.

Z

zemstvo (zemst′vō), *n., pl.* **-stvos.** a local assembly that managed the affairs of a district in pre-revolutionary Russia.

Zollverein (tsôl′fer īn′), *n.* a union set up by the Prussians in 1834 to deal with tariffs.

Index

The Index tells you where to find maps *(map)*, illustrations *(illus.)*, definitions *(def.)*, and pronunciations *(pron.)*. Pronunciations are respelled in the familiar Thorndike Barnhart pronunciation key, which is shown on page 732. For many foreign words in *History and Life*, the pronunciation given is not the local pronunciation but an Anglicized version, one acceptable to educated Americans.

591, 660, *illus.* 537
war with Israel, 662, 663
war with Libya, 664
Einstein, Albert [1879-1955], 628, *illus.* 525
Eisenhower, Dwight D. [1890-1969], 624
Eitoku (ā′tō kü′) [1543-1590], painting by, *illus.* 317
Elba, 456
Electricity, discoveries in, 434-435, 491
Eliot, George (Mary Ann Evans) [1819-1880], 497, *illus.* 494
Elizabeth I, of England [1533-1603], 342, 365, 366, 373, 374, 375, 376, 377, 445, *illus.* 366
Enclosure acts, 485
Encomienda (en′kō mē en′də), 414
Encyclopedia, 439
Engels (eng′glz), Friedrich [1820-1895], 509
Engineering: Roman, 125
Engines. *See* specific kinds
England
civil war in [1642-1649], 446
Glorious Revolution in, *illus.* 447
Hundred Years' War, 336, 337, 345-346, *map* 345
Magna Charta, 340
Restoration in, 446
split with Roman Catholic Church, 369, 373-374
War of the Roses, 343
See also Britain; Great Britain
English East India Company, 379
Enlightenment, 384, 502
Entente Cordiale, 551
Epicurus, (ep′ə kyur′əs) [342?-270 B.C.], 105
Equiano, Olaudah (ō lou′də ē′kwē ä′nō) [1741-1797], 253, 254, *illus.* 253
Era of Warring states, 75
Erasmus (i raz′məs) [1466?-1536], 363-364, 365, 370
Eratosthenes (er′ə tos′thə nēz) [276?-195 B.C.], 105
Ericson, Leif [c. 1000 A.D.], 392
Erie Canal, 488, *map* 489
Eskimos, 260
mask made by, *illus.* 220
Essay on the Principles of Population, 505-506
Este family, 354
Estonia, 182, 563, 614
Etesian (ē tē′shən) winds, 21
Ether, value of, 493

Ethiopia, 231, 539, 598, 609. *See also* Abyssinia
Etruscans, 111-112
Euclid (yü′klid) [c. 300 B.C.], 105
Euphrates (yü frā′tēz) River, 1, 19
Euripides (yủ rip′ə dēz′) [480?-406 B.C.], 107
European Economic Community, (Common Market), 707
Evans, Sir Arthur [1851-1941], 89
Eware (ə wä′rē) the Great [c. 1400s], 252
Ewedo (ə wä dō) [c. 1300s], 252

F

Faberge Easter egg, *illus.* 572
Fabian policy, 115
Fabius Maximus (fā′bē əs mak′sə məs) [?- 203 B.C.], 115
Factory system, 485, 487
Fahrenheit (far′ən hīt), Gabriel [1686-1736], 434
Family
in China, 76, 303-305
in India, 58, 289
in Japan, 327-328
in Rome, 113
Faraday, Michael [1791-1867], 491, *illus.* 496
Farouk (fä rük′), of Egypt, [1920-1965], 660
Fascism, 597, 609-610
Fashoda incident, 548-549
Fatehpur Sikri (fät′ə per si′krē), 292
Fatima (fə tē′mə) [606-636], 197
Fatimads, 197
Faust, 496
Fell, Barry, 392
Ferdinand of Aragon [1452-1516], 347
Ferdinand I, Holy Roman emperor [1503-1564], 375
Ferdinand II, Holy Roman emperor [1578-1637], 377
Fertile crescent, 28, 32
Feudalism
in Europe, 154-156, 337-338
in Japan, 321-327, 533
Fielding, Henry [1707-1754], 440
Fiji Islands, 536
Fillmore, Millard [1800-1874], 533
Finance capitalism, 491
Finland, 182, 382, 563, 614
Five Nations. *See* League of the Iroquois
Five-year plan, in Soviet Union, 578
Flanders, 345
Flaubert (flō bār′), Gustave

[1821-1880], 497
Florence, 349, 354, 355, 359-360, 361, 400
Florida, discovery of, 393
Flying shuttle, 485
Foot binding, 305
Forbidden City, 588, *illus.* 588
Forum (Rome), 114, *illus.* 114
Fourteen points, 561, 562, 563
France
in Africa, 537, 538
and Common Market, 707
and Congress of Vienna, 464
constitutional monarchy in, 452
and the Crimean War, 469, 470
democracy in, 706
under the Directory, 453
First Republic, 452-453
and the Franco-Prussian War, 473, 476
and the French Revolution, 450, 452-454
and the Hundred Years' War, 336, 337, 345-346, *map* 345
under Louis Philippe, 467, *illus.* 466
under Napoleon I, 454-457, *map* 457
under Napoleon III, 468, 469-470, 471, 473
in New World, 395, 396-397
as nuclear power, 709
restoration of Bourbon monarchy in, 466
and the Seven Years' War, 386, 528
socialism in, 508, 514
social legislation in, 513-514
in Southeast Asia, 535-536
Third Republic, 476-477
and the Thirty Years' War, 377, 378
unification of, 343-346
in World War I, 554
post-World War I, 562, 563, *map*
pre-World War I, 550, 551 560
in World War II, 614, *map* 617
post-World War II, 637, 706
See also French Revolution
Francis Ferdinand, of Austria-Hungary [1863-1914], 553, *illus.* 553
Francis Joseph I, of Austria-Hungary [1830-1916], 479, 554
Franciscans, 161, 370
Franco, Francisco [1892-1975], 582, 609-610
Franco-Prussian War [1870-1871],

Roosevelt, Theodore [1858-1919], 543

Roosevelt corollary, 544

Roses, Wars of, 343

Roundheads, 446

Rousseau (rü sō'), Jean Jacques [1712-1778], 438-439, 496, *illus.* 439, 440

Rubaiyat, 214

Rubens (rü bənz), Peter Paul [1577-1640], 365

Rurik (rùr'ik) [?-879], 180

Russia
  under Alexander I, 568-569
  under Alexander II, 569
  under Alexander III, 569
  beginnings of, 172, 347-348, *map* 182-183
  under the Bolsheviks, 567, 574, *illus.* 567
  under Catherine the Great, 568
  communism in, 597
  and Crimean War, 469, 569
  Decembrist revolt [1825], 569
  desire of, for ice-free port, 381, 382, 383, *map* 382
  emancipation of serfs, 569
  and control of Finland, 382
  and Great Northern War, 381, 382, 383
  and Japan, 382
  early Mongol rule of, 183-184
  and Napoleonic wars, 456
  and Nazi Germany, 617
  1905 revolution in, 570
  1917 revolution in, 568, 574
  in 19th century, 568
  under Nicholas I, 569
  under Nicholas II, 568, 569-570, 571, 576
  and Ottoman Empire, 382, 480, 549
  under Paul I, 568
  under Peter the Great, 381, 382, 383
  provisional government of, 570-571
  and Russo-Japanese War, 535, 549, 570
  and Siberia, 535
  spread of Christianity to, 173
  time of troubles in, 348, 381
  pre-World War I, 550-551
  in World War I, 554, 560-561, 571, 576
  See also Union of Soviet Socialist Republics

Russian Orthodox Church, 179, 381, 574

Ryukyu Islands, 707

S

Saar (sär), 562

Sadat (sä dat'), Anwar [1918-1981], 662, 664, 665, *illus.* 665

Saif (sef), 250

St. Augustine [354-430], 140, 146

St. Bartholomew's Day Massacre, 376, *illus.* 376

St. Bede, 147

St. Benedict [480?-543?], 147

St. Boniface (bon'ə fäs) [680?-755], 146

St. Francis Xavier [1506-1552], 150, 324

St. Helena, 456

St. Lawrence River, 395, 396

St. Patrick [389?-461], 146

St. Paul [?-67?], 139

St. Paul's Cathedral, *illus.* 615

St. Peter's, Rome, 362, 371

St. Petersburg, 381, 382, 570

St. Thomas Aquinas (ə kwī'nəs) [1225-1274], 167, 214

Sagento, 115

Sakhalin, 535

Sakharov (sä'kä rof), Andrei [1921-   ], 702

Saladin (säl'ə dən) [1138-1193], 162, 198

Salamis (sal'ə mis), battle of [480 B.C.], 97-98

Salvation Army, 514

Samurai (sam'u rī), 315, 322, 327, *illus.* 325

Sanchi, *illus.* 63

San Martín (sän'mär tēn'), José de [1778-1850], 459

Sanskrit (san'skrit), 59, *illus.* 78

Santa Anna, Antonio Lopez de [1795-1876], 459

Santo Domingo, 409

São Paulo, 691

Sardinia, 115, 471

Sargon I [c. 2500 B.C.], 30

Satire, 440

Saudi Arabia, 595, 660

Savanna, 225, 228-229

Saxons, 143, 144

Saxony, 382, 464

Scandinavia, spread of Lutheranism to, 372
  See also specific countries

Schiller, Johann Friedrich von [1759-1805], 496

Schmidt, Helmut [1918-   ], 706, *illus.* 706

Schubert (shü'bərt), Franz [1797-1828], 497

Science: in Greece, 105; during the Middle Ages, 167; in the Roman empire, 127-128. *See also* specific sciences

Scientific method, 429-430, 436-441

Scientific revolution, 429

Scientific socialism, 509

Scipio (sip'ē ō) the Elder [237?-183 B.C.], 115

Scholarship: in China, 300, 310-311; role of monasteries in preserving; *See also* Education

Scotland, 341

Scott, Sir Walter [1771-1832], 496

Sculpture
  African, 224, 236-237, *illus.* 224, 230, 236-237
  Chinese, *illus.* 83, 84
  Greek, 107, *illus.* 92, 95
  Incan, *illus.* 271
  Indian, *illus.* 67
  Italian Renaissance, 360, 361
  Mayan, 264, *illus.* 264
  Minoan, 90
  North American Indian, 273

Sea of Marmara, 173, *map* 177

Sekigahara, battle of [1600], 324

Seleucus I, (sə lü'kəs) [358?-281 B.C.], 102

Self-determination, 466

Seljuk (sel'jûk), 198

Seljuk turks, 161, 198, 199

Seneca Indians, 260

Senegal, 672

Senegal River, 241

Senghor (saN gôr'), Leopold [1906-   ], 672

Sepoy (sē'poi) rebellion [1857-1858], 528

September Massacre [1792], 452-453

Serbia, 553, 554

Serbs, 479

Serfs, 155-156, 157, 381, 383
  emancipation of, 569

Sesshu, 323-324

Seurat, Georges [1859-1891], painting by, *illus.* 498

Seven wonders of world, 103

Seven Years' War [1756-1763], 528

Severus, Lucius Septimius [146-211], 123

Seymour, Jane [1509-1537], 373

Shaba province, 670

Shah Jahan, 292, 293, 294

Shakespeare, William [1564-1616], 127, 365-366

Shang dynasty, 43-44, 75

Shanghai, 608

302-305, 307, 308;
art of, *illus.* 301, 303
Sun Yat-sen (sun′ yät′sen′)
[1867-1925], 586-587
Surgery, advancements in, 493
Susa (sü′sə), 30, 36
Suttee (su tē′), 289, 529
Sutton Hoo, tomb of, *illus.* 142
Swahili city states, 247, 248, 249,
map 247
Sweden, 347, 377, 382, 383
Swift, Jonathan [1667-1745], 440
Swiss Reformed Church, 373
Symphonies, 497
Syria, 102, 193, 207, 564, 594,
660, 662, 663, 664

T

Tacitus (tas′ə təs) [55?-120?], 111,
126-127, 137
Taghaza (tə gä′zə), 241-243
T'ai Tsung (tī′dzung′), 82
Taiwan, 67, 534, 653, 711
Taj Mahal (täj′ mə häl′), 293, 294,
illus. 281, 293
Tale of Genji, 321
Talleyrand-Perigord, Charles
Maurice de [1754-1838], *illus.*
463
Tamerlane [c. 1336-1405], *illus.*
281
Tamil land, 65
Tamils (tam′əlz), 65
Tang (täng) dynasty, 82-84, 299
Tanganyika (tang′gə nyē kə), 672
Tanka, 321
Tanks, use of, in World War I, 558,
illus. 556
Tanzania, 6, 238, 248, 672
Taoism (dou′iz′əm), 78
Tarik, 193
Tarquin the proud [534-510 B.C.],
112
Taung (tä ung′), 6
Taxes
of the American colonies, 449
and the French Revolution, 450
graduated income in China, 307
progressive income, 518
Taxila (tak si′lə), 53
Tchaikovsky, Peter Ilich
[1840-1893], 499, *illus.* 495
Telegraph, 492
Telephone, 492, *illus.* 492
Telescope, 430, 434
Telford, Thomas [1757-1834], 488
Tennis Court Oath, 452
Tenno, Jimmy, 317
Tenochtitlan (tā nŏch′tē tlän′),

265, 268, 410, *illus.* 410
Teutonic knights, 183
Textile industry, 485, 487
Thackeray, William Makepeace
[1811-1863], 497
Thailand, 64, 67, 617
Thatcher, Margaret [1925-   ],
703, *illus.* 705
Thebes (thēbz), 22, 101
Theodora (thē′ə dô′rə) [?-548],
illus. 178
Theodoric (thē od′ə rik), king of
the Ostrogoths [454?-526], 144
Theodosius I (thē′ə dō′shē əs)
[346?-395], 124, 140, 173
Thermoluminescence, 306
Thermometer, 434
Thermopylae (thər mop′ə lē),
battle of [480 B.C.], 98
Third World countries, 713-714
Thirty Years' War [1618-1648],
377, 378, 384
Thor, 143
Thrace (thrās), 97
Three Principles of the People, 587
Threshing machine, 488
Thucydides (thü sid′ə dēz)
[460?-400 B.C.], 105-106
Tiahuanaco (tyä′wä nä′kō), 268
Tiberius (tī bir′ē əs) [42 B.C.-
37 A.D.], 117, 121
Tiber (tī′bər) River, 111, 120
Tibet, 73
Tigris (tī′gris) River, 1, 19, 195
Timbuktu (tim buk′tü), 211, 228,
244, 245, *illus.* 245
Time capsules, 122
Time lines, 2-3, 50-51, 134-135,
222-223, 280-281, 334-335,
426-427, 524-525, 634-635
Timur (ti mur′) the Lame
[1333?-1405], 184, 284, 290
Tintoretto (tin′tə ret′ō)
[1518-1594], 361
Tiryns (tī′rinz), 90
Titian (tish′əN) [1477?-1576], 361
painting of, *illus.* 360
Tithe, 159
Tito (tē′tō), (Josip Broz)
[1892-1980], 643, 648, *illus.* 643
Tiw, 143
Tlaloc (tlä′lok), 267
Tokugawa (tō kū gä′wä)
Shogunate, 322, 325-327, 328,
533
Tokyo, 325, 326
Toledo, 207
Toleration Act, 447
Tolstoy (tol′stoi), Leo [1828-1910],
487
Toltecs (tol′teks), 262, 265, 267,

map 266
Tordesillas, Treaty of [1494], 391
Torricelli (tôr ə chel′ē),
Evangelista [1608-1647], 434
Tory party (Great Britain), 446,
447, 507
Totalitarianism, 523, 602
Totem pole, 260, *illus.* 261
Tours, 193
battle of, 148, 732
Towaddud, 203-204
Towns, development of medieval,
163-165, *illus.* 164, 336, 344
See also cities
Toynbee, Arnold J. [1889-1975],
111
Trade: Aegean, 89-90; African,
241, 243; 255; Byzantine
empire, 176, 177, 178; China,
76, 81, 302, 309; Greek, 92-93,
map 93; Indian, 60, 65; Islamic
empire, 208-211; in Italian
Renaissance, *map* 354; silent,
241, 243; Roman empire, 65;
Stone Age, 15; during Middle
Ages, 156, 163
Trade associations, 209
Trafalgar, Battle of, 455
Tragedy, in Greek drama, 107
Trajan (trā′jən) [53?-117], 121
Trans-Jordan, 564, 594, 595
Transportation: improvements in,
488-490, 518; growth of mass,
503; river in Africa, 232; in the
Sahara desert, 226
Trans-Siberian Railroad, 535, 551,
576
Trevithick (trev′i thik), Richard
[1771-1833], 489
Triana, Rodrigo de, 389
Tribunes, 114
Triple Alliance, 550, 555
Triple Entente, 551
Trotsky (trot′skē), Leon
[1879-1940], 576, 577, *illus.* 567,
577
Troy, 90
Truman Doctrine, 641
Truman, Harry S. [1884-1972],
628, 641
Tsetse fly, 230
Tsingling (ching′ling′) Mountains,
73
Tuberculosis, 493, 503
Tudor dynasty, 343
Tughlak (tug lak′), Firuz Shah
[1308-1388], 284
Tunisia, 193, 228, 538, 660
Turkestan, 299
Turkey, 480, 595, 665-666, 668
Turks, 283

Acknowledgments

Quoted Material

9 Cited in O. D. von Engeln, Ph.D., and Jane McKelway Urquhart, A.B., *The Story Key To Geographic Names*. New York: D. Appleton and Company, 1924. (All the book features called "What's in a Name?" are cited in this source, except the one on book p. 580.

19 From *The Literature of the Ancient Egyptians*, trans. by Aylward M. Blackman. (London: E. P. Dutton & Co., 1927, pp. 146–149).

26 From *The Book of the Dead*, Oliver J. Thatcher, ed., *The Ideas That Have Influenced Civilization*, Milwaukee, 1901.

31 C. H. Johns, ed., *Babylonian and Assyrian Laws, Contracts and Letters*, "Library of Ancient Inscriptions" (New York: Charles Scribner's Sons, 1904), pp. 44—67 passim.

37 *Herodotus*, trans., H. G. Rawlinson, rev. and annotated. A. W. Lawrence (London: Nonesuch Press, Ltd., 1935), p. 735.

44 Reprinted by permission of G. P. Putnam's Sons and Macdonald and Jane's Publishers Ltd. from *The Ancient Worlds of Asia* by Ernst Diez, trans. by W. C. Darwell. Copyright© 1961 by Macdonald & Co. (Publishers) Ltd.

60 From the *Bhagavad Gita* trans. by Sir Edwin Arnold, (Boston 1885).

61 Bottom cited in H. G. Rawlinson, *India: A Short Cultural History* (London: Cresset Press, 1937).

62 Quoted in Percival Spear, *India: A Modern History*, (Ann Arbor: University of Michigan Press, 1961).

65 J. Legge, trans. and ed., "The Travels of Fa-Hsien," in *Chinese Literature* (London: Cooperative Publishing Co., 1900), p. 230.

68 Quoted in K. M. Panikkar, *A Survey of Indian History* (London: Meridian Books, Ltd. 1948), p. 130.

78 From *The World's Great Religions*. (New York: Time, Inc., 1957).

83 "The Moon Over the Mountain Pass" by Li Po., which appeared in the anthology *The White Pony*, ed. by Robert Payne. Permission granted by Bertha Klausner International Literary Agency, Inc.

87 From *The History of the Peloponnesian War* by Thucydides, edited by Sir Richard Livingstone. (New York: Oxford University Press, 1966).

88 Thucydides: *The Peloponnesian War*, trans., Rex Warner (Middlesex: Penguin Books, Ltd., 1954), pp. 118, 119.

98 From *Herodotus, History of the Persian Wars*, trans., George Rawlinson in *The Greek Historians*, Vol. I, ed. Francis R. B. Godolphin, p. 378. (New York: Random House, Inc., 1942).

106 *Thucydides Translated into English*, Benjamin Jowett, ed. and trans., Vol. I (Oxford: The Clarendon Press, 1900),

p. 16

137 From *The Complete Works of Tacitus*, Translated from the Latin by Alfred John Church and William Jackson Broadribb. Ed. Moses Hadas. (New York: Random House, Inc., 1942) p. 716.

173 Marcus Nathan Adler, trans. *Itinerary of Benjamin of Tudela*. (New York: Philipp Feldheim, Inc.).

176 Quoted in J. F. C. Fuller, *A Military History of the Western World*, Vol. I, (New York: Funk and Wagnalls, 1954), p. 522.

179 *Procopius*, Vol. I, trans., Henry B. Dewing, Loeb Classical Library (Cambridge: Harvard Univ. Press, 1914), pp. 231 — 233.

181 Samuel H. Cross and Olgerd P. Sherbowitz-Wetzor (trans. and ed.), *The Russian Primary Chronicle* (Cambridge: Harvard University Press, 1930, 1958).

183 From *Medieval Russia's Epics, Chronicles, and Tales* translated and edited by Serge A. Zenkovsky. Copyright© 1963 by Serge A. Zenkovsky. Reprinted by permission of the publishers, E. P. Dutton & Co., Inc.

191 The Koran, trans. by M. M. Pickthall in *The Meaning of the Glorious Koran* (New York: Mentor Books, 1956), pp. 438 — 439. Reprinted by permission of George Allen & Unwin Ltd., London.

214 (left) From *A Literary History of the Arabs* by Reynold A. Nicholson. Published by Cambridge University Press, 1966. Reprinted by permission.

214 (right) From *Rubaiyat of Omar Khayyam* trans. by Edward Fitzgerald. (Boston: Houghton Mifflin, 1898).

233 "Hymn of Propitiation" from *People of the Small Arrow* by J. H. Driberg. Published by Payson & Clarke, 1930. Reprinted by permission of Routledge & Kegan Paul Ltd.

240—241 From *Narrative of Travels and Discoveries in Northern and Central Africa, In The Years 1822, 1823, and 1824* by Major Denham, Captain Clapperton and Doctor Oudney. (London: John Murray, 1826), p. 63.

245 From *Ancient African Kingdoms* by Margaret Shinnie. (New York: St. Martin's Press, Inc., 1965).

248 Quoted in *Discovering Our African Heritage* by Basil Davidson. (Boston: Ginn and Company, 1971), p. 119.

259 Hakluyt Society, *Works Issued by the Hakluyt Society*, 196 vols. London, 1847 — 1951.

283 Sir H. M. Elliot and John Dowson (eds. & trans.), *The History of India as Told By Its Own Historians* (London: Trubner & Co., 1871), III, 182 — 185.

301 Quoted in Elizabeth Seeger, *The Pageant of Chinese History*, (London: Longman Group Limited, 1934, 1947).

303 Quoted in Dun J. Li, *The Ageless Chinese*. (New York: Charles Scribner's Sons, 1971).

311 E. Backhouse and J. O. P. Bland, *Annals & Memoirs of the Court of Peking* (Boston: Houghton Mifflin Co., 1914).

315 Mikiso Hane, *Japan a Historical Survey* (New York: Charles Scribner's Sons, 1972).

316 Reprinted by permission of Hawthorn Properties (Elsevier-Dutton Publishing Co., Inc.). From *An Outline History of Japan* by Herbert H. Gowen. Copyright 1927 Appleton-Century; 1955 by Herbert H. Gowen.

317 From *History of Japan I* by James A. Murdoch, 1964. Reprinted by permission of Routledge & Kegan Paul Ltd.

321 (top and bottom) Edwin O. Reischauer and John K. Fairbank; *East Asia: The Great Tradition*, p. 497, 652. Copyright© 1958, 1960 by Houghton Mifflin Company.

321 (middle) Reprinted from *The Manyoshu* (New York, 1965), page 283, by permission of Columbia University Press.

355 *Machiavelli: The Prince and Other Works*, trans. by A. H. Gilbert (Chicago: Packard and Co., 1941).

389 Hakluyt Society, *Works Issued by the Hakluyt Society*, 196 vols. London, 1847 — 1951.

408 Bernal Diaz del Castillo, *The True History of the Conquest of Mexico*, trans. by Maurice Keating, 1800.

428—429 From *Memoirs of the Life, Writings, and Discoveries of Sir Isaac Newton* by Sir David Brewster (Edinburgh: Thomas Constable and Company, 1855).

445 Quoted in R. R. Palmer, *The Age of the Democratic Revolution*, Vol. I, *The Challenge*. Copyright© 1959 by Princeton University Press; Princeton Paperback, 1969. Reprinted by permission.

484 Quoted in Paul Joseph Mantoux, trans. by Marjorie Vernon, *The Industrial Revolution in the Eighteenth Century*, (New York: Harper & Row, 1961).

512 Quoted in J. H. Hexter & Richard Pipes, *Europe Since 1500*. (New York: Harper & Row, Publishers, 1971).

547 Viscount Grey of Fallodon, *Twenty-Five Years*, Vol. II (New York: Frederick A. Stokes Company, 1925), p. 20.

562 Woodrow Wilson, *War and Peace: Presidential Messages, Addresses, and Public Papers (1917 — 1924)*, ed. Ray Stannard Baker and William E. Dodd (New York: Harper & Brothers, 1927). I.

567 Quoted in N. N. Sukhanov, *The Russian Revolution, 1917: A Personal Record*, Joel Carmickael, ed. (New York: Oxford University Press, 1955), p. 273.

580 Cited in Great Soviet Encyclopedia, 3rd ed., Vol. 14

585 Bal Gangadhar Tilak, *His Writings and Speeches* (Madras, India: Ganesh & Co., 1923).

605 From *Mein Kampf* by Adolf Hitler,

translated by Ralph Manheim. (Boston: Houghton Miffin, 1943).
636—637 Lucius D. Clay, *Decision in Germany* (New York: Doubleday & Co., Inc., 1950), p. 360.
659 Peter Abrahams, *A Wreath For Udomo.* New York: Alfred A. Knopf, Inc., 1956, p. 135.
682 Albert Baltra Cortés, "Nuestra América y sus problemas," pp. 3-27. Trans. by ed., Benjamin Keen in "The Crisis of Latin America," LATIN AMERICAN CIVILIZATION: THE NATIONAL ERA, Vol. 2, 3rd ed. (Boston: Houghton Mifflin Company) 1974, p. 439.
700 Richard Bell, Associated Press Writer. "U.S.-Iran Crisis Thrusts Japan Into Oil Politics" as appeared in THE CINCINNATI ENQUIRER, Dec. 15, 1979.

Illustrations

Positions of photographs are shown in abbreviated form as follows: top (t), bottom (b), center (c), left (l), right (r). All photographs not credited are the property of Scott,Foresman.
Cover: Pete Turner/Image Bank
xviii Gerald Clyde/Alpha/FPG
2 (1a) The Danish National Museum (1b) Courtesy Field Museum of Natural History, Chicago (2) Courtesy The Oriental Institute, University of Chicago (3) Courtesy French Government Tourist Office (4) Courtesy of the Trustees of the British Museum
3 (6) Directorete General of Antiquities, Baghdad, Iraq (7) National Museum, New Delhi (8) University Museum, University of Pennsylvania (9) Farrell Grehan/Alpha/FPG (10) Musee de l'Homme, Paris (11) The Metropolitan Museum of Art, Brisbane Dick Fund, 1954 (12) Nelson Gallery-Atkins Museum, Kansas City, Missouri (Nelson Fund)
4 Musee des Antiquites Nationales, Musee de St. Germain
7 Courtesy American Museum of Natural History
10 (t) Rene Burri/Magnum (bl,br) FPG
12 (t) Courtesy Field Museum of Natural History, Chicago (bl) Musee de l'Homme, Paris (br) Archives Photographique
15 Soprintendenza all Prehistoria e All'Etnografia, Rome
18 Maynard Williams/Shostal
22 Jim Howard/FPG
23 John G. Ross/ARAMCO Magazine
24 (t,cl) Courtesy of the Trustees of the British Museum (cr) Edwards/FPG (bl) Courtesy of the Trustees of the British Museum (br) Courtesy The Oriental Institute, University of Chicago
26 Courtesy of the Trustees of the British Museum
30 University Museum, University of Pennsylvania
31 Archives Photographique
33 (t) Musee du Louvre, Paris (c) University Museum, University of Pennsylvania (b) Courtesy The Oriental Institute, University of Chicago
35 (l) Shostal (r) Detroit Institute of Art
36 Bettmann
37 (t) George Holton/Photo Researchers (b) Courtesy The Oriental Institute, University of Chicago
39 Pakistan National Museum
40 (t) Museum of Fine Art, Boston (bl) Reproduced by permission of The Director of The India Office Library and Records (br) National Museum, New Delhi
42 Courtesy of The Cultural Relics Bureau, Beijing,and The Metropolitan Museum of Art
43 Courtesy of the Smithsonian Institution, Freer Gallery of Art, Washington, D.C.
44 East Asian Library, Columbia University
48 Roloff Beny
50 (1) Virginia Museum of Fine Art, Richmond (2) Dennis Stock/Magnum (5) Rene Burri/Magnum (6) Don Marvine (7) Courtesy of the Trustees of the British Museum
51 (8) The Metropolitan Museum of Art, Rogers Fund, 1943 (9) Bettmann (15) Courtesy of Seattle Art Museum, Eugene Fuller Memorial Collection (16) Courtesy Field Museum of Natural History, Chicago
52 D. von Knobloch/Shostal
55 S. Fiore/Shostal
58 (l) J. Allen Cash/Photo Researchers (r) Alice Schalek/Three Lions
59 Courtesy Museum of Fine Arts, Boston
61 Courtesy of Seattle Art Museum, Eugene Fuller Memorial Collection
63 (l) Brown Brothers (r) Robert Frerck
66 (tl,b) Robert Frerck (tr) John Drake/Photo Researchers
67 Courtesy The Field Museum of Natural History, Chicago
68 R. Gruberg/Shostal
71 (both) Courtesy of The Cultural Relics Bureau, Beijing,and The Metropolitan Museum of Art
72 FPG
76 Courtesy of The Cultural Relics Bureau, Beijing,and The Metropolitan Museum of Art
79 (t) Courtesy of the Trustees of the British Museum (l) Courtesy The Oriental Institute, University of Chicago (c) University Museum, University of Pennsylvania (b) Courtesy of the Smithsonian Institution, Freer Gallery of Art, Washington, D.C.
80 Courtesy of The Cultural Relics Bureau, Beijing,and The Metropolitan Museum of Art.
81 The St. Louis Art Museum
83 University Museum, University of Pennsylvania
84 (l) Courtesy The Field Museum of Natural History, Chicago (r) Courtesy The Art Institute of Chicago
87, 89 Hirmer Verlag Munchen
91 (l) Art Reference Bureau (r) Deutsches Archaologisches Institut
92 Hirmer Verlag Munchen
94 Ray Manley/Shostal
95 Wadsworth Atheneum, Hartford. J. P. Morgan Collection
98 Alinari/EPA
99 (tl) Art Reference Bureau (tr) The Metropolitan Museum of Art, Fletcher Fund, 1931 (b) Ashmolean Museum, Oxford
102 Scala/EPA
104 (l) Anderson/EPA (c) Bettmann (r) Scala/EPA
106 Donald Seymour/Magnum
110 National Archaeological Museum, Naples
113 Villa Giulia and A.F.L. Naples
114 Dennis Hallinan/FPG
116 (t) Courtesy of the Trustees of the British Museum (cl) Alinari/EPA (bl) Courtesy of the Trustees of the British Museum (br) Giraudon
118 Anderson/EPA
119 Courtesy of the Trustees of the British Museum
120 Anderson/EPA
122 National Archaeological Museum, Naples
123 Shostal
125 Eric G. Carle/Shostal
127 Shostal
128 Alinari/EPA
132 Cathedral Treasury, Aachen. Photo by Ann Munchow
134 (1) Courtesy of the Trustees of the British Museum (2) Anderson/EPA (3) Universitetets Oldsaksamling, Oslo (4) Marilyn Silverstone/Magnum (5) Giraudon (6) Courtesy of Edinburgh University Library
135 (8) Courtesy of the Bygdoy Museum, Oslo (10) Universitetets Oldsaksamling, Oslo (11) Musee de l'Homme, Paris (12) Bettmann (16) Bibliotheque Nationale, Paris (17) Courtesy Newberry Library, Chicago
136 Manuscript page 34V from the *Book of Kells.* Board of Trinity College, Dublin
138 Pontifical Commission on Sacred Art/Art Reference Bureau
141 (t) Andre Held (b) Marburg/Art Reference Bureau
142 (all) Courtesy of the Trustees of the British Museum
144, 146 The Curators of the Bodleian Library, Oxford
147 (l) National Museum of Ireland (r) Rheinisches Landesmuseum, Bonn
150 Cathedral Treasury, Aachen. Photo by Ann Munchow
153 Courtesy of the Trustees of the British Museum
157 (tl) Archives Photographique (tr) Bettmann (c, br) Courtesy of the Trustees of the British Museum (bl) The Pierpont Morgan Library
158 Bibliotheque Nationale, Paris
159 Courtesy of the Trustees of the

British Museum
162 Bibliotheque Nationale, Paris
164 (tl) Scala/EPA (r) Giraudon (bl) Courtesy of the Trustees of the British Museum
166 Historical Picture Service, Inc., Chicago
169 (t) Anderson/EPA (b) Giraudon
172 Scala/EPA
178 (l) Alinari/EPA (c,r) LIFE Picture Service, Time, Inc.
179 Erich Lessing/Magnum
181 Bibliotheque Nationale, Madrid
184 (t) Courtesy Newberry Library, Chicago (c,b) Bettmann
187 Courtesy The Art Institute of Chicago
189 Edinburgh Library. Courtesy Newsweek Books
190 (t) The British Library Board (b) Staatliche Museen zu Berlin
192 Bibliotheque Nationale, Paris
196 Anderson/EPA
200 Photo from the National Portrait Gallery, London. From the collection of the Earl of Yarborough, Brocklesby Park
203 Bibliotheque Nationale, Paris
205 (both) Mehmet Biber/Photo Researchers
206 (t) The Metropolitan Museum of Art, Rogers Fund (c) Erich Lessing/Magnum (b) The Metropolitan Museum of Art
210 (t) The British Library Board (b) Bibliotheque Nationale, Paris
211 (l) Reproduced by permission of The Director of The India Office Library and Records (r) The British Library Board
213 (both) Bettmann
215 (l) Reproduced by permission of The Director of The India Office Library and Records (r) Bibliotheque Nationale, Paris
216 Shostal
220 Lee Boltin
222 (1,2) Erich Lessing/Magnum (3) Courtesy Field Museum of Natural History, Chicago (4) Emil Muench
223 (5) Courtesy of Detroit Institute of Arts (6) Courtesy The Art Institute of Chicago (7) Joe B. Blossom/Photo Researchers (8) Ann and Myron Sutton/FPG (9) Courtesy Field Museum of Natural History, Chicago
224 Courtesy of the Trustees of the British Museum
226 Bruno Barbey/Magnum
230 Courtesy Field Museum of Natural History, Chicago
231 Musee de l'Homme, Paris
234 (t) Lepsius, Denkmaler . . . . 1860 (b) PIP photo by Paul Pipper Ltd.
236 Courtesy of Federal Department of Antiquities, National Museum, Lagos, Nigeria
237 (l) Museum of Primitive Art, New York (r) Courtesy of the Trustees of the British Museum
240 The British Library Board
245 BBC Hulton Picture Library
249 Authenticated News International
251 Courtesy Newberry Library, Chicago

253 New York Historical Society
254,258 Lee Boltin
261 David Muench
262 (t) Shostal (bl) D. Grew/Alpha/FPG (br) Karl Kummels/Shostal
264 Museo Nacional de Antropologia, Mexico
268 Library of Congress
270 Lee Boltin
271 (l) Courtesy The Art Institute of Chicago (r) Lee Boltin
274 New York Public Library
278 Detail, "Peach Blossom Spring" Ch'iu Ying, 1530. Handscroll, ink and colors on silk. Courtesy The Art Institute of Chicago
280 (1) Detail of six fold screen, Genji Monogatari. Courtesy The Art Institute of Chicago (2) Drawing by John Christiansen from Joseph Needham, *Science and Civilization in China*, Vol. 4, Pt. 2, Fig. 650
281 (3) Detail, "Efficacy of Repeated Invocations to the Amida Buddha." Courtesy The Cleveland Museum of Art. Purchase, Mr. and Mrs. William H. Marlatt Fund, John L. Severance Fund and Edward L. Whittemore Fund (4) Detail, handscroll, "Street Scenes in Times of Peace." Courtesy The Art Institute of Chicago. Kate S. Buckingham Collection (5) John Massey Stewart, London (6) Reproduced by permission of The Director of The India Office Library and Records (7) Gerald Clyde/Alpha/FPG
282 Musee Guimet, Paris
286 (tl) Ray Manley/Shostal (tr) Robert Frerck (b) Lawrence L. Smith/Photo Researchers
288 (tl) Crown copyright, Victoria and Albert Museum (tr) Reproduced by permission of The Director of The India Office Library and Records (b) Robert Frerck
291 Courtesy of the Smithsonian Institution, Freer Gallery of Art, Washington, D.C.
292 Alice and Nasli Heeramaneck Collection, New York
293 (l) H. Armstrong Roberts (r) Helen and Frank Schreider/Photo Researchers
294 Red Fort Museum, Delhi
298 Detail, "Spring Festival on the River" Ming dynasty scroll. Metropolitan Museum of Art, Fletcher Fund 1947. The A.W. Bahr Collection
301 Detail, hanging scroll by Yuan Chiang. Courtesy The Art Institute of Chicago
303 Courtesy of the Trustees of the British Museum
304 (t) Emperor Hui-tsung: "Ladies Preparing Newly Woven Silk," Sung dynasty. Courtesy Museum of Fine Arts, Boston. (b) Detail, Ladies playing "double sixes." Sung dynasty. Courtesy of the Smithsonian Institution, Freer Gallery of Art, Washington, D.C.
306 Brooklyn Museum
310 The University Museum,

University of Pennsylvania
314 Detail, "Tale of Genji," 6-fold screen, Genji Monogatari. Courtesy The Art Institute of Chicago, gift of Robert Allerton
317 Eitoku: "Izangi and Izanami Standing in Clouds and Creating Island Out of the Sea Water," late 19th century. Courtesy Museum of Fine Arts, Boston
320 Sakamoto Photo Research Laboratory, Tokyo
322 The Tokyo National Museum
323 World Publishing Company
324 Detail, Sesshu: "The Four Seasons." Courtesy The Art Institute of Chicago
325 Detail, "The Burning of the Sanjo Palace" 13th century. Courtesy of Seattle Art Museum
326 Detail, Masanobu: Interior view of the Nakamura Theatre in Edo, 18th century. Courtesy The Art Institute of Chicago
327,328 Courtesy Museum of Fine Arts, Boston
332 Scala/EPA
334 (1) Kunsthistorisches Museum, Vienna (2) Erich Lessing/Magnum (4) Bibliotheque Nazionale, Venice
335 (5) Direzione Belle Arti del Comune, Genoa (6) Musee de l'Homme (7) Courtesy of the Trustees of the British Museum (9) Museo Nacional de Historia, Mexico
336 Scala/EPA
340 Crown copyright, Victoria and Albert Museum
341 Bettmann
342 E. Streichan/Shostal (tl) Marmel Studios/FPG (bl) Shostal
344 (l) Musee Conde de Chantilly
346 Giraudon
348 Historical Picture Service, Chicago
349 Dortmund Museum of Art and Cultural History
352 Scala/EPA
357 Museum of London
358 (l) Royal Library, Windsor Castle. Reproduced by Gracious Permission of Her Majesty The Queen. Copyright reserved. (r) Shostal
359 Museo Civico, Padua, Italy
360 (l) Alinari/EPA (r) Reproduced by courtesy of the Trustees, The National Gallery, London
364 (t) EPA (b) The Greater London Council as Trustee of the Iveagh Bequest, Kenwood
365 Kunsthistorischen Museum
366 The New York Public Library
369 The Folger Shakespeare Library
372 (l) Giraudon (r) Jean Arlaud, Musee Historique de la Reformation, Geneva
373 Isabella Stewart Gardner Museum, Boston
376 (l) Bettmann (r) The Granger Collection, New York
378 Giraudon
381 Historical Picture Service, Chicago
383 Courtesy Hillwood Museum, Washington, D.C.
386 (l,r) Brown Brothers

609 Three Lions, Inc.
610 Pablo Picasso: "Guernica." 1937, May-early June. Oil on canvas. 11' 5½" x 25' 5 ¾". On extended loan to The Museum of Modern Art, New York, from the artist
612 Camera Press, Ltd.
615 Associated Newspapers Ltd., London
616 Wide World
617 H. Roger Viollet
620 (l) UPI (r) World Federation of Bergen-Belsen Association
621 Imperial War Museum
622 Robert Capa/Magnum
623 (tl) Imperial War Museum (tr,bl) U.S. Coast Guard photo (bl) Defense Dept., U.S. Marine Corps
624 UPI
625 Franklin Delano Roosevelt Library
626 (t) Bettmann (b) Library of Congress
627 (tl) Wide World (tr) Culver (bl) Sovfoto (br) UPI
628 UPI
632 Robert Langridge, PhD. Computer Graphics Laboratory, University of California, San Francisco
634 (1) Courtesy of United Nations (2) U.S. Air Force (3) Cecil Beaton, London
635 (6) UPI (7) Gamma/Liaison (8) UPI (9) NASA (10) Romano Cagnoni/Magnum (11,12) UPI (13) Courtesy International Olympic Committee (14) UPI
636 Wide World
638 (l) Courtesy of United Nations (r) World Health Organization

641 (r,l) UPI
643 Camera Press, Ltd.
644 (l) Paolo Koch/Photo Researchers (c) Brian Brake/Photo Researchers (r) Novosti/FPG
646 (both) NASA
647 Susan Greenwood/Liaison (bl) USSR Magazine from Sovfoto
648 Erich Lessing/Magnum
650 J.P. Laffont/Sygma
651 Bernard Lipnitzki/Magnum
652 UPI
654 U.S. Army
655 (t) China Pictorial (bl) Photo by John Dominis © Time Inc. (br) Magnum
659 Marilyn Silverstone/Magnum
661 Courtesy Johnson Publishing Company
664 A. Chauvel/Sygma
665 White House photograph
666 (tl) Allen Green/Photo Researchers (bl) The National Foundation for Infantile Paralysis
667 British Information Service (tr) D. McCullin/Magnum
668,669 Ledru/Sygma
673 (t) Marc & Évelyne Bernheim/Rapho Guillumette/Photo Researchers (c) Dr. Philip Kahl/Black Star (b) Robert Frerck
674 UPI
675 Marc Riboud/Magnum
678 W. Campbell/Sygma
679 Hugues Vassal/Liaison
682 Bruno Barbey/Magnum
684 Melloul/Sygma
685 UPI
686 (t) Jackson Pollock: "Greyed Rainbow, 1953." Collection The Art Institute of Chicago (b) Romare Bearden: "Evening, 9:10, 461 Lexington Avenue." Cordier and Ekstrom, Inc., New York. Photo by Robert S. Crandall
687 (tl) Roy Lichtenstein: "Torpedo . . . Los." 1963 Courtesy of Mrs. R. B. Mayer, Chicago (tr) Robert Smithson, Utah USA: "Spiral Jetty." Photo Georg Gerster/Photo Researchers (b) Louise Nevelson: "American Dawn." Collection The Art Institute of Chicago
689 Bettmann
690 UPI
695 U.S. Marine Corps
696 UPI
697 James Montgomery/Gamma Liaison
700 T. Schmitt/Sygma
702 (l) James Andanson/Sygma (r) Magnum
704 J. P. Laffont/Sygma
705 (tl,tr) UPI (tc) Wide World (cl,cr) Wide World (c) UPI (b) Michel Artault/Gamma Liaison
707 (l) Marc Riboud/Magnum (r) Regis Bossu/Sygma
708 Rapho Guillumette/Photo Researchers
710 Sovfoto
711 White House photograph
712 Raymond Depardon/Magnum
713 Alain Nogues/Sygma
715 (l) Dan F. Connolly/Time Inc. (r) Georg Gerster/Photo Researchers
717 Courtesy Solar Energy Research Institute